NEWSWEEK CONDENSED BOOKS

PAUL DICKSON
<hr>

'ADAM SMITH'
<hr>

MARCIA SELIGSON
<hr>

DAVID HALBERSTAM
<hr>

THE GREAT AMERICAN ICE CREAM BOOK

SUPERMONEY

THE ETERNAL BLISS MACHINE

THE BEST AND THE BRIGHTEST

NEWSWEEK BOOKS, New York

NEWSWEEK CONDENSED BOOKS

Kermit Lansner, Editor

The original editions of the books in
this volume are published and copyrighted
as follows:

The Great American Ice Cream Book
Published by Atheneum Publishers
Copyright © 1972 by Paul Dickson

Supermoney
Published by Random House, Inc.
Copyright © 1972 by 'Adam Smith'
Condensation by special arrangement with
Random House, Inc.

The Eternal Bliss Machine
Published by William Morrow & Company, Inc.
Copyright © 1973 by Marcia Seligson

The Best and the Brightest
Published by Random House, Inc.
Copyright © 1969, 1971, 1972 by David Halberstam
Condensation by special arrangement with
Random House, Inc.

CONTENTS

THE GREAT AMERICAN

ICE CREAM BOOK

A condensation of the book by

PAUL DICKSON

CHAPTER 1

THE CREAMING OF AMERICA

A ny minor interruptions to the Great Depression of the Spirit now
upon the land are worthy of attention for no other reason than that
they divert us from the mess at hand and offer us a chance to enter
realms at once uplifting, comprehensible, and determinedly irrelevant
in this age of relevance. No further apology is needed for concerning
ourselves with the ongoing American ice cream revival.

Wall Street was awash with ice cream, and the hottest rumors heard
there concerned "free sprinkles" and "outasight maple walnut." One
large vendor claimed to be dipping a cone a second in the area. Further
uptown some of the nation's highest-paid executive talents spilled
out of their glass and concrete lairs onto the streets to demand their
chocolate, vanilla, and strawberry in "sugar cones"—a delicacy previously known only to the *cognoscenti* that drew on a weekly allowance
rather than a corporate expense account. Across town and into outer
boroughs and suburbs, long lines appeared in front of signs marked
Barricini, Barton's, Fannie Farmer, and Howard Johnson's.

Meanwhile, relief was on its way from the hinterland: H. P. Hood
and Sons of Boston was sending a fleet of six hundred ice cream
vending trucks to the city to supplement the beleaguered forces of
Mister Softee and Good Humor; Baskin-Robbins was completing its
march from the West Coast and was about to take New York; dipping
equipment and ice cream were being moved into locations ranging
from twenty-seven new Yum Yums to nine established Zum Zums.
Established parlors like Hicks and The Flick were more popular than
ever, and their proprietors were keeping a competitive eye on the
dozens of new independent parlors under construction. A turn-of-
the-century parlor was discovered intact in Haverstraw, New York,

and, with the painstaking care normally associated with archaeological excavation, was being taken apart, packed up, and removed to Third Avenue to emerge as Agora. Reliable sources told of marble counter-tops being designed into an ice cream parlor which was to be located in the staid lobby of the Plaza Hotel. Summing it all up, Gael Greene wrote in a *New York* magazine cover story on ice cream in August, 1970: "New York is in the full throes of an ice cream renaissance."

While it was manifested most dramatically in New York, where it started during the summer of 1970 and continued to flourish through 1971 and into 1972, it was hitting all over the country as well. It is hard to determine exactly where it began, but cities ranging from Boston to San Francisco had seen earlier evidence of revived interest in high-quality ice cream, sparked by a variety of catalysts. Nationally, the movement of forces like Bresler's and Baskin-Robbins was signifi-cant—and then there were the local sparks. In New York, for example, people attribute great influence to the decision of the Barricini chain to bolster lagging candy sales by installing dipping counters. In San Francisco the steady parade of flavors coming out of the area's 31-store Swensen's chain and the must-be-seen-to-be-believed Ghirardelli Soda Fountain in Ghirardelli Square were of great importance, while in Boston most believe it was prompted by a combination of established entities—such as the remarkable Bailey's and Cabot's fountains—and new emphases: for one, Howard Johnson's was using its Boston-area stores to experiment with the long-overdue idea of again giving star billing to its fine ice cream rather than such things as its less-than-mediocre egg salad sandwiches. Nor was all of this restricted to urban and suburban America. There were also expanding pockets of rural excellence, such as Miller's ice cream parlors in Michigan and the Deering chain moving across Maine and into New Hampshire.

Lest there be any confusion about this ongoing revival, it has thus far had no significant impact on the quantity of ice cream being sold; today the average American consumes about the same amount of the stuff as he or she has every year since 1950. The revolution taking place is subjectively measured in terms of flavors tested, respect ac-corded, consumer behavior (meaning that ice cream cones were to be found clutched in the hands of an increasing number of adults, as anyone walking down any major urban street during the last few summers could see), and, most important, quality demanded. Children of all ages have begun to opt for good ice cream over that miracle of chemical engineering and technical expertise that has been passing for ice cream for so long. Despite the much publicized contemporary worry about the dollar and the calorie, droves of Americans are deserting the anemic 69-cent half-gallon for a 35-cent double-scoop of rich, full-bodied, fattening ice cream.

Added to these delightful goings-on were all the attempts to ex- lain the sudden adult rediscovery of quality ice cream. Opined *The Nation's Restaurant News:* "Behind the change in consumer consciousness lies the youth culture, nostalgia and recessionary economics." The trade biweekly backed up its assessment with quotes gathered from restaurant owners and ice cream eaters across the country, which alluded to such specifics as "rebellion against the machine culture," the demise of "phony sophistication," "sensual pleasure," and a "desire for the good old days." *Look,* in one of its last ventures into pop psychology, tried to explain the sudden addiction this way: "Perhaps it's nothing more complicated than mother's milk—in 28 flavors, and you get to choose." William Holmes, Atlantic Coast manager for Beatrice Foods (a combine which owns a diverse stable of ice cream labels, including the prestigious Louis Sherry brand), says: "There is something about hard times that brings out an urge for simple pleasures like ice cream." He adds, with the trained eye of an ice cream marketer: "Of course, there is a very simple thing at work here too. Long ago, ice cream left downtown for the shopping mall and supermarket and now it's back. A lot of people never ate ice cream cones on their lunch hour simply because they couldn't get them." Said Gael Greene in *New York* magazine: "In these harsh and uncertain times, as the establishment cracks and institutions crumble, it is no wonder we reach out to ice cream. It is a link to innocence and security, healing, soothing, wholesome. . . ."

Everyone was getting into the act, including those who pushed beyond analysis to application. Dr. David Reuben, author of *Everything You Always Wanted to Know about Sex but Were Afraid to Ask,* told *Woman's Day* readers in 1971 that the sure-fire way of nailing a man was to serve him milk, cream, or ice cream. Reuben offered this as his keystone theory to the man/woman relationship:

For every man the world of the subconscious is ruled by the symbol of milk. Milk shakes, ice cream, even alcoholic beverages . . . carry the theme of Mother's milk throughout every day. The six-foot, two-hundred pound man sipping a cup of coffee with cream is emotionally only moments away from the ten-pound baby happily drinking from his bottle. . . . When a woman establishes herself as the *provider of milk* she literally makes herself part of her man's unconscious mind. If she wants him to marry her, all she has to do is inject enough milk (or milk substitute) into their relationship.

11

Enjoying this profundity and analysis most were those of us who had *actually* got the whole thing going. We were the ones who had sought out, supported, and freely advertised high-quality ice cream when it was in hiding. Among ourselves we could argue for hours over who had the best vanilla fudge; but with others, ours was a solid front, and we worked hard to convert those who could look on ice cream as "all the same." Like wine nuts and their vineyard towns in Burgundy, we had our dairy towns to dote on and dally in, and would send others to places like Westminster, Maryland, where even gas stations sell home-made ice cream. We knew that if we were ever in Philadelphia we would head straight for Bassett's in the Reading Terminal. It was Petersen's in Chicago, Gifford's and Avignone Frères in Washington, Bailey's in Boston, the Chocolate Shop in Kalamazoo, and Wil Wright's in Los Angeles. Besides memorizing names, we developed an ability to sniff out new finds. For instance, it was axiomatic that most universities with dairy schools have a good ice cream shop on the premises. Ours was a cult with leaders, such as Jane Howard who brought us together in her *Life* article, "Confessions of an Ice Cream Eater," in which she spoke for all of us when she said, "I'd drive five hours, and recently did, for a good cone of chocolate chip. I'd make an inconvenient side trip between Kansas City and Chicago, and recently did, for a dish of maple pecan." Her confession was ours, and when she said, "I am an unregenerate ice cream fetishist," we applauded from each nook and cranny of the nation.

In the final analysis, it mattered little whether a dip in the economy or some unconscious mammalian lactic urge was behind it all. To the ice-creamaniac what did matter was the lip-smacking reality of the movement to good ice cream spreading across the nation with the firm determination of a glacier. A new ice cream age had begun.

CHAPTER 2

UP FROM THE ICE AGE

It is typical of man that he collectively records and remembers far more about his detractors and destroyers than about those who innovate in his behalf. Thus we can put our hands on all sorts of information on plundering armies, rampaging hordes, and lunatic despots, but we have no idea who cranked the first pint of ice cream. About all that we can estimate is that this remarkable person or persons appeared somewhere in Europe—probably in Italy, maybe in England—in the fifteenth or sixteenth century. We do know, however, that ice cream did not originate in the United States as so many unthinking geocentrics have long assumed. Like apple pie (brought from England along with apple seedlings) and certain other edible symbols of America, ice cream had an alien genesis although it was popularized in the United States.

The first known use of a substance even vaguely resembling ice cream occurred during the rule of Nero Claudius Caesar (A.D. 54-68). Nero periodically sent teams of runners into the mountains for snow, which was relayed back to his table where it was flavored with honey, juices, and fruit pulps. Although this is all that is known, the emperor's dessert was obviously the forerunner of the modern fruit ice. Roman writings of the second century after Christ mention, but never describe, a dish called mecla—and it has perplexed scholars ever since the Renaissance. Several have advanced the thesis that it was a frozen or chilled milk concoction.

For the next thousand years there is no recorded mention of anything even suggesting ice cream. Then, at the end of the thirteenth century, Marco Polo returned from the Far East with a recipe for frozen dessert which included milk and, as far as we can tell today, resembled modern sherbet. The popularity of ices and sherbets grew in Italy and probably evolved into ice cream sometime in the sixteenth century. One description of Italian foods written in 1560 refers to a "food from milk which is made of milk sweetened with honey and frozen. . . . Some persons call it the flower of milk, some call it cream. . . ." If flower of milk was not ice cream it was certainly something close to it.

Frozen desserts are believed to have been brought to France in 1533 by Catherine de Médicis and her retinue when she left Italy at the age of fourteen to marry the Duke of Orléans, who later became Henri II. Through the cooks and chefs she brought with her, she introduced ices and sherbets and possibly ice cream itself to France.

Ice cream reached England at an early date, and just possibly may have predated its appearance in Italy. A manuscript describing the coronation of Henry V mentions a third-course delicacy in the coronation banquet called "crème frez," which at least sounds as though it could be ice cream. If not, ice cream was certainly in Britain in the early seventeenth century when "creme ice" appeared regularly at the table of Charles I. An oft-told, but perhaps apocryphal, story says that Charles was so pleased upon first tasting the dish that he gave the French chef who introduced him to it a pension of twenty pounds sterling a year on the condition that the formula for it be kept secret. The story goes on to say that after Charles was beheaded in 1649, the chef sold the secret to a consortium of noblemen who had long coveted it. James II, Charles's son, apparently shared his father's passion, as the accounts of the Lord Steward's department for 1686 show an entry for "a dozen dishes of ice cream" which were purchased for James while he was camped at Hounslow Heath and priced at an unconscionable one pound per dish.

Although frozen desserts were becoming common in regal circles, not until 1670 when the Café Procope opened in Paris did "iced creams" and sherbets spread to the masses. Founded by a Sicilian, Francesco Procopio dei Coltelli (Procope for short), the café not only introduced the new type of dessert but was credited with being that city's first coffeehouse, or café. Coltelli had opened his trend-setting establishment after a long career as a Paris *limonadier*. At the time he was one of 250 master *limonadiers* who were organized as a trade guild, suggesting that perhaps the city was glutted with lemonade and that he shrewdly opted for something novel with a more promising future. Café Procope is still in operation today on the rue de l'Ancienne Comédie, as is the Caffè Florian on the Piazza San Marco in Venice, among the first of the Italian coffeehouses and reputedly Coltelli's source of inspiration. During the next hundred years a succession of new cafés appeared in Paris, many of which had their own house ice cream specialty. From the Café Napolitain on the Boulevard des Italiens came the macaroon, rum, and ice cream concoction named for its proprietor, an Italian named Tortoni.

During the eighteenth century ice cream began appearing in other parts of Europe. From Vienna, Beethoven observed in a note in 1794: "It is very warm here. The Viennese are afraid that it will soon be impossible to have any ice cream, for as winter is mild, ice is rare."

The first record of any sort indicating the presence of ice cream in America is a letter, written in 1700 by a guest of Governor William Bladen of Maryland, which states: ". . . we had dessert no less Curious; among the Rarities of which it was Compos'd was some fine Ice Cream which, with the Strawberries and Milk, eat most Deliciously."

So far as is known, the first public advertisement of ice cream anywhere in the world was paid for by Philip Lenzi, a confectioner, who announced in the New York *Gazette* of May 12, 1777, that his ice cream "may be had almost every day." It can be assumed that ice cream was gaining a toehold in New York during the 1780's, because other ads began appearing in the New York papers. In 1781, a Lenzi competitor named Joseph Corre was the first to advertise the words ICE CREAM in large conspicuous letters, and an announcement in the New York *Post Boy* (1786) read: "Ladies and Gentlemen may be supplied with ice cream every day at the City Tavern by their humble servant Joseph Crowe." Commenting on the significance of these early ads, two American dairy historians, H. A. Schuette and Francis J. Robinson of the Laboratory of Foods and Sanitation at the University of Wisconsin, wrote in 1933: "But quite apart from the antiquarian interest which attaches to these advertisements is the fact that they were in a sense prophetic of the day when the adopted home of ice cream was to outstrip the countries of its origin in the degree to which it was to be developed and in the popularity accorded it. . . ."

Within a few years, the French gourmet Anthelme Brillat-Savarin returned from a trip to New York to report that the ice cream ladle was helping to create an American *nouveau riche*. In his classic *La Physiologie du Goût*, he devotes a chapter to French nobility in exile who made their living from food, and wrote: "Capitaine Collet made a great deal of money in New York, during the years 1794 and 1795, by selling ice cream and sherbet to the inhabitants of that busy city. The ladies especially never tired of a pleasure so novel to them; nothing was more amusing than to watch them smirk and simper as they tasted it. They could not understand how it could be kept so cold. . . ."

Considerable evidence has come to light indicating that George Washington possessed more than a passing fancy for ice cream. It is known that he was served ice cream by Mrs. Alexander Hamilton at a dinner party in 1789 and that the inventory at his home in Mount Vernon contained "two pewter ice cream pots." The fact has also been unearthed that when he was in Philadelphia attending a meeting of the Society of the Cincinnati, he bought something called a "Cream Machine for Making Ice"—which sounds as though it might have been some sort of an ice cream-producing device. Most impressive of all, however, are the records of an ice cream merchant on Chatham Street in New York, which show that Washington ran up a tab of £51/6s./2d.—about $200—for ice cream during the summer of 1790. Similarly, Thomas Jefferson has left evidence of a proclivity for ice cream, which includes his own eighteen-step recipe for ice cream and a favored way of serving it enclosed in warm pastry.

While ice cream had graced the tables of presidents before, it was Dolley Madison who glamorized it by first serving it at the White

House at state dinners. An impressionable guest describes it with convincing effect: "Last night I was bid by our President to the White House, and it was a most unusual affair. Mrs. Madison always entertains with Grace and Charm, but last night there was a sparkle in her eye that set astir an Air of Expectancy among her Guests. When finally the brilliant Assemblage—America's best—entered the dining room, they beheld a Table set with French china and English silver, laden with good things to eat, and in the Centre high on a silver platter, a large, shining dome of pink Ice Cream."

For many years ice cream was a dish of the very wealthy in America. Not only was ice difficult to come by during most of the year; even with an ample supply of ice, ice cream was ever so difficult to make. Commonly it was made by the "pot freezer" method, an especially awkward process in which the mixture was vigorously beaten in a pot at the same time that the pot was shaken up and down in a large pan of salt and ice. Two early nineteenth-century developments changed the situation.

First, "ice harvesting" and the insulated icehouse became widespread, and that precious commodity became much more common. The number of confectioners who sold ice cream increased and ice cream parlors began appearing in major cities. Second, in 1846 Nancy Johnson, an innovative woman about whom we know little, invented the hand-cranked ice cream freezer, but for reasons that have never been made clear, did not patent her invention. On May 30, 1848, William G. Young registered it with the Patent Office. Young at least had the courtesy to call his product the "Johnson Patent Ice-Cream Freezer."

The familiar "Johnson-Young" crank-and-paddle freezer in a bucket was an immediate sensation, bringing ice cream making into the realm of the average citizen. The popularity of the device was such that Young was given a run for his money. Within a few years, there were many imitations and "improved" versions on the market, and dozens of other patents had been issued on hand-cranked freezers. An 1851 Philadelphia cookbook gave added credence to the fact that ice cream was coming into its own, as it contained recipes for no less than thirty-four different ice creams and eighteen different water ices.

Ice cream had become popular in the United States by mid-century —so much so that Ralph Waldo Emerson was prompted to write of the national character, "We dare not trust our wit for making our house pleasant to our friend so we buy ice cream." The stage was set for the birth of a full-fledged ice cream industry.

16

CHAPTER 3

THE ANNALS OF AMERICAN ICE CREAM (1851-1941)

Today the American ice cream industry is a mammoth entity annually producing more than enough ice cream to fill the Grand Canyon. Each American man, woman, and child consumes a yearly average of twenty-three quarts of ice cream, ice milk, sherbet, ices, and other commercially produced frozen dairy products. Except for Australians, Canadians, and New Zealanders, no other people eat nearly half that much. In fact, if the average annual intake of two Frenchmen, two Austrians, an Italian, a Belgian, and a Briton were added together, the total would still be two pints and a few Good Humors short of the American average. This giant American industry got off to a humble start over one hundred years ago when the average American tongue could expect to taste less than a teaspoon of it a year.

The ice cream industry began as a problem of supply and demand was solved. A moderately successful Baltimore milk dealer named Jacob Fussell had long been finding himself oversupplied with cream. The problem stemmed from the fact that his dairies were giving him a constant supply of it whereas its pattern of sales was highly erratic. By 1851 the problem was such that it threatened Fussell's business and he was hard pressed for a solution. After exploring several possibilities, he decided that his surplus could be profitably disposed of as ice cream for 25 cents a quart, which compared dramatically with the prevailing price of 65 cents a quart charged by city caterers and others who made and sold ice cream in very small quantities.

In short order, Fussell found that his ice cream business was more profitable than milk, and he lost no time in converting his entire plant to the production of ice cream, thus making him the first full-fledged manufacturer/wholesaler in the field. By 1856 he had prospered to the point where he set up another plant in Washington; within a few years he opened one in Boston and, finally, founded the first wholesale ice cream operation in New York. While Fussell inaugurated the ice cream industry in the East, he also had a direct impact on the westward movement of the industry. Perry Brazelton, a banker and close friend who had fallen on hard times, was taken in by Fussell and tutored in the business. Like a latter-day Johnny Appleseed, Brazelton successfully moved the industry to the Midwest.

Despite the early success enjoyed by Fussell, Brazelton, and others, the industry grew very slowly and many populous states did not have their first ice cream company until 1880 or later. Ice cream fanciers in such states as Delaware, Arkansas, and Montana did not see their first factory-made ice cream until the early 1900's. The reason for this sluggishness was that as late as the 1880's, the ice cream plant was little more than a very large hand-cranked freezer. F. D. Hutchinson, who opened Iowa's first ice cream plant, recalled some years later: "I remember that on the Fourth of July in 1890 we shipped out three hundred gallons of ice cream—all frozen by hand."

Not until the turn of the century did the industry begin to grow dramatically, which it did for about a decade, when the pace accelerated from dramatic to phenomenal. A five-million-gallon-a-year babe in 1899, industry production shot up to thirty million gallons in 1909 and topped 150 million gallons in 1919. This remarkable growth was occasioned by a quick, steady procession of technical developments which transformed the ice cream plant to a practical profit-promising operation. One after another, mechanical and technical revolutions occurred. First came practical steam power, then mechanical refrigeration, the homogenizer, electric power and electric motors, sophisticated test equipment, packaging machines, new freezers and freezing processes, new insulation concepts, and the motorized delivery van. The net result of all of this was that by the early 1920's the ice cream plant was nearly as modernized as the ones that exist today.

Ice cream was fast becoming what industry leaders liked to call it, "America's typical food." It was dispensed everywhere, from the corner drugstore soda fountain to the Pullman car. The ice cream soda, sundae, and banana split seemed to grow more popular each day and the particularly American craft of the soda jerk was coming into its own as an indigenous folk art. Everyone was eating ice cream and noteworthy Americans extolled its virtues. In the world of sports, for example, the incomparable Walter Johnson boasted that all he ate on the day he was to pitch was a quart of ice cream. Others—among them Babe Ruth, Ty Cobb, and Pablo Nurmi, "the Flying Finn"—gave unsolicited testimonials to their favorite dish. In keeping with the prohibitionist litany of the era, a popular story asserted that when the fast, lithe, ice cream-stoked "Gentleman Jim" Corbett defeated the great booze-loving John L. Sullivan, the latter reformed and ate ice cream until his dying day.

That the nation was opting for ice cream instead of beer and liquor was looked upon in the industry as a heartwarming development. Not only were the pooh-bahs of ice cream pleased with the promise of new profits, there was the added dividend of smug self-righteousness associated with weaning the nation away from the hard stuff onto the cold stuff. During the early days of Prohibition the trade journals regularly compiled lists of breweries that had been turned into ice cream plants, and the leaders of the industry proclaimed their zealous satisfaction in verse and prose.

The 1920's, an era of prosperity and frivolity, saw ice cream expanding into new territory and gaining new popularity. Indicative was the 1921 decision by the Commissioner of Ellis Island to treat all immigrants to a taste of something truly American upon arriving in the land of promise: as part of their first meal in America they were served ice cream. Reporting on a meal for 1,700 new arrivals, *The Ice Cream Review* said that many were tenderly spreading this sweet, cool "new butter" on their bread with knives. Ice cream was moving into every nook and cranny of the land. For instance, in the Missouri and Arkansas Ozarks it had long been a delicacy and the ice cream social a major event. Ice cream was a rare commodity there, since its production was completely dependent on the vicissitudes of weather. Thus the winter social could be held only after harsh periods when mountain streams had frozen, and in the summer it had to be hastily arranged after hailstorms covered the land with enough large, hard pellets to be collected and used. Traditionally, Ozark ice cream had been made by agitating tin sorghum buckets placed in boxes filled with salted ice. This all changed in the 1920's as the ice cream truck began nosing its way into the hills.

In addition others of missionary zeal found new markets for American ice cream overseas. One such citizen, Paul S. Crawley, introduced ice cream to China by way of his shop in Shanghai, and during his first year in operation sold nine thousand gallons of ice cream and over a million Eskimo Pies. Complete soda fountains—replete with Tennessee-marble counters and banks of syrup pumps—were exported in volume to nations as far away as Japan and Chile. Ice cream mixes and equipment were bringing the cool dish to South America, and American technicians went to Europe, the cradle of the frozen dessert, to help bring production techniques out of the nineteenth century.

By 1929 Americans were downing an unprecedented nine quarts apiece per year and ice cream had steadily grown as a vital commercial force in its own right. The small plant, the street vendor (or Hokey-Pokey man, as he was called in many cities), and the dairyman selling home-made ice cream from his barn on weekends were giving way to large dairy combines and corporations listed on the New York Stock Exchange.

So important was the product and the shifting fancies of the American ice cream consumer that economies of smaller nations were virtually dominated by the American soda fountain and ice cream parlor. Vanilla became a hot item of international commerce, and there was rejoicing in several republics as the banana split became the thing an American bought when he wanted to splurge after the movies. This *de facto* ice cream imperialism reached such a stage in the late 1920's that the United States Department of Commerce was able to report that the fantastic popularity of the Eskimo Pie and other chocolate-jacketed novelties lifted the cocoa-dependent economy of Ecuador out of depression into a period of recovery. But Ecuador's respite was short-lived, for as America awoke to the Great Depression, the nickels and dimes needed for ice cream became harder and harder to shake loose.

Not only did the Depression itself have an adverse effect on the ice cream industry, but on its heels came a series of events and conditions that compounded the problem, with the net result that by 1933 the per-capita production had dropped to almost half its 1929 level. Frozen custard, or "frozen fluff" as it was then called, emerged as one major "new menace" to ice cream sales.

In 1933 the Twenty-first Amendment, repealing Prohibition, was ratified, thus setting off considerable panic in the industry, which believed that ice cream would be the major casualty in an impending national binge. Industry leaders cautioned against despair and sought out ways to rebound when beer and liquor hit the streets. In a typical pep-talk of the period the industry was asked by the editors of *The Ice Cream Review*, "Are we going to sit around and cry on each other's shoulders and assure each other that the industry will now surely go to the bow-wows?" The editors answered with a resounding No! and called for creative thinking, even going so far as to suggest new strategies ranging from billing ice cream as a "morning after" remedy to the creation of unlikely mergers in drinks containing liquor and ice cream or sherbet. Best-forgotten concoctions like "Iced Tea Tango," "The Bêrmuda Sling," and "Cherry Nectar" were unveiled to ensure ice cream's part in the upcoming booze bath. But repeal was a strong blow and sales were affected, as *The Ice Cream Review* reported sadly in late 1934: "The dime that went for soda now frequently goes for beer."

But despite booze and bad times, the industry was showing signs of recovery. While 1935 was not another 1928 saleswise, 1937 was.

Of all the ice cream boosting in the 1930's none could compare with what was coming out of Hollywood. Fred Astaire and Ginger

Rogers tied up with Borden's to promote the "Hollywood Lunch"—the noontime repast of a sandwich and a malted—and thirty thousand soda fountains carried huge cutouts of the popular couple promoting their favorite lunch together with the film *The Gay Divorcée*. Then there was the giant boost accorded by *Kid Millions* starring Eddie Cantor, which came out in 1934 and treated an estimated twenty million moviegoers to an all-color, talking picture with an extended ice cream fantasy for its finale. The scene takes place in a most extraordinary ice cream factory where a chorus of beautiful girls carries chocolate, vanilla, and strawberries to a mammoth freezer as another troop of scantily clad lovelies skates across the freezer top and still others coast about on huge slabs of Neopolitan ice cream. Stage center is young, philanthropic Cantor treating hundreds of waifs to an opulent ice cream banquet while a reformed gangster shoots cherries onto each youngster's helping from a machine gun. "Kid Millions" sodas and sundaes were a big item nationally and then-mayor Jackson of Baltimore declared a special "Ice Cream Week" in his city.

Right through the 1940's ice cream and celluloid proved to be an inspired match. On the screen the small-town soda fountain became an important setting for action in family-oriented films of the Andy Hardy genre, and the real life soda fountain was the place to go after the movie. The fountain at Schwab's Drugstore at Hollywood and Vine was Hollywood incarnate, and it was to this shrine that ambitious beauties from Middle America came to be discovered. *The Ice Cream Review* was able to boast one string of four magazine covers which went from Madeleine Carroll to Bette Davis, Claudette Colbert, and finally Dorothy Lamour—each eating ice cream.

Other breaks for ice cream just happened or were made to happen by industry leaders and innovators. President Franklin D. Roosevelt publicly confessed in 1935 that he liked to have ice cream at least once a day. Infant airlines like Pan Am, Eastern, and TWA began booking ice cream on their flights. Sales gimmicks galore appeared, ranging from the Ice Cream Telegram—a molded ice cream replica of a Western Union telegram delivered to the home—to sundaes with hot toppings to sell in the slack winter months. National dairy and ice cream associations traded on the healthy nature of ice cream, pushing it as an item high in nutrition and low in cost.

The effect of much of this promotion did not translate into sales because the nation went on war rationing and shortages sharply limited the supply. However, this did not mean that the nation was not thinking about ice cream.

CHAPTER 4

ICE CREAM AND THE MODERN ERA (1941-1971)

As early as 1789 the American soldier looked upon ice cream as something special. Historian Harry Emerson Wildes wrote that, after victory at the Battle of Fallen Timbers, Major General "Mad" Anthony Wayne and his officers sat down to a feast that ended with "dishes of ice cream, a dainty which the Army had not seen since it left the East."

Later, during the Civil War, none other than Jacob Fussell was selling ice cream to Union supply officers from his Washington plant. It was during World War I that ice cream first got official army endorsement as a "morale food," and no less a person than the Secretary of War made periodic announcements as to the availability of ice cream for American troops. So popular was ice cream that firms were founded near large domestic bases just to supply them, and the situation was such in late 1917 that the military was buying so much ice cream that it became a matter for "competitive bidding," thereby elevating it to the status of an important wartime matériel. On the home front, ice cream was officially decreed an "essential foodstuff" and none of its components were rationed within the industry.

Much later, during the 1950's, the Pentagon was prompted to come out foursquare on the side of ice cream as food for its fighting men. The policy question was raised by the late General Lewis B. "Chesty" Puller, who led the First Marine Regiment in the early months of the Korean War, when in a Patton-like gesture he announced that his marines "don't get ice cream." Puller stated that the nation's troops were being pampered and suggested "beer and whiskey" as the proper fuel for what he disdainfully termed "the ice cream and candy Marines." Organizations ranging from the Women's Christian Temperance Union to veterans' groups howled at Puller's intemperate remarks, with the general feeling being summed up by a VFW commander, who was quoted in *The New York Times* as saying, "Puller is 100 percent wrong. Ice cream doesn't make a man a sissy. It's in the American tradition." In April, 1952, shortly after the original statement, the Pentagon moved to close the debate by announcing a scheme by which ice cream would appear in Korean mess lines at least three times a week.

By the time of the war in Vietnam, military ice cream production had developed to a level of sophistication that began to seem more like a McNamara weapons system than a dessert production. Included in the ice cream arsenal was everything from a big Foremost Dairy plant near Saigon to a compact little freezer, built to military specifications for use in remote areas, that could crank out 2.5 gallons of ice cream in ten minutes. Ice cream had become such an element of military planning that a scheme to install thirty small ice cream plants in the Pleiku area by 1968 was given the martial code name of "Operation Deep Freeze."

Despite all this attention to ice cream during other periods of national stress and mobilization, none can compare with World War II, when ice cream was at once an edible symbol for good morale, for what was being fought for, and for America itself. It represented home and all that was wholesome and happy, and for that reason was what GI's wrote home about, what their pin-ups lapped from cones, and what the boy-heroes of the era's motion pictures dreamed about in their innocent dreams.

During World War II the symbol of ice cream was flashed home in all shapes, sizes, and tones as the press carried a steady diet of ice cream stories. The nation was told that for every pilot rescued from the water by an escort destroyer, aircraft carriers would give the smaller ship a twenty-gallon reward. Newspaper after newspaper carried quotes from hometown boys, like this one from the Altoona, Pennsylvania, *Tribune*:

The first thing I'm going to do when I get back in the good old USA is to find the prettiest girl in town and sit myself down to a mess of hamburgers with everything on them, and divide my time looking at her and wolfing down hamburgers with dishes of ice cream on the side.

And from the narrator in *Thirty Seconds over Tokyo*, when it first appeared in *Collier's*, we learned:

One of the things I often thought about during the tough days . . . was ice cream and apple pie. Kid stuff, but it preyed on my mind so much that I swore that if I got out to a big city I'd eat myself glassy-eyed on apple pie à la mode.

The popularity of ice cream in the armed services was such that in 1945 the navy commissioned the world's first "floating ice cream parlor" for service in the western Pacific. Built at a cost of over one million dollars, the parlor was a concrete barge capable of producing ten gallons of ice cream every seven seconds. If the floating parlor was evidence of the navy's official recognition of ice cream as a very special substance, it could not compare with the spontaneous testimonial delivered by the crew of the aircraft carrier *Lexington* when it was mortally damaged and the order was given to abandon ship. Someone remembered that the ship was carrying a large stock of ice cream and suggested that the crew get its licks in before the ship went down. Word spread quickly and the cans of ice cream were hustled up onto the carrier's flight deck. The sailors dug in and many were still eating ice cream as they scrambled down the nets cast over the side of the ship.

The navy was not alone in its ice cream bias, for each service seemed to be vying for the title of most determined admirer, most avid consumer, and most ingenious provider of ice cream. Word came via *The New York Times* in 1943 that airmen based in Britain had stumbled upon a novel means of production. These men were placing ice cream mixtures in large cans stowed in the rear gunner's compartments in B-29's where the combination of the plane's vibrations and the freezing effect of high-altitude flying yielded an especially smooth and creamy ice cream.

Not only was ice cream the symbol for all that was good in America, its absence was a symbolic reminder of all that was wrong in the world. As the clouds of war gathered during the summer of 1941, the warlords in Tokyo let it be known that ice cream was to be dispensed with. In true totalitarian style, authorities dropped the controlled price of ice cream sodas and sundaes from 20 sen to 13—a move calculated to force vendors out of business, thereby ridding the nation of a needless luxury. On the Allied side, the demands of war had produced shortages of such severity that in 1942 ice cream was banned outright in Britain. In the United States ice cream was still available to civilians, but limited by stringent rules and conditions. The industry cut itself back to twenty flavors to simplify distribution, deliveries were reduced to conserve rationed truck tires, and the government was forced to reduce the milk and sugar available for ice cream. Shortages were common and many a neighborhood soda parlor found itself without ice cream intermittently.

This era was brought to a close with the symbolic 44-foot-high, 16-foot-wide, 3,500-cubic-foot helium-filled balloon shaped like a triple-decker ice cream cone that appeared in Macy's 1945 Thanksgiving Parade. Billed as the world's largest cone, its image was carried by wirephoto to papers across the nation, signaling the end of a period in which ice cream was adored in the abstract and the beginning of a period of ice cream consumption never equalled before or after.

As rationing ended and raw materials became plentiful again, the nation started upon an unprecedented ice cream orgy. In 1946 over twenty quarts of ice cream were produced for each American. This was twice that being produced at the beginning of the war, and though recent years have seen per-capita production for all frozen desserts —ice cream, ice milk, sherbert, etc.—go over twenty quarts, there has never been a year to compare with '46 for consumption of straight ice cream.

If 1946 had been a great year for ice cream, 1947 was a very good one, and 1948 was a pretty good year. The postwar passion for ice cream had died down to a relatively steady urge, which has been relatively steady ever since. The orgy was over and the industry was settling into maturity. Significantly, the industry celebrated its centennial in 1951, one hundred years after Jacob Fussell had opted for ice cream over milk.

The biggest of the centennial events took place in June in Baltimore at the exact spot where Fussell's business had first stood. It was a festive affair of the first order. Free ice cream was dished out, and the youngsters of Baltimore mingled with hundreds of industry bigwigs and VIPs who had come to mark the occasion. Piper Laurie and Tony Curtis were crowned "Sweethearts of the Ice Cream Industry," songs were sung, proclamations were read, and Mrs. Carrie Fussell Craft, the 84-year-old daughter of Jacob Fussell, unveiled a bronze tablet in honor of her father, which still stands embedded in concrete at the corner of Hillen and Exeter streets. Though festive, it was also an intensely patriotic celebration. This tone was set by Thomas D'Alesandro, Jr., as he opined, "Ice cream, to my mind, is a symbol of American living," and was carried to its extreme by Senator Herbert R. O'Conor (D.-Md.), who called the ice cream industry something that could happen only in America, the product of individual initiative and private enterprise, an integral part of the American way of life. Topping it all off, O'Conor exhorted his listeners to "drive away from America the enemies who would destroy these things that make such a centennial possible."

If O'Conor was worried about a Communist assault on ice cream —just the kind of thing that legislators worried about in the 1950's —he could have saved his breath, for ice cream had long before been quietly adopted in the Soviet Union and was flourishing as an adored industry there. The agent for this cultural transfer was Soviet diplomat Anastas Mikoyan, who fell in love with American ice cream in the 1930's and went home to help get an industry started. Today there are seven ice cream plants in Moscow alone, and though ice cream is still uncommon in many parts of the U.S.S.R., the average Muscovite eats more ice cream than the average American.

As it turned out, the American ice cream industry was in for some upheaval, prompted, however, by the vagaries of the capitalist marketplace, not by any international Communist conspiracy. In fact, as O'Conor spoke, one of the most venerated of all ice cream institutions was being undermined.

Although the 1950's saw the industry as a whole doing well, it saw a dramatic dropoff in the population of drugstore soda fountains. According to industry sources, fountain removals had reached the rate of 1,200 a year during the early 1950's, while new stores were being planned and built without them. The problem was not lessened consumer demand but stemmed primarily from the advent of hot proprietary items like "wonder drugs," nylon-stocking racks, and—perhaps most important—exhaustive lines of cosmetics. From coast to coast beloved Pop's and Doc's opted for bottled miracles and Revlon displays over large, often unprofitable, fountains with their particular breed of "operational problems"—verbal shorthand for such specifics as gum under the counter; Hygeia-straw wrappers dipped, blown, and cemented to the ceiling; un-cost-effective soda jerks; syrup spills; the 3:15 school let-out; drugstore cowboys and rituals like "Mister, can I have another cone? Mine fell on the sidewalk." True to the laws of supply and demand, the slack was picked up elsewhere. The ice cream-marketing structure changed; ice cream consumption shifted from the fountain to the supermarket.

For lovers of good ice cream, the change was not welcome because the large chain supermarkets, which at first had accepted quality ice creams, soon began to favor what the trade has come to call "private labels." In almost every case, these brands pushed the laws of economics and dairy standards to the limit, combining low cost and high profits, low butterfat and high overrun (i.e., the air pumped into ice cream to fill the carton). America now had its ice cream *ordinaire* selling for 69 cents the half gallon. In the name of economy, people were starting to buy ice cream so infused with stabilizers and so inflated with air that it tasted like vanilla (or chocolate) Styrofoam.

The 1950's was the decade in which soda fountains fell by the wayside; the 1960's proved to be the decade in which inefficient plants (many producing marvelous ice cream) and small companies died or were absorbed in droves. U. S. Department of Agriculture figures told of 1,656 plants closing between 1957 and 1969, and as the number of firms grew smaller, entities like Foremost, Beatrice Foods, and

Sealtest grew bigger. It was a time of consolidation; the merger and conglomerate instincts were upon the land and small ice cream companies were traded around like so many Popsicle sticks.

Competition was fierce and its results were both good and bad. As the weak, airy supermarket blends became more common some manufacturers responded by creating quality ice creams to carve out a market among those who wanted superior ice cream. And as the drugstore soda fountain continued to decline, drugstores started stocking quality ice cream again, but this time to be taken home from their floor freezers. The decade also witnessed the proliferation of a new breed of ice cream parlor/store featuring high-quality ice creams. Some of these were strictly local operations, while others like Baskin-Robbins and Bresler's moved across the land.

Meanwhile, on the cultural and political fronts it was an intriguing decade for ice cream. Andy Warhol created a TV ad for Schrafft's featuring the Warhol Sundae portrayed in wavering tones of puce, magenta, chartreuse, and mauve. Three Presidents in a row expressed their love of ice cream, with Richard Nixon going so far as to have his favorite flavor, macadamia nut, flown to the mainland from the Kahala Hilton in Hawaii. Within moments of the Apollo 13 touchdown on the moon, Baskin-Robbins unveiled "Lunar Cheesecake" ice cream in its stores. Sheikh Bader Mulla of Kuwait went to California and bought an ice cream plant which was removed to his country, the Japanese figured out a way to dip ice cream in batter and deep-fry it like tempura, Sealtest successfully moved ice cream in Vienna (something like moving California wine in Paris), and the Swedish government began storing that nation's ice cream surpluses in deep underground caves—suggesting a place for survivors to start a new world order should there ever be a thermonuclear war. The era also saw ice cream thrust into a symbolic role for the first time since World War II. In 1963 *The New York Times* and other leading periodicals took to talking about the "Ice Cream Congress." The term was coined in reference to the prevalent opinion that about the only constructive thing the U. S. Congress had done during early 1963 was to repeal a 1921 law that had prohibited the sale of solid milk products in packages of smaller than a half pint in the District of Columbia. Congress, in all its might, had taken the Eskimo Pie and the Dixie Cup off the contraband list, and LBJ signed the bill into law a year later.

With this broad sweep of ice cream history behind us, it is essential that we examine the great phenomena of ice cream. After all, where would it be without the cone, the soda, the float, the sundae . . . ?

CHAPTER 5

FROZEN ASSETS

I ce cream cannot be fully appreciated in a vacuum; it must be seen in light of the many glorious forms in which it is presented to us. Scant attention has been paid to these edible institutions in the past— unfair, since many of us grew up knowing more than we wanted to know about Eli Whitney and his cotton gin (1793, right?) and nothing about the then more relevant Eskimo Pie or sundae. To rectify this educational injustice, the stories behind some of these lip-smacking institutions have been assembled. Sadly, several defy historical sleuthing and seem to have just appeared around the turn of the century. Such is the case with the ice cream sandwich, the banana split, and the float—and for lack of data the songs of their hero-inventors must go unsung. Fortunately this is not the case with the ice cream soda, the sundae, the cone, and ice cream on a stick.

The generally acknowledged creator of the ice cream soda is Robert M. Green, who fathered it in October, 1874, at the semicentennial celebration of the Franklin Institute in Philadelphia, where he was a concessionaire selling soda fountain drinks from a three-foot-square dispenser. At the beginning of the exhibition he was serving a popular drink of the time which was a mixture of sweet cream, syrup, and carbonated water. During one of the early days of the celebration, however, he ran out of cream and began substituting vanilla ice cream. The customers gave their hearty approval to the new drink as evidenced by the fact that Green, who had been averaging $6 a day with the first drink, was taking in over $600 a day for ice cream sodas by the end of the exhibition. Green went on to make a fortune as a soda manufacturer, and when he died in 1920 his will called for a large monument to be erected over his grave with the inscription: ORIGINATOR OF THE ICE CREAM SODA. His firm, Robt. M. Green and Sons, continued to flourish until after World War II, when national priorities turned against the amenity of the soda fountain.

Two years after Green's soda first appeared, it had become such a sensation that James W. Tufts, another pioneer soda fountain manufacturer, paid $50,000 for the sole right to dispense ice cream sodas at the Philadelphia Centennial which was held to commemorate the one hundredth anniversary of the Declaration of Independence. By 1893 an American magazine had heralded the ice cream soda as "the national beverage" and it was being served in every corner of the land. Similarly, by 1892 the ice cream soda had clearly moved across the Atlantic, for in that year a British analytical chemist named G. H. Dubelle had published his *Soda Fountain Beverages*, which contained a formula-laden chapter on the new drink.

In no time at all the ice cream soda became a fresh new menace for the more excitable members of the American clergy. As Stewart H. Holbrook observes in his *Lost Men of American History:* "In the author's native town of Newport, Vermont, as late as 1890, a powerful sermon was preached against 'sucking soda' and eating ice cream in drugstores on the Sabbath; and in certain Midwest towns laws were passed against the abomination, and the selling of soda water on Sunday was prohibited." Such actions begged for another fountain concoction—one that would be so construed as to skirt the intolerant Sunday blue laws legally.

The ice cream sundae emerged in the late 1890's and became extremely popular around the turn of the century. This popularity was substantially aided by laws prohibiting the sale of sodas on Sunday, and for this reason the concoction was first known as the "Sunday" or the "Soda-less Soda." The more elegant *-ae* ending probably came about when those who orated from the pulpit on the sinful soda went to work on the sacrilegious use of the name of the Sabbath for its stand-in.

As for the specific birthplace of the dish, two possibilities emerge as the most likely among many contenders. The first claim goes back to the 1890's in Evanston, Illinois (then widely known as "Chicago's Heaven" or "Heavenston"), where civic piety had reached such a state that it became the first American community to recognize and legislate against the "Sunday Soda Menace." This prompted confectioners to create Sundays so that they could do business on the Sabbath. Ironically the soda was later given a strong boost from this community when the Evanston-based Women's Christian Temperance Union (WCTU) championed it as a pleasant alternative to alcoholic drinks.

The Two Rivers, Wisconsin, claim goes back to the same era and, so the story goes, was created when a youth named George Hallauer went into Ed Berner's soda fountain for a dish of ice cream. As the ice cream was being scooped, the daring Hallauer spied a bottle of chocolate syrup normally used in sodas and asked Berner to pour some of it over his ice cream. Berner sampled the concoction and liked it enough to begin featuring "ice cream with syrup" in his shop for the same price as a dish of ice cream. The name *sundae* was given to the dish when George Giffy, an ice cream parlor proprietor in nearby Manitowoc, was forced by customer demand to serve the popular Berner concoction. Giffy was convinced that the nickel dish would put him out of business and at first served it only as a Sunday loss leader. In Manitowoc it soon became known as "the Sunday." Giffy soon found that he was making money on the dish and began advertising his "Ice Cream Sundaes," with the spelling changed so that it would lose its Sunday-only association.

Regardless of the origin, by 1900, midwestern soda-fountain supply salesmen were carrying samples of tulip-shaped "Sundae Specials." Within a few more years they would be carrying an even hotter item: the World's Fair Cornucopia, later known as the ice cream cone.

On April 28, 1954, the pooh-bahs of the cone and ice cream industries assembled in St. Louis to celebrate the golden anniversary of the ice cream cone. Under the sponsorship of the International Association of Ice Cream Manufacturers (IAICM), the two-day celebration/convention was held at the Chase Hotel, built atop the very spot where the Association had determined that the first cone had been made.

It was a festive affair honoring the late Ernest A. Hamwi, a Syrian who had come to St. Louis from Damascus in 1903. Based on the IAICM's investigations, the birth of the cone goes like this. In 1904 the St. Louis Exposition—also known as the St. Louis World's Fair and the Louisiana Purchase Exposition—opened and Hamwi obtained a concession there to sell zalabia, a crisp waferlike Persian pastry baked on a flat waffle iron and served with sugar and other sweets. Close to Hamwi's stand was an ice cream concessionaire who was selling his product in 5-and-10-cent dishes. One extremely busy day, the ice cream stand ran out of dishes and the alert Hamwi rolled one of his wafers into a cornucopia, let it cool, and put a scoop of ice cream in its mouth. The ice cream vendor was intrigued with the idea and the "World's Fair Cornucopia" was born. It was an immediate hit at the Fair.

This version of the birth of the cone was confirmed by Association research, the testimony of Hamwi's relatives, and the eyewitness account of Stephen H. Sullivan who, as a young man, had been at the Fair and witnessed the historic marriage of waffle and ice cream. The Hamwi story became the official version and news of it was carried across the land by the press.

During the very year that the cone anniversary was being celebrated, *The New York Times* carried the obituary of Italo Marchiony, an Italian immigrant who until his death had pushed to advance his claim as inventor of the cone. Ironically it was his obituary that brought him to public attention. The *Times* article, which appeared on October

29, 1954, stated that Marchiony had been making cones and selling them as early as 1896 and that he applied for a patent on his cone mold, which was issued on December 13, 1904—well before the Fair opened. The mold was described in the patent application as being "split in two like a waffle iron and producing several small round pastry cups with sloping sides."

Since the Marchiony-Hamwi row of 1954 at least two other contenders have emerged. In 1965 another *Times* obituary brought the name David Avayou into the contest. The *Times* reported that Avayou, a native of Turkey and long-time operator of a string of Atlantic City, New Jersey, ice cream shops, had long claimed to have invented the cone while working at the St. Louis Fair. He claimed that he had first seen cones in France, where ice cream was eaten from *paper* cones, and had applied the idea in edible form at the Fair. Even more recently the name of Abe Doumar has been introduced into the controversy. The Doumar claim has been advanced via a paper (and a set of photographs) written and circulated by his son, Al. The mimeographed monograph, entitled *The Saga of the Ice Cream Cone*, had an immediate impact in ice cream circles. *The Western Ice Cream News* went so far as to tout the revisionist document in a 1971 article entitled "The Ice Cream Cone Revisited." The Doumar version begins with Abe Doumar and a partner leaving their home in North Bergen, New Jersey, to hawk Holy Land souvenirs at a section of the St. Louis Exposition called the Old City of Jerusalem. At the Fair, their hottest item was a 50-cent glass paperweight filled with "Jordan River Water." According to the Doumar manuscript, the cone was born as follows: "The 'Jerusalem Streets' closed daily at 6:00 P.M. but the entertainment section stayed open until the crowds thinned. A certain waffle shop was the gathering place for the workers and concessionaires. Nightly, Abe could be found there chatting with other Syrians and Lebanese. . . . One night at the waffle stand, Abe took one of the French waffles in much the same way as he would have taken the top part of a round Syrian loaf and rolled it up to form a scoop or horn. He went next door and put some ice cream in it and told the waffle man that this would increase both the sales of waffles and his gross per unit sale. The waffle man told him to be his guest and try it out. This Abe did nightly, after 6:00 P.M. They called them Cornucopias and sold them with success. The waffle man was delighted and gave Abe one of the waffle irons to take home with him at the end of the season."

The cone gained popularity quickly. Before the Fair was over, St. Louis foundries were banging out baking molds for making the World's

Fair Cornucopia, and those who played a part in its introduction fanned out to popularize and profit from the novelty. By 1924 an estimated 245 million cones were produced. The competition to create best-seller cone designs became fierce. There were cones with a side-pouch for an extra scoop, spiral cones, cones that stood on the table, those that looked like rocket ships (or Gothic spires), and those that borrowed from turn-of-the-century bathtub designs, and "dripless" models of every description. One of these dripless cones contained an elaborate system of annular troughs while another featured a patented built-in candy catch-basin.

The decade-long flurry of intense creative activity, when inventors throughout the land dreamed of originating *the* great American cone, is half-forgotten history. Today all we are offered is a basic cake-and-sugar cone, with a few minor variations from firm to firm. The cone has become the Volkswagen of the ice cream world.

One afternoon in 1919 a young boy entered a candy store in Onawa, Iowa, and ordered an ice cream sandwich but then changed his mind and ordered a candy bar. Christian Nelson, the proprietor, asked the boy if he really knew what he wanted, to which he replied, "Sure I know—I want 'em both, but I only got a nickel." The lad's comment prompted Nelson, a Danish-born schoolteacher who ran the candy store as a sideline, to conclude that there was probably a market for a confection that combined chocolate candy with ice cream. He experimented with the idea but got nowhere because he was unable to make chocolate stick to ice cream. Weeks later he learned from a candy salesman that cocoa butter improved the clinging ability of chocolate, and he tried again. He succeeded on the first try and dubbed his chocolate-covered creation the "I-Scream Bar." The first five hundred bars were taken to the Onawa Firemen's Tournament, and all were sold.

Convinced that his was a money-making creation, Nelson applied for a patent and set out to sell it in Omaha. In 1921, after months of failure during which he was reduced to racking balls in a pool hall for $20 a week, he met an Omaha ice cream company superintendent named Russell Stover who liked the idea, and a partnership was established. Stover felt that there must be a better name for the confection than "I-Scream" and he came up with "Eskimo Pie," which he thought had more commercial appeal. The early Eskimo Pie, a small 1½-ounce stickless bar, was introduced during the summer of 1921 in Des Moines, where it was an immediate sensation. In Omaha later in the same summer, Stover and Nelson put a quarter of a million bars on the market and they were all sold within twenty-four hours. A national office was set up in Chicago and area franchises sold like so many Eskimo Pies. In less than a year over 1,500 licenses to make the pies had been issued.

By the spring of 1922 sales were averaging a million pies a day and Nelson, who was collecting $30,000 a week in royalties, was being compared to Horatio Alger's most meteoric heroes. But just as the pie took off and the money started rolling in, problems emerged, and by 1923 the company was fast going broke. Those who wanted more than their fair share of the pie were not paying royalties, and dozens of imitators freely infringed on the patent. The company was spending $4,000 a day to defend the patent. Stover became so upset by the situation that he sold his share to Nelson for $30,000 and went on to Denver where he used that money to open the first Russell Stover Candy Store. Meanwhile Nelson went looking for help and found it in R. S. Reynolds, who ran the U.S. Foil Company, which is today known as Reynolds Metals. It was a natural combination, since Reynolds's company was working around the clock to produce the gleaming foil wrappers for the Eskimo Pie, and Reynolds had told Nelson on their first meeting, "Young man, I've just made a million dollars on your idea." In 1924 they merged and Eskimo Pie became a U.S. Foil subsidiary. Thereafter, Nelson, who did not enjoy marketing chores, concentrated on research.

Although the Eskimo Pie patent was declared invalid in 1928, the company kept a large share of the market and prospers today. Latest word from its headquarters (the Eskimo Building in Richmond, Virginia) is that 750 million pies are being sold annually. There are Eskimo Pie factories in Luxembourg, England, France, and Canada, and expansion into Japan, Holland, and Australia is anticipated.

One of those who heard of Nelson's original 1919 discovery that melted chocolate could be made to adhere to ice cream was Harry Burt, a confectioner and ice cream parlor operator in Youngstown, Ohio. Burt, who had successfully marketed a lollipop called the Good Humor Sucker, was always looking for new ideas, so in 1920 he decided to try to replicate Nelson's feat. After a series of failures, late one night Burt emerged from his hardening room and presented his new ice cream bar to the family to taste. His daughter approved but thought the bar "too messy" and asked why he did not put it on a stick like his famous lollipop. Father Burt went back to the hardening room and tried a new prototype model with a stick in it. A bond was formed by ice crystals interlocking with the wooden handle and it stuck. He immediately applied for a patent on the Good Humor Ice Cream Sucker. Burt liked the name "Good Humor" because it expressed his belief that the humors of the mind were regulated by those of the palate.

After three years of waiting, the Good Humor patent had still not come through, so Burt's son, Harry, Jr., was sent to Washington with a five-gallon can of Good Humors which he carried to the Patent Office. Young Harry literally forced his evidence into the mouths of patent officials, who then agreed that it was an original idea and granted the patent.

Before the patent was issued the Burt family had begun selling Good Humors. Harry, Sr., convinced that his unique product needed unique marketing, outfitted a white truck with a set of bells (from the family bobsled) and dressed the driver in white. Soon there were a dozen of these trucks jingling around Youngstown. The Good Humor was a local success with potential as a national product, so in 1926, when Harry Burt died, all rights to the Good Humor were quickly snatched up by a group of Cleveland businessmen who formed The Good Humor Corp. of America. Their idea was to sell Good Humor franchises for a $100 down payment. A young Tennesseean, Tom Brimer, bought a group of these franchises, opened first (and prospered) in Detroit, and then went on to Chicago.

One of the early breaks for Good Humor came at the hands of mobsters. No sooner had Brimer opened his operation in Chicago in 1929 than he was issued the then-common ultimatum of "$5,000 for protection"—or else. Brimer ignored the demand but did increase the insurance on his equipment. A few days later eight Good Humor trucks were blown up. The cost was covered by insurance and the explosions put Good Humor on the front pages, with the result that sales shot up. At the end of 1929—a bad time for things financial —Brimer paid his stockholders a very impressive 25 percent dividend.

This dividend attracted the attention of a Wall Sreeet speculator named Michael J. Meehan, who had bought some shares in Brimer's operation based on a tip. Meehan was so impressed that he called Brimer to New York and after consulting with him told him to go to Cleveland and secure national rights to the Good Humor. Meehan paid close to $500,000 and acquired a 75 percent share of the company.

As it quickly evolved, the company took on a distinct caste with strong paramilitary overtones. It kept tight rein on its flotillas of spotless vans and its white-uniformed troops, with their shiny Sam Browne belts, who, in the 1930's, were required to raise their caps to women customers and issue snappy salutes to men. Such was the discipline, reported *Business Week* in 1932, that the man who said, "Good Humor ice cream" instead of the official "Ice cream Good Humor" might find himself drummed out of the corps. To stay in line, drivers studied their manual, *Making Good with Good Humor,* which not only contained stern rules but paternalistic advice—a sample: "Eat regularly at a good restaurant with your mind free from worry. . . ."

The third member of the great novelty triumvirate of the 1920's was born on a cold eureka-shouting morning in New Jersey in 1923. The inventor was Frank Epperson, who made lemonade from a specially prepared powder that he sold at an Oakland, California, amusement park. While visiting friends in New Jersey, he prepared a batch of special lemonade and inadvertently left a glass of it on a windowsill with a spoon in it. The temperature went down below zero during the night and in the morning Epperson saw the glass. He picked it up by the spoon handle and ran hot water over the glass, freeing the frozen mass. In his hand was the first Epsicle, later to be known as the Popsicle. Epperson saw immediately the potential of what he held in his hand and applied for a patent, which was granted in 1924. He was fortunate, because research conducted by *The Ice Cream Review* in 1925 revealed that a major ice cream company was experimenting with "frozen suckers" at the time of the windowsill incident, and as far back as 1872 two men doing business as Ross and Robbins sold a frozen-fruit confection on a stick, called the Hokey-Pokey.

Epperson later sold his patent to the Joe Lowe Corporation (now called Popsicle Industries), which went on to create the Twin Popsicle, Creamsicle, and other members of the Sicle family. Today three billion of these products are made each year, hammered out in more than four hundred ice cream plants.

Since the brief period during which Nelson, Burt, and Epperson sent their patent applications to Washington, there have been thousands of discoveries and inventions in the world of ice cream, but most of them have been either variations on earlier themes or technical advances (which, we shall see, are not always advances in the direction of better ice cream). Ranged alongside such creations as the cone, the ice cream soda, the sundae, and the ice-cream-on- a-stick family, they are minor. In fact, what may be the most significant development since the discovery of ice cream itself predates the discoveries covered in this chapter and goes back to the laboratory of Joseph Priestley and to an enthusiastic nineteenth-century American, John Matthews. Through them the soda fountain emerged.

CHAPTER 6

JERKS AND BUBBLE MERCHANTS

Naturally carbonated waters have forever been seeping up from the ground, offending animals and causing humans to build resorts around them. The first recorded instance of man himself carbonating water came in 1767 when Joseph Priestley, the English Unitarian divine and discoverer of oxygen, created it in his laboratory by charging water with carbonic-acid gas collected from brewery vats in Leeds. Other scientists of the era experimented with the process and then, in 1770, Swedish chemist Torbern Bergman pushed the Priestley discovery one step further by coming up with a means of producing carbonic-acid gas in commercial quantities. It remained something of a laboratory curiosity until the beginning of the next century in the United States where several forward-looking scientists began to see its commercial possibilities. Benjamin Silliman, Yale University's first professor of chemistry, began bottling and selling it around New York in 1807 and a year later Dr. Philip S. Physick, the University of Pennsylvania's first professor of surgery, added minerals to carbonated water and began selling it. By 1810 in New York City it was selling briskly as a cure for obesity.

It was not until 1832 when young John Matthews arrived in New York from England to seek his fortune that carbonated water became an industry of consequence. Matthews knew how to make carbonic-acid gas and reasoned that there was a market for such a skill in New York. He began by supplying carbonated water to New York stores, where it was consumed cold and straight, and then he began manufacturing a compact dog-house-sized apparatus for carbonating water which was soon widely known as the fountain. In time several others entered the field—including such soon-to-be-giants of the field as A.D. Puffer of Boston and John Lippincott of Philadelphia—and an industry was born to supply America with straight, unembellished seltzer.

Matthews was a soda booster of the first order and helped to popularize seltzer water in America through his own prose. He wrote in one of his catalogs: "Youth as it sips its first soda experiences the sensations of which, like the sensations of love, cannot be forgotten but cherished to the last." And in another advertisement he claimed: "... nearly all physicians are consumers of this beverage. Among the most civilized and cultivated of mankind, its consumption is rapidly increasing."

Besides contributing to the growing literature of bombastic claims for carbonated water, Matthews advanced the art of soda-making. He pioneered in new ways of producing the needed carbonic-acid gas and was the first to liberate it by mixing sulfuric acid and marble chips. Matthew's firm secured the rights to picking up the scrap marble produced by the construction of St. Patrick's Cathedral in New York, which in itself was enough to carbonate twenty-five million gallons of water.

In addition to Matthews and other manufacturers there were others who had a profound influence on the development of the fountain. One was a French immigrant who in 1825 opened the first "modern" drugstore at the corner of Sixth and Chestnut streets in Philadelphia. He was Elié Magliore Durand, a pharmacist in Napoleon's army, who correctly reasoned that the American pharmacy was ready for a new incarnation. Not only did his store have an entire glass front and feature mirrors, marble-topped counters, and mahogany display cases, but he sold cigars and featured soda water—the first to appear in a drugstore. National attention was focused on Durand's unique drugstore when Lafayette, then on a triumphal tour of America, stopped in Philadelphia to see two old friends: Joseph Bonaparte, Napoleon's brother, and Durand. This first corner drugstore in the modern sense quickly became a center for the physicians, scientists, and literati of Philadelphia who were drawn there by the combination of sparkling water and the erudite and well-connected Durand.

The next person to have seminal influence on the fountain was another Frenchman immigrating to Philadelphia. Eugène Roussel, a perfume dealer who sold soda in his shop, was the first to make the connection between soda and syrups, and in 1838 or 1839 began adding flavors to his soda. The idea spread quickly and within a few years it was common for a soda fountain owner to carry an arsenal of syrups, normally including such fashionable flavors as birch beer, pepsin, ginger, lemon, kola, cherry, sarsaparilla, champagne, and claret. The result of the perfumer's discovery was the establishment of a much larger market for carbonated water.

Next to make his mark on the fountain was Gustavus D. Dows, of Lowell, Massachusetts, the first to bring marble and other ornate touches to the normally drab apparatus of soda dispensing. In 1858 Dows first offered a small cottage-shaped combination fountain and ice shaver in a white Italian marble housing for $225. We know little more about this Cellini of the fountain than that he did a brisk business in Boston and was successful enough to exhibit his fountain in Paris.

Dows's influence was nonetheless great, for he touched off interest in the fountain as an artful object. Though Dows's small "cottage" fountains were models of cool restraint, his followers soon lapsed into the ultra-ornate, embellishing their fountains with such items as cathedral spires, Doric columns, gargoyle spigots, sphinxes, and goddesses. Often the total object was a hodgepodge of allegorical reference set in an awkward stew of decorative styles.

Finally, Robert Green came along and gave the industry the ice cream soda, which served to bring ice cream to more soda fountains. For a while it had been common for druggists to store and sell ice cream from the ice compartment of their fountains; with the advent of the ice cream soda it became all but obligatory.

In 1903 a new fountain came on the market. It did not stand against the wall but was actually a counter which one could stand behind, there to work with an array of draft arms, syrup pumps, and deep ice-packed wells containing ice cream. The first of these was installed at the Broad Street Pharmacy in Philadelphia, and within a few years hardly a town in America was without a modern fountain. Although not as ornate as earlier models, the new fountains did not skimp when it came to fine materials and elegant trappings like glass umbrella-shaped lampshades, sculpted light standards, and fine glassware. However, the counter itself was the center of attraction and many a corner druggist went into debt to compete with a white Italian marble, alabaster, black slate, or Mexican onyx fountain top.

As styles changed and technical developments came along, the fountain changed, although never radically, and by the 1920's it was a well-entrenched full-fledged American institution. It was the social, if not cultural, center of numerous small towns, and many a footnote to twentieth-century American history was created in it. For instance, over sodas at Robinson's Drugstore in Dayton, Tennessee, on May 5, 1923, a young teacher named John Thomas Scopes was persuaded by a freethinking businessman to test publicly the state's ban on teaching "theories that deny the divine creation of man." Later, after the Scopes trial began, Robinson's became the meeting place for the likes of H. L. Mencken and Clarence Darrow.

During the 1920's and into the 1930's the fountains being built were no less artful than their predecessors. Fountain-building was spurred by Prohibition as many a hotel and cocktail lounge converted their bars to fountains for the duration. In *Playboy* style, *Soda Fountain* magazine devoted its centerfold to the great new fountains of the era as they came on the line. Many were huge by any standard. In back-to-back issues of 1932 the magazine featured the fashionable 800-seat Broadmoor fountain on Madison Avenue and the gargantuan 1,200-seat fountain built into Chicago's Merchandise Mart. Others were featured for reasons of style rather than size, such as the ersatz Louis XIV fountain in the Ambassador Hotel in Los Angeles, Gilchrist's Marble Spa in Boston—as much a museum of rare alabasters and marbles as a fountain—and Bullard's in Chicago, a 97-foot-long display of ornate tilework.

The flamboyance of the new fountains was matched only by the creations being served in them. Such was the fervor of concocting in 1932 that a guest editorial by an ice cream manufacturer appeared in *Soda Fountain* protesting the "Hodge Podge at the Fountain." Alluding to such excesses as "The Flapper's Experience" and the "Chocolate Enchilada" (many of which were being promulgated in the magazine), the author said, "They disrupt my mental digestion and arise to haunt me with terrible potentialities. I freeze in vari-colored gobs of ice cream; smother in oodles of whipped cream; wallow in oozy marshmallow. Floods of syrup engulf me. I am bombarded with pecans, walnuts and peanuts. I seem to become at one with them."

The fountain continued to grow and prosper through the 1940's; at the end of that ice-cream-gorging year of 1946 the Soda Fountain Manufacturers Association in Chicago reported that there were 120,000 fountains in the nation, which during that unprecedented year had done over a billion and a quarter dollars in business. As we already know, the fountains' days of glory were limited and they exist today only in small numbers. The nation did not lose just the fountain but also an American craftsman and folk hero of considerable proportion.

Called soda clerk, dispenser, "the Professor," or soda jerk (after the practice of jerking the draft arm on the fountain), he, and occasionally she, rose and fell with the fortunes of the fountain itself. For years his stature was akin to that reserved today for the rock musician, and young men often worked months—even years—in the syrup room or as a dishwasher or broom pusher to get their chance behind the counter. Except for small out-of-the-way fountains, they worked in pairs and shared a multitude of roles—innovator, linguist, entertainer, stylist, neighborhood counselor, and, above all, concocter. They ranged in age from teenagers to the elderly, and for a long time it was as much a calling and profession as that of the druggists they often worked for. During the 1920's and into the 1930's when the great, fashionable urban streets boasted scores of fountains and ice cream parlors, there was the dream of mobility as the small-town soda jerk waited to be discovered and then installed as the new phenomenon of Broadway, Harvard Square, or downtown St. Louis. He became as much a particularly American figure as the cowboy or the lumberjack and was honored in song, poem, short story, joke, and film. His epic was a film serial of 1932 called *Fighting Blood,* starring George O'Hare as a tender but tough soda jerk who defends the honor of the innocent, becomes a champion prizefighter, and goes on to make a fortune with a drink he invents at his fountain.

The soda dispenser was not without technical advice: the first forty years of this century saw dozens of manuals and formularies created to pass along the hundreds of recipes required to be known by the professional. Aside from formulas, these handbooks gave tips on developing style and grace as a dispenser and told of the rewards waiting at the top of the profession. Said E. F. White in his *Spatula Soda Water Guide* of 1919: "Dispensing soda water as it exists today is an art and really good dispensers, either men or women, are scarce. Those at the top command good salaries. . . . [However] true excellence takes years of practice." The best could not only expect financial reward but a certain degree of fame. Men like Ralph Hersch, chief soda clerk at the Waldorf Astoria during the 1920's and soda jerk to such notables as Sir Thomas Lipton and the young Prince of Wales, and C. L. Taylor, a jerker who had risen from the ranks to become the nation's ranking expert on chocolate concoctions, enjoyed nationwide reputations for their skills. Others who did not get written up in the mainstream media were honored in "Who's Who in the Soda Fountain World," a regular feature of *Soda Fountain* magazine. Typical of the entries in that section was this one for a highly seeded Pennsylvania soda jerk, which began:

Not so many years ago a young newsboy wandered up and down the streets of Chambersburg, Pennsylvania, and every time he passed a soda fountain he looked longingly through the window and dreamed of the day he would become a soda man. Thirteen years ago that dream came true, and since then Donald Haller has made a real place for himself in the soda fountain world.

Though gone from the scene today, much of the art and science of the soda jerk has been saved through the aforementioned handbooks and trade magazines published during their reign.

As has been true of other trades and crafts, soda jerking produced its own jargon. In this case it was a particularly distinct and rich manner of speaking, which was the result of a variety of factors. It had functional uses. It was a system whereby a deadbeat leaving without paying his bill could be quickly and unobtrusively identified with the call, "Ninety-five." The fact that the boss was on his way could be signaled with the term "White Bread" or the number "Ninety-eight," and the feelings of a customer were spared as "Mary Garden" or "M. G. Cocktail" was passed on as an order for citrate of magnesia. Complex orders could be telescoped into quick calls, and the bizarre terms themselves served as memory aids. Perhaps the most important factor was that it gave the soda jerk an identity and a chance to show off for an audience. The jerker was usually a young but special person who, like the railroad man or hobo, saw his as a calling requiring an argot of its own. Unlike other jargons, however, it was meant for showing off, and for that reason there was a host of terms for almost everything. For example, an order for a cup of black coffee became such calls as "Mug of murk," "Draw one," "Leg off a pair of drawers," "In the dark," "Midnight," and "No cow."

Scholars are at a loss to pinpoint the time when the language began to take shape, but there is evidence that it was in the nineteenth century. For instance, it is known that preacher/orator Henry Ward Beecher (1813-1887) was intrigued by it and never missed a chance to test its dexterity. Beecher often told of going into a fountain and ordering two fried eggs on toast, which was relayed as the classic call, "Adam and Eve on a raft." Beecher then puckishly asked that the eggs be scrambled and without hesitation the counterman added, "And wreck 'em."

The vitality and universality of the tongue more or less followed the course of the fountain itself, appearing at its strongest from the beginning of the century through the mid-1930's. The ability to speak this national tongue—once as important a criterion for a fountain job as knowing the difference between the Tulip Sundae Dish and the Crimped Parfait—is practically nonexistent today. Its long and agonizing death began in the late 1930's when Columbia University linguistics specialist W. Bentley observed, "The craze for this sort of fountain entertainment seems to be on the wane. Indeed the practice is frowned upon in many fountains, particularly those owned or operated by large chain organizations or department stores." It was a smart, cocky tongue which at its most outlandish included calls like "Bellywash," "Maggot," "Dog," and "Graveyard Stew"—terms that apparently did not sit well with the policymakers employed by emerging giants of the Whelan/Walgreen ilk.

Luckily Bentley and several others paid attention to the now moribund tongue and recorded it. Two works are especially important: Bentley's "Linguistic Concoctions of the Soda Jerker" (*American Speech*, Vol. II, No. 1, February, 1936) and Michael Owen Jones's "Soda-Fountain, Restaurant and Tavern Calls" (*American Speech*, Vol. XLII, No. 1, February, 1967). Bentley's ambitious work was based on a year's observation in New York soda fountains, while Jones's compilation emerged from interviews with Paul Sinclair who was associated with the Jayhawk Café in Lawrence, Kansas, from the late 1930's to the mid-1960's. The old calls had held on at the Jayhawk long after they died elsewhere and Sinclair was able to recall them for Jones.

Based primarily on these two works and leaning some on others, such as H.L. Mencken's *The American Language, Supplement II* and John Lancaster Riordan's "Soda Fountain Lingo" (*California Folklore Quarterly*, Vol. IV [1945], 50-57), an abbreviated list of calls is assembled here. The presentation is made to display the vitality of that lost tongue and to offer a guide to those wishing to revive it.

ADAM'S ALE   Water

ALL THE WAY   Used when ordering chocolate (or fudge) cake with chocolate ice cream

AND ANOTHER   Coffee

A-PIE   Apple pie

BABY   Glass of milk

BARKED PIE   Pie with upper crust

BELCH WATER   Glass of seltzer

BLACK AND WHITE   Chocolate soda with vanilla ice cream or chocolate malted milk

BLACK BOTTOM   Chocolate sundae with chocolate topping

BLACK STICK   Chocolate ice cream cone

BLUE-BOTTLE   Bromo

BOTTOM   Ice cream in a drink

BREAK IT AND SHAKE IT   Put eggs in a drink or whatever

BRIDGE   Four of anything (sometimes stated, A bridge party)

BUCKET OF . . .   A large scoop

BUCKET OF HAIL   Small glass of ice

BURN   A malted milk shake, chocolate unless otherwise specified

BURN IT AND LET IT SWIM   Float

BURN ONE ALL THE WAY   Chocolate malted with chocolate ice cream

CANARY ISLAND SPECIAL   Vanilla soda with chocolate ice cream
CAT'S EYES   Tapioca
CHASE   Pass (verb)
CHICAGO   Pineapple soda, but sometimes pineapple sundae
CHOC IN   Chocolate soda
CITY JUICE   Water
CLEAN UP THE KITCHEN   Hamburger or hash
C. O. HIGHBALL   Castor oil
COFF   Coffee or coffee ice cream
COKE PIE   Coconut pie
COLD SPOT   Glass of iced tea
CONEY ISLAND CHICKEN   Frankfurter
COW JUICE   Milk
C-PIE   Cherry pie
CROWD   Three of anything (believed to have derived from "Two's
   company and three's a crowd")
DOG AND MAGGOT   Cracker and cheese
DOG or DOG BISCUIT   Cracker
DOG SOUP   Water
DRAW ONE   Cup of coffee
DROP   A sundae
DUSTY MILLER   Chocolate sundae with malted milk
ECHO   Repeat the order
EIGHTY-ONE   Glass of water
EIGHTY-SEVEN AND A HALF   Attractive female approaching.
EIGHTY-SIX   We don't have or are out of the item ordered (Jones
   suggests that this term was taken from railroad jargon, where
   it was used in telegraphy to say that a yard was unable to fill
   an order.)
EIGHTY-TWO   Two glasses of water
FIFTY-FIVE   Root beer
FIFTY-ONE   Hot chocolate
FILET   À la mode
FIRST LADY   Spare ribs
FIVE   Large glass of milk
FIX THE PUMPS   A customer with large breasts
FIZZ   Carbonated water
FLY CAKE   Raisin cake
FORTY-ONE   Lemonade
FOURTEEN   A special order, listen carefully
FREEZE ONE   Chocolate frosted

GENTLEMAN WILL TAKE A CHANCE   Hash
GEORGE EDDY   Customer who leaves no tip
GLOB   Plain sundae
GO FOR A WALK   To take out
GORP   Greedy eater
GRAVEYARD STEW   Milk toast
GROUND HOG   Hot dog
H2O · Water
HANDFUL   Five (Handful plus one, A pair, Crowd, etc., used for
   six, seven, and so forth)
HEMORRHAGE   Ketchup
HIGH YELLOW BLACK AND WHITE   Chocolate soda with vanilla
   ice cream
HOBOKEN SPECIAL   Pineapple soda with chocolate ice cream
HOLD THE HAIL   No ice
HOPS   Malted milk extract
HOT CHA   Hot chocolate (also, Hot cup and Hot top)
HOT SPOT   Tea
HOUSE BOAT   Banana split
ICE THE RICE   Rice pudding with ice cream
IN   Soda
IN THE AIR   A large glass
IN THE HAY   Strawberry milk shake
INHALE   To drink
JAVA   Coffee
JERK   An ice cream soda (This term derives from the jerking of
   the fountain lever forward to make the carbonated water spray.)
L. A.   À la mode
LOAD OF   Plate of anything
LONG COKE   Large Coke
LOOSENERS   Prunes
L-PIE   Lemon pie
LUMBER   Toothpick
M. D.   Dr. Pepper
M. G.   Dose of citrate of magnesia
MAIDEN'S DELIGHT   Cherries
MAKE IT VIRTUE   Cherry Coke
MARY GARDEN   Dose of citrate of magnesia
MODE MODE   Two scoops of ice cream with pie or cake
MOISTURE   Water
MUD   Chocolate ice cream

MYSTERY   Chocolate and vanilla sundae
NATURAL   7-Up (from the combination of 5 and 2, which is a natural in craps)
NERVOUS PUDDING   Jell-O
NINETY-EIGHT   The manager (sometimes, the assistant soda man)
NINETY-FIVE   Called when a customer is walking out without paying
NINETY-NINE   Head soda man
NO COW   Without milk
OH GEE   Orangeade
O. J.   Orange juice
ON   All sundaes
ON WHEELS   To go
ONE IN ALL THE WAY   Chocolate soda with chocolate ice cream
ONE ON THE CITY   Water
ONE ON THE COUNTRY   Buttermilk
PAIR   Two
PAIR OF DRAWERS   Two cups of coffee
PATCH   Strawberry ice cream
PEST   Assistant manager
PINK STICK   Strawberry ice cream cone
PITTSBURGH   Toast, or something, is burning
POP BOY   Soda jerk who doesn't know his business
RHINELANDER   Chocolate soda with vanilla ice cream
RIFFLE   Refill the order
SALT WATER MAN   Ice cream mixer
SAND   Sugar
SCANDAL SOUP   Tea
SCOOP   Spoon
SHAKE ONE   Milk shake, chocolate unless otherwise specified
SHOOT IT YELLOW   Lemon Coke
SHOOT ONE   Coke
SHOOT ONE FROM THE SOUTH   Especially strong Coke
SHOT   Small (6-ounce) Coke
SINKERS AND SUDS   Coffee and doughnuts
SODA CLERK   Soda man in top-rated fountain
SPLA   Whipped cream
SPLIT ONE   Banana split
SQUEEZE ONE   Orange juice
SQUIRT   Soda dispenser
STRETCH ONE   Large Coke

SUDS   Root beer
THIRTEEN   One of the big bosses is around
THIRTY-ONE   Lemonade
THROUGH GEORGIA   Chocolate syrup added
TO THE LEFT   Lemon flavor, which traditionally appeared to the
   left of the Coke syrup pump
TO THE RIGHT   Cherry flavor, which was dispensed from the right
   of the Coke
TOOLS   Table utensils
TWENTY-ONE   Limeade
TWIST IT, CHOKE IT, AND MAKE IT CACKLE   Chocolate malted with
   egg
VAN   Vanilla ice cream
VANILLA   There's a pretty girl out in front
VIRGIN COKE   Coke with cherry
WESTERN   Coke with chocolate flavor
WHITE COW   Vanilla milk shake
WHITE ONE   Small (6-ounce) milk
WHITE STICK   Vanilla cone
YUM-YUM   Sugar

Armed with this admittedly small sampling of the total vocabulary,
the challenge is putting the terms into the full rhythmic calls of the
soda jerk. With a little practice, three strawberry milk shakes become
"Shake a crowd of patch," while three large glasses of ice are, "Hail
a crowd in the air," and four chocolate sodas translate to "Jerk a bridge
through Georgia."

CHAPTER 7

THE ANATOMY OF ICE CREAM

A lthough the precise food value of ice cream depends on the value
of its component parts, it is a nutritious and caloric frozen dessert
which the federal government officially classifies as a "food." On the
average it has more fat (3 to 4 times more) and more calcium (about
15 percent more) than plain milk. Though rich in calories as a "food,"
it is relatively low in calories as a "dessert"; for example, a half-cup
of ice cream is about equal in calories to a plain cookie three inches
in diameter.

Generally speaking, ice cream is a blend of dairy products, sugar, flavoring, sometimes eggs, federally approved additives, and air. The latter "ingredient" may come as a surprise to some, but without it ice cream would be an icy lump rather than ice *cream*. Needless to say, there are limits: too much air yields a heavy, soggy mass which experts say resists flavoring. However, today's consumer need not worry about getting too little air. Within this basic framework of ingredients there is a broad range of alternative possibilities from fresh-from-the-farm flavors to synthetic ones, from sweet cream to powdered milk, and from vegetable to chemical additives.

There are almost as many commercial ice cream formulas as there are brands of ice cream. As a result any of the following may be present: sweet cream, frozen cream, plastic cream (not what it sounds like, it is actually a very rich dairy cream), whole milk, skim milk, buttermilk, butter, butter oil, nonfat dry milk, several varieties of condensed milk, evaporated milk, powdered whey solids, malted milk, cane sugar, beet sugar, sucrose, brown sugar, honey, corn sweeteners, corn syrup, corn-syrup solids, dextrose, maltose syrup, fructose, fresh eggs, frozen eggs, powdered eggs, salt, colorings, a wide variety of natural and man-made flavorings, and a long list of items known as emulsifiers and stabilizers.

The last two terms require some explanation. Stabilizers and emulsifiers are extras added to most commercial ice creams in very small quantities. Stabilizers are used to prevent ice crystals from forming in the ice cream and are of two general types: gelatins, from animal sources, and vegetables ranging from Irish moss to oat gum. Emulsifiers are a relatively new class of additives which smooth, fill, and render ice cream more whippable. Most of them derive from either natural glycerides or hexahydric alcohols, glycol, and glycol ester. Alabama prohibits their use and several other states impose stricter limits on their use than federal standards permit. Although few commercial ice creams do not have both stabilizers and emulsifiers, ice cream expert Dr. Wendell Arbuckle pointed out in his textbook *Ice Cream:* "Excellent ice cream can be made and considerable amounts are made without the use of a stabilizer or an emulsifier. Since milk and milk products contain natural stabilizing and emulsifying materials . . . mixes of certain composition and processing treatment may be stabilized by the effect of these natural materials." Emulsifiers have been a matter of some controversy and not just among natural food devotees. *Consumer Bulletin* reported in 1962 that certain ice cream emulsifiers and their chemical relatives approved by the Food and

Drug Administration had produced severe illnesses in laboratory animals when administered in large doses.

The difference between ice creams is directly tied to the quality, richness, and freshness of all of the aforementioned ingredients and the way they are blended and cared for. An "economy" ice cream will rely more heavily on dried products, air, a low percentage of milk fats (10 to 12 percent), and will normally contain the maximum amount of stabilizers and emulsifiers. A high-quality ice cream will rely on fresh whole products, be less airy, contain 16 to 20 percent milk fat, and employ additives sparingly. To the connoisseur these differences are dramatic. "Ice cream is like wine," said Gael Greene in *New York* magazine. "It ranges from the meanest *vin ordinaire* to the *grand cru* yield of the great châteaus." The analogy is perfect; however, the ice cream lover is at a monumental disadvantage over his or her cork-sniffing counterpart in that there is no detailed label or classification system to help in selecting the "right ice cream." As Dr. Arbuckle says in *Ice Cream:* "Market grades or classes have not as yet been accepted in the ice cream industry in spite of the fact that many consumers would welcome a system of market grades."

Not only is ice cream exempted from laws that require ingredient labeling, but those things that do appear on the carton are not very helpful and are occasionally deceptive. Investigative reporter Coleman McCarthy of the Washington *Post* wrote of going to an ice cream plant and asking to see where the company's top-of-the-line "hand packed" ice cream was packed (McCarthy, like all ice cream buffs, knows that hand packed is the best). McCarthy found that the "hand packed" ice cream was hand-held under the filling machine on the assembly line like most regular ice creams. Confronted with this, a company official told McCarthy, "We say 'hand packed' not 'hand dipped.' That's pretty clever, isn't it?"

The help that we do get is the federal provision that requires artificial flavors to be so noted with terms like "vanilla flavored" and "artificial vanilla added." Also, by federal law, only ice cream with eggs in it can be called "French." Although as far back as 1914 there was a movement afoot in the nation's newspapers to get ingredients listed on ice cream cartons, the organized industry has batted down every labeling proposal since then (including that of adding ice cream to the recent Fair Packaging and Labeling Act) and is still actively doing so. In the July, 1971, issue of *Up to Date,* the newsletter of the Milk Industry Foundation and the International Association of Ice Cream Manufacturers, it was reported that the two groups were working against a group of Washington law students (calling themselves "Label Inc.") who were trying to get the government to insist on lists of ingredients on *all* products. Said the newsletter: "For a number of sound reasons, such labeling is totally inappropriate for many dairy products. It's an impossible requirement for ice cream as an example, because of the many, many optional ingredients available. Moreover labeling names of some ingredients and the amounts would likely be misleading in many ways to consumers."

Second only to the long-waged war against ingredient labeling is that against sale by weight, which has also been waged for many years. The sale of ice cream by volume, of course, predominates. Federal standards require that ice cream weigh at least 4.5 pounds a gallon or it is not ice cream; however, this minimum grants considerable latitude. While homemade ice cream or truly deluxe commercial brands will weigh in at close to twice the minimum, most low-grade supermarket brands come so close to the 4.5 pound minimum that if one of these weighs in higher it is probably an indictment of your scale rather than cause for thanking the manufacturer. Today's commercial ice creams range from a robust 20 to 40 percent air to an anemic 50 percent or more, but ice cream manufacturers do not like to talk about such things as air and weight, and only a few will divulge their air percentages.

This obfuscation of the content and condition of ice cream is not just the handiwork of the industry and its powerful Washington lobby, but has government as an accomplice. Ice cream, along with a few other privileged products such as soft drinks, is exempted from ingredient labeling and other nuisances because the government has granted it what is termed "a standard of identity." This means that if a product meets those standards, it is ice cream, whether it is a superior blend of fresh ingredients or an inferior airy substance hardly worthy of the name—that is, hardly worthy of the name outside the corridors of the Food and Drug Administration. These standards were established after *twenty-four years* of give and take between government and industry, which provided lots of time for give on the part of the government, as the 38,000-page hearing record shows. As it is put quite candidly by Robert North, who heads the International Association of Ice Cream Manufacturers, "Our organization really got started fighting federal standards and now we fight to maintain them."

Besides saying that ice cream must weigh 4.5 pounds per gallon, the government says it must contain 10 percent butterfat, and goes on to permit a broad variety of ingredients including small amounts of chemical dyes, stabilizers, and emulsifiers. One of the main reasons that the industry balks at labeling is that it fears consumer reaction to the names of these federally approved additives. But the industry's concern for our sensibilities is little solace to the ice cream consumer looking for blends of fresh cream, cane sugar, and eggs rather than tetrasodium pyrophosphate, dried cheese whey, polysorbate 80, propylene glycol, seaweed derivatives, dried corn syrup, and the like. In short, we have no way of knowing who has taken the advice of the American Food Laboratories, whose ads in *Dairy and Ice Cream Field* magazine read: "Imitation Products, Real Profits."

This lack of frankness and bewildering array of additives is beginning to attract some deserving attention. *Consumer Bulletin* says, "The proverbial purchaser of a pig in a poke had nothing on the buyer of ice cream in our modern age of palatial supermarkets." The influential Gael Greene was moved to conclude, "Most ice cream sold today is sadly 'mock.'" Observed Dow Jones's *National Observer* in reviewing supermarket ice creams, ". . . it comes as close to being completely synthetic as it legally can." Within the industry *Ice Cream World* has been pushing for an overall upgrading of ice cream (even though that might spell the end of the 69-cent half gallon) and a few manufacturers have begun to brag about their dedication to "natural" and "fresh" ingredients— a trend which has others in the ice cream industry (not to mention the chemical industry) upset. Perhaps most telling were the remarks delivered in 1969 by Mrs. Virginia Knauer, Special Assistant to President Nixon for Consumer Affairs, to a group of ice cream manufacturers. She said, in part: "but to say that the consumer is confused is putting it mildly. If there's a Federal standard for it, he can't even be sure of the exact ingredients. . . . Perhaps we in the Federal government should take a new look at our entire food standards requirements." She added: "I . . . believe the consumer should be better informed on the use of food additives. The average person eats about 3½ pounds of assorted additives a year. The use of chemical food additives—for flavor, for color, and for other purposes —has increased 50 percent in the last few years, so that we now have nearly 3,000 additives on the market. How many more will we have five or 10 years from now? What are we going to add to the additives?" The industry reacted negatively to the Knauer remarks. (Carped *Dairy and Ice Cream Field:* "As far as the dairy industry is concerned, one thing remains clearly evident—housewives, including Mrs. Knauer, need more education about how ice cream is made and what it costs. . . .") Since the speech nothing has changed and the consumer is still "protected" from nasty-sounding ingredients. What is puzzling about all this is the remarkable lack of information the industry gives out. Who knows, maybe seaweed and locust-gum are better for us than the traditional ingredients, but the industry is conspicuously silent when it comes to making its case for them or letting us know that we are eating them.

Yet amid all this there are many superior ice creams on the market today—ice cream as good as has ever been served—and indications are that their number is increasing.

How then do we know which are these superior brands? The only real way is to taste them and subjectively judge, just as the wine taster must ultimately do (despite labels, in the final analysis, of course, it is the wine and not the florid label that we taste). The combination of fresh ingredients, real robust flavoring agents, high percentage of butter fat, and avoidance of such indiscretions as "heat shock" (that careless treatment of ice cream which causes globs of ice to form in reaction to jarring differences in temperature) will almost always win out. Though imperfect, price is another useful guide. Needless to say, there are some inferior ice creams over-priced and some excellent ones (often found in rural areas) which are pleasantly inexpensive. Generally, however, you pay more for such brands as Louis Sherry, Baskin-Robbins, Swensen's, Häagen-Dazs, Petersen's, Friendly's, Schrafft's, Howard Johnson's, and the like because they range from very good to great. Mrs. Anita Stickney, who heads the small northeastern chain of Deering Ice Cream Shops (which, for what it is worth, sells an ice cream that the author and his wife contend is the best they have ever tasted), says that there are many criteria for judging ice cream, but none is more important than the use of *fresh* ingredients, blended without scrimping and sped to the mouth of the consumer with care. She adds, "About the best way to tell if fresh ingredients are in the ice cream is to taste it. If an ice cream has a lot of stabilizer, for example, it simply won't taste fresh and good." What bothers Mrs. Stickney and others who produce high-quality ice cream is that much of the good ice cream is being bought by adults for themselves and their guests while a half gallon of *ersatz* ice cream is brought home for the kids. As she puts it, "I'd hate to see the day when young people can't tell the difference because they've never tasted good ice cream."

It is perhaps too much to hope for, but the revival of interest in good ice cream may help upgrade the general level and tone of American ice cream to its highest level ever. Meanwhile we can be thankful that there are superior ice creams, that there are at least some federal standards (for a long while there were none), and that the average bowl of new-fashioned ice cream is much cleaner than its old-fashioned counterpart.

A reward accruing to the ice cream researcher is that, within the moldy texts and dog-eared dairy industry periodicals which are searched, there are formulas and bits of technical derring-do leaping from the musty pages begging to be reintroduced and enjoyed anew in this more complicated era. A small selection of these discoveries follows. While these samples represent only a small fraction of the thousands of great concoctions in the literature of ice cream, it is hoped that they will be enough to help renew interest in creative concocting and expert soda jerking, whether amateur or professional.

THE CATAWBA FLIP—1903

Originally published in 1863, *The American Dispenser's Book ... Containing Choice Formulas for Making Soda Water Syrups and Fancy Drinks, or: How to Make a Soda Fountain Pay* was one of the first of many books to launch the emerging soda fountain industry into sophisticated glory. Many of these original formularies have been lost—eluding even the acquisitive grasp of the Library of Congress —and are known by reputation only. The 1903 edition of *The American Dispenser's Book ...* was found, revised, and republished in 1971 as a joint effort of Howard Johnson's and Winter House Ltd. (It sells for $1.95 in bookstores and at Howard Johnson's.) By permission, here is one formula from the 1903 (1971) edition.

1 ounce ice cream   *A sufficient quantity of*
1 ounce grape syrup   *chipped ice*
1 egg

Put all into a shaker, and mix thoroughly. Strain into a glass, fill with soda water, dust some nutmeg over the top, and serve immediately. Sells like hot cakes.

THE BANANA SKYSCRAPER—1936

The 1930's were big years for the banana split, which was especially popular among the college crowd. The "Skyscraper" was a famous variation, first served at the Penn Pharmacy near the University of Pennsylvania campus.

½ ounce syrup, any flavor
1 scoop vanilla ice cream
1 banana, quartered
1 scoop chocolate ice cream

1 ounce syrup, any flavor
Whipped cream
½ maraschino cherry

Place one-half ounce syrup in bottom of tall tulip sundae dish. Add scoop of vanilla ice cream. Quarter one ripe banana by cutting once lengthwise and once crosswise. Place quarters upright on ice cream with points of banana upward and cut side next to glass. Place scoop of chocolate ice cream on top of vanilla ice cream between pieces of banana. Cover ice cream with one ounce of syrup, then top with whipped cream and cherry.

THE WASHINGTON MONUMENT SUNDAE—1947

Let's Sell Ice Cream was the last of the great ice cream formularies. It was first published in 1947 by the Dairy Training and Merchandising Institute and featured established ice cream classics as well as original creations from specific establishments. One such house specialty was this from Weile's—a long-established parlor of note in the nation's capital.

6 different flavors of ice cream
Chocolate syrup
Raspberry syrup
Nuts in syrup

Bananas
Whipped cream
Candy decorettes (blue and red)
Whole cherries

Into a *very* tall glass put ½ ounce chocolate syrup and 1 large dipper vanilla ice cream. Add raspberry syrup and 2 or 3 slices of banana. Then continue by alternating with syrups, nuts, and ice creams of different flavors, using a total of 6 dippers of ice cream. Place a half banana upright in center on top, forming the height, and cover with plenty of whipped cream. Sprinkle with red and blue candy decorettes and 5 whole red cherries around the top edge of glass. Insert small American flags.

TRIPLE ICE CREAM BOMBE WITH FLUFFY
CHOCOLATE-NUT SAUCE—CIRCA 1960

As the fountain went into decline and concocting became less of a fountain art, the creative pendulum swung to the American kitchen where elaborate frozen desserts became more popular. Aiding the trend has been the Thursday-newspaper food section where "canned" articles on ice cream desserts appear with regularity, supplying some of the textual material that keeps supermarket ads from running over each other. A prime canner of such "articles" is the American Dairy Association, which researches them in its Chicago test kitchen and then presents them to papers replete with pictures, captions, headline, and exclusive area rights to the piece for a year. This practice, employed by other large food promotion groups, has all of the journalistic authenticity of the televised Bayer Aspirin press conference, but it has produced some good formulas, such as this one from the ADA's arsenal of "articles."

1½ cups vanilla crumbs (40 wafers)	1 pint chocolate ice cream, softened
¼ cup (½ stick) butter, melted	1 pint cherry ice cream, softened
1 pint vanilla ice cream, softened	

In a small bowl combine crumbs and butter; press evenly against bottom and sides of 6-cup mold to about ½ inch from top. Freeze. Spread vanilla ice cream evenly with back of spoon over crumb shell. Freeze. Repeat with chocolate ice cream. Freeze. Spoon in cherry to fill mold. Freeze. Unmold by dipping into warm water and turn out onto chilled plate. Makes 10 to 12 servings.

Serve with Fluffy Chocolate-Nut Sauce, which is prepared as follows:

1 package (6 ounces) semi-sweet chocolate pieces	1 cup whipping cream ½ cup chopped nuts

In a small saucepan combine semi-sweet chocolate pieces and ½ cup whipping cream. Heat over low heat, stirring constantly, until chocolate melts and mixture is smooth. Cool. Whip remaining ice cream; fold into chocolate mixture along with nuts. Yield: about 2 cups.

BANANA SPLIT PIE—1970

This is the formula for one of those luscious items that show up in the display cases of Baskin-Robbins shops. It appears in *Scoops*, the B-R dealer magazine, and won the coveted Baskin-Robbins engraved Golden Scoop for its designer, who is Martha Hunter of Columbus, Ohio.

9-*inch graham cracker pie shell*
8 *ounces fresh strawberry ice cream*
8 *ounces chocolate ice cream*
8 *ounces vanilla ice cream*
1 *banana*

Crushed pineapple
Chocolate syrup
Crushed almond bits
Maraschino cherries

Slice slightly more than half of the banana and lay slices in bottom of pie shell. Place a layer of strawberry ice cream on banana slices and smooth. Let freeze for 30 minutes. Remove from freezer and smooth layer of chocolate ice cream on top of the strawberry ice cream. Place layer of crushed pineapple on top of chocolate and let freeze for another 30 minutes. Remove from freezer and smooth on layer of vanilla ice cream. Freeze for 30 minutes. Slice rest of banana and place on top of vanilla ice cream. Dribble chocolate syrup throughout the banana slices. Spear a maraschino cherry through each banana slice. Sprinkle with 1 ounce crushed almond bits. Freeze for 30 minutes.

SUPERMONEY

A condensation of the book by

'ADAM SMITH'

CHAPTER 1

SUPERMONEY: WHAT IS IT? HOW DOES ONE GET IT?

I think it was Gertrude Stein's cousin, according to Miss Stein, who said that money is always there, but the pockets change; it is not in the same pockets after a change, and that is all there is to say about money. Well, maybe.

We have a capital market that is a great national asset, like the wheat fields of Kansas and the Grand Canyon. Some of the Yankee monopoly in technology and management techniques has been broken, gone to Wolfsburg and Milan and Toyota City. But Tokyo and Amsterdam and Frankfurt and Buenos Aires do not have that great, deep capital market, ready to handle the world's investable funds, so everybody still has to come to New York, and when they come, they bring money not only for what they buy but also for commissions, tips, and shoeshines.

What happens to the money community has some relevance to the large drifts of our society, for that community is in charge of much of the liquid wealth of the country. The money community's health affects our savings and investments, the assets of university endowments and foundations, the cost of government, and whether the pension money will be there when the employees are ready to retire.

In turn, some of the changing attitudes about work and play and people and the uses of the present are going to affect the money community and what it shepherds. Economists start with a basic definition of money: money is M_1, all the coins and currency in circulation outside the banks, plus demand deposits (i.e., checking accounts) in the banks. To this, most economists add M_2, which includes savings accounts and time deposits in banks. This can be spent almost as easily as M_1. Everyone does not cash in his savings account on the same day, but all you have to do is transfer your savings account to your checking account to get M_2 to M_1, and that's pretty easy. Some economists add short-term government bills to this, since they are also practically cash.

To this I suggest we add M_3, Supercurrency. Supercurrency is the before-and-after of a stock going public, in at book and out at market. That act of going public creates additional currency, just as switching a savings account to a checking account moves M_2 to M_1. To get M_3 to M_1, you buy at book, sell at market, peel off some stock, move it to your checking account, and presto! M_1, you are rich.

We have a somewhat skewed income pattern in American society. There are people below or outside the level of M_1. They have problems earning any money at all, because they are badly educated or not motivated or they can't get to where they have to go. They have no money to speak of, whether currency, coins, or checking accounts, and many of them are on welfare. Then we have the vast majority of people, earners of M_1. They go to work; their employers pay them; they spend the money at the grocery store, mail checks to the druggist, pay their taxes, stash a little into M_2, and struggle on. And finally we have the Supercurrency holders, the serene owners of M_3.

The poor innocents among us do not realize the impact of a superior currency around. They still think the green stuff in their wallets is money. We can all huff and puff and work overtime, but there is no way we can catch up, because there is nothing to capitalize our earnings. But Supercurrency compounds beautifully, given a bit of time. The Rockefellers may be smart, but the gap between our smartness and theirs is not equal to the difference between our currency and theirs, by several light-years.

It used to be, in the imperfectly developed securities markets of days of yore, that if a company had some assets, it could sell stock to the public. The common stock then had some claim on these assets, after the bonds and the preferred. But that style has changed and the love of assets has been left far behind; it now is the income stream—and the market's readiness to capitalize it—that matters. For instance, Uncle Harry's company will "go public," and in fact, its goal is not just to take care of Uncle Harry and Aunt Edna and that worthless hippie Cousin Eugene, but to make it to the public marketplace; the company will merge, borrow, and doll itself up to that end objective. If the company is marginal, there are years when it may have to wait, but the commissions are fat on underwriting original issues and generally there is always a hungry underwriter.

Let us make up a capricious example. There are two Park Avenue doctors swabbing childrens throats. They are doing a land-office business. Together they make $100,000 a year. (They could make even more, but taxes are high, they like to ski, and they do not like children.) With their $100,000, they pay taxes and grocery bills, and maybe put something in the savings bank.

They form Pediatricians, Inc., meet the hungry underwriter, and sell the stock to the public at thirty times earnings. Their after-tax net is $50,000, so their stock is worth $1,500,000. Now when they want to pay grocery bills, they peel off some of the $1,500,000, as much as the market can stand. They have moved into the Supercurrency class. If their auditors had made a statement of their net worth before, it would have consisted of stethoscopes, fluoroscopes, and a jar of lollipops. Now their net worth is $1,500,000—partly in cash, which they sold to the public, and the rest of their stock. Their old net worth—the sum of stethoscopes, fluoroscopes, and lollipops —came, let us say, to $10,000. Their new net worth is $1,500,000. The difference of $1,490,000 is new money to the economy, just as if the Federal Reserve Bank had printed it, and should be included in all the calculations of the money supply.

You have to have a good market to sell Pediatricians, Inc., but perhaps the example really is not so capricious. Advertising agencies consisting of three hot talents, two typewriters, four crayons, a telephone, and a line on some zippy accounts have made it into the Supercurrency class, thereby turning the $60,000 made by the participants into a multiple thereof.

In 1972 we had a good example of Supercurrency. The Levitz brothers—Ralph, Gary, Leon, and Phillip—of Pottstown, Pennsylvania, were furniture retailers whose company netted $60,000 or so a year. Then the company noticed that sales were terrific when they ran the year-end clearance sale from the warehouse: furniture right in the carton, cash on the barrelhead, 20 percent off. The idea was very successful, they added more warehouses, and the company went public—in fact, superpublic. At one point, it was selling for seventeen times its book value, one hundred times its earnings, and Ralph, Gary, Leon, and Phillip had banked $33 million of public money for their stock, and they still held $300 million worth. (History will tell, of course, whether selling furniture from warehouses is really worth 100 times earnings, but the $33 million is safely in the bank.)

Paul Newman is going public, along with Shirley MacLaine and Sidney Poitier. That is not the end of the line by any means.

I have an ambivalent attitude toward this. On the one hand, there is no question that hungry underwriters have sold lots of junk to the public. Should they be policed in some way? We get then to the other hand. In almost no other country do small enterprises have such easy access to capital, and easy access to the public markets is part of this, a great national asset. *Caveat emptor*: the odds are better than at the track. Small enterprises keep the Establishment on its toes, and sometimes even grow into great enterprises.

Does Mrs. Rudkin bake good bread at her home in Fairfield, Connecticut? She does indeed. But after her business expands into a bakery called Pepperidge Farm, the Rudkins want to trade it in for the real money (Supercurrency brings more than cash almost every time), so they trade the bakery for $28 million of Campbell's Soup, very good Supercurrency. With the broad stock exchange listing of Campbell's Soup, they can peel off some, turn it into cash, diversify, and start behaving like rich people. In fact, you can go through the Supercurrency-history exercise right in the kitchen: you can see the food families' trading right up there on the label, because usually the family name was well enough known that the Supercurrency company kept its own identity to a quiet little line somewhere. Is there some Hellmann's mayonnaise? Obviously there once were some Hellmanns in the mayonnaise business: that is not a name an ad agency would think up. The Supercurrency ultimately turned up as CPS, formerly Corn Products, via Best Foods. Dannon is not a family name, but Isaac Carasso, a Spanish businessman, named his product after his son Daniel—hence Danone, later Anglicized to Dannon. At some point Dannon was traded in for Beatrice Foods, a billion-dollar dairy Supercurrency. Is there some Breakstone cottage cheese? The Supercurrency is Kraft.

Finally, all of the following were good businesses on their own, and they all have something in common: Avis Rent a Car, Cannon Electric, Federal Electric, Sheraton Hotels, Howard W. Sams (a publisher), Continental Baking, Grinnell Corporation (pipes and pipe fittings), Hartford Fire Insurance Company (a major insurer), Rayonier, Pennsylvania Glass Sand, Southern Wood Preserving Company, and Levitt and Sons, the famous builders of Levittowns. What do all of these thriving enterprises have in common? Their owners all traded up for the *same* Supercurrency, ITT, formerly International Telephone and Telegraph, which has been the prime example of how a Supercurrency company uses its premium currency to buy what it stalks.

Corporations sell stock to retire debt, to build new plants, or what have you. That is not Supercurrency, because on the books of the company the money received turns into the new plant. But when the Selling Stockholders dispense of their equity, they move into the Supercurrency class, at capital-gains rates.

There are other ways of compounding wealth, usually involving borrowing on the asset—the real property or the oil in the ground—and buying some more. But the most easily accessible form is Supercurrency, obtained as close to the source as possible. That is your number, M3, and if riches are your goal, at least you know where they are.

While there are other forms of wealth, Supercurrency is the superior currency of the country, because if they make a profit, even the oil deals and the real estate deals and the farm deals will be brought to market and sold at a multiple of their earnings so that their participants can get the real stuff, traded paper.

Obviously, the laws and mechanisms of the country are built around the protection not just of currency but also of Supercurrency. It would not be the same society—whichever way you like it—without the structure and mechanisms that support the currencies, both Super and regular. Yet a very short time ago, the structure and mechanisms went through some perilous times. The shaking of the structure was a much nearer thing than anyone realizes—anyone except those who were in at the countdown—and there are lessons to be learned.

The structure swayed perilously the weekend the United States almost ran out of money. Most investors turn only to the stock-market page, but the stock market does not exist all by itself. There are also bond markets, commercial-paper markets, commodity markets, a banking system, and so on. None of these is self-contained: money does flow and the markets are interdependent. Any disaster or near disaster brings a search for villains, who fleeced the lambs, and so on. In the Crunch, the villains were very widely dispersed; in fact, the crisis point came from a rather broad sweep of history.

CHAPTER 2

THE DAY THE MUSIC ALMOST DIED—PART ONE

Everybody could tell, that June weekend in 1970, that a Crunch was on: it was difficult for small borrowers to breathe, and their ribs hurt. If you wanted to buy a $40,000 house, five years previous you might have put up $6,000 in cash and paid 5.5 percent for twenty-five years. Now, in the late spring of 1970, the savings and loan wanted

$15,000 down and 8.5 percent, if it would make the loan at all, and some did not. Some smaller businesses were even worse off. They had been, let us say, used to taking out a bank loan for taxes, and then repaying that loan over a year. Now they were told the loan would be cut down or out, and if they went to other banks, the other banks said they weren't taking any new clients. That meant the small borrower was out on the street, hustling for money wherever he could find it.

Interest rates were at their highest levels in a *hundred years.* The prime lending rate at banks had been as high as 8.5 percent, and some said there was no reason it could not go to 10 or 12 or 15 percent. If the prime rate is at 15 percent, that is such a new ball game that the Dow Jones averages could nearly be predicted to sell at 002.

There are bankers around who say there was no crisis in 1970; you could always get money if you wanted it—you might have to pay 20 percent interest for it, that's all. Or maybe take it in blocked dinars. As that June weekend begins to fade, the crisis seems less acute. By the time of the annual report of the Fed's Board of Governors, the language applied to the events had changed from "crisis" to "serious uncertainties."

The liquidity crisis of that time didn't have much to do with the inability of buyers and sellers of stock to find each other and touch fingertips. Liquidity in this case meant usable funds, borrowable funds for American business. A decade ago nobody could imagine that money in the United States was finite. It was like all the rest of our natural resources: there was plenty for everybody, you could get what you needed, and you certainly didn't have to worry about running out. The discovery that the supply of money was limited seems to have had a profound social effect as well, for, as with middle age, it does mean that you may be able to think of what you would like to do, but that does not mean you get to do it.

There were two popular off-the-top-of-the-head rationales for the Crunch, and both of them were true. One was that nobody had bothered to finance the Vietnam war. There were no major increased taxes to pay for Vietnam, for reasons well spelled out by political commentators. It was not supposed to last that long, and increased taxes would endanger the Great Society program. The second reason was "inflation psychology," which meant that you had better buy it today, because tomorrow it, whatever it might be, would cost more. Right after the summer the money almost ran out, I had a long talk with the treasurer of the telephone company in one of our major industrial states. The telephone company has excellent credit, and even in a Crunch it can borrow. This particular treasurer—and his appropriate committee —committed his company to pay more than 9 percent for twenty years. If he had waited through the crisis, it might have cost his company only 8 percent or even less. One percent on many millions of dollars can buy a lot of telephones. I wanted to know if he felt dumb, though I didn't put the question quite so baldly. He said he didn't, and he had worked out a nice rationale. He had had a leeway of only six or eight months, he said, in which to borrow the money.

"The rates were eight percent, so I decided to wait a bit," he said. "Then they went to eight and a half. That is historically very high, so I wanted to wait until the rate came back to eight. Then the rates were nine—more than nine—and there was talk that they might go to ten or twelve. We needed the money, and I had run out of time. So I had to do it."

It still sounded dumb to me, but then I have never had to borrow money for the telephone company, and quarterbacking is easier from the grandstand, especially after the game is over.

The story of what happened can be seen from the Federal Reserve table called *Funds Raised, Nonfinancial Sectors.* Vietnam and inflation were indeed the causes of the Crunch, but from the Federal Reserve's figures we can see that the stage was well set, for the demand for credit had increased by more than twice the savings that could supply it.

In the early sixties, the demands for money were more or less consistent with the growth of personal and corporate savings. But by 1964 the demands for credit by business and by state and local governments had begun to increase. After a period of fairly slow economic growth, business began to spend for new capacity and new technology. By 1965 corporations had more than doubled their 1960 borrowing, from $14 billion to $29.6 billion. State and local governments increased their borrowing 40 percent. And in consumer credit and mortgage, individuals and households increased their borrowing 72 percent.

All this was against an increase in the gross national product of 36 percent and in personal savings of 40 percent. Against that 40 percent, the total of credit demands by all borrowers moved up 90 percent. So that even before the escalation in the Vietnam war, much of the flexibility in the credit system had been lost. The demand for funds was already pushing the available supply.

Then between 1965 and 1968 the Federal government increased its expenditures by *$60 billion*—about half of it related to defense—without raising the taxes to cover this burst of spending. In 1966 the Federal Reserve made one stab at an anti-inflationary policy by restricting the money supply; then, its fingertips burned by the brief "crunch" of that year, during the two years following it let loose a $24 billion addition to the money supply. In mid-1968 Congress passed a 10 percent income surcharge, which was supposed to take the steam out of the economy that had been supplied by all that new money.

By that time the momentum of inflation had really taken hold. Much of the borrowing was short-term, because the borrower didn't want to commit himself to a lifetime of high interest rates. It was a dumb corporate treasurer who had not borrowed at 4.5 percent back in 1964. Besides, borrowing was a way to boost the earnings per share of the stock, and that was what the stock market wanted—increased earnings per share. So off to the market they went, better late than never. And individuals did not cut back on spending as much as all the econometric models suggested they would, because they had no choice. Their spending was more for the essentials of life than for the so-called discretionary items. The cost of those essentials increased faster than personal income. If you wanted a house, the mortgage cost that much more—if indeed you could get a mortgage—and if you needed a doctor or a hospital, that cost a lot more. The state and local governments had to meet increases in teachers' salaries, in paving contracts, and so on.

American business, impressed with the ugliness of cash as an asset, increased its borrowing to $47.9 billion in 1969, almost three and a half times the 1960 total. The banks had about loaned out the amounts they were permitted to by the Fed; they went to Europe and borrowed Eurodollars—dollars that had been generated abroad or taken abroad—and then reloaned them here.

The Federal Reserve figured inflation could be cut back if borrowing could be cut back, and it began to restrict the borrowing of its associate banks. It even moved to cut off the borrowing of Eurodollars. But the lead time of the corporations did not permit them to turn around so quickly. The money was committed to be spent. So the corporations, in aggregate, borrowed up full at the banks, edged out of the long-term debt market, and began to sign IOU's: short-term commercial paper.

Some say the Federal Reserve indirectly encouraged the growth of this paper by forbidding banks to pay the going interest rate on large time deposits. Some say the banks steered their clients into paper because they couldn't accommodate them; certainly the dealers in that paper sold their products aggressively. Commercial paper is just that: an IOU. It says that Sears Roebuck or Chrysler or what-have-you promises to pay you, in thirty or sixty or ninety days, the face amount. Most commercial paper does not have a maturity of more than ninety days, and much of it matures in under thirty days. The buyers of commercial paper are big buyers: the smallest customary denomination is $25,000, and some pieces run $1 million. Some pension funds and banks buy commercial paper, but most often the buyers are corporate treasurers who want to put money to work for just a few days at a higher rate than Treasury bills and similar instruments will yield.

A company treasurer or a country banker buying commercial paper expects to get his money back in a few days, plus interest. If the U.S. Treasury will pay him 7 percent for those days, he may get 8.5 percent from commercial paper. Obviously he believes the commercial paper is a good risk, or he could not take a chance with all that money for only a few days' worth of extra interest. Traditionally, a company is supposed to have bank credit equal to its outstanding commercial paper. After the debacle, or near debacle, questions were asked and lawsuits filed: how come the credit behind the paper hadn't been thoroughly analyzed? The answer will not be found here; the question is part of the feeling of the time. But obviously the buyers once thought all the paper was good; they were wrong about a small part of it; then for a time, they thought no paper was good.

With the banks tight and their ability to sell bonds limited, American corporations sold IOU's, commercial paper. From 1966 to 1970, the amount of outstanding commercial paper more than quadrupled, from $9 billion to nearly $40 billion. For the twelve months up to the June Crunch weekend, it had doubled.

The lack of liquidity in the economy had its roots half a decade back. Much of the borrowing done by business had been under at least some assumptions that sales would be good, but they were disappointing. The flow of cash in corporations was 10 to 30 percent below expectations, and that in itself built up the necessity to borrow.

By June of 1970 the sixth largest enterprise in the United States and the largest railroad in the country, the Penn Central, was busted, busted enough to be very slow in paying the conductors on its trains. It was having trouble renewing, or rolling over, its maturing commercial paper, and it had $200 million outstanding. For weeks, the Penn Central's bankers had worked night and day on an emergency loan to be guaranteed by the U.S. government. The Administration lobbied in Congress for the loan. On Friday, June 19, the bankers were so confident that they gathered in the Northwest Conference Room on the tenth floor of the Federal Reserve Bank of New York to sign the papers as soon as word came from Washington that the government guarantee would be in effect. But the word did not come.

Congressional disapproval had been hardening. The $200-million loan, said Wright Patman, chairman of the House Banking Committee, would be "only the beginning of the welfare program for this giant corporation." It would risk "hundreds of millions of the taxpayers' money in a highly questionable scheme." (Later, Patman told Congress that the Administration had asked the Federal Reserve Bank of New York to check out the loan; the Bank replied that the loan "would provide no significant relief to the Company," that it "could not recommend approval of the proposed loan on the basis of factors normally considered in appraising credit risks," and that it did not see how the taxpayers would ever get their money back. But the Administration, said Patman, did not bother to give Congress that report when it was lobbying.)

Shortly before 5 P.M., a government official, the intended guarantor of the loan, told the assembled bankers in New York that there would be no approval.

"The bankers who had been working on the project so intensely," said the notes of a later Federal Reserve meeting, "were shell-shocked but not resentful. They left our building and went to the uptown office of the First National City Bank, where they tried to figure out how they could protect themselves."

In Philadelphia, the Penn Central's lawyers began to draw up the bankruptcy papers; they would rather, they reasoned, march in orderly under a white flag than have some creditor put them into bankruptcy. The Penn Central's chairman, Paul Gorman, and three of his directors went to Washington to see Patman on Saturday. Patman had not changed his mind. The directors went back to Philadelphia. The Penn Central's board met again in Philadelphia on Sunday and threw in the towel; one of the lawyers drove to the suburban home of U.S. District Judge C. William Kraft, Jr., with the papers. Sunday is always a good day to go busted.

Once the Penn Central had handed over the papers, it did not have to pay its debts, except under reorganization. Most important for this story, it would not pay the holders of its IOU's, its commercial paper. They could paper their bathrooms with all $200 million. The corporate treasurers who had thought they would put money out at a better rate than Treasury bills would get back neither interest nor principal, at least not without lengthy lawsuits. They would lose *all* the money they had put up. The Walt Disney Corporation lost $1.5 million that way, American Express $4.8 million, Homestake Mining $1 million, and so on. (The paper holders eventually sued everybody in sight, and some settled for a fractional reimbursement from the dealers.)

There were some other very large American corporations also in a state of gasping illiquidity. It is not polite to name names, but you could start with Lockheed, Chrysler, TWA, Pan American, and LTV. In particular, two finance companies, Chrysler Financial and Commercial Credit, had commercial paper out far in excess of their approved credit at banks.

The worriers began to see the following script: the holders of the Penn Central's commercial paper would be busy papering the bathroom and calling their lawyers. Like Mark Twain's cat, who sat on a hot stove, and then would not sit on any kind of stove, hot or cold, investors would not exactly be reaching for more commercial paper. The commercial paper from other companies had short maturity: some would come up Monday, some Tuesday, and so on.

There was $40 billion of commercial paper outstanding, and if nobody was to sit on that particular stove again, where would $40 billion come from as the notes matured, day by day? Not from the stock market: the stock market was flat on its back, and anyway, it takes time to register to sell stock. Not from the bond market: the bond market was in disarray, and the bond dealers were still working off inventories from weeks previous. Not from the banks: the banks were all loaned out.

"I was on a summer weekend in Cape Cod," says the economist of a major New York bank. "I went to town to get the paper, and I just stood there reading it in the grocery store. I could see the U.S. banking system might have to pick up an extra fifteen billion dollars, and it just didn't have it to give. I remember thinking to myself, *This could be another Credit Anstalt.*"

The Credit Anstalt was the Austrian bank that failed in 1931, and turned out to be the first domino to fall; it triggered a whole series of bank failures and helped to bring on the world-wide depression.

Wasn't that a bit extreme? I asked the senior economist.

"The sixth biggest enterprise in the United States goes broke," he said, "but it's a railroad. There are special provisions for railroads, left from the 1930's; they keep operating. But you let half a dozen major U.S. companies default on their short-term debts, their creditors throw them into the courts, their suppliers and contractors are afraid they won't get paid and *they* rush for the courts, and meanwhile everybody tightens up and cuts operations and starts laying off people. You could have a real panic that would snowball, a panic that would feed on itself. It's happened in this country before."

But, I said, in this day and age, that wasn't likely.

"You've never lived through a panic," he said.

But there is a lender of last resort; that is why we have a Federal Reserve system. Congress, by the Constitution, can create money, and Congress gave that money-printing function to the Federal Reserve in 1913, when that agency was created. The Fed reports to Congress once a year; it is an independent agency; its seven governors are appointed by the President for terms of fourteen years apiece. This is not the place for the college-freshman-economics-course explanation for the mechanics of the working of the Fed. Suffice it to say it can turn money on and off. By the way it turns the faucet, the Fed hopes to speed up the economy when it slows down, and slow down the economy when it gets overheated. It used to believe that if the cost of money went up, buyers would drop away. At this point, however, the Fed was working more with monetary aggregates, which one Fed official described as "roller-skating on three wheels—it will work, but you need new body movements."

There is a philosophy that the way to cure inflation is to get everybody to stop reaching out. You want them to curl up in a fetal position and stop breathing for a while; that cures enthusiasm. Then things cool off. The Fed had had the money valve largely off, because inflation was certainly roaring. The Fed itself had been criticized: for cutting off money too abruptly in 1966, for increasing it too fast in 1967 and early 1968.

Fed meetings are not public, but the two possible positions were fairly clear. The first position said thus: only *we* can print money. Once we print it, we can't control how it is used. Printing money has to be part of an overall plan, involving foreign balances, taxes, and so on. Our Official Policy is one of restraint, and if we depart from it, not only are we not able to control where the money goes, but the news of a sudden change might have a reverse effect and scare everybody to death.

The second possible position for a Fed governor was to worry about Monday morning, and to treat the weekend as something special in history. The issuers of commercial paper would not be able to sell any more; they would go to their banks; the banks would say, sorry; the issuers would be brought into the courts by the people to whom they owed money; the issuers would start to lay off people and cut back operations; everybody could stake out a corner for an apple stand, if the corner wasn't already occupied by a fried-chicken stand. The notes of a Fed official to a Fed meeting later that summer uses this language: "inability of the issuers to pay their paper at maturity would have dire consequences for the issuers, the commercial paper market, other financial markets, and the banking system." *Dire consequences* is a phrase not used lightly.

The Monday-morning worriers won.

Alfred Hayes, the president of the Federal Reserve Bank of New York, was in London; acting for him was a sixty-three-year-old former Wall Street lawyer, William Treiber, now the executive vice-president of the New York Fed. Treiber is a pleasant, white-haired type, given to conservative three-piece suits, just as you would expect from a Columbia College, Columbia Law, Sullivan and Cromwell executive vice-president of a Federal Reserve bank. Treiber left the massive Federal Reserve building, modeled after the Strozzi Palace in Florence, at the same time the shell-shocked Penn Central bankers went up to the First National City's offices. Treiber drove to his weekend home, a two-hundred-year-old farmhouse in East Winchester, Connecticut. He called the First National City Bank; at 10:30 P.M., the bankers were all still there and still in a state of shock.

Treiber got on the phone. Over the weekend, that was all he did. He moved a card table with a phone on it into the dining room of his farmhouse. He talked to Arthur Burns, chairman of the Board of Governors and captain of the Monday-morning worriers. He called the head of every major bank in New York at home, or the next in command if the chief executive couldn't be found. (David Rockefeller of the Chase Manhattan was on his boat, off Bar Harbor, Maine.) Treiber couldn't leave his card table, except briefly, because the farmhouse only had one line, and frequently he had to leave word. His daughter took a picture of "Daddy's weekend office." In the dry language in which these things are reported, it was said the bankers were told that "the use of the discount window would be appropriate," which does not mean everyone got a cut rate.

Sunday night Treiber flew to Washington; the Fed's Board of Governors met Monday at 9 A.M. By Monday night, phone calls had gone out through the twelve Federal Reserve banks to every bank in the system—not just to big city banks, but to small-town banks all over the country. The Fed's index finger was beginning to bleed from all the dialing. The message was the same: if anybody comes into your bank and wants a loan, *give it to him*. Then if you're all loaned out, come to us and we'll see that you have the money.

I began to speculate: What would have happened if teen-agers tied up the home phones? Or if the Fed's own Paul Revere were unable to get through? The Penn Central's lawyers are driving through suburban Philadelphia looking for the judge's house, nervously thumbing the paper, and the line is busy.

I could see the following scene. After all, school was out.

"Hello, Mr. _____, please."

"This is Timmy."

"Hello, Timmy, can I speak to your father?"

"No."

"Please, Timmy, it's important."

"No."

"Why can't I speak to your father?"

"He's not here."

"Where is he?"

"He's outside practicing his golf swing."

"Could you go get him?"

"No."

"Why can't you go get him?"

"I'm not allowed to leave the kitchen until I finish my lunch."

"This time it's all right. I'll fix it for you, I promise."

"I have to finish my lunch."

"How long will it take to finish your lunch?"

"I don't know. I don't like carrots. But I have to eat them."

"Could you call him from where you are?"

"No."

"Is anybody else home?"

"Yes."

"Who? Let me talk to them."

"Arthur can't talk."

"Who can't talk? Why can't they talk?"

"He's a dog."

"Timmy, listen closely. I want you to *put the carrots in Arthur's dish*, and then go get your father."

"They'll find out. Arthur doesn't eat carrots."

"Just do it. Listen, Timmy, would you like a new football helmet?

Would you like an autographed picture of Arthur Burns? *In uniform?*"

"Yes."

"Good boy. Just do what I say."

After an appropriate interval, the banker makes it to the phone. "Hello."

"Rodney, this is the Federal Reserve calling. I'm sure you know why."

"Uh, I think my kid got the message garbled, he said you said to put the carrots in the dog's dish."

The Fed official says, sorry to call him at home, but that if anybody wanders into his bank, dispense money. Rodney thanks him and reminds him: "Don't forget the autographed picture of Arthur Burns."

On Monday, June 22, Arthur Burns, the Fed's pipe-smoking chairman, pressed not only for the additional reserves but to do away with Regulation Q, which would permit the banks to take in large short-term time deposits. The Fed had taken those large time deposits away from the banks as an anti-inflation move. Now it decided to worry about inflation some other time, and gave them back. After an all-day debate, Burns won his point.

From that point on, events followed the script. The Penn Central went broke, but no one else did. Six billion dollars fell away from the commercial paper market, as buyers recoiled in horror. The companies that were going to sell the commercial paper and were unable to do so went to their banks and begged for money. The banks went to the Fed, the Fed loaned them the money, and the banks reloaned the money to the would-be insurers of IOU's. In one July week alone, the banks lined up for $1,700,000 at the Fed window. More than $2,000,000,000 in bank money went to companies whose commercial paper was coming due. Not only that, with Regulation Q wafted away, the banks took in $10,000,000,000—ten billion dollars—in time deposits, just in case anybody needed more money. Some of the bankers who had stayed awake that summer, fretting that if anybody added up the losses in their bond portfolios they might think the bank was busted, were stunned to find that they were having a very good year.

The Fed was pleased. Not only had there not been a crisis, but the money had been recycled. It had been there as debts before and it was still there; now, however, it was owed to banks, not to individual borrowers, and with the banks, the borrowers could have some breathing room to sit down and work repayments out in an orderly way. And there was no great inflationary addition to the supply of money. Gradually, there began to be faint, faint cheers for the Fed's actions from all of the seventeen people who understood them. A New York banker said the Fed had done "a classic job." *Business Week* said "a wrong move by the Fed could have allowed Penn Central's financial distress to infect the nation's financial system . . . touching off a chain reaction of corporate failures."

As the Crunch abated, the bankers and the Fed performed the equivalent of the pro football touchdown ritual: lots of fanny-patting, jumping up and down, and hugging the ball-carrier. I can see it all in a ghostly, silent instant replay, except that the stadium is empty. It is empty because nobody knows it happened—not only Mr. and Mrs. America, who think that the Fed is the FBI, but all the readers of those papers that carry financial pages. It is all too abstract, and too hard to explain. A razzle-dazzle touchdown in absolute silence.

William Treiber's September 10 report to New York Fed directors contained some sense of satisfaction. "The commercial paper market was in a near crisis situation," he said. "The banks stepped into the breach promptly to provide credit . . . aided, of course, by . . . the expressed desire of the Federal Reserve to assist the banks in avoiding a crisis. The commercial paper market is now calm."

Treiber had to add a final sentence. "It was an interesting," he said, "at times, a highly *exciting* experience."

I have to figure the crisis of June 19-23, 1970, as a very near miss, because the normal language of banks—and especially of the Fed —is dry, abstract, full of passive tenses, and unemotional. Things are not supposed to be "interesting" in the banking business, and when they become "highly *exciting*," I begin to hold my breath.

Something else bothered me. Why was everybody cheering the Fed? Did not some people say that the Fed's stop-go policies had helped *cause* the Crunch? Was it not their job to do just what they did? I asked the Fed.

"It seems to me," I said, "that the Fed did just what it should. That is why we have a Fed, so we do not have the panics that we had in 1873 and 1893 and 1907, with banks failing and markets collapsing and everybody out of work. It's like having a fire. You call the fire department."

The Fed officer leapt at the metaphor. I guess Fed officers are so used to saying, "The discount window might be appropriate," that a metaphor has seductive charm for them.

"Exactly!" said the Fed officer. "Exactly! The fire department! *This never happened before!* And it worked! The engines, and the hoses, and the water pressure, and the foam—it works! It all works!"

And why is this drama relevant to understanding what went wrong in the stock market?

Any investor has a choice: he can buy a stock or he can buy a bond. If bonds are yielding 2 percent, he may well figure he can do better in the stock market. If bonds are yielding 10 percent, he may just settle for that. If you are running a pension fund, and all you need to supply the pensions is a return of 4.5 percent, and you can buy a telephone bond at 9 percent, you buy the telephone bond and play golf until you retire, for your job is over. When there isn't enough credit, people will bid up the price of money, and telephone bonds will sell at 9 percent.

Then the money that could go into stocks will go into bonds instead. Or stockholders—professional and individual—will sell their stocks and buy bonds. And that means that everybody who bought an 8 percent telephone bond at 100 finds it marked down to 97 when there is a new telephone bond at 100 that yields 9 percent. When there is a 9 percent telephone bond, everybody that owns an *old* bond, even a week old, has a loss.

That is a description of an uneasy bond market, and why it is bad for the stock market. If you add to that a real Crunch, with the possibility of major companies not paying their bills and their payrolls, nobody will buy stocks. Maybe some other time, maybe they will be cheaper later: maybe we will get a chance to buy Chrysler at the 1933 prices, if there still is a Chrysler. If you add to that just a few rumors of a bank holiday—well, it does something to the atmosphere.

All the banks have been reminded of the name, address, and telephone number of the lender of last resort, and all the bankers' children know that if the phone rings on Sunday and it is a man from the Fed sounding breathless, it is perfectly okay to go outside and get Daddy without finishing your lunch.

CHAPTER 3

THE DAY THE MUSIC ALMOST DIED—PART TWO

If there was a lesson learned from the Crunch, it was that illiquidity snuffs out a stock market. People who need money bid the price up, and then bond yields go up, and then other people take their money out of the market and buy bonds, and the market goes down. Nice and simple. So you have to look one page past where your stocks are listed, to the bond page. If well-rated bonds are yielding 7.5 percent, that is an amber light. If they are at 8 or 8.5 percent, you can start to get nervous. By the time they get to 9 percent, it is probably too late.

There were people, respectable people, who thought the bear market was going to last for five years or ten years or maybe forever. That was how long it was going to take to get liquidity restored. Corporations needed $50 billion, and states and cities and the Federal government—well, they would never be through with the money demands at all. But once the cycle was cracked, the treasurers—both public and corporate—who once had hurried to market because next week the rate would be higher, held off. Now if they simply waited a month or two, they were rewarded with lower rates, and that brought back the more normal supply-and-demand flow.

But the liquidity crunch was not the only near miss in the Big Bear. Wall Street itself almost collapsed from its own mismanagement. It is possible to write a near-miss, equally hair-raising script about the last day of American capitalism, and focus it on good old Wall Street, which itself had been so used to judging the rest of corporate life.

The middle sixties was a euphoric period for the broker types. It should be said right away that some people kept their houses in order and did not get their names into the paper, and both of them are still happy. One hundred and twenty firms went out of business.

The center of this drama is a piece of paper, the stock certificate. In the old days, under the buttonwood tree, one Knickerbocker would hand over the coins and the other would hold forth the piece of paper. That was in a time when all the trading was over by morning-coffee time. A century and a half later, the mechanism was still the same.

The people who got into trouble were the so-called retail brokerage houses. They dealt with the public, and the public was in the market. The name of the game was "production," which meant "writing tickets." To do that you opened a new branch office, hired some new salesmen—bored housewives, failed accountants, dropout aluminum-pan salesmen—and told them to call everybody they knew with the hot new stock ideas. The ex-aluminum-pan salesman's Aunt Mary and his lodge brothers opened accounts, the production went up, and the tickets went up. That was where the trouble started. For Wall Street, by and large, was like a beautiful, fan-tailed, Detroit Belchfire Eight with leather seats, remote-control windows, color TV in the back seat, and under the hood—six perspiring squirrels running on a treadmill. The branch offices were equipped with beautiful quote machines, that great promotional device, the "tape"—now probably in orange symbols electronically flashing on a black background—and a Dow Jones ticker so demure it went *clack muffle muffle clack* instead of *tocketa tocketa*.

When the lodge brother bought a stock, the transaction would be recorded in the back room by a gentleman wearing gym shoes and a jacket indicating the freshman basketball team of Cardinal Hayes High School, who would lick his pencil as he recorded the trade. With such personnel it was not uncommon to have mistakes. The securities, if they could be found, would be delivered to the brokerage firm by another gentleman in a Salvation Army overcoat, a nine-day growth of beard, and a certain air of muscatel, California 1973. Sometimes he would get where he was going, and sometimes he would not. Sometimes his parcel would get there with him, and sometimes it would not.

Business was very good. You could walk into a teller's cage and walk out with securities. They were lying on the floor, on the tables, all over the place. Did not bad people then take the securities away, and never bring them back? Yes, they did. In 1971 they took $500 million worth. Sometimes good people did too. It was commonly assumed that The Mob was responsible for all the missing securities. It was very easy to put in your very own man. You could dress him in a Salvation Army overcoat if you wanted to get the securities that way, and you could dress him in acne and a Cardinal Hayes letter sweater if you wanted them that way. If you wanted to move him up one step in sophistication, you put a man in the clerical department as the bank transfer agent, or in some other record-keeping capacity, and then nobody could figure out the records. One step up from that, you took the securities to a country bank in Limburger, Ohio, put them up as collateral, took out a loan, and then simply left them there forever—why not? Not your stocks.

I was having a drink one evening with a governor of the stock exchange who had worked very long and hard hours on the problem.

"The Mafia couldn't possibly have stolen that much money," he said. "Good people had to steal too. The temptation was too great."

The FBI—the other Fed—apprehended some bad people and located some missing securities, to wit, some 3,400 shares of IBM belonging to a well-known brokerage firm. Plucky public servants that they are, they called up the firm and told them to be happy, their IBM was found.

"We're not missing any IBM," they were told. (Months later, when the records were a bit more straight, the firm sheepishly asked the FBI if it could have the IBM back. The FBI said yes. It is not recorded what else they said.)

Not all the securities, of course, were stolen. Many were not there in the first place; they were clerical errors. In fact, most of the discrepancies probably belong in the bookkeeping category. Firms lost physical control of the pieces of paper. At the peak of the troubles, "fails to deliver" totaled $4 *billion*. Nobody could find four *billion* dollars' worth of stocks.

The New York Stock Exchange has certain requirements. A firm is supposed to have a certain amount of capital in relation to its obligations. Never mind that the obligations were getting out of hand. There was trouble on the capital end, too. If you had put capital into a Wall Street firm, you could take it out—sometimes in ninety days, sometimes in a year. Few other businesses have such an ease of exit. Some of the capitalists took their capital out. And the remaining capital—well, that was frequently in the stock market, and many of those stocks were melting away in market value.

Back to the near miss.

As firms began to fall grossly behind in their capital requirements, they would be suspended from dealings by the New York Stock Exchange. Except for very big firms. There was indeed a prejudice in favor of size. Said Robert Haack, president of the exchange, "We simply can't afford to have a major firm fail." Much later, the stock exchange gave three justifications for its prejudice in choosing to try to save the major firms, while letting lesser firms fail. The great number of customer accounts, they said, would not have allowed an orderly liquidation. Suspension of the firms would have lost them their technical clerical staffs at a time of intense competition for such people. And the announcement of a suspension of a major firm might cause a run on all brokers, even ones in good shape, by worried customers.

The stock exchange had established a trust fund early in the sixties, at the time of the salad-oil scandal which put Ira Haupt & Company out of business. Those funds were to provide an orderly liquidation for a failed firm so that the customers would not lose their money and maybe spread the word that you could lose all your money without even making a mistake in the market. That leads to the calling up of congressmen. As the major firms began to teeter, the exchange would authorize its members to increase the trust fund: the amounts increased from $10 million in 1965 (with an additional $15 million in stand-by credit), to a maximum of $55 million in 1970, to $75 million in January 1971, and finally to $110 million, with $30 million set aside in a customer-assistance program for Merrill Lynch's obligations in its Goodbody & Company rescue. At each increase, some of the surviving members would ask, "Why don't we just let the bastards go down the tube?" And Felix Rohaytn, a soft-spoken governor of the exchange, a merger specialist from Lazard Freres (who had bought a number of companies for ITT), would say, "That is not an acceptable risk."

At 8:30 A.M. on September 11, 1970, Hayden, Stone was out of business. It had followed the classic pattern: increased production, disorganized record-keeping facilities, its capital impaired by being invested in falling securities, and a large number of fails. (At one time, it had been said that Hayden, Stone was so disorganized that "you could peel the wallpaper off the wall, deliver it to Hayden, and get paid.") Rohaytn and Bernard Lasker, chairman of the governors of the stock exchange, had applied all their merger-making talents to finding a firm that would take over the lagging giant. The problem was a group of Hayden, Stone's noteholders, who were reluctant to go along with the marriage arranged, by shotgun and persuasion, with Cogan, Berlind, Weill & Levitt.

"If the Hayden merger didn't go through," said an exchange governor, "that could have been the ball game."

The end of the ball game might have had the following script:

The opening bell rings. Hayden, Stone is declared in liquidation. A minumum of $25 million from the trust fund would have been needed to pay the overhead and clear up the records while the firm's affairs were straightened out. The firm's overhead had been running at $5 million a month; even reduced to $2.5 million, the costs of liquidating it would more likely have been $40 million to $70 million over eighteen months, perhaps as high as $100 million. Hayden, Stone's 90,000 customers would have been frozen in place, unable to buy or sell for many months. The cash and securities owed by Hayden, Stone to other firms would have forced those firms under; perhaps another fifty firms could have gone out of business. As those firms sold securities to raise cash, the Dow Jones average need not have stopped at 630, or indeed anywhere short of 400 or so, and broader market averages would have suffered equally.

But worse: the confidence of millions of investors, already impaired by the bear market, would be dealt a final blow by the sight of Hayden's immobilized and screaming customers. They would all race to their brokers and demand their cash and their securities. Wall Street had for years used its customers' cash, and many of the securities were very likely nowhere to be found. There would be a classic run—not on the bank, but on the brokers.

And beyond *that* loomed a specter so frightening nobody wanted to think about it. There was $50 billion out there in mutual funds. A mutual fund can be redeemed in one day; you simply bring the papers in and say, Sidney, I want the money. The mutual funds had had a cushion: every year their salesmen sold more fund shares than fundholders redeemed. So they had to sell stocks only as a market strategy: if they thought the market was going down, they might want 10 percent in cash; if they thought it was going up, they might want to be fully invested. (Statistics show, parenthetically, that that is what they did when they thought those thoughts, but the market generally went the other way, rather perversely.) They did not sell stocks to give cash back to worried redeemers.

What if the holders of mutual funds got scared and started to cash in? Already fifty brokers were going out of business, hundreds of thousands of accounts were tied up, a run on the brokers was going on, brokers were selling stocks to beef up their capital accounts—and now, what if the mutual funds were *forced* into sales to raise cash to pay off nervous redeemers of their shares? To whom would they sell their stocks?

"I thought about that a lot," said my friend who was the exchange governor. "We would have had to close the exchange."

"Close the New York Stock Exchange?" I said. "What happens then?"

"I don't know, because it's never happened like that," he said. "But certainly you would have the government step in, and when the exchange finally reopened, things would be very, very different."

"Maybe like the Yugoslavia Stock Exchange," I suggested.

"Maybe," he said.

At 8:30 A.M. on September 11, 1970, the script was ninety minutes away from the bomb in the suitcase. To get Hayden, Stone merged safely away took the approval of 108 noteholders of the company. Not only did the Hayden, Stone officials scramble to get the signatures; so did Robert Haack, the president of the New York Stock Exchange, and the ubiquitous and worrying governors, Messrs. Rohaytn and Lasker. By Friday, September 4, when the deal was supposed to have been set, all but a few of the noteholders had said they would go along. The merger was supposed to be delivered to the exchange's board of governors on Thursday, September 10, but one of the note-holders still had not signed. By the exchange's own rules, Hayden, Stone should have been suspended some time before; now the board of governors voted a reprieve of a few hours. The holdout was an Oklahoma City businessman named Jack Golsen, who had put $1.5 million in the firm only the previous March, believing, he said, that the firm's statements were up-to-date and that the New York Stock Exchange would not have allowed him to invest in a firm that was about to go busted. Golsen said he'd rather go into liquidation; maybe the tax consequences were better, and anyway, he was tired of being pushed around.

Having been given a few hours' reprieve, the Cogan, Berlind people, who were to take over the merged firm, raced for the Teterboro Airport, chartered a Lear jet, flew to Oklahoma City, and sat up all night with Golsen. At dawn Golsen was still shaking his head. At 8 A.M. Rohaytn and Bunny Lasker got on the phone in a conference call. "They hit me with a whole trainload of social responsibility," Golsen said. The government, said others, was aware of the situation. Golsen capitulated. At 9:55 A.M., five minutes before the liquidation would have been announced, the Dow Jones ticker flashed the news of the merger.

But the duties of Rohaytn, Lasker, and the other worriers were far from over. Two other great firms were taking on water fast: Francis I. du Pont, with 275,000 accounts, the third largest brokerage house in the United States, and Goodbody & Company, 225,000 accounts, also one of the largest in the country. It did not take an adding machine to figure that if they both went down, the exchange's trust fund would be out of money and then some, and the whole run-on-the-bank script would be back in operation. Both of these stories have been rendered elsewhere in the press. You could make a book out of all those adventures alone, or better yet, a successor to *Mission: Impossible*, with a cliff-hanger each week ending at the last commercial

It was not easy to get people to take over Wall Street firms that were losing millions of dollars a month. Remember the alternate uses of money: you could get 9.35 percent a year, every year, in that good old telephone bond, and never worry about another thing. But in a takeover you had to put up more than money. You had to have the expertise to take over and, if necessary, shut down branch offices; you had to take over and straighten out the tangled records and finances; in short, you had to take over and run a large and failing business. Who needed that! Obviously, only a major financial institution could do it. There had been pressure from mutual funds and insurance companies to join the exchange, but that pressure had been resisted by the existing members, the brokers, for fear it would hurt their own businesses. So the exchange had no institutional members. Only two or three brokers could take over someone as big as Goodbody. It was decided that Merrill Lynch—by far the biggest broker—should have the new acquisition. Merrill drove a hard-nosed bargain: the exchange community was to put up $30 million against losses incurred in straightening Goodbody out, and absolutely no other firm should fail or   That left du Pont, and the du Ponts of Wilmington, Delaware, were in no mood to help. The candidate on the white horse was clear: it was a Texas billionaire called Ross Perot. Perot was not at all the traditional loud, cigar-chomping, super right-wing, cartoon Texas oilman. His money was all in shares of Electronic Data Systems, or EDS, a computer software company. Perot was so straight and H. Alger-like that even stricken Wall Streeters could not believe it. As a boy, he had gotten up at 3:30 A.M. and ridden twenty miles on horseback to deliver the *Texarkana Gazette* to poor neighborhoods that no one else wanted to service. He was an honors graduate of the Naval Academy. His billion came from the high price at which EDS shares sold, but he said often that the day he became an Eagle Scout was more significant than the day he became a billionaire, and he gave several million to the Boy and Girl Scouts. He had joined IBM as a salesman and had met his yearly quota by the third week in January. He started EDS with $1,000, and was turned down eighty times before he made his first sale. Perot is five feet six, has a crew cut, and wears straight ties. His night life is playing basketball with his wife and five children, or taking everybody out for a hamburger.

Perot first came into the news because of his efforts to take Christmas packages to prisoners in North Vietnam; his chartered planes had gotten as far as Laos.

The Nixon Administration knew both Wall Street and Perot. Attorney General John Mitchell was a partner in a law firm specializing in municipal bonds; Richard Nixon himself had been a senior partner of that firm. Peter Flanagan, a special assistant to the President, had been a partner in Eastman, Dillon. Mitchell had managed the 1968 campaign, to which Perot had been a contributor. Furthermore, Perot certainly knew Francis I. du Pont and Company, even if he did not know Wall Street; EDS had been hired to do the computer work for the firm.

"John Mitchell was very helpful in getting Perot involved," said an exchange governor. That whole story need not be recounted here. The cynics said that if EDS revenues were $50 million, and 15 percent of that came from the du Pont contract, then it should have been worth a $100 million to keep that business alive, and anyway, maybe Perot wanted EDS to take over all the computer work for the stock exchange and a lot of other firms. The believers say Perot wanted to save Wall Street and the system that had been so nice to him. One friend of mine who knows him well says that Perot is "half Boy Scout and half horse trader, totally sincere at both, and very good at both."

Perot took over du Pont. First he put in $10 million; then he put in another $30 million; so far, he has had to put up about $50 million.

Taking over Hayden, Stone had involved teams of people; taking over Goodbody had enlisted the biggest firm in Wall Street; the final role—and it is so extremely rare that this falls to one man—had fallen to a single individual, who said that if Wall Street had been impaired, "even temporarily, the consequences would have been dire, not only for industries, but for the cities, counties and school systems of the country."

Everybody knows what happened. Wall Street survived, No other major firms went out of business. Congress, mindful of the 1,500 letters a month the SEC was getting, and of its own mail, passed the Securities Investor Protection Act of 1970, which created an agency that could borrow up to $1 billion from the U.S. Treasury, if necessary, to protect customers against losses if it became necessary to liquidate the firm in which their securities and cash balances were held. That took the pressure off the industry and off the New York Stock Exchange, and restored some public confidence.

The piece of paper—the stock certificate—is still at the center of the transaction, and delivery is still made by gentlemen in Salvation Army overcoats. That is still troubling, but the mechanism of transaction, it is safe to say, has everyone's attention. Securities in the "fail to deliver" class dropped from $4.1 billion at the end of 1968 to $1 billion at the end of 1971. And, said the chairman of the SEC, "looking down the road a little, the time will come when the execution of a trade will be electronically conveyed to a point where securities are transferred by electronic record with paper print-out and payment is made by similar electronic means."

The future of the New York Stock Exchange is not totally clear, but what is clear is that it will not be moving to Dubrovnik.

CHAPTER 4

THE NAME OF THE GAME IS COMMON SENSE

O ne of my functions within the investment community, and one which I enjoy, has been to be a moderator at seminars and conventions. There is one in particular, an annual meeting that attracts the largest number of bank trust officers and mutual fund managers. We assemble the investment types with the best records, and they tell what insights led them to their triumphs, what stocks they have just bought and therefore would like the audience to buy, and what they see ahead. Of course, it is not always genius that earns an investment type a slot on this panel. He may have taken undue risks; he may be down 90 percent in the next year; he may have done the equivalent of flipping heads fifty-one times in a row. No matter; the figures are in, and up to the dais he comes. I have never found one who was inarticulate, and in fact most are willing to comment on the investment significance of foreign policy, economic policy, sociological changes, and other subjects usually reserved for Eric Sevareid. It has become a minor tradition that I needle the panelists gently, reminding them perhaps of a sour stock they had confided to me some other time—rather like the slave in the Roman chariot assigned to whisper to the garlanded conqueror that glory is fleeting.

I thought it would be a nice psychological purge, after the worst year of the Big Bear, if some of the previous winners would get up and confess their sins. Every one of the professionals in the audience, after all, harbored some dark secret, his own block of National Student Marketing which he had dropped behind the paper-towel bin in the men's room, hoping no one would notice. There they were, these professionals, walking around harboring these unconfessed misdeeds. Who could tell the damage being done to the collective unconscious of the investment community?

So I think I had in mind a group therapy session for fifteen hundred investment professionals. Previous winners would get up, face the audience, and say that not only had they bought National Student Marketing, they still owned it—in case anybody would like to buy it—and furthermore they had put it into their children's accounts. In Alcoholics Anonymous, you are supposed to be on the road to cure if you can face your peers and say, "My name is John Jones and I am an alcoholic." Not only would my session benefit the confessors, but the audience would identify and go through something of the same process. Some of them might feel the spirit and rise from their chairs, crying, "I bought Four Seasons Nursing Homes!" The audience would respond with the business-school equivalent of "Glory!" Everybody would leave feeling cleansed and free.

For a while it worked. Two of the previous winners talked with good temper about what they had done and would not do again. They would no longer have such a limited view of history; the limited view of history said that you don't sell good stocks in a decline because they'll come right back. They would no longer go into illiquid situations, no matter how great the promise. They would no longer fall in love with stocks, forgiving the first lapse, and then the second lapse, and so on all the way down.

"We didn't pay attention," said one speaker, which was to say everybody had paid attention to ten or fifteen stocks but not to Vietnam and Cambodia and the Federal Reserve and Washington and the world at large. Another speaker was going to laugh if somebody said, "There is only a limited supply of stock." And still another speaker was going to disregard his clients, or potential clients, especially the ones who, when you were bearish, would say, "Call me when you're more optimistic."

Snug in its chairs, the audience was warm and responsive. It was all going well. Then I tapped David Babson. I should have known better what was coming. Babson is a crusty, amiable New Englander who heads the sixth biggest investment-counseling firm in the country. He was then just turning sixty. For a couple of years he had been preaching and scolding. The stock market, he had said, was becoming "a national crap game." If the sinning didn't stop, he had told other groups, if the whole "gigantic pari-mutuel operation" didn't stop, there would be government intervention.

Babson had told me once that when he brought good grades home from Harvard to the family farm in Gloucester, Massachusetts, his father was down in a vegetable garden. The Babsons are 1630 New Englanders, but Yankees, not Brahmins. In addition to running the farm, Babson's father was the local veterinarian. Babson walked the length of the field and told his father the news. "That's good," said his father, "but you been home ten minutes and you still don't have your overalls on."

Babson had not always been scolding; in fact, his weekly letters proved him to be a cheery optimist and a bull on America in the late forties, a time in which the surrounding opinion was quite gloomy. He had started the weekly letter because, when he began his counseling service in 1940, "there was no line outside the door." In Babson's

view, the most prized virtues were hard work and common sense
—not smartness or cleverness, but common sense—and these virtues
would triumph in the long run. Babson read off a list of eleven villains,
which I will come back to in a moment. I picked him up on a statement:
Was this terrible market due to the professionals?

"Of course, " he said. "Nobody else. The professionals, people who
ought to know how to manage investments, got sucked into speculation."

"What do you think we ought to do about this?" I asked.

Babson looked over his glasses at the audience.

"Some of you should leave the business," he said.

There was nervous laughter. I asked him if he had anybody in
mind.

"Some of them have offices near here," he said.

I said I didn't know anybody with an office near here.

"Some of them are sitting quite close," he said. "When a prospect
for a new account asks how much growth he can expect, and we
tell him ten percent, and he says somebody else has promised him
twenty percent a year, we ask him which Fred promised him that."

By sheer coincidence, there were some very well-known aggressive
portfolio managers named Fred. We had one, by another coincidence,
sitting with us. (Later, each of the Freds was to express resentment
at having been lumped in with the other Freds.)

"Too many Freds," I heard Babson mutter, and then he said, "Should
a manager who put Parvin Dohrmann into a client's account be allowed
to advise anyone again?" Dohrmann had gone from 142 to 14.

"I have a list here," Babson said. He pulled it out and began to
read.

"Four Seasons Nursing Homes," he said. "The high was ninety-one
and the low is bankrupt. Anybody that went to bed with Four
Seasons—"

"David," I said gently into the microphone. The audience was beginning to rustle. You can tell something has happened to the good
feelings when the water pitchers start to clink nervously against the
water glasses in a rising cacophony.

"Commonwealth United," he said. "The high was twenty-five and
the current price is one. Susquehanna, the high was eighty and the
current price is seven. Unexcelled, the high was sixty-eight and the
current price is four. All great institutional favorites."

"Don't read the list," I said.

The audience was beginning to scrape its chairs. My massive group therapy session had taken a sour turn. Nobody was going to confess if they were being accused.

"Computers," Babson said. "Management Assistance, forty-six to two. Levin-Townsend, sixty-eight to three."

"David," I said.

"Leasco Data Processing, fifty-seven to nine. Data Processing and Financial General, ninety-two to eight."

"David," I said, "you have passed the pain threshold of the audience."

He stopped. The audience was absolutely silent. Well, I remember thinking, maybe catharsis was the wrong idea anyway. Maybe Sinners in the Hands of an Angry God is more appropriate.

"Thank you, Jonathan Edwards," I said.

Babson did not get a standing ovation.

We had questions from the audience. There was one rather plaintive one for Babson, which showed that my original idea had taken hold.

"Isn't there just *one mistake* of yours that you could point to?" the questioner asked Babson.

That got the applause.

Babson said he could find a few if he dug hard, but no serious ones. Babson's own fund had taken seven years to double when others were doing that in months, but it had held its ground while the others melted away.

"My host asked me what my strategy is," he said. "It is the same this year as for any year. To try to use our common sense."

I asked all my other winners whether the game was coming back. They all said that sooner or later it was. Except Babson.

"No greater period of skullduggery in American financial history exists than 1967 to 1969, " he said. "It has burned this generation like 1929 did another one, and it will be a long, long time before it happens again."

"The day I went to work in 1932," Babson said later, "steel mills were running at eight percent of capacity. I remember days when the trading was so slow people played ball on the floor of the exchange. The ticker didn't move at all, and then Armour crossed at $4 a share.

"After the war, I pushed growth stocks when today's performance managers were in their playpens. The Census Bureau predicted the U.S. population would be a hundred and sixty-five million—in 1990! I was a radical then, and maybe I'm a curmudgeon now—times change, the economy changes—but another group has to grow up ... and the scars have to heal before you do it all again."

I said that was pretty optimistic.

"Maybe so, but common sense will go a long way to help."

Here is Babson's list of villains:

1) The conglomerate movement, "with all its fancy rhetoric about synergism and leverage."
2) Accountants who played footsie with stock-promoting managements by certifying earnings that weren't earnings at all.
3) "Modern" corporate treasurers who looked upon their company pension funds as new-found profit centers and pressured their investment advisers into speculating with them.
4) Investment advisers who massacred clients' portfolios because they were trying to make good on the over-promises that they had made to attract the business.
5) The new breed of investment managers who bought and churned the worst collection of new issues and other junk in history, and the underwriters who made fortunes bringing them out.
6) Elements of the financial press which promoted into new investment geniuses a group of neophytes who didn't even have the first requisite for managing other people's money—namely, a sense of responsibility.
7) The securities salesmen who peddled the items with the best stories—or the biggest markups—even though such issues were totally unsuited to the customers' needs.
8) The sanctimonious partners of major investment houses who wrung their hands over all these shameless happenings while they deployed an army of untrained salesmen to forage among even less trained investors.
9) Mutual fund managers who tried to become millionaires overnight by using every gimmick imaginable to manufacture their own paper performance.
10) Portfolio managers who collected bonanza incentives of the "heads I wind, tails you lose" kind, which made them fortunes in the bull market but turned the portfolios they managed into disasters in the bear market.
11) Security analysts who forgot about their professional ethics to become storytellers and let their institutions be taken in by a whole parade of confidence men.

This was the "list of horrors that people in our field did to set the stage for the greatest blood bath in forty years," Babson said.

The doctor in Pocatello, Idaho, did not by himself think up the idea of buying Liquidonics and Minnie Pearl, and the man on Main Street didn't decide on his own hook to buy "a new El Dorado mutual fund which has since flushed half its assets down the drain."

Well, that is a handsome list of villains. I have the feeling that in Babson's part of New England the stocks they put you into for not having common sense are the wooden ones down on the village green that are very uncomfortable for the hands and feet. In retrospect, there is nothing wrong with Babson's list except that the villains do overlap and the excesses are seen as totally within the industry. There were some macro-villains that also helped to set the stage: there was the unpaid-for Vietnam war with the concomitant inflation, and those responsible for that; and there was the antiquated structure of the securities industry, and those responsible for that. Four of Babson's eleven villains were investment managers guilty of one sin or another, and three were people in other roles in the securities industry proper —partners, analysts, salesmen—who ignored their professional responsibilities.

I brought Babson's list in here to show that there was a lot of finger-pointing within the industry, and that if you have a secret hurt, so did a lot of the professional managers. If you bought an "El Dorado mutual fund," you may have hurt right along with those managers.

Which brings up a pertinent point: suppose that all this business about the Federal Reserve and the market and the swings makes you too nervous. Suppose you want to leave it all to the pros. You go to your bank and let them manage the money. Or you buy a mutual fund. How would you have done? (For, after all, it should be pointed out that many funds were not "El Dorado" funds, and that the vast majority of American securities by market capitalization were not promotions but mature American companies. They may not have produced gains for their investors, but that may be due to other reasons having more to do with their own basic natures and the broader market forces.)

A simplistic answer has to precede the statistical one. If you bought a mutual fund that went up, you did well. There were such funds. If you bought one that went down, you did badly. There were such funds, too. And there were banks that made money for people, and banks that lost money for people, and investment counselors that did the same. This point is brought up for a very obvious reason: you have to do something with the money, and just because you invest it does not mean you have to be the median or the average. Somebody has to be first and somebody has to be last.

Now to the sources. They are familiar to those in the industry who care about such things, and they include the obvious: *The Institutional Investor Study Report of the Securities and Exchange Commission*, especially Volume 2; *The Comptroller's Staff Reports* from the Office of the Comptroller of the Currency; *Bank Trusts: Investments and Performance;* and the work done by several academic institutions, notably the Wharton School of Finance at the University of Pennsylvania. From the latter came the best-known statistical job: sponsored by the Twentieth Century Fund, it is published as *Mutual Funds and Other Institutional Investors,* by Irwin Friend, Marshall Blume, and Jean Crockett. In addition, there are a number of academic papers, usually heavy in mathematics and statistics, published in such professional journals as the *American Economic Review,* the papers of the American Statistical Association, and so on. And you can take your own samples from the Lipper computer runs of funds, since those have been done, and the Weisenberger statistics from the mechanical age. For various reasons, I have had to go through much of this material as it came out, and I have talked, though not extensively, to the authors.

This battery of citations is a defensive measure, for—as you might have guessed—the news is not so good, and some very well-paid manager might just come up to me in the shuttle line at the airport and swing if we say that managed funds with well-paid managers do about the same as a totally random portfolio. For that is what the statistics say, and we are back with our old friends from the freshman course, the random walkers. Here is a key sentence from the Wharton study led by Irwin Friend:

Virtually all the published government and academic studies have indicated that the investment performance of mutual funds in the aggregate is not very different fron that of the stock market as a whole.

The Wharton study compared the mutual funds with random portfolios in New York Stock Exchange stocks:

Mutual funds as a whole in 1960-68 seemed to perform worse than equally distributed random investments in New York Stock Exchange stock, but, except for low-risk portfolios, did better than proportionally distributed random investments.

It isn't necessary to go into the comparisons with the funds here —whether the random portfolios were weighted or unweighted (the Wharton people tried both) and the so-called beta coefficients, or degrees of volatility, in the portfolios. For some of the period of the

Wharton study, the higher-risk funds—those so asperically charged by Babson—helped the overall performance of the fund industry, because the Wharton study ended in September 1969, before those funds took their biggest bath, and a horseback guess would be that by factoring that in now, you would once again come out about even. These statistics do not count the sales commission of the fund (if it has one), so if you pay that, you have to start that much further behind.

In other words, a random portfolio is just as good as the average mutual fund. Chicago's Harris Trust tried another way: comparing funds with the Dow Jones average and the Standard & Poor's 500 stock average, for the twenty-five years ending in 1970. For half of that time, the median common-stock fund came in last, behind the averages. "There is no evidence," says Professor Friend, "that any group of funds can beat the averages."

Of course, you cannot buy a statistically random portfolio, even though your portfolio may have a very random look about it. And you cannot really buy the Dow Jones average or the Standard & Poor. If you are going to buy a fund—or the equivalent slice in a bank-managed common trust—you have to buy that, and you hope that your fund or your bank is at the top of the list, helping the team against the randoms, and not at the bottom.

There is at least one other important point in the Wharton study from the potential fund investor's point of view. Adjusted for risk, the performance correlation in funds between one time period and another is zero. In Professor Friend's words, expressed also in the study: "There may be no consistency in the performance of the same fund in successive periods."

In other words, a fund that performed well in 1966 and 1967 may not perform well in 1969 and 1970.

This is important, because many new investors came to buy funds for the first time, or were sold them, within the last five or six years. The funds that took in the most money the fastest from investors were those that had the hottest records for a short period of time previously. The investors who in 1967 and 1968 bought funds that had shown big increases in the year or two previous did unusually badly, worse than they had any statistical right to expect. Gerry Tsai's Manhattan Fund, up 39 percent in 1967, went down 6.9 percent in 1968, 10.15 percent in 1969, and 36.8 percent in 1970. The Gibraltar Growth Fund, ranked third in 1968, ranked 481st in 1971; it threw in the towel and was taken over by the Dreyfus organization.

The conclusions seem obvious. If you want to buy a fund, buy it, do not be sold it. There are magazines and publications—*Forbes* among them—which rank mutual funds over a period of years in all kinds of markets. You do not need more than a year or two to judge a record, and it does take some investigation, a small enough price to pay.

CHAPTER 5

WHEN MY SWISS BANK WENT BROKE

In early September of that bad year, 1970, I was riding into New York on one of the Penn Central's surviving trains when a story in *The Wall Street Journal* caused some hot flashes and palpitations. Nothing alarming; in 1970 it was impossible to read *The Wall Street Journal* without having hot flashes and palpitations. This story was not even on the front page, and I am sure was passed over by many of the newspaper's readers. UNITED CALIFORNIA BANK, read the headline, SAYS SWISS UNIT INCURRED LOSSES THAT MAY HIT $30 MILLION. Swiss unit? United California Bank? That was *my* bank!

I don't mean it was my bank in the sense that the Bank of New York is my bank because I have a checking account there, or that people have a friend at the Chase jmanhattan because that is where they owe the payments. I mean *it was my bank because I owned it.* There was no public stock in this bank; it was the biggest, solidest, and safest investment I had ever made. A lockup, as they say. And only months after I bought this hunk of the bank, my judgment seemed to be confirmed. The majority interest was bought by the great United California Bank of Los Angeles, one of the fifteen largest in the United States, second largest bank on the West Coast, itself the flagship bank of Western Bancorporation, *the largest bank holding company in the world.* Big brother.

Clifford Tweter, senior vice-chairman of United California and president of its parent, Western Bancorporation, last night declined to explain how the loss occurred. He said he hoped to be able to provide more data once an audit at the Swiss bank is completed. That would be within the next few days, he added. "We think we should speak in general terms at this time," Mr. Tweter said.

The troubled institution, United California Bank in Basel, is 58% controlled by United California Bank . . . the other 42% is held "by a variety of investors, mostly individuals," Mr. Tweter said.

It was a good year when I bought into my Swiss bank. I had a popular book on all the best-seller lists. Now you take the average American male who has a fat year or a windfall, and there are a lot of ways to spend the money in tune with fantasyland. He could buy a beautiful sloop (not to mention yawl, ketch, and cutter) and cruise around the world. He could get fitted for a Purdy in London or a Wesley Richards .375 and go shoot an elephant in Kenya while they are thinning out the herds. He could buy a pro football team—or at least part of one—and buy and sell 280-pound tackles, and have a modest little speech prepared when the television cameras roll into the locker room amidst the victory whoops, the champagne, and the wet towels. Not me. I had to buy a Swiss bank. Overexposure to early Eric Ambler, I guess, when if you really wanted to know what was going on, you certainly didn't watch the newspaper headlines because they didn't tell you anything; you watched the rise of the dinar and the fall of the drachma, and those barely perceptible flutters told you that Peter Lorre and Sidney Greenstreet were in a compartment on the Orient Express on their way to Istanbul. They were looking for Demetrius, and you remember the trail led right back to Switzerland, good old Switzerland, where the master spy was in his château playing a Bach fugue on his magnificent organ.

So it wasn't all safety and solidity that attracted me, though what could be safer than a Swiss bank? It was a hedge against the troubles of the dollar, and a friendly place to call upon in Europe, and the prospects of a lot of fun, and maybe even a very good investment to boot. The United California Bank of Los Angeles didn't buy into the bank because of Eric Ambler. American business was expanding in Europe. There was big merchant banking to be done. American banks were expanding in Europe—opening branches, chartering banks. Dollars had piled up overseas and there was a big business in Eurodollars. American banks sought to start banks in Europe, but that was hard, and took time; it they could buy one, that would put them right in the middle of the action. We junior partners were delighted when the United California Bank took over; obviously our bank was to be part of the big expansion in Europe. We were in for a great ride.

When I got to my office that September day the story came out, I dialed 061 35 94 50, the number of the bank's office in Basel. I remember that I was worried but not stricken. No one likes to see his biggest investment have a bad year. But with the great United California Bank as a senior partner, could anything really go seriously wrong? It was like owning a great ship in partnership with Cunard. The *Titanic* is unsinkable. If you hear that it has had a little brush with an iceberg, you are annoyed that maybe some paint has been scraped off and now the damn thing is going to need a new paint job when it gets to New York.

After only a few moments, 061 35 94 50 answered, but the bank's office seemed to be in some confusion. I asked for Paul Erdman, the thirty-eight-year-old American president of the bank. Previous calls had gone right through, the voices across the Atlantic sounding clearer than a local call. Both Paul Erdman and his secretary seemed not to be there. There was some chattering in German on the other end.

Finally a male voice said, "Mr. Erdman is not here. He is not with the bank any more."

Since when? I wanted to know.

"Since yesterday," the voice said. I asked where I could reach Erdman, and the voice said to try him at his home in Basel, which I did. Erdman sounded cheerful as usual.

"I've resigned," he said. "But I'm staying on as a consultant. There's a bit of a mess. Maybe you heard."

I told him I had just read about it, and what exactly was the problem?

"There's a shortfall in the trading account of thirty million dollars."

Thirty million dollars?

Unlike American banks, Swiss banks act also as brokers, and can trade for their own accounts. The assets of our bank were reported to be $69 million at the end of 1969, but of course there were liabilities against those assets. The capital of the bank was less than $9 million. A loss of $30 million would have busted not only our bank but two more the same size, except for our giant parent. I brought this up.

"UCB will keep the bank open," Erdman said. "They have to—their reputation would be damaged if they closed it."

Where is the thirty million dollars? I wanted to know.

"It's lost," Erdman said. "We lost it trading. A commodities trader lost it."

"Listen," I said. "I have seen guys lose one million dollars. Two million dollars, even. But there is *just no way to lose thirty million dollars*. No way."

"Well, it's lost," Erdman said. "The UCB will make it up. You're going to suffer some dilution. But the bank will go on."

"How come you resigned?" I asked.

"The buck has to stop somewhere, and I was in charge," he said.

94

At that point I began to feel some sympathy for Erdman. For me the bank was an investment; for him it was a personal creation, something he had spent years building up. I said, "This must be tough."

"I'm all right," he said. "I'll be at the bank tomorrow, helping to clean up the mess."

But he wasn't. Shortly thereafter, the Basel police picked Erdman up, as they did all the directors of the bank who were in Switzerland. The two directors they did not pick up were the chairman of the board, Frank King, who was also the chairman of the United California Bank in Los Angeles and, in fact, of Western Bancorporation, and Victor Rose, a vice-president of the Los Angeles bank. Both of them were in Los Angeles. It seemed somehow very Swiss to put the board of a bank in jail. I never heard of it happening here.

Erdman was to spend ten months in the Basel prison, much of it in solitary confinement. *Habeas corpus* is an Anglo-Saxon institution. In Switzerland they can keep you in jail as long as they see fit, for investigation. The Swiss say it's very efficient.

I called Erdman's house a few days later, and talked to Erdman's attractive blonde wife, Helly.

"It's like a nightmare," Helly said. "No one will speak to me. They won't let me talk to Paul. I am afraid the house is being watched. It's like a bad criminal show on TV."

How could they simply hold someone without a charge?

"In Switzerland this is very serious," she said. "More serious than murder."

That, incidentally, is true. Long jail sentences do not meet the Swiss standard of justice. There is a gentleman at this moment in the Basel jail who caved in his wife's skull with a blunt instrument. She was a nagging wife, he said, and she liked to boss him around. One day he had had all he could stand, and he dispatched her. Then he went downtown and mailed a letter. Murder one, five years, with a year and a half off for good behavior. In Switzerland almost everybody gets off for good behavior, because almost everybody is well behaved.

On September 16, 1970, at 2 P. M., the United California Bank in Basel AG closed its doors and posted a notice on its premises at St. Jakobsstrasse 7. According to the papers, the losses were closer to $40 million than $30 million. Representatives of the United California Bank in Los Angeles presented a plan to the Swiss banking authorities in Bern. They would, they said, make good to the depositors and creditors. In a report to its own stockholders, the California bank explained that a great international bank has deposits from other great international banks, and if it were to welsh it couldn't continue in business. The loss, it said, would be treated as an ordinary and necessary business expense, and it applied to Internal Revenue for a tax saving of half the loss. Furthermore, insurance might cover $10 million. On the New York Stock Exchange, Western Bancorporation went down two and a half points, and then back up two points. In 1969, Western Banc had had a net profit after taxes of a bit more than $60 million, so a $10 million or even a $20 million loss, while quite an inconvenience, was not a serious impediment to doing business.

Western Bancorporation was a publicly traded company; the United California Bank in Basel was held privately, by the Los Angeles bank and a few of us faithful junior partners. No one called the junior partners —at least no one called me, and I certainly left my phone number in enough places. There seemed to be nowhere to get information. I called an investment officer I knew professionally at the UCB in Los Angeles. He clucked sympathetically, said he didn't know anything that hadn't been in the papers, and suggested that the best use for my stock certificates was as wallpaper.

"Write it off," he said.

"Off what?" I said.

Finally I began to play a little game. I would call the office of Frank King, the chairman of the United California Bank, and explain carefully why I was calling, what it was in reference to, and that it was a call from the junior partner to the senior partner. Frank King's office would say they would take the message and he would call back. Then he wouldn't call back. We tried this thirty-one times and then gave up. I had to conclude that nobody wanted to talk to me. We were, after all, in the same boat, and we did have something to talk about, but when there is trouble, bankers get very tongue-tied, and this incident was a real conversation-stopper, bankwise.

My calls were over several weeks. Paul Erdman's salary stopped instantly, and since his only real possession was the bank stock, Helly got a job as a secretary. Teams of auditors moved onto the premises of St. Jakobsstrasse 7, but no one had any clear idea of how $40 million could disappear from a modern banking institution. Especially a *Swiss bank*.

Paul Erdman was in a small single cell, with a toilet, a fold-up bed, and a table.

My bank was busted.

Paul Erdman had come to my office one summer day in 1968. He was lean, tall, and bespectacled. I forget now who sent him; we were seeking to expand our knowledge of European banks, and Paul Erdman was to tell us about the Swiss, who are not eager to tell about themselves. We went to lunch, and Erdman began to tell me not so much about the rest of the Swiss banking establishment—he would introduce me to someone who could do an even better job than he could—but about his own small bank in Basel. I liked Paul.

Furthermore, I have an interest—or a weakness—for and in small companies that have big ideas. You would never consider running General Electric to be *fun*. It might be something else, but not fun. But you take a couple of guys with a sheet of yellow paper and an idea, and the idea is right, and they have an itch to make something happen, to build something that grows—that's quite exciting. If it works, it's exhilarating and—though the word is inadequate—fun, almost as much fun as anything else you can think of. The odds against success are quite long: the idea does have to be right, and the money—enough money—has to be there, and then more money has to be available, and then you have to have the counter-strategy ready when the existing establishment feels the sting and starts to growl. And most important, you have to have the right combination of people, and they must all bring out one another's positive qualities to the optimum. This is hardest of all, because people are the most valuable resource of any quickly growing operation, and the fellow who first started musing on the sheet of yellow paper is likely to have a very big ego along with his imagination, and a corresponding lack of sensitivity to the people the company needs.

I suppose I have been involved in about a dozen of these amateur venture capital situations, and the record is no worse than anybody else's. It used to be, when the venture business was easier, that in the morning you expected to find a couple of your colts stiff, their feet in the air, but that one or two would turn out to be great winners, ten or fifteen for one, and that would more than make up for the losers. In the early sixties I was in a company that made radar antennae so successfully it went broke. It doubled its sales every year, and the Navy loved the antennae, but they sold for less than they cost, somehow, and the company ran out of money. It barely managed to sell its stock to the public before it went broke. Then there was the electronic grading machine that was going to be used in every school in America—a lot of them were sold before they found all the bugs in the machine—and the company that made the typewriter that talked back to three-year-olds when they pressed a key.

There was one outfit that was designed to relieve office overtime. No need to hire expensive temporaries for, say, peak insurance work: you just dictated into the attachment on your phone, and Dial Dictation would have it for you the next morning. The company hit some foul weather, and at night the president used to call me in California, where I lived at the time, to talk to me. Finally I asked him why he was calling me; I wasn't a very big stockholder and I wasn't a director.

"Nobody else will talk to me," he said.

There were a couple that worked: Control Data bought the laser company, and the company that made the radiation equipment for atomic tests not only made it to the public-offering starting gate but was given a very nice ride in the 1967 enthusiasm. So—no great fortunes, but a lot of interesting entertainment, and my basic conviction was still unshaken: you don't get rich owning General Motors, because General Motors has already grown up. What you should do with General Motors is inherit it. What you look for—at least before technology became a bad word—was "the next Xerox." A lot of people have gone down swinging trying for that one.

Typewriters that talked back to three-year-olds; attachments for telephones. I had never thought about a Swiss bank.

I took Paul to lunch at the restaurant of the American Stock Exchange, and he told me how he had started his bank.

"Swiss banks," he said. "The most common concept is the secrecy—numbered accounts, tax evasion, South American dictators, all that. But Swiss banks are universal banks. They operate everywhere and they are used to processing information from all over the world. But did you ever do business with a Swiss bank? Cold, formal, snooty, extremely cautious, very conservative, eh? I could see the age of the multinational corporation arriving, Polaroid and IBM building plants in Europe, Swiss drug companies expanding in the United States. The services offered by Swiss banks weren't up to those offered by American banks. I thought, What about an *American* bank in Switzerland, eh? A bank that would have American management techniques and American aggressiveness, but that was operating in Switzerland under Swiss laws, with Swiss universality. With maybe some of the dynamic qualities of a top-flight British merchant bank, *eh*?"

Paul was an American, but enough of Basel had rubbed off on him so that he frequently ended his statements with a Baseler interrogative, *ja*? Certainly if anyone was going to start an American bank in Switzerland, Paul was uniquely qualified, except that, with hindsight, maybe his knowledge of bank operating procedures was a bit sketchy. *The Wall Street Journal* was to describe him later as "a personnel man's dream." He was born in Stratford, Ontario, where his father, an American Lutheran minister, had been called to a parish. Paul's father is now a vice-president and administrator of the Lutheran Church in Canada, responsible for such activities as Lutheran hospitals and Lutheran insurance. Paul was sent at fourteen to a Lutheran "gymnasium" boarding school in Fort Wayne, Indiana, and then to Concordia College in St. Louis, where he met Helly, a native Baseler.

After he graduated from Concordia in 1953, Paul enrolled at the School of Foreign Affairs at Georgetown University, thinking he might be interested in the foreign service. He worked part-time as an editorial assistant at the Washington *Post* and graduated with an M.A. in 1955. Still not sure of a vocation, but wanting to study abroad for a while, Paul and Helly returned to her native Basel, where Paul enrolled at the University of Basel; one of his professors there later remembered him as a brilliant student. He received a second M.A. and then a Ph.D. in 1958, and his dissertation on Swiss-American economic relations was published in 1959. His academic credentials got him a job with the European Coal and Steel Community; in collaboration with a German economist, a friend of his, Paul produced another book, this one in German, called *Die europäische Wirtschaftsgemeinschaft und die Drittländer*, a study on the European Economic Community. Now his visibility was such that the Stanford Research Institute of Palo Alto scooped him up as a European representative. For three years he commuted from Basel to the Stanford Research office in Zurich, but, he told me, "I wasn't there much. I was all over Europe, consulting on business problems. We did a study for Alfa Romeo on their trucks, another for a Dutch steel mill that wanted to know whether and how to build large-diameter pipe, and so on." Stanford Research moved him back to Palo Alto, but consulting began to pall. He wanted to do more. Through Neil Jacoby, dean of the UCLA Business School and a director of Stanford Research, he met Charles Salik, a San Diego businessman who had formed an investment company called Electronics International, Inc. Salik sent him back to Basel to monitor European companies, and then bought the idea of a brand-new, American Swiss bank.

"What'll we call the bank?" Salik asked, and after some toying with words such as Swiss and American, Paul suggested Salik Bank.

"Why not?" Paul said. "It was his money." Salik and his family put up $600,000, and the bank began in two rooms.

No one could accuse the Salik Bank of being formal or snooty. Paul himself hustled customers all over Europe, and at one time the bank claimed to be Basel's second biggest Swissair customer, even though Basel is headquarters for several of the world's great drug companies. The Salik Bank not only took deposits and made loans—short-term collateralized loans in this case—but like most Swiss banks, it dealt in portfolio management, commodities, and foreign exchange. Its resources grew apace: from 13.7 million Swiss francs ($3.5 million) at the end of 1966, to 37.8 million Swiss francs ($9.8 million) at the end of 1967, to 142.5 million Swiss francs ($37 million) in mid-1968.

Paul's particular interest was in currency speculation. In many ways, this is the headiest speculative game of all, for it involves anticipating the moves of central banks, watching the trade balances of countries, and assessing both gossip and political intelligence. Basel itself is an arena for such talk, because the Bank for International Settlements, the clearing house for nations, sits in an old converted mansion opposite the railroad station. The headiness of the speculation comes from the large sums and high debt involved, because one side of the transaction has a floor.

For example: let us say, as it was in 1967, that the Bank of England is committed to buy and sell pounds at roughly $2.80. That is where the value of the pound was arbitrarily pegged. But Britain has a trade deficit; no one wants to hold pounds; there are more sellers to the Bank of England than buyers. You decide that the pound is weakening; sooner or later it must be marked down to a level where international trade will once again support it, and where once again it will reflect the realities of that trading.

So you sell, for future delivery, a million dollars' worth of pounds. You have already sold them, so to deliver them you will have to buy them back at a future date. You have sold them at $2.80; you know that you can buy them from the Bank of England close to that price. You need put up only $50,000 or so; your only expense is the commission on buying and selling, and the interest charges on your obligation. You hope, of course, to buy the pounds back cheaper, marked down.

But ripeness is all. Those interest charges can begin to mount.

Analysts of World War II like to point out the influence of *kendo*, the Japanese bamboo-stave fencing, on Japanese military strategy. A lot of parrying, watching for the perfect moment, and then victory in one devastating, lightning stroke—thus, Pearl Harbor.

Paul's mentality was something like that. Not for him a slow, quiet, dust-covered compounding in some vault.

In the fall of 1967, Paul was watching the sterling situation closely. A number of customers of the Salik Bank sold pounds for future delivery at $2.80. When Britain devalued the pound to $2.40, the customers bought their pounds in at $2.40 and delivered them, cleaning up. One client made $80,000 over the weekend. The coup, the shattering *kendo* stroke, had worked. Paul's reputation on currency matters rose, and he enjoyed the role of the currency critic. He wrote papers on gold and the dollar, signed by *Dr. Paul Erdman, President, the Salik Bank, Basel.* Not only is there something heady about currency speculation, but there is an element of the ultimate judge when one in effect says to a whole country: "Get your inflation in check and your trade balances up, or down goes your currency." That is the role not only of the Bank for International Settlements opposite the railroad station in Basel, but of the currency speculator.

Paul also wrote for *The International Harry Schultz Letter,* a breezy investment advisory letter from London with Winchell-like tones:

"Hi-lo ratio is negative but mkt not ready for a real kachunk . . . $ trading in Germany hectic . . . frustration with biz expectations causing a rise in nationalism." While the Winchell gossip might have been about starlets and entertainers, Schultz's concerns trade deficits, currencies weakening, and cryptic bulletins on world markets:

"*Austria:* sell into strength . . . *Holland:* buy, *Italy:* avoid, *Japan:* hold (reread HSL 254) . . . "

Schultz had been a California newspaper publisher, and is the author of several investment books, including one on Switzerland and Swiss banks. He likes to compare the United States to ancient Rome in its decadence; debasing of the currency is a favorite Schultz leitmotif; he considers it not the symptom but the *cause* of national decline.

Schultz's letter was a boost for Paul. It ran his short articles, detailed in one-liners some of Paul's travels and thoughts, and even identified some customers for the bank. It was one of Schultz's tenets that in the face of the weakening dollar, investors should not hold cash in U.S. savings or bank accounts. Instead, they could profit from the revaluation of the harder currencies: the Dutch guilder, the Japanese yen, the German mark, and Belgian and Swiss francs. Accounts in a Swiss bank could, of course, be invested in any of those currencies, and in fact an account could be left in a Swiss bank in a time deposit and denominated in Swiss francs.

Because of the corruption of the dollar, the faithful also saw exchange controls coming. Soon you would not be able to take dollars out of the country. After all, the English had once roamed the world, and now they were restricted at the borders to a few measly pounds and could scarcely travel abroad. The same could happen to Americans; the faithful, by getting their money out ahead of the lowering boom, could assure their future mobility. They would still be able to travel, to buy a house in France or a ski lodge in Switzerland; their foresight would be rewarded. Denuded of the rhetoric, the faithful were, of course, right. The dollar has been devalued, some say not for the last time. Specific taxes have been laid on to discourage American investment abroad, and the first limitations on transferring capital abroad have been imposed. Your bank keeps a record of each transfer into another currency of more than $5,000, and in fact you are supposed to report any such transfer to the IRS. Brand-new law. Presumably the IRS can thumb through all the microfilm any afternoon it feels like looking for fleeing capital.

Schultz ran a short list of Swiss banks in his letter, with the Salik Bank conspicuously on the list. After one Harry Schultz seminar in London, an excursion to Switzerland was formed, with Paul and his fellow Salik Bank employees entertaining the excursioners in Basel. Paul said he did not always agree with Schultz's apocalyptic notes, and he disparaged some of the Schultz faithful as "right-wing Texas kooks, who eat that stuff up," but he was glad to have them as clients. For a small bank in Switzerland's second city, the bank had an unusual number of Texas clients, and reportedly some of the clients became shareholders.

When Paul came to see me, he was not seeking another shareholder; he was seeking a friend for the bank. He did this naturally, as an active promoter, a selling president. He sought friends everywhere, and found them. Economists, business-school deans, currency experts, commodity dealers—all found him interesting and agreeable. He even cultivated the press—unlike, I am sure, any other bank president in Switzerland. Other Swiss bankers went to lengths to avoid the press. Paul courted friends for the bank everywhere. If he were asked to write an article on currency for a magazine, he was glad to do that; if, as we did, someone requested more information on Swiss banking, he would set us up with people who could help us.

But he could sense my enthusiasm. A dynamic young bank that had increased its resources by a factor of fifteen in less than three years—that was exciting to me. Coincidentally, the bank had grown so fast that it needed more capital, and it was just in the process of raising it. Paul himself had written the prospectus, and while the prospectus, representing a Swiss corporation, naturally did not need to be registered with the SEC in Washington, it was "just like a prospectus for the SEC, because we want to do everything right; we may come to the U.S. some day, and a New York law firm is going over it completely."

"It occurs to me," Paul said, "that you would be a very good shareholder for us to have."

I said I was very interested. We shook hands, mutually impressed, and Paul returned to Basel. The prospectus arrived a month later.

"From the beginning (1965)," said the prospectus, "the Salik Bank was conceived as a bridge between conservative Swiss banking—characterized by extreme caution, stability, and a unique expertise concerning financial matters on a worldwide basis—and modern corporate and financial management techniques usually identified with the United States." The bank had, the prospectus reported, recruited talent in the fields of portfolio management, foreign exchange, and commodities, and a Swiss financial newspaper had reported that the bank was the fastest-growing banking institution in Switzerland.

The bank, the prospectus reported, acted as a broker and dealer in foreign exchange, metals, and commodities. "This field of activity," said the prospectus, "is usually reserved to the large commercial banks, since the private banks of Switzerland seldom have sufficient expertise in this rather esoteric area of international finance." "The Salik Bank has sought," it added, "to move beyond the usual areas of money management offered by many of the more traditional private banks in Switzerland, and to provide 'total money management' by building its capabilities related to type of investments other than the usual stocks and bonds."

Little did I know, but those paragraphs contained the potential for disaster. But like the hidden figures in the child's puzzle—how many animals can you find?—my eye could not see anything but good.

The bank was also to open a subsidiary in Brussels; then within three to five years, there would be an international bank holding company, which could make other acquisitions "on a larger scale in other areas of Europe, as well as perhaps the Far East and even Australia."

The Far East and even Australia! The sun would never set on the Salik Bank!

I asked some of my pals on Wall Street for their counsel. I said I had a chance to buy a rapidly growing Swiss bank at a quarter over book value. Would they do something like that?

"How much can you get me?" they said, to a man, and they offered to take any left over. Of course, they were basically gunslingers, attracted to such situations. They didn't get any of the stock, but that didn't help them. The nursing home and peripheral computer companies they bought did just as badly. My enthusiasm grew. I decided to go to Basel.

You would have to say that as a European city, Basel is undistinguishable but likable. Green trams seem to run everywhere. You can sit by the Rhine watching the barges and sip pleasant Swiss wines—or even pleasanter German ones—and there are some nice parks and squares. For a city whose main industry is a series of drug and chemical complexes, it seems remarkably clean. At first, when you walk the streets, you can't quite define what's missing, and then you realize: it's the garbage bags, spilling over on the sidewalks, that you see so consistently in New York and London. And where is the litter? Where are the wrappers underfoot, the cigarette butts, the old newspapers? I never could figure out whether everybody peel-strips his butts and throws the tiny shreds into a container, the way they bring you up at Fort Dix, or whether the Turks and Spaniards and Italians who clean Basel just do a good job.

Paul picked me up at the airport, and we had lunch with the gentleman who was to fill us in on the background of Swiss banking—the subject that had brought Paul and me together. And after lunch we went to St. Jakobsstrasse, one of the main thoroughfares of Basel. There it was, all glass and metal and shiny: my Swiss bank.

Paul had worked with the architect, designing the circular staircase that connected two floors. Otherwise it looked like—well, what can you say? It looked like a bank—like an American bank, all open and bright and shiny, with tellers and people in shirt sleeves, and calculators. Which is to say that it did not look like a private Swiss bank, with its corridors and guards and its general air of reticence.

We sat in Paul's office, with its impressive desk and conference area—the right dimensions for a proper *Bank-präsident*—and I met a variety of people. Now I can only remember one of them, and that is perhaps because I met him a number of times later: Louis Thole, a pleasant, blond Dutchman in his thirties, scion of an Amsterdam banking family, who was going to handle the bank's portfolio-management activities.

"The Deutsche mark looks a bit stronger," said one of our staff.

"Let's buy another million Deutsche marks," Paul said.

Louis Thole wanted to know if I had looked at Japanese convertibles. I hadn't.

"The Hitachis are coming next week," Louis said. "They are beautiful. They are quite sexy."

"Silver," Paul said. "Silver is going to go through the roof."

I knew the silver story.

"I'm doing a report on silver," Paul said. "The U.S. Treasury will run out of silver at some point, and then, *whoom*. We have a man in Beirut who is very good on silver."

And gold—well, the world was not going to stand for long for all these jerry-rigged paper currencies, depreciating every day as their governments printed more paper.

Then another pleasant gentleman came in, whom I will call Alfred because I can't remember his name. Alfred had with him the forms to open an account. I said I was going to become a stockholder, not a depositor. Alfred said most of the stockholders were also depositors, and didn't I know all the advantages of a Swiss bank account?

I don't know what made me hesitate. Swiss bank accounts seemed appropriate for Las Vegas gamblers, South American dictators, Mafiosi, and people with cash incomes—some doctors, say—or with incomes abroad who weren't about to tell the government their foreign earnings because they considered taxes a personal injustice. I didn't see myself as the holder of a numbered account. Where would I keep the number? Tattooed on my heel? And what would I put in the account, anyway?

"I don't need an account," I said. "I already have a checking account. In the United States."

Alfred looked a little weary. Obviously that was not the right thing to say. I began to think the other visitors to the bank must have arrived with cardboard suitcases full of currency.

"Look," I said. "I'm very excited by the bank as an investment, but I pay my taxes."

Alfred looked absolutely blank at that. I was still apologetic.

"My income," I said, "is totally visible, and they take the taxes right out. And anyway, if you don't want to pay your taxes right away in the United States, you put your money into tax shelters, and then you don't pay them—at least that year. All legal and approved by the government."

"You do not have to have a numbered account," Alfred said. "You can have an account as public as you like. I am happy you like to pay your taxes. In Switzerland we feel that what happens between a gentleman and the tax agents of his own country is his own business.

In Switzerland we cooperate fully with other countries in pursuing criminals, but by Swiss law tax evasion in another country is not a crime. But let me ask you: are you married?"

I was married.

"Happily married?"

Happily married.

"Now," said Alfred, "you are happily married, you have insurance on your house. You naturally believe you will always be happily married, but you know that statistics do not bear this out, especially in America. And we know what happens in American divorces. They are famous. The woman keeps the house, she continues to live the same life; the lawyers and the courts take the husband's income and permit him to live on seventy dollars a week, in poverty. You are happily married now, but no man knows the future, five, ten, twenty years away. You think you will always be happily married. But do you not owe yourself a little insurance?"

"What are you saying?" I asked.

"With an account here, you need do nothing illegal. You can pay your taxes, you can buy stocks on any exchange in the world, you can buy and sell commodities anywhere in the world, and *no one need know about it*. And someday, when your wife's lawyers are trying to take away the money you have worked for twenty years to build up, you will have a private reserve."

Alfred must have met Americans before. Like a master insurance salesman, he closed in. Even the happiest of husbands would have paused for a moment.

"Nothing illegal," Alfred said. "There is nothing illegal in trying to strike a more equitable bargain with your wife's lawyers. That is nothing to do with you and your government."

Now that the matter was not between me and the government but between me and my wife's lawyers, those sonsabitches who were going to make me live on $70 a week, I began to loosen up. I could see them, the ferret-faced wretches—Bardell and Pickwick, crackling at their rolltop desks, rubbing their bony hands together as they dispatched me to some roach-infested garret with winos lying in the hallway and junkies shooting up under a ten-watt bulb. Why? What did I do?

"It's not illegal not to tell my wife's lawyers?" I said, forgetting for the moment that my wife had no lawyers nor any need of them.

"You don't owe your wife's lawyers anything, do you?" Alfred said. "They are going to try to prove you a criminal—that is the nature of American divorce justice: one party must be a criminal, an adversary proceeding. A criminal in fiction, mind you—mental cruelty, lack of attention, what-have-you—things that would make a European laugh. When an American wife behaves in a manner that would cause her to be *shot* if she were married to a European, the American stands still like a patient lamb to be fleeced."

"I've seen some tough cases," I said. "A friend of mine just went through it. They left him one shirt and one cuff link."

"Another thing," Alfred said. "Your dollar is declining. Your Vietnam war is bleeding it. Your government mishandled its finances. That is going to cost you dearly as a citizen."

"I've been saying that for three years," I said.

"Good," Alfred said. "Now, you pay your taxes, so you are already paying for your government's political sins, but why should you pay for its fiscal sins, when you yourself warned against them? Your account here will be in Swiss francs, so when the dollar falls apart, you will still have some currency with some value."

"Terrific," I said.

"Sign here," Alfred said, holding the pen out for me.

"Wait a minute," I said. "I don't need a number. Just a name."

"That number is for us," Alfred said. "Not secret. Your own account in America has a number. All bank accounts have numbers. Computers can't work with Roman numerals."

"Okay," I said.

Alfred held the pen out. I signed the form.

"No secret number," I said firmly.

"As you wish," Alfred said.

I had a Swiss bank account. I put $200 in it.

"No alarm clock," I said. "No toaster? No bonuses for signing up? Do I get pretty checks? A winter scene?"

Alfred did not seem to know about the American banking tradition of giving away two-dollar appliances for new accounts, and he indicated as long as the account was that size I would probably not need checks. The bank charges for the various bookkeeping transactions of deposits and checks were higher than in the United States. Paul came back into the room.

"You have a new depositor," I said. "But no number."

"Good," Paul said.

"Now that I'm part of the family," I said, "tell me. Do we have any South American dictators as depositors?"

"Oh, for heaven's sake," Paul said.

"I bet we must have one Mafioso. What's a Swiss bank without at least one Mafia account?"

"For heaven's sake," Paul said, "we want to go *public* with this bank."

We walked out through the bank, and Paul pointed out various of the officers. One was working in a small room with a desk calculator. Paul said he was from a wealthy family; he himself was a multimillionaire. Then why, I asked, was he working in a bank?

"First of all," Paul said, "in Switzerland everyone works. We have no playboys. If you are going to be a playboy, you have to go to the south of France or to London or New York or wherever they have that environment. St. Moritz is for foreigners. And second, in Switzerland you never know how much money anyone has. There are families in Basel whose net worth must be a billion dollars. But you never know. If you ever get to anyone's house, and through the front door, sometimes you see it on the walls—Picassos, Renoirs, and so on. And when they take a vacation they take a good vacation—a safari in Africa, a visit to South America, and so on. But you must leave Basel to spend the money. The houses are solid and square, not ostentatious. In Switzerland it is not only the money you *have* that is important, it is the money you *get*."

On the way to his house, Paul drove up to the cathedral, and we stood in back of it, overlooking the Rhine. We walked around among the gabled houses of old Basel, some of them centuries old.

"Basel's skills came from the Catholic persecutions," Paul said. "The Protestants who fled here had two skills. One was that, not being Catholics, they could lend money and change currencies, and that grew into banking. The other skill was in dyeing, dyeing textiles. During the nineteenth century the skill of mixing dyes grew naturally into chemicals, and during the twentieth century there was a natural transition from chemicals into drugs, and that is how Basel became one of the great chemical-drug complexes of the world."

Paul lived in a pleasant American-suburban-style house with a cathedral ceiling and books in three languages overflowing the shelves. The house was located in a solid residential section of Basel. The Erdmans did not live elaborately; they had an Alsatian girl who helped with their two daughters.

"It's nice to have somebody for dinner," Helly Erdman said. "In America you do that all the time. In Switzerland you just don't do that. Visits inside the house are inside the family. You go out to dinner only to see your own relatives."

"Once a year," Paul said, "maybe you will go to someone's house —another banker, let's say. Then it is very stiff, very formal. Dinner jackets. You send flowers to the hostess ahead of time."

"The conversation is very stiff too," Helly said.

"There are no backyard barbecues in Basel that I know of," Paul said. "Switzerland is built on privacy."

We talked about the plans for the bank. There would be a branch in Zurich, and then another in Geneva, and a subsidiary bank in Brussels; eventually the bank would sell its stock to the public in Europe and spread its activities far beyond Switzerland.

"Paul is involved in every detail," Helly said. "I can't tell you—he even debated with the architect over where that stairway should go in the bank."

The next morning we went back to the bank, and I went over various reports on European issues and European currencies. I also used my new bank to make an investment.

The Bank for International Settlements is the international clearing house for the central banks of governments. It is through this bank that government currency swaps are engineered, and also through this bank a government that is going too deeply into deficit in its international accounts is told to shape up. The stock of the bank is held by the member governments: the United States, Germany, France, Japan, Italy, and so on. Every once in a while there seem to be a few stray shares floating around, and so there was this day. For something like $1,100, I bought one share. Then the stockholders were the United States, Germany, France, Britain, Japan, Italy, and Adam Smith. I think I had in mind going to a meeting of the stockholders, or having some conversations with them, but I never got around to it.

Paul had a present for me. It was a diseased cocoa pod; someone had brought it to him, and there had been a section on cocoa in my book which Paul liked. We took pictures of each other holding the cocoa pod in front of the Bank for International Settlements. In the light of what was going to happen, it was the ultimate in irony.

I got on the train for Zurich. Swiss trains were supposed to run with the precision of watches; the train was to leave at 11:59, and I had just had my Swiss watch set. Starting at 11:57, I watched the sweep of the second hand. The train left ten seconds early.

In Zurich I had appointments with several major banks. Sometimes, peripherally, I would drop the name of my new bank into the conversation just to test the reaction. There wasn't much of one. Those who had heard of it didn't know much about it; one banker who had, thought the bank was "very aggressive," which in Switzerland is not a term of praise.

In Zurich the visceral feeling I had about Switzerland and money began to be confirmed. Now, I do realize that a week spent in banks does not provide a very broad background for generalizing about a country. You could spend a week on the ski slopes and come away with a different feeling, or a week in the chocolate factories, or some time with watchmakers or with the cuckoo-clock guild. Nonetheless, there is something about Switzerland and money that makes it ultima Thulen the country that provides one definitive end to the spectrum. After all, why *Swiss* banks? Most Western industrialized countries have well-developed banking systems, and a number of countries —Lebanon, the Bahamas, and Uruguay—have imitated the Swiss system of secrecy. Lebanon even used the Swiss banking code as a model. Still, for its size and per capita income, Switzerland leads the world in this profession. Why? It is the Swissness of the Swiss, and it might be interesting to take a moment to see how they got that way. Even though my new bank was not very typically Swiss, it gave me a feeling of confidence against fiscal dangers unknown, a home away from home.

By rights, Switzerland ought to be one of the world's losers. The popular image of Switzerland is mountains, and the popular image comes pretty close to being right. Only 7 percent of Switzerland can be farmed, and the country can't feed itself. Unlike much of Europe, it has no coal, oil, gas, iron ore or other industrial amenities, and no access to the sea. It had, of course, William Tell, a symbol of pragmatism, technical competence, and an unwillingness to be pushed around. Being mountainous, Switzerland had no large estates, no large convenient political divisions. Each valley community had to survive by itself. That led to a certain amount of hard-headedness. It isn't a Swiss proverb that says if you have an ugly face, learn to sing, but it might as well be.

In the late Middle Ages, the small Swiss towns found themselves astride a German-Mediterranean trade route, handling sugar, salt, and spices, discounting the gold from Venice and the silver from the Rhineland. According to one author, T. R. Fehrenbach, the Swiss burghers also had little use for medieval Christianity. For the Swiss businessmen already honored hard work, individual effort, and money, and medieval Christianity denigrated all of these things. *Gott regiert in Himmel und's Galt uf Erde*, went a Zurich proverb. *Für Galt tanzt sogar de Tuufel.* "God rules in Heaven, and money on earth. Even the Devil dances for gold."

John Calvin and Ulrich Zwingli changed the course of Switzerland. Gold was the sober gift of God and work was holy. Calvinism, according to the historian Tawney, is "perhaps the first systematic body of religious teaching which can be said to recognize and applaud the economic virtues."

Thus banking became one of the Protestant fine arts. According to Fehrenbach:

Zwinglianism did not reconcile Christ and Mammon. Zwingli and his rational spiritual descendants never saw any conflict. The Swiss did not learn to love money ... The Swiss *respects* money, a very different thing. Respecting it, a Swiss pursues, handles, and husbands money as an end in itself, which is utterly different from German materialism with its emphasis on things or American status-seeking, with its drive for power or prestige ... respecting money, the Swiss made its handling not a miserly trait but more a priestly calling. He erected ritual rooms and bare confessionals, guarded one and gave the other secrecy.

For four hundred years, the Swiss stuck close to the proverb. Money rules on earth. No political passions, no religious crusades. When the Swiss went to fight a war, it was somebody else's war. Something like two million Swiss soldiers left Switzerland to fight all over Europe—but always for money. The Swiss mercenary became a factor in the military history of the world.

Hard-headedness, pragmatism, and a distrust of new ideas; if the Swiss had had General Motors, they would have erected a statue to Charley Wilson for saying that what was good for General Motors was good for the country. Feudalism and Catholic Christianity weren't good for business; nor was despotism, anarchy, nationalism, a strong central government, socialism, Marxism, or even female suffrage. All of those winds have swept over the mountains without effect. (Only recently did the ladies get the vote. But Switzerland is still a male-chauvinist-pig country. If community property is involved, any husband can request information on his wife from a bank, but no wife can get such information on her husband without his consent.)

Non-Swiss seem to have been affected most by two factors in the Swiss banking code. One is the Swiss attitude toward taxation. In the Zwinglian Protestant society, honesty was not only the best policy, but work and the reward of work were holy. There was no strong central government, only a confederation of states, so by any world standard, national taxes are not particularly high. Therefore you get what you pay for, and you pay your taxes; taxes are a part of duty, and duty is a part of life. In the 1300's, the Austrian Hapsburgs had made life tough for William Tell, and sent the nasty agent Gessler, still booed in schools. Swiss society is structured to leave the individual Swiss alone. No Swiss government has ever made the evasion of taxes a *crime*. Americans shook off the stamp tax and the tea tax imposed by the Crown and went on, independently, to taxes of their own. The Swiss, having gotten rid of the Hapsburgs, saw no need to complicate life further: that lesson was learned.

Most governments in the world today cooperate with each other in apprehending criminals—but only if they agree on the crime, or on what is a crime. A crime in Soviet Russia or in Mao's China might not be a crime in the United States. A tax matter in Switzerland is an administrative detail between the state—that is, the canton—and the citizen. Not a crime. But if you rob a bank and send the money to a Swiss bank, the Swiss government is delighted to cooperate, take the lid off the bank account, check the serial numbers, and help send you to jail. Everybody agrees that bank robbery is a crime.

The other factor in the Swiss banking code that has endeared Swiss banks to foreigners is secrecy. But secrecy is nothing new to banks; in fact, the lack of secrecy is something relatively new, a part of contemporary nationalism. Roman banking law, Germanic civil law, and the laws of the northern Italian states, where banking flourished during the late Middle Ages, all contained secrecy provisions. Europeans are still a little startled by the way an American department store—or worse, the American government—can call up your bank and find out your fiscal habits. Until the 1930's, a Swiss bank account was properly secret, but it was up to the Swiss banker to preserve the secrecy.

As Germans—particularly German Jews—began to send their money out of Germany under Hitler, Gestapo agents tried to follow the money. Some of them simply bribed or cajoled the employees of Swiss banks, but others came up with a more ingenious device: they tried depositing money in Swiss banks, in the names of various wealthy Germans. The Swiss bank that accepted the Gestapo agent's ruse as a courier, and accepted the deposit, confirmed the fact that there was a bank account, and the unlucky German was whisked to a concentration camp, from which he asked the Swiss bank to send his money back to Germany, and then was tortured and executed. Much of the money that left Germany was never recovered and is still in the Swiss banks, and by now it belongs to the banks themselves, since under Swiss law if no one has claimed the deposit after twenty years it escheats to the bank.

The Swiss government was annoyed enough by the Gestapo's tactics to ratify the Banking Code of 1934, which made bank secrecy a part of the penal law. It took the moral burden off the banker by making it a crime to reveal any banking secrets, and it reassured foreigners that foreign deposits were protected by Swiss law.

The final appeal of the Swiss bank is not in the Swiss banking code, but in the Swiss banker. From his neutral perch, he has seen the world on the horizon go to war for seven hundred years. Castles are sacked in war, chieftains are scattered far, kings are deposed, governments fall, currencies become worthless, families break apart, wives leave husbands, husbands leave wives, children turn on their parents, mobs swirl in the streets—all like one of the Brueghels in the Swiss museums. If governments were not corrupt, if paper currencies did not depreciate, if taxes were fair, if there were no wars, if humanity were not so fallible—if the world were like Switzerland —then there would be no need of Switzerland. But the world is like that, and if Switzerland did not exist, to paraphrase Voltaire, it would have to be invented. The money in the bank is there in solid Swiss francs, backed by gold. Never mind the people who brought it there; it is the money that is immortal, to be tended like a delicate flower by God's own anointed gardeners. Even that simile is not quite accurate, for it is more important that the money be *preserved* than that it grow. Thus the honored calling: to preserve the incremental lump, the evidence that somewhere, sometime, someone pleased God with some work that was rewarded: husbanding the lump—that stewardship is an elite-enough calling.

And incidentally, very profitable. Can anything profitable be all bad?

In the month following my first visit to the bank, Paul and Louis Thole came to New York. Paul was eager to get the bank established in underwritings—that is, to be one of the group selling securities to the public, a function usually done by brokerage houses in the United States. Paul also wanted the bank to get more deeply into money management, running portfolios for clients.

Those were the heady days of "offshore" funds, led by Bernie Cornfeld's IOS. The funds were headquartered in "tax havens" such as Curacao and the Bahamas. These are countries equal to the United States, Britain, and West Germany in legal status, but their laws gov-

113

erning taxes, investment policies, and the ability to borrow on the funds were (and are) more relaxed than those of more developed countries. Paul and I talked about a hedge fund to be operated by the bank, as an additional service to its clients. We tried the hedge fund for a brief period on a "pilot" basis—that is, with a very small amount of money but with the pretense on paper that it was really full size. We washed around in some of the popular stocks of the tail end of the bull market, but it was plain to see that there was something nervous in the market: it simply did not behave with any degree of health. We discontinued the experiment after a few months with a small loss.

In the spring of 1969 I got a jubilant letter from Paul. Now the stationery was different: it bore the bold words *United California Bank in Basel,* in the same type face used by the United California Bank in Los Angeles. It also had a familiar monogram: UCB, familiar to me because I had once lived in California, and the UCB had a very catchy commercial all over the television channels.

"Now we can proceed with a number of projects," Paul wrote. "You will see by our new stationery that we have changed our name and made a great step forward. The United California Bank has bought a majority interest in the bank. UCB itself is the flagship bank of Western Bancorporation, one of the biggest bank holding companies in the world. Frank King, the chairman of both the UCB and Western Bancorporation, has become our chairman, and I am vice-chairman. We have a number of very exciting plans."

But for the next year, I was not in very close touch. We ran a seminar on American investments at the Savoy in London, attended by a number of European institutions, major banks, mutual funds, and insurance companies from Britain, Switzerland, France, the Netherlands, Belgium, Germany, and Italy. Paul and Louis came as invited guests, but I did not have much chance to speak to them.

In the spring of 1970 our Basel bank offered additional shares to its shareholders. I called Paul. He said things were going well, that the expansion was continuing, but that 1969 had been a disappointing year due to losses in the securities markets. That was not surprising; 1969 was not a good year anywhere. But now we had a new and additional important shareholder: the Vesta Insurance Company of Bergen, Norway, and through them, perhaps twenty Scandinavian banks. Scandinavia was to be a new and fertile field, and our Scandinavian shareholders would send us a lot of reciprocal business.

Bear-market gloom was upon Wall Street, and brokerage houses tottered. There wasn't much time to think about Basel or the United California Bank, but presumably things were going well. That was all I knew.

The Basel bank was indeed one of the fastest-growing financial institutions in Switzerland. In the United States such an image would have been welcomed; in Switzerland it was considered not sound and a bit pushy. For one thing, it was not easy to find qualified, competent people. Hiring away from another bank is something not readily done in Switzerland. To manage the bank's portfolios, Paul recruited Alfred Kaltenbach, an affable, nattily dressed Swiss with uncharacteristic long sideburns.

But the prize catch was Bernard Kummerli, an intense, near-sighted, rather olive-skinned foreign-exchange specialist. Jummerli was a native of Reinfeld, a small Swiss town near Basel noted for its spa and medieval old section. Kummerli's father was the banker in town. Kummerli had been educated in the local schools and in a private Catholic school, and then had worked for the Crédit Suisse, one of Switzerland's Big Three banks. Paul found himself at the Bank Hoffmann, a smaller, private bank, where Kummerli was the head of the department that traded currencies. Kummerli was very ambitious. His reputation was that of a walking computer, a man who could transact millions in foreign exchange in his head, the essence of cool. Kummerli is described as emotionless, which can scarcely be true for someone with that kind of fire in his belly, but that was the description extant. Kummerli could effect $10 million trades without the flicker of an eyelash. Three or four young traders came with Kummerli from the Bank Hoffmann, one of them Victor Zurmuhle. The -li or -le suffix in a Swiss name is a diminutive; Swiss-German abounds in diminutives. When Paul's trading department got going, Kummerli and Zurmuhle became known to the currency and commodity traders in Europe's financial centers as the "-li boys" or "Lee boys."

Paul had assembled a staff of young executives—almost all of them in their thirties—but not without some cost. The Big Three banks of Switzerland sent Paul a rather stiff, formal, four-page letter. It was not done to go raiding for employees, said the Big Three, and Paul was to stop it.

Kummerli arrived in mid-1968 and took a characteristic plunge into silver futures. The bank and some of its customers had already been into silver, and Paul had put out a letter in May suggesting that silver was a sale. But if his executives and his customers wanted to speculate—well, the customer was always right.

The rationale for the silver play was that the U.S. Treasury had stopped selling silver. Industrial uses of silver were growing. Therefore, with the U.S. Treasury no longer selling and industrial uses growing, silver had to go up. Right?

There was only one problem with that reasoning, and that was that the story was too old. Speculators had already anticipated all the events. I myself had culled out the dollar bills that came to me when breaking a ten or a twenty and saved the ones that said "silver certificate" on them, and in fact I had taken nineteen of them to the U.S. Treasury and traded them for a baggie full of silver. At this point there were no more dollar bills that were silver certificates, and the price of silver had in fact gone from 91¢ an ounce to $1.29, the price at the time that the Treasury had stopped selling, all the way to $2.50, the point at which the Basel geniuses discovered it. But so had all the people who had patiently bought silver for years, awaiting just such a rise; certainly the last 30 percent of the rise had been sheer speculation. By the end of 1968 the speculators had begun to cash in, and silver was down to about $1.80. In a commodity trade, the cash the investor puts up can be as low as 10 percent, so a drop of 25¢ an ounce on $2.50 silver would wipe out the account; long before that, there would be margin calls.

By June of 1969 silver had dropped further, to less than $1.60, but the bank had recouped some of the losses by quick trades on both sides. For its own account the bank made back its losses, but its customers who had been in silver were, needless to say, quite unhappy, and some of them complained to Paul.

Since May 1968, Paul had disassociated himself from the silver trades. He believed, he said, in giving his staff full rein, in leaving them complete autonomy. Paul felt badly about some of the accounts with silver losses. "Those guys," he said of his staff, "put some people in who had no right to be in. Not exactly widows and orphans, but practically. That was wrong." Especially after his form letter predicting just such a decline. So the bank did an extraordinary thing: *it canceled some of the silver trades, taking the losses onto its own books.* "We looked over the list," Paul said, "and we figured if it was a sophisticated guy, he was big enough to take his own lumps. But some of the accounts weren't, and we took the losses ourselves." The losses on the silver accounts were more than two million Swiss francs.

If it had become known that my Swiss bank was guaranteeing its clients against loss, it soon would have become the most popular financial institution in the world. Yet it was to do this twice more.

Once it was in an over-the-counter stock called Leasing Consultants, Inc., a Long Island computer-leasing company which financed aircraft and computer equipment. There was a plethora of such companies in the late 1960's; they based their existence on a bank loan for, say, an IBM-360 or a jet plane, something that could be readily leased. Then they sold the management of the company to the public. By the time Alfred Kaltenbach had found this company, it was already late in the game. Leasco, Data Processing, Financial General, and Levin-Townsend were on their way to Mr. Babson's booby list. An analyst in Oslo, Norway, told our sideburned and nattily dressed Kaltenbach about Leasing Consultants, proving that distance from Roslyn, Long Island, lends enchantment. For the bank's account, Kaltenbach bought letter stock, which was restricted and which the bank could not sell for a number of years, at prices around $12 and $13 a share.

Not only did the bank buy Leasing Consultants for its own account, but it circulated a report on its own stationery recommending its purchase. Nineteen of the bank's clients bought the stock through the bank. Unfortunately, Leasing Consultants went the way of many such companies. Its income had been overstated, and early in 1970 it admitted it. The stock dropped to 7. By August the company had filed for bankruptcy, and the stock was 37¢ bid.

Again, the bank was distressed at the losses of its clients. This time the major loss was in the bank's own account—in fact, the loss was to total $2 million—but the nineteen clients got their money back. In *The Wall Street Journal* Ray Vicker reported that "one startled customer" had said "this was the first time anybody ever reimbursed me for a bum trade."

Meanwhile, Kummerli had found a new field for his talents: cocoa futures. But by the time Kummerli was really rolling, our bank was part of the great United California Bank.

In 1968 Paul had been on a trip to the West Coast, and had looked up his friends from the Stanford Research Institute. Over drinks one night, Paul met Edward Carter, the chairman and chief executive of Broadway Hale, one of the nation's major department-store chains. Carter, who was on the board of both the United California Bank and its parent, Western Bancorporation, later called Cliff Tweter, the vice-chairman, who set up a meeting for nine the following morning. Tweter was joined by the senior vice-president for international affairs of the bank, Victor Rose, then sixty-five. Within ten minutes, according to Paul, Rose had said, "Can't we buy that bank?"

In October, shortly after my own visit to Basel, Paul had met Frank

King, the chairman of the United California Bank, in the London Hilton. King, then seventy-one, had started as the assistant cashier of the first National Bank of Sparta, Illinois; he had been president of the United California Bank for twenty-four years. "We want to buy your bank," King said. King had three prerequisites: first, that the United California Bank in Los Angeles have absolute control; second, that Charles Salik and his family retain no further interest; and third, that the management team stay on. In January King came to Basel to look over the bank. There seemed to be no question of his fascination with Paul Erdman. In March of 1969 there was a handshake agreement between King and Salik, and the lawyers went to work. The deal was complete in May; the Basel bank was valued at $12 million. What the UCB sought, among other things, was the Basel bank's toehold in Switzerland and Europe, and even more important, its dynamic young executives. "We bought the bank to get Paul Erdman," said a UCB official at the time. And according to Ray Vicker of *The Wall Street Journal,* King regarded Paul "almost as a son."

The United California Bank put two men on the board of its new acquisition. Frank King became the chairman of the board, and Victor Rose became a director. The California bank was quite proud of its acquisition. It changed the name almost immediately to The United California Bank in Basel. In its glossy annual report for 1969, it discussed the acquisition of the Basel bank as high among its achievements for the year, and listed it as a subsidiary.

Paul had thought the affiliation with a powerful bank would bring in new business, but apparently it did not. Paul was to report directly to Frank King, and in their discussions they went over a potential international program. In particular, now that he had Scandinavian stockholders, Paul had planned his end run around the dominant banks of Scandinavia. There were no American banks in Scandinavia; now, with his new Scandinavian connections, he could meet middle-sized businessmen in those countries and recruit their accounts before they moved from their country banks to the major banks of the Scandinavian capitals.

At the time the California bank took over, it had sent in its own auditors, who reported how the bank had taken over the customers' losses on silver, and also that there was a substantial exposure on margin accounts. But this did not get in the way of the merger. In fact, according to Paul, there was little communication with the parent bank. "Occasionally," Paul said, "a visiting fireman from Los Angeles would come through. He would ask where the good restaurants were, and whether we would get him a reservation at the two- and three-star places over the border in France." There was no general plan, and no external budget, and only slowly did the Basel bank come on stream into the California bank's reporting system.

Meanwhile, Bernard Kummerli was on his way to buying *half the cocoa in the world.*

Even to this day, I find the incident which brought down the bank totally and personally incredible. I had received the write-up on Leasing Consultants, and in fact had asked Louis Thole where they had come up with such a turkey at such a late date. But no one ever told me our bank was going into *cocoa.* What was to follow was as bizarre an example of nature imitating art as could ever be found.

Our bank had already dabbled in cocoa for the accounts of some of its customers. "A few contracts, nothing more," Paul said, and in the noble tradition of our bank, when the market went against the clients the bank, of course, took over the losses. "Small stuff, only a hundred thousand dollars or so," Paul said. "I thought we had only a few contracts." All that, according to Paul, had been audited by the United California's Bank's own auditors when the Los Angeles bank bought the majority interest.

The bank, of course, was eager to have a coup. It had a reputation for brilliance and aggressiveness, and Paul's own style was the *kendo* stroke. The mistakes in silver and the securities market needed to be made up.

Somebody must have told Kummerli the world was about to run out of cocoa. So he took off for Ghana to become an expert. Later I asked Paul what Kummerli had done in Ghana.

"Damned if I know," he said. "Drank a lot of beer. I think he got to know some of the fellows who were experts, commercial attachés, people in the cocoa trade, and so on."

In mid-July of 1969, there was some sort of interdepartmental intrigue going on in the commodity department of our bank. Kummerli was on vacation, and the other one of the Lee boys, Victor Zurmuhle, came to Paul to report that Kummerli had been speculating. According to Paul, Zurmuhle discovered three thousand cocoa contracts, all betting on chaos, riots, no spray—and Black Pod, a dreaded cocoa disease. What did they do? "We traded them out." Heretofore there had been no limits on the commodity traders; now Paul told the young Swiss accountant on his staff, Helmut Brutschi, to set controls. Apparently Brutschi never got started, and even Paul, out on the frontiers wooing the Scandinavians, began to realize that better operational controls were needed. He hired such an officer from a Swiss unit of National Cash Register, but "he didn't work out." And by the time another such officer was brought in, this one from the Volkesbank, the books had been doctored.

When Kummerli returned from vacation in August 1969, he promptly fired Zurmuhle. Zurmuhle, he said, had been speculating without authorization.

What follows is perforce a bit hazy, and it may safely be said that probably no one knows exactly what happened. Since the bank closed its doors teams of auditors have been sorting out the Byzantine mess, and to compound the usual Swiss secrecy, a trial is impending and much of the information belongs to the prosecuting attorney, who is tight-lipped even for a Swiss and a prosecuting attorney.

Somewhere along the line the United California Bank in Basel bought 17,000 cocoa contracts—*seventeen thousand* cocoa contracts —with a face value of $153 *million*. That is quite a chunk for a bank with a net worth of $8 million or $9 million. The contracts were sold by major commodity brokers: Merrill Lynch; Hayden, Stone; and Lomcrest of London. Normally, brokers would not extend a total of $153 million in credit to an institution with $8 million in assets, but our stationery did say that we were the United California Bank in Basel, and the United California Bank itself had assets of more than $5 billion.

Our bank's exquisite timing extended to cocoa. It managed to buy at the highs, something like 48¢ a pound, and the market promptly began to erode. By June of 1970 it was close to 30¢ a pound, and on 10 percent margin, the bank had lost three or four times its stake, maybe more, and was desperately insolvent, except for whatever its California parent cared to put up.

Only, nobody knew it, since by now the books were really doctored. "The balance sheet was undeniably falsified," said Max Studer, an auditor from the Swiss Society for Bank Inspection. But the chicanery had begun before. The bank had not exactly taken all its loss on the Leasing Consultants fiasco. "That was just too big a loss," Paul said. "No one writes off five million Swiss francs in one quarter. That was too big a hunk. You spread it over a longer accounting period. It would have looked very bad." What Kaltenbach did was to get a letter from the Norwegian firm that had first recommended the stock, promising to buy it at its $25 cost, even though by then the stock was down some 40 percent. In return, the bank promised to make good the Norwegian firm's purchase so that they would lose no money on it. In other words, the two institutions would trade worthless pieces of paper. "The Norwegian guarantee is meaningless," Paul told the California bank. "As long as it keeps the auditors happy," said L.A. Apparently that was all right with the California bank.

The auditors were a company called Gesellschaft für Banken-revision; the auditing firm itself was owned by two of Switzerland's Big Three: the Swiss Bank Corporation and the Crédit Suisse. Not only were the auditors happy, but they approved and certified a balance sheet that was already short by about twenty million Swiss francs.

Kummerli and crew rather desperately tried to straddle cocoa as it fell; some auditors, that is, tried to minimize losses by contracts covering short-term fluctuations with different delivery months, but even the straddles misfired. On the rare occasions there was a cocoa profit, that went onto the books. When there was a loss, the con-firmations went into Kummerli's desk drawer.

Later—in fact, the day after Paul got out on bail—I asked him how, in an age of computers and organized record-keeping, all this had been possible.

One mistake, he said, was that the commodity department ran from under the same roof as the foreign exchange trading and the money desk, where interbank deposits were made and accepted in a multi-plicity of currencies. "The Big Three banks controlled the foreign exchange market," Paul said. "We were very aggressive. We had built up until we were fifth in Switzerland, and we were turning over five billion Swiss francs a day in exchange. The bank's own positions in currencies, forward and spot, added up to more than two billion dollars. When you have that much out, nobody cares much about a few million dollars." The brokers who sold the UCB cocoa contracts were paid out of the foreign exchange department. The California bank had spot-checked its bumptious subsidiary, and suggested that maybe a position of $2 billion in foreign exchange was a bit much for a bank that size; it suggested that perhaps only $1 billion in foreign exchange be held.

Paul and I sat there on an apartment terrace in Basel discussing this just as if we were management consultants analyzing the process.

"Say," I said, "you remember the thing I wrote about cocoa?"

"Sure,"Paul said. "That was good."

"You remember you gave me a diseased cocoa pod as a present when I first came to Basel?"

"Sure."

"You remember what it said at the end of the story? That there are serious pros in cocoa? Hershey and Nestle and like that? When you are tempted to speculate in cocoa, *lie down until the feeling goes away.*"

Paul shrugged. "These fellows said they knew what they were doing."

"How about Kummerli? Did he read that story?"

"No, it wasn't out as *Das grosse Spiel ums Geld* yet, and Kummerli didn't read English."

For the first time, I lost my temper.

"He bought the cocoa in English, didn't he?" I said.

There was an awkward silence and the cordiality dropped away.

"He bought the cocoa in English." Paul shrugged again. "I'm sure he never read the story."

We went back to discussing the decline and fall.

How could it happen, I asked, in a modern, twentieth-century Swiss bank that so much money could disappear unchecked simply by putting the losses into a desk drawer? After all, this was not a robbery, not an embezzlement, and as far as was known, no money actually went in anyone's pocket.

"We should not have combined the commodity money market and foreign exchange departments," Paul said again. "That made it too easy to cover by simply listing a time deposit from another bank. And if a department gives an order, the confirmation should go somewhere else, to be double-checked. Every position in the balance sheet should be verified, and it wasn't."

"Shouldn't the outside auditor come in and check, at least once or twice a year?"

"They should, but Swiss auditing firms only care that the numbers you give them match up, not that there is anything behind the numbers. There's one more thing."

"What's that?"

"The chief executive of a bank should know the operations side of a bank—all the procedures, the accounting processes, and so on. I thought I had people covering that, but I didn't, and I certainly didn't do the job myself."

I wanted to know what Kummerli's motivations were. I could see how anyone could bite on the cocoa story; I had myself. After all, in any given year, the world can run out of cocoa, although it has never happened yet. But from there to putting the losses into a desk drawer, and thence to busting a bank, is quite a step.

"I think at first he wanted to impress his own traders. He had a big ego, a reputation for being very smart. When the losses were a million or two, he just couldn't admit it. He was like a man at a roulette table, doubling up and doubling up again, waiting for the final double up that would break him even. Finally—I don't know, maybe he saw the handwriting on the wall and decided as long as he was going to get nabbed at some point, he would put something away for the day he got out of jail. I don't know. To do that he would have had to have confederates somewhere else, someone working in one of the commodity houses."

One day in the summer of 1970 Paul was preparing to go on vacation. At that point, he had condoned the jiggle of Leasing Consultants, and knew that there was speculation going on in commodities, but the depth of the trouble lay ahead. He stopped by the office of the bank's chief accountant, who said he had a question. It was a small piece of pink paper with a debit of twenty-five million Swiss francs. The accountant said it must be a mistake; Paul hadn't a clue.

"I knew something was wrong," Paul said. "I knew I should stay and sort it out. But the family hadn't had a vacation in a long time."

One of the items on Paul's desk was a partial translation of the annual report, done internally. Foreign exchange, foreign currency, and margin positions for commodities had been lumped together in one big number. There was that mysterious pink slip for twenty-five million Swiss francs, apparently a realized cocoa trade. Paul deleted the reference to "margin" in the report, even though it had already circulated in German and had been approved by the Swiss Banking Commission. "Why wave a red flag if you don't have to?" Paul said. "We needed time to clear things up."

The family took off for Marbella, Spain, but Paul did not enjoy his vacation.

"I didn't sleep very well," he said. "I had a tummy ache."

Paul decided that the vacation just wasn't going to work, with unanswered questions floating around. Why had that accountant given him a chit for twenty-five million Swiss francs and then asked what it was? What else was wrong?

"Something wasn't right, and I wasn't facing it," Paul said, a bit belatedly. Back to Basel went the family and behind Kummerli's back.Paul started a low-key investigation. There were, it seemed, huge losses in the commodity department. So, according to Paul, he called Kummerli in, and something like the following dialogue took place:

Paul: What's going on?

Kummerli: Losses, losses.

Paul: I know losses, but how much?

Kummerli: I don't know.

Paul: Why not?

Kummerli: I lost control. I just lost control.

Paul: How much are the losses? Five million?

Kummerli: More than that. I lost control.

Paul: Ten million? Fifteen million?

Kummerli: More than that, I think.

Paul: Twenty million?

Kummerli: Somewhere around there, I think.

Kummerli kept muttering "Losses, losses" and "We lost control."

At twenty million, not only was the bank gone but so were one and a half more banks the same size. Paul decided that he had better carry the message to Los Angeles personally, and he caught the daily Swissair early bird from Basel to Paris and then an Air France flight over the pole to Southern California.

Paul and Helly checked into the Century Plaza in Los Angeles. Neil Moore, a senior vice-president of the UCB, met them. "Don't give me the details," Moore said. "Just tell me the loss, down to the penny."

On Sunday, August 30, Frank King led the group of UCB officials who met with Paul in a conference room at the Beverly Hilton. The president of the bank, according to Paul, was philosophical. "Win some, lose some," he said. The one concern was to keep the affair secret to avoid a run on the bank. "How many people know about this?" Paul was asked. "Can we keep it all a secret?"

The bank's chief auditor was worried about the extent of the loss. "We could handle five million dollars," he said. "But twenty million—twenty million could mean trouble even for Frank King."

Two days later, Paul and Helly and Neil Moore and an attorney for the bank flew back to Basel. "Nobody said much across the Atlantic," Helly recalls. Outside auditors went to work on the bank's books; the losses seemed to be closer to $30 million than to $20 million. In Los Angeles, Paul had tendered his resignation, but he was to remain as an executive and consultant to "straighten the mess." The idea was that the bank would remain open, still the United California Bank's Swiss unit; the parent would work out a scheme to protect depositors and creditors.

On September 6 there was a board meeting of the United California Bank in Basel, but Paul did not stay long. He was asked to leave the room and told that he was fired. "I went home and had a Scotch."

Paul was about to come down to breakfast on Wednesday, September 9. He was wearing loafers without socks and was in his shirt sleeves when two Basel policemen appeared at the door. They said he was wanted for questioning. Paul expected this; he would be there, he thought, two or three days. The Basel police also picked up the Lee boys, Kummerli and Zurmuhle, as well as Helmut Brutschi, the accountaint Beat Schweitzer, Louis Thole, and Alfred Kaltenbach.

The UCB officials went to the Swiss Bank Commission in Bern, and presented their plan to reimburse the depositors and creditors. The Swiss Bank Commission naturally was worried about the reputation of Swiss banks; the word around Basel was that once that was protected, they were glad to see an American-owned bank get a black eye; now it would be easier to keep the foreigners out of Switzerland. The details of what went on between the UCB officials and the Swiss Bank Commission are not known; again, there were rumors that the commission told the UCB that if it would make good and get out of Switzerland, it would be kept out of the trial to follow as much as possible. On September 10 the bank suspended operations, and on September 16 at 2 P.M. it posted notices on its doors saying it was bankrupt.

The United California Bank in Basel AG was by no means the first Swiss bank to go broke. In the Depression of the 1930's, three of the top seven Swiss banks folded, just as banks everywhere did. Swiss banks were overinvested in Germany, and suffered from the German inflation of the 1920's and the rise of the Nazis, and then from the impact of World War II on their German investments. In more recent years, the Germann Bank has folded because of bad loans, and the Aeschen Bank and Arbitrex on speculation, and the Sligman Bank had bought a huge tract of land south of Rome without clearing the building permits, and expired, suffocated by illiquidity. So busted banks were not new to Switzerland.

But my bank goes in the almanac—it is the biggest Swiss bust ever.

Meanwhile, back at the ranch in New York, I called Abe. I should have done that first anyway. Abraham Pomerantz is sixty-nine, portly, and has a nice white mane. He is also the name that scares banks most, not to mention mutual funds and other financial institutions, because Abe is the Ralph Nader of the investment business. There are differences, of course. Ralph Nader lives in a boarding house and operates from a pay phone down the hall. Abe lives in a penthouse and operates from the senior partner's corner suite of a prosperous midtown law firm. Ralph Nader burns with righteous zeal; Abe thinks there are many defects in the society which can be corrected through legal action, and he gets enormously well paid for the corrections when they work.

One day in the early 1930's, when Abe was a struggling young lawyer, the widow of his high school gym teacher came to see him. The widow Gallin's husband had left her twenty shares of the National City Bank. Once they had been worth $400 a share, and now they were worth only $20 a share. "I remember telling her there was no law against losing money," Abe said, and the widow Gallin went away. Then the Senate Committee on Banking and Currency, identified usually by its counsel, Ferdinand Pecora, began to investigate the skullduggery that had gone on in some of the nation's board rooms: the excessive compensation, the dealing in corporate assets, and so on. Charles Mitchell and some of the directors of the National City Bank seemed to be high on the list, in a famous case adequately chronicled elsewhere. Abe filed suit on behalf of the widow Gallin against National City Bank—and hence its stockholders—in a derivative action, so called because the stockholders derived their rights from the shares in the corporation they own. The stockholder who brings the suit brings it on behalf not only of himself but of his class—that is, his fellow stockholders.

The courts awarded the widow Gallin $1.8 million, of which Abe —and the lawyers and accountants who worked on the case—took $472,500. Abe became a champion of the minority stockholder. The Chase Bank was next—$2.5 million for a Mrs. Gertrude Bookbinder.

Abe went on to test the way mutual funds used the commissions derived from buying and selling their portfolios to pay for the selling of their funds; excessive sales loads for mutual funds; using the commissions to buy research, and so on. In the courts, he questioned the way banks use the commissions from their trust departments to gain deposits for themselves. Eventually he even got to the drug companies on the price-fixing for tetracycline, which resulted in a judgment against the drug companies of $152 million. Since it was impossible to pay back the individual consumers of the drugs, that amount was spread out among the health departments of the fifty states. Most of Abe's efforts, though, were in the securities and investment fields, and the structure of that industry was hardly the same for having known Abe.

So I called Abe. Normally, and at this stage of his career, Abe does not take phone calls from private citizens, however grievously wounded, but in our peregrinations through the securities business, our paths had crossed. Abe had already read about it. He told me to come right up. "Makes me feel young again," Abe said.

I had made up a list of questions. If a big bank bought a little bank, and hence had the power to hire and fire people, and in fact the right to name the whole board, weren't they responsible for proper procedures? They did have that power; they had, in fact, fired the president in ten minutes one Sunday, without even telling us junior partners. So wasn't the big bank guilty of *ungetreuen Geschäfts-führung* ("Suspicion of Untrue Management"), even if they weren't guilty of *Urkundenfälschung* ("Falsification of Documents")? And the outside auditors certified all the *Urkundenfälschung* and the *unget-reuen Geschäftsführung;* Price Waterhouse and Peat Marwick had gotten into a lot of trouble for less. Weren't the auditors liable too? And the board: naturally, the board.

When I went to see Abe, he was in a sober mood. He had read through some research, and he looked up from the papers.

"If this had happened in this country," he said, "this would be worth a hundred million dollars as a class action. But it happened in *Switzerland* and everything in Switzerland is a secret. We don't even know who the stockholders are. Switzerland is a very backward country. They have never heard of a class action. So the answer to all your questions is yes. Yes, the board is clearly liable, but the management of the bank is in jail and clearly busted, except for the two Californians from the parent. And yes, if it were *here,* the auditors would be culpable. And yes, if it were *here,* the controlling bank would have a liability. But it wasn't here. So I can't take the case, but I like you and you like me, and out of all the people that the UCB doesn't want to have overhanging the cleanup of this, the two of us have to be at the top of the list. I have a reputation as an ogre in this field, and so I will write them on my ogre stationery, and we'll offer them your stock, at cost. Maybe they'd like to buy out a partner, just to clean things up. Their name was all over the prospectus, after all."

But the United California Bank didn't seem eager to buy any more stock. We got a stiff letter from O'Melveny and Myers, the lawyers for the United California Bank. The entity to which we referred, they said, was a *Swiss bank.* Funny it had the same name, but clearly, how could they be involved?

"I was afraid of that," Abe said. "You see, that's the trouble. This whole damn thing is *in Switzerland.* The Swiss won't even tell you

127

the telephone number. You'll have to sue in Switzerland, and the trouble with that is, there is no bank left in Switzerland, so there's nothing left to sue. And the United California Bank itself is in Los Angeles."

"Is there no justice?" I asked.

"That's a metaphysical question," Abe said. "I don't know if there is or isn't justice, but I do know one thing: there's no class action in that damn backward country over there. You know, I had a client once who put me into a sure thing in commodities."

"What happened?" seemed to be the proper inquiry.

"I lost my shirt," Abe said. "I've never made a penny on an investment. It's good I've been lucky in the law."

After a while, the bank's management was released from prison on bail. Louis Thole had a nervous breakdown, was released, and went to Belgium. In the early summer of 1971, Paul was released on bail of half a million Swiss francs, raised from Henry Schultz, Helly's family, and some friends. Paul went to England to work for the Harry Schultz letter. All the prisoners were out on bail except Kummerli, and the word was that Kummerli—pending, of course, his guilt or innocence at trial—would be in custody a long time. Paul had had one confrontation with Kummerli before the investigating magistrate. Kummerli said that everyone knew the books were doctored, and that he got his orders from Los Angeles. "He might as well have said from Joan of Arc, or Jesus," Paul said. There was some speculation around Basel as to whether Kummerli had really gone off the deep end in jail, or whether this was a foxy act so that he would be allowed to serve his time in a mental institution rather than in prison.

I went over the prospectus once more. There it was, "the bridge between conservative Swiss banking and modern corporate and financial techniques, usually identified with the United States."

The present situation, then [it said], is that the Bank is a subsidiary of United California Bank of Los Angeles, a bank with total assets of $5.2 billion at the end of 1969. United California Bank is, in turn, affiliated with Western Bancorporation, the world's largest bank holding company, embracing twenty-three full service commercial banks located in eleven western states of the United States. United California Bank itself is the full owner of an international bank in New York City, and has branches, representatives or affiliates in England, Belgium, Switzerland, Spain, Lebanon, Japan, Mexico and Greece. It has direct correspondent relations with ... banks throughout the world.

The music began to rise again. The sun would never set on our fast-growing Swiss bank. I was trying to abstract some lesson from the experience, but I knew that if tomorrow someone brought me the fastest-growing financial institution in Switzerland, with that kind of affiliation, and with a dynamic young management, I would probably do it all over again. There was one thing that bugged me the most.

"When I called you," I asked Paul, "and asked you how the bank was doing, at the time the bank was raising more capital, you knew that all was not well, and you didn't say a word."

"We were opening new branches in Zurich and Geneva," Paul said. "We were going to have banks in Brussels and Luxembourg. We had a little problem with the balance sheet, but who would have thought we couldn't work things out?"

Paul had started to write a novel during his ten months in prison. I asked him what he was going to do next.

"I don't think I'll be the president of a bank," he said.

I didn't think so either.

I read the first sixty pages of Paul's novel. Belatedly, maybe I did learn something. It was set in the near future. The world was involved in a financial crisis. Treasury officials from various countries were flying from capital to capital. Among the characters were a Russian from the Narodny bank, a titled Englishman from the Bank of England, a bluff American, a safe-cracker named Sammy, a Basel policeman, and a stiff, austere Swiss banker who was about to pull off an audacious and entirely legal currency coup which would result in a profit to his bank of one billion dollars. *One billion dollars.* The greatest *kendo* stroke of all time.

CHAPTER 6

SOMETHING ELSE IS GOING ON, OR
"I AM NOT GOING TO BUST MY ASS FOR ANYBODY"

I think it was about five o'clock in the afternoon and the snow was getting worse and I began to ask myself what I was doing in the Pink Elephant Bar in Lordstown, Ohio. The Pink Elephant is on the highway, Route 45, the one that goes by the new $250 million General Motors plant that makes Vegas on the world's most automated assembly line. My friend Bill and I go up, cold, to these various characters, some of them indeed with mustaches and long hair and sideburns, and there we are: boy social scientists, amateur pollsters. Can we talk to you? Can we buy you a beer? Rolling Rock or Genesee? Do you work in the Vega plant? Is that a good place to work? I mean, would you tell your brother or your son to get a job there? What do you do there? Does your wife work? Do you want another beer? When you get your paycheck, what do you spend it on? Do you spend it in stores, for things, or do you pay it to people—doctors, barbers, plumbers? What do you think of the kids in the plant? The old guys? The blacks? The foremen? The management? Do you want another beer? What do you want to do with your life?

At one point this character in a leather jacket comes up behind us who looks like an old pro football player gone a bit soft—not a tackle; a guard or a linebacker, maybe six-three, two forty-five—and he says, "I heard you talkin'."

We wait. Some tension in the air, momentarily.

"Air you fum West Vihginyuh?"

We are not from West Virginia. Bill is from Detroit and I am flown from the canyons of Gotham.

"I knew you wasn't fum here. You talk lahk you're fum another country."

Well, yes, I say, it is another country.

"Good, lemme buy you a beer, I lahk to talk to people fum other countries."

What do you make per hour? Would you rather have overtime or the time off? Is there a generation gap? Would you buy one of the cars you make? What does the union do for you? Why do you work there? What would you rather do? Do you think things are working properly in the country?

You can see all the contemporary social science bits going on: Attitude/Authority? Agree/Disagree? Sick Society? Attitude/Work?

Our ambitions are very modest. Bill is doing a story. Maybe he can get another Pulitzer, why not have two? And as for me—why, I am just looking for clues, see, The Future of American Capitalism. I am going through the money-management macro bit in an untraditional way. The man running the money comes into his office, puts on his green eyeshade and his sleeve garters, and says: How goes the world today? And how will it go in six months? A year? But what does he know then? He reads reports and numbers, but what do they tell?

Are we really then back to normal, a big sigh of relief and business as usual? Or is there Something Else Going On? Maybe the system is changing, maybe our view of reality was distorted all the time. The very bright people were in charge of the government, and making the world safe for democracy, and not only is the world not safe for democracy, it is not even safe in Central Park and downtown Detroit and nobody wants to go out after dark. We put the money into public housing and it turns into disasters such as Pruitt-Igoe in St. Louis, and twenty-two downtowns look like Berlin in 1945. We did put men on the moon, but do we really know how to manage, and how to perform?

The estimable white-haired and pipe-smoking chairman of the Fed, Arthur Burns, comes to report to the Joint Economic Committee of Congress. Clutched in his hand is the Fed's report for the year, and its promises for the future. But before Burns delivers the report, he has to make some remarks that are not in the report. Maybe "old-fashioned remedies"—that is, those available to Arthur Burns: the levers of credit—can't do the job. Businessmen aren't responding in the usual ways. Consumers aren't responding in the usual ways. "Something has happened to our system of responses. Troubled times have left a psychological mark on people. Americans are living in a troubled world, and they themselves are disturbed."

What can the matter be? Well, "a long and most unhappy war," and busing, and the youth vote, and campus disorders, and urban race riots, and the fact that "women also are marching in the streets." Oh my God, women are marching in the streets.

"If only life would quiet down for a while," said the chairman of the Fed. The classic economic policies would have a better chance of working *if only life would quiet down for a while.*

So said the chairman of the Fed, hardly one of your bomb-throwing radicals.

Something has happened to our system of responses. If only life would quiet down for a while.

Poor Arthur Burns, you press the levers and the right things don't happen, and the problem is life itself. But maybe that is life; maybe that is the way things are going to be from now on. Good God, women marching in the streets, nobody responding in the usual ways. Mindboggling.

So that is one of the reasons I am getting a bit bloated on Rolling Rock beer in the Pink Elephant Bar on Route 45 in Lordstown, Ohio. If you simply read the financial pages, you would find no hint of anything different. The type face is the same, the language is the same, and the reports are all of prices: bonds are up, the dollar is down, retail sales are up—sheer minutiae. So everything is back to normal, we had a bad turn there at the end of the sixties, we had to hold our breath a little, but now we can go back to the old stand. Has the symphony of progress come back? Or does Arthur Burns really have something to worry about?

They say, for example, that the good old Protestant Ethic has died away. Whatever happened to work? Doesn't anybody want to? And growth: the whole system is geared to growth, that is its justification, it *works* better. What is all this about no-growth, zero population growth, zero economic growth? There is only so much stuff in and on the planet, and at the rate we are using it up in x years there will be no planet. Apocalyptic literature arrives not only on the ecological side but on the cultural side. "There is a revolution coming," writes Charles Reich. "It will not be like revolutions of the past. It will originate with the individual and with culture, and it will change the political structure only as its final act . . . this is the revolution of the new generation."

If *any* of this is true, we simply go back to where we were. Radical change is very hard for most people to contemplate, and money managers are no different. Their attitude is: Sure, changes, we sell something and we buy something else to fit the changes. You say work is going out of style? We'll buy play. Here are my six Leisure Time stocks, and let me tell you how long I've owned Disney. Money managers operate on the theory of displacement: the framework will be the same, but inside you move things around. My favorite is a gentleman I ran into after I got back from the Vega plant. I told him that one problem among others in certain localities was dope addiction, and at one plant—though the number sounded very high to me—the rate was reported to be 14 percent.

"Well," he said, "I haven't owned an auto stock for years. But fourteen percent! Geez, *who makes the needles?*"

The Chairman was pleased to report sharply higher profits for the year, due to increased sales of the entire line of hospital supply equipment. The reasons for the record profitability, said the Chairman, were Medicare, Medicaid, and the sharply increased use of the company's new handy throwaway needle by the burgeoning heroin addiction market.

Now it may be that displacement is all we have to consider. Ah, *things* are out, quality of life is in, back to the countryside; there is a waiting list for ten-speed bicycles, who makes the ten-speed bicycles? Ah, the ecologists are gaining strength, where is our list of water-pollution companies?

That is probably good thinking on the tactical level, but there is also a strategic level, and the strategic level has to consider what the more profound changes are, and in fact it ought to even without the rather parochial justification of buying and selling.

So this is why I am in Lordstown, just as one stop, looking for the sources of Arthur Burn's angst: Will life quiet down?

In the automobile industry, to consider the parochial side for a moment, rewards and punishments are very tangible, and since the automobile industry is such a fantastic part of America, that would affect us all. General Motors—my God, nobody can comprehend the *size* of General Motors; it makes one out of every seven manufacturing dollars in the country; its sales are bigger than the budget of any of the fifty states, and of any *country* in the world except the United States and the Soviet Union. But even General Motors has problems. As Henry Ford II said, *the Japanese are waiting in the wings.* Someday, he said, they might build all the cars in America. The problem, or one of them, is that imports keep rising, in spite of the theology of Detroit, which always maintained: little cars, fah! Americans won't buy them; Americans want power, a sex symbol, racing stripes, air scoops for nonexistent air, portholes for nonexistent water; they want to leave two big black tire marks going away from the stoplight, rubber on the road. And the names went with the technology: Firebirds and Thunderbirds, Cougars and Barracudas and Impalas, *growrrr*, nothing about driving a handy little car there—so the handy little cars sold were foreign.

Eventually enough handy little cars were sold that the balance of payments continued its sickening ways and even Washington began to lean on Detroit, and Detroit figured, Okay, we'll build a handy little car. General Motors was not about to have any more of the problems of urban Detroit; it put its $250 million Vega plant in the middle of an Ohio cornfield. And then this work force showed up, the youngest work force around, and *look* at them—hair down to the shoulder blades, mustaches, bell-bottoms, the whole bit; it looks like Berkeley or Harvard Square.

It was a Ford official who wrote the following paragraph, but the same thing applies not only everywhere in the automobile industry but probably in much of factory work. The memo is from an industrial relations man to his superiors, and he is talking about the present

133

and the future. This gentleman is nobody's fool, and his memo should be in the sociology texts, not in the filing cabinets. (The memo was xeroxed, and a friend of mine got a xerox and xeroxed it again, so I have one, and I guess the UAW has one, because its vice-president Ken Bannon used some of the same phrases word for word in an interview. Communication by *samizdat:* think what Xerox will do in Russia when it gets going.) The rate of disciplinary cases was going up; turnover was up two and a half times; absenteeism was alarming on Mondays and Fridays. (Hence the useless advice, never buy a car built on a Monday or a Friday. But your dealer will tell you *his* cars are built only on Tuesdays and Thursdays.) Furthermore, the workers weren't listening to the supervisors. And why?

For many, the traditional motivations of job security, money rewards, and opportunity for personal advancement are proving insufficient. Large numbers of those we hire find factory life so distasteful they quit after only brief exposure to it. The general increase in real wage levels in our economy has afforded more alternatives for satisfying economic needs. Because they are unfamiliar with the harsh economic facts of earlier years, [new workers] have little regard for the consequences if they take a day or two off ... the traditional work ethic—the concept that hard work is a virtue and a duty—will undergo additional erosion.

General Motors was going to outflank that stuff with the newest, most automated plant; machines would take over a lot of the repetitive jobs; the plant would be in that cornfield in Ohio, near Youngstown, away from all those problems of the, uh, you know, core city. Everything at Lordstown would be made in America, no imported parts, the apogee of American industrialism. The head of Chevrolet buzzed in for a Knute Rockne pep talk. *America* was going to make the small car, by golly, and that was the end of the elves in the Black Forest and the Industrious Yellow Peril in Toyota City, who thought they had been in the small-car business. Planeloads of newsmen were flown in. The line is going to do a hundred cars an hour, lots of it without any people; *kachunk* goes the machine that pops the wheel rim into the tire, *pffft* goes the machine that blows up the tire.

So what is all this about trouble in Lordstown? The line is not going at a hundred cars an hour—at least not much of the time—and there are all these characters, all good UAW Local 1112, average age twenty-five, the youngest work force practically anywhere, peace medals, bell-bottoms, and hair like Prince Valiant, and the union president is twenty-nine and has a Fu Manchu mustache like the one Joe Namath

134

shaved off, and GM is going up the wall. Where is the *productivity?*
Curtis Cox, the supervisor of standards and methods, is getting apoplec-
tic. "I see *foreign cars* in the parking lot," he says. "The owners
say they are cheaper. How is this country going to compete?" The
GM people practically weep when they think about Japan: all those
nice, industrious workers, *singing* the alma mater in the morning ("Hail
to Thee, O Mitsubishi"); whistling on the way to work like the Seven
Dwarfs, for God's sake—never a strike, never a cross word; playing
on the company teams; asking the foreman if it is okay to get engaged
to this very nice girl as soon as the foreman meets her.

So I ask General Motors quite routinely if I can go see this apogee
of American industrialism, say, Tuesday, and General Motors says
no, never.

I admit to being a bit stunned. Do they not fly planeloads of people
there all the time? Did they not fly alleged same planeloads at the
end of the GM strike, together with appropriate refreshment, to watch
the first Vega come off the line, with a handout about how the Vega
was going to Mrs. Sadie Applepie, library assistant of Huckleberry
Finn, Illinois, with a quote all ready from Mrs. Applepie: "Oh, I
have been waiting so long for my Vega, I can't believe it's finally
here. I'm so excited," did they not? What do they mean, No, not
that guy? Who the hell do they think I am, Ralph Nader? I begin
thumbing my other notebook that has the number of the pay phone
in the hallway of Nader's boarding house, and it's off to Lordstown.

So we are walking around the plant at Lordstown, all $250 million
of it very visible, like an iron-and-steel tropical rain forest with the
electric drills screaming like parakeets and the Unimate robot welders
bending over the Vegas like big mother birds and the Prince Valiants
of Local 1112 zanking away with their new expensive electrical equipment. Vegas grow before your eyes. Beautiful. I recommend it, next
time you take the Howard Johnson tour across the land of the free.

But what are these cars waiting for repair, marked *no high beam
signals, dome lite inoperative, no brakes* ... no brakes? *no brakes.*
But what is this on the bulletin board?

Management has experienced serious losses of production due to poor quality workmanship, deliberate restriction of output, failure or refusal to perform
job assignments and sabotage.

Efforts to discourage such actions through the normal application of corrective discipline have not been successful. Accordingly, any further misconduct
of this type will be considered cause for severe disciplinary measures, including dismissal.

"Corrective discipline"? My God, you can get *court-martialed* in this place. They should have an industrial psychologist read the language on the bulletin board. I can hear the Glee Club louder, "Hail to Thee, O Fair Toyota."

Hi there.

Hi.

What is that?

That's the window trim.

Is this a good place to work?

Well, it will be, as soon as we get it shaped up.

Would you buy one of these cars?

Sure, if it wasn't so expensive; it's a well-engineered little car.

Wouldn't you rather be out on your own, say, a garage?

Naw, a garage don't have no benefits.

Say, I don't want to bother you, two of those Vegas just went by without window trim.

Well, they all go by without somethin', this line is moving too fast.

That's productivity, man.

Oh, is that what they call it?

I can give you a few notes of our brilliantly unscientific survey of Lordstown, but they are just that. Our people would rather have had the time off than the overtime. But their wives worked because they needed the extra income. They would tell their brothers to get a job there, and in fact some of them did. Supervisors bugged everybody. Sabotage? Beer cans welded to the inside of a fender? Well, there might be a few hotheads, but that's silly, man, the Vega is our bread and butter—the more Vegas they sell, the better for us. If the foremen bugged our people too much, they would get another job somewhere else; they took for granted there would be such a job.

We asked the older types if the young bucks were any different. They said, "Yes. They're smarter. They don't put up with what we did."

Our favorite Prince Valiant haircut said: "I am not going to bust my ass for anybody. I don't even bust my ass for myself, you know, working around the house."

But beware. One has to be an epistemological agnostic considering any such report, whether done by journalists or social scientists. How do we know the people who talked to us are representative of a work force of ten thousand? Further: journalists and social scientists are verbal, conceptual people. They would probably score very low in electrical repairs around the house; unconsciously they feel: How

136

do they stand it? I wouldn't like to work here. They did not sleep through senior year in high school with Sister Maria Theresa droning on about Wordsworth and look at the plant as a relief from that.

So all right, it makes sense to have a demurrer for the statistical discipline, but the *feeling* is there, Something Else Is Going On: the world is not necessarily going to settle back, with life all quieted down. The key phrases are from the xerox of the xerox of the xerox of the confidential memo at Ford; the next key phrases are from the banks of the Charles River. Lordstown is the biggest and bestest example from industrial America, and the Harvard Business School is the West Point of capitalism, or at least so its denizens tell each other, and certainly the place has provided one of the great Old Boy networks of modern times. Let a Business-School-type foul up out there in the world and he need not fear: another Business-School-type will come to his rescue and they will call it merger, or recapitalization, or synergy, or something. I have two straws in the wind to submit from the West Point of capitalism.

Admittedly, these come from an unusual time. Two years before, the greedy little bastids in Investment Management could hardly wait to get going on their first five million. Now there is a new crop of greedy little bastids; naturally, the course is still wildly popular, but outside, the Cambodian invasion has been timed neatly with my spring visit. The feeling that all is not well in the world has even penetrated the clouds of greed in my three sections. Around Harvard Square the graffiti was getting political; nobody had written *Heloise Loves Abelard* in quite a while; instead this flowed in large letters for a third of a block: JOHN HANCOCK WAS A REVOLUTIONARY, NOT AN OBSCENE LIFE INSURANCE SALESMAN. But that, of course, was on the College side of the Charles River, where the life style is different —beards and mustaches and poor-boy clothes, almost as much a uniform as the gray flannel jackets and khaki pants of a generation before. But across the river at the Business School, the budding *apparatchiks* are coming to class in Brooks Brothers suits and button-down white shirts, looking like sub-assistant secretaries in the Nixon Administration.

There is no revolutionary chatter in the course catalog at the B School. You find one of the major preoccupations of the catalog is control: "The field of control deals with the collection, processing, analysis, and use of quantitative information in a business." In a previous year, when an SDS faction took over University Hall in the College and there was a big bust, the College as an institution seemed very confused, but the Business School had a Contingency Plan in a fat binder with colored index tabs. I had the classes at that time, too, and one B-School faculty member, fearing some Dickensian carmagnole in the streets, Paris, 1789, said of the dissenters: "They'll never make it to this side of the river. We'll blow the bridges first."

So: this is not the Last Bastion, it is not Bob Jones University or even Utah State; it is where they grow the *apparatchiks*, the technicians who sop up the top spots of a generation hence, and if Something Else Is Going On, these types will either lead it or fight it or try to take it over after it gets going.

First straw. *Notes from A Class.*

The Guest Lecturer has posed a Case. You are running a portfolio of a hundred million dollars. Company A is a notorious polluter, but its profits are unimpaired. Company B is buying antipollution equipment that will depress its profits for years. Other things being equal, which do you buy, A or B? The Case was not too far from reality. Ralph Nader's Project on Corporate Responsibility was trying to put some people on the General Motors board, and Harvard owns 305,000 shares of General Motors. Harvard's treasurer reportedly said he was going to vote for management "because they are our kind of people," after which both faculty and students generated a furious debate. The Case is not only limited to pollution; the same principles of the social purpose of investment can be applied to defense contractors, the makers of napalm, companies with investments or branches in South Africa, and so on.

All right, you want to achieve performance in your portfolio, and this performance is being measured competitively. It may affect your career. Do you buy Company A, the profitable polluter, or Company B, the unprofitable antipolluter?

Student One: I would try to evalute the long-term effect ... because in the long run Company B is going to have a better image.

Student Two: But in the long run you would have lost the account. I think you have to know the wishes of the constituency. If it's a fund, how do the fundholders feel? What do they want?

(Scattered boos. The class begins to chant, "A or B, A or B.")

Several other students offer comments, all trying to hedge, to keep both the profit and the social purpose.

Student Three: I buy the polluter. *(Cheers, then scattered boos.)* It isn't the business of a fund manager to make a social decision, or to discriminate between companies on his own ideas of some social purpose. That could be dangerous. If we want to combat pollution, let society vote for it, and have a consensus. I doubt that consumers really want to pay the price. You can't ask profit-making organizations to subsidize society.

The Radical Student (The Radical Student is only radical by standards of this side of the river, which is to say that he is neatly shaven but is wearing a colored shirt and a tie that is e bit zide than the 1955 width.): Meybe that's the problem. Everything in this school is geared to the purpose of the corporation, and thet purpose is maximized profit.

We ask the Radical Student: "What are the goals of a corporation, if not to maximize profit?"

Silence, a rustling of papers. The idea is very confusing.

What are the goals of a corporation, if not to maximize profit?

Not a hand goes up. It is just too hairy a question. We ask it once more. More shuffling, an occasional left wrist shoots out from the cuff with the wrist watch exposed.

The Radical Student: You know the trouble? It's the way we look at it. We're concerned with property rights.

At the Law School, say, they talk about civil rights. We're objective, but maybe objectivity has been overdone. Is our one purpose to measure *things?*

My second straw is the Resolution. This was, as I said, an emotional time. The Business School voted and passed this, then bought an ad in *The Wall Street Journal* to publicize it. The Resolution called for American withdrawal from Southeast Asia, not startling for a student resolution at that time. But this was the Business School, normally heavily Republican, heavily Republican in 1968, and it was the *language* juxtaposed to the source that was startling:

We condemn the administration of President Nixon for its view of mankind [its view of mankind?] and the American community which:

1. Perceives the anxiety and turmoil in our midst as the work of "bums" and "effete snobs";

2. Fails to acknowledge that legitimate doubt exists about the ability of black Americans and other depressed groups to obtain justice;

3. Is unwilling to move for a transformation of American society in accordance with the goals of maximum fulfillment for each human being and harmony between mankind and nature.

Harmony between mankind and nature?

I asked the former dean of admissions what was this about harmony between mankind and nature; when had that crept into the Business School?

"I don't know," he said. "I guess it means they're not going to work for Procter & Gamble and make those dishwasher soaps that don't dissolve and smother the lakes. They don't want to work for big companies anyway, or so they say; I'd like to see what they say a couple of years out. The big companies treat them as objects, they say. In the fifties, the guys here all wanted to get to the top of Procter & Gamble. In the sixties it was finance."

"Last year," I said, "my classes all wanted to go right to work for a hedge fund. You couldn't even offer them twenty thousand a year, because they were going to run five million into ten in a year and take twenty percent of the gain. I used to say, 'Good morning, greedy little bastards.' "

"The guys in the fifties," said the ex-dean, "wanted to run the Big Company, and the guys in the sixties wanted to be Danny Lufkin, make a big bundle by the time you're forty and run for something."

"And now?"

"And now, they're just confused. I've never seen such malaise. I don't think the big companies have gotten the message yet, and maybe the *Fortune 500* can run without the Harvard Business School, but I have the feeling something will give on one side or the other."

More recently, I talked to the same ex-dean, who now teaches a popular course, and asked him what changes there had been. Were the current B-School classes still holding out on the big corporations? Were the big corporations bending at all?

"They're bending to the extent that they don't come and interview the wives and tell them they have to fit to corporate life, and move fourteen times in fifteen years," he said. "But other than that, all you can say is that they're conscious of some change. As for my students, I think they have an acceptance of corporate life and they're looking for something inner. I hear a lot about life styles, how they want a non-anxious working life. They don't want to have what one of them called a dumbell life, which is to say a blob of work at one end, a blob of home life at the other, and a conduit between, a railroad or a freeway. There's a lot of stuff about walking on the beach, that the worthy cause is themselves, and that work should fit life, not the other way around, and they talk a lot about intimate relationships, wives, children, and so on.

"So if I had to divide the decades again, I would still say that the fifties produced the corporate man who would rise to the top and die seventeen months after retirement, leaving a beautiful estate; the sixties students wanted a piece of the action; and currently the fantasy is a balanced life—just *enough* success to include it all; they want to run things but not at any cost; they still want power but now they want love too."

Maximum fulfillment for each human being? Harmony between man and nature? That's not the *old* Business School. How do you put those things into a balance sheet? Can we operate a corporate society without objectivity, or at least what has passed for objectivity? I write: *Will General Motors believe in the harmony between man and nature? Will General Electric believe in beauty and truth?*

It is not, of course, a revolutionary idea in the limited history of capitalism in this country to make something for less than a maximum profit. First of all, profit was not necessarily something that could be controlled; it came like the rain on the crops, between the costs and the market. Moreover, when the bulk of business was family-owned, its purpose was to take care of the family—sons, nephews, and so on—and of the product's reputation, if it had a reputation of value. So a wagon-maker could simply make a good wagon, and a book publisher could publish simply because he wanted to. What we have come to call social purpose was a matter of individual integrity, randomly and haphazardly applied.

But these businesses sold out to bigger ones, and those in turn to bigger ones. Supercurrency! That New York Stock Exchange listing, that broad market with the stock selling at a fancy multiple, the sons of the Founders with Caribbean estates, and the grandsons in their pads all secure to blow their minds with 3K electronic guitar apparatus and not worry about work because the Supercurrency has been salted and peppered into hundreds of trusts so the tax man cannot get it. Only the Supercurrency has to stay Super, the profits have to keep growing, the multiple has to up, and the accountants can't do it all.

Multimillion-dollar businesses can't be run by intuition or seat-of-the-pants engineering. There has to be objectivity, whatever that is, and the continuous quantification of results; we have to have what the course catalog at the school calls "a rigorous and systematic approach," that is, the collection, processing, analysis, reporting, and use of quantitative information. But there is competition, maybe, and the judgment of those crazy crapshooters up in New York; if the earnings go down they will bomb the stock, and then what will our report card as a manager look like?

For our man in the green eyeshade asking how goes the world, how will it go, the harmony between man and nature becomes an important question, and not just a spiritual one.

Nobody is against such harmony. When ecology first crept into the scene, industry seized it as an advertising opportunity; not a filter was bought that the buyer didn't take an ad about cleaning up the rivers and waters. In fact, at one point someone figured out that more was spent drumbeating about cleanup than on the equipment. Industry began to sense that the public belief that more was better was beginning to fall away. Union Carbide dropped its slogan, *There's a Little Bit of Union Carbide in Everybody's Home.* They wanted you to think of the plastics and the sandwich bags, and instead a Little Bit of Union Carbide meant: the wind's shifted, here it comes again, shut the doors, close the windows, you know what it cost to have the curtains cleaned last time. President Nixon gave an Ecology Speech, and somebody slipped him a real good quote from T. S. Eliot. "Clean the air! clean the sky! wash the wind!"—that's what we are going to do, said the President, not realizing that the very same quote went on, "Take stone from stone and wash them ... Wash the stone, wash the bone, wash the brain, wash the soul, wash them, wash them!" Not ecology at all, but the blood of murder in the cathedral.

But while everybody agrees that mankind and nature should live in harmony, few agree on what that means, or how the cost shall be borne. They have not changed the consciousness of the way they think. To paraphrase University of Colorado economist Kenneth Boulding, man has lived through history in a "cowboy economy" with "illimitable plains" and "reckless, exploitative, romantic, and violent behavior." Consumption was "linear"—that is, materials were extracted from supposedly infinite resources, and waste was tossed into infinite dumps. But we are shifting to a "spaceman economy." The earth is becoming finite, like a closed spaceship; consumption must become "circular"—that is, to conserve what we have, resources must be continuously recycled through the system. Air and water have always been free, and few realize that we are approaching the point in our cowbody ways when we will wrench the earth's ecology out of shape. In *The Closing Circle*, biologist-ecologist Barry Commoner writes that we have to reconsider the true value of the conventional capital accumulated by the operation of the economic system: we have not considered the true cost.

The effect of the operation of the system on the value of its *biological* capital needs to be taken into account in order to obtain a true estimate of the overall wealth-producing capability of the system. The course of environmental deterioration shows that as conventional capital has accumulated, for example in the United States since 1946, the value of the biological capital has *declined*. Indeed, if the process continues, the biological capital may eventually be driven to the point of total destruction. Since the usefulness of conventional capital in turn depends on the existence of the biological capital—the eco-system—when the latter is destroyed, the usefulness of the former is also destroyed. Thus despite its apparent prosperity, in reality the system is being taken into bankruptcy. Environmental degradation represents a crucial, potentially fatal, *hidden* factor in the operation of the economic system.

So we do not even have a true picture of how well we have done. This parallels the arguments of the British economist Ezra Mishan. If a wage earner dies sooner because of exposure to mercury, radiation, and DDT, but doesn't have extra medical bills, is there not still the cost of the lost earnings from the extra years? They have to be assigned a value, even if the human anguish of the missing years is ignored.

According to Commoner, intense environmental pollution in the United States has come with the technological transformation of the productive system since World War II. Production based on the new technologies has been more profitable than the older technologies they replaced; that is, the newer, more polluting techniques yield higher profits. We could, of course, survive with new technologies, new systems to return sewage and garbage to the soil, retire land from cultivation, replace synthetic pesticides with biological ones, recycle usable materials, and cut down the uses of power. That would cost about six hundred billion, or a quarter of our current capital plant.

Placed in the kind of terms used in the analysts' societies, this debt-to-nature means there is suddenly a liability on the balance sheet we didn't know was there. It must have been in the footnotes, in fine print. We have been very profitable, but the plant is falling down. We can build a new plant, but we are going to have to amortize the charges against earnings for a long time.

Ah, but then we have a spanking new plant. Isn't that good? Not in the terms, necessarily, that we have been used to considering as good. Of course, if we survive, that's good. And perhaps even prevent life from getting more noxious, that's good. But we have been measuring good as profitable. New capital expenditures are—at some point —supposed to increase the profits. That is why the class is so confused when asked what the purpose of the corporation is. Good is profitable; profitable is new technology; new technology has been pollutive *and* profitable. Killing whales is very profitable until the day when there are no more whales, because we have only been amortizing the ships and the radar and the depth charges and harpoons. We haven't amortized the whales, and anyway, how do you replace whales?

But the debt to nature, paid, does not increase either productivity or profitability. Thus, probably the corporation is not going to pay up unless the society compels it, induces it, inveigles it, or brings it about some other way. The vision of good is simply too far removed from the vision of what has been perfectly good in the hundreds of years of cowboy economics.

This is going to be true not just for the United States and not just for capitalism. The Cellulose, Paper, and Carton Administration of the Ministry of Timber, Paper, and Woodworking in the U.S.S.R. is going to have its problems, too. It has its quotas, and the boys at the Ministry get their satisfactions from churning out the stuff, and ecology freaks are everywhere. This is from Professor Marshall Goldman's account of the pollution of Lake Baikal, the world's oldest lake and largest body of fresh water by volume. The manager of the plant at Bratsk is asked why a new waste filter has not been installed. Says he: "It's expensive. The Ministry of Timber, Paper, and Woodworking is trying to invest as few funds as possible in the construction of paper and timber enterprises in order to make possible the attainment of good indices per ruble of capital investment. These indices are being achieved by the refusal to build purification installations."

The finite-earth argument leads almost inexorably to a call for an end to growth, both in population and industrial output. Growth in industrial output is one of the justifications for both capitalism and socialism, each to each. When Khrushchev talked about burying us, he was bragging about increases in industrial production. Increases in our Gross National Product have been hailed as the triumph of our system. (Leave aside for a moment what GNP measures. It does measure only quantity; so if everybody goes and buys triple locks for his doors because crime has increased so much, the GNP goes up, though the quality of life may have gone down. There are those who believe we should attempt to measure such quality.)

The most dramatic assault on growth came from a group at MIT headed by Dennis Meadows, which built a mathematical model of the world system with the interrelationships of population, food supply, natural resources, pollution, and industrial production. The Meadows group produced a doomsday equation: the world is out of business in less than a century, unless the "will" is generated to begin "a controlled, orderly transition from growth to global equilibrium." Even new technologies, such as nuclear power sources, said the group, wouldn't help much. The team doubled the resources and assumed that recycling cut the demand to one-fourth; even optimistic estimates didn't put the day of doom off longer than 2100. We are going to stop growing one way or the other, said the group, the other being the collapse of the industrial base through depleted resources, and then lack of food and medical services.

This report did not lack for critics. One economist said it was "Malthus, with lights and a computer"; others said the base was too skimpy for the assumptions, and that future science and future technology were unknown. If you had assumed our population growth in 1880 without the automobile, you could have assumed asphyxiation by horse manure. If materials were going to become visibly scarce, would not the prices begin to anticipate scarcity? And would not new materials and new power sources be developed? The representatives of less developed countries who considered the report at a Smithsonian symposium were particularly alarmed, because freezing growth without some sort of world distribution of income would keep them at their current levels. The poorer nations, said the Indian ambassador, would "slide down to starvation." At another international conference, the Malaysians said: "Some of us would rather see smoke coming out of a factory and men employed than no factory," and "We are not concerned with pollution but with existence."

At the laissez-faire end of the spectrum, economists like the University of Chicago's Milton Friedman think that in arguments over social issues "there is a strong tendency for people to substitute their own values for the values of others." The current pollution concern is "an upper-income demand—the high-income people want to get the low-income people to pay for something that the high-income people value . . . people move from the clear, clean countryside to the polluted cities—not the other way around—because the advantages of the city outweigh the disadvantages." Left alone, "people are more likely to act in their own interests, to evaluate the costs and benefits of their own activities."

It is, of course, hard to legislate changes in consciousness. But most economists are unwilling to give up growth as a goal. World population is certain to grow for many years to come, an extra billion between 1960 and 1975, three more billion in the next quarter-century. Even if that rate of increase is slowed, you need growth just to keep pace. In a world of no growth but more people, you only accomplish one person's well-being, or one nation's, at the expense of another. That is the kind of redistribution of wealth we had before there was any surplus wealth to compound, when people in skins hit each other over the head with mastodon thighbones to accomplish the redistribution. Presumably we have only recently outgrown such activity, and the record of social maturity is not a record anybody would trust to the application of economic problems. So the doomsday equations at least get people to think about the problems of a finite earth; it will take long enough to do something about it anyway.

It is from the increments that poverty is alleviated and the goals of the society met. If there are social problems—such as pollution—that can't be met by the market mechanism, they can be met by a pricing system: penalizing the polluter, let us say, or giving a tax incentive to achieve the desired end. This is not a net gain to growth in the traditional ways we have measured growth, because the stimulus from investments in pollution control is outweighed by the price rise in the end product, hence a damper on total demand. A study prepared for the Council on Environmental Quality, a government office, indicated this could be done for a small percentage of annual GNP, less than 1 percent, for air and water.

What is the impact of all of this on the man in the green eyeshade considering how goes the world? In the short run—and the short run is all that is considered by many of the men in green eyeshades—he can continue to play the game of displacement: who makes the needles. (If the Meadows model were to be true, and we were to be closer to doomsday, and the pricing mechanism were left alone, the man in the green eyeshade could make incredible killings by buying up commodities on the eve of their disappearance.) But in the longer run, the demand for social purposes, whether in pollution control or health, education, and welfare, is going to come out of the savings flow. (*Institutional Investor* magazine polled forty-one of the nation's leading academic, governmental, and business economists, and two-thirds of them believed that (a) growth should continue, with a change in priorities, and (b) that additional "income-wealth redistribution is required.") If the government borrows in the capital markets to deliver, it tips the balance. If it raises taxes to deliver, that comes at least partially out of profits. And if it, in effect, prints the money to deliver, then inflation also will cut into profits. As is often said in this sort of discussion, there ain't no such thing as a free lunch.

There are some items to be balanced against this. One is the growing role of services in the economy; by 1980 the Department of Labor says more people will be employed in services than in manufacturing. Services are non-pollutive, but the productivity curve also begins to flatten because there are no economies of scale from doctors, teachers, barbers, and string quartets.

The man in the green eyeshade is a capitalist and a manager: "The capitalist and managerial classes may see," writes Robert Heilbroner in *Between Capitalism and Socialism,* "the nature and nearness of the ecological crisis ... and may come to accept a smaller share of the national surplus simply because they recognize that there is no alternative."

Some conclusions are inescapable. Even if the ecological crisis is overstated and far away, even if social problems can be solved with the existing mechanism—both of these points arguable—the consensus is moving away from the market as decision-maker and from the business society. As soon as you get all the articulation of "goals" and "priorities," you are moving from decision-making by market to decision-making by political philosophy. "What's good for General Motors is good for the country," said Charley Wilson, one of Eisenhower's businessmen Cabinet members. It would be interesting to see, year by year, what percentage of the people agree with that, and to watch the change.

So the money manager in the metaphorical green eyeshade will no longer be operating in a world where the market determines totally what is produced (and induced), nor in a society run by business decisions. Capital is scarcer and profits are thinner. He is still looking for three stocks that will double, but the range of his options is less. He has always looked not just at profits, but at the rate of change in estimated profit, and in the long run *his expectations are diminished.*

Open-ended expectations are an integral part of the markets we have grown up to know. Without them, the calculators can calculate the rates of return, and everybody can be on their way home at 10:05 A.M. to work on their Leisure Time, or more likely, to attend some committee meeting that will take up the remaining hours.

Keynes said that "in the long run we are all dead" and that the conventions by which we operate were a succession of short terms —those looking at the long run did so at their own peril. We have a marketplace in which it is possible to float all the services as well as the manufactures, and so probably many happy hours of playing with the displacements await our men. But if we are to give up the "illimitable plains" of the "cowboy economy," the new and smaller horizon is going to affect our ability to believe that we can compound and extrapolate with impunity, that the three hot ones we heard about at lunch today can go from 5 to 100. We have already lost our gunsling ers, and if our Big Sky goes we will have to give up some of our fantasies. But they always were fantasies anyway, and maybe there are other energies to make our wheels spin.

Having thus dispatched the spirit of capitalism, let us see what we can do with the Protestant Ethic. That phrase describes a devotion to thrift and industry, postponed pleasure, and hard work—the hustle as approved by the Lord. It accompanied the Puritan temper, a rather forbidding and pleasure-shy view of life, and is aptly described in the confidential Ford memo together with the complaint that it is disappearing: "the traditional work ethic—the concept that hard work is a virtue and a duty—will undergo additional erosion." (We have already seen the seeds of conflict, because if Prince Valiant at the Pink Elephant says, "I am not going to bust my ass for anybody, I don't even bust my ass for myself," it is safe to say he does not believe that "hard work is a virtue and a duty.")

We may keep using the phrase Protestant Ethic—everybody does —but for the record we should now split Protestant from Ethic. We call it that because Max Weber called it that in one of the classic works of political economics, and the sociologists and political economists are still sending students to the paperback stores for Max Weber, and not just for the *Protestant Ethic and the Spirit of Capitalism.* The textile families of northern France—Catholics all—sent letters to their sons, and to each other, that could have gone right into *Die protestantische Ethik.* Weber did not say, of course, that Protestantism was the sole cause of capitalism. In his commentary on Weber, Julien Freund says that the *Protestant Ethic* was at least in part a reaction against Marx's solely economic motive. Embryo capitalism had existed in other societies—Babylonian, Indian, Chinese, and Roman—but the "spirit" of capitalism only developed with the mystery-less, magic-free character of Protestantism, with its rationality and rationalization. (This will come up again in a moment in the counter-culture's objections.) The accompanying asceticism of Protestantism said that you worked hard in your calling to succeed—a sign of election by God—but did not spend the wealth created, because only sobriety pleased God. "Thus the Puritan came to accumulate capital without cease." Even Keynes's assumptions in *Essays in Persuasion* seem to be based on a kind of Protestant society, where wealth increases because the margin between production and consumption increases.

Talk about industry, thrift, and the way to salvation, the Protestant Ethic has found its happiest current home in a very non-Protestant country—at least in name—Japan. A while back, on a visit, I would ask the people of Japan: How much vacation do you take a year? And the answers would come back: two days, one day, three days. Why so little? Well, if you work on your vacation you get paid more, and the beaches are too crowded anyway. And I remember sitting with the translator of my own book, himself a distinguished director of the Bank of Japan, everybody cross-legged, a sliver of raw fish poised between his chopsticks, a garden scene framed perfectly by the door.

"In the 1960's," said the honorable director, "our total output passed Italy, France, Germany, and England; at this rate we will pass the U.S.S.R. in 1979. How? Our people save twenty percent of their wages. No other country saves so much. In the U.S. it is closer to six percent."

It is indeed, and when sour years come and the people clutch a little and the savings rate goes up to 8 percent, the President gathers his economic advisers to Camp David and wants to know what the hell is wrong with the Consumer, how do we get him to loosen up?

"Of course," said the director's research assistant, "we will not pass the United States until ..." and everybody stopped talking because that was not courteous.

"Sometime in the 1990's," said the director, "and many things could happen by then: we have social overhead building up."

"But we have done this without resources, without oil, and without surplus food," said the assistant, "with industry and thrift, industry and thrift."

The voices in Osaka rise to haunt the finite-earth model builders, in the morning alma mater:

> For the building of a new Japan
> Let's put our strength and minds together
> Doing our best to promote production
> Sending our goods to the people of the world,
> Endlessly and continuously,
> Like water gushing from a fountain.
> Grow, industry, grow, grow, grow!
> Harmony and Sincerity!
> Matsushita Electric! Matsushita Electric!

Industry and thrift, dedication, and devotion; you could imagine the United States without them, but not without the mythology and ethic behind them. What is at stake is the happiness of Arthur Burns, whether we will always have a cost-push inflation, whether we stay Nation Number One like President Nixon wanted.

Once again, the Ford memo:

For many, the traditional motivations of job security, money reward, and opportunity for personal advancement are proving insufficient.

Insufficient! Security, money, and personal advancement? Do you know what we have to throw off to get to this point?

I give you the honorable Cotton Mather:

There are *Two Callings* to be minded by *All Christians*. Every Christian hath a GENERAL CALLING which is to Serve the Lord Jesus Christ and Save his own Soul ... and every Christian hath also a PERSONAL CALLING or a certain *Particular Employment* by which his *Usefulness* in his Neighborhood is Distinguished ... a Christian at his *Two Callings* is a man in a Boat, Rowing for Heaven; if he mind but one of his *Callings,* be it which it will, he pulls the *Oar* but on *one side* of the Boat, and will make but a poor dispatch to the Shoar of Eternal Blessedness ... every Christian should have some *Special Business* ... so he may Glorify God, by doing *Good* for *others,* and *getting of Good for himself* ... to be without a *Calling,* as tis against the *Fourth Commandment,* so tis against the Eighth, which bids men to seek for themselves a comfortable Subsistence ... [if he follow no calling] ... a man is *Impious* toward God, *Unrighteous* toward his family, toward his *Neighborhood,* toward the *Commonwealth* ... it is not enough that a Christian *have* an Occupation; but he must *mind* it, and give a *Good Account,* with *Diligence* ...

and so on to *Poor Richard's Almanac:* A sleeping fox catches no poultry; one day is worth two tomorrows; diligence is the mother of good luck; early to bed and early to rise provides a man with job security, money reward, and opportunity for personal advancement.

The extension of this ethic into industrial America was a real triumph. The Ford vice-president has a distinct problem: it is very hard to think of working on the line as a Calling. Cotton Mather's listeners did not take this lightly, nor did he: "Man and his Posterity will Gain but little, by a Calling whereto God hath not Called him"; a Calling was to be *Agreeable* as well as *Allowable.*

It is a wonderful Inconvenience for a man to have a *Calling* that won't *Agree* with him. See to it, *O Parents,* that when you chuse *Callings* for your *Children,* you wisely consult their *Capacities* and their *Inclinations;* lest you Ruine them. And, Oh! cry mightily to God, by *Prayer,* yea with *Fasting* and *Prayer,* for His Direction when you are to resolve upon a matter of such considerable consequence. But, O *Children,* you should also be *Thoughtful* and *Prayerful,* when you are going to fix upon your *Callings;* and above all propose deliberately *Right Ends* unto your selves in what you do.

It is a bit hard to imagine, then: "Ma, I have fasted and prayed and sought the wisdom of God. I know my Calling, and I am going to work on the line at Ford, $4.57 an hour, as an assembler."

It seems almost simplistic to suggest, but you are more likely to bust your ass when everybody has been fasting and praying for you and what you are doing and your oar of the boat on the way to the Shoar of Eternal Blessedness than if none of those things are true; and if you are Ford, you have an extra problem if that spirit has departed.

Not that it has departed everywhere. It is still in the literature. Ralph Waldo Emerson's "Self-Reliance" and "Wealth" are in a direct line from Cotton Mather and Poor Richard; be not only industrious, be clever, absorb, and invest. Bishop Lawrence, doyen of the Episcopal Church at the turn of the century, really did say, "In the long run, it is only to the man of morality that wealth comes. Godliness is in league with riches." Some of our major corporations have institutional advertising even today that could have been written by the Social Darwinists, and Dale Carnegie courses run on principles that were devised by Benjamin Franklin. The Man Who Gets Ahead in Business Reads *The Wall Street Journal* Every Business Day. (Did you ever see the television commercial about The Man Who Gets Ahead in Business? Business is a field event, pole-vaulting, and the bar is set at about a hundred feet, and the poor bastard is there in his business suit and his Knox hat and his briefcase, and he looks up nervously at this bar a hundred feet high and fingers the pole uncertainly. After knocking the bar off the first time, he makes it the second, presumably because he has read *The Wall Street Journal. The Wall Street Journal* may be one of the best papers in the country, but I suggest that anyone who sees his job as a hundred-foot pole vault with no track shoes is in the wrong Calling and should pray for guidance.)

While the literature of the Protestant Ethic has been exhorting everybody for three hundred years in this country to be industrious and thrifty, sober and wise—to "postpone gratification," in the words of the scholars—another literature has sprung up. It is literature really only in the McLuhanesque sense, but it is with us every day, and that is advertising. The purpose of the advertising is not to get you to produce and save but to spend, to buy the goods, and this has been the case since at least fifty years ago, when mass marketing and mass advertising really got going. Now we have commercials in living color, and the populace spends far more time with them than the old populace did with Cotton Mather. What do we see? First of all, we never see anybody *working* except when they are candidates for medication: aspirin, pain relievers, tranquilizers, cold remedies. At least not office or factory work; the White Tornado and the Man From Glad will come and help with the housework. The rest of the time, people are at play: is it possible to sell soft drinks without running into the surf? You only go around once in life, says the beer commercial, so you have to grab everything you can; that character is hanging precariously onto the rigging of his boat because one hand is clutching a beer can. And the airlines—well, there is the bell tolling the end of the Protestant Ethic: Fly now, pay later, Pan Am will take you to an island in the sun where you can be a beachcomber (not a Calling approved by Cotton Mather) and Eastern wants to fly you and Bob and Carol and Ted and Alice *all* to your own little love-nest in Jamaica.

The message of capitalism has been schizophrenic: at work, be hard-nosed, industrious, single-minded, frugal, and thrifty, and once you leave work, *whoopee,* have you seen Carol *and* Alice in their bikinis? It may be that some doers can step into a telephone booth and emerge as Clark Kent, but I doubt if it works for a whole society.

The second literature of exhortation, advertising, sometimes recognizes this, and tries to say that the deferred gratification of the Protestant Ethic is a matter of hours, not lifetimes and generations. "You've worked hard, you deserve this," says the clever ad, whether it is a beer, the reward for the day, or a vacation, the reward for a season, or whatever: buy, try, fly.

The less intensive attitude toward work also applies to play. In the winter of 1972 Columbia barely managed to find a basketball team for its Ivy League opener; it could send only six men to Providence to play Brown. "Four members," *The New York Times* reported (January 6), "had resigned, making it a particularly dramatic example of student unhappiness with organized extracurricular pursuits ... Several other college teams have suffered similar player shortages in the last month." Said the team's second-highest scorer as he departed: "My father thinks I'm just a degenerate hippie now, because when I left high school I had all these fantastic ambitions for wealth and fame—and I wanted to be the greatest lawyer in North Carolina. Now I just don't have that."

Oppose this to that paragon of the extreme ethic, Vince Lombardi. You could say, of course, that this is not quite fair: soldiers and professional football players are supposed to win. But the example is not frivolous. When Lombardi died, his death was a major front-page story in all—including the most serious—of newspapers, and personally grieved the President of the United States. Lombardi's hold on the country and the President was that for ten years the teams he had coached had either won championships or come in second. The ethic according to Lombardi, all from *Lombardi* and *Run to Daylight:*

Winning is not everything. It is the only thing.

The will to excell and the will to win, they endure. They are more important than any event that occasions them.

To play this game, you must have that fire in you, and there is nothing that strokes fire like hate.

And from Lombardi's players:

He had us all feeling that we weren't going to win for the Green Bay Packers, but to preserve our manhood ... and we went out and whipped them good and preserved our manhood.

Vinny believes in the Spartan life, the total self-sacrifice, and to succeed and reach the pinnacle he has, you've got to be that way. The hours you put in on a job can't even be considered.

He treated us all equally—like dogs. I don't think I'd want to be like Lombardi. It takes too much out of you. You drive like that, you've got to give up a lot of time with your family, and you lose a lot physically. ... Still, now that I'm in business, I'm applying Lombardi's principles. I sent my secretary home crying my first three days on the job. One gal retired on me. I was putting them through training camp. I walked in and the first thing I said was, "Your job is on the line. If you don't make it, you're through." I said to the secretary, "What the heck you been doing all day? I don't see anything you've done." And if she gave me a letter and there was one mistake in it, I'd make a big X all the way across it and say, "Type it again." It worked out pretty well. They're organized now ... I'm strict. A lot of him has rubbed off on me.

And the players on the changes:

If you were told to beat your head against the wall, you did it .... I think we're entering a different period now. I think we now have to give youngsters a good reason to get them to beat their head against a wall.

Kids today don't fight like we did. They can play football and basketball like hell, but they're very gentle, very kind. They're out playing for fun, and its not going to interfere with their demonstrations for the week or with the things they consider important ... Those kids don't look at it like the whole world is going to fall apart if you don't beat the Bears.

153

The examples are so eloquent they need no comment.

Someday we may have such technology and science-and-compound-interest that whether people work hard or not would be marginal, but meanwhile there has been a lot of talk about alienation and unhappiness and The Blue-Collar Blues and, for that matter, The White-Collar Blues. Industry notices this because of absenteeism, turnover, and the lack of candidates for foreman, but nobody really *knows*.

I suspect that two things are true in this country. One is that there are certainly a lot of jobs in this country that are boring, not built to the human spirit or the human body, or not fulfilling in some other way, and that most of American industry is only beginning to pay attention to this. The second is that people like to work, as opposed to not working or hanging around the house. They like to work, or at least they like to go to the place where work is, because they see their friends, they have a beer afterward or a coffee break during, and it gets them into motion, and anyway we have not developed the tradition of playing the lute and counting that as a good afternoon. Given any degree of pleasantness, encouragement, and satisfaction, they would go to work even without the exhortations of the Ethic and the prospect of the Shoar of Eternal Blessedness.

It is almost axiomatic in the literature of work that part of the problem comes of bending the men to the machines. But computers are machines too; the pay may be less than that around nonelectronic machinery; yet the blues are not so much heard from this sector, and among the differences may be style and air conditioning.

How hard, or with what care, people work is something else. William H. Whyte, Jr., and the other observers of the fifties told us of the crossover: the executives were working the seventy-hour week and taking work home while the blue-collar hours were going down.

The difference is that both the executive and the blue-collar worker are now conscious of *options* that heretofore they did not think they had. Conscious only, for relatively few have acted on the alternative; behavior and attitude do not necessarily go immediately together. Most of the attention has been paid to the younger generation; at least the future executives were thinking about a balanced life, and the corporations were getting a bit shyer about telling them how demanding corporate life was going to be. Whatever the terrors that haunted the Man in the Gray Flannel Suit—not Making It, not having the House in the Suburb—the terrors do not have quite the same intensity that they used to. The terrors are also less for the industrial workers. For one thing, if you have a house and a car, another house and another car become much less urgent, however pleasant or convenient. (There is a lake within cruising range of the Vega plant in industrial Ohio which is, to put it baldly, a blue-collar lake, which is to say most of the boats belong to union workers from the plants. If they put five more boats on that lake you will not to able to see the water for the boats; thus if you are an industrial worker and don't have a boat to take the kids in, the chances are you have a friend who does, or maybe your old man will lend you his.)

A lack of *things,* unless those things are food, clothing, and shelter, does not provide terror except for a Man in a Gray Flannel Suit who has bought a distortion of the old ethic, its tangible evidences without its spirituality. Back to the Ford memo:

> Because they are unfamiliar with the harsh economic facts of earlier years, [new workers] have little regard for the consequences if they take a day or two off.

That's about as succinct as one can be. The harsh economic facts of earlier years were an unpleasant but effective motivator. You do not even have to have gone through a Great Depression yourself, if you heard enough talk about it while you were growing up. Now it has been more than thirty years since the end of the Great Depression, and not only do the Prince Valiants in the plant not know about it, they have not even heard that much about it because granddad does not live with them. I had a series of chats with Daniel Yankelovich, social scientist and the head of the leading market research and social science research firm that bears his name, a firm that polls continuously in this area for corporate clients. Only in the last five years has this change in attitude taken place so strikingly. The changing of work goals from salary to interpersonal relationships to content of work has also been documented by Professor Ray Katzell, chairman of the Psychology Department of New York University, and others. It took that long—almost two generations—for the motivation by economic fear to fade.

Granted, all the moonlighting to make ends meet at the current levels; granted, all the places and pockets that have been missed, and some of the unemployment which persists. Mass employment is not a political possibility—almost everyone would agree to that—and the economic whiff of grapeshot (what this country needs to shape up these deadheads is a good depression) has gone out of the lexicon of bargaining. What Yankelovich calls the "sacrifice consensus" is

155

breaking down. The sacrifice part of the phrase means that deferrals for something else are not as popular or necessary: I am doing this for my family, I am working so that my son has a better life than I do. And the consensus, obviously, is that there was agreement that this was a right and proper way of life. The breakdown of this sacrifice consensus does not mean that it is replaced right away with something else, only that now there are many elements present—some sacrificers; some not, but no agreed-upon consensus.

("If women's lib breaks the equation between masculinity and being a good provider, what does that do to motivation? And, say, to insurance?" Yankelovich asked at one point, which started something that made us both late for dinner.)

So: our productivity curve begins to flatten not only because we are becoming a service economy, but because some of the motivations —the spirit and the fear—have gone out of the producers. And maybe our inflation is persistent. If you want the dank side of the extrapolation; some of the workers retire right there on the job and wait for their pension, some take Fridays off. The servicing of all our *things* (and indeed even the services themselves) becomes so erratic and sloppy that the manufacturers have to work to make them service-free, no checkup for ten thousand miles, and the consumers get so irritated they transfer that irritation into political channels and gladly accept more government regulation of business.

So: it is affluence itself that has taken the edge off our edge. But the President need not exhort us to get out and return to the honesty of a day's work for a day's pay, which he has done on several occasions. Nation Number One will not be unique, because these elements don't stop at the water's edge; at different times, but for the same reasons, they will take place in all the Western industrial countries. The exhortations of Charman Mao may be to a different end than the Shoar of Blessedness, but the tone is the same. In the capitalist industrial countries, it is the first generation off the farm that provides the longest hours and the most uncomplaining workers. Somebody who has spent sixteen hours a day looking at the wrong end of an ox for sub-subsistence on a patch in Poland may not complain at all when he emigrates with a paper suitcase to a steel mill on the south side of Chicago, but his grandson may not think it is a good deal. We are the furthest off the farm. Japan had a generation that made its industrial reputation, those glee-club singers in the Matsushita plant think Matsushita is about the most dazzling thing that ever happened, but meanwhile the Germans are using Turks and Spaniards—again, fresher from the farm—to fill out the ranks in the Volkswagen plants. All of which does not solve our problem, but gives us company.

Perhaps that just gives us a challenge. Adolph Berle, among his other activities, was co-author with Gardiner Means of the granddaddy classic in all this line of thinking, *The Modern Corporation and Private Property*. In one of his later books, *The American Economic Republic*, Berle suggested that we had a flexibility of response which he called the Transcendental Margin, those qualities that accounted for the prosperity of Israel but not Iraq, of the Netherlands but not Bulgaria—a certain creative energy. It propelled our system not toward profits but toward—are you ready?—beauty and truth. In a younger and more optimistic America that did not seem so strange. If we still have it, or something like it, it should be possible to make of work something fulfilling that does not need either spiritual exhortation or economic fear to motivate it. This is a tall order and a big challenge, but our luckier citizens who have experienced something like it know that under those propitious circumstances it can be fun to bust your ass.

We ignore revolutions at our peril. Current evidences may or may not lead to profound changes, but we know that even when changes seem to happen quickly the ideas behind them have been hanging in the air for a long time. Our man at the desk considering how goes the world, had he been in the city of London in 1913, would have been one of the merchant princes of the world: to him for capital came the Moscow Power and Light Company, the breweries of Bohemia, the trolley lines of Shanghai, the apples of Tasmania, the oil of Mexico, the ranches of Texas and Arizona, the tin mines of Malaya, the hemp of Tanganyika, and the railroads of absolutely everywhere. Half a century later our man was still at his desk and still at work, a bit shabbier, but his role and the world had changed.

At this point the metaphor is going to break down, because revolutions do not come neatly across a desk; if the change is profound enough, the frame through which we have looked at this scene will go away, and the chair will still be there but nobody will be sitting at the desk.

But once again, a degree of skepticism is in order. In going through an inordinate amount of the literature, for example, I found one phrase a number of times: "Our youth is in revolt." The writer is a verbal, conceptual person, usually an academic, and what he *means* is "*My graduate students are in revolt*"; or, "My students have just worked their way through some Marcuse and they have had it with the System."

157

The Faculty of Engineering is not so prompt to report that the students are in revolt.

This is not at all to write off small numbers of people. They may have a symbolic value to everybody else articulating what larger numbers feel. But I think it is important to distinguish the flavor of what has been done: greenhouse people have reported on greenhouse people, which is to say that academics and book writers have talked about students, who may not end up being greenhouse people, protected from the storms and freezes of life, but who are in a stage of life—being at school—where they are protected from what shapes everybody else. Just the simple *numbers* have gotten so much bigger. Twenty-five students here and there do not make the impact that a "counter-culture" of a million makes, but that million counter-culture is possible because of a trillion-dollar economy and, among other things, a student population of eight million. When everybody has to spend sixteen hours a day behind an ox, there is no counter-culture.

Obviously, in spite of the looseness of the ways in which we have learned, Something Else Is Going On. I belong to a Club housed in a magnificent old building in New York which is supposed to be made up of Distinguished Intellectuals, because I suppose, somebody had written *The Wealth of Nations* as an achievement by my name. The club has been infiltrated by foundation executives and downtown lawyers, and the average age of the members is 94.3, because foundation executives and downtown lawyers are very long-lived. Anyway, following the precepts of intellectual inquiry, we had a debate one night on Charles Reich's *The Greening of America*. This is the most talked-about of the revolutionary tracts. Corporate America—an idea, incidentally, from the old Berle and Means classic—has taken over the country, to the mindless end of its own perpetuity. "This apparatus of power has become a mindless juggernaut, destroying the environment, obliterating human values, and assuming domination over the mind and lives of its subjects." We are not only an incredibly rich country, but a desperately poor one, because we have disorder, corruption, hypocrisy, war, distorted priorities, an artificiality of work and culture, powerlessness, absence of community, and a loss of self. (Apologies for the abruptness of the summary.) But out of biological necessity, a new consciousness "has emerged out of the wasteland of the Corporate State like flowers pushing up through the concrete pavement." The revolution is individual and cultural, and only changes the political structure as its final act.

I did my homework quite properly and intensively, because there was much that was not only naïve but diffusely derivative, some of it funny: seven times Mr. Reich stated that there was no more chunky peanut butter; the Corporate State had the power to deliver only homogenized peanut butter. The Corporate State gave us snowmobiles "instead of snowshoes, so that the winter forests screech with mechanical noise," yet four times the author celebrated light motorcycles "to restore a sense of free motion," and he obviously never tried to read or think near a quiet road patrolled by a kid with a new Honda. Moby Grape was celebrated for the positive feelings of "It's a beautiful day today," which did seem to me to ignore "Oh, what a beautiful mornin'" (Consciousness I) and Peggy Lee's "Now it's a good day" (Consciousness II). That was fun and games, my real barbs came for the greenhouse thinking.

Yet, five minutes after the discussion started, I threw my notes away, because there wasn't a debate. My distinguished seniors had read the book and they were so furious they weren't even *listening*; their faces were becoming purple over their white wing collars. What in the world could be so *threatening?* On the spot I had to switch sides and become the public defender, because the argument from the other side was: *It does not exist.* And the point I have been making is that however imperfectly assessed, Something Else Is Going On.

Jean-François Revel's tract, largely a pamphlet to needle his fellow Frenchmen, says that only in America can the true revolution take place: "It is *the* revolution of our time ... it is the only revolution that ... joins culture, economic and technological power, and a total affirmation of liberty for all in place of archaic prohibitions." (It is nice of somebody to say we are still trying.) And he mentions some of the political activities that have taken place: sit-ins, civil-rights marches, student strikes, and so on.

But it is important to separate out, for this discussion, the *political* aspects. Martha Mitchell may have looked out the window and seen the milling students as the 1917 St. Petersburg mobs, but few others did. And it becomes important to separate out what is *style*. Long hair may or may not represent something profound, but if you compare yearbook pictures of the class of 1872 and 1972 the beards and the sideburns look much the same; the only difference is that in 1872 Daddy had a beard or muttonchops too. If we leave out politics and style, that brings us back to behavior; within that, loosely there *is* a revolutionary idea. And that is: Where did all those bright people get us, anyway? Weren't McGeorge Bundy and Robert McNamara two of the smartest people walking around? "Consciousness II," wrote

159

Reich, "rests on the fiction of logic and machinery; what it considers unreal is nature and subjective man .... Consciousness III is deeply suspicious of logic, rationality, analysis, and of principles."

We don't have too look very far for a prime example of the causes of a suspicion of logic, rationality, and objectivity. If we do not stop the Communists in Vietnam, they will think we are chicken, they will take over Asia, and so on. We analyze the problem. We will send x number of men, we will drop y numbers of millions of tons of bombs. Every day our television screens will carry the body-count report: *Them, 5357, Us, 422; Villages pacified today, 324.* The next day the score is the same, and the next. They see the score and we see the score. Therefore we win the war and achieve our principles, and the Communists will learn the lesson. It is all there, measured in what Yankelovich called the McNamara fallacy:

> The first step is to measure whatever can be easily measured. This is okay as far as it goes. The second step is to disregard that which can't be measured or give it an arbitrary quantitative value. This is artificial and misleading. The third step is to presume that what can't be measured easily really isn't very important. This is blindness. The fourth step is to say that what can't be easily measured really doesn't exist. This is suicide.

Thus the use of feeling, emotions, ritual, and magic by the unconscious revolutionaries as a rebellion. "The marked tendency," says Theodore Roszak in *The Making of a Counter-Culture* (a literary essay which isn't really about that at all), "has been to consign whatever is not fully and articulately available in the waking consciousness for empirical or mathematical manipulation to a purely negative catchall category (in effect, the cultural garbage can) called the 'unconscious' or the 'irrational' or the 'mystical' or the 'purely subjective.' "

Reich:

> Accepted patterns of thought must be broken; what is considered "rational thought" must be opposed by "nonrational thought" — drug-thought, mysticism, impulses. Of course the latter kinds of thought are not really "nonrational" at all; they merely introduce new elements into the sterile, rigid, outworn "rationality" that prevails today.

That is the *real* end of the Protestant Ethic—not only everybody *stoned,* man, but the end of the *rationality* that led to the burgeoning of capitalism.

"It is as if," Yankelovich wrote, "the great victories in succeeding centuries won by Protestantism, individualism, rationalism, science and industrialization all were gained at a terrible cost—the sacrifice of community." And to define *community* he quoted from still another sociologist, Robert Nisbet:

Community encompasses all forms of relationships which are characterized by a high degree of personal intimacy, emotional depth, moral commitment, social cohesion, and continuity in time. Community is founded on man conceived in his wholeness rather than in one or another of the roles, taken separately, that he may hold in a social order.

Max Weber, one of the founders of sociology whose phrase gave us the melody for this sonata, and who was the masterful historian of rationalism, wondered whether all the secularization and rationalism would not strip life of its mystery, charm, and meaning.

But obviously—and "obviously" is admittedly a rational adverb—the complex technological society is not going to go away. Some small numbers of people may try to go away from it, to manage on communes with *The Last Whole Earth Catalog* as a textbook. (I wouldn't knock that, and I found myself inordinately tickled to have a book of mine included in the catalog among the kerosene lamps and potter's wheels.) The rest of us are left to cope, to try to reintegrate what is missing into what we have. We can use a seeming-rational approach to try to assess, for our own rational and managerial ends, what the changes in ethic and spirit mean, but totally to accept a nonrational world is to say goodbye to our role.

Anyway, irrationality and mystery and magic are no strangers to us in the money markets. That was one of the points of *The Money Game,* to show that while the language of the game was built on rationality and precision, the Game itself was played by behavior, and with all sorts of totems and taboos that would do credit to any tribe in New Guinea with an anthropologist in residence.

Changes do not occur overnight. The moral code which accompanied the accumulation of capital for the past several hundred years has encouraged us to applaud and honor purposiveness. In his remarkable and extraordinary essay "The Economic Possibilities for Our Grandchildren," Keynes wrote:

Purposiveness means that we are more concerned with the remote future results of our actions than with their own quality or their immediate effects on our own environment. The "purposive" man is always trying to secure a spurious and delusive immortality for his acts by pushing his interest in them forward into time. He does not love his cat, but his cat's kittens, nor, in truth, the kittens, but only the kittens' kittens, and so on forward for ever to the end of cat-dom. For him jam is not jam unless it is a case of jam

161

tomorrow and never jam today. Thus by pushing his jam always forward into the future, he strives to secure for his act of boiling it an immortality.

It may be that the era of purposiveness, with its inherent dictum of sacrifice, is winding down, however slowly. That does not mean another era of something else is immediately at hand. The counter-culture may not be a proper guide to the future because it is defined by its opposition; it is easier to describe what it is against than what it is for. But it may serve to stimulate some sort of synthesis, to make us broaden the idea of what is "rational," to help crack the consensus. Long before the term "counter-culture" came to be bandied, Keynes had delineated the lopsidedness of the accumulative society. "We have been trained too long to strive," he said, "and not to enjoy." Perhaps in a hundred years, he wrote—a hundred years from 1931, that is—the chief problem of mankind would be to live agreeably and wisely and well.

What would bring us to that point? Science and compound interest, incremental technology and accruing wealth. Some of the members of our affluent and post-affluent society are already into that spirit, as we have seen.

But alas, our views of both science and compound interest are changing. Science is no longer the unmitigated good the late Victorians saw, the radio added to Pasteur added to the electric light added to the steam engine. There is even some doubt about how incremental scientific growth is: in *The Structure of Scientific Revolutions,* Thomas Kuhn argues that each generation of scientists rewrites its textbooks to make everything a continuous flow. And as for compound interest —well, Keynes did say, in a phrase usually overlooked, "assuming no important wars and no important increase in population." Compound interest does not solve our economic problems if population compounds faster, because *per capita* is our divisor.

Unexpected turns in the road do have a way of materializing; it was only a generation ago that some of our industrial societies were worried about how to get the birth rate *up.* If we could indeed count on the cushion of science and compound interest, then indeed we could look forward to the day when (Keynes again) "there will be great changes in the code of morals . . . All kinds of social customs and economic practices, affecting the distribution of wealth and of economic reward and penalties, which we now maintain at all costs, however distasteful and unjust they may be in themselves, because they are tremendously useful in promoting the accumulation of capital, we shall then be free, at last, to discard."

But what do we do on Monday morning?

All of these exercises come under the perilous heading of long-term expectations, and we know that the long-term investor must seem —Keynes again—"eccentric, unconventional and rash in the eyes of average opinion." If the long-term investor succeeds, that confirms the belief in his rashness, and if he does not, "he will not receive very much mercy. Worldly wisdom teaches that it is better for reputation to fail conventionally than to succeed unconventionally."

If we are left with capital and not community, we still have to do our best to make our garden grow. Even the Enlightened One said that some hours must be spent in chopping wood and carrying water. But it would be folly not be *aware*, even for parochial purposes, of the changes going on around us, and that awareness is not a traditional sensitivity in the rational preciseness of a game played with numbers.

Meanwhile the mechanism and the structure of the markets in which our game is played have survived. The currency and the Supercurrency are still there. Maybe some of the players have gotten a little heavier. All of us have to make choices on the uses of our energies; some things are as they are and not as they ought to be, but this is the way the world is. If you are still for the Game, why, may you prosper; I wish you the joys of it.

THE ETERNAL
BLISS MACHINE

A condensation of the book by

MARCIA SELIGSON

WILLIAM MORROW & COMPANY, INC.

INTRODUCTION

I first discovered that there is something hilarious about weddings when I was a bridesmaid at Dee Dee Epstein's, during the summer of my nineteenth year. She was the first of our crowd to get married and it was my debut as a bridesmaid, so excitement ran absolutely amuck for months and months prior to the Big Day. (So, I should add, did jealousy and hatred for our bosom pal Dee Dee, who was not only getting married and being unspeakably smug about it but was also having a colossal super-extravaganza circus of a wedding—The Dream of Dreams.)

I have never forgotten one moment of Dee Dee's wedding, and its indelible imprint on my brain is probably the single factor responsible for this book. It took place at an oceanfront beach club on Long Island, near the suburban town where I grew up. A vulgar nook, it had somehow succeeded in convincing the world that, by virtue of its six (yes, six) swimming pools, it was the apex of CLASS. What I remember most vividly about the El Patio Beach Club is that no matter how far out into the ocean you swam, you could always hear cha-cha music. It was the perfect spot for Dee Dee's wedding.

Five hundred revelers crammed the El Patio that hot Sunday in June. Upon entering, each had been handed a newspaper entitled *The Epstein-Horowitz Gazette*—a ten-page printed journal recounting the lives of Dee Dee Epstein and Malcolm Horowitz, our groom. The climax of the bacchanal was the arrival of the wedding cake—a fourteen-foot mountain of stark white goo. Against the cake was placed a ladder which Dee Dee daintily climbed, brandishing a long silver knife. At the peak, she dramatically slashed into the sugar hulk, thereby releasing a battalion of anxiety-ridden white doves.

Six months later Phyllis Nussbaum (who was marrying Harvey

Cohen) successfully one-upped Dee Dee—with an eight-foot-long replica of a cruise ship made out of chopped liver, green olives for the portholes, and pimientos spread along the bow spelling out *S.S. Cohen*. Then, before the ten-course dinner, we gathered to watch home movies of the couple's respective childhoods.

Because of my own background, I believed—prior to writing this book—that only Jewish weddings were funny and grotesque and wildly absurd. But in the last two years I've traveled all over this country and attended 45,000 weddings (or so it seems), and clearly I was wrong. Whatever it is about weddings that makes people go a little bananas—construct ships out of chopped liver or dye mashed potatoes pink to match the bridesmaids' dresses—it transcends ethnic division and crosses state lines.

Being a reporter at a wedding is a little like being a reporter at an orgy—you don't know quite where you fit in. Sometimes, depending on the ambiance and my own zest, I would participate—drink champagne, mambo with granddaddy, glut myself on the goodies. At other times I remained A Reporter—cordial, questioning, slightly aloof, and probably rather menacing. Occasionally I felt moved, frequently I found myself giggling, and sometimes I was repelled.

All to be expected, I guess. The only response that truly surprised me happened when I was standing in the rain on the White House grounds watching little Tricia march down the aisle on the arm of her beaming father, and suddenly, astoundingly, I felt a small tear form. But that's the thing about weddings. They're very tricky.

CHAPTER 1

THE AMERICAN WAY

The wedding, they say, is a dodo bird. Extinct. They say that America's children are abandoning established American values. Marriage is in its terminal stages, gasping for its dying breath as the new breed of youth shuns wedlock for cohabiting, or one-to-oneness for the communal clan. Those few who are still choosing to get married, everybody insists, are certainly not doing it the way their parents or even older sisters and brothers did—that is, in the traditional, conventional fashion of flowing white lace, "Oh, Promise Me," and a week in Bermuda. That's what everybody says about weddings in America.

They are dead wrong.

Consider these facts:

—In 1971, there were 2,196,000 marriages in America, 648,000 more than in 1961. In those ten years the steady increase paralleled the population growth, that is, 1 percent of the population got married every year.

—Seven out of eight first-time couples are married in a church or synagogue.

—Seven out of eight first-time brides receive an engagement ring.

—In 1971, 80 percent of all first-time weddings were formal; in 1967, that figure was 73 percent.

—In 1971, 96 percent of marrying couples held a reception; in 1967, 85 percent.

—84.5 percent of first-time brides wear a formal bridal gown.

—The wedding industry represents $7 billion a year to the American economy.

Making generalizations about American youth has of late become a thorny dilemma. Woodstock makes headlines, as do marijuana busts,

169

freaky outfits, and the wedding on a Big Sur cliff where the bride and groom arrived on horseback—nude—and all the guests peeled off their jeans and tie-dyed shirts in a whooping tribal celebratory dance. One makes vast assumptions based on *Time* magazine covers and the seven o'clock news, but the question always remains: How many? How many kids are dropping out, dropping acid, dropping their drawers at their weddings? Many, many fewer, I believe, than we think.

A Louis Harris poll of American high school and college students in *Life* in 1972 unearthed some surprising opinions from youth—surprising in their "straightness" for a generation that is often presumed to be spending much of its waking life prone. "Is it perfectly all right to enjoy sex for its own sake?" posed one question. Forty-four percent of college kids said "No." "Should any girl who wants an abortion be allowed to have one?" "No" from 45 percent. One-half replied "No" to the question, "Will sexual experience before marriage contribute to happiness later?" And—what to me seemed the most astonishing revelation—52 percent of the respondents answered "Yes" to "Do young men still consider virginity until marriage important in a woman?"

That is not to say that *nothing* has changed; it is, rather, a claim that the transformations in lifestyle and values among America's youth are not yet as widespread or as dramatic as one frequently assumes. It is also a claim that whatever shifts *are* occurring in this country, there is at least one stronghold in which tradition will rule—almost, statistically, every time. The American Way of Wedding.

The fact is that we Americans are getting married almost precisely as we did a hundred years ago. And although there is no such thing as "the typical American wedding"—as many styles of weddings exist as the styles of citizens giving them—every single one possesses the same ritualistic ingredients, the same replay of ancient custom and primeval symbolism, the same predictable plot and standard players. A wedding is, after all, a wedding.

But that very fact—the suspenseless, every-wedding-is-just-like-every-other-wedding truth—bespeaks some fundamental human need. A minister in Atlanta says: "People simply *crave* weddings—the guests as well as the families. Although they are all the same, in a sense, they are all profoundly different, and somehow crucial to us."

Like a newborn baby. We automatically find it irresistible and unique despite its resemblance to all the babies surrounding it. Babies and weddings both seem to tap in us a wellspring of emotion that is as ever-present as it is mysterious. Both are, surely, metaphors for the beginning of new life, emblems of hope and continuity. In the case of a wedding, all connections to reality are suspended as the radiant bride floats down the flower-decked aisle and we feel ourselves choke up (by my informal tally, 80 percent of all wedding guests choke up). It simply does not matter who she is, whether we know her well or even like her much. Our knowledge of the perils of marriage, the zooming divorce rate, the possibilities of emotional bloodbath—none of it has any place at a wedding. The wedding is wired in to other needs that are monumental and timeless.

One of those innate psychic hungers is for ritual—prescribed and repeated systems of observance, "a sense of formal, sanctified public ceremonial" (as defined in an essay in *Time* magazine). Boy Scout parades are rituals, as are political conventions, Christmas cards, football games, funerals. Ritual provides our lives with a point of stability, an equilibrium and consistency, a bridge with the past.

"Rituals are society's unwritten permission for civilized man to express primitive emotions: fear, sexuality, grief," continues *Time*. They invite people "to be more human in public—more themselves—than they dare to be in private."

As American life gets more fragmented, our drive to create new ceremonial observances and to strengthen the old becomes heightened. Especially fierce is our hookup to the most primitive of all rituals—the rites of passage.

Every culture, in every time throughout history, has commemorated the transition of a human being from one state in life to another. Birth, the emergence into manhood, graduation from school at various levels, birthdays, marriage, death—each of these outstanding steps is acknowledged by a ceremony of some sort, always public, the guests in effect becoming witnesses to the statement of life's ongoingness. To insure the special significance of the rite of passage, its apartness from any other event of the day, these rituals usually require pageantry, costumed adornment, and are accompanied by gift-bearing and feasting. We wear black to funerals, bring presents to christenings and birthday parties, get loaded at wakes, eat ourselves sick at bar mitzvahs. Birth, marriage, and death, to be sure, are the most elemental and major steps, and as there is only one of those ritual commemorations for which we are *actually,* fully present, the wedding becomes, for mankind, its most vital rite of passage.

And it is, historically, a public, not private, event. "The wedding is a doorway to new status. It is the announcement of a new relationship between two persons, a relationship in which society, as well as the two individuals themselves, is interested," writes the author of *Marriage for Moderns*. Society's interest exists to protect established moral standards, to legitimize children, and to safeguard property rights, and "for this reason there are a ceremony, records, a public expression of willingness on the part of the couple, witnesses, sanction of the state and frequently of the church. . . ."

What, then, does it all mean to the individuals concerned—the girl, the boy, and the families? To ask this question of the people involved, folks who are dedicating more money, time, energy, and emotion to this one day, indeed these few hours, than to any previous or future activity in their lives—is to receive a series of answers that are but variations on the same theme: THE WEDDING IS THE MOST IMPORTANT DAY IN LIFE.

—"The most beautiful thing about my wedding was the look on my dad's face. He felt this was the height of achievement of his whole life."

—"I had always dreamed about being a beautiful bride for as long as I could remember. I just loved every single minute of it, and even though it was ridiculously expensive and there were months of aggravation, I would go through it again in a minute."

—"I eloped, and I made myself a promise that my daughter would have a lavish, absolutely gorgeous wedding. I planned it from the day she was born."

To the bride's family, those who actually create the wedding, it becomes a symbol of the fulfillment of their roles as parents. Mama, the nurturer, devotes her life toward preparing her daughter to follow in her footsteps—wifehood, motherhood. On the wedding day the proof is right out front that she has succeeded in her big job. A classic illustration of maternal power is the California woman who was so thrilled with her daughter's sweet-sixteen party at the posh Bel-Air Hotel that, right then and there, she made a reservation for five years hence—the girl's twenty-first birthday—for her wedding. Those five years were spent making certain it all came about as programmed. Sure enough. . . .

Daddy, too, has satisfied *his* ordained role as the provider by being able to splurge on such a splendid razzle-dazzle. And the heroine of this family drama, the bride, is exhibiting to the world that she turned out all right, was transformed overnight from frog to princess, from flawed adolescent to flawless woman, and now she's doing what she's supposed to do. Everybody fulfills his destiny at The Wedding.

According to Barbara Donovan, the editor of *Bride's* magazine, "The American girl is married long before she is even in high school. Her images of her wedding day begin when she's *practically* an infant." As evidence, take The Bride Game—a board game like Monopoly or Sorry, but this highly popular item is for girls aged eight to fourteen. On the box is a picture of a bride decked out in long white veil, bouquet—except she looks to be about eleven years old. "The object of the game," assert the instructions, "is to be the first girl to get her complete matching wedding party along with the necessary accessories for the wedding ceremony." She gets wedding cake cards, bridal bouquet cards, ring cards, and she moves with dice rolls from bridal salon to pastry shop to jewelry store—to the aisle. The winner of The Bride Game is the first tot to reach the spot marked "Ceremony." Eight years old and she already *knows,* by God, that she must acquire her diamond and her garter and all her THINGS before she can get to the altar. She also knows that *she* is the superstar of the wedding, the sole subject of all the attention and adoration. There is not, in The Bride Game, a solitary man, nary a mention of the groom.

Ladies in ancient Greece computed their age from the day of their marriage, not from birth. Our view of the wedding day as the true beginning of a woman's existence is only slightly more insidious. About two years after I graduated from college, I visited a school pal in her New York bachelor-girl's apartment, which she shared with two other young single women. There was scarcely a stick of furniture, not a plant to perk up the barrenness. I asked her why and she replied: "Oh, I'm not going to fix up an apartment until my REAL life!" I knew immediately what she meant and I never forgot the remark. Nor what it revealed about how women experience their lives.

It's the old Cinderella mythology. While little boys are dreaming heroic dreams of conquering worlds, little girls are yearning for transformation—becoming beautiful, becoming a woman, becoming a mommy. As marriage is the single event which will presumably guarantee that metamorphosis, it is, naturally, the day for which her entire life has been in preparation. She is, today, the fairy princess, queen for a day, Miss America floating down the ramp. For a man, marriage is but a continuation of growth and change; for her it is the REAL beginning. The prince is, classically, passive and fairly indifferent toward an occasion that does not represent to him what it does to his lady; he goes through with it because she wants it, the families want it, society wants it, and it is payment of his last dues as a "child." The groom, as it turns out, does not even partake in the processional to the altar, but sort of sneaks in, inconspicuously, through a side door, and is—somehow—just THERE.

The bridal apparel industry has special corporations for bridesmaids' garb, mother-of-the-bride dresses, even flower girl doodads. The men—even though there are as many male attendants as female—must rent, borrow, steal their outfits—who cares anyway? Their job is basically to escort the women, to be appendages to the princess and her ladies-in-waiting.

The American Way of Wedding is a glaring reflection of the American way of life. Primarily, it is a metaphor for our two paramount, lifelong concerns as a people—Love and Money.

Does anybody doubt the immeasurable strain of romanticism lurking in the American head? It tends to lie dormant; we hardly realize—in the steely face of our computer technology—what marshmallows we are in our souls. But then, periodically, we are confronted with cultural phenomena the message of which is undisguised and unavoidable. Rod McKuen, the crown-prince mush huckster of all time, sells seven million books of poetry, even more record albums, standing-room-only concerts, and all that he's hawking is loneliness and misery and MUSH. Erich Segal pens an éclair about wondrous love and exquisite dying and lo and behold . . . one of the hugest-selling books, biggest-grossing movies in history.

"Oh, to be a June Bride. You've dreamed of it since you were a little girl. You've seen yourself wrapped in clouds of white gliding up a rose-strewn aisle toward an altar bathed in summer sunlight." This molasses from an old issue of a bridal magazine says it all. The American wedding is nothing if not profoundly romantic, pure magical fantasy. And, whatever the simplicity or exorbitance—it is theater. A dramatic ritual of romance in which the same "plot" is enacted each and every time, the same "characters" in their inevitable "costumes" appear, and only the "sets" change, depending on the style of the pageant. It can be a musical comedy, a Wagnerian opera, a rodeo, a carnival, a vaudeville, or burlesque. The same elements emerge. Opening night, stage fright, and an audience. The unfolding and outcome are, as we've said, without suspense, but, on the other hand, so is *Gone with the Wind* the fourteenth time you've seen it and still Rhett's final exit evokes from us the same teary, sentimental response every single time. And the wedding quells the same hunger as all theater—it spirits us away from daily life with its banalities and drabness and downright reality for one golden, unblemished moment in time.

In order to perpetuate our romantic passion for love and weddings, the industry has solely dedicated itself to the first-time bride. Although 25 percent of our marriages consist of people making their second or third trips, they are utterly ignored by the forces of the bridal business. In part, the dismissal is realistic—old hands tend not to throw immense wedding spectaculars or purchase entirely brand-new rigs of furniture. But what concerns us here is illusion, not reality. The bride-figure can feed our *Love Story* fevers only by her symbolic innocence, her non-tarnishment, her utterly pure belief in the perfection of love and marriage. A bride who has been through the *Sturm und Drang* of divorce is—well—stained. The demon Reality is the number one killer of romance, so let's simply obliterate the demon and get back to that divine wedding with The Vision in white organza.

Americans spend fortunes on weddings, borrow thousands from banks, hock the family jewels, sacrifice next summer's vacation. They arrange productions so lavish, so SHOW BIZ as to put Darryl Zanuck out of work. Thousands of people, in fact, spend more on getting their children married than on their education. Okay, we understand why The Wedding as ritual is a central part of the culture. But why the chopped liver cruise ships, the kitsch, the hilarious/grotesque extravaganza? If a wedding is a wedding—and they all are made up of the same components, fill the same personal needs—then why does a nice girl from a nice family having a nice wedding at the Waldorf-Astoria Hotel in Manhattan hire a live horse to dance the "Blue Danube Waltz" with its trainer? (The horse, incidentally, added several other unexpected touches to the evening.) Why does a simple middle-class family in Woodstock, Illinois, build a special knotty-pine wedding chapel—with stereo, mind you—in their backyard, tearing it down immediately after the wedding?

It's all about MAKING IT. Making it, that is, in the American sense of being able to acquire GOODS, showing off POSSESSIONS, upward mobility on the THING scale, asserting your escalating status to your friends with SYMBOLS. The concept, of course, is strictly middle-class American, where the structure is always fluid, the challenge is to rise and rise, and the possibilities are seemingly limitless. (The upper and lower classes have a fixed place resting on their birth that is not generally mobile and is denied by the middle class.) The wedding —simply because it *is* such an emotional happening, such a terrific reason for all sorts of outpourings—is a quintessential vehicle for letting-it-all-hang-out materialism. The ostentation overkill present in so very many weddings is obvious only to the outsider. To the host, it is his validation as a man, a father. And the realization of The American Dream.

Certainly, more pure motives exist for the gigantic wedding jamboree. We tend today to be cut off from our roots, disconnected from community life. The nuclear family has replaced the extended family or clan environment, and we are isolated, lonely. There are few enough occasions left in life for communal gathering, the wedding and the funeral being the primary two, and it is only the wedding that permits opportunity for rejoicing and feasting with folks we care about.

But there is no such animal as "The Typical American Wedding," even though the subcultures that make up our populace are becoming increasingly homogenized. Neighborhoods are not so strictly "black" or "white" or "Greek" anymore; corporate life is no longer quite so WASP, cops not so Irish, all psychoanalysts are not Jewish. But weddings are different. Anchored in historical group traditions, plus reflecting the subtle and not-so-subtle position and values of the group on the American ladder, American weddings are a true smorgasbord. Middle-class Jews do it differently than middle-class Italians; weddings in South Carolina are not much like weddings in Iowa. Hotel fiestas bear little resemblance to those at the local Kiwanis Club.

And nobody—but NOBODY—tosses a wedding blowout barbecue like the folks in Texas, Nosirreebob.

CHAPTER 2

IN THE BEGINNING

A lmost all of the wedding customs operative today are merely echoes of the past—everything from the presence of flowers and a veil to the bridesmaids and processional. At one time every last ingredient bore a very specific and vitally significant meaning. Today, although the original substance is lost to us, we incorporate them into our weddings because—well, just because. Because they're traditional and ritualistic and we mortals crave tradition and ritual. And because—as the man said about the mountain peak—they're THERE.

Anthropologists have argued for decades about the origins of marriage, whether in fact it was sexual instinct that bound men and women together, or survival considerations, or an emotional craving for protection and permanency. One popular view—and that espoused by the most renowned marriage and wedding rite historian, Edward Westermarck—is that wedlock originally came about as a result of the helpless-ness of the newborn child, *its* need for family nurture and protection. Thus Westermarck claims that "marriage is rooted in the family rather than the family in marriage."

Among early peoples, *everybody* married, bachelorhood being considered a crime against nature. As the main issue was children, *not* to bear offspring was to be denied entrance into the Gates of Paradise—a notion persisting today in many cultures. Of the three forms of pairing—monogamy, polygamy (a man with many wives), and polyandry (a woman with many husbands)—monogamy has been historically the most perseverant, although probably not by natural impulse so much as practical motivations. And until very recently matrimony has taken place, especially for girls, at a very young age, often at the onset of puberty. (A Lady Mary Villiers, we are told, was a widow at the age of nine.) People didn't live very long, for one thing. Then, as we shall see, marriage was often a buy-and-sell arrangement perpetrated by the girl's family for profit, the bride being the commodity for sale, and a young lamb—strong, a virgin, easily shaped to the master's will—could bring the better monetary deal.

The earliest known form was Marriage by Capture, in which a man invaded another tribe and kidnapped a woman. Although this barba-rism became obsolete with the birth of Christianity, it remained legal in England until the thirteenth century and occurred periodically among southern Slavs until the 1800's. (Westermarck says that the Yahgans and the Onas of Tierra del Fuego are still doing it today.)

The most common and longest-lasting system was the Marriage by Purchase. Still in evidence today throughout the globe, this method both reflected and perpetuated the growing strength of patriarchy, in which the male of the family had supreme control, a woman had no more legal status than a child and could be sold and traded like the prize sow. A marriage helped to make the patriarchal father an even more powerful influence in his community, as it was planned in order to heighten his economic station and as an alliance between important families. In theory, the father was losing valuable labor by his daughter's exit and thus he must be well compensated; and, too, she—and the offspring that she would bear—would be her hus-band's most valuable "possession," so he should be willing to pay for her in the same way that he would pay for a sturdy new plow.

The word "wedding," in fact, refers to the "wed"—the "bride price." That is, that amount of money, goods, or property paid to the lass's father for her purchase. The level of negotiations would depend on the wealth of the families and the qualities of the girl—her beauty, strength, and abilities. As she was considered more salable if pure, chastity became a big virtue. (In parts of Morocco, today, a workingman pays $70 to $100 for a virgin, only $30 for a widow or divorcée.) Proof of virginity became a necessary part of the wedding ceremonial—inspection of the bridal sheets the morning after or, as in Greece, the bride's stained nightgown left hanging in the window for days.

The bride, naturally, had no voice whatsoever in the arrangements. Neither does a goat when it is being sold to the farmer next door. And once she was married she had no more autonomy as a wife than she did as a child. Even the liberty of deciding divorce was confined to men, who could legally abandon their wives for being barren or for being rotten cooks—or for virtually any other failing in servitude.

The husband paid the bride price to his future father-in-law; the bride came to the marriage with a dowry, a gesture of repayment to the groom. Our bride received nothing. Daddy got the bride price; hubby got her dowry and complete control over her person. Even in later eras, when marriages for love were being made, lots of haggling took place over the components of the dowry, and receipts were exchanged immediately following the ceremony.

In societies where chastity was not a particular virtue (some Algerian tribes, or among the aborigines of Nicaragua), the young girl was expected to earn her dowry by prostitution.

During the entire time span from the primitive Marriage by Capture to the late Middle Ages, religion played little part in the wedding ritual. As an alliance between families, a wedding was simply a family and community folk fest, an extraordinarily joyous frolic. It began generally as a "processional" of an entire village or tribe, led by the bride's father, making its merry way to the groom's habitat where the lass was turned over to her new master. *That* transfer alone comprised the legal wedding rite. Feasting, music, and dance followed, often for days. (The Vikings, in fact, celebrated each wedding for a continuous month.)

The early Christian fathers, you see, were opposed to the whole idea of marriage, preaching that celibacy was surely man's highest striving. Affairs of the spirit were distinctly more important, for one reason; for another, the end of the world was clearly imminent, so it was futile to think about propagating the species. Then, as the Church assumed more power in general, word began to spread that God's blessing was a good thing for wedlock—although any marriage was certainly lawful without it—and couples, as part of the ritual, would go to the church for benediction *after* they were wed.

By the thirteenth century, weddings had fallen under religious control and the Church then insisted on the mutual consent of the newlyweds as a condition. Marriages, in practice, were still arranged by the families; nonetheless, the rule of mutual consent was, in philosophy, a gigantic step forward in marital history.

The Council of Trent in 1563 declared that any marriage not performed by a priest was null and void, and it was then not until the eighteenth century—with the French Revolution and moves for independence in the American colonies—that the pendulum swung back and matrimony once again became thought of as a private and civil venture.

It was also not until the eighteenth-century Enlightenment that the odd concept of romantic marriage caught flame. Lovers' passion had naturally always existed but had had nothing at all to do with the business of wedlock. It was only with the slight psychological elevation of woman's status that conjugal affection could begin to substitute for sheer enslavement. To date, Marriage for Love has been the shortest evolutionary stage of conjugal history.

Most of today's wedding customs predate the Church; they are moored, rather, in magic and superstition and paganism. But the most common means of celebrating the marriage throughout history has been by feasting, the custom of eating together having always symbolized the public bringing together of families, affirmation of the strongest kinships.

Surrounding the actual wedding were the preparatory and final rituals. Then, as marriage always implies sexual intercourse and procreation, the wedding night was as much public participation as the events preceding. Guests would follow the couple into the bedroom, the male attendants undressing the groom and tussling to capture the bride's garter; the parents would make elaborate fertility toasts over the bed, and cowbells, having been surreptitiously affixed to the mattress, would make joyful noise unto the activities that followed. It was not unusual for the "witnesses" to hang about outside until the first consummation was completed and the husband gave some public sign of its satisfactoriness.

Every ingredient within the marriage rite, born of primitive magical belief, symbolizes one of, or several of, four ideas: fertility, female submission, separation from one family and union with another, or the protection from evil. There is much overlapping and much anthropological nitpicking about which element falls within which category, whether—for example—the Russian father's beating of his daughter primarily signifies male mastery over women or is, in fact, an act to expel the evil spirits from the bride's body. All in all, one senses that ancient peoples were so cradled in superstition that each act probably bears many meanings simultaneously—rather like carrying a rabbit's foot AND not walking underneath a ladder.

Badges of fertility, to insure both consummation and reproduction, are woven through the wedding. The presence of food and flowers is symbolic of fruitfulness and the continuance of life. In France, wheat is showered over the newlyweds; in America it is rice, and in Greece nuts and dates. All are gestures of the bride's contact with seed-bearing plants. Slices of wedding cake are given to guests to take home to guarantee their own fecundity. And fragile objects are broken to indicate the breaking of the bride's hymen: in parts of England a plate containing salt is smashed over the groom's head, and Jews traditionally stomp on a glass.

The woman's submission to her husband has been established since the dawn of marital history, and some of our most durable wedding traditions find their sources in this state of affairs. The most conspicuous emblem of maidenly chastity and subservience is the veil. After the bride was bargained for and the terms set, she was then veiled, as an announcement to the world that she was "sold" and that no man but her master could gaze on her.

Among primitive people, the dread of evil spirits pervaded each society with a profound force. All ritual—whether joyous or mournful, so long as it was significant—remembered the omnipresent need to appease, or drive away, or trick the malevolent influences that were supposed to be always hovering about. Young brides and grooms were believed to be the most vulnerable and endangered, due to their innocence and happiness, and the history of wedding rites is permeated with symbolic means for protecting against the unseen powers. In Russia, for example, the doors, windows, and chimney were shut tight for the ceremony; shooting off guns was a common practice in central Europe; Arabic grooms would lay a sword on the bridal bed and a pistol under the pillow prior to the wedding. It was also believed that the presence of great quantities of food would pacify or seduce the demons.

One means to safeguard the couple was by deception—the wearing of masks or disguises. In Moorish weddings the bride and groom were painted all over with henna, as to be virtually unrecognizable;

bridesmaids and groomsmen originally dressed precisely like the bride and groom in order to outfox the spirits. And in Denmark the couple would wear old clothes of the opposite sex—guaranteed to utterly baffle *everybody*. The dangers were assumed to be lurking either above or below the earth, so appropriate precautions were taken: carrying the bride over the threshold to protect her from the ground monsters (also a mark of enslavement); paths strewn with flowers; the Jewish "chuppa" (pronounced "huppa"), or canopy, offering the couple sanctuary from evil above.

The mythical idea is that only first-time brides and grooms are considered to be in a state of peril as it is only they who are passing into a new state of life and who are therefore innocent. It is the ancient explanation of why only first marriages and not subsequent ones are attended by such elaborate hoopla and are so full of symbolization.

What cannot be ignored in this historical tapestry of marriage and the wedding, the theme that occurs and reoccurs throughout the ritualistic reenactment of centuries-old customs and patterns, is the subjugation of women, the view of women as chattels, as nonpeople.

Despite the gigantic inequities operative today where women are concerned, it is not, I grant you, easy to regard Miss American Bride as oppressed. The wedding, of course, is a matriarchal totalitarian event, in which men have no more relevance than the elevator operator on a self-service elevator. The bride is the Virgin Fairy Princess Star; her groom is—okay, let's say it—mere woodwork, attracting less interest than the parsley surrounding the chicken breasts.

Rampant female chauvinism? It would certainly seem so, but on closer examination the truth becomes clear. The bride is the central figure because the real change in status is hers. She changes her name to her husband's, prepares to have children, follows him wherever he goest because his work is assumed paramount. He continues his growthful journey through the real world as before, with the addition of a new appendage, a wife; she is transferred from economically dependent child to economically dependent "adult." The language says it succinctly: "wife" originally meant "woman"; "husband" meant "master of the house." And this day is her one brief breakout between anonymities. She poses on pedestals, glides through misty clouds of mauve stage lighting, glorifies the cover of *Modern Bride*, becomes enshrined in chicken salad.

But pedestal sitting is far removed from eyeball-to-eyeball equality. Deifying women in the abstract has been a repeated historical pattern: ancient goddesses were worshiped for fertility and sexual allurement, while ladies on the earth were dominated and demeaned; the age of chivalry and courtly love romanticized and idealized women, while still allowing them no rights. The process is simply called dehumanization, and it is the same game whether she is being stared up at or looked down upon.

CHAPTER 3

THE LOVE MACHINERY

On this very day, experts estimate, 5,641 American girls will become engaged to be married to a like number of American boys. Mere minutes after the "Okay, let's" or the "YIPPEE THANK GOD AT LAST" is uttered by one of the parties, the love machinery goes into operation. All the cogs and wheels of American enterprise are mobilized into action as this new consumer entity—the About-To-Be-Newlyweds—is born. It will dump $7 billion into the economic pot between day of engagement and six-months wedding anniversary. Six hundred million of that will find its way to the engagement ring boys, $1 billion to the trousseau brokers (luggage, lingerie, apparel, and cosmetics), $3.5 billion to the home furnishings and appliance merchants. The new entity will be enriched by $200 million worth of gifts.

If one were to follow a bride—hand-in-hand with her mother, tailed at ten paces by the groom—through the ritualistic parade from engagement to honeymoon, one would be struck by the ever-spiraling web of detail and expenditure in which the participants are caught. Engagement announcements; the ring; the wedding invitations; the wedding preparations; the trousseau; the bridal showers; the registering for gifts; the new home and massive catalog of accompanying purchases; the wedding itself; the honeymoon. And each category is inevitably and inextricably shackled to outpouring of money.

A girl in my college dormitory got engaged and instantaneously assembled a three-ring looseleaf notebook which she called "My Marriage Book." Although it exactly resembled a standard classroom notebook, the dividing categories were not "French" or "Trigonometry" but, rather, "Stemware," "Linens," "Sterling Silver Flatware," and on and on. She carried this bible with her *everywhere*, for eight months, neatly pasting in ads from magazines and inserting notes to herself on objects she would see on her daily shopping trips. "My Marriage Book." A rumor ultimately spread through the dorm that Annette actually slept with it under her pillow in case a vision of The Perfect Ice Bucket should come to her in a dream.

Part of the wedding choreography is the obsession to do it *right*. It is why dreary books on wedding etiquette proliferate, why the job of "wedding consultant" is such a juicy one, and why the bridal magazines devote a section of every issue to the Umpteen Commandments of weddingdom.

Having decided the where and when of the wedding arrangements, the next paramount step is the invitations. *Bride's Book of Etiquette* says: "There is no procedure connected with a wedding which is more bound by tradition and etiquette than the issuing of invitations and announcements. Ingenuity and individuality have no place here. The wording is set by the laws of etiquette, as are the stationery and the engraving." Not to mention the addressing, the folding, the sealing, the stamping, and the timing of the mailing.

Bess Harris, the invitations saleswoman with Cartier in New York for the last thirty years, is ramrod rigid in her bailiwick. Engagement announcements, she insists, are outré. ("It's bad etiquette. Only Jews and Italians do it.") If the wedding is in church, one must say, claims Miss Harris, so-and-so "requests the honour of your presence," but if in a hotel, it's "the pleasure of your company." She quakes at the mere mention of informality. "We're very firm about etiquette. An invitation with the Cartier imprint assumes perfection; that's why people come to us."

As American family life gets more complex, so accordingly do wedding invitations. Unbendable rules exist to cover the wording variances of an invitation being issued by the bride's divorced mother, or by the bride's divorced and remarried mother, or the bride's widowed mother, and on and on and on. Then, too, there are military laws for the reception cards, the will-be-at-home cards, the church admission cards (to avoid crashers), pew cards, and of course the occasional cancellation notices—which must certainly be as Emily Postian as anything else.

For very large weddings, Cartier peddles gift acknowledgment cards: "Miss So-and-so acknowledges the receipt of your wedding gift and will take pleasure in writing you herself in the near future."

Bess Harris is trapped in the eye of an invitation revolution that she clearly finds appalling. "Years ago we'd make you walk out of the store if you asked for a colored invitation. Now people have become psychedelic and we're allowing the *most* ridiculous things. Blue printing instead of black." In a what-is-this-world-coming-to slump, she

183

continues, unhappily: "It used to be that if the text was in bad taste, we wouldn't do it. If the girl's parents were divorced and both wanted to be on the invitation anyway—well, it's just dead wrong—but now we'll do it if the client fusses a lot. I don't approve at all."

Love—to the jeweler—means $1 billion a year shelled out by the matrimonial set for articles falling into the "Jewelry Industry" playpen: that is, rings, silver, china, and crystal. Of that sum, $750 million, in 1971, was spent for weddings and engagement rings, a soaring increase over the $600 million spent the previous year.

Startlingly clear proof, it seems, of how truly little is being dismantled of the American way of wedding is the statistic that 87 percent of all American brides receive engagement rings, and four out of five of those are diamonds. The diamond, in our society, possesses symbolic values and implications that are inescapable; it is, perhaps, the key status object. Elizabeth Taylor, the empress of consumption overkill, already owns everything in the world; as her peak act of self-aggrandizement, she thus purchases the largest diamond boulder in existence, 69.42 carats, costing well over $1 million and which she is permitted to wear—according to insurance regulations ($66,000 a year in premiums)—only twenty times a year. The fact that the little shopgirl, whose life will never bear any resemblance whatsoever to Elizabeth Taylor's, can also possess a diamond, albeit a microscopic cousin, is terrific status.

At the time in history when brides themselves were purchased, the engagement period was specifically meant for the exchange of tokens—the girl's father putting up security that the marriage would take place, the groom making a down payment of food, cattle, or jewels. The diamond ring, as token, did not make its appearance until the fifteenth century when Archduke Maximilian of Austria—in a great frenzy to get married and rush back to the wars—presented Mary of Burgundy with the first of its kind. (Women, in general, were not permitted to wear jeweled rings.)

Even as diamonds came into engagement ring fashion, they were still rare and, therefore, the prerogative of the very rich. It was not until the mid-nineteenth century that huge quantities were discovered in South Africa and not until the 1900's that they were cut into tiny stones and mass marketed. Today the average "little shopgirl" in America gets half a carat, at an average cost of $328.85.

In New York City I went to visit two corporations with grand claims: Zale is, they say, the largest jeweler in the world; J. R. Wood and Sons (Art Carved Rings), the biggest in "the fancy wedding ring business." Wedding ring sales tally to approximately $107 million a year. For 90 percent of our newlyweds, that means two rings per couple (it's an old tradition in Europe, but did not spread in the United States until World War II, when men were separated for long periods from their wives).

In its building on Thirty-third Street, near the Hudson River, Zale purports to have more money stored, in jewelry, than any bank in the world. The only outfit that buys rough diamonds, cuts the stones itself, and then grinds out two thousand engagement rings every day, Zale also has a network of 950 retail stores around the country. J. R. Wood, by contrast, manufactures only wedding rings—700,000 a year—and since approximately three million a year are sold, they capture a solid wedge of the pie. Apparently, I am given to understand, more changes are being executed in the ring business than in any other wedding category. "Kids are more sophisticated today," says Allan Ginsberg, from Zale. "They don't come in anymore with their hats in hand, not knowing what they want, insecure. They're more discerning, and the biggest trend that I notice is the dying of the classic, klutzy bread-and-butter look." (That look, he explains, means the center diamond in the white gold setting.)

Since 86 percent of all first-time brides—more than four out of five—read either or both of the bridal publications, *Modern Bride* and *Bride's,* and since both conduct frequent and exhaustive market research studies worthy of a nervous Presidential candidate, one can assume that they know their girl. Inside and out. They know, for example, that 67 percent of their readers live at home until they get married, that three out of five have attended college, that 73 percent expect to work full time during the first year of marriage. They know, too, that she averages out to 20.3 years old, her guy is 21.8, and together they earn $7,900 a year. They know that most young women read bridal magazines before they are even engaged, and that prospective brides, on the average, will look at a particular page of interest exactly 12.1 times. It stands to reason, then, that one can discover a lot about the American bride of today by looking at what the experts feed her.

Bride's says their magazine deals with three areas: "(1) how to be sure the wedding and wedding trip will be perfect in every detail; (2) how to make her husband happy through knowledge of him and understanding of herself; (3) how to successfully plan and furnish a first home to suit both new members of the family as well as their guests." "Our target girl," says Barbara Donovan, "is between eighteen and twenty-four, getting married for the first time and changing her lifestyle and place of residence. All the information gathered between our magazine's covers is to help her make the transition between two very different lives. To that end, *Bride's* is basically a textbook."

"A bridal magazine has the relevance of a Sears Roebuck catalog," from the slightly more cynical George Morrissey, publisher of *Modern Bride*. "Our girl isn't special. She's any girl who is getting married in a formal ceremony and moving to a new home." What his girl is, certainly, is utterly unprepared to deal with the tidal wave of purchasing under which she is being swept, the buying bout that will surpass, statistically, any other period of her life. Though she has undoubtedly been dreaming of this golden time since childhood, what on earth does she know of carats and baguettes and electric brooms and Alençon lace?

That's what the magazines are for. *Modern Bride* boasts more advertising pages than any other consumer magazine in America (not to mention the first contraceptive ads in a national publication). Hundreds of ads for bridal gowns, sterling silver, luggage, mattresses, tuxedos, honeymoon resorts, linoleum, sex manuals, eye makeup, china, and vaginal douche powder. The feature subjects in every issue are standard: where to go on your honeymoon; detachable booklets on wedding etiquette; first-home furnishing and hostessing hints—everything from the basics of how-to-set-a-perfect-table to the basics of how-to-whip-up-a-perfect-paella; columns on beauty advice ("How do I make my feet look divine for my wedding?") and columns on etiquette ("Can my bridesmaids carry parasols as late as September 3?" The answer, by the way, is yes. Summer was not officially ended, that year, until September 4). In *Bride's* especially, there is the *de rigueur* monthly article on sex, but the weight of the feature material is placed on bridal fashions.

After reading a truckload of *Bride's* and *Modern Bride*, I came away with a strong sense of our American bride being astonishingly ignorant about *most* adult concerns, in addition to the silver-china-vacuum cleaner issues. In an article in *Bride's* of June, 1972, entitled "Questions Brides Ask About Sex," the first query is "What will happen when my husband and I have sex?" And the author really-truly explains, à la my seventh-grade social hygiene class, about foreplay ("Usually lovemaking starts with the couple kissing, touching and stroking each other"). Shockingly elemental, in a magazine that advertises vaginal foam. In the very next month's issue appears a piece called "This Is the Way to Wash Your Clothes." The bride is—at least as the magazines perceive her—not only inexperienced in the realms that we would expect ("How You Go About Buying a House" seems like an obviously pertinent story), but fundamentally helpless.

She is also deeply romantic about her wedding, most particularly in how she wants to look for it. And she clearly believes that marriage is the most glorious and rapturous state on earth. All activities, when one is married, are divine. That is the key message.

George Morrissey says *Modern Bride* is identical now to what it was ten years ago. "Every issue is primarily the same; we haven't done anything different really since the inception except for more travel interest and the contraception ads."

Barbara Donovan, by sharp contrast, sees subtle shifts in focus and attitude of her publication—the mirror of changes around us. She says: "We've gone from showing the spectrum of concrete objects to showing a spectrum of abstract thoughts. We say, 'You don't need to conform either to the submissive housewife role or the new liberated role. You can develop your own wife-style.' And we talk about the total range of wife-styles." ("Wife-style" is jargon invented at *Bride's*.)

On the other hand, *Bride's* is having an obvious psychic conflict. They want to deal with reality, with the shifting of women's position, but, like *Cosmopolitan*, they're not sure if too much reality isn't bad for business. So they tend to get cute. A feature called "How to Solve Problems of Two Working Partners" is very WITH IT in tackling issues of liberation from the defined marital roles. But the solution is sugary, simplistic, Pollyanna. Just-talk-about-it-and-it-will-go-away-because-you-love-each-other-to-death.

The ever-skyrocketing success figures of both *Bride's* and *Modern Bride* indicate the robust health of the industry; ad revenues and circulations increase every year. But their strength also provides a clue to the perpetuation of our romantic mythology about weddings and marriage, in which life is just a sterling silver bowl from Oneida, Ltd., overflowing with yummy Bing cherries from our adorable together jaunt to the supermarket.

At no other time in one's life does such an unrelenting purchasing marathon take place. The newlywed bride spends an average of $3,500 to furnish and equip her first home—more than any other homemaker in America. Extensive market research conducted by the bridal magazines indicates that she enters her married life with 120 major new products and plunks an annual $3.5 billion into the strongboxes of the home furnishings and appliance makers. The figure has soared 45 percent since 1964.

(It should be pointed out that the subjects of these research studies are readers of *Bride's* who—as a category—buy the magazine primarily as a shopping guide, so are perhaps more acquisitive than nonreaders. However, four out of five American brides read it, so the figures are fairly generalized.)

What she doesn't get under her own purchasing steam the bride will acquire through marital largesse. Two hundred million dollars' worth of wedding gifts are bought each year—and not merely one gift per couple, which would seem the reasonable state of business. Some brides—the very rich, the very social, *or* the very ethnic—have as many as eight showers tossed for them. I attended a shower for 120 ladies at the Bridgeport, Connecticut, American Legion Hall—a six-course dinner *avec* fifteen-piece orchestra. The evening's jollies consisted of the bride's opening each of the hundred-odd shower gifts that literally engulfed the stage, including two vacuum cleaners, a king-sized bed, and THREE color TV sets. Undoubtedly an expression of the wedding psyche that believes the new household must be completely stocked at its inception. Insurance for the marriage.

Two hundred million dollars spent on wedding gifts each year, and the corpulence of that sum *must* be abetted by the genius who invented the Gift Registry. What happens is that the bride—sometimes with groom, more frequently with Mama—goes to a department store or housewares shop, or several of each, in which she selects every goody she would like to own. Starting out with her silver patterns (sterling and "everyday"), china (fine and "everyday"), and glassware, she then gets into linens and cookery and "accessories" (her crystal jam pot and silver vegetable warmer and electric wok). Then, with the abiding help of the store's bridal consultant, she registers the hundreds of nest-feathers on an interminable form sheet. After Aunt Hazel purchases the jam pot, the store will check it off the registry sheet, so duplications cannot occur. It's a brilliant scheme for everybody—the store gets all that gift loot, Aunt Hazel doesn't have to devote days to picking out something she's basically sure the girl will loathe, and Our Bride gets everything she's ever wanted.

I myself thought the practice of gift registry was dead. Who cares about sterling silver anymore? Bone china? I agreed with *The New Yorker* writer who, in covering the wedding gift shopping scene, said: "It is not the business of youth—especially of today's youth—to gloat over silver and crystal. Why, then, do well-wishers continue to ply young couples with decanters and asparagus servers of Cartier and Tiffany and Baccarat and Buccellati, instead of with the meat grinders and manure spreaders of the Whole Earth Catalog?" Why indeed? Because the givers know something that I didn't, namely that 86 percent of all readers surveyed by *Bride's* anticipated the acquisition of crystal stemware, 84 percent fine china dinnerware, and 58 percent sterling silver flatware.

Six out of ten brides still register, and experts say the figure would be exceedingly higher if every town had the facilities. J. L. Hudson's, in its nine Detroit and suburban stores, has sixty-one consultants and, using computers that update the forms three times weekly, registers 22,000 brides a year. A middle-class bride in St. Louis registered at four local emporiums and the bonanza started streaming in the instant invitations were received; two years later, as laughingly reported by the girl herself, over a hundred gifts lay, still in their original boxes, in her mother's basement.

Happiness, you see, is ordained by the objects we purchase, marital bliss ensured by the right choice of china pattern. That the quality of the marriage is, in some way, substantially connected to the 120 major new products obsessively accumulated by the newlyweds is clear. It is the fundamental message of the wedding industry.

CHAPTER 4

THE ETHNIC ETHIC: KEEPING THE FAITH

At a veterans' hall in Pittsburgh a young Polish couple throws a wedding for 450 that lasts the entire weekend. The sausage and beer are continually replenished while folks go home, nap, and return for more. The orchestra plays marathon polkas for two days.

At another Polish bash on New York's Lower East Side the bride replaces her veil with a babushka and whirls around the floor with the male guests, each of whom pins a dollar on her dress. The groom dons an apron with oversized pockets, for the same purpose. They rake in $650.

An Italian father, a factory foreman in Duluth, gives each of his four daughters a $10,000 wedding replete with two bands (one Neopolitan, one rock), six varieties of pasta, and a $600 gown.

The famed Priscilla of Boston claims she has to design special, super-hardy trains for the bridal gowns of her Greek girls, to deal with the boundless frenetic dancing. She also admits she personally prefers "ethnic weddings" to your "boring, uptight society affair."

She has a definite point. "Ethnic weddings," that is, Italian, Polish, Chinese, Ukrainian, Mexican—the strains of minority culture in America—do seem to possess more color, joy, flamboyance, food, music, tradition, and terrific fun than the typical American rite. As these minority pockets have remained more tightly knit, less diffused than in WASP America, the wedding to them becomes life's most momentous celebration. Thus it is not unusual to find a Greek or Puerto Rican family who begins socking away pennies for a daughter's wedding on the day she is born. They will frequently abandon the alternative of sending her to college for four years in order to provide the infinitely more meaningful value—The Wedding.

If he must, the father will borrow money. (A major New York bank, which lends up to $6,000 for this purpose, does a booming wedding business.) In any case, he will not scrimp. He will invite *everybody* (as, historically, anyone who was passing through the village or within galloping distance was welcome to the festivity). In comparison with his WASP neighbors, his daughter will have more bridesmaids, a more elaborate, lacier, more expensive gown; her wedding will continue on for more frolicsome hours and will be more reminisced about for years to come.

Too, the ethnic groups have retained a clearer connection to their roots, so the wedding will be a closer approximation to the original rituals, the pure folk celebration, unaltered customs (like the pinning of money to the bride's dress) from wedding history.

We do, however, live in America and not in the sixteenth-century Ukraine. With growing acculturation and the passage of time, authenticity has been lost. Or almost lost. There is perhaps one subsociety in this country that has remained startlingly untouched by most aspects of twentieth-century life. They have stayed utterly loyal to their historical lore, still living by the ancient, unchanged codes of the past. These are the Orthodox Jews, approximately one million strong in America.

Attending an Orthodox wedding is like stepping into a time capsule and emerging somewhere around the eleventh century in middle Europe. It is the essence of the true ethnic wedding—abounding with passion, primeval symbolism, rollicking joy, solemnity, and history. It is also filled with undisguised sexist horror.

I don't know what to expect as the subway train on which I am riding plunges farther into the bowels of Brooklyn, heading toward the first Orthodox wedding I've attended. As a Reform Jew manqué, my only contact with my holier brethren has been on brief jaunts through Manhattan's Lower East Side, where one would invariably pass a gaggle of unhealthy-looking young fellows on their way to or from school or the synagogue ("too much time spent at the Torah," I always thought about those sun-deprived, icky white complexions). You knew they were Hasidim (major Orthodox-niks) by the curlicue sideburns ("payess") and the shapeless, too-big black suits. In New York and Brooklyn, the Hasidim live in self-created ghettos much like nineteenth-century Europe; they study Torah and the Talmud, become rabbis, or go into particular businesses like diamond merchanting; they seem to attend synagogue all the time, speak Yiddish most of the time.

So, recalling my only associations with Orthodoxy, by the time I arrive at the Aperion Manor hall on King's Highway ("Exclusive Glatt Kosher Catering"—very haute kosher, to you), I feel like a goy. Instantly I make two profound errors: I have stupidly worn a miniskirt —a shocking exposure of thigh—and, even worse yet, I shake hands with Mr. Pruzansky, the owner. Men, you see, are not permitted to touch flesh with *any* woman other than their wives, so I have committed a Glatt Sin by my aggressive, automatic greeting. Were it not for the fact that I am A REPORTER, I would be banished forever to the Brooklyn streets. As it is, I become the star of the evening, only slightly less fascinating than the bride herself, nineteen-year-old Judith Bucksbaum, the Hebrew teacher.

To the Orthodox Jew, marriage has always been the symbol of existence—both of providing structure to life (the home being second in importance only to the synagogue) and of literal survival. *Every* Orthodox person gets married, without fail. According to Jewish law, it is actually a religious duty—a man who doesn't marry is guilty of diminishing the image of God, and in the past, a single man over twenty could be ordered by the court to take a wife. As one eighteen-year-old girl at this wedding, still unattached but blithely confident, said to me: "Being married, raising a family, running the house, is what we were born for. It's what gives meaning to a woman's life." In the same way that my suggestion of alternative lifestyles is unthinkable, so is anything except a huge razzle-dazzle of a wedding. A young Rockefeller would be more likely to tie her knot in City Hall than a lass of the Orthodox faith; if her parents can't afford it, all the friends and relations will chip in, without shame, to provide The Great Day.

Knowing all this ahead of time, I don't drop dead with shock when, upon entering the reception hall, the first object my eyes fasten on is the bride—perched on a golden throne. Let me describe the setting. The Aperion Manor is your basic catering hall, found in cities and towns all over America. It is furnished in a style that can only be termed "Bridal Baroque"j8that is, a decor peculiar to institutions dealing with weddings: lots of red velvet, wall-to-wall mirrors, chandeliers, crystal doodads, marble statuary. The style might also be called "Bronx Apartment House Lobby Rococo," but its most pervasive ingredient is the Gilt Complex—EVERYTHING is phony gold.

The Aperion Manor can handle three weddings simultaneously on its three floors, but tonight there is only one, the reason being its size. There are degrees of Orthodoxy, depending on how closely one adheres to the thousands of strictures, and on a scale of one to ten, the owner tells me, tonight's gala would measure a solid nine. A true Hasidic wedding would never be held indoors, regardless of weather, the notion being that the couple's children should be as numerous as the stars in the sky, thus one should be close to them. An acceptable approximation for Orthodox Jews has been provided by the Aperion Manor: in the room where ceremonies are held, a small hole has been cut out through the ceiling and the roof above.

Back to Judith on her gilt throne. There are two receptions taking place simultaneously, prior to the ceremony, in the cavernous room divided in half by a floor-to-ceiling velvet drape. Each half has its own bar and mammoth smorgasbord, and the guests do not move from one section to the other. At the "Bride's Reception," the princess is surrounded by girlfriends, people approach the throne to pay court, admire her ornate gown (by Priscilla of Boston, I learn). To the earthy music of a six-piece band—no Miami Beach mambo, but true deedle-deedle-dai-dai Yiddish folk stuff—the folks dance in large circles, the hora, the miserloo. Women with women, men with men. At no time do the sexes intermingle. This band, I am told, the most sought after on the Orthodox circuit, won't work a wedding where there is heterosexual dancing.

The pervading aura of European old-worldliness is caused largely by the music and by the way in which the assemblage is dressed. All the men and boys of all ages wear those pawnshop black suits and either yarmulkes (skullcaps) or black George Raft fedoras. The women's garb runs from "goin'-to-meetin'" dresses to bespangled satin gowns. But decorously covered, you betcha. Not a bare arm, hint of a breast or thigh in the joint. The young maidens truly look maidenly, curiously old-fashioned, unstylish, virginal—the reason being, as we will explore in a moment, that they are all, indeed, virgins. As it registers on my consciousness that the majority of women have exactly the same hairdo—that Pat Nixon plaster-of-Paris bouffant—I remember. These are wigs. Nobody has real hair. Orthodox women are required to shave their heads upon marriage and to wear wigs forevermore in public.

The food is overpowering, leaden, sensational. And, of course, Glatt Kosher. Long tables with cold salads, smoked fishes, fruit, challah; bubbling caldrons of stuffed cabbage, veal stew, kasha varnishkes (don't ask me to explain), noodle pudding, pot roast, chow mein. As it is, traditionally, the Orthodox feeling that wine should be taken to help rejoice but not to cloud the head from one's studies, people are drinking very little—but attacking the food with unbound fervor. Dinner, after all, won't be served for an hour yet.

I am waiting for Moshe Pruzansky, the thirtyish, overweight (small wonder), highly Orthodox proprietor, to return to me from his overseeing chores, so that I may peek in at the "Groom's Reception," on the other side of the barrier drape. That's where all the heavy action is taking place. Where the marriage contract, or Ketubah, is being negotiated and approved. It is probably the most critical segment of the whole wedding ritual.

Historically, a Jewish man and woman were considered married if any one of the following took place: (1) an article of value, such as a ring, was given to the bride, as a gesture of her purchase; (2) a document was drawn up specifying how much the groom was paying and for what (200 silver denarii for a virgin, 100 for a widow); (3) sexual intercourse, with the intention of consecration. The first two were to be executed in front of two adult, Jewish, nonrelated males. For the third, the witnesses were to wait outside the groom's tent. At an Orthodox wedding today all three conditions must be met, literally or symbolically.

On the male side of the partition no women are permitted. For the heathen reporter, an exception is made. A flock of rabbis, the groom, both fathers (the groom's father is himself a rabbi), and the witnesses are poring over the Ketubah with the intensity of deliberation of WASP corporation attorneys arranging a major merger. In fact, the deed is a business transaction, stating, among other fine points, that Judith is a virgin and specifying what she is entitled to in case of divorce or widowhood. There is nothing mock-serious or automatic about this ritual. It takes two hours this night to agree on terms, to proofread, haggle, and recheck for errors.

Suddenly there is a great bellowing shriek from the men. The Ketubah has finally been signed. The Hasidic music at once becomes louder and more frenetic, and then, in an explosion of the most primitive exuberance and passion, the young groom—a thin, pallid twenty-three-year-old rabbinical student—surrounded by his black-suited comrades, dances into the bride's domain. Everybody—six hundred strong—joins in, in exultant, foot-stomping, shouting joy, whirling with him across the room as he goes to claim his bride. When he reaches the throne on which she is demurely poised, he covers her face with a white veil, thereby asserting that she is now his alone, is never again to be gazed on by men other than himself. Until this moment he has not been permitted to see her for seven days. It is now time for the wedding ceremony to begin.

To comprehend Orthodox life, one must understand the concept of the separation of women from men. In synagogue they must sit on opposite sides; at social events they do not mingle; men and women never dance together, even husbands with their own wives, except in some ultra-liberal sects where each will dance holding the opposite ends of a handkerchief, so as not to touch. They are not permitted any physical contact with a member of the opposite sex, save for their own mates. I am startled to realize, at this incredibly ecstatic wedding, that there is barely any talking, any mingling at all between men and women. And yet the atmosphere is heavily charged with sexuality. How to understand this?

Some days later it is explained to me by Rabbi Bruce Goldman at Columbia University. "Among the Orthodox Jews," he says, "there has always been a keen recognition of the power of sex. If a man is praying in synagogue or studying Torah and a woman were to be sitting next to him, he wouldn't be able to concentrate. In the same way, people have nothing to do with any but their own spouses because presumably they'll respond to others, be attracted to them, which will disrupt the home and family. Obviously, this must have been, historically, a problem, for the rabbis to lay down all these injunctions about separation. You don't prohibit something unless there's difficulty."

For the ceremony, men and women take their places on opposite sides of the pseudo-synagogue, a grand room one flight down from the reception hall. There is minimal resemblance to other wedding ceremonies: no bridesmaids or best man, no "Here Comes the Bride." Instead, the groom enters, wearing a white robe over his suit to illustrate his purity, walking between his parents, carrying lit candles. The bride and her parents then march to the floral chuppa placed directly under the hole in the roof and walk seven times around the groom, indicating the seven days a week that she will serve him.

The Hasidic band plays—now on flutes and accordions only—very peppy tunes, a surprising incongruity for so solemn a shindig. No English is spoken at all; everything is in Hebrew. A neighbor interprets the goings on for me: now the rabbi is reading aloud the marriage contract; now a little blessing over the wine, and Judith and Yisroel sip together; now each of the honored rabbi guests, thirty in all this night, comes up to add his blessing; now another sip of wine. On and on . . . .

After seven standard blessings are recited—chanted, really—comes the climax, the most poignant and joyful moment of every Jewish wedding service. The groom stomps on a glass, breaking it, and the couple is wed. The meaning of this gesture is not entirely clear. The standard explanation is that a Jew, in every instance of happiness, must remember the destruction of the Temple by the Romans and the suffering of all Jews. Another is the symbolic breaking of the bride's hymen. Many cultures have an equivalent—Moroccan Jews throw raw eggs at the bride so that she should bear as plentifully and easily as a hen. At any rate, with this merry sound and the spontaneous shouting of "Mazel Tov!" everybody storms the chuppa, the music becomes frenzied, the same unbridled jubilation as when the Ketubah was signed. The message one gets from this moment, and many moments throughout the evening, is ancient and tribal and profound. Infinitely deeper than the vibrations at today's typical weddings —"Isn't this sweet, isn't she pretty in white, isn't the roast beef tender?" Tonight, deep in the heart of Brooklyn, there is a sense of people fulfilling a primordial destiny. It is not just a splashy, expensive wedding. It is, at least to the participants, a Dance of Life.

As the couple walk back down the aisle, almost enveloped by shouting, embracing, dancing, sweating well-wishers (note: there is still no inter-gender hugging or kissing), they fulfill the last part of the ceremony, a ritual that, to my knowledge, exists only among Orthodox Jews. Led to a tiny room down the hall, in which a bit of food has been laid out, Judith and Yisroel are secluded alone together for twenty minutes. In the old days this custom of "Yihud" was, in fact, meant to consummate the marriage, the final validation. Today it's not sexy but sweet and, to be sure, practical. For this Orthodox couple barely know one another; they have had only a few dates, a very short engagement, and in all likelihood have *never* been alone. They have both fasted for twenty-four hours, in order to cleanse and purify themselves for their future together, so in the Yihud they break fast together, spend their very first moments alone, begin this ordained new life.

A few words about purity: virginity is still a primary prize in this peculiar universe. The Orthodox wedding invitation reads, "We invite you to the marriage of the virgin Deborah." The insistence upon brief, chaperoned courtships is to minimize sexual temptation. (Boys are not required to be virgins, but since they hardly pass the time of day with ladies anyway, they mostly are.) The whole gestalt of separation between the sexes is related to this focus on purity, as is the accepted Orthodox doctrine of woman as "unclean."

My fur begins to bristle as the zaftig, earthy, bewigged woman sitting on my left at the ceremony explains "uncleanliness." Evidently there are several hundred religious laws—literally several hundred—regarding a woman's status during her menstruation. These are the basis of all Orthodox marital codes of behavior, the premise being that she must be ostracized while "unclean." If any of them are broken, according to a terrifying little manual called the *Code of Jewish Family Purity*, "awesome, frightening punishment, also reserved for such capital sins as incest and violation of the Yom Kippur Fast, cuts off the sinner's soul from the immortality enjoyed by other souls and cuts off from life the generations which have been conceived in sin."

I ask my neighbor how she feels about (1) being considered virtually leprous for two weeks a month and (2) being able to make love only two weeks a month. To the first question she regards me blankly. She knows nothing else, is so shockingly estranged—indeed ghettoized—from the forward motions of twentieth-century American life surrounding her on every corner that nothing has seeped in of how others live today.

But my neighbor tells me the period of abstinence is splendid for the sex life: "The anticipation makes it like a honeymoon every month. It's always like the first time all over again." She's been married for twenty-four years, and there is something about her—some quality of contentment and self-caring—that makes me believe her. And yet intuitively I know that if you think a woman is untouchable and dirty you do not love her, and on the deepest levels you must not—cannot—enjoy her sexuality.

Meanwhile, back at the wedding, passion is pudding-thick. A tenfoot-tall partition, cloaked in greenery, has been erected, dividing the room into male and female halves. (At Level Ten Glatt Orthodox weddings the rabbis will sit at a table in the corner and put up a barrier around their very own table, so that there is nary a possibility of even catching a glimpse of woman flesh.) The dinner is heavy and unceasing—the historical product of a people who obviously believed every meal to be their last. Everybody gorges (how? what stomach pocket possibly remains unoccupied?) but indifferently. It's the nonstop dancing, building orgasmically in its fervor, that is turning on the whole joint. In one number, the groom sits on a chair that is then hoisted atop several pairs of shoulders and whirled about dizzyingly. On the bride's turf, the dances are less macho but equally as impassioned, breathless. There is never a time when the music stops, when the fever lulls, when the folks sit down and relax. Old men gambol about with old men, grandmas with tiny girl children. It builds and builds and builds. How odd to suddenly realize that the young couple for whom this tribal revelry is being celebrated will never in their lives, never once, dance together. How odd and anachronistic and—ultimately—how unfathomable.

If the Orthodox Jewish culture has been bizarrely immune to any influences from the world, what can you say about a black wedding in Harlem where the soloist croons "Oh Danny boy, the pipes the pipes are caw-all-ling"? And where a bevy of lady guests are gussied up in blond wigs?

To begin with, you can say the obvious: that the black population has been tragically bereft of its own ethnic identity, its linkage to black history and culture. The emergence of an Afro-American sense is very new, very limited. Then you can make a direct parallel to white society and that peculiar truth about weddings: most "Consciousness III" youngsters, kids who have rejected, at least for the moment, the values of their parents, return to the fold for their weddings. Black kids—whatever their personal goals and politics—do not, statistically, don the dashikis and bone up on African tribal rites for their nuptials; they rent a catering hall, spread out the roast turkey and potato salad, and the band plays "Theme from Dr. Zhivago."

Among the poor, where there is little enough romance or pageantry in their daily existences, The Wedding is easily life's only rainbow. But in the striving middle class, the psychology is like the middle-class Jewish one: the wedding is less a manifestation of life's continuum than it is an undeniable demonstration of the family's success.

Barbara Boggs, a professional wedding consultant in Washington, D.C., makes the observation that in her city, where there is a large, continually expanding black population, "the big money these days is being spent on black middle-class affairs. The white society is toning down spending—because of the recession and the fact that there are so many parties in this town nobody's much impressed by flashy hors d'oeuvres anymore—but among the blacks, we see more and more tented weddings for five hundred. For them, it's the period of social arrival."

At the New Covenant Baptist Church, in New York City's Harlem, on a cool Saturday afternoon in September, Catherine Richmond is marrying Curtis Trueheart. She is a social worker, twenty-nine, and he is a union troubleshooter of forty-two. Although this is her second marriage (his first), she's having a big blowout. Six ushers, six bridesmaids, ring bearers and flower girls, two hundred guests, Cadillac limousines to shepherd folks to the reception at a catering establishment across town.

A half hour before the ceremony is to begin, a black face and shoulders hang out of every tenement window on the block. Silent, gleaming black limos rim the curb. Excited kids run back and forth, peering inside the dark, empty vehicles, anticipating the action. Poised on the narrow Harlem street is the ramshackle old church, and from a block's distance one can spot a fierce explosion of color—pinks and purples—on its steps.

There are the six ushers, ushering, and they're gorgeous. Double-breasted maroon velvet Edwardian frock coats, shocking-pink ruffled shirts, black silk bow ties, bell-bottoms. Seventy dollars to rent for the day, one tells me.

And the guests, starting to arrive now, bearing gifts in hand, gigantic, fancy-wrapped parcels. What a parade, what costumes! Sequined, jangling, beaded, chiffoned, starched. Mink stoles, gold spike-heeled shoes, bare midriff, maxi-mini-midi, fringe, spangles, orange hair, blond curls, an occasional Afro, kiddies with ribbons flowing from everywhere. Eye-boggling cleavage, twenty bracelets on one arm. *Quelle* contrast to the barren, bleak church, with hardly a flower, windows too dirty to see through, and a portable fan perched on a table set between the pews. The organ is broken today so a lady from the congregation plays a not-too-healthy piano and then another lady sings 'Ohdannyboythepipesthepipes. . . ."

Is there one person here who isn't taking pictures madly? Flash-bulbs, the whir of a movie camera, snap, wind, focus. The bridesmaids making their appearance. Gorgeous too, in shocking pink flowing to the floor, matching cloche caps, dainty white pearl earrings. Dynamite knockouts they are. Now the bride's Cadillac pulls up and she is swarmed over by the street audience. Catherine's the celeb today; because of her there's fuchsia and limousines come to Harlem.

"It's just a big dress-up, that's what it's all about," claims the best man. "How often you get decked out like this and have a big blast?

The main draw is the reception and then the parties afterward, goin' on all night. You're in the groove anyway, so it's a ball!"

"A weddin' is heartwarming," says the woman sitting next to me in church, wrapped in battle-scarred silver fox. "There aren't too many warm things left in life. No matter how short the marriage lasts, the weddin' is a beautiful thing."

Directly behind the Baptist minister, on the altar, hangs suspended a five-foot color framed photo of himself. His sermon lasts twenty-five minutes ("Sweet and long," I hear whispered at its dramatic high point). His singsong emotionality is punctuated all the way through by the congregation's noisy agreements. "Amen" . . . "Say so" . . . "That's right, Lawd" . . . "You tell 'em."

"We're here to join in holy matrimony which is mighty nice. Man gets mighty lonesome." "A-men" to that one. He immediately launches into what apparently is his pet topic of the moment—woman's place. "The Bible says, 'Wives, submit yourselves to your husbands.' That's where you wives get off base, not wanting to obey your husbands. The wife needs to look up to her husband, reverence him, be obedient to him." ("That's right, right . . . .") "The husband is the head, the wife is the foot. The head tells the feet what to do, and I wanna tell you somethin' right now. Anythin' with two heads isn't normal." ("A-men, Lawd.")

He bellows a lot about divorce, instructions to avoid it. "This is what breaks up a home, in-laws who cling too close. The mother and father's hands have to leave go of their children." Loudly paying tribute to life's tragedies and tribulations, he gets better every minute, and the wedding guests really begin to jive.

The ability of the black culture to verbalize suffering is much keener than other groups'. It is clear from this ceremony that blacks hold few fantasies about marriage and the perfect glories therein. ("I now pronounce you man and wife and you go on about your business," is his closing.) Have I ever before heard the existence of divorce acknowledged in a wedding service? Certainly not. But here it is spelled out up front, with helpful hints for prevention.

To the blacks the wedding ritual has less to do with the acting out of notions about flawless, till-death-us-do-part ecstatic future than some other momentous human need. In these gray surroundings, with the aluminum fan whirring an accompaniment to the proceedings, I sense that it's all much closer to a hunger in one's life for color, splendor, spectacle, drama. "No matter how short the marriage lasts," says the realist, who's seen no more carnage than the rest of us, but hasn't learned to confuse The Wedding with Wedded Bliss, "the wed-din' is a beautiful thing." To the struggling black middle class, the wedding represents the classic tale of Doing Everything Just Right. Nice people. Respectable. Making-It Americans.

CHAPTER 5

MEMBERS OF THE WEDDING

Within the supermarket of wedding styles, the jumbo array of choices—shall we have it at home, in a hotel, on a hilltop, in church, at the country club, on Uncle Herman's putting green, on the Staten Island ferry?—certain elements are fixed, essential, ubiquitous. Nobody, but nobody, has a wedding wingding without a photographer or a cake or flowers. It may be the Bachrach studio or Aunt Beverly with the Brownie Reflex. The vittles may be in quantity to stuff the population of Vermont for a week, or able to be seen only through a high-powered microscope. No matter. The American wedding does not take place without them.

A combination of tradition, spiritual need, and external pressure demands it. And so a battalion of servicemen—the caterer, the cake maker, the florist—thrive on the wedding fiesta. Many grow exceedingly plump and some, like tapeworms, fatten while their host starves. Who they are, how they operate, their relationship with clients form a key chapter of the American wedding story.

Two seemingly incompatible qualities epitomize the wedding specialists: extreme romantic sentimentality about weddings and the compulsive, cynical thrust to make you spend more than you want to or can afford. I have seen both in operation: a bandleader in Los Angeles who, after twenty years of wedding-working, actually displayed tear-filled eyes as an unspectacular bride trooped down the aisle at the Brentwood Country Club; I also saw a caterer convince a customer that her frolic would be utter schlocksville if the caviar were to be, as she wished, something humbler than beluga.

The vulnerability, you see, is monstrous. One is not buying a pair of rubbers or a new freezer where minor emotional baggage is attached to the purchase, where the salesman is peripheral and the product crystal clear and if it doesn't work you simply return it. The involvement between wedding fixer and wedding giver is more like patient and doctor. So you trust. And what you are buying is a dream.

In this case you are placing your "life" in the hands of a florist or a baker. A mother told me how the floral arrangements on the dais at her daughter's wedding were terribly skimpy, how it ruined the whole day as far as she was concerned. Her lips were pinched in the telling, her eyes visibly moistened just remembering it. And this catastrophe took place twelve years ago. Too much pepper in the vichyssoise and it's declared a National Disaster. A band that plays too loud or too slow, and Mama's life is over.

From terror, or insecurity, or childlike faith, the wedding thrower tends to leave everything in the mavins' hands—which is precisely where they wish the power to reside. The fingers, then, tend to stretch out and grasp more than just their allotted share. The iffy-piffiest caterer in Los Angeles, Milton Williams, will go shopping with the bride for her gown; a florist in Denver also handles the invitations and hires the parking valets; *everybody* considers himself a consultant, coordinator, and four-star general.

Then, of course, there is the Kickback. It works at all levels in the wedding industry: you, the caterer, recommend your buddy the photographer and your other pal the rentals-supply man and they in turn express their gratitude to you. The bridal consultant in the department store has her palm greased by the florist, who in turn gets a little something from the bandleader. The professional wedding consultant, lucky her, gets it from all directions, since she hires EVERYBODY. According to an executive at Bradford Bachrach, the well-known portrait photography studio, "Every girl in America could get married for twenty percent less if this practice stopped." The funny fact is that every pro admits the existence of the system, deplores it, and assures you that he's the only virgin in America.

The caterers, I must tell you, are the most fun to talk to. Appropriate words like "juicy" and "spicy" apply. All obsessively devoted to food, they are, for the most part, fat. Obviously they adore what they do, even the bad ones. And they will be able to recall instantaneously every menu of their lives, as many a fashion freak can tell you precisely what she has worn to every memorable occasion of the last ten years.

The near-favorite story of Milton Williams, a warm and handsome black of about forty, is of a society wedding he catered some years back on chic Harbor Island, with guests arriving from all over southern California. Let him tell it: "The hostess's idea of a wedding was a cucumber sandwich and a glass of champagne. I said, 'How can you have the audacity to ask people to drive four hours for a piece of watercress? Is that all you think of your guests?' Well, she gave in and we wound up with three round buffet tables of schnitzel paprikash, barley soufflé, watercress and endive sandwiches, and oysters in saki cups, plus cheese and fruit. It was superb."

Milton ("*everybody* calls me Milton") is an elegant connoisseur of good food and good living (he is also a decorator and lives in a spectacular home in the Hollywood hills). He swears, and one absolutely believes it, that he has never created the same menu twice; his phone number has been unlisted for seventeen years, and I have heard him referred to, by worshipful clients, as both "the Tiffany of caterers" and "the Messiah." Which may seem a little exalted for a chef, but then in southern California folks are very dependent on their helpers.

Because of his power in the catering sphere, Milton gets away with murder. For Danny Thomas' daughter's wedding at the Century Plaza Hotel—a caterer's services are really superfluous in this case—he went in and cooked with the chef. "It's not allowed," he admits. "Most of these guys are European and, you know, they think they wrote the book." When he does a hotel gala, he brings in his own staff —twenty-two people who work for him as bartenders, waiters, and cooks—"to keep our standards up." Also forbidden. And he frequently argues with banquet managers when he feels the liquor bill has been unduly escalated.

His anecdotes all reflect the quality of his needing you infinitely less than you need him: "A very rich, social-climbing woman called me to do her daughter's wedding. She said she wanted pastrami, salami, lox, and cream cheese. I simply said, 'I don't do this sort of thing. Why don't you call a delicatessen?' She said, 'No, no, Milton, I must have *you*.' So I suggested a smorgasbord with a man slicing Nova Scotia salmon to serve on hot rolls and brioche. Plus some beautiful cold meats if she wanted. But cole slaw, *never*. She said she was convinced, then I told her the price and she was appalled. Do you know this nebbish called back at six A.M. to beg me to do the wedding? I refused, naturally."

In the old days, people "catered" their weddings themselves, or with the help of family and friends. Or they had servants who did it. Now, with the disappearance of both traditions, a new career category has arisen—the Party Professional. People who are paid to help other people entertain. Yet another in the grab bag of technological achievements that cuts us off from our activities.

There are, obviously, caterers and caterers. The Milton Williamses who cook in their own kitchens, shop personally for every item, rearrange the client's furniture, invent ever-zingier party gimmicks, are practically members of the family (a Beverly Hills hostess says it's not uncommon in her circle for a guest to enter, shake her hand, and kiss the caterer). And who never, but never, solicit business, but on the contrary, make you feel positively *blessed* if they agree to take your case.

Ruth Factor, also in Los Angeles, is the more usual breed of caterer. Operating from an office-cum-professional kitchen, one section of which is for take-out hors d'oeuvres, she tells you immediately that she is the "resident caterer" of Temple Beth-El, an apparent coup. I go to see her one morning, posing as a bride in search of a chef; subsequent to my visit, for the following month, I receive several letters from Mrs. Factor soliciting my supposed soiree.

Caterers generally charge by the person, $25 a head being nifty-high, $15 closer to the average. The admitted profit is around 20 percent. The kind of food that's most popular depends, among other aspects, on the area of the country. Los Angeles is more meat-and-potatoesy than San Francisco or New York; in Houston—according to caterer David Moncrief—it's real "Amurrican," with a flash of Mexican. "Egg rolls and sweet-and-sour chicken is about as exotic as we ever get. I do stuffed grape leaves occasionally, but a lot of people think they're old green cigars." Moncrief, I should point out, is the only saintless wedding professional I have spoken to, the only man in the industry who will 'fess up to taking kickbacks from everybody he deals with.

Getting a florist to describe to you how he puts together a wedding is rather like asking a Mafia magnate to tell you about his day at the office. It's not only the reluctance—which is considerable. It is also the fact that, for most of us, it is as impossible to comprehend forty thousand pink American Beauty roses as it is $100 million. I know what three dozen roses are, but forty thousand? And those are the numbers in which they deal.

Throughout history, the presence of flowers at weddings has been paramount—one of the primary earmarks of ongoing life. Orange blossoms, for example, embody the highest of all virtues—innocence, purity, lasting love, and fertility—and thus the greatest good fortune. (At least according to the Chinese, Greeks, Romans, and the Crusaders who introduced them to northern Europe.) However, the bridal bouquet was not originally composed of flowers at all, but of a potent combination of garlic, rosemary, bay leaves, and other strong herbs, the purpose being to drive away evil demons threatening the couple's happy state.

Today, flower power is a $1.5 billion a year industry, $250 million of that sum gleaned from weddings. How much flowers cost depends, obviously, on who you are and where the wedding is being held. Many churches around the nation have outlawed botanical excess under the theory that it has nothing to do with religion. (A florist in Denver told me about a Catholic wedding where the family wanted extravagance and the priest forbade it. They planned the ceremony, thus, for when he would be away, and installed $3,000 worth of flowers. Except that he came back unexpectedly the night before and had them remove every last daisy.)

Hotels, on the other hand, revel in gluttony. The banquet manager at the Pierre in Manhattan tells me "you can't do it properly for under three thousand dollars," implying that one will desecrate his sanctuary by spending a cent less. I viewed the finished decorations for a wedding at the Plaza—a simple but quite lovely forest setting, mostly greens and very few flowers—and watched the banquet manager's frozen assessment of the room, as if he were peering at one of his buffet tables piled high with bologna sandwiches.

Home weddings can be the least exorbitant, unless you are the Beverly Hills tobacco czar who transmogrifies your humble estate into a southern plantation for your daughter's wedding, by gluing billions of magnolia blossoms to the elm trees. Then, too, a half million white roses and five thousand orchids decorate the library for the twelve-minute ceremony; the flower bill is $150,000 and the happy couple is divorced four years later.

In any case, the flowers are the most variable and flexible of all wedding costs, depending on the season of the year, the part of the country, the quantity, the containers, and the dexterity of the florist. Many floral bills should rightly win the Pulitzer Prize for fiction. Some fellows use artificial greenery on the walls and ceilings of a room but charge for real; some, reports the banquet manager of a Detroit hotel, use seconds (day-old flowers) from the wholesale market, which are already in their terminal stages before you reach the peach melba; still others charge for yellow roses but furnish the room with yellow daisies, assuming rightly that the hyper-excited family won't notice.

Even the very reputable boys can't estimate what the price will be. Stanley Kersten, a Los Angeles florist, goes to the flower market in the wee morning hours but can never be sure what posies are available that day or if it's a good crop. Kersten, who charges the cutomer $4 for every $1 he pays, admits that often he has to make out a fake bill for the father, sending the real tab to the mother, who will then pay him the difference over a period of months, from her own pocket.

Florists, more than the other arms of the wedding tree, are experiencing changes in taste. Kids are more attracted to field flowers and informal greenery than staid arrangements. Enormous flowing bridal bouquets are on the decline and, if you believe Mel Atlas, the movie *Goodbye, Columbus* has killed—or at least permanently maimed—the blossom trade. "That movie murdered us," he says with hysteria. "Now all the time I hear, 'Don't give me a *Goodbye, Columbus* wedding,' from the mothers as well as the daughters. That damn movie is responsible for simplicity becoming In. My average big wedding used to run six thousand dollars in flowers. Now it's a helluva lot less." Atlas' reaction is perhaps so violent not only because his wallet is a bit less bulgy, but because *he* is the villain responsible for the wildly elaborate floral decorations in *Goodbye, Columbus*.

CHAPTER 6

THE DREAM BROKERS

For actor Jack Webb's wedding reception at the Ambassador Hotel in Chicago, the cake was decorated entirely with police badges made out of sugar icing and was so immense that it had to be sawed in half to fit through the door. At a summer stock theater in Massachusetts, where Mickey Rooney was starring in a play called *Alimony*, replicas of his six wedding cakes were displayed in the lobby. Fountains gushing champagne from the peak of the cake are beginning to blossom into popularity. (Nobody can seem to explain to me why the cake doesn't become soaked.) And Sammy Davis, Jr.'s, most recent wedding sported a three-tiered psychedelic cake, topped by bride and groom figures in icing overalls.

There is no wedding without a cake. Liquor is optional, food not inevitable, but cake—always. It was one of the most ancient parts of the nuptial rite and one of the primary fertility objects. The early Romans prepared a cake—actually a loaf of bread made of barley—as an offering to the god Jupiter. After sharing a wedge, the groom broke the remainder over his bride's head, signifying both the breaking of the hymen and the dominance of the male over the female.

In early Anglo-Saxon weddings, bread was replaced by small hard biscuits, in turn replaced in the Middle Ages by sweet small buns, brought by the guests themselves and stacked in a high mass in front of the newlyweds. It was in the Restoration period that the transition was made from sweet bun to solid confection: Charles II, returning to England from exile in France, brought with him French pastry chefs who completed the cake evolution by icing the solid squares with a crust of hardened sugar, then topping the mound with toys and figures. What we think of today as the wedding cake is actually the "bride's cake"—frilly, decorative, not meant to be eaten. The "groom's cake" was dark, a fruitcake, practical, substantial. The sexist implications rise like the yeast.

I cannot tell you why, but all the professional makers of wedding cakes whom I have met are the most colorful characters in the bridal business. Perhaps it's the repeated exposure to all that confection and goo that makes one a bit more whimsical than one's fellows. Paradoxically, the creators are infinitely more flamboyant and bouncy than their creations. Wedding cakes are not only visually indistinguishable from one another, but all taste—no matter what the proclaimed ingredients—like wet wallpaper.

In Houston, Texas, one lady bakes every middle- and upper-class cake in town and she is—like Neiman-Marcus—a household word. Mrs. Steude (rhymes with "booty") was the first woman ever to graduate from Rice University with a degree in chemistry: how and why she made the leap from test tube to cake pan is apparently a private saga, but she's been at it now for forty-four years, whipping out an average of 150 cakes a year.

She possesses a dedication and high integrity about her craft. "I never send out a cake unchaperoned," she says. "Either my daughter delivers it or my friend from college whom I've known for forty years and I can really trust. And I *always* go to the wedding myself. You know, people at a reception drink or get a little carried away and they can assassinate or mutilate a cake. I'm a troubleshooter." And she's serious besides. She will let no other person cut or serve the cake, executing the surgery with a silver knife festooned with flowers ("We never touch anything with our fingers," she prides) and with the solemnity of a Houston heart transplanter.

She outlines her *modus operandi*. "First," she begins, "I interview the customer for two hours before taking the job. To make sure I like the people. I do everything myself, you know, and it's very important. Some weeks I bake for a thousand people, which means I could use ninety dozen eggs. You know how many eggs that is to break yourself?"

Mrs. Steude has two kitchens, $1,000 worth of cake pans which she designed herself, and diagrams every cake on paper. "Just the setting up of the cake is an engineering project," she says, "but it's all a matter of organization." She begins working on Monday for cakes due the following weekend, by ordering the eggs and chopping the pecans. She makes only two kinds, white and chocolate, her own recipes, decorating them with handmade sugar orchids or stephanotis. "I always turn off my hearing aid when I start to bake," she says, "and sometimes I forget to turn it on again." She prefers, above all, Jewish weddings, where "there is served a complete repast."

I would like to be able to tell you that Mrs. Steude's cake was as delicious as she. It was not.

Gary Hansen is the U.S. Steel of southern California bridal baking, what with four chefs, a basic "line" of a hundred different models, and a Beverly Hills showroom in which a pretty young girl hands you a brochure describing flavor choices—"Pure Bridal White, Daring German Chocolate, Classic Italian Marble, and Secret Danish Gold" —and leads you to the cellar where a hundred plastic replicas of the styles reside on tables, each looking, to my eye, exactly like its neighbor. Nonetheless, Hansen, who descends from six generations of pastry chefs, including one who baked for the King of Denmark, believes that a great revolution is taking place in wedding cakedom. He speaks about his subject with the exhilaration of an architect who has just invented the skyscraper. "We're making really big break-throughs," he says, barely able to bottle his enthusiasm. "We're going to be using fresh flowers on our cakes, for what we call our 'flower children cake.' It started as a joke, you know, but now we're really excited. Kids are rebelling against their parents' traditions and want something truly revolutionary.

"You know, we innovated chocolate wedding cakes in L.A., to keep up with the new freedom of expression. But it really upset some people. It's wild what we're doing, but who says it has to be the same old four-tiered white cake year after year? The times are changing, you know? We just hope people will accept such far-out ideas."

Hansen, whose family started this business thirty years ago, makes cakes priced from $3 to $1,000 (the average is $150) and claims he has done and can do *anything*. Frogs cut out of cake, Boeing 707's. He created Governor Reagan's birthday cake, which duplicated a portrait of the ex-movie star in icing; the cake for Marlo Thomas' twenty-first birthday was seven feet tall, with crowns, fountains, and an icing pillow.

"Every year we come up with styling changes," says the cake pioneer. "This year we're stressing water fountains very heavy and next year our big push is the chocolate. We consider ourselves culinary artists." To accompany this grand vision, he is in the process of installing, behind the kitchen, an art department with draft ng boards, and hiring artists to create new designs.

Hansen bubbles about the NOW wedding cake: "We've gone to artificial plastic roses, the petals all hand-shaped, to look like the sugar roses of fifty years ago. We're using advance styling methods to get back to the grand days of culinary art, to get that wonderful elegant look. With labor costs today, you can't do the real thing anymore. We're putting the pilot model in the showroom now."

I am agog, cannot wait to glimpse the outcome of this cultural revolution. He shows me the color transparencies of his new models, the cake contribution to future shock, and again, all twenty-four numbers look to me just like every wedding cake I've ever seen. "Like cars, we go into a model change every year," he says with uncontained excitement, but it's all the same old Edsel to me.

Pity the poor photographer. He is, not uncommonly, the most detested presence at the wedding. The pain-in-the-neck intruder. He arrives as the bride is dressing, hovers over the events of the day like a relentless bill collector or—to quote one disgruntled groom— "an anxious buzzard." In some extreme cases he has been known to poise himself mid-aisle, like some wedding guest gone berserk, commanding *"Hold it right there"* to the advancing attendants, snapping, clicking, popping flashbulbs. Sometimes he slinks up behind the altar, in back of the clergyman, and shoots blindingly into the couples' face amid the "I do's." But solemnity is not his business. Making pictures is.

There are more photographers in the wedding business than in any other sphere of photographic work in America. Competition, therefore, is bloody ferocious. When a girl's engagement announcement appears in *The New York Times*, before the ink is dry on the page she will receive a phone call from a representative of Bradford Bachrach, the biggest operation in the East. Heaven alone knows where the salesperson (they prefer "bridal consultant") gets the telephone number—but brides report the pitch to be fierce. One says the lady guaranteed her Bachrach wedding photo would appear in the *Times* (Bachrach denies this, insisting, "All we say is that we have better glossies than other photographers, and if that's an influence, well. . . .").

Fred Winchell, a remarkably tall vice president of Gittings, the largest portrait photography outfit in the West and Southwest, claims: "We have to go after our business more aggressively than other people because brides don't think about photography as a necessity. People spend thousands on flowers and music and booze—the things that will show and impress—and then have Uncle Marty come to the wedding with his Instamatic. We have to convince them that in future years they'll want a marvelous permanent keepsake of the wedding."

Gittings ("Candid coverage from garter to getaway"), with traveling door-to-door salesladies in sixty-five cities, is primarily in the portrait business, only 20 percent of their volume coming from weddings. "But that's where it all starts, that's the cornerstone," explains Winchell. "We photograph the bride, then she has children and we photograph them. Then the graduations, debuts, family portraits, et cetera." Apparently the industry is on the wane: more amateurs are becoming camera hobbyists, preferring their own candid account of Junior's evolution to the formal studio approach.

This is perhaps the moment to mention how Winchell (as well as every other wedding photographer) "preserves happy times." Each album bears the same standard triteness: bride and groom sipping champagne from the same glass, the cutting of the cake, rice-throwing, riding away in the car. Winchell says it's because the same things go on at every wedding. "We're not making cliché pictures, but pictures of clichés. . . ."

Financially, most photographers operate in fairly standard manner. You must guarantee a minimum order, and they guarantee a minimum number of shots. Bachrach will take at least eighty; you must purchase thirty prints. For Jack Huff, in Los Angeles, the minimum is $175; William Figge in Glendale charges $185 for twenty 8 x 10's.

None of that, however, matters in the slightest. *Everybody* orders more than he has to. "What we're selling," says Jack Huff, "is sentimentality. The bride's mother looks at the proofs, all the glorious memories come flooding back, and she wants pictures of it all. We have to depend on her being sentimental, or we don't make money."

A mother of the bride in Milwaukee talked to me the morning after her daughter's wedding. Recalling, ecstatically, every detail of the event, she said: "I just can't wait for the pictures to come so I can live it all over again." Her memories would, as they do, dim. The flowers were already buried, the champagne digested. The only indelible record of all that toil and money—all those dreams and plans—the only permanent keepsake of the wedding would be the photographs.

CHAPTER 7

DEEP IN THE HEART OF EXCESS

Why does everything—the quality of life itself—seem bigger, noisier, richer, in Texas than anywhere else in the country? One hears of fabulous weddings, oil-gusher extravaganzas that could happen only in a paperback novel. Or in Texas. They're still chattering about the Blaffer shindig—Blaffer, as in Humble Oil—a mock Italian Renaissance court pageant, music by the Houston Symphony, costumes by Mr. John, who flew down from New York for last-minute nips and tucks. Or the John Mecom (also oil) wedding, where one thousand nearest and dearest were served a sit-down filet mignon dinner and a thirty-foot wedding cake, and the flower bill alone came to $28,000. Or the Cone affair in Lubbock, for which a Manhattan hairdresser and two assistants were imported for one week prior to W-day (at $1,500 a day) to do daily coiffure repairs for the four hundred lady guests from all over America who were being treated to seven days of breakfast, teas, and golf.

Or the double wedding in Houston, a prominent doctor's two daughters, for 1,400 guests. One of the grooms was from Madrid, so a jet was chartered to cart over his Spanish guests, along with a fifteenth-century carved-wood pulpit—a priceless church relic purchased just for the ceremony.

A Houston caterer, who has of late been doing divorce-announcement dinner dances for six hundred, tells of the most lavish wedding in his history, held in a home "already as big as a country club." In order to accommodate the eight hundred invitees indoors, the host added a ballroom on to the house, which cost $20,000 to build.

Even White House weddings—normally the models of solid burgher respectability—took on a Texas flair under L.B.J. If Tricia's was like a Grosse Pointe country club dance, Luci and Lynda Johnson's had about them at least a smidgen of San Antone rodeo. Luci and her twenty-six attendants marched down an aisle the literal length of a football field plus a basketball court, in the largest Roman Catholic church in the United States. Its 56-bell carillon pealed for one full hour before the ceremony. Lynda Bird's fete, truly humble by comparison, cost $62,000 and was preceded by twenty-one prenuptial parties.

In much the same way that the ethnic wedding—the classic celebration of the culture—speaks volumes about the history, tastes, and values of that culture, so do the ways in which people marry in various parts of America reflect the character and idiosyncracies of our geography. As regional cooking has a distinct entity, so do regional weddings.

Washington, D.C., a town devoted to hearty socializing, is not knocked out by yet another big party with yet more leaden cheese puffs. Ellen Proxmire, a Washington wedding consultant, describes Washington nuptials as "simple as they can be. Washingtonians don't use a wedding as an excuse to produce a spectacle. The kinds of splashy weddings that are *de rigueur* elsewhere would be considered grotesque here." A "typical" wedding in D.C. would be held in a church with a hotel reception afterward (hotel catering is considerably cheaper here than in other cities), a light buffet, and quiet music for quiet dancing. Good Taste.

By contrast, take Los Angeles, cuckoo capital of America. Where else, except in this nest of paradoxes, could you attend a wedding where, following the eight be-pinked bridesmaids down the aisle, marches the family white toy poodle in a pink organdy "dress," and at the dinner the mashed potatoes are also dyed pink; where, for a Pasadena society bash, the bride's mother decides that the green interior of the church doesn't groove with her yellow plans, thus paints the entire church yellow the day before the ceremony, repaints it green the day after?

The lifestyle in southern California is, even within its most rigid social castes, freer, more eclectic, crazier than in the East. The fact that, at a Hancock Park/Gentile/oil/conservative wedding, the couple and their friends interrupt the sedate ceremony to sit down in a circle and toss the I Ching coins does not make Grandma faint or necessarily find its way into the local society column. In Philadelphia folks would be dining out on that shocker for the entire winter, but in L.A.—even haute Hancock Park—it's a mild yawn.

San Francisco, on the other hand, is light-years farther away from L.A. than its 425 miles. A tradition-bound, staid town, it is characterized, by a knowledgeable local caterer, as "still a village. There are only ten thousand people who run the city, spend the money, dominate the cultural and social life. Their emotional ties are with New York and Boston and they'd rather die than be linked with Los Angeles in the same breath."

In San Francisco people spend their loot at one-third the rate of citizens elsewhere. A wedding in this area is graceful and elegant, bereft of poodles and tricky lighting. While the kids of the rich are sometimes going the peasant route in dress—how quaint, really—and getting married under the trees, their weddings often resemble the one at a Walnut Creek ranch. The entire barn was decorated with field flowers (not *actually* hand-picked in the field, mind you, but purchased from a chic florist), French champagne was poured, a barbecue pit with electric spit was constructed, and whole lambs skewered therein, all to the tune of a string quartet from the Oakland Symphony. The tab was $60,000—for 160 guests. San Franciscans who attended love to describe that gala as a "hippie wedding."

Now there's Texas. Witness a Texas wedding—your average middle-class home-garden wedding. Could be happening, at that same instant and without much variation, in Larchmont or Dubuque. Only here, in Houston, on a steamy Friday evening in August, there's a difference: the guests number 1,200. Twelve hundred bodies and that's not even ranked, in Texas, as a circus maximus.

"My biggest problem in planning this affair," says Mrs. Quisenberry, mother of the bride, "was in cutting down the guest list." She's not kidding, one sees, as she continues: "Ah have hundreds and hundreds of deah, deah girlfriends—from college, from various clubs and organizations and from working on political campaigns. Many of them Ah haven't seen in ten years, but they're still mah very good friends." And what better place to gather them together—all of these "deah, deah" buddies from twenty-five years ago's Theta Chi house—than in your Ferberesque jamboree/barbecue of a daughter's wedding.

The fact that a "friend" is defined as somebody you knew three decades ago, haven't kept in touch with, but wouldn't dream of throwing your daughter's wedding without, is distinctly Texas mentality. The famous Texas hospitality tends to be indiscriminate, the cordiality instantaneous, the warmth expansive but skin-deep. There is about this state a profound flat emptiness that begins with the land and ends with its citizens.

Mrs. Quisenberry tells me she is invited to at least one wedding a week, two or three in the height of the season. She expresses amazement at my amazement: "But that's our whole social life. That's what we do on Friday and Saturday nights. Where else would we go?" And it perpetuates itself, naturally. If you have 1,200 folks at your clambake, you can expect at least one wedding invitation back from each of them over the next few years. Yep, that's sho' a lot of busy—if interchangeable—Saturday nights.

One would expect the Quisenberry celebration to be a rollicking, hog-stomping, yip-yip-yipping, shoot-'em-up Texas jubilee. Wrong. The ceremony is held at 8:30, the bride and groom disappear at 10 (after *not* being greeted by a majority of the stranger-guests), and by 10:45 the tents are de-escalated. Hardly anybody dances, gets drunk, becomes obnoxious, or appears to have a particularly peachy time. A traditional, bland, pretty, lifeless American wedding. A big TWO on the Terrific Party Scale of ONE to TEN.

CHAPTER 8

ALL DECKED IN WHITE

When I was between the ages of six and eight, my best friend, Lois Brenner, would come to my house every Saturday morning. We would go to my room, shut the door, turn on the radio to Archie Andrews and "Let's Pretend," and we would draw. Hour after hour, sprawling amid papers and crayons, we drew one thing and one thing only—girls in wedding gowns.

Then, for many years, I also had my bride and bridesmaid dolls, with little dresses that my mother would periodically take off and wash and iron so that they always looked fresh. For my birthday one year she bought me a completely new bridal wardrobe for my synthetic friends.

That's how it all begins. Way back in those early days when we get the messages about what's important and when the playthings that engage us are working to shape our future lives. A few months ago, in the bridal salon of a Cleveland department store, I saw a young girl come in wearing her jeans-and-sneakers uniform, but there to shop for her wedding gown. The bridal directress brought several long white rustling garments into the dressing room, politely advising the girl to comb her hair and apply makeup before proceeding. She did, slipped into the first dress, peered at herself in the mirror for a long moment—and burst into tears. "I can't believe it," she sobbed joyfully. "I've always dreamed of being a bride and looking just like this, and it's really come true. Is this really *me*?"

At a bridal specialty shop in Chicago, when the young customer tries on a wedding tog, she then models it for the entire staff—emerging through a curtain to float down a long ramp, while an organ recording plays "The Wedding March" and the salesladies gasp and sigh, as per instruction. One such saleswoman reports that eight out of ten girls buy the very first gown they don—so overcome are they with the initial vision of themselves.

We never, in our childhood play, concerned ourselves with the flowers and decorations, or gave a thought to the gifts. Even the man —aside from possessing several of the combined perfections of our various movie gods—was unclear. How we would look walking down the aisle with all eyes upon us was the essential fantasy. And for almost every young woman getting married in America today, it still is. She is transformed, this day, from whatever she was to utter radiant beauty. She doesn't need a nose job, silicone, or Weight Watchers. She only needs a flowing white wedding gown—that exquisite embodiment of all the romantic dreams of her life.

Item: the largest of the bridal manufacturers, Alfred Angelo, receives hundreds of letters each year with the same theme: "I've been carrying around this picture from *Modern Bride* of one of your dresses for five years. Now I've finally met a guy and I'm getting married. Do you still have it?"

Item: the Brides and Bridesmaids Apparel Association (a trade organization of manufacturers) held an essay contest a few years back for recent brides, on the topic of "Why I Chose My Gown." *Nobody* answered "because it was stylish." Over 90 percent replied, "It made me look like a fairy princess," or similar sentiments.

To the extent that marriage and weddings are involved with idealized departures from reality, the wedding dress is the key metaphor. "Happiness is getting married in just the look you want," claims *Bride's* magazine, in describing a bridal frock on its pages; a recent Alfred Angelo collection was called "Garden of Dreams." Experts say the key word is "memorable": every bride wants, above all else, to look memorable, that is, to remember this supreme experience for the rest of her life. What she will recall most vividly, and most wistfully, in the years to come is not the peach melba or the pink petunias but how utterly beautiful she looked—indeed what a vision she was—on her day of days.

Eighty percent of all first marriages in the United States in 1972 were formal weddings. That is to say, 1,411,200 girls got married in bridal gowns, as opposed to pants suits or street dresses. Eighty-seven percent of these garments were floor length, the average price was $164 (including the headpiece), and 94 percent were white or ivory.

The color white, so deeply glued to our current notions of bridedom, has not always been used and, in fact, is not today in other cultures. During the American Revolution brides wore red, the symbolic color of rebellion; Chinese girls today don red as an expression of happiness and permanence. Spanish peasants wear, of all things, black, and in

Norway green is the most popular shade. White, however, has historically been connected to joy—not purity, mind you, until the Victorian era, but rather to celebrate great joyous events. The early Romans decked themselves in white at births and for feast days; the Patagonians painted white decorations on their bodies for every happy occasion, and on the eve of wedding ceremonies they simply covered their entire bodies with white paint. Today the Japanese bride wears white, but the message is dual: also a mourning color, it indicates that she is "dead" to her parents and that she will never leave her husband until she goes to the grave.

Now, of course, we have come to associate white with chastity, and the symbolism hangs on with a deathlike grip. The fact that wedding etiquette will staunchly not permit a second-time bride to wear white implies, naturally, that first-timers are virgins. Flying in the face of what we know to be true. Tradition nevertheless will out.

Hear George Morrissey of *Modern Bride*: "A very significant statistic is the one which shows that each year there is even a higher rate of white wedding gowns sold than is accounted for just by the increase in the number of marriages. More and more people are having formal weddings every year. It astonishes even me."

Bridal consultant Mary Ann Maxwell says: "I was out of the bridal business for three years recently and when I came back I could have sworn I'd just been out to lunch."

Granted, the media deceive us. It would clearly be dreary for the woman's pages to repeat incessantly the same fashion story. Much flashier copy is a piece on the bridal apparition in leather jump suit or mammoth crepe tent. And a candid manufacturer will tell you he only designs these bizarrenesses tongue-in-chic—showpieces brought out for fashion shows and on television, meant to carry the message that the company is "with it," "now," but then sent off in cartons to the used-clothing drive.

"The most important thing to remember about the bridal field," says an executive of Alfred Angelo, "is that the worst-selling dresses are the up-to-the-minute fashions." A peculiar atavistic reversion seems to take over in almost all young women. Regardless of their lifestyle at the moment, when it's time to get married they harken back to some ancient tribal voice. Store after store reports: lass enters as a tie-dyed hippie, leaves as a vanilla ice cream cone.

Two-thirds of all wedding dresses are purchased—the rest are borrowed, hand-sewn, handed down, or rented—and sales of bridal finery totaled $150 million last year. In a fundamental sense the bridal apparel

biz is as far removed from the operations of the ladies' garment industry—whose gabardine ghetto on New York's Seventh Avenue it shares
—as it is from the workings of Campbell's soups. First of all, it is
a tiny subcategory, less than a hundred manufacturers in all. Then,
it is dealing with a one-time customer. The bridal guys can figure
out, from population statistics, the finite number of potential customers
each year. And, for them, it's now or never.

As one dramatic result, there is a desperate competitiveness among
bridal clothiers not unlike a battle to the death for the last seat in
the lifeboat. Another contributant to ferocity is the difficulty in making
head or tail of the market. If you manufacture, say, little basic $100
cotton shirtwaist dresses, you know whom you're selling, whom you're
excluding; you know what towns and what stores in those towns in
which to place the garments. But, in bridal wear, it is often the poorest
girls who spend the most money. And they have totally disparate
taste from wealthier girls and do not shop at the same emporiums.
So what kind of $500 dress do you design to suit both mentalities,
and which store will buy it?

The biggest contrast, however, between the bridal kingdom and
the rest of fashion is that it is *not* a ready-to-wear business. Except
for the low-end dresses—those under $100—every gown is more or
less custom-made. Mori Lee is the exception. The second largest house
($6 million a year), their togs retail from $50 to $125, their major
customers are J. C. Penney and Sears. Functioning exactly like their
ready-to-wear cousins, they cut and ship 3,000 carbons of one style
at a clip, no custom craft whatsoever. They sell 80,000 gowns a year—a
very hefty portion of the bride population—and claim that 90 percent
of the girls in Omaha get married in their dresses.

The Alfred Angelo line is more to the point. With gowns ranging
from $100 to $295, the only garment produced in advance is the sample,
sold one to a store. The customer's actual getup for her wedding is
cut after she places the order. Not only to be altered to her size,
but to accommodate her styling changes as well—a longer train, a
little lower in the neckline. In addition, most of the dress is actually
hand-made. Beading, lacing, the lining are separate processes,
executed *for every individual gown* by ladies sitting in huge factory
rooms sewing on tiny beads, one at a time. It is, in an era of no-
human-hands-have-touched-this-product, a startling concept. It also
explains why the markup is 100 percent or more, as opposed to the
ordinary ready-to-wear escalation of 42 percent.

Buying bridal finery is the sole experience with the luxury, the elitism, of custom-made clothing that most American girls will ever have. Hence it is no accident that the bridal salon is often the fanciest nook in the store. Nothing hangs limply on racks, nobody shoves, salesgirls do not sniff or grump.

The bridal apparel industry is native to the United States, and only of the last thirty years. Before that gowns were not manufactured at all but were either hand-made by dressmakers or handed-me-down by grandmas. Then the small bridal specialty shop was developed, where several seamstresses were employed to concoct each costume from scratch; one-half of all purchased bridal dresses today come from these marts. (In Europe there is still no wedding gown industry to speak of.) Until the end of World War II, only twelve or fifteen manufacturers existed and those few were in serious danger of extinction when the government rationed fabrics of "nonessential" industries. Luckily, the bridal powers convinced Uncle Sam that there is hardly anything MORE essential during wartime than the stability of marriage, so the quota was removed. As the war ended, the marriage rate soared (1947 is still the biggest year in history), and with it came the frock factories.

Sometimes termed the General Motors of the field, Alfred Angelo, Inc., is the oldest, as well as largest, corporation. It has seven subdivisions and covers every inch of the bridal globe—economically and culturally. Its total volume is over $10 million a year. To study the workings of Alfred Angelo is to uncover a fascinating story of American sociology, of who gets married and how in our country.

It's a mama-and-papa candy store that "just growed"; Alfred Angelo is Alfred Piccione, who began a bridal shop thirty-five years ago. Today, between him and his wife, Edith, and their four children (who have worked on and off since age seven), their operation comprises three factories, 750 employees, four wedding dress lines, two for bridesmaids, one for headpieces.

"Each of our companies has its own special market," explains Edith Piccione, as we trudge through the massive confines of her main factory in North Philadelphia. "To understand bridal design you *must* understand the background, the religious connections, the economic status, of your girl." With that, we sit down in her airy office, strewn with pencil sketches of females in long gowns (she does it too, eh?), and watch a fashion show—a one-hour parade of models in white. At the beginning every doodad appears virtually the same to my virgin eye, but by the time sixty or so costumes have passed by, Mrs. Piccione has—to her credit—conveyed her extraordinary knowledge of the game.

We start with the gowns from Bridallure, their budget and volume company, prices ranging from $50 to $110. Bouffant, sequined, lacy, these are, without exception, highly gingerbreaded dresses. Yards and yards of train, layered skirts that stretch three feet away from the body. My first reaction is surprise that the cheapest, those that are *not* custom-made, but factory-produced en masse, should be so elaborate. Edith clears my head: "The customer of Bridallure is the girl who cannot afford a five-hundred-dollar wedding dress but it has to look that way. This girl is undoubtedly from a background of foreign-born parents or a group of people who hang on to all of the old traditions. On the West Coast she is probably Spanish; in the Midwest she is from a really small town and is likely to be Polish or Italian. She wants ruffles, glitter, the top-of-the-wedding-cake look. That's her image of a bride."

She is a girl, according to Edith Piccione, who is not influenced by or even exposed to fashion trends. She is a movie magazine reader, is very affected by television—Edith does a lot of local TV fashion shows to reach her—and doesn't get to department stores to shop. She is strongly knit to family convention and will have a gigantic wedding, for which her parents will have been saving for years. If she's Italian, the groom's family will pay for part, so it's got to be even more extravagant. The Bridallure bride has hardly, if ever, worn a formal gown before; she is the most vulnerable to purchasing the very first she dons due to the socko impact of witnessing herself in so much lace and a train longer than the Super Chief.

Again vogues in fashion don't at all affect this line. "When we try something new, it frequently bombs," says Edith with regret. "We're always looking for something different, but it doesn't work, these girls don't want it. We have one dress that we've kept in the line for ten years, and it's still one of the heaviest sellers."

Bridallure dresses are always pure, snowy, virgin white.

The Alfred Angelo line—$100 to $295—is, by contrast, 50 percent white, 50 percent ivory. The fabrics are of finer quality: imported chantilly laces (it's domestic in Bridallure), imported organza instead of nylon, silk-faced peau de soie. The big difference between the lines is the fashion styling. Straight or A-lines replace the Scarlett O'Hara look, trains are short or nonexistent.

The Angelo bride reads the bridal publications, *Vogue*, and *Seventeen*; she's more likely to be in college than the Bridallure girl; and although her dress will be more expensive, her wedding will be smaller and simpler.

The two couturier lines are Piccione Bridal and a series of gowns, inaugurated in 1970, by Oscar de la Renta. (Wedding rigs designed by French biggies are a new wave—and thus far not a very successful one. They do not seem to understand, with Mrs. Piccione's clarity, the American girl.) Whereas Edith alone creates all the Bridallure and Angelo robes, a young designer named Ron LoVice chisels the Piccione line, selling from $250 to $600. "We started Piccione three years ago," says Edith, "in response to what we sensed was a great need for the highest up-to-date fashion in quality gowns. We use, here, the finest silk fabrics, hand beading, and laces that I design myself."

It is in the elite dresses, from *all* manufacturers, that one tends to observe whatever leaps from convention are being taken. The girl in this bracket is very modish and devoted to looking original. *Not* micro-mini-plastic-peekaboos, mind you, but distinctly memorable and even—God help us—sexy! Eleanor Robbins, a young dynamo who has revolutionized the dreary bridal department of New York's Bonwit Teller since taking command two years ago, says: "My girls want uniqueness. They want to feel they're onstage, and naughtily provocative. My kids are kicky!" Her kicky kiddies are among the few in America who will buy pantaloon outfits and mid-length gauchos.

The man from Mori Lee—second only to Alfred Angelo in yearly volume—capsulizes this business neatly for me: "I could take a Piccione four-hundred-dollar dress and copy it down to sixty dollars—and I couldn't give it away. The sixty-dollar girl has a completely different vision of how she wants to look and it doesn't matter that she's getting a bargain. She wants something that *looks* expensive, and in her book that means with a whole lot of goop all over it."

One cannot, I suppose, explore the bridal apparel game without mentioning the superstar, Priscilla Kidder—Priscilla of Boston. Because she has achieved prominence through her association with White House affairs (she befrocked Luci Johnson and Julie and Tricia Nixon), there are those who believe Priscilla to be the *only* bridal designer in the country. She herself may be one of the staunchest believers.

Priscilla is without doubt the savviest go-getting promoter in an industry not known for its zip. Her company creates not only the usual array of variously priced attire, but also a line of mother-of-the-bride dresses, flower girl dresses, duds for the under 5'3", and Priscilla Veils. She owns two retail stores in Boston, acts as wedding consultant for her more socially notable clientele, and jets around the country running three-hour fashion showings and preaching that no store should employ a bridal buyer over the age of twenty-five. Other manufacturers, as to be expected, think Priscilla's designs old-hat, matronly, and "gloppy"; other manufacturers, on the other hand, have not been asked to create historical splendor in the White House.

The bridal gown biz is infinitely more personal than any other huge industry. If you purchase your finery in a department store, the salon ladies will, statistically, spend four and a half times longer with you than any other salesgirl with any other customer. In Houston, you will very likely purchase your gown, and those of your attendants, at Foley's, because everybody knows Mary Ann Maxwell is the hippest bridal dame in town and for no extra charge she'll coach your whole extravaganza right through to the wilting end. In New York, Monica Hickey at Bergdorf's is so "in" that Piccione will invent special laces *just* for her clients. And across the street, at Bonwit Teller, I witnessed the arrival of a Santa Fe oil tycoon and his daughter, who flew there because the news has spread about the new terrific bridal buyer.

But half of the brides in America will acquire their robes from wee-sized bridal shops, like Rose de Paola's Bridal Aisle, on Fourteenth Street in Manhattan. Rose, who earns around $70,000 a year, and caters primarily to Italian, black, and Puerto Rican working girls, is a rare leftover from the days when Grand Street—in the Italian ghetto of the Lower East Side—was the wedding garb nucleus of New York and everything was hand-sewn by the little women in the back room. She has been in this profession for forty years and in all that time has never accepted any payment but pure cash. A fat chunk of her business is still custom-made—and those dresses start at $350. "I won't buy a Priscilla dress," she says. "I'd rather copy it myself and make a bigger profit." Rose has noticed, in four decades, only microscopic changes but one solid consistency: "Once a bride-to-be sets her heart on a dress she usually buys it, no matter what the cost."

CHAPTER 9

IN THIS HOLY ESTATE: THE CATERED AFFAIR

The scene is a chapel. A wedding ceremony is in progress; the attendants have made their entrances and are in position, waiting. The three hundred guests are silent, the organ throbs softly, and the lights are dim. Suddenly a misty red spotlight appears, focusing on the side wall where there seems to be a round pedestal, raised seven feet off the ground. It is enveloped by a filmy net curtain behind which there is a person poised, an ethereal silhouette with its back toward us. As the organ begins a long crescendo, the pedestal starts revolving, very, very slowly until the figure is facing us, bathed in a warm rosy glow. The curtain opens then to reveal none other than—The Bride. As she steps down, her father is there to escort her up the aisle. En route, her feet activate a treadle mechanism hidden under the carpeting which causes flickering colored lights to play on her face and gown all the way to the altar.

No, we are not on a movie set. We are at the Huntington Town House on Long Island, and we have just witnessed a real-life production that will be repeated approximately twenty times this same weekend. The Town House and its cousins—Leonard's of Great Neck, the Narragansett Inn, the Fountainhead, about fifteen in all—are a mushrooming phenomenon of the eastern seaboard. They are an outgrowth of the increased spending capability of the suburban middle class and the rise to power of a new breed of American, The Caterer.

If you live on Long Island, or in New Jersey, or lower Westchester, and you want your daughter to have a bang-up blowout for three hundred of your nearest and dearest, where do you go? Well, you can go to a Manhattan hotel, the Plaza or the Waldorf, say. That is, if you have $20,000 to spend and are Jewish. (Christians always hold their ceremonies in church, and it's a far trek from West Orange to Fifty-ninth Street.) You can do it at your country club, that is, if you belong to a country club. Or on your back lawn, if you happen to live on a football field. But why not choose a place like The Manor, a grand catering establishment decked out like the Vatican—"where the Hospitality of the Old South meets Continental Cuisine for gracious dining in suburban New Jersey"—where weddings are sold as budget package deals ($19.95 per person includes not only unlimited drinks, hors d'oeuvres, and a cha8teaubriand dinner but candelabra for the head table and a dressing room for the bride) and everything, but everything, is arranged for you.

They are immense, these palazzi. Leonard's—the Taj Mahal of catering temples—cost $5 million to build, has twelve banquet rooms, can handle 1,000 folks for each party, and plays host to 30,000 revelers a month. The Town House holds 850 cars in its parking lot and does 1,500 weddings a year. The Manor, resting on twenty acres, pays a light bill of $6,000 a month and figures annual glassware breakage at $16,000. Any way you slice it, that's a lot of chopped liver.

Let me describe the ambiance. Several of the palaces were designed by the same New York architect, Richard Bellamy, inventor of the Materializing Bride—a geniusness inspired by the Metropolitan Opera production of *Lohengrin*, in which the swan boat glides out of the mist and onto the stage. He calls his style "eclectic"—"English Regency, French Provincial, Louis XIV, and sometimes all three together." The philosophical premise of this school of decor is that nothing should be left simple, everything that *can* be painted gold *must* be painted gold. Leonard's is populated, both inside and out, by naked marble cupids with water spouting from any one of the various orifices; The Manor is a "Southern Plantation" with a fake greenhouse, fake stained-glass windows, a fake Torah, and a Greek love temple on the lawn for outdoor ceremonies.

Crystal chandeliers are a big number. One could perform open-heart surgery by the light of the chandeliers in Leonard's lobby, and the Town House boasts a custom-made one that cost $56,000, copy of an original in the Schönbrunn Castle in Austria, with crystals arranged in tiers thirty feet deep. Balconies are good, grinning marble cherubs are classic, fountains very crucial, as are ornately spiraling stairways. The aim of the decor, explains architect Bellamy, is "to create a Cinderella-like setting for the bride and her handsome prince."

Not that weddings are the only activities, bear in mind. At the Huntington Town House, although nuptials comprise 75 percent of their business, they do lots of organizational fetes on weekdays ("We have the Heart Fund, the Mentally Retarded. We've had Nixon and Agnew. They all come here," brags the manager) and bar mitzvahs, sweet sixteens, and anniversary parties on weekends.

Each palace has its own package deal, but they're just variations on the same theme. At Leonard's they stress the "yarmulkes-are-included" feature, at The Manor you get seconds in your main course ("We're the only ones who offer that bonus"). The Fountainhead, in New Rochelle, does an original theatric: "We bring in a gigantic bowl of salad, instead of serving it on individual plates. We lower the lights and then the spotlight hits the chef in his white hat as he tosses the whole salad right in front of you. It's *very* exciting." At several places, if you buy the most expensive package, your waiters will wear white gloves. At budget prices their hands go naked.

Here's the basic at the Fountainhead, explained to me by the pudgy salesman as I posed as a potential customer: "First you get your drinks and smorgasbord. Now, you can have that after the ceremony, in which case people are often too full to do justice to the really fabulous seven-course sit-down dinner. Or you can have it before, in which case you miss it because the bride's not allowed to be seen.

"Anyway, the butler serves the hot hors d'oeuvres. All good items. Egg rolls, kreplach, your Nova Scotias and herrings, your egg foo yung, and your sweetbreads Regency. All nice. Incidentally, there's a bubbling fountain in the middle of the smorg table. Very exciting.

"Then we go in for dinner. For your appetizer we've gotten away from the fruit. It's a cliché by now. We go for a hot appetizer, like your duck flambé is a good item."

Ultimately one reaches the main course—which accounts for the greatest variance in the price of the package. Chicken is the cheapest, prime ribs the dearest, with turkey, pot roast, squab falling between. Nobody chooses chicken, I am told, because all his friends know what it costs.

Prices also depend on the number of guests (they go down the more you invite), the day of the week (a reception for 250 can be $1,100 cheaper on a Thursday than a Saturday night), and the time of the year (summer months are most expensive). Photography and music are not included in the deal, but—surprise, surprise—all the joints have photographers and orchestras on the premises.

So the packages run anywhere from $11 to $22 a person, infinitely cheaper—perhaps one-half the price—than any fancy hotel. The sum includes all the food and booze (unlimited liquor), minimum flowers, the ceremony—although some charge extra for this—wedding cake, personalized matches, waiters' tips, and cigarettes. Most customers, however, choose some of the splendid extras: the "intermezzo" (a sherbet between courses) for $1 per person; fruit cup sitting in a carved Rome apple instead of silver bowl, 50 cents; ice lovebirds, $25 to $50 apiece; Viennese coffee table (a giant buffet of pastries, served immediately after the wedding cake, which is served immediately after the Cherries Jubilee) at $1.95 per head.

Volume is the key, of course, and business is colossal. Witness the basement banquet offices at Leonard's of Great Neck on a rainy September Sunday afternoon. I am waiting my turn—again a poseur—in an anteroom jammed with folks planning social do's. Thirty-five minutes pass before I am ushered into an office by one of the five banquet managers, each wearing a different-colored ruffled shirt —fuchsia, gold, robin's-egg blue—a shiny black suit with velvet bow tie. The telephone, ringing incessantly, is overseen by a tough, ash-blond receptionist who knows everything in the world. "I can only tell you, madam, that whatever your budget is we can give you a party for it, but I can't discuss any more on the phone." Bang. Despite her "catering," Leonard's is booked solidly for the next three months and hardly an hour is available for June—nine months away.

In a home, hotel, or church wedding there are a zillion decisions to be made. Blue candles or yellow? What kind of flowers? It is imperative that one's wedding be perfect, so every choice engenders the deepest of anxieties. A party on such a grand scale is utterly out of sync with the manner in which most people live. Which of us can bear the possibility of making fools of ourselves, being social klutzes? Mrs. Heathersnit from Newport was reared to throw little galas for five hundred. The suburban housewife fears her inadequacy in this department, and yet it is even more urgent to *her* that she create an impeccable, spectacular occasion. Comes along, on his white horse, toting his tray of forty hot-'n'-cold hors d'oeuvres, Big Daddy the Caterer who promises to take care of everything.

At Leonard's, the salesman whisks me on a rushed, impatient tour beginning with the three chapels—one on each floor, one for each of your major faiths.

Wedding palaces cater to both Jews and Gentiles, with the scales slightly tipped toward the Jewish. Is it odd then that *all* the food is kosher? And that the Town House has on the payroll several rabbis who, by some Talmudic law or other, must be present to supervise the kitchen whenever it's in operation? "The Gentiles don't mind," assures Vinnie Ferraro, operational manager. "They never complain about no butter on the table, and we use a coffee mix instead of cream, which they never even notice."

"Let's face it," confides a Fountainhead salesman, "the Christians aren't interested in the smorg. They're looking for the whiskey and the beer." All the managers make the same distinction. At The Manor, where they have computed the median liquor consumption to be 2.9 drinks per person, higher for you-know-who, the man claims: "In a Polish wedding they drink like they're going to the electric chair. The Irish drink with both hands. The Jews, on the other hand, eat anything that isn't nailed down."

Let me take you then to the Huntington Town House on a Saturday evening in early September. It is 7 P.M. and hundreds upon hundreds of people are streaming into the main lobby. Comparing the crush to Wrigley Field ten minutes before a World Series gamen or Penn Station on the Friday night of July Fourth weekend, would not be inappropriate. Only everybody here is rhinestoned to kill and an odor of perfume permeates the entire vastness. Some of it, granted, is residue from the afternoon fireworks, in which four weddings, three bar mitzvahs, and an anniversary party took place. Tonight, beginning shortly and continuing until 2 A.M., are scheduled one bar mitzvah, seven Gentile wedding receptions, and three complete Jewish weddings. The respective ceremonies will occur in the chapel at eight, eight-thirty, and nine, exactly.

The airport aura is certainly not diminished by the fact that the loudspeaker is never silent. "Will all the guests of the Schwartzberger affair please return to the Windsor Room? Your dinner is being served," it commands. "The O'Riley cocktail hour is now beginning in the Hampshire Room," it proclaims. It is an atmosphere of barely contained chaos. And the noise, oh my friends, the relentless stereophonic cacophony of feet thundering, bands trumpeting, party voices squealing and shrilling, dishes clattering. One of the ancient weapons to drive away evil spirits believed to be threatening newlyweds was that of loud noise. I think to myself that with the volume here, there couldn't possibly be an evil spirit still breathing anywhere east of the Rockies.

"Everything goes off like clockwork," claims the manager. "We have to keep that feeling of smallness, intimacy, the sense that there is only one affair going on at a time in the building. After all, brides certainly want their privacy on this day." Management is very sensitive to the "Wedding Factory" label, the assembly-line stigma that would be bad for business. That's why they lie. Why they insist that the activities are so brilliantly staggered that no two parties are waiting in the lobby at the same time. Why they insist you can't hear the music from one room to another.

It is time for the first of the three ceremonies of the evening. I am blessed with permission to attend all of them. The chapel-in-the-round is enveloped in artificial flowers and rimmed with fake stained-glass windows that also turn out to be fake windows. The chuppa—which the management also titles "the gazebo," depending on your persuasion—graces an altar that is lit by dozens of phony candles. Off to the side, you remember, is the whirling pedestal. The crowd is chattering noisily—unaware for some reason of the holiness of this setting—and has a small glow-on from the cocktail hour which has just preceded. The lights go dead. It is time. Pandemonium barely diminishes a decibel as the double doors creak open and enters the rabbi wearing—you'll just have to believe this incredibleness, too—a SEQUINED prayer shawl.

The processional is uniquely grotesque for a number of reasons, not the least of which is a perspiring photographer who has stationed himself right in the middle of the aisle and snaps and gallops to new positions without cease. Another horror is the opening and shutting of the big twin doors for each member of the wedding party. Apparently the din in the lobby will not allow for doors to remain open more than an instant, but these creak and crash without mercy. Enter the groom and his parents. CREEEEEAAKKK. CREEEEEEAAKKKK open for the maid of honor. CRRRRRRUUUUUNNNNCH shut. The ultimate offense is the organist who clearly received his training at a roller skating rink and thus deems it fitting suddenly to change the music without warning, to prevent boredom, I suppose. As each bridal party member enters through the clanking doors he strikes up a new tune—despite where he was in the previous one. So that at one instant he is booming an up-tempo martial ditty for the bouncy best man, abruptly switching to "A Pretty Girl Is Like a Melody" for the bridesmaids, followed immediately by a tune from *Fiddler* as Grandma and Grandpa toddle down the aisle.

Luckily, everything seems to progress very fast; indeed, it is like a mini Keystone Cops movie. But of course we must be out in exactly twenty minutes and thirty-five seconds for the next ceremony.

At the dance of the revolving bride the audience makes the required gurgles despite the evidence that most have seen this ritual scores of times. Incidentally, this part of the service is optional; your bride can also arrive in the normal fashion. But, they tell me, only one out of five hundred passes up the pedestal.

As the folks file out the next shift is already waiting. Same procession, seedier crowd. In this wedding the maid of honor sobs her eyes out. The sequined rabbi from the previous scene plays cantor in this one, with a voice rather like Frankie Laine chanting "Mule Train."

In-out-in-out. Twenty minutes and thirty-five seconds later it's over, right on the nose, precision timing (although the rabbi *did* have to scurry through the last part of his blessing in order to make the schedule).

The next crowd—250 of them—is mucho gay and some new summit in noise pollution is achieved. Even when the lights go off and the photographer, who is now sweating absurdly, begins his snapping and the doors begin their crashing, the gang *still* won't knock it off. It takes an organ blast of "Pomp and Circumstance," outvoluming them into submission, to provoke silence. This rabbi has an accent that hovers between British, Old Testament, and the west side of Chicago, and calls the bride Margery instead of Marilyn.

On to the merrymaking. The manager leads me from sanctum to sanctum, cha-cha to cha-cha. Each cave that we enter swells and bursts with eatables and there is never a minute in the five-hour marathon when the celebrants are not eating. The quality of the fare may fall somewhere between economy-class airplane and summer-camp dining hall. But never mind. Look at the array, table after table, silver tray upon silver tray. It just keeps coming, and besides, what we miss in gourmetdom we more than make up for in conspicuous consumption and sheer show biz. In the Madison Room a picnicking army awaits the arrival of the duck flambé. Lights dim, folks are commanded by the PA to "Please be seated while your course of duck is being served." The band strikes up a sprightly "Bridge on the River Kwai," the cue for the entrance of two waiters hoisting flaming spears of carrots, leading a parade of ten waitresses bearing fiery trays of duck and rice. Everybody applauds wildly.

When it's cake time, we get the same popular choreography. The wedding cake arrives—an astonishing gooey replica of an altar, with a cake priest, cross, and cake bridesmaids. Oddly enough it's called the Cathedral Cake, is one of the Town House super deluxe extra goodies, and there is apparently a Semitic version. Its entrance is marked by climactic music, and the top of the cake flaming away.

I ask a new bride, an eighteen-year-old Italian girl marrying her sixth-grade sweetheart before 275 witnesses, how she likes the Wedding Palace. "Oh, I love it! Everything is so beautiful and you get so much for your money. I just loved standing on the pedestal and whirling around. It's just like Hollywood here!"

One can go no further than the Wedding Factory to escape the ancient marriage rituals and customs. The feast of joy in which everybody participated and contributed has given way to the impersonal hand of the caterer.

CHAPTER 10

THE AMERICAN SPECTACLE: HOLLYWOOD AND THE WHITE HOUSE

Hollywood is both a reflection of and the cradle for American values. Certainly we've acquired much of our wedding psyche from Hollywood. The wedding day is *the* chance that Miss Average U.S.A.

gets to play Star, this one moment possessing all the excitement and anticipation of a Broadway opening night, minus the pain. No chance the audience won't love her, no possibility of bad reviews; the bride is a sure-fire smash hit. She is Miss America and the Academy Award winner and the about-to-be-crowned princess and Judy Garland at the Palace, all at one moment. The closest she will come to fulfilling the impossible golden dream of Hollywood.

If Hollywood so colors our fantasies, what about its citizens? Well, everybody loves a wedding, Hollywood adores a spectacle, so why not combine the two?

Celebrities' weddings, like their lives, are frequently bigger than life. Johnny Cash's *fifteen*-year-old daughter decides to get married, and eight days later Hendersonville, Tennessee, is rocked by a gala for six hundred in which participate a maid of honor, eight bridesmaids, three junior bridesmaids, a best man, a head usher, six ushers, one junior usher, a Bible boy (five-year-old Kevin Carter Jones—in tails), two candlelighters, two guest registrars, two program attendants, and nine hostesses. At the reception later held at the Cash lakeside mansion, no liquor is served, only grape juice flowing from an electric fountain.

What are we to say about Tiny Tim tiptoeing through ten thousand tulips imported from Holland, as he takes his vows with his seventeen-year-old Miss Vicki before twenty million devotees of the Johnny Carson show? Perhaps, simply, that it is sensational, crucial publicity.

Is it different from the heyday of the fan magazines when *Photoplay* paid for Janet Leigh and Tony Curtis' wedding, in exchange for an exclusive story? Or when one of the Lennon Sisters recently allowed a photographer to come along on her honeymoon, the deal being that he foot the bill in exchange for all the pics he wanted?

For some, the wedding is not just an extension of the hoo-hah attendant to their careers; it's the only splash they will ever get, so all the stops are pulled. A dancer on the Lawrence Welk Show was marrying the accordionist's daughter on Valentine's Day. On the show the prior Saturday the entire nationwide audience was extended a "personal" invitation to the wedding. Every senior citizen in Long Beach showed up at the church. Thousands milled outside where they could hear the actual ceremony, due to the thoughtfulness of the groom who had arranged for a PA system. As the rite drew to a close the minister's voice boomed over the PA: "Ladies and gentlemen, Mr. and Mrs. Bobby Burgess. You may applaud."

In Hollywood's prime time, the glorious golden years from the twenties through the early fifties, weddings reached a pinnacle of extravagance. Never again will the world witness—no, be a part of—a pageant like the marriage in 1928 of movie idols Vilma Banky and Rod LaRocque. The couple had originally planned a simple elopement, but her boss, producer Samuel Goldwyn, took command and produced a Real Life Spectacular, with who else but Cecil B. DeMille (Rod's boss) as best man and a regiment of cops to keep under control the fifteen thousand waiting, swooning, crazed fans. A gargantuan reception boasted mammoth hams and turkeys that later revealed themselves to be plaster-of-Paris creations, specially prepared, as was the wedding itself, for the photographers and press. The studio's aim, in staging a wedding, was for more and greater publicity, and the fans—having been hyped to believe in the intimate connection between their idols and themselves—assumed they would be included in on the festivities.

Thus, when Elizabeth Taylor married Nicky Hilton, it became a worldwide circus. Hollywood veteran costume designer Edith Head remembers it as "the charge of the light brigade, thousands and thousands of fans—many in evening gowns or tuxedos—waiting outside the church for even a glance at the gorgeous, rich, magic couple. People fainted, screamed, the press went utterly berserk."

For Grace Kelly's wedding—a gala that combined all the splashy elements of Show Biz with the *haute* regality of a European coronation—the princess's gown was "produced" by the MGM costume department. Thirty-five seamstresses spent six weeks in its execution, confronting 300 yards of lace and 450 yards of satin.

Edith Head, whose office on the lot of Universal Studios is drowning in Oscars and whose memory bank is overflowing with luscious tales from historic Hollywood, has designed hundreds of wedding dresses —in movies and in real life. "The further back you go, the more colorful and dramatic the weddings were," she says. "As the star system disintegrated, as the studios declined, so did the Hollywood wedding."

She reminisces fondly about one which she costumed—that of Veronica Lake to millionaire Andre9 de Toth. "It was in the days—the early forties—when you still took weddings very seriously in this town. She was at the height of her career and it was the superstar in the superdress in the superwedding. It was held in a Bel Air mansion with pools and sunken gardens. Everybody in town was there and the whole house was lit with candles. Veronica was a great beauty, he was dark and dashing—a truly romantic, beautiful Hollywood couple. When she came floating down a long winding flight of stairs in a candlelight-white satin medieval gown, well—it was just absolutely perfect." Enrapt with her emotion-filled recollection, I suddenly realize I am watching this scene, in my mind's eye, as if it were a movie. A divine, sublimely romantic, 1940's Hollywood saga, in which this magic moment is the final scene. The music swells, the screen blackens, and we all go home, thrilled to death. Needless to add, the couple lives happily ever after.

"It was simply another era," Miss Head continues, "the era of extravagant living, extravagant movies, extravagant clothes. Those kinds of big palatial weddings would be incongruous now, have nothing to do with the current way of life in Hollywood."

Naturally, there are periodic exceptions to the fabulous-weddings-are-dead rule. But they exist primarily among the offspring of celebs. Dinah Shore's daughter's wedding (*only* $12,000 for flowers, grumps Harry Finley, Beverly Hills' chicnik florist), Danny Thomas' daughter (800 for dinner at the Century Plaza Hotel), Lucie Arnaz (the hot awaited moment was when Mama Lucy danced with ex-hubby Desi).

Two Hollywood weddings of recent vintage stand out; both brides were the offspring of stars. Bob Hope offered his daughter, Linda, $25,000 instead of a wedding. She refused. So he sent out a three-page press release, detailing the flowers ("white orchids flown from Hawaii"), the attire of the wedding party, and the guest list (Ronald Reagan, Spiro Agnew, and Toots Shor). Bob Berman, the rentals man, recalls: "It was the largest wedding ever done under a tent. Every rentals person in the country competed for this job, and the fee to us came to over twenty thousand dollars. It was all done on Hope's own golf course."

Insiders talking about Nancy Sinatra's wedding to producer Hugh Lambert like to describe it as "simple," "unpretentious." Perhaps for the Sinatra clan it was. Perhaps compared to her opening-night party at Caesar's Palace, where Harry Finley's decorations cost $65,000, it was. After all, it was not even her first wedding and she *was* married in a Palm Springs church that used to be an army hospital. Understated, yes; but then the bride wanted a candlelight ceremony at two in the afternoon so in order to transform a daytime infirmary into a nighttime cathedral, the entire building—windows and all—was covered with vines and shrubbery, $25,000 worth (well, okay, that *does* include 10,000 white roses at the altar).

Come with me on a brief trip through an understated Hollywood wedding, as told to me by a Hollywood costume designer named

230

Donfeld, who not only designed the garb for *The Cincinnati Kid* and *They Shoot Horses, Don't They?*, but also for Nancy Sinatra, her mother, and her kingpin father, for her wedding. "She didn't want to do the klieg lights number," he says. "She wanted a tasteful, quiet affair, like a nineteenth-century country wedding. I did twenty-five sketches of her gown before she accepted one—a silk Georgette over a slip of white crepe-backed satin. Fifty different kinds of laces. All made by hand." This country maid's frock tallied in at $3,000.

The reception for two hundred was held at the Sinatra compound in Palm Springs—five houses in all. Sinatra's three jets flew Donfeld in from L.A., a hairdresser from Las Vegas (each had his own bungalow on the estate), and the guests from who-knows-where.

Barbara Stanwyck said it was the most beautiful wedding she'd ever seen. Another guest observed it was "a sleepy gathering for a Sinatra vaudeville."

Other countries have royalty; we have movie stars for heroes. Other cultures have bigger-than-life political figures, with total power and longevity; we have politicians who are here today, gone next November, and are generally lower than extras in the celebrity hierarchy. The Kennedys, of course, were movie stars—beautiful, rich, young, perfect. Captivated by every last, minute detail of their days, we molded them into super culture heroes, invested in them a portion of ourselves never before or since granted to our first families. But most Presidents and their families are not movie stars.

We rarely get glamour and exotica from the White House. Except in one situation: the White House Wedding. It is the one event in the President's private orbit to which we can relate with passion.

It can do as much good for a President's current popularity as a quick troop withdrawal or a little minimum-wage boost. Indeed, after Tricia Nixon's blowout, her father's image went soaring, say the pollsters. On that day the President was Everyman—the bumbling, blushing, semireluctant, wistful daddy losing his firstborn to another man's hearth. Touching, you'd have to call him. More vulnerable and appealing than we ever witnessed him, before or since.

Tricia Nixon's wedding did have a tremendous effect, at least temporarily, on certain aspects of American life. Votes in the bag for Daddy, money in the till for the bridal gown manufacturer who threw together an instant copy of Tricia's dress, available in stores three days later, and sold thousands upon thousands to upcoming young brides. There was a sudden run on the California champagne served at the reception, and a New York psychiatrist reports that every single female patient, the week following, was fixated on discussion of Tricia's wedding—mostly with envy.

There is, naturally, an American tradition of White House weddings, Tricia Nixon's being the sixteenth. The first, Maria Hester Monroe's in 1820, was attended by forty-five guests and recorded with a concise thirty-five words, two days later, in a Washington newspaper.

The most sumptuous White House bash to date—Tricia's has been labeled a "simple spectacular"—was that of Alice Roosevelt to Nicholas Longworth, in 1906. One thousand guests crammed the East Room, and there were no bridesmaids as Miss Roosevelt was highly competitive. She need not have worried: all eyes were fastened on the two, not-one-but-two, diamond necklaces adorning her throat, gifts from the groom. According to a newspaper report, "Miss Roosevelt looked as pretty as she ever did in her life and that's saying a good deal. As for the sturdy and good-humored fellow who won her, he was one broad beam of sunshine from that much-advertised bald head to his feet."

The subject of wedding gifts has always had heavy political significance in the White House. But at no time was this as keenly felt or exaggeratedly exhibited as in the Roosevelt picnic. The President of France sent a $25,000 Gobelin tapestry, the Pope sent a mosaic table, and the city of Cincinnati delivered a team of horses. The government of Cuba planned on giving San Juan Hill to the couple, then decided instead on a $30,000 pearl necklace.

A White House wedding often reflects the social personality and tone of the Presidency. Luci Johnson's wedding was a classy Texas barbeque to which, as comedienne Edie Adams quipped, "only the immediate country was invited." There were 700 guests, a 100-voice male choir, a 300-pound cake, Peter Duchin, cold beef sirloin, and the gang had a nifty time. The same for Lynda Bird's. "The Johnsons loved yippee parties," says Washington's Ellen Proxmire. "They had more of them than the Kennedys, less glamorous, of course, but most people said theirs were more fun."

The interesting—okay, incredible—aspect of Tricia's wedding—the third interchangeable White House rite in only four years—is that, on June 12, 1971, it was the biggest news event in the world. Why? Certainly not due to the personnel. Tricia was not one of the more colorful young women on the American scene, and Edward Finch Cox was, as far as we knew, a nice, bright, clean rich boy.

No matter. Our First Family is aristocracy—in a kind of ho-hum pumpkin pie way—so anything that concerns them personally becomes of public consequence. We do not require adoration of the participants. We just worship the pageantry.

What can I tell you about the wedding? The media made the message in several zillion words, and you know it all. A White House wedding has about it the aura of history, and like all affairs of this sort, this one became a magical, irresistible business. There certainly have been, compared to Tricia's, weddings more elaborate, original, kookier, more jolly. But whether it's the family who borrows from Chase Manhattan to provide their daughter with her promised one day in white, or the White House family determined to provide the nation with a day of historical significance, a wedding is—after all—a wedding.

On the other hand, when guest Alice Roosevelt Longworth was asked if Tricia's wedding brought back the past, she sniped: "It didn't bring back one goddamn memory." So there you are.

CHAPTER 11

WHITE BREAD AND UPPER CRUST

Would you be surprised to know that the very rich—at least the very rich who are also High Society—spend less money on their weddings than both the middle class and the working class? That a father who begins to save from the day of his daughter's birth (and perhaps has to hock something of value and borrow from the bank besides) in order to create the most memorable day of everybody's life—that he is very likely spending *more* than the gent who only has to scribble out a check, which hardly alters the balance in his account?

The Wedding, for most Americans, is a psychologically loaded event, heavily weighted with fantasies of status, Making It in the community, and being—at least for a tiny time period—bigger than one really is. Daddy Thoroughbred, with a family tree whose roots stretch way back into American history, is already a Brahmin; he adds not a single inch to his image by purchasing every nasturtium currently alive in the world. Mumsy is ho-hum used to swell parties—last night the Beri Beri Ball, today lunch at Le Haut Snob.

Then, too, his daughter's wedding is perhaps the nonrich father's one chance in life to experience the luxury and affluence that the rich take for granted. The single occasion when he can unpress his nose from the glass and actually partake of the greatest of American dreams—extravagance, even waste.

Speaking of that nonrich daughter, what does the formal wedding mean to her? To the average girl, it means everything. Absolutely everything. The society miss, on the other hand, is rather inured to buying zippy expensive clothing and having public attention paid her and going to spiffy shindigs. She has undoubtedly been to Dubrovnik and the Bahamas, not to mention 138 weddings of her classmates from Miss Finch's Finishing Farm. Because she's proud and secure with her heritage, she will even wear Granny's old wedding dress —Miss Average would rather go naked. Also, she gets to participate in another momentous ritual that generally occurs several years before her wedding. The Debutante Cotillion—the formal introduction of young women into society—possesses all of the "princess" elements of the wedding. White gown, getting to play movie queen, moving from childhood to womanhood. For the mass of womankind, by contrast, The Wedding is their debut.

But a massive delusion is in operation. We have no real contact with how the aristocracy lives—we drive by their gigantic mansions and all we can glimpse are eighty-five windows and the silhouette of a pool. Little do we realize that the interior is peppered with peeling wicker rockers and Great-Granny's antimacassars, so we are left to our fantasies. When we plan that wedding of ours, we emulate what we believe to be the opulent style of upper-class life. Obsessed with the need to do it RIGHT, the way *they* would do it, we somehow confuse gaudy with classy, gilt with gold, quantity with quality. The truth is, of course, that patricians thrive on watercress tea sandwiches on Wonder Bread with the crusts cut off and would sooner fall on their swords than wear a single sequin.

Society folk, more than the rest of us, live according to rules of behavior. The undefined, intuited codes of good taste, or the spelled-out-to-the-nth doctrines of etiquette. Laws for where to place the dessert fork, ordinances for how to monogram the silver ("Three letters are standard and tend to look best. Two are permissible but seem somewhat inadequate," proclaims *Vogue*). As you might suspect, the statutes concerning the ceremonial rites of life make the Koran read like a Donald Duck comic, and their weddings, thus, are just ever so slightly less fixed than plays. There is a proper hour (four o'clock ceremony, reception five to eight is the most chic, and Saturday the smartest day); there is a breakdown of correct attire, depending on the place, day, and time of day, that is so stern that a Los Angeles wedding consultant threatened to quit midstream of a big society Do where the groom wanted to wear a tuxedo. To hear her tell it, with righteous outrage: "*Naturally* a tuxedo isn't proper in the afternoon. I told him I wouldn't do the wedding if he insisted on wearing it. It's a terrible reflection on me if I allow that. Of course, he backed down."

I spent a morning in the company of Anita Farrington Earl, the aforementioned consultant, as she consulted with the tense mother of an upcoming bride. She works from her home in Palos Verdes Estates, a clifftop community on the ocean, south of L.A. Heavily populated with top corporate types and homes that begin at $75,000, Palos Verdes is almost entirely Christian and about medium-high to medium-well-high on the social ladder.

Blanche DuBois, I think to myself at the door, as Mrs. Earl floats toward me in a floral hostess gown, yellow hair, and purple eye shadow. But the voice changes that image, with a uniquely cultivated way of speaking that someone once labeled "Larchmont Lockjaw" because it emerges from a mouth that looks to be frozen into an unmoving smile and teeth that seem clenched together for dear life. It is a voice that is bred exclusively in the upper class and handed down from generation to generation.

Anita Farrington Earl believes in Etiquette the way some people believe in God. For her it provides structure, reassurance, and answers to some of life's major questions. "But," she insists, "you can never really learn the codes adequately, no matter how many books you read. You have to be born to it." Mrs. Earl was. On the mimeographed promotion sheet that details her personal services as wedding coordinator, we get a brief bio—title "QUALIFICATIONS"—as follows: "Undergraduate schooling in private schools in the East. Graduate of Skidmore College, B.S., Fine Arts. Descendent WsicE of Old American family dating back to pre-Revolutionary days. Listed in the New York Social Register and the California Register . . . . Thoroughly grounded in all aspects of Etiquette." Blood the color of the sky.

Her job consists of handling *everything* for a wedding. She goes to the ceremony and reception, making sure it all comes off without a single hitch, without the most minute digression from perfect form. She takes enormous pride in the fact that nothing unexpected ever occurs at an Anita Farrington Earl wedding.

This morning she is having one in a series of run-throughs with Mrs. Pillsbury, who refers to her husband as "Pill." The wedding is two weeks off, for three hundred people at a local church, followed by a reception on the grounds of a friend's estate. The girl is eighteen, her fiance9 twenty-two, both students in a small college in northern

California. There will be sixteen attendants and there have already been five harried months of preparation. Later on, after the woman leaves, Mrs. Earl will confide to me that this whole affair is, according to her standards, tacky. "We're doing things I don't approve of at all. A green and white tent instead of a white one, just to save a few hundred dollars. Really shocking . . . ."

For now, they consort like Pentagon chieftains whose subject matter is no less than the future fate of the entire planet. "I want the ushers at the church an hour ahead of time with their boutonnieres in place," orders the general. "Don't forget—with cutaways they must wear gloves." The lieutenant takes frantic notes.

On to the first dance, to occur immediately after the receiving line. A decree as to who starts, who then cuts in with whom, when and for how long. Ten minutes of floral discussion: has Mrs. P. ordered the corsage for the vocalist, for the guest-book girl, the bride's "going-away" corsage, flowers for the cake table and the base of the cake? Don't forget the underskirt for the cake table, don't forget the special cake for the groom's mother whose birthday is the same day, but when should it be served and should they use special candles?

"Who pays for the out-of-town guests' hotel accommodations?" asks the befrazzled hostess. Mrs. Earl snips, "Why, you do, of course." Imagine not knowing that, how positively hoi polloi. Mrs. Pillsbury is put in her place with an icy gentility that makes it utterly clear who's the more *haute* of the two women. Mrs. P. continues sheepishly: When does the bride toss the bouquet, before or after she changes to leave? (For Gentile girls, it's before; after for Jewish. I have no idea why.) Is the guest book signed at the church or at the reception? Mrs. E. doles out orders. Hire a detective to guard the gift display. Make sure the parking service is bonded and insured. Find out how many reserved pews the groom's side requires. Mrs. Pillsbury leaves eventually, a bit bent under the weight of both the ceaseless details and her implied inadequacy, and Anita Farrington Earl regales me with wedding tales. Mostly about catastrophes which may not, to you, seem like much on the sliding scale of possible life catastrophes, but in her realm are indeed calamitous. A bridesmaid's bouquet missing, so that she has to pluck a flower from here and there to construct one; the bride's tipsy father leaving the marriage license in the rented limousine, which has already been dismissed; the disappearance of the ring bearer's pillow.

Another responsibility of the social consultant is publicity—making sure the engagement and wedding announcement, cum photograph, reaches prominence on the society pages of the local newspaper. Often a more substantial concern than the wedding itself (a party's just another soiree, but fame—well, my lambies), this is becoming increasingly problematic. Once upon a time the society pages were just that—a newsletter to let one Brahmin know what his friends were up to. From a quiet dinner *en famille* to a garden luncheon where elegant ladies held elegant chitchats in their elegant new bonnets, to a charity gala for the Albanian monsoon victims—every such happening was reported, obviously considered of fascination to *all* castes.

In smaller cities, or cities in which the population is not particularly transient, little has changed. Often the cover of the Sunday section, especially in the Midwest, is devoted to society brides, and more than one nervous squire has been known to attempt bribery. In San Francisco a social consultant reports: "Wedding announcements in the *Chronicle* are very essential to people. Sunday is for the key people, Saturday for non-society, when nobody reads the paper anyway."

Remarkable, but predictable, changes have been occurring recently. Houston was growing so rapidly that both newspapers entirely abandoned wedding announcements over three years ago. Nowadays you have to pay, like a classified ad (a good-sized story can run $150), so *naturally* it's In to be Out. Nobody who's anybody BUYS space.

The move, among many large papers, has been toward egalitarianism. Merit ranks higher—they claim—than pedigree. Charlotte Curtis, Family/Style Editor of *The New York Times*, says, about choosing whose announcement is fit to print: "We feel strongly about kids who make it on their own. If your father is a garbage man and your husband's father is a street cleaner, but you and your fiancé are Phi Betes at Harvard and Radcliffe, you can be sure it'll get in." When pressed, she cheerfully admits that that tale will get in more readily and with more spatial prominence than if those same two Phi Betes have elite ancestors. "It's a more interesting news story this way," Miss Curtis confesses.

She has been known, in this spirit, to crash a wedding and call the story as she sees it. Thus, despite having been expelled by the ushers at George Plimpton's nuptials, she wrote up the announcement: "Mr. Plimpton was married here last night, not to Mrs. John F. Kennedy, Queen Elizabeth II, Jean Seberg, Ava Gardner, Jane Fonda, Princess Stanislas Radziwill, or Candy Bergen, all of whom he has escorted at one time or another, but to Freddy Medora Espy, a wisp of a photographer's assistant."

There is, certainly, a definable entity called a High Society wedding.

Let us first talk about what it is not. It is not, under any circumstances, a regatta in which we will find doves, revolving pedestals, or sequined clergymen. There will be no rollicking, no frenzied dancing, no weeping or heavy sweating.

Lest you be confused, a wedding such as Sharon Percy's to John D. Rockefeller IV, at which she wore a Mainbocher gown, and the 1,800 guests were serenaded by the Chicago Symphony Orchestra, is not typical—although the cast of characters was certainly tip-top. Nor is the case of the two society sisters getting married at the Los Angeles Country Club one night following the other. The Friday night flowers cost $5,000; Mummy insisted that not a day-old leaf remain, so Saturday morning another $5,000 worth of posies—brand-new —was installed.

Characteristically, an upper-birth fiesta takes place in a church. Episcopal, probably, but with the current breakdown of previously unmovable lines, a thimbleful of Presbyterians and Catholics have filtered into the ranks. No Jews, however. The church will be decorously adorned with flowers and the organ will play traditional wedding ditties. As the Episcopal church is rigorous about maintaining the basic form of service, you will have heard these particular vows five hundred times. Afterward you will make your way, for the reception, to a gracious home or private club (the Colony or Cosmopolitan in New York) or country club (the Burlingame in San Francisco or Piping Rock on Long Island). There you will crawl through a polite receiving line, sip vintage champagne, and dance to the cultivated strains of Lester Lanin or Peter Duchin. Then you'll munch a bit of wedding cake and be home precisely three hours later. You will not have drunk too much—getting sloshed is definitely *outré*—and the whole experience will be remembered in future years, by all concerned, as "Nice."

Professionals who serve the rich perpetuate notions of proper behavior with a stringency that borders on rigor mortis. They—the social consultants particularly—are haughtier, snobbier, and much more elitist than even the loftiest of their clientele. Their standards of what's Right and what's Wrong (not morally, mind you, but tastewise—a force far stronger than Good and Evil) are totally clear cut. And out of this vision emerges an interesting language. One dame talks about "People That Matter"; another breaks her categories down into "Nearly Everyone" and "No One."

"Nearly Everyone," of course, refers to approximately eleven people in America.

Nonetheless—in spite of the strict statutes—one sees some of our hippest hippies among the offspring of the 400. Although the "New Wedding" is primarily a manifestation of middle classism, the upper class has always had place for the eccentric, the oddball. Mrs. Pruneface may trudge to Bergdorf's in her ratty old fur, sure of herself and what is her purchasing power. Mrs. Babbitt, more self-conscious with her position, daren't. It is therefore likely that she will freak out if her daughter wants to get married in tie-dyed overalls.

Patrician kids are not only less nervous about the rules but are lately appalled by the outdated performances of their elders. The Debutante Cotillion, the entire process of Coming Out, is in its death throes. Especially on the east coast. Within the last five years the official list of debutantes in the Boston area has declined from three hundred names to a paltry ninety-two. A young Bryn Mawr freshman, from credentialed stock, who last year eschewed making her debut, says: "I would be mortified to go through that farce, all that snobby crap which is just another way of separating yourself from the great unwashed. It's absolutely irrelevant and immoral in today's world."

But even in nooks where the debut is still in swirling swing—San Francisco, for instance—the New Weddings are a big item. Social consultant Jean Fay Webster explains it: "San Francisco society has a hold on its children until the age of eighteen—coming-out age—so they go along with the debut tradition. But by the time they're ready to get married, they're freer thinkers. So you see more and more so-called hippie weddings, on mountaintops or in glens, or at the beach. It's becoming *very* smart to serve organic food and white wine."

But, often, what one finds is the grand compromise. The parents accede to an outdoor, simple ceremony with peculiar vows and funny clothes, and the kids then come down off the mountaintop to a fashionably dreary reception at the club.

CHAPTER 12

THE ODD COUPLES: WATER SKIS, CEMETERIES, AND THE NEON NIGHTMARE

There are folks who, by some inexplicable behavioral quirk, some aberrant psychological force, do not get married the way everybody else does in America. In a country where the urge for Le Grand Wedding seems to be as timeless, as sweeping, and as innately imbedded as the other heavy hungers, we find a smattering of defiers.

Water-skiing freaks in Miami did it on skis, with the reverend shouting the vows from the back of the boat; a stewardess was married on Northeast Airlines Flight 52 from Miami to New York (they had met on the same flight three years before); two equestrians wed on horseback in Syracuse, New York, with the minister and six attendants also mounted. (The bride's horse bolted after being hit in the face by a carload of confetti.)

Then there are those who dispense with plans, preparations, that intense portion of the ritual that—like the state of pregnancy—is often as emotionally essential and satisfying as the Big Day itself. They do it *fast*, in county courthouses, city halls, at a justice of the peace, or in Las Vegas. Not appearing to care about the environs, they rent a bridal gown or wear a T-shirt and chinos, maybe have a party afterward or maybe not, perhaps honeymoon, or not.

Are all of these defiers less romantic about marriage than most of our countrymen? Are they less American in their fantasies and expectations of life's one perfect day? Or is it all ultimately the same, regardless of the surroundings? Is a wedding still a wedding, whether it takes place in St. Patrick's or atop a Ferris wheel?

As our culture has always made room for the quirky character—we accept him for what he is and just go on about our business—there is a tradition for the offbeat wedding that, while obviously not widespread, is worthy of consideration.

—In 1964 a couple was married in the Vineland, New Jersey, roller rink, on skates. The service was executed by the town mayor, also on skates, as were the four attendants. The couple had met there, two years prior, and he had later proposed in the same spot. Is that, or is that not, romantic?

—The bride wore a powder-blue gown over ski pants as she and her childhood sweetheart were spliced on Squaw Peak, in California, at a height of 8,700 feet, in a raging snowstorm. Both wore skis.

—A manicurist in Louisville was married in her beauty shop.

—In Corpus Christi, Texas, a nineteen-year-old go-go dancer was married topless during the floor show, wearing a veil and traditional white gown—*sans* front. The maid of honor wore topless blue.

—Two amateur sky divers jumped from a plane holding hands, followed by the priest who married them where they landed. The bride wore white leather jump boots, a white crash helmet, and white satin overalls.

—In San Francisco, a couple was married by a priest of Satan, who asked the blessings of Lucifer and used, as an altar, a naked woman lying on a leopard skin on the mantel. The ceremony was conducted by candlelight—candles stuck in human skulls. The marriage was later declared illegal.

Increasingly blossoming on the cuckoo scene is the nude wedding, the first publicized one occurring in 1934 in Chicago at the World's Fair Garden of Eden. The six attendants were bare, but the presiding bishop wore a goatskin. At a more recent naked nuptial in California, the pastor (whose friends call him Tony the Tiger) proclaimed: "You're married, as long as you dig it." More to the contemporary point, perhaps, was the wedding on Jones Beach, Long Island, where after the ceremony the couple consummated the event in front of the 150 guests. "They are trying to achieve a feeling of unity," the minister explained.

Odd couples seem to get married in settings that—unlike hotels or churches—have something to do with their real lives. And since, historically, the wedding is a public statement of private commitment, a declaration to the community, there seems to be a sense of relevance in the offbeat caper that is undeniable.

But how to comprehend the unfathomable notion of choosing to get married in a cemetery? Let me tell you about Forest Lawn Cemetery in Los Angeles, one of the true unnatural wonders of the earth and one of the great bizarre institutions of southern California. Besides being in the burial biz, it is profoundly immersed in the tourist biz and the wedding biz. In the early 1920's, the story goes, "a bride-to-be and her fiancé walked through the sunlit glades of Forest Lawn. Coming upon a charming old-world church in a setting of green lawns and tall trees, she exclaimed, 'Look!—a storybook dream come true!' Then and there they decided that this was where they wanted to be married."

Since this fortuitous discovery fifty years ago, more than fifty thousand weddings have taken place at Forest Lawn—either at the main arm in Glendale (just east of Los Angeles) or at the three branch "stores." As many as five or six ceremonies may take place a day, compared to twenty-five funerals a day. "Weddings are not a thing that we make money on," quoted a spokesman for Forest Lawn in a *Los Angeles Times* article, the implication being that it's a public relations service provided so that satisfied bridal customers will remember Forest Lawn with fondness later on, if you know what I mean.

Forest Lawn is—yes, let's admit it—beautiful. If you didn't know what it is, what it contains, you would drive through the curving, hilly lanes and walk the sea-green meadow grasses believing yourself to be on some luxurious rolling Kentucky estate. And the chaps at Forest Lawn have done everything possible to make you forget. Not a vertical tombstone exists to disturb the vista; they are all flat with the land and barely visible except when walking on them—thousands upon thousands (over two million in all). The grave sections are titled Rest Haven, Inspiration Slope, Lullabyland. Babyland is encircled by a heart-shaped drive.

Forest Lawn considers itself one of the finest art museums in America, with more than a thousand bronze and marble statues, and boasts that it is "the only place in the world where one can view all the major sculptural works of the greatest Renaissance artist, Michelangelo." No matter that they are copies and, as Jessica Mitford says, look "like the sort of thing one might win in a shooting gallery." This place is the embodiment of the California dream/reality where life—and, apparently, death—is one terrific jolly barbecue with plastic forks and franchised fried chicken.

One day I go to visit Mrs. Bobbe Bennett, the "Wedding Hostess," a saccharine, fairly spooky lady with a mountain of bleached platinum hair and very pale skin and the predictable black dress. Pretending bridedom, I ask a million questions which she answers in canned speech that flows so speedily I can hardly get it all down. "The basic cost is thirty-five dollars with five or six guests, plus the services of the hostess, or one hundred and fifty dollars for the deluxe; the organist is fifteen dollars, and that includes a uniformed attendant to clean the church and set up the flowers. We suggest a twenty-dollar minimum fee for the minister." (He is, incidentally, Methodist or Baptist; they cannot get a Catholic priest, and Jews are not exactly given the royal carpet at Forest Lawn.)

The whole thing is, naturally, a terrific bargain as weddings go. Sort of like buying a haunted house. You can really get good value.

When pale Mrs. Bennett ends her routine, I ask her if I can see the wedding chapel. "Oh, yes, of course," she perks. "Unless there's a funeral service going on."

Why do people want their weddings at a cemetery?

One apparent motive, a fairly common one, is that a parent or favorite relative is buried there and the family wishes to be close to him on this day. But surely that doesn't explain all. "Our couples have grown up with Forest Lawn," says Mrs. Bennett, which at first hearing sounds ridiculous, but on later thought seems more real. If you grow up in Los Angeles, and listen to your radio and drive a car, Forest

Lawn is as much a part of your conditioned experience as the presence of the Pacific or movie stars or the smog. As the repetition of a single word over and over makes that word lose its meaning, so it is with Forest Lawn. It's not what it is, a graveyard; it's merely a California fixture, another recreation area. Still, I must confess to you, I do not *really* understand and doubt that I ever will.

Las Vegas is a place so tawdry, so evil, and so unnatural to man that one would not want to do anything *real* there. I cannot envision cooking dinner in Las Vegas or taking my towels to the laundry or reading a book or having a tooth filled. Getting married in Vegas is a notion the awfulness of which I cannot begin to entertain.

But last year almost fifty thousand marriage licenses were issued in Las Vegas (a 3 percent climb over the year before)—100,000 lovers came here, to America's shlock city, to sanctify their bond. It's a town that thinks in these terms—in hard cash—so they estimate that weddings bring in $60 million a year. Peanuts compared to the crap tables and slots, but a hefty penny in any real world.

Nevada makes it very easy to spend your money simply by having different laws than the other states (though they already have the loosest divorce rulings, an attempt was made recently to change the waiting period from six weeks to one day), so getting married here takes ten minutes, the whole shebang. No blood test, no waiting period. Proof of age (girls, eighteen; boys, twenty-one); that's it. You just hop over to the county courthouse—downtown near the low-end sleazy casinos—open, like everything in Vegas, twenty-four hours a day. Pay your six bucks for your license (on weekdays, nine to five) or your sixteen bucks (weekends and odd hours). Hop to an office room in the back and in four minutes flat, you're wed.

Or if you want a little class, a little romance, saunter down the strip to one of the town's twenty-six "wedding chapels," like the Silver Bell (CALIF. CHECKS OK, PHOTO, FLORIST, DRESSING ROOMS, proclaims the flashing sign in front), wake up the proprietor (it's okay, he's open round the clock too) who'll phone and wake up the minister (he guarantees to be there, in black suit, within eight minutes).

Then, while you're digging out your $25 or so, depending on the elegance of the joint (plus $12 if you want a roll of black-and-white photos, $5 for a tape recording, $3 for a plastic daffodil or $10 for a live orchid), the proprietor will be sizing you for rings ($15 for one, $25 for two, unless you want a special saying engraved inside, like "Forever Yours" or "Love Is a Many Splendored Thing." Most folks don't bother with those extras. Takes too long).

Before you can say "Frank Sinatra," you'll be back at the Thunderbird casino stuffing quarters into the old one-armed bandits, waiting for the Big Killing. Married.

Vegas is a town that should exist only at night, when the flashing neon hides the pores, when the gambling fever seems sexy and not so sordid. The darkness can support delusions and it's okay, somehow. A roll of the dice may, after all, change everything. But during the day it's a totally different place, hideous and naked under an unyielding sun that burns away all hope.

On a scorching Saturday in May some nine hundred hopefuls come to town, mostly from other states, to get married. You stand outside the county courthouse and watch them file in and out, an endless stream of traffic that never diminishes through the day and night. The action is as brisk as at the tables and the faces as varied.

—A motorcyclist in jeans, fringed suede vest, no shirt. His lady in hot pants and over-the-knee black boots.

—A middle-aged couple with eight friends and her two small children.

—Two young couples from San Diego who decided to elope together. After both ceremonies are finished, one boy turns to his companions, saying, "O.K., now you want to go to Caesar's or the Sands?"

—A three-hundred-pound woman, with bouffant white hair, and her nondescript boyfriend.

—A scrubbed boy in a ten-gallon hat and cowboy boots. His girl sports a fancy white lace minidress, bleached, teased, and sprayed hair, and her parents snap Brownie pictures without stop.

—A Mexican boy of eighteen and his Anglo bride of nineteen; he has an affidavit of consent from his father, but her parents don't know they're eloping.

There is no way to categorize the couples, just as there is no way to generalize about who comes to Vegas itself. But everybody has a story. The first couple I speak with, outside the courthouse where they have just been married, is from Santa Ana, California. The boy is Mexican-American, twenty-four; his nineteen-year-old wife is Anglo. They drove down for the day with his mother, and the bride says the five-minute ceremony was "beautiful to me, just as exciting as in a church and more convenient." They will have, she says, a church wedding and honeymoon in the future, but can't afford either right now and couldn't wait to get married. On a sharp second glance at her Empire dress, I notice that she is pregnant.

Another couple has been married fifteen years. They come to Las Vegas periodically to gamble, and this is the fourth time they've repeated the wedding procedure, in order "to renew our romance."

I meet a couple—Jim and Dee—in front of the courthouse and decide to tag along as they look for a chapel and Dee—having quite suddenly gone sentimental and decided she must wear white instead of her green pants suit—a gown. They are from Phoenix, Arizona, in their mid-twenties; he is a lab technician, she's a secretary, both Methodist, both previously married and divorced. Neither has any family. At eleven o'clock last night they decided suddenly to get married and drove straight through the night to Vegas. They have been going together for two months. "Everybody gets married in church," according to Jim. "It's different to do it here." When I approach them he is bent over, taping homemade crayoned signs to his 1969 red Datsun that read. SHE GOT HIM TODAY, HE'LL GET HER TONIGHT; CANDY IS SWEET BUT SEX DON'T ROT YOUR TEETH. Sweet, jittery, and touching, they have somehow picked up the Vegas tough uglies and make jokes about it's-all-a-big-crap-game. They laugh, I laugh.

On our chapel shopping tour the first stop is the Little Chapel of the Flowers, a small white house with a phony church spire, nestled between a Texaco station and the Yucca Motel. Like its competitors, it has two rooms, the anteroom-lobby where the plastic accoutrements are sold, and the chapel itself—wooden benches, two stained-glass somethings masquerading as windows, which they clearly are not, a sparse sprinkling of artificial flowers (known in this part of the world as "perpetual plastic"). Music? "For your listening pleasure we have a high-fidelity lifetime recording," the owner answers.

We move on to the next. The Chapel of the Stars has lavish displays of white plastic carnations and electric candelabra. The minister mentions God, or not, as you request; you can purchase a license covering with a white bow, a rose corsage (real, as opposed to perpetual), and a special courtesy provides a car to pick you up at your hotel, take you to the courthouse for your license, wait, then drive you back here for your wedding. No muss, no fuss. Thirty-five minutes.

Right next door, on the same premises as the Holiday Motel, is the world-famous Chapel of the Bells where, as the owner immediately tells us, Keely Smith was married. He also informs us that he once appeared on the "David Frost Show" and asserts that "this is the most famous chapel in the world," which I certainly would not think of refuting. "I don't want to say anything derogatory about the other chapels," he says, "but they're all dumps compared to the 'Bells.'"

In fact, his place *is* sweller than the others we've visited. It has more vinyl couches and more plastic posies.

Jim and Dee finally settled on the Little Church of the West, definitely the class operation in town. A dice-throw away from the Frontier casino but nonetheless snuggled into a little patch of fake New England grass. Looks like the spot where Great-aunt Sophie is buried, but rumor has it that Elvis Presley got married here. Next, a quick stop at the Stage Bridal Shop, where the sign reads: ASK US ABOUT ONE-HOUR TUXEDO AND BRIDAL GOWN RENTALS." We do, and the charges—$12.50 to $50 for a dress, $10 to $25 for a tux—suddenly seem prohibitive and foolishly romantic. With a shrug that conveys both oh-what-the-hell and disappointment, Dee keeps on the pants outfit she's been wearing since yesterday morning in Arizona.

Lovers tie the knot in Las Vegas with the same speedy indifference that they toss away thousands they can't afford at the tables. I serve as legal witness to several marriages this busy Saturday—most couples come to town alone and the chapels charge anywhere from $2 to $6 to furnish witnesses, so I am in popular demand as maid of honor to these utter strangers. As dreary as are the chapels, courthouse weddings are a notch bleaker. Cold, bureaucratic, listless.

One-third of Vegas weddings take place at the courthouse, and as a result of a recent law prohibiting justices of the peace from performing marriages (they were each raking in $150,000 a year in fees), the job of Commissioner of Marriage was created, enabling the money to be kept in the Nevada coffers. Five deputies do the deeds, on three shifts—"the day shift, the swing shift, and the graveyard shift," one explains. He himself works four ten-hour days, does ninety or a hundred quickies on a Saturday and insists he is romantic about weddings. "I've been married for thirty-eight years. It hasn't been all beautiful, mind you, but mostly it has."

The wedding I witness takes place in his office—a tiny cubbyhole populated only by a steel-gray desk with a box of rubber bands on it, a floor vase of white plastic lilies of the valley and one painting on the wall, a desert landscape, with a card taped underneath reading: "Title: Landscape; Price: $10.00 plus tax." The couple is in their fifties, have been common-law married for years, now are "doing it right." One aches, of course, to know the whole saga, why after all this time they are prompted to legally cement themselves, and in this setting. But the ceremony is beginning. And then it is ending. The deputy drones relentlessly for three minutes in a bad southwestern twang (it is, let's be kind, his forty-eighth marriage spiel of the day, and he has four hours left on duty) and mispronounces their names. But a curious thing happens. The bride's hands tremble throughout, the groom's temples get damp, and they regard each other with a kind of starry-eyed adoration one sees in engagement ring ads. Or among children getting married in the divinely romantic church surroundings that fulfill their lifetime's fantasies.

CHAPTER 13

CONNUBIAL BLINTZ

I t was to be the most razzle-dazzle super-extravaganza of all time. All the forces of the Fontainebleau Hotel in Miami Beach were commandeered into feverish action for weeks ahead, preparing the Grand Ballroom for the wedding of twenty-year-old Susan Grenald to Ronald Rothstein, a law student at the University of Miami. "This is exactly what I've wanted since I was a little girl," whispered the dewy-eyed blonde surveying the specially built, twenty-seven-foot, pink-carpeted stairway down which she would float, trailed by thirty feet of white train. To the accompaniment of strings, she would first emerge from behind a curtain through a celestial white cloud— provided by a specially built white cloud machine—which would then envelop her in soft mist as she levitated to the altar. As her mother explained: "Susan will look like she's coming from heaven." Where, as we know, all good Jewish Princesses originate.

After the ceremony the three hundred guests would munch Oysters Rockefeller, a small mountain of Iranian caviar, and filet of beef. When the bride sliced into the eight-tiered, six-foot-tall cake, two lovebirds would be released, to soar with ancient symbolism through the heavenly upper reaches of the ballroom. The couple would then depart for their eighty-three day round-the-world honeymoon, leaving Daddy to pay $25,000 worth of bills.

Mama, six months before, had tried to hire THE society wedding coordinator in the area, who refused the assignment. "What you need is a Broadway producer," he sniffed. As he tells it, she was elated: "Oh yeah? Where do I get one?" Most probably she *didn't* hire one, but the Fontainebleau public relations department, sensing the show to be a sure smash hit, gave it a title—as one would *any* Broadway spectacular. "Wedding Fantasia" was to be covered by a team from *Time* magazine, and although the reportage was not quite as planned, the event did indeed make nationwide headlines—the groom chickened out, making a panicky celestial exit the night before and leaving behind a hysterical bride and a carload of stuffed mushrooms to die an unnatural death in the Fontainebleau kitchen.

Such a burlesque has, of late, been tagged the *Goodbye, Columbus* wedding—in honor of the scene in the film where Brenda Patimkin's brother gets married in a lavish and jazzy hotel festival. It has become a shorthand for the kind of wedding celebration that characterizes middle and upper-middle-class Jewish life in America, to wit: the twelve-hour fete in the gardens of a Beverly Hills mansion—the only daughter of a prominent Jewish psychiatrist—where a different meal was served every hour and two authentic gondolas navigated guests back and forth in the swimming pool; the affair at a Westchester country club—a carpet manufacturer's offspring—where Papa had his mills produce a special rug, emblazoned with the words "Sandy and Norman," to cover the entire lobby; the real-life Joseph E. Levine production in New York's Plaza Hotel, in which his daughter wanted a synagogue wedding but Mrs. L. didn't, so—as a glorious compromise—the Terrace Room was transformed into a chapel. For a service that lasted one-half hour, they had made twelve Plexiglas replicas of the Chagall windows—each six feet wide and twelve feet high.

Jews are no different than any other minority culture, in that the gigantic wedding is symbolic of having succeeded in the community. If one can afford—I suppose the logic goes—to throw away thousands on something as temporary as flowers, one must really be a mensh. Food is a permanent, a staff of life; never mind that we provide such an overabundance—the Cossacks may come tomorrow, who knows when we'll eat again? But flowers? Here today, gone tonight, and you can't even eat them. What *real* and awesome extravagance. . . .

The wedding is one of the few occasions in life at which Jews feel justified in getting drunk, so it is unrestrainedly, relentlessly gay. The measure of the success of the Jewish wedding is in the joy of the guests: if Bertha, the spinster sourpuss of the family, got a little loaded, danced with all the men and whooped and hollered, *that's* a smashing wedding. And since the Jews have never cultivated the Oriental love for silence, or the American Gentile value for understatedness, the volume keynotes that success.

A bandleader in New York says: "At a Jewish wedding, if you play soft and pretty background music, the bride's father storms up and screams, 'What's the matter, didn't your men show up?'" Then, of course, the band has a master of ceremonies, a stand-up comic who not only bellows forth a stream of running sexy jokes but also announces every wee event of the evening as if he was proclaiming THEWINNERANDHEAVYWEIGHTCHAMPIONOFTHEWORLD: "*And now,* Morty and Judy have their first dance. . . ." "*And now,* the maid of honor's sister dances with the groom's brother-in-law. . . ." "*And now, ladies and gentlemen, the Baked Alaska. . . .*" To boot there is the ceaseless clatter of dishes as the marathon plunges ahead into its sixth straight hour.

It's also true that Jews function heavily on the concept of "shonda"—shame. The expression, "It's a shonda for the neighbors," tossed at me throughout my childhood as criticism for all varieties of bad public behavior, is as firmly etched into my psyche as "Thou shalt not kill." What the neighbors will think of us—indeed, the assumption that they are *always* observing and judging us—molds our actions, and what on earth will they think if we do not provide our daughter with a proper wedding? That we're paupers, or cheapskates, or—horror of horrors—Bad Parents.

The most dread accusation of all to a Jew, worse yet than being a failure in business, is to be a bad parent. In Jewish lore, what that means, specifically, is not providing your offspring with the best of everything, the creamiest that money can buy. It's like the food obsessions: the historical deprivation of rights and privileges taken for granted by everybody else is so ingrained in the Jewish genes that only outlandish excess will wash the memory away. Thus bursts forth the new generation of Have, the Jewish Princess—she who is denied nothing, to whom every material luxury is not a luxury at all but a life's-breath necessity. Daddy must—as his proof to the world and himself that he has done right by little Shirley—furnish her with the most lavish send-off available to modern man.

Jewish weddings have become so copiously overdone, so laughably jazzy, precisely because of this: in order that the fabled "neighbors" shouldn't talk. There is simply no choice about whether or not to play the game. Your friends have given big blowouts, your business partner did it, and all the ladies in your wife's Mah-Jong club. You must not only do it, but it invariably has to be a four—compared to the Feinbergs' three—ring circus.

At the Hampshire Country Club in New York's Westchester County the average wedding costs $10,000, but they not infrequently soar to double that amount. (The producer of *Goodbye, Columbus* belongs to Hampshire and apparently patterned the wedding scene on all the shindigs he's witnessed there.) Pete D'Angelo, the club's manager, tells more riotous stories about nuptial ridiculousness than anyone I've met. "The competition is murderous," he explains. "At one wedding the whole ceiling of the ballroom was covered with silk fabric, to look like billowing clouds, and tiny bulbs were planted above, twinkling through like stars." At another he had to have all the linen dyed gold to match the bride's mother's gown, to the tune of $3,000. Two hundred and fifty pineapple shells sprayed powder blue, champagne fountains where the wastage is 25 percent—small but key (and highly visible) symbols of going your neighbor one better.

Pete recalls: "One man, a furrier, insisted that all the scotch be at least twenty-one years old; it cost us eighteen dollars a bottle and we charged him fifty. A month later his best friend's daughter got married and they had to do something to top *that* number, so they threw a breakfast for three hundred the morning after their gigantic wedding."

This sort of Jewish fiesta is the prime illustration of the it's-all-for-the-parents syndrome. Of all the recently married couples I have interviewed, it is *only* the Jewish girls from moneyed families who reported that they loathed their weddings, never wanted such a Mardi Gras, but felt overwhelming parental pressure (funny, Daddy thinks he's doing it for *her*) and not only acceded, but abandoned total responsibility. Would David Merrick allow his fledgling assistant to produce *Hello, Dolly!*? Certainly not. *This* production is staged, controlled, shaped by that mythic figure, the Jewish Mother. The sole function for her daughter is to go for fittings, write thank-you notes, and prevent her skin from breaking out before the big day; the groom is a phantom, and Daddy writes the checks.

Small wonder the kids relinquish: the stakes are simply too high. Poker is jolly fun when it's nickles and dimes but another game entirely when the bets are pot limit. Once the wedding machinery is set into operation, the accumulated tensions over the months of planning become volcanic. Every decision becomes so fraught with weighty implications that one senses there is clearly something much heavier at stake, for the family, than just the load of money being spent and the fever to create a memorable barbecue. It seems to represent an affirmation, a validation of one's total life. Christians—the majority culture, the true Americans—do not, I believe, bear this need. The American Jew of immigrant or second-generation stock knows, on some level, the limitations of his options: he cannot be President, either of the country or of its most powerful enterprises. What *is* open to him is acquisition of the symbols and their display for the world.

The ghetto black goes hungry to buy the Cadillac and the color TV. The Jew, obviously more privileged but still an outsider, and with the same needs, just exhibits more symbols—the hoopla wedding being among the most mighty.

It is for the parents, *their* affirmation, thus the guests will be primarily Daddy's business associates, Mother's Hadassah clique, or the family ancients who surface only for funerals and weddings. Leftover space will be filled in with a scattering of the couple's friends.

Like the Fontainebleau fiasco, couples not infrequently break up as a result of the escalating strains. One twosome, who eloped to Las Vegas midstream in the preparations for a Beverly Hills Hotel spectacular, talk about how their love story degenerated into a sequence of daily squabbles over the centerpieces, the napkins, whether the cigarettes should be plain or menthol. Now married four years, the girl recalls: "One night, three months before the wedding, we sat there with our parents arguing about should the tablecloths be pink or yellow. Jerry snarled at me, 'I can't stand pink. If the tablecloths are pink, I'm not going through with it.' And I thought, 'I can't marry this jackass. He hates pink.' At that moment I knew we'd better elope or we'd never get anywhere near the altar." They did, that weekend. Three months later, never having told their parents, they went through with the hotel rodeo as planned.

When I asked her what this little charade cost, she chuckled. "It could have cured cancer."

The *Goodbye, Columbus* wedding does more than its share to support the industry. The average American reception (according to *Modern Bride*) costs $601.21, and the largest percentage of families spend between $1,000 and $2,000; while no available statistics break down these figures ethnically, the industry experts agree that the Jewish middle class spends at least ten times the nationwide norm.

The cost of the average diamond engagement ring (half a carat) is $328.85. Our Jewish Princess wouldn't be caught dead on the line for her unemployment check in less than two and a half carats. The national bride spends $164 on her bridal gown; Marjorie Morningstar tosses those pennies away on three sets of Pucci underwear. And whereas only one percent of American brides get married in hotels, approximately one-third—again according to estimation from the pros —of all Jewish couples tie the knot in these establishments. Most hotels calculate that at least 50 percent of their total banquet business comes from weddings. And, of that, anywhere from 60 to 85 percent are Jewish. Jews being the only religious group permitted to hold

251

their ceremonies outside of the home or a house of worship—as long as the setting is spiritual, say the ordinances—*every* hotel ceremony is Jewish. As is virtually every sit-down dinner.

Although most Jewish girls still get married in synagogue, in large cities where the hotels have adequate banquet facilities an increasing number pick this particular "spiritual setting"—the most expensive and statusey of all. An elegant hotel, after all—the Beverly Hills, say, or the Regency in New York—offers a kind of nonreligious prestige that the neighborhood temple just can't match.

Hotels that cater to the wedding trade range from the high-elite to the ever-spreading chain commercial establishments. All that's really needed to compete for a piece of the silver pie are a couple of rooms of varying sizes to accommodate the demands of the tiny, private affair or the super-soiree—and those falling somewhere between. The premise of the hotel wedding is at opposite poles from the wedding palace. At Leonard's the whole shebang comes in a package, a set price, and your only decision is the chicken-or-roast beef one; the hotel fiesta is geared for the matriarch who wants, *needs*, to maneuver EVERYTHING—absolutely everything. From the style of engraving on the personalized matchbooks to—and this is ultimately the costliest, weightiest choice—the quality and quantity of the liquor.

Each item is charged for separately. Scan a bill from the Plaza Hotel for a recent Jewish pageant for 220 guests, the total cost $10,013.07 —and this doesn't include photography, music, or any of the other nonhotel purchases. The dinner, châteaubriand at $23 per guest, came to over $5,000—the major expense. But then there was $68.75 for Don Diego cigars passed "to the gentlemen with their café," pink cathedral candles at $1.25 each, 4 per table (for a total of $56), $100 for extra-fancy gold water glasses, and $30 to the washroom attendants.

It is on the booze that the hotel makes its fattest profit (65 percent as opposed to 30 percent on the food, says the banquet manager of the Beverly Hilton) and for which all accusations of hotel cheating—like bathtub gin being poured into the Beefeater bottles—are leveled. Most establishments charge either by the bottle ($10 to $25) or by the drink at $1.15 each. There are ways to economize—subtle to the outsider but sore-thumb visible to the cognoscenti. Instead of rolling bars, the top extravagance, you can have a stationary bar, where one has to exert some effort to get a drink. (The average consumed per person then drops over the course of the evening.) Or you can cut off the hard booze right before dinner, from then on serving only champagne. Or—El Multo Cheapo—you can decide precisely how much you will spend and close down the drinking when that sum has been reached. In general, the guilt-edged Jewish ego will not permit any of these frugaling measures. You and I, if neophyte wedding-goers, would probably not notice the cutback; the eagle eye of the "neighbors" will, no doubt, and the mind boggles to consider how lightning fast that tidbit will spread—plaguelike—through the beauty shops and golf foursomes.

All of this paranoia and guilt derives not only from Jewish heritage, the Bad Parent terror, and dread of the serpent-tongued neighbors. It is fed and nurtured by that outstanding figure of hotel wedding life—the Banquet Manager.

Every hotel has one. He is to the Jewish regatta what the wedding consultant is to the *haut monde* Gentile; that is to say, he coordinates, oversees, advises, and makes you feel your own tragic ineptitude. As you become more dependent on his experience, superior tastes, and aggressiveness, he becomes increasingly in charge of *your* party. His purpose is not so much a gratuitous ego/power trip as a quite deliberate means to a businessman's end—getting you to shell out as much money as possible. That is his job, after all. Not unlike funeral directors who convince us that we are horrible humans for considering the burial of a loved one in a plain pine box, that somehow love means planting Aunt Nellie in mahogany. Vulnerability to the un-spoken accusation is equally as operative for weddings as funerals —the crucial rites of passage. You may not be sending your Princess daughter off to the great hereafter, but you *are* sending her off. How American that the commodity, the judging scale, is the dollar. A bad parent spends few, a good and noble parent spends the contents of Fort Knox. Or more.

There is not a banquet manager worth his smoked sturgeon who does not understand this psychology and exploit it. On a warm spring afternoon I made an appointment to consult with one of the managers at the Beverly Hills Hotel, the lovely and smart haven for show busi-ness types on expense accounts from New York and local royalty getting bar mitzvahed or married. Posing as a future bride auditioning hotels, I learned—instantly—the name of the game: Intimidation.

This particular lady—very Teutonic, ultra chic—from the moment I entered her domain, appraised me blatantly. With one piercing glance that traveled down my body as if she were reading a map of New Jersey looking for Weehawken, but in fact was computing labels and price tags of my pants suit, shoes, jewelry, and underwear, she succeeded wordlessly in making me feel abysmally shabby. Poor.

Unworthy. And it only took twenty seconds. At that instant I would have done *anything* to reverse her judgment. "Are you on a budget?" is her first question, and I feel, by my "yes" answer, that she envisions me living in a subway station. Obviously, I assume, no one who has ever taken up one moment of her time has ever been on a budget. One could, of course, respond: "Yes, I don't want to spend a nickel over four hundred thousand," but that would still not justify having a budget to begin with. Tacky. Tacky, tacky.

Plainly repelled by me, she rushes me through a tour of the Crystal Room and the Maisonette Room, all with the impatient spirit of the *grande dame* showing her mansion to the new maid. She doesn't suspect I'm a reporter—it's not that; it is my insistence on asking what everything costs that revolts her. I am in and out of the Beverly Hills Hotel in twenty minutes, certain that if I were to rush back and say, "Okay, I want to have my wedding here," I would be rejected.

Banquet managers come in different styles, but they all play Intimidation. And it absolutely works to perfection. Gerd Ries is in charge of banquet activities for New York's very nicest hostelry, the Regency. A small, quiet, utterly iffy-piffy establishment, only ten years old, you will rarely spy a movie star in the lobby. In fact, you will hardly ever see a famous face at the Regency, unless you happen to be able to recognize kings, presidents of countries, or the top financial monarchs in the world.

With banquet provisions less extensive than the Plaza, St. Regis, or the Pierre—the Regency Suite can accommodate only two hundred with no dancing—their wedding image is soaring among Jewish parvenues who require "Quiet Elegance"—that interesting WASP expression that used to be used a code for resorts that didn't allow Jews.

Mr. Ries is a terribly personable European who seems to be, although he isn't, wearing white gloves. He hates noisy frolics and rolling bars, permits only French service—each item is served individually, as opposed to bringing out the already piled plate *à la* dinner on an airplane—and all his waiters wear high-winged collars and gloves.

I am permitted to be present for his prenuptial conference with a thirty-year-old schoolteacher named Rita who is three months hence marrying a wealthy stockbroker from an our-crowdish family. It is obviously a heavy Jewish status number. She is, as a result, insecure and desperate. Ries is the super-elegant gourmet pro daddy. Although he could not be more soft-spoken, polite, and genteel throughout the interview, it becomes more than clear that, by the nature of the game, he could sell her the Throgs Neck Bridge for her wedding cake.

It is to be a small affair, sixty guests, with a buffet supper and dancing. The purpose of this meeting is to plan the menu. Watch the game in action. Rita has been suggesting dishes; Ries has, in response, been blanching, frowning, all but groaning audibly. "In order to keep up with the expectancies of the Regency and yours also," he commands, "*this* is the environment I think you should have." Whereupon he suggests two esoteric dishes that I have never heard of, and to judge by her terror, neither has she.

But the real crisis of the day arises when Rita mentions that she has hired some uncle or other to do the flowers. Ries becomes pinched and—so quietly that one can barely hear the words—tells her she *must* use the Regency florist, it is a hotel ruling, and he will be severely criticized by management otherwise. (This is a general dictum among the finer inns throughout America.) Things get murderously tense for a long silent minute while Rita fearfully calculates how much more this will cost than Uncle Sidney's wholesale daisies. Guess who surrenders? Guess who does Rita's flowers?

Rita's wedding, they estimate, will cost $3,000, or $50 a person. And that is for a mere buffet ($10-$20 a head), not the sit-down dinner ($15-$25). What her tip will be, in cash, to Mr. Ries, for his abiding help and taste, is hard to know; a gargantuan picnic can easily bring the banquet manager $500 from a grateful parent.

There is apparently no way to control the skyrocketing costs of the hotel wedding. As the good father cannot tell his guests to cool it with the drinking, so can he not ask them to leave after the standard four hours—just because it will cost him up to $250 for the room for each additional hour, plus hundreds more for the musicians. In some hotels he must use not only their florist but one of the few photographers and bands that management finds acceptable.

The need for spectacle, the urge to produce an unforgettable, knock-'em-dead extravanganza, has resulted in Jewish musical comedy—the *Goodbye, Columbus* wedding. What makes jollier sagas the morning after than an adventure in gross excess? Venetian gondolas floating down a Jewish swimming pool? Hilarious. Princesses materializing from cloud puffs? A howl. Chagall windows? The best. Hollywood does it on a huge screen and we adore the flamboyance, get high on the overdose. Why not, then, in real life?

Well, perhaps the jaded banquetman says it: "What bothers me most is looking at the thousands of dead flowers piled up the next day, waiting for the garbage man. It's such a damn incredible, astonishing waste. Such a waste."

CHAPTER 14

THE NEW WEDDING OR POWER TO THE PEOPLE

A rocky cliff overlooking the ocean in Big Sur, California, was the scene of the wedding of Ms. Myrna Schwartz of Beverly Hills to Mr. Foster DeWitt III, of Nob Hill in San Francisco. Ms. Schwartz, the daughter of renowned physician Dr. Harold Schwartz ("the brain surgeon of the stars," as he is popularly known), was, until her recent arrest for the attempted assassination of David Susskind, a student in business administration at Yale. Mr. DeWitt, otherwise known as "Eldridge," is a former student at Sarah Lawrence and the son of Foster Hubbard DeWitt II, president of United Oil, Steel, Motors, Steamship and Broadcasting Corporation of America.

The wedding, which took place at precisely 5:22 in the morning ("We want to commune with the sun, man—you know—birth, resurrection, the whole bit," articulated Mr. DeWitt), was what is today called a "New Wedding." The ceremony, performed by a defrocked priest, Father Patrick "Blow-em-up" O'Shea, had been created by the bride and groom and included readings from "Schizophrenia and Capitalist Society." Michael "Mao" MacGregor IV served as best man; Mrs. Irving Lipschitz, sister of the bride and president of the Scarsdale Radical Feminists, was matron of honor.

This wedding, which may or may not ever have happened, certainly *could* have happened and surely would have been hailed by the media as the style that is sweeping the country. Rumor and *Time* magazine to the contrary, the New Wedding is hardly an epidemic on the American scene. But, just as a crystal-spangled extravaganza at the Huntington Town House reflects the values of the folks giving it, so the New Wedding is an emblem of the youth counter-culture.

Almost. But not quite.

Illustration: Bergdorf Goodman devoted one of its front windows recently to a bride in an Indian crewel gown, wearing no shoes—the exactly correct costume for a New Wedding. It cost $500. Franklin Simon has opened a bridal salon entitled "The Barefoot Bride."

Further illustration: a very fashionable caterer of the Jewish horsey set in the suburbs of Chicago is publicizing his new service—elegant menus for the Hippie Wedding. The absolute divinest of vegetarian casseroles (eggplant and zucchini flown in from the ends of the earth) and homemade organic bread. Since silver service would simply be déclassé for the mod squad, he boasts a pantry of imported French country crockery on which to serve the darling nibbles.

Radical chic in action? Another cutesy-poo idea for a party when we've "done" the mariachi bit and the omelet maker and the whole lambs roasted on the spit and the soul food? Certainly, but let's not be confused. The New Wedding, in its pure form, is a very real—if still infant—metaphor of change in this country.

The New Wedding, like the counter-culture itself, is, in the main, a syndrome of children from the successful middle class. (One Boston minister reports most of his offbeat "cases" are kids from Ivy League schools who are in psychoanalysis.) The offspring of folks who have "made it" in our traditional American terms and in whose bosom bloodless revolution is tacitly permissible, and small rejections are understood not to rend the family fabric. The rebellion is against what the kids consider a dearth of values and values of the wrong kind. It is a rejection of plastic, of false emotion, of obsession with material things to validate who we are. In theory, the New Wedding is spontaneous, without artifice, and "personally relevant" (an expression that is used as often in this crowd as is "dearly beloved" in the black-tie set). Sometimes even in practice. It is often, this sort of pageant, moving and irresistible and indeed "personally relevant." Sometimes it is self-conscious and ludicrous. I have seen both.

The key word in the New Wedding is "meaningful," and what seems to be most "meaningful" to the new breed is the beauty of an outdoor setting. Beaches, hilltops, meadows. Free space. Serenity. The *Goodbye, Columbus* revelers spent $5,000 transforming the Plaza ballroom into a forest; these kids simply use the forest. And the setting naturally dictates the tone of the fete. One cannot quite summon up visions of haughty white-gloved waiters trooping through the sand dunes with silver trays of miniature quiche lorraine. Thus the New Weddings are natural and informal.

So is the food. Wine or even milk has killed off Jack Daniels, and the vittels are so virtuous as to make one pant for ravioli. Organic everything is the order of the day. Goat cheeses, soybean concoctions, stone-ground bread, One would kill for a knish. "The hardest thing for me to get used to in these new weddings," says one minister in San Francisco, "is how lousy the food is. The kids may like all this organic stuff, and I'm sure it's good for you, but I just can't face honey on *everything*."

(At a wedding on a hilltop outside Denver, an array of various salads was created and we guests commanded to eat with our fingers, right from the huge communal bowls. The only liquid available was a tragic blend of wine and beer.)

Since the New Wedding is, in spirit, a statement about who the bride and groom are, dress is often of the anything-goes school, and men—as a FIRST in wedding history—are encouraged to groove. I attended one dune-top frolic where the boy, clad in the smashingest getup of white satin bell-bottoms, white boots, and a balloon-sleeved silk shirt that didn't omit one color in the entire spectrum, received the awed gasps classically reserved for the bride. She, you see, was bedecked only in your ordinary white suede hooded monk's robe and was completely overshadowed.

A new wedding is an exercise in Do-It-Yourself. And not just for the bride, but also the guests, who are thought of as significant participants, instead of passive audience. One doesn't invite fringe people to this intimate day—none of Father's business accounts or Mother's bowling team will clutter *this* hilltop with indifference. Only true loved ones to share and care.

A prominent New York psychiatrist's son married the girl he had been living with for three years and the wedding consisted of an encounter group where the twenty-odd guests all sat on the floor in a circle and shared anecdotes from their own relationships with the couple, as a gift in understanding. Much hugging and crying and primal kissing took place, and it was remembered as "a beautiful ceremony."

On a beach in New Hampshire the minister encouraged the guests to express anything they felt about the bride and groom during the ceremony. The response was spontaneous, to be sure—one young woman burst forth with the news that she had always, until this moment, believed her friend had made a terrible choice and that the groom was a jerk, but she was beginning to change her mind.

The notion of Do-It-Yourself (with a little help from your friends) begins from the beginning—with the invitations. Sometimes they are in the form of a scroll, sometimes a mobile. They are generally hand-made and highly personal. "We have found ourselves in each other and want you to share the ceremony of commitment to our love," stated the hand-printed prelude to a classic new wedding held in Los Angeles' rustic Topanga Canyon. Linda, the bride, made her own white peasant dress and her groom's white pants festooned with yellow ribbons; she composed a song for the ceremony and together they wrote their vows; each of their friends contributed some organic tidbit to the feast, and folk dancing to the music of an Autoharp continued long into the night. "All the work that went into it," reminisces Linda, "was a true labor of love and we felt that the wedding expressed the feelings that all of us have for each other."

The conventional middle-class American wedding serves as a reconciliation—at least for one day—of disparate elements within the family. Folks who in normal life have nothing much to say to one another today somehow find a commonality. And the inevitable, inexorable war of the generations is called to a temporary cease-fire on this meeting ground. But the New Wedding stretches the parental/offspring generation gap into a continental divide. When I was in college the most defiant gesture I could make, the apex of rebellion against my background, was to date a black boy (who was then called a Negro). Today, I am told, what with liberal guilt, that act is no longer guaranteed to send a white Mother to the Nembutal. The announcement, however, that you are abandoning her lifetime plans for The Wedding and having a barefoot gypsy fest on a Big Sur rock will.

The most commonly seen denouement of the drama is that the folks relinquish, bitterly, and finally attend this peculiar happening. I would like to tell you that they get caught up in the spirit, groove on the jubilation and freedom, and ultimately understand and accept. Mostly, I am sorry to say, they do not. Mostly they hate every moment.

Not too long ago I attended a New Wedding in the woods of Malibu Canyon, just north of Los Angeles. Virginia and Ken, the couple, are in their early twenties and have lived together for about a year; he is a film editor and she works in a plant store; they are both from L.A. and Jewish. Although Virginia's family knows that she has been living with Ken, they still expected her to have a veritable Barnum and Bailey spectacular, and a great rift followed her declaration of wedding intentions. But tempers eased and now both sets of parents are present, along with a dozen or so close relations and fifty of the couple's friends.

One has to park the car at the bottom of a rolling grassy hill and walk for about half a mile. Lining the path and sitting poised in several trees are young friends playing soft rock tunes on flutes, guitars, and harmonicas. The scene is idyllically beautiful and the aura of open friendliness and joy is pure, untrammeled by the robot presence of banquet managers or the rigor mortis of etiquette edicts. I saunter up the hill, feeling the magic of the day, and almost immediately have my first confrontation of many with the generation chasm. Behind me the bride's Aunt Florence, wearing a pink brocade Hadassah gown, has caught the heel of her pink satin shoe in a tree root and now she wants to go home. I don't know whether I feel like laughing or sympathizing, so terror-stricken is she about this wedding.

But then, nothing that occurs this day bears any familiarity for Aunt

Florence. The bride does not march down an aisle; she is standing on the hill when we arrive, wearing a long peasanty dress made of patchwork tablecloths, no shoes, and a coronet of daffodils. Ken is splendid in orange-and-yellow-striped bell-bottoms and a fringed Apache vest and a matching daffodil headpiece. All the friends are dressed flamboyantly, exuberantly. Bare midriffs, leather shorts, gypsy wildnesses. The elders, of course, are in their spiffiest wedding finery.

People are talking, drinking wine, joints are being passed with some discretion (nobody hands one to Aunt Florence), and both sets of parents are trying, they are really trying—desperately. Soon a rabbi appears—one of the "hippie rabbis," as they are known around L.A., not because they themselves are hippies, but because they do this kind of wedding—and the joints are extinguished. (This cleric has insisted ahead of time that no pot smoking take place while he is on the premises.)

At some point everybody casually sits down on the grass (chairs have been provided for Aunt Florence, et al.) in a circle around Ken and Virginia and the rabbi, and easy rapping just sort of flows into the "ceremony." The rabbi recites some familiar lines from *The Prophet*: "Love one another but make not a bond of love. . . ."

Virginia speaks a Carl Sandburg poem, looking lovingly into Ken's eyes. Now, so far everything is terribly romantic and touching and even the elders are moved. After all, Ali and Ryan in *Love Story* read Elizabeth Barrett Browning to each other in their nuptials, so it must be sort of okay.

But then the recitation takes a turn away from the schmaltzy, a bizarre turn with Ken and Virginia together reciting the Fritz Perls "Gestalt Prayer": "I do my thing, and you do your thing./I am not in this world to live up to your expectations/And you are not in this world to live up to mine." The families start to glance around at each other in unspoken *you-see-I-knew-it* looks of anger.

Then something incredible happens, something awful, the coalescence of everybody's terrors of how this debauchery would turn out. Suddenly this strange ceremony—not even a word of Hebrew, or a "for better or worse"—suddenly it gets POLITICAL. Virginia stands up and reads from Emma Goldman on Woman's Suffrage, all about "asserting herself as a personality and not as a sex commodity" and "refusing to bear children, unless she wants them" and "refusing to be a servant to God, the State, society, the husband, the family. . . ." And the kids shout *"Right on, sister,"* and the family drops dead.

In ancient Jewish lore, when a girl marries a Gentile, she is declared dead by the father and, in effect, is treated as such forever. Virginia—I see by the faces of the judges—has just been pronounced a corpse.

The party following is jolly, with lots of group singing and folk dancing and the playing of games like Spin the Bottle and Pin the Tail on the Donkey, and an organic feast which includes homemade breads, the invariable honey-in-the-comb. The only incongruous note is the presence of a whole roast suckling pig, which reclines dead-center in the mélange of food—like a gigantic middle finger pointed upward.

The pig is just one more stab to the older generation, who have not yet recovered from Emma Goldman, and their rage and confusion suffuses the otherwise joyful ambiance. I am saddened by the real depths of the breach—they cannot step down off their chairs and the kids cannot understand or lessen their pain.

Mother tries hard throughout the day but finally falls apart, goes limp. I go over to her as she is sipping some rose-petal soup and it is as if she is in shock. "I don't know what to do here," she mourns, "and to tell you the truth, I don't really believe they're even married."

What the lady doesn't realize, of course, is that the New Wedding is a direct throwback to the past, to the style in which *everybody* got married before the entrance of the church and the caterer. All weddings took place outdoors, were cooperative ventures with the whole tribe or village sharing in the experience, the feast and gifts and decorations hand-wrought. The rebel youth, it appears, in their rejection of their parents' vision of The Good Life, have instinctively turned back to pure folklore, to a sense of the communal and a way that seems to them richer, more natural.

Undoubtedly, more New Weddings would take place if religion was more flexible. Most churches, however, are governed by rigid dogma from which individual clerics cannot swerve and for which reform comes slowly. But then the overwhelming majority of American kids, we know from statistics, *want* to be married in church or to have a sacramental service, even in a hotel. So the old ways carry on with little alteration.

The most radical changes have been in the Catholic Church where, since 1970, religious intermarriages can be performed at a Nuptial Mass, by both the Catholic priest and the minister of the other faith. Then, too, the non-Catholic no longer has to make formal promise to raise his children Catholic. For the ceremony, four choices of vows now exist and thirty different scriptural readings. The declaration of consent by the bride and groom becomes central, instead of the priest's interrogation, and fidelity is now for the first time an obligation of the husband as well as his wife.

For Reform and Conservative Jews, the wedding service is entirely a matter of custom. There is no ceremony which must be followed to the letter. Tradition dictates the key features—sipping of wine, Hebrew benedictions, the breaking of the glass. Among Orthodox Jews, a New Wedding is, of course, as likely as a B.L.T. on toast.

The fastest-growing church in America is one called the Metropolitan Community Church, in existence only since 1968 but already with branches in thirty-four cities. This new church, ministering to all Christian denominations, reflects another swelling social tide taking place today—the movement toward liberation and equality. Metropolitan Community Church is run for and by homosexuals.

When Troy Perry, a young Pentecostal minister in Florida, was expelled from the church for divorcing his wife of ten years and admitting he was gay ("Ministers believe you can't be gay and a Christian too," he says), he came to Los Angeles, placed an ad in the local homophile newspaper for a church service to be held in his home, to which twelve dubious individuals came and contributed a total of $4.18. He now commands a huge church building in Los Angeles, ten thousand members throughout the country, and says, "We would be even bigger if we could find enough gay ministers." (All of M.C.C.'s pastors were once establishment clerics—the Reverend Sandmire in San Francisco was a Mormon, the Chicago minister a High Anglican —and secret homosexuals.)

The function of this church is that of the gay liberation movement: to eliminate guilt, to lead homosexuals out from the closet and into the mainstream, to engender political change. In this new spirit of openness Perry and his fellow ministers have been performing an increasing number of marriage ceremonies between homosexuals.

In most states there are no laws against two people of the same sex marrying. But public feeling has thus far prevented all attempts of gay couples to marry in the eyes of the state. Where they have tested—that is, gone to City Hall and applied for a license—they have been rejected on the grounds of "tradition." In Kentucky, where the laws against sodomy have been invoked as prevention, a couple who had been refused a license went to the state Supreme Court and was again turned down.

As it is not legally recognized, and since none of the practical purposes for marriage apply—no children, no protection of property, no tax benefits (although the Reverend Perry says gay couples have been getting away with filing joint returns, "since the computer is not yet set up to differentiate between a straight and a gay tax form")—why do it? Why, in this day when lots of folks who *could* get married are choosing to live together instead, go through the motions of a mock wedding ceremony?

The answers are as complex as for any heterosexual twosome. For the Reverend Perry, a militant activist, it's political: "I want to be able to do anything that any other citizen of the United States can do, whether it's work for the government, or serve in the army, or get married." But most of his flock, including several with whom I've spoken, verbalize hungers for stability and respectability that clearly outweigh abstract concerns.

"The words 'we're married' take away some of the stigma of homosexuality, the belief that we're just promiscuous cruisers. At least with other gay people they do." Bob, who has spoken, is fingering an ornately carved gold wedding band, the twin of which is worn by Hank, sitting across the room. We are in their small apartment in Venice, California—a beach town noted for its huge homosexual population. They were married two weeks ago by the Reverend Perry in an urgent move to hold their affair together.

Bob and Hank are young, exceedingly attractive, and never unaware of that attractiveness in themselves and in each other. In their particular corner of the world, an affair that lasts a month is cause for flagwaving; most of their friends are unattached and "have" a remarkable average of ten different guys a week, wherein sex is fleeting, instantaneous, and singularly obsessive. The center of life is the gay bar, its *raison d'être* solely for making sexual connections, and its proliferation through Venice making it harder to avoid sex than to find it. "The guys in there don't care if you say you're in love with someone else," bemoans Hank, "even if they see the ring on your finger. They say, 'Oh, come on, it's just for the moment,' and you think, 'Why not, it's just for the moment.' After all, you don't have kids, no plans for the future, nothing to really tie you down or give you a sense of permanency."

So the ring becomes a chastity belt—enforced faithfulness when internal fortitude isn't enough. Like taping one's mouth with Band-Aids when on a diet.

When I recount this story to Pat and Jan, two women in their late twenties who are about to get married in a few weeks, they are slightly contemptuous—with that people-like-that-give-us-a-bad-name annoyance. They, by contrast, lead a quiet social life in which most of their friends are other gay couples who have been together for a while, are faithful to one another, and do not go to bars.

Pat and Jan are churchgoers, active members of M.C.C., and their wanting to be married stems from a desire to have their love blessed in the eyes of God. They are having a small, informal wedding, and neither of their families is being told. (Both of these women and Hank and Bob were heterosexual until their mid-twenties; two have been married heterosexually, and Bob has two children.)

Right after I meet with Pat and Jan, I attend a wedding of two women in the church sanctuary. Besides myself, there are only four guests in the cavernous room, two female couples both in the old-fashioned lesbian role-playing tradition: one member is "feminine," the other is a "butch" in men's garb.

As the ceremony begins, the minister (the Reverend Perry's assistant) enters in a long black robe, and from the side, appearing with customary groom's anonymity, two men enter, middle-aged, broad and swaggering. One wears a white cutaway, the other is in matching yellow. It is several minutes before I realize that they are both, in fact, women and that the person in white is the "groom."

The processional starts. A lady in long yellow chiffon, carrying a bouquet of carnations, steps stiffly up the aisle, trying to hold back the dam of tears that has just exploded and that will build to flood line by the end of the ten-minute service. She is the "bride's" mother. Following her in parade are a teen-ager—the bride's sister—and an aunt, both in flowing, graceful yellow gowns. It is obviously a very traditional wedding.

Then the organ strikes up "Here Comes the Bride." And down the aisle, on the arm of an elderly husky man in a tuxedo, floats an uncommonly beautiful, tiny angel in white lace. She cannot be one minute over seventeen and could easily be the winner of the Miss High School America contest. She is—astoundingly, bizarrely—the embodiment of the perfect fantasy American bride. Radiant, in love, as glowingly happy as any bride in America today. As she passes me, I suddenly realize that the man on whose arm she is leaning—the father about to give her away—is also a woman.

The wedding ceremony is the standard one from the *Book of Common Prayer*, with three alterations: "Do you, 'Jane,' take 'Mary' to be your wedded spouse" (instead of "husband" or "wife"); "I pronounce you married" (instead of "man and wife"); and "so long as you both shall live" is replaced by "as long as there's love."

As the newlyweds kiss with tenderness, Mama breaks into great heart-lurching sobs. I find myself more involved with the mother in her pain than with the couple, wishing that I could somehow explain to her what I cannot fully understand myself.

It is not, I think, the notion of homosexual marriage that shocks or even mystifies me particularly. It is the Gothic quality of the scene, the role playing—tragic and unnecessary aping of the "straight" world —the need to play "The Big Strong Man" and "The Little Woman" that saddens and appalls just as it saddens these days when enacted *in extremis* by men and women.

The bedrock of society shifts slowly, imperceptibly. But it does shift. What the homosexual wedding and the New Wedding express in common is the budding claim for Self, for dignity, and for alternatives. The one constant, in all of this, is our undying hunger for the wedding ritual. Even the New Wedding in its insistence on "personal relevance" is beginning already to fall into the predictable, repetitive mold of its conventional cousins: ho-hum, another sunrise ceremony in a cow pasture, yet another crunchy granola soufflé, yawn, those same old weary passages from *The Prophet* that we've heard at the last three weddings. In ten years will we have to reserve cow pastures six months in advance? And are the different drummers ultimately just banging out the same old beat?

That, as they say, remains to be seen.

THE BEST
AND THE
BRIGHTEST

A condensation of the book by

DAVID HALBERSTAM

A cold day in December. Long afterward, after the assassination and all the pain, the older man would remember with great clarity the young man's grace, his capacity to put a visitor at ease. He would remember the young man's good manners almost as clearly as the substance of their talk, though it was an important meeting.

In just a few weeks the young man would become President of the United States, and to the newspapermen standing outside his Georgetown house, there was an air of excitement about every small act, every gesture, every visitor to his temporary headquarters. They felt themselves a part of history; the old was going out, the new was coming in, and the new seemed exciting, promising.

On the threshold of great power and great office, the young man seemed to have everything. He was handsome, rich, charming, candid. The candor was part of the charm: he could beguile a visitor by admitting that everything the visitor proposed was right, rational, proper—but he couldn't do it, not this week, this month, this term. Now he was trying to put together a government, and the candor showed again. He was self-deprecating with the older man. He had spent the last five years, he said ruefully, running for office, and he did not know any real public officials, people to run a government, serious men. The only ones he knew, he admitted, were politicians, and if this seemed a denigration of his own kind, it was not altogether displeasing to the older man. Politicians were needed to run the government, but the world? What did they know about the Germans, the French, the Chinese? Experts were needed for that.

The older man was Robert A. Lovett, the symbolic expert, representative of the best of the breed, a great surviving link to a then unquestioned past, the Stimson-Marshall-Acheson war and postwar years.

He was the very embodiment of the Establishment, a man who had a sense of country rather than party. He was above petty divisions, so he could say of his friends, as so many of that group could, that he did not even know to which political party they belonged. He had been good, very good, going up on the Hill in the old days and soothing things over with recalcitrant Midwestern senators; and he was soft on nothing, that above all—no one would accuse Robert Lovett of being soft.

They got along well, these two men who had barely known each other before. Jack Kennedy the President-elect, who in his campaign had summoned the nation's idealism, but who was at least as skeptical as he was idealistic, preferring in private the tart and darker view of the world of a skeptic like Lovett.

In addition to his own misgivings he had constantly been warned by one of his more senior advisers that in order to deal with State effectively, he had to have a real man there, that State was filled with sissies in striped pants and worse. That senior adviser was Joseph Kennedy, Sr., and he had consistently pushed, in discussions with his son, the name of Robert Lovett, who he felt was the best of those old-time Wall Street people. For Robert Lovett understood power, where it resided, how to exercise it. He had exercised it all his life, yet he was curiously little known to the general public. The anonymity was not entirely by chance, for he was the embodiment of the public servant-financier who is so secure in his job, the value of it, his right to do it, that he does not need to seek publicity, to see his face on the cover of a magazine or on television, to feel reassured. He was the private man in the public society par excellence. The classic insider's man.

He was born in Huntsville, Texas, in 1895, the son of Robert Scott Lovett, a general counsel for Harriman's Union Pacific Railway, a power man in those rough and heady days, who eventually became a member of the Union Pacific board of directors and president of the railway. His son Bob would do all the right Eastern things, go to the right schools, join the right clubs (Hill School, Yale, Skull and Bones). In World War I he commanded the first United States Naval Air Squadron. He married well, Adele Brown, the beautiful daughter of James Brown, a senior partner in the great banking firm of Brown Brothers.

At Brown Brothers, starting at $1,080 a year, a fumbling-fingered young clerk, he rose to become a partner and finally helped to arrange the merger of Brown Brothers with the Harriman banking house to form the powerful firm of Brown Bros., Harriman & Co. So he came naturally to power, to running things, to knowing people, and his own marriage had connected him to the great families. His view of the world was a banker's view, the right men making the right decisions, stability to be preserved. The *status quo* was good, one did not question it.

He served the government overseas in London, gaining experience in foreign affairs. He saw the rise of Hitler and the coming military importance of air power; when he returned to America he played a major role in speeding up America's almost nonexistent air defenses. He served with great distinction during World War II, a member of that small inner group which worked for Secretary of War Henry Stimson and Chief of Staff George C. Marshall ("There are three people I cannot say no to," Lovett would say when asked back into government in the late forties, "Colonel Stimson, General Marshall, and my wife."). That small group of policy makers came from the great banking houses and law firms of New York and Boston. They knew one another, were linked to one another, and they guided America's national security in those years, men like James Forrestal, Douglas Dillon, and Allen Dulles. Stimson and then Marshall had been their great leaders, and although they had worked for Roosevelt, it was not because of him, but almost in spite of him; they had been linked more to Stimson than to Roosevelt. And they were linked more to Acheson and Lovett than to Truman. Though Acheson was always quick to praise Truman, there were those who believed that there was something unconsciously patronizing in Acheson's tones, his description of Truman as a great little man, and a sense that Acheson felt that much of Truman's greatness came from his willingness to listen to Acheson.

In 1947, after Acheson had resigned as Undersecretary of State, Marshall (who was then head of State) chose Robert Lovett as his successor, and in 1950 he became Secretary of Defense. Now as the sixties were about to begin, Lovett seemed to represent a particularly proud and successful tradition. For the private men felt they had succeeded admirably: they had taken a great dormant democracy, tuned it up for victory over Japan and Germany, stopped the Russian advance in Europe after the war, and rebuilt Western Europe under the plan whose very name was more meaningful to them than to most others. There was, given the can-do nature of Americans, a tendency on their part to take perhaps more credit than might be proper for the actual operation of the Marshall Plan, a belief that *they* and not the Europeans themselves had worked the wonders. Just as they had predicted, the

Russians proved untrustworthy and tried to expand in Europe, but Western democratic leadership had turned them back. They were not surprised that a cold war ensued. The lesson of history from Munich to Berlin was basic, they decided: one had to stand up, to be stern, to be tough.

The men of that era believed, to an uncommon degree, that their view of history had been confirmed; only a very few questioned it. One of their eggheads, George F. Kennan, became in the fifties increasingly disillusioned with the thrust of American policy, believing that those men had exaggerated Soviet intentions in Western Europe, and had similarly exaggerated their own role and NATO's role in stopping them. But Kennan was too much of an intellectual; he had been useful to them in the early part of the Cold War, but he became less useful as his own doubts grew. Besides, he was not a central member of their group—Lovett was.

So that cold December day Kennedy was lunching with a man who not only symbolized a group, the Establishment, and was a power broker who carried the proxies for the great law firms and financial institutions, but was also tied to a great and seemingly awesome era. If Kennedy, as he always did in that period, complained that he knew no experts, that was no problem; the Establishment had long lists, and it would be delighted to cooperate with this young President, help him along. It was of course above politics. More often than not it was Republican, though it hedged its bets. A few members were nominal if cautious Democrats, and some families were very good about it—the Bundy family had produced William for the Democrats and McGeorge for the Republicans—and it was believed that every major law firm should have at least one partner who was a Democrat.

Kennedy believed in the Establishment mystique; there had, after all, been little debunking of it in early 1960. Rarely had there been such a political consensus on foreign affairs: Communism was dangerous, there was of course the problem of getting foreign aid bills through Congress, which would help us keep the Third World from the Communists. Besides, he was young, and since his victory over Nixon was slimmer than he had expected, he needed the backing of this club, the elitists of the national security people. And he felt at ease with them: after Chester Bowles and Adlai Stevenson and all the other Democratic eggheads pushing their favorite causes, Lovett, who seemingly pushed no causes and had no ideology, was a relief.

The two took to each other immediately. When Kennedy asked

Lovett what the financial community thought of John Kenneth Galbraith's economic views (Galbraith being one of the President's earliest and strongest supporters), he was much amused when Lovett answered that the community thought he was a fine novelist. And when Lovett told Kennedy that he had not voted for him, Kennedy just grinned at the news, though he might have grinned somewhat less at Lovett's reason, which was Lovett's reservation about old Joe Kennedy. In a way, of course, this would have made Lovett all the more attractive, since much of the Kennedy family's thrust was motivated by the Irish desire to make these patricians, who had snubbed Joe Kennedy, reckon with his sons; this meeting was, if anything, part of the reckoning. ("Tell me," Rose Kennedy once asked a young and somewhat shocked aristocratic college classmate of Jack Kennedy's back in 1939 as she drove him from Hyannisport to Boston, "when are the good people of Boston going to accept us Irish?")

The meeting continued pleasantly, Caroline darting in and out, emphasizing to Lovett the youth and the enormity of the task before this man. Lovett had a feeling that he was taking too much of the President-elect's time, but he found that just the opposite was true. Kennedy tried hard to bring Lovett into the government, to take a job, any job. Lovett, who had not voted for Kennedy, could have State, Defense, or Treasury ("I think because I had been in both State and Defense he thought he was getting two men for the price of one," Lovett would later say). Lovett declined regretfully, explaining that he had been ill, bothered by severe ulcers, and each time after his last three government tours he had gone to the hospital. Now they had taken out part of his stomach, and he did not feel he was well enough to take on any of these jobs. Again Kennedy complained about his lack of knowledge of the right people, but Lovett told him not to worry, he and his friends would supply him with lists. Take Treasury, for instance—there Kennedy would want a man of national reputation, well known and respected by the banking houses. There were Henry Alexander at Morgan, and Jack McCloy at Chase, and Gene Black at the World Bank. Doug Dillon too. Lovett said he didn't know their politics. Well, he reconsidered, he knew McCloy was an independent Republican, and Dillon had served in a Republican Administration. At State, Kennedy wanted someone who would reassure European governments: they discussed names, and Lovett pushed, as would Dean Acheson, the name of someone little known to the voters, a young fellow who had been a particular favorite of General Marshall's—Dean Rusk over at Rockefeller. He handled himself there very well, said Lovett. The atmosphere was not unlike a college faculty, but Rusk handled the various cliques very well. A very sound man. Then a brief, gentle, and perhaps prophetic warning about State: the relations between a Secretary of State and his President are largely dependent upon the President. Acheson, Lovett said, had been very good because Truman gave him complete confidence.

Then they spoke of Defense. A glandular thing, Lovett said, a monstrosity. Even talking about it damaged a man's stomach. In Lovett's day there had been 150 staffmen, now there were—oh, how many? —20,000; an empire too great for any emperor. Kennedy asked what makes a good Secretary of Defense. "A healthy skepticism, a sense of values, and a sense of priorities," Lovett answered. "That and a good President, and he can't do much damage. Not that he can do much good, but he can't do that much damage." They discussed men of intelligence, men of hardware, men of the financial community, men of driving ambition. The best of them, said Lovett, was this young man at Ford, Robert McNamara. Lovett had worked with McNamara in government during the war, and he had been terrific: disciplined, with a great analytical ability, a great hunger for facts.

Then the meeting was over, and the young man guided the older man through the throng of waiting reporters, saying that he had asked Mr. Lovett to come have lunch with him to see if he could get him for State, Defense, or Treasury. Since it was cold and there were no taxis, Kennedy gave Lovett his own car and driver, having failed to give him State, Defense, or Treasury.

CHAPTER 2

K ennedy had decided early on to be his own Secretary of State, a decision which was much applauded, since he was obviously well read (followers of newspapers and magazines were regularly apprised of what he and Jacqueline were reading); he had served on the Senate Foreign Relations Committee (largely thanks to Lyndon Johnson, who did not so much want to put Kennedy on the committee as he wanted to keep Estes Kefauver *off*); and he was, in Washington terms, considered conversant with the great problems of the world.

This confidence in his ability had not always existed; indeed, Kennedy had not been a towering figure in Washington, one main reason being that since 1956 he had almost never been there, always dashing out of town, meeting delegates, in preparation for the 1960 campaign. Lyndon Johnson was considered a more formidable force, in part because he was highly visible, a definitive man of Washington who reveled in the city's intrigues, its power, whereas during much of the late fifties Jack Kennedy was a figure darting into the airport, sending an aide to the paperback-book counter to buy something for the trip, preferably history. There was a great Trevor-Roper phase in 1958, an aide remembered; one learned too little from fiction. But the 1960 campaign had changed his reputation in Washington. He had won the nomination and had been given the chance to run for the Presidency.

Sometime in the middle of the campaign he had hit his stride. Suddenly there was a new confidence in his speeches, even the timbre of his voice seemed to change. That harsh New England tone seemed to soften a little at the very same time that the nation began to find it distinctive and began to listen for it. He seemed to project a sense of destiny for himself and for his nation. Even Walter Lippmann sensed it; Lippmann, who more than any other man determined critical Washington's taste buds. He began to hail this young man, who as no one since Franklin Roosevelt had caught and stirred the imagination of the American people. Day after day, columns in this vein appeared until finally the *other* venerable columnist, Arthur Krock, stormed out of his office, smoke belching from his cigar, saying, "Well, I may be getting old and senile, but at least I don't fall in love with young boys like Walter Lippmann." But Lippmann and the rest of the Washington community had watched the 1960 campaign and approved; Richard Nixon had never been their particular favorite, to say the least. In Kennedy they had found a man worthy of the city, the job, the decade ahead. So when it became clear that he wanted to be his own Secretary of State, Washington did not dissent. The idea was appealing: a strong President towering over his Secretary of State, whoever he might be. But to an extraordinary degree the very process of that choice would mark what the Administration was, and what many of its more basic attitudes and compromises were.

Whoever else the Secretary was, it would not be Adlai Ewing Stevenson. Stevenson wanted the job, almost too much. He had played a historic role for his party, twice its Presidential candidate, the first time running against impossible odds in 1952, at the height of the Korean War and McCarthyism, with the party already decaying from the scandals of twenty years in power. Running against the great hero of an era, Dwight Eisenhower, Stevenson had lost, of course, but his voice had seemed special in that moment, a voice of rationality and elegance. In the process of defeat he had helped give the party a new vitality, bringing to its fold a whole new generation of educated Americans, some very professional amateurs who would be masterly used by the Kennedys in 1960. If Jack and Robert Kennedy seemed to symbolize style in politics, much of that was derived directly from Stevenson. He had, at a particularly low point for the party, managed to keep it vibrant and vital, and to involve a new kind of people in politics. The Kennedy brothers' gratitude for these offerings was limited. It was all right, they thought, to present an image as the citizen-leader rather than the politician who made deals, but it was dangerous to believe it yourself. The Kennedys regarded him as weak and lacking in toughness, despite the fact that the races against great odds in 1952 and 1956 might historically be viewed as acts of courage (similarly, Kennedy would regard him as soft during the Cuban missile crisis, although Stevenson consistently stood alone against an enormous onslaught of hard-line detractors). Stevenson, of course, had not named Jack Kennedy his running mate in 1956, but worse, he had opened the choice to the convention, which had made him seem indecisive.

Yet for all this, there were many times in 1960 when he could have been chosen Secretary of State. There were overtures letting him know that if he came aboard, State was his; the Kennedys knew he had a powerful hold over many articulate elements in the party, and though the primaries were going well, the nomination was not locked up by a long shot. Stevenson seemed crucial. He might block them at Los Angeles. Even as late as the day after the Oregon primary in May, the idea of State was still open, and Kennedy himself, visiting with Stevenson in Libertyville, Illinois, on his way back East from Portland, asked friends of Stevenson's if he should make the offer right then and there. The aides said no, they thought it would offend the governor at that moment. The next day, when Stevenson was apprised of the offer, he seemed more reluctant than ever to join the team. If the Kennedys thought him weak and indecisive, he in turn thought them arrogant and aggressive ("That young man" he would tell friends of Jack Kennedy's, "he never says please, he never says thank you, he never asks for things, he demands them."). Yet the offer stayed open through Los Angeles, though it closed there; the Kennedys found they could do without him, and his due bills evaporated overnight.

Even though Stevenson had not played their game, he was hoping, long after the convention was over, that he would get State; he believed himself best qualified. So when Kennedy offered him the post of ambassador to the United Nations, he was appalled. He would not take it, he said privately, it was an insult, he had had that job before. "What will you do if you don't come aboard?" an old friend asked him. "What I've been doing all along," he answered. "And have your speeches printed on page forty-seven of *The New York Times*?" the friend said.

Kennedy was annoyed by Stevenson's refusal to accept the offer immediately. He had decided upon Rusk as Secretary and asked Rusk to call Stevenson. Kennedy took no small amount of pleasure in recounting to friends how Rusk had hooked Stevenson. "Adlai," Rusk had said, "the President has asked me to take this job and it is a sacrifice, but I have decided I cannot refuse. I cannot say no. I feel all of us have a loyalty greater than our own interests. We need you, the country needs you. I hope you will serve as he has asked you to serve." In retelling the story to friends, Kennedy would chuckle and say, "I think old Adlai was really impressed."

There was an aura of thinly veiled contempt toward Stevenson at the White House; he was someone to take Jackie to the theater. It was all a humiliating experience. It was not surprising that in early 1964 Stevenson began to praise Lyndon Johnson extravagantly. "We have a great President now," he told a friend in Washington. The friend was somewhat surprised, since the Stevenson-Johnson friendship had never been that close. But as Stevenson described his meeting with Johnson, it soon became clear why he was so enthusiastic: as soon as he had walked into the President's office, the latter had risen, pointed to his chair, and said, "Governor, by all rights you should be sitting in this chair and in this office."

But Kennedy wanted to be his own Secretary of State, and above all he did not want a Secretary who already had a constituency worthy of a President, rather he wanted Stevenson's constituency, both here and abroad. Kennedy knew that he could not really perform as a President until he had taken Stevenson's people away from him. This he proceeded to do with stunning quickness, depending more on style and grace than policies. Nonetheless, when Stevenson died in 1965, a year and a half after Kennedy, he seemed a forlorn and forgotten figure, humiliated by his final years; his people mourned the loss of Kennedy more than of Stevenson. It would only be later, as the full tragedy of the Vietnam war unfolded and a Stevenson disciple named Eugene McCarthy challenged Johnson, as humanist values seemed to be resurgent and regenerative against the rationalist values, and the liberal community looked back to see where it had gone wrong, that Stevenson would regain his constituency. Posthumously.

So it would not be Stevenson. Nor J. William Fulbright, whom Kennedy had worked with on the Senate Foreign Relations Committee. Fulbright impressed him—the intelligence, the range, the respect he commanded on the Hill as the resident intellectual. They had worked well together, even though Kennedy had not been the most diligent member of the committee. On the rare occasions when he was present, he seemed to spend much of his time autographing photos of himself which were to be sent out to fervent young admirers. To Fulbright's credit was the fact that his constituency was the Hill rather than the New York intellectual world, so that his coming aboard would be an asset rather than a liability, as in the case of Stevenson. But there was the problem of Fulbright's position; he was chairman of the committee, and thus could do Kennedy and his policies a great deal of good sitting right where he was.

Nor would it be McGeorge Bundy. Walter Lippmann and others were pushing him for high jobs, and Kennedy, listening to their recommendations, had thought, well, if he was that good, why not State itself? Bundy's credentials were impeccable; he had support from the intellectual community, if not by dint of articles or books, at least by virtue of standing. He had taken no wrong positions, he was not soft, and though he was a Republican, even this could be dealt with. For a time Kennedy considered him for State, and flying down to Palm Beach right after John, Jr., was born, he told a group of trusted reporters that State was still a problem. He didn't know what he was going to do, but he wished he could make Bundy Secretary of State. "Why can't you?" asked Sander Vanocur, one of the pool reporters. "Because he's too young. It's bad enough that I'm that young, but if there's a Secretary of State that young it'll be too much. Besides, he's a Republican and Adlai will never serve under him." Which was true. Stevenson might bury his disappointment about not getting State and might serve in the Department, but he had demanded at least some say in the choice of his boss. He had retained, if nothing else, something of a veto power. This he used against McGeorge Bundy, brilliant intellectual, great liberal, who had voted for Tom Dewey over Harry Truman, and twice for Dwight Eisenhower over Adlai Stevenson. If there were limits to Bundy's liberalism, there were also limits to Stevenson's tolerance.

Nor, finally, David K. E. Bruce—rich, patrician, the classic diplomat, his assets including a very wealthy wife. He had haunted the great chambers of Europe for two decades, a man with a great sense of where power was and how to deal with it. He was well connected in the Democratic party hierarchy, in part because of many generous past contributions. Against Bruce was his age, sixty-two, which made him almost twenty years older than the President he would serve. Nor was he helped by his own close ties with Stevenson; Kennedy had heard that Bruce's wife had burst into tears when Kennedy had been nominated at Los Angeles.

What it came down to was a search not for the most talent, the greatest brilliance, but for the fewest black marks. The man who had made the fewest enemies in an era when forceful men espousing good causes had made many enemies: the Kennedys were looking for someone who made very small waves. They were looking for a man to fill the most important Cabinet post, a job requiring infinite qualities of intelligence, wisdom, and sophistication, a knowledge of both this country and the world, and they were going at it as Presidential candidates had often filled that other most crucial post, the Vice Presidency, by choosing someone who had offended the fewest people. Everybody's number-two choice. Thus their choice would be determined by neither talent nor brilliance, but to a degree by mediocrity. It was a sign of the extent to which the power of the Presidency had grown that this was applauded in many quarters. That the man they turned to was virtually unknown was revealing in itself, for if he had really done anything significant in his career, then he would have a record, for better or for worse.

Dean Rusk. He was everybody's number two. At the height of the selection process, Kennedy had turned to Chester Bowles and said, "If you were Secretary of State, what kind of organization would you set up?" Bowles, who was on the board of the Rockefeller Foundation, had answered that he would begin by naming Dean Rusk Undersecretary. "Dean Rusk?" Kennedy said. "Isn't he the head of the Rockefeller Foundation?"

Everyone spoke well of him. Good qualities. Hard working. Patient. Balanced. Steady. A good diplomat. Lovett admired him. Acheson, the Secretary of State emeritus, put in a strong word: Rusk had been loyal and reliable. Fulbright spoke well of him, a fellow Southerner and a fellow Rhodes scholar. Everyone spoke well of Rusk, for he was always courteous, hard working, and thoughtful. Only one person, McGeorge Bundy, was strongly opposed to Rusk. They had met several times when Bundy was the dean of Harvard and Rusk ran the Rockefeller Foundation and held the purse strings. Bundy did not like Rusk (the Rusks of the world do not, except under extreme provocation, permit themselves the luxury of liking or disliking; God did not create public servants for the purpose of liking or disliking) and had decided that there was something missing, something second rate. Kennedy's future adviser on national security affairs cast a vote against Rusk, but it was not that important, anyway, since Bundy would be working in the White House and not at State.

And so Dean Rusk slowly sidled into the prime position. Rusk was a quiet man of enormous self-control, his ambition carefully masked. It did not flash naked for all to see like a Bundy's or McNamara's, but it was there nonetheless. He had campaigned for the job cautiously in his own veiled way; through the Establishment's channels he had sent up a few cautious signals to acknowledge that he was, well, available. He had taken Bowles aside so that Bowles could tell the Kennedys that Rusk had been working for them up there in Scarsdale. Though he was not known for his published work, he had published an article, a rare act indeed, in *Foreign Affairs*, the official journal of the Council on Foreign Relations, which was not given to turning down articles by heads of major foundations. The article, which was not entirely by chance published in the spring of 1960, dealt with the role of the Secretary of State. It called for the President to make a lot of decisions in foreign affairs and for the Secretary to travel less (no Secretary would travel as widely as Rusk). Similarly, Rusk had, just by chance, a willing citizen duly concerned, written a letter to the President-elect, dated November 22, 1960, on the subject of the electoral college, which also said that the President should work to heal racial scars ("As a Georgia-born citizen who believes that the Supreme Court decision on integration was long overdue. . . ." the letter began). There seemed to be a mild element of lobbying.

Thus the coming of Dean Rusk. One pictures the process. The Establishment peers sit around and ponder who its candidates should be. Slowly, varying possibilities are checked off. Most of the best known are too old or are not Democrats. And finally the name that comes to the fore is Dean Rusk, a man who is nominally a Democrat (he holds his job at the Foundation not so much through the courtesy of the Rockefellers as through John Foster Dulles, who got it for him). Knows the military, knows strategy, plays the game. So, quietly, the campaign for Rusk was put together and his qualifications tallied: not too young, not too old; a Democrat, but not too much of one;

a Southerner, but not too much so; an intellectual, but not too much so; worked on China, but no problems on that—in fact, good marks from the Luce people, who watch the China thing carefully. The acceptable man.

The Kennedy investigation into Rusk was marginal. There were a few phone calls, one from Richard Goodwin, a bright young man on the White House staff, to a reporter who had served in the China-Burma-India theater, a vast area which had contained the then Colonel Rusk. What about Rusk? Well, he was considered a good guy out there, not making enemies with the British like Stilwell, soothing tempers when Stilwell ruffled them, but he disapproved of the way the British treated the wogs. And he had a slight reputation as a ladies' man. "Great, Kennedy will love that." The first and last hint of Dean Rusk the swinger. An enigmatic figure before entering the government, he was to be an enigmatic figure during it.

By chance, Rusk happened to be with Bowles at a Rockefeller Foundation meeting in Williamsburg when he got his call from Kennedy.

"What do you think he wants to talk to me about?" he asked Bowles in a note.

"He's going to ask you to become Secretary of State," Bowles wrote in answer.

Rusk met with Kennedy the next day and later phoned Bowles. "Forget it," said Rusk. "If the idea of my being Secretary of State ever entered his mind, it's dead now. We couldn't talk to each other. It's all over."

"I doubt it," said Bowles.

They were both right.

After Rusk had been offered the post as Secretary of State, he retained one doubt about accepting, which was financial. Unlike most good Establishment candidates, he had no resources of his own, neither by inheritance nor by dint of working in a great law firm for six figures a year. Rusk mentioned this problem to Averell Harriman, and while it was not a situation which Harriman had ever faced personally, he enjoined Rusk not to worry. "For God's sake, man, when you leave State you'll be overwhelmed with offers, you'll be rich." But Lovett was aware of the financial problem, and he moved quickly to bolster Rusk's position. Rusk, he said, was entitled to some termination allowance in view of accrued pension rights which he would abandon by leaving the Foundation. A very generous settlement was made, and sped by both the Establishment's connections and resources, Rusk left for Washington.

On being told that Chester Bowles would be his Undersecretary, Rusk had said again and again how pleased he was with the news. Not surprisingly, a Rusk-Bowles relationship never developed. When they did communicate it was not always happily (when Bowles returned from Southeast Asia in 1962 and suggested the neutralization of Vietnam, Rusk turned to him, quite surprised, and said, "You realize, of course, you're spouting the Communist line"). It ended very badly, with Bowles being driven from the Department with no small amount of humiliation involved. One attempt to fire him failed. The second attempt, in the reorganization of the State Department late in 1961 (which subsequently became known as the "Thanksgiving Day Massacre"), was a bit more successful, though just as messy, Rusk telling Bowles that he hated to do it, but that Kennedy was behind it, and Kennedy telling Bowles he hated to do it, but Rusk was behind it. Bowles was shifted to a meaningless post at the White House and eventually to his second tour as ambassador to India, an ideal place in the eyes of the Kennedys, since he could listen to the Indians and they to him. He served once again with distinction, and when he retired in 1969 a small group of old friends and enemies gathered at the State Department to bid him farewell. The last toast was proposed by Dean Rusk, in a speech of extraordinary grace in which he talked about Bowles' constant, relentless youth, the freshness of his mind, and the fact that he had more ideas in a day than most people have in a year.

The Kennedy years, which were so glittering for everyone else, were a time of considerable pain for Rusk; more than any other senior official he was not on the Kennedy wavelength. There was no intimacy; the President never called him by his first name as he did the other senior officials. The Washington rumormongers, who sensed these nuances with their own special radar, soon turned on him. They claimed that Rusk would go, a rumor mill fed by Kennedy's own private remarks reflecting doubt upon the Secretary. Even today the photographs of that era bear testimony to the incompatibility: the Kennedy people standing at attention waiting for some foreign visitors, all young and flashy, and Rusk—surprisingly tall—and his wife, both dowdy and older and more tired, looking like the representatives of a previous Administration, or perhaps simply the chaperons at the party. There was other, subtler evidence too: Jackie Kennedy's intimate, graceful letter to Ros Gilpatric, thanking him for a book of beautiful poems and mocking the idea that a gift of such rare sensitivity might have come from "Antonio Celebrezze or Dean Rusk."

The Kennedy-Rusk relationship failed on more serious levels. Rusk, who always did things through channels and by the book, was never able to adjust to the freewheeling, deliberately disorganized Kennedy system. In almost every sense the relationship was exactly what Lovett had warned Kennedy that it should not be. Years later, as the war progressed and Rusk seemed to many of the Kennedy people a betrayer of the Kennedy dream, he would be attacked by the very people who had praised the brilliance of the Kennedy selection process. There could be no one to blame but the President himself, and those who had applauded the idea of the weak Secretary of State had gotten what they wanted and deserved. Those years would show, in the American system, how when a question of the use of force arose in government, the advocates of force were always better organized and seemed to have both logic and fear on their side, and that in fending them off, a President would need all the help he possibly could get, not the least of which should be a powerful Secretary of State.

Thus had the liberals lost the important job in the Administration, though of course they could never admit this. In the main literature of the era (Schlesinger, Sorensen), there is no note of how Kennedy manipulated the liberals and moved for the center, partly because of a desire to see the Kennedy Administration as they would have it, and partly to claim Kennedy for history as liberal.

CHAPTER 3

It was a glittering time. They literally swept into office, generating their style, their confidence—they were going to get America moving again. There was no time to wait, history did not permit that luxury. Everyone was going to Washington, and the word went out quickly around the Eastern universities and political clubs that the best men were going to Washington. The challenge awaited and these men did not doubt their capacity to answer it. Even the campaign quote of Jack Kennedy seemed to keynote it. He had used it again and again, moving swiftly through small towns in the New Hampshire winter, closing each speech with the quote from Robert Frost: ". . . But I have promises to keep, And miles to go before I sleep, And miles to go before I sleep." History summoned them, it summoned us: there was little time to lose.

We seemed about to enter an Olympian age in this country, brains and intellect harnessed to great force, the better to define a common good. It seems long ago now, that excitement which swept through the country, or at least the intellectual reaches of it, that feeling that America was going to change, that the government had been handed down from the tired, flabby chamber-of-commerce mentality of the Eisenhower years to the best and brightest of a generation.

The new Kennedy men were tough—"hard-nosed realists" was a phrase often used to define them, a description they themselves had selected. They had good war records; they were fond of pointing out that they were the generation which had fought the war, that they had been the company commanders, had borne the brunt of the war and lost their comrades. This gave them special preparation for the job ahead; it was the company commanders replacing the generals, and even here was seen virtue. Actually, most of it was a myth. It was Walt W. Rostow, Bundy's deputy, who had made this point, and typically, he had not been a company commander—he had picked bombing targets in Europe. Rusk had been a staff colonel in the service; Robert McNamara had been a semicivilian doing statistics in the War Department; McGeorge Bundy had been an aide to a family friend who was an admiral (of the top people in national security, only the President had a distinguished war record). But their image was of virility; they played squash and handball to stay in shape, wrote books and won prizes (even the President had won a Pulitzer Prize), climbed mountains to clear their minds.

Day after day we read about them, each new man more brilliant than the last. The social columns of the major newspapers were closely read to find out who went to which cocktail party. We soon found out, however, that they did not go to many cocktail parties. They didn't have time for idle chitchat.

The President himself was of course the object of the greatest fascination, and we craved details on what he read, what he ate, where he and Jackie went; all of that was news, and started, or ended, trends. It caused James MacGregor Burns to write with some irritation:

He is not only the handsomest, the best dressed, the most articulate, and graceful as a gazelle. He is omniscient; he swallows and digests whole books in minutes; his eye seizes instantly on the crucial point of a long memorandum; he confounds experts with superior knowledge of their field. He is omnipresent; no sleepy staff member can be sure that he will not telephone—or pop in; every hostess at a party can hope that he will. He is omnipotent; he personally bosses and spurs the whole shop; he has no need of Ike's staff apparatus; he is more than a lion, more than a fox. He's Superman!

McNamara, Bundy, Rostow, Arthur Schlesinger, Sargent Shriver. Did they need a Texan? Everyone who met Bill Moyers came away impressed—a Kennedy-style Texan, with perhaps too much of the Bible in him, but that would change. A general? They had Maxwell Taylor, a *good* general, soldier-statesman, an intellectual who had written a book. They said he had resigned in the Eisenhower years in protest against the archaic defense policies, but they were wrong —he had retired after serving the full four years, and then he had written his book. But the book was so critical that it seemed as if he had resigned—a small but important difference which went unnoticed at the time.

It was an extraordinary confluence of time and men, and many people in the know quoted Lyndon Johnson's reaction to them at the first Cabinet meeting. He, the outsider, like us, looked at them with a certain awe, which was no wonder, since they had forgotten to invite him to the meeting, until the last minute. They were all so glamorous and bright, but the one who impressed him the most was "the fellow from Ford with the Stacomb on his hair." The fellow from Ford with the Stacomb on his hair! A terrific line, because it once again delineated Johnson, who, Vice President or no, seemed more a part of the Eisenhower era than this one. What was not so widely quoted in Washington (which was a shame because it was a far more prophetic comment) was the reaction of Lyndon's great friend Sam Rayburn to Johnson's enthusiasm about the new men. Stunned by their glamour and intellect, he had rushed back to tell Rayburn, his great and crafty mentor, about how brilliant each was, that fellow Bundy from Harvard, Rusk from Rockefeller, McNamara from Ford. On he went, naming them all. "Well, Lyndon, you may be right and they may be every bit as intelligent as you say," said Rayburn, "but I'd feel a whole lot better if just one of them had run for sheriff once."

So they carried with them an exciting sense of American elitism, a sense that the best men had been summoned forth from the country to harness this dream to a new American nationalism, bringing a new, strong, dynamic spirit to our historic role in world affairs. It was heady stuff, defining the American dream and giving it a new sense of purpose. Not everyone, of course, was stirred by it. There were intellectuals who felt a more modest, limited sense about their own nation and its possibilities.

In 1961, when the Kennedy team was already on board and there was great enthusiasm over the new theories of counterinsurgency and

Vietnam had been chosen as a testing ground, David Riesman, the Harvard sociologist, had lunch with two of the more distinguished social scientists in the Kennedy government. On the subject of Vietnam the others talked about limited war with the combativeness which marked that particular era, about the possibilities of it, about the American right to practice it, about the very excitement of participating in it. Riesman became more and more upset with the tone and the direction of the conversation, until finally he stopped them and asked if they had ever been to Utah. *Utah!* No, they said, not Utah, but why Utah, had Riesman ever been there? No, Riesman answered, but he had read a great deal about the Church of the Latter-Day Saints, and it occurred to him that his friends did not know much about America, about how deep the evangelical streak was. "You all think you can manage limited wars and that you're dealing with an elite society which is just waiting for your leadership. It's not that way at all," he said. "It's not an Eastern elite society run for Harvard and the Council on Foreign Relations."

He left them after lunch, uneasy about the direction the country was taking. He had made a hobby of studying the American Civil War, and he had always been disturbed by the passions which it had unleashed in the country, the tensions and angers just below the surface, the thin fabric of the society which held it all together, so easy to rend.

It was only natural that the intellectuals who questioned the necessity of American purpose did not rush from Cambridge and New Haven to inflict their doubts about American power and goals upon the nation's policies. So people like Riesman, classic intellectuals, stayed where they were while the new breed of thinkers-doers made the trip, not doubting for a moment the validity of their right to serve, the quality of their experience. They were men who reflected the post-Munich, post-McCarthy pragmatism of the age. One had to stop totalitarianism, and since the only thing the totalitarians understood was force, one had to be willing to use force. They justified each decision to use power by their own conviction that the Communists were worse, which justified our dirty tricks, our toughness.

Among those who felt that way was Walt Whitman Rostow, who had authored one of the best of the campaign phrases—"Let's get this country moving again"—and he was now safely ensconced in the White House. Kennedy had intended to funnel him to State, but Rusk, who had accepted most of Kennedy's other appointees, had finally put his foot down. He found Rostow particularly irritating—this verbose, theoretical man who intended to make all his theories work. So Rostow was shifted to the White House, under McGeorge Bundy.

Bundy, the former dean of Harvard College, had been made Special Assistant to the President for National Security Affairs. By the force of his personality, intelligence, and great and almost relentless instinct for power, he was to create a domain which by the end of the decade would first rival and then surpass the State Department in influence. Since his support of Kennedy during the campaign had been somewhat less active than other professors', and though he was not a great admirer of Rostow, he quickly paid a debt to Kennedy by adding Rostow to the White House staff, sure that he could handle him there.

For there was no doubt in Bundy's mind about his ability to handle not just Rostow, and the job, but the world. He was the brightest light in that glittering constellation around the President, for if those years had any central theme, if there was anything that bound the men, their followers, and their subordinates together, it was the belief that sheer intelligence and rationality could answer and solve anything. If this was the quality of the young President, then no one else exemplified it more than Bundy.

Bundy was a man of applied intelligence, a man who would not land us in trouble by passion and emotion. He was an aristocrat, a Brahmin, and yet he had gone beyond that closed little arena to play in a larger sphere. He had been a legend in his time at Groton, the brightest boy at Yale, dean of Harvard College at a precocious age, and perilously close to being president of it ("*Sic transit gloria Bundy*," quipped the classicist John Finley when Nathan Pusey was chosen). The early Washington years seemed to confirm the Bundy legend. He was at the center of things, darting in and out of the President's office. He was a Kennedy favorite, that was clear, and in 1962, when he was offered the presidency of Yale (a job which might have tempted him in another time, and which eventually went to his close friend Kingman Brewster), Kennedy was, there is no other word for it, effusive about not losing him. In a rare show of emotion, Kennedy declared that the possibility of Bundy's leaving the White House was *out of the question*.

He was above self-interest, as others, politicians, labor leaders, Negro leaders, were not. In contrast to the austere quality of his work style, he was considered charming at dinner parties, and people marveled at the difference between the professional Bundy and the social Bundy. He was all steel and drive and work, the smile was hard, almost frozen, and at times there seemed to be a certain cruelty about

him, the rich, bright kid putting down the inferior. When in 1961
Daniel Ellsberg at Defense discovered that the Joint Chiefs of Staff
had a war plan, which told how they would go to war, and more
important, that they had carefully hidden this fact from civilians,
including among others the Secretary of Defense, he was dispatched
to the White House by his superiors to inform Bundy. Feeling that
the manner in which he had uncovered the plan and the secrecy
around it were almost as significant as the plan itself, Ellsberg began
by trying to explain how he had come across it. Bundy quickly snapped,
"Is this a briefing or is it a confessional?" It was the kind of put-down
that many others in the government would feel, and thus in later
years, when Bundy began to develop his problems and his reputation
slipped, there was a surprising number of people who took no small
pleasure in it.

Yet these stories would surface later; if one was put down by Mac
Bundy in those days, he did not boast about it. That would have
been a sign of being on the outside, for Bundy was a favorite of that
predominantly liberal part of Washington which sets the tone of the
city, deciding who is in and who is out, who has power and who
does not. He made himself accessible to the right elements of the
press, columnists linked with the establishment, such as James Reston
or Joseph Alsop. That this small segment of the press did not constitute
the press itself did not bother him, and some of the newer journalists
like Sander Vanocur, the White House correspondent for NBC, complained regularly that Bundy snubbed reporters representing such
proletarian outlets as the National Broadcasting Company.

Men like Vanocur did not come to love Bundy at all, and there
was a feeling of many in Washington that Bundy was in all his dealings
too much the elitist. But even here, he was a cool operator who held
most of the press at bay, and yet at the same time saw his reputation
grow, so that at the height of those years, just before it all began
to sour, Joseph Kraft, one of the best political writers in America,
a taste maker himself and Bundy's kind of columnist, would in an
article declare him a fit subject for Milton's words:

> A Pillar of State; deep on his
>   Front engraven
> Deliberation sat, and publick care;
>   And princely counsel in his face . . .

That, of course, was the high point, written in the summer of 1965
and published in the fall. By then the war was deepening, and the

doyens of the Establishment were already losing control. Only a few years later, Kingman Brewster, the president of Yale, was to make a different assessment of his friend. "Mac," said Brewster, "is going to spend the rest of his life trying to justify his mistakes on Vietnam."

Bundy is from Boston. The rest of the world which is not from Boston thinks of him as being very Boston and the name as being very Boston. This is not true, since the Bundys are from Grand Rapids, Michigan, and by Boston standards he is not a Bundy but a Lowell, on his mother's side. Katharine Bundy is also a Putnam, which by Boston standards is very good too, but the pedigree is on the Lowell side, as is much of the determination and the drive. The family descended from Percival Lowle, who came to America in 1639 and sired a great family which became noted for its inventiveness, shrewdness, industry, its success and, by the nineteenth century, its dominance of Harvard College and the New England textile mills. A crusading minister of the 1840's, Theodore Parker, wrote of the Lowells and the other first families of fortune: "This class is the controlling one in politics. It mainly enacts the laws of this state and the nation; makes them serve its turn. . . . It can manufacture governors, senators, judges to suit its purposes as easily as it can manufacture cotton cloth." They were also families which had a fine sense of protecting their own position, and they were notorious for giving large grants to Harvard College, which was *their* college, and just as notorious for doing very little for public education.

John Amory Lowell, the great-great-grandfather of McGeorge Bundy, was a towering figure of his era in Boston, having picked no fewer than six presidents of Harvard. Augustus Lowell, his son, increased his share of the family inheritance six or seven times, and in addition produced a remarkable family even by the standards of a Lowell: Amy Lowell the poet, A. Lawrence Lowell the educator, and Percival Lowell the astronomer. The fourth child was Elizabeth Lowell, who married William Putnam and gave birth to Katharine Lawrence Putnam, who later married Harvey Hollister Bundy.

"Mother never forgot for a minute that she was a Lowell," Bundy's sister, Mrs. G. Andelot Belin, wife of a Boston lawyer, said to reporter Milton Viorst. "She was one of those people who believed that there are three classes in society—upper, middle, and lower—and you know which one she belonged to. We sometimes kidded her about it, but it was assumed in the family that none of us would want to become bus drivers." Mrs. Belin added, "We were a noisy family, and Mother was the noisiest among us. For her, things were black and white. It's an outlook that descends directly from the Puritans and we all have it. But Mac has it more than the rest of us."

By contrast Harvey Hollister Bundy was a mild, reserved figure. A friend spoke of him as being a "Bostonian not born in Boston. Coming from the Midwest, he surprised those who supposed that rigid adherence to principle is an exclusive Boston characteristic. . . ."

Harvey Bundy graduated from Yale in 1909 with high honors, and was later first in his class at Harvard Law, an achievement which brought him an appointment as law clerk to Oliver Wendell Holmes. He returned to Boston in 1915 and here the Lowell connections did not hurt. In Boston in those days one of the chief industries was taking the vast fortunes of the great families and turning them into trust funds in order to avoid taxes, and Harvey Bundy became the lawyer for many of them. A few years later he also became a close friend and confidant of Henry Stimson's, "Colonel Stimson" as he liked to be known after he reached that rank in World War I. Stimson had been very close to Teddy Roosevelt, and at Roosevelt's urging even ran (unsuccessfully) for governor of New York in 1910, served under Taft as Secretary of War in 1911 as a Taft gesture to the Roosevelt wing, though when the 1912 split came, he stayed loyal to Taft. Stimson was firmly linked to the tradition of Teddy Roosevelt: an aristocracy come to power, convinced of its own disinterested quality, believing itself above both petty partisan interest and material greed. The suggestion that this also meant the holding and wielding of power was judged offensive by these same people, who preferred to view their role as service. ("First-generation millionaires," Garry Wills wrote in *Nixon Agonistes*, "give us libraries, second-generation millionaires give us themselves.")

Harvey Bundy was typical of this era. He served Stimson loyally as an aide when he was Hoover's Secretary of State. In Stimson's opinion Franklin Roosevelt, running for the Presidency in 1932, was an untried and untested figure, and Stimson found the general public antagonism toward Hoover surprising, though he noted that "the people of sobriety and intelligence and responsibility" were on Hoover's side. He would eventually meet with Roosevelt and find to his surprise that the new President was intelligent and competent, and a few years later, when Roosevelt was in the subtle process of preparing the country for European intervention, he brought Stimson back to the government as Secretary of War, since Stimson was a strong and forceful advocate of preparedness. ("In our house," Bill

Bundy, Mac's brother, once noted, referring to the Stimson tie, "the State Department and the Pentagon were interchangeable," a comment not just about his family but about an era, which he himself would confirm in 1964 by moving from a job as Assistant Secretary of Defense and taking a comparable one at State.)

As Secretary of War, Stimson worked with Frank Knox, who was Secretary of the Navy, a man who had been a friend for more than twenty-five years, since he had first shown up in Stimson's office with an introductory note from Teddy Roosevelt saying: "He is just our type!" At War, Stimson's first assistant was Robert Patterson, and after him came John McCloy, Robert Lovett, and Harvey Bundy.

The Stimsonian tradition of public service and power, and the Stimsonian philosophy of preparedness and force, had made a deep mark on the Bundy household; it is Stimson's photograph which sits on Bundy's desk to this day. After the war, when Stimson decided to publish his memoirs and wanted some help, he naturally chose as his literary aide McGeorge Bundy, the bright and ambitious son of his friend Harvey Bundy; together they produced his biography, *On Active Service in Peace and War.*

The Bundy youth was not unlike that of the Kennedys in some respects; lots of children everywhere, lots of intellectual and physical competition. There were violent games of their own lawn sport, a somewhat more physical form of croquet, with Mrs. Bundy leading the pack. According to friends of the family, she seemed to center her hopes on Bill, two years older than Mac; in fact, some of Mac's old friends attribute his intense drive and competitiveness, the combination of what they feel is calm on the surface and considerable seething tension underneath, to boyhood competition with an older and slightly favored brother.

Mac Bundy was born in 1919. He attended Groton, the greatest prep school in the nation, where the American upper class sends its sons to instill the classic values: discipline, honor, a belief in the existing values and the rightness of them. Coincidentally it is at Groton that one starts to meet the right people, and where connections which will serve well later on—be it Wall Street or Washington—are first forged; one learns, at Groton, above all, the rules of the game. *Cui servire est regnare* is Groton's motto. "To serve is to rule." The overt teaching was that the finest life is service to God, your family, and your state, but the covert teaching, far more subtle and insidious, was somewhat different: ultimately, strength is more important; there is a ruling clique; there is a thing called privilege and you might as well use it. That is the real world and it is going to remain that way, so you might as well get used to it. Bundy was of course part of this and has always accepted the special privilege that his advantages offered, working perhaps discreetly to change it from within (but never so much as to be tabbed as something odd, like a reformer), but accepting it nonetheless, an acceptance which has made some outsiders a little suspicious. If he is really that egalitarian, what is he doing in all those clubs? At Yale, for instance, where his friend Kingman Brewster turned down the secret societies, Bundy joined (the best, naturally) Skull and Bones, and later, in Washington, he would similarly resist requests from friends that he resign from the Metropolitan Club, which ten years after the great storm about its membership in 1961 was not noticeably more egalitarian.

At Groton, Bundy was something of a legend in his time, as he would be everywhere he went. Louis Auchincloss, a contemporary at Groton, has said that Bundy was ready to be dean of the school at the age of twelve. Richard Irons, the school's best history teacher, said that even then it was astonishing to read Bundy's essays; they were always better than the books he had used as reference. The story is told of a group of outstanding students asked to prepare a paper on the Duke of Marlborough. The next day Bundy was called upon to read his composition in class. As he started to read, his classmates began to giggle and continued all the way through his reading of a perfectly excellent paper. The teacher, pleased by the essay but puzzled by the giggles, later asked one of the students what it was all about. "Didn't you know?" said the student. "He was unprepared. He was reading from a blank piece of paper."

After Bundy graduated from Groton when he was sixteen—summa cum laude, of course, just as Bill had before him—he went to Yale. The very choice of Yale was somewhat unorthodox, since Bostonians usually sent their children to Harvard after Groton, but the Bundys had decided that after both Boston and Groton, Yale might be somewhat broadening. On arrival, the freshmen were summoned to a mass meeting where the dean announced that there were two distinguishing features about the class: first, it comprised 850 students, which was the desired number; second, one member of the class was the first Yale student to get three perfect scores on his college entrance exams. Bundy of course.

Bundy was class orator and also became a columnist for the *Yale Daily News*, refusing to try out for the paper, as most young men did, because it was too time consuming, but because of his special abilities, he was allowed to write for it, anyway. And he was a member of Phi Beta Kappa. Altogether he was a formidable figure on the campus, so much intelligence harnessed to so much breeding, all that and the competitive urge as well. The Yale yearbook for 1940 noted: "This week passed without Mahatma Bundy making a speech." He was—not surprisingly, given his background, the ties of his family to Stimson—already deeply involved in foreign affairs, a committed internationalist and interventionist. In 1940 in a book called *Zero Hour*, in which young writers discussed the threat to the United States, Bundy, writing in a style which reflects the sureness of his upbringing and the values instilled in him, said: "Let me put my whole proposition in one sentence. I believe in the dignity of the individual, in government by law, in respect for the truth, and in a good God; these beliefs are worth my life and more; they are not shared by Adolf Hitler."

From Yale, Bundy went to Harvard, but hardly as a struggling graduate student. Rather, he was a Junior Fellow, a member of the select Society of Fellows, the chosen of the chosen. The Society had been founded by his great-uncle A. Lawrence Lowell, who set aside millions of his own money to endow the program and who told each new Fellow, "You will practice the virtues and avoid the snares of the scholar." The Society was a special program at Harvard designed to spare supremely talented people the drudgery of normal doctoral work. (It means, among other things, that Bundy is not Dr. Bundy. Of course, anyone can get a Ph.D., but very few can be Junior Fellows.) The fact is that he has in his lifetime done almost no serious scholarly work. Of his two major books, the first is the collaboration with Stimson on his memoirs, the second is the edited speeches of his brother's father-in-law, Dean Acheson. The Stimson biography is a good and serious book, and perhaps in a way more reflective of that elitist viewpoint than it intended to be, but it is hardly pioneer work. The important thing is how easy it all was for him; very few young men in their twenties, with no previous literary credentials, are offered the job to share in the writing of the memoirs of such a distinguished public servant. He was bright, but he was also so well connected that things came to him much more readily than to his contemporaries (like a girl who is both prettier than the other bright girls and brighter than the other pretty girls, it was almost unfair), and along the way he picked up less wisdom, less scar tissue than other men.

While he was a Junior Fellow at Harvard, Bundy made his one attempt to run for elective office, and the way in which he became involved is somewhat revealing about the way things are done for those who have a certain head start in life. "Henry Shattuck, who was a very powerful and important figure in Boston in those days, called me and asked me if I wanted to run for his place on the Boston City Council," he once told a reporter. "He told me that for a young man with an interest in public life it was a splendid way to begin. He assured me that the election was a formality, no one but a Republican had ever won before, and he would assure the support of the Republican Ward Committee, and since it was a very heavy Republican area, I agreed. I had an opponent, he did his work and I did not, and I got licked and I deserved to be beaten." Bundy never ran for public office again.

He left Harvard for the war. Although he had been rejected by his draft board because of weak eyes, he managed to memorize the eye charts, and he ended up serving as an aide to Vice Admiral Alan Kirk, a family friend. On board the *Augusta*, Admiral Kirk's flagship, he participated in much of the planning for the D-Day landings. He was remembered for his intelligence and audacity, and those who were aboard said he was not afraid to correct General Omar Bradley on minor matters. The brashness was clearly there; on June 9, when Bradley was leaving the ship, Bundy reminded the general that when he was gone, Captain Bundy would once again become the ranking Army officer aboard the *Augusta*.

When the war ended, he returned to civilian life and worked for a time on some of the postwar planning that went into the Marshall Plan, became a political analyst for the Council on Foreign Relations, wrote speeches for John Foster Dulles in his New York Senate campaign, and eventually ended up at Harvard as a lecturer in government, where he also did some discreet recruiting for the CIA. (This was not surprising—brother Bill being in the Agency and Allen Dulles being a good friend of the family's—since the CIA needed the right people on the right campuses to find the right young men who knew the rules of the game.)

He spent the fifties at Harvard and they were happy years for him. He was immensely popular with the undergraduates, he was very accessible and not at all pompous; rather, he was considered open and challenging. He loved taking on students, combating them and their ideas, challenging them, bright wits flashing back and forth, debate almost an end in itself.

His major undergraduate course, Government 180: The United States in World Affairs (his successor in teaching it was, fittingly enough, a young German émigré intellectual named Henry Kissinger), was taught with great style and enthusiasm. His Munich lecture was legendary at Harvard, and when word got out that it was on the day's schedule, he played to standing room only. It was done with great verve, Bundy imitating the various participants, his voice cracking with emotion as little Czechoslovakia fell, the German tanks rolling in just as the bells from Memorial Hall sounded. The lesson was of course interventionism, and the wise use of force. This was known as the ultrarealism school. Its proponents believed that force must be accepted as a basic element of diplomacy. Toughness bred toughness; Stalin had been tough in Eastern Europe, so the West would be tough somewhere else. The Communists legitimized us; force met force. John Kenneth Galbraith, a friend and colleague of Bundy's, later remembered that he and Bundy always argued at Harvard and later in Administration days about the use of force, and Bundy would tell Galbraith with a certain element of disappointment, "Ken, you always advise against the use of force—do you realize that?" Galbraith would reflect on that and then note that Bundy was right, he always *did* recommend against force, in the belief that there were very few occasions when force can be used successfully.

Bundy was a genuinely popular figure at Harvard. Despite his breeding and traditions he was not a blue blood in style. If he did not rebel against that which produced him, he seemed not to take it too seriously, he did not rely on it; it did certain things for him, and he was sure enough of its authenticity and value not to flaunt it. When in 1953 James Conant left Harvard to become United States High Commissioner to Germany, there was considerable talk that Bundy might succeed him. If ever there was a faculty candidate for the job, it was Bundy. Instead, Harvard chose Nathan Pusey, since the university was under severe attack from McCarthy and since the prospect of a deeply religious figure from the Midwestern heartland was somehow reassuring to alumni. Bundy became merely dean of the College, inspiring a Yale colleague to pen this doggerel:

> A proper young prig, McGeorge Bundy,
> Graduated from Yale on a Monday
>   But he shortly was seen
>   As Establishment Dean
> Up at Harvard the following Sunday.

By the standards of very tough critics, Bundy was a magnificent dean. It was a virtuoso performance, designed as much as possible to open up the university, to bring it greatness despite the usual bureaucratic restrictions. David Riesman (social sciences), Erik Erikson (psychiatry), Laurence Wylie (French civilization)—all were brought in by Bundy despite the opposition of the departments to which they would be assigned. Lillian Hellman, the playwright and a good friend of Bundy's, remembers being with Bundy in Cambridge one night when he suddenly said to her, "Why don't you come up here and teach?"

"Oh," she said, "the English department wouldn't want me."

"We'll see about that," he said. Off he went and in about an hour he called her. "It's all set."

"But I don't know how to teach," she protested.

"But you know something about writing," he answered. "Give them some real work. Teach them how to take from what's really around them and how to use it."

Even the slight nastiness, which has from time to time been a Bundy trademark, was an advantage; he had the ability to be unfair, to go after special men and give them special privileges, people like Riesman and Erikson who did not teach as much as other members of the faculty. Perhaps a less aristocratic, less arrogant man with a greater sense of fairness and a greater sense of risk (the name Rusk comes to mind, Rusk would never have broken the rules) might not have done it. Bundy took the complex Harvard faculty—diverse, egomaniacal—and played with it, in the words of a critic, like a cat with mice. He was brilliant at learning things in conversation, in absorbing. The great skill of his mind, the training in classics and math, allowed him to see and understand how other people's intellectual processes work. He was a deft bureaucratic politician; he knew the men around him, whom to flatter, whom not to. "He was so good," said one of his friends who knew his strengths as well as his weaknesses, "that when he left I grieved for Harvard and grieved for the nation; for Harvard because he was the perfect dean, for the nation because I thought that very same arrogance and hubris might be very dangerous."

Mac Bundy was a good and true Republican (Bill was the family Democrat) and had voted twice for Eisenhower, but in the late fifties he began to forge a relationship with Jack Kennedy, in which Arthur Schlesinger served as the main intermediary. Bundy and Kennedy got on well from the start, both were quick and bright, both hating to be bored and to bore, that was almost the worst offense a man could commit, to bore. Rationalists, both of them, one the old Boston

Brahmin, the other the new Irish Brahmin, they seemed to be free of the prejudice of the past. (Indeed, the achievement of a close relationship between his son and a Lowell-Bundy was what it had been all about for Joe Kennedy.) If they had much in common, Jack Kennedy still had some advantages. He had traveled a far longer and harder road than Bundy; he had triumphed in electoral politics and had thus created a real base for himself, whereas Bundy had no personal base. If he was to play a role in American policy making he would have to be dependent upon someone like Kennedy. He had to sense Kennedy's moves, his whims, his nuances. To an uncommon degree, Bundy possessed that capacity to sense what others wanted and what they were thinking, and it would serve him well.

And so he joined the new Administration. He came full blown, a man of definite characteristics. By a curious irony he arrived, in Washington's mind, a full-scale intellectual, though in Harvard's mind the super administrator. (Eventually in Washington some of the men around him would realize that he was, above all, the administrator, the supreme mover of papers. "Clerk of the world," said Mark Raskin, a disenchanted man who once worked for him on disarmament.) He was bright and he was quick, but even this bothered people around him. They seemed to sense a lack of reflection, a tendency to look at things tactically, rather than intellectually; they believed Bundy thought that there was always a straight line between two points. He carried with himself not so much an intellectual tradition as a blood-intellectual tradition, a self-confirming belief in his origins. It was the Establishment's conviction that it knew what was right and what was wrong for the country. In Bundy this was a particularly strong strain, as if his own talent and the nation's talent were all wrapped up together, producing a curious amalgam of public interest and self-interest, a strong moral sense of propriety, and a driving, almost naked thrust for power. McGeorge Bundy, then, was the finest example of a special elite, a certain breed of men whose continuity is among themselves. They are linked to one another rather than to the country; in their minds they become responsible for the country but not responsive to it.

Thus, foreign policy was not a chord running through the country and reflecting the changes, and in 1964 and 1965 when Martin Luther King, Jr., began to make public speeches criticizing the war, the entire Establishment turned to silence him. They assured him that he knew about civil rights, but not about foreign policy; he was not an expert and they were. He remained bitter about this put-down to the day he died, feeling that he had in effect been told that, Nobel Prize or not, there were certain things that were not his business. Others who were in the Administration felt similarly excluded. "Those of us who had worked for the Kennedy election were tolerated in the government for that reason and had a say, but foreign policy was still with the Council on Foreign Relations people," Galbraith would recall years later. "We knew that their expertise was nothing, and that it was mostly a product of social background and a certain kind of education, and that they were men who had not traveled around the world and knew nothing of this country and the world. All they knew was the difference between a Communist and an anti-Communist. But that made no difference; they had this mystique and it still worked and those of us who doubted it, Goodwin, Schlesinger, myself and a few others, were like Indians firing occasional arrows into the campsite from the outside."

The other strain running through Bundy, not surprisingly, given the first strain, was a hard-line attitude which was very much a product of the fifties and the Cold War, the ultrarealist view. That this attitude also made one less vulnerable to attacks from the right about softness on Communism did not hurt; it dealt at once with totalitarians abroad and wild men at home. Force was justified by what the Communists did; the times justified the kind of acts which decent men did not seek, but which the historic responsibilities made necessary. This was very much a part of Bundy, a willingness to accept the use of force and to concentrate his energies on operational tactical questions.

As Special Assistant for National Security Affairs, Bundy soon became the invaluable man in the Kennedy Administration. Keeping the papers moving, protecting the President against people who wanted his time but were not worthy of it, making sure that people who needed his time got it, learning quickly what the President's tastes, needs, reservations were, always moving things. In his own words, the traffic cop. Doing it with style, which would show at an early press conference. Kennedy usually did well on these occasions, but this time he was hampered by a lack of news to reveal. Someone suggested that Kennedy's decision to reverse the last Eisenhower decision—to bring home the dependents of United States troops overseas—would be a dramatic announcement. But the Kennedy decision had not yet been cleared through the bureaucracy, and normally something like that takes weeks and weeks. While others were talking about whether it could be done, Bundy was on the phone, calling Douglas Dillon at Treasury and then the Pentagon and then State, saying, "The President would like to announce today that . . . . Do you see any objections?" In five minutes he was back, it was all cleared, all very nifty.

He was invaluable, functioning very easily. At meetings the President would ask him to sum up, and then, looking for all the world as if he had not even paid attention, Bundy would instantly give the quickest, most incisive, summing up imaginable. He was a great list man, too. They always needed prospective names, and Mac of course had the list, a job here, a committee there. Mac knew who should go on it, how far left or right it could go, who was acceptable, who was not. Mac was a terrific memo writer, facile, brief, and incisive. It was not, as publication of documents would later prove, exactly something which would make the literary world envious, but to be a good memo writer in government was a very real form of power. Suddenly everyone would be working off Bundy's memos, and thus his memos guided the action, guided what the President would see.

State was of course large and unwieldy (Acheson liked to tell of how much it had grown; when he became Secretary he had gone by to see Cordell Hull and had suggested that that venerable gentleman come by and meet the Assistant Secretaries. "Well, Dean, you don't mind if I refuse," Hull answered. "I never was very much good in a crowd. . . ."). This natural clumsiness, coupled with Rusk's cautiousness, soon created a problem in the bureaucracy. Kennedy was quickly dissatisfied with State, and Bundy, sensing the vacuum, moved deftly to fill in. He began to build his own power, looking for his own elite staff, a mini State Department of very special experts who could protect the President and give alternative answers. They could move papers quickly, something State could never do, and through an informal network at Defense and CIA, they could exploit sympathetic friends and thus create an informal inner network in the government. State, after all, was given to missing deadlines with papers and then answering with last year's myths. Bundy created an extraordinary staff, bright young men summoned from all areas of the government and academe. They were Robert Komer and Chester Cooper from CIA, Carl Kaysen from Harvard, Jim Thomson from Bowles' staff, Michael Forrestal, Francis Bator. He worked well with them, and exhibited the rare quality in Washington, in Thomson's words, "of being able to evoke whatever excellent existed in a person. Every encounter was like a mini Ph.D. exam."

Bundy tried to hide his disdain for Rusk as best he could, though in rare moments it would slip through. (It was said that Rusk held his counsel so closely that no one, including the President, was privileged to hear it, and sometimes Bundy would tell the story about a meeting of the six top officials, with Rusk asking all the others to leave so he could talk to the President. When they were alone the President asked Rusk what it was, and Rusk said, "Well, if there weren't so many of us in the room. . . .") Rusk, the least incandescent member of the group, bore it well. He resisted the impulse to react to stories being told about him, but at times the anger and irritation would flash through. "It isn't worth being Secretary of State," he once told Dick Goodwin, "if you have a Carl Kaysen at the White House." Substitute for the name Kaysen the name Bundy.

The latter, of course, did not worry about the rumors of his growing power and influence; he delighted in them, knowing that the reputation that you are the man to see feeds on itself, and makes you even more so. He loved power and did not shrink from it, rather the opposite was true, there was an enormous thrust for it. He was known at the White House as a tough infighter; at the beginning of the Administration, Schlesinger and some of the other intellectuals had pushed for Bundy's Harvard colleague Henry Kissinger to serve as a special consultant on European questions, since Kissinger was said to be very good on the Germans and the Germans always needed reassuring. For a time Kissinger traveled from Cambridge to Washington, though he was not entirely sure whether he wanted to be in or out, and Bundy did not, to say the least, encourage Kissinger's visits. Eventually they stopped. In 1969, when Kissinger arrived permanently in Washington under Nixon to take the same seat that Bundy had held, it was also announced that Dr. Richard V. Allen, a right-wing figure of some renown, would be Kissinger's assistant. Asked by friends how he would treat Dr. Allen, who was considered somewhat warlike (in those days Kissinger was not considered warlike), Kissinger answered, "I will handle him the way Mac Bundy handled   The early White House years were golden years for Bundy. He seemed to gloss over the problems of the world, it was a dream realized, the better for him, the better for the nation. Some of those who knew him felt his thinking and performance were too functional and operational, he was not considering the proper long-range perspective, instead he was the man who did not want to wait, who believed in action. He always had a single pragmatic answer to a single question, and he was wary of philosophies. But pragmatic thinking is also short-range thinking, and too often panic thinking. A government is collapsing. How do we prop it up? Something is happening; therefore we must move. Thus, in 1965 Bundy was for getting the country into the Dominican mess, because *something* had to be done, and then very good at extricating us when he realized that extrication had become the problem, though as he and the men around him would learn, not all countries were as easy to get out of as the Dominican Republic.

CHAPTER 4

F or all the style and excitement of the new team, and all the great promise, 1961 was a terrible year for the Kennedy Administration. America might move again at his demand, but in which direction? And in what way could he move it? He was the first of a new kind of media candidate flashed daily into our consciousness by television during the campaign, and as such he had manged to stir the aspirations of millions of people. It had all been deliberately done; he had understood television and used it well, knowing that it was his medium, but it was done at a price. Millions of people watching this driving, handsome young man believed that he *could* change things, move things, that their personal problems would somehow be different, lighter, easier with his election. As President, Kennedy was faced with that great gap of any modern politician, but perhaps greatest in contemporary America: the gap between the new unbelievable velocity of modern life which can send information and images hurtling through the air onto the television screen, exciting desires and appetites, changing mores almost overnight, and the slowness of traditional governmental institutions produced by ideas and laws of another era. In his first major struggle, the great battle to expand the House Rules Committee, a classic conflict of the two forces, Kennedy finally won. But his victory was more Pyrrhic than anything else; it exposed the essential weakness of his legislative position, the divisions in his party, and as such, enemies on the Hill would feel encouraged in their opposition. The lesson, not immediately discernible, was that it was easier to stir the new America by media than it was to tackle institutions which reflected the old order. In a new, modern, demographically young society, this was symbolized by nothing so much as congressional control by very old men from small Southern towns, many of them already deeply committed, personally and financially, to existing interests; to a large degree they were the enemies of the very people who had elected John F. Kennedy. He was caught in that particular bind.

But there were other problems too. In terms of the Cold War, 1961 would be a difficult year: there was the Bay of Pigs in April, followed by the escalation in the arms race, the bullying by Khrushchev in Vienna, the growing tensions in Laos, the outbreak of violence in the Congo, the almost daily conflicts over the Berlin Wall, the preliminary reports that Vietnam might be a problem. All this took some of the edge off the excitement of the job, and Kennedy's oft-quoted comment was that the most surprising thing about coming to office was that everything was just as bad as they had said in the campaign. A less quoted remark, underscoring the difficulties inherent in events outside his control, came when Carl Kaysen, a White House expert on disarmament, brought in the news that the Soviets had resumed atmospheric testing. The President's reaction was simple and basic. "Fucked again," he said.

All the setbacks would seem minor compared to the Bay of Pigs, which was a shattering event, both within the Administration and outside. It would seriously disturb the balance of the first two years of the Kennedy Administration; it would almost surely necessitate a harder line both to prove to domestic critics and to the Russians that despite the paramount foolishness of this adventure, his hand was strong and steady. By necessity, an Administration which had entered almost jaunty, sure of itself, would now have to be more belligerent both for internal and external reasons, and it would not be for another eighteen months, when the Kennedy Administration had already deepened the involvement in Vietnam, that it would begin to retrieve a semblance of its earlier balance.

In a way it was a test run for the Vietnam escalations of 1965, and it would be said of John Kennedy and Lyndon Johnson that both had their Bay of Pigs, that the former's lasted four days and the latter's lasted four years. But the component parts were there: serious misreading of aspirations of a nonwhite nation; too much secrecy with too many experts who knew remarkably little either about the country involved or about their own country; too many decisions by the private men of the Administration as opposed to the public ones; and too little moral reference. And finally, too little common sense. How a President who seemed so contemporary could agree to a plan so obviously doomed to failure, a plan based on so little understanding of the situation, was astounding.

There were men who opposed the invasion and, to a degree, they were the same men who would later oppose the Vietnam commitment. One was General David M. Shoup, Commandant of the Marine Corps. When talk about invading Cuba was becoming fashionable, General Shoup did a remarkable display with maps. First he took an overlay of Cuba and placed it over the map of the United States. To everybody's surprise, Cuba was not a small island along the lines of, say, Long Island at best. It was about 800 miles long and seemed to stretch from New York to Chicago. Then he took another overlay, with a red dot, and placed it over the map of Cuba. "What's that?" someone asked him. "That, gentlemen, represents the size of the island of Tarawa," said Shoup, who had won a Medal of Honor there, "and it took us three days and eighteen thousand Marines to take it." He eventually became Kennedy's favorite general.

Significantly, two of the men who might have been Secretary of State knew of the plan and were opposed (a third, Stevenson, did not know of it, but presumably would have opposed it), and both were Democratic party professionals who also knew something of foreign affairs. Senator J. William Fulbright and Undersecretary of State Chester Bowles, public men with a sense of public responsibility, were objecting to a clandestine operation organized by private men who seemed to be responsible to no one but their own organ zations, with even that responsibility so secret that it was difficult to define whether it existed. (In secret organizations, a subordinate's failure reflects badly upon his superior as well, so there is a very strong instinct on the part of both to cover it up.) Bowles heard of the plan at the last minute, agonized over it, and wrote Rusk suggesting he fight it, noting:

. . . Those most familiar with the Cuban operation seem to agree that . . . it [is] a highly risky operation. If it fails, Castro's prestige and strength will be greatly enhanced. . . . I realize that this operation has been put together over a period of months. . . We should not, however, proceed with the adventure simply because we are wound up and cannot stop.

If you agree that this operation would be a mistake, I suggest that you personally and privately communicate your views to the President. It is my guess that your voice will be decisive.

The man who had been chosen as Secretary of State, Dean Rusk, a Democrat but a private man, was against the invasion. He expressed doubts but did not really oppose it.

In the aftermath, the crux of the matter was not whether the United

States should have provided the counterinsurgents with air power, but how the United States government could have so misread the Cuban people. Had there been even the beginning of serious anti-Castro feeling in the country, nothing would have rallied the average Cuban more quickly to the cause of Fidel than to have an invasion sponsored by the United States. The least of the mistakes were the ones most frequently commented on, the tactical ones, the question of the air power, but these were the mistakes which were fastened on: General Maxwell D. Taylor was called in to conduct a special review which centered on the tactical faults (too few men in the brigade assembled in Guatemala, too few pilots in the air arm, too few reserves, too little knowledge about uncharted reefs).

There was far too little questioning of the moral right to launch the attack: after all, the Communists did things like this all the time, that was the way it was, the way power was used. A vast number of people felt it had failed because too little force had been used. The President himself probably began to learn important lessons about institutional wisdom, but among his advisers there seemed to be little learned. Nothing very important, nothing very serious. "A brick through the window," McGeorge Bundy would tell friends. Part of the fault, the Administration believed, was that the advice had come from relics of the Eisenhower years, Allen Dulles at CIA and General Lyman L. Lemnitzer, Chairman of the Joint Chiefs of Staff, and the departure of both would be precipitated, the idea being that people more loyal to the President should head those institutions and thus make them more Kennedy-like.

Rusk's weak stand left the Kennedy people more frustrated by his performance than anything else, and left both Kennedy and Rusk wishing that he had spoken up more clearly. But Rusk had, after all, not been chosen because Kennedy wanted a strong man. Thus a voice which might predictably have been strongly opposed to this kind of military adventure was muted. On the other hand, the overt opposition of Bowles and Fulbright did not do them much good. Although it strengthened Fulbright's reputation in Washington as the chief Hill intellectual, it did not bring him any closer to the Kennedy circle, in part because of his own growing doubts about the men now in the executive branch.

For Bowles it would be a good deal worse. Somehow the word got out that he had been against the invasion. Soon there was a story going around Washington that Bobby Kennedy had come out of a meeting, jammed his fingers into Bowles' stomach, and told him, that he, Bowles, was for the invasion, remember that, he was for it, they were all for it. The Bay of Pigs debacle seemed to symbolize the futility of Bowles and to seal his end; he was talky, a do-gooder. He was too ideological, while they, of course, were all pragmatists. In the early days of the Administration that particular word had been used so frequently that David Brinkley noted that at a Washington cocktail party a woman had gone around the room asking each of the hundred people there if he was a pragmatist.

In May, a month after the Bay of Pigs, when a variety of lessons might have been sinking in, Bowles wrote one of the most prophetic analyses of the new Administration in his private diary:

The question which concerns me most about this new Administration is whether it lacks a genuine sense of conviction about what is right and what is wrong. . . .

Anyone in public life who has strong convictions about the rights and wrongs of public morality, both domestic and international, has a very great advantage in times of strain, since his instincts on what to do are clear and immediate. Lacking such a framework of moral conviction or sense of what is right and what is wrong, he is forced to lean almost entirely upon his mental processes; he adds up the pluses and minuses of any question and comes up with a conclusion. Under normal conditions, when he is not tired or frustrated, this pragmatic approach should successfully bring him out on the right side of the question.

What worries me are the conclusions that such an individual may reach when he is tired, angry, frustrated, or emotionally affected. The Cuban fiasco demonstrates how far astray a man as brilliant and well intentioned as Kennedy can go who lacks a basic moral reference point.

At the end of May an incident occurred which certainly contributed to Bowles' downfall. While both the President and Rusk were in Europe with De Gaulle, there was a crisis in the Dominican Republic following General Rafael Trujillo's assassination. A group headed by Bobby Kennedy, but including McNamara and a few others (with Rusk, Kennedy, and Bundy out of town, they represented the highest officials in the government), wanted to effect an immediate, though somewhat limited American intervention. They had some CIA contacts who promised that the right kind of Dominicans would rally and thus save the republic. Bowles, acting as Secretary, held the line against intervention because he doubted the legality of what they wanted to do. The others argued that speed was of the essence. Bowles suggested they find out a little more about which way events were moving.

At that point Bobby Kennedy, still in his hard-nosed incarnation, the tough guy of the Administration, unleashed a cascade of insults about Bowles' being a gutless bastard, which made some of the others in the room wince. Later in the day Bowles went on the phone to the President in Paris, explaining what the activists wanted to do and why he objected. Kennedy concurred in the objections.

"Well, I'm glad to hear it," said Bowles, "and in that case, would you clarify who's in charge here?"

"You are," the President said.

"Good," said Bowles. "Would you mind explaining it to your brother?"

By early July, 1961, a somewhat embarrassed Rusk was offering Bowles a job as roving ambassador, preferably to rove out of town, and admitting that it was Kennedy's idea. Bowles called up Kennedy and asked for a meeting. A curious conversation ensued. Kennedy began by saying that perhaps it had been a mistake not to make Bowles Secretary of State and that if so, things might have been different. But Rusk *was* Secretary of State, and changes had to be made. Would Bowles like Chile? No, Bowles would not like Chile. They decided to meet together in a few days, on July 17.

Washington seethed with rumors that Bowles was on his way out. He had become the perfect target for the conservatives. The liberals, uneasy about the direction of the Kennedy Administration, began to rally round him. For the first time the split personality of the Kennedy Administration seemed to show itself. Stevenson, Walter Reuther, Soapy Williams all rallied and told Bowles not to leave without a fight. At the July 17 meeting he showed up armed with memos on Cuba, China, and related issues, which incorporated far more new ideas than the Kennedy Administration was prepared to handle. He told Kennedy he did not intend to take Chile. Later that day Press Secretary Pierre Salinger held a briefing and said no, Bowles' resignation was not currently expected, but he added that off the record, he was not expected to be around very long.

There were others in the Kennedy circle uneasy with the decision-making processes used in the Bay of Pigs. Shortly afterward Arthur Goldberg, the new Secretary of Labor, asked the President why he had taken such a narrow spectrum of advice, much of it so predictable. Kennedy said that he meant no offense, but although Goldberg was a good man, a friend, he *was* in labor, not in foreign policy.

"You're wrong," Goldberg replied, "you're making the mistake of compartmentalizing your Cabinet. There are two people in the Cabinet you should have consulted on this one, men who know some things, and who are loyal to you and your interests."

"Who?" Kennedy asked.

"Orville Freeman and me."

"Why Orville?"

"Because he's been a Marine, because he's made amphibious landings, and because he knows how tough they can be even under the very best circumstances. He could have helped you."

"And why you?"

"Because I was in OSS during the war and I ran guerrilla operations and I know something about guerrillas. That they're terrific at certain things. Sabotage and intelligence, nothing like them at that. But they're no good at all in confronting regular units. Whenever we used them like that, we'd always lose all our people. But you didn't think of that—you put me in the category of just a Secretary of Labor."

"A brick through the window." Windows are easy to replace, and the Bay of Pigs did not change the basic direction of the Kennedy Administration in foreign affairs. It was still activist, anxious to show its muscles, perhaps more anxious than before. Kennedy would soon have a chance to show whether he was worthy of his mandate, at the upcoming conference with Nikita Khrushchev in Vienna in early June, a meeting scheduled so soon after the Bay of Pigs that the very holding of it was dubious. But he went through with it, and the outcome, rather than lowering tensions, increased them. The President left Khrushchev in Vienna feeling that he had been bullied, more determined than ever to show Khrushchev that despite his youth, despite the Bay of Pigs, he was someone to conjure with. He would call up the reserves, and flex American muscle in many ways.

Perhaps, just perhaps, it need not have been that way. Averell Harriman had long felt that a meeting between Khrushchev and Kennedy was inevitable, and he had carefully prepared himself for it. He was then sixty-nine years old, and a supreme party warhorse. Although something of a failure in domestic politics (in 1958 he was beaten badly by Nelson Rockefeller in the New York gubernatorial race; and he had wanted his party's Presidential nomination but never came close to it), he was one of the most forceful players at governmental politics of a generation, relentless, restless, and ruthless, expert in the care and feeding of Presidents of the United States. In 1960, after his defeat in New York, he had fallen from grace and activity as only a defeated American politician can.

Even at this low point, Harriman had been projecting a future role for himself. Sensing that there was a good chance of a Democratic President's being elected in the fall, and wanting to specialize in Soviet affairs, exploiting the most personal kind of expertise that went back to his boyhood, he had written to Khrushchev suggesting that the Premier invite him to Moscow (which would be a marvelous piece of wampum to barter with a new President). Khrushchev, who understood the game, of course, and who knew what Americans did not know, that a Harriman was just as much a Harriman out of office as in office, immediately invited him. They spent two days together, twelve good long hours, and at the beginning Khruschev, as was his wont, bullied Harriman, threatened, stomped, the voice rising: if the Americans did not move out of Berlin the rockets would fly, the tanks would roll, and he, Citizen N. Khrushchev, could not be responsible for all the terrible things which would happen. Harriman listened and then quietly rejoined that rocketry was a two-way avenue, that there were now few shelters left on either side, that the Soviet industrial might was just as vulnerable as American might and had been built up at just as high a national price. That done with, they had subsided into long and profitable talks about other subjects, the possibility of coexistence, the aims of the Chinese, a very pleasant exchange which had lasted the two days.

Harriman came back from that trip believing that there was a possibility of a deal with the Soviets, that history had finally converged to a point where both nations were ready, that the Soviet fear of the Chinese radically changed their national security problems. He felt in this winter of a long career that this was the special contribution he could make, particularly to a young President. To the Kennedys he was someone who had once been Democratic governor of New York, someone they ought to do something for. He had a serious hearing problem, which would not have been a problem except that he also had a serious vanity problem, which precluded a hearing aid. At the first meeting with Kennedy after November, 1960, he had been at his worst; asked what he thought about a complicated question of Soviet intentions, he had answered "Yes." Later, Kennedy had taken Michael Forrestal, Harriman's protégé, aside and asked if there was someplace they might talk privately. Forrestal suggested the bathroom, and they went in there, locking the door, Forrestal delighted, sure that his own big job was coming, at least an assistant secretaryship. "Do you think," asked Kennedy, "that you can get Averell to wear a hearing aid?"

In February, 1961, Harriman was made roving ambassador, a particularly low level in the governmental hierarchy when one considers the many distinguished posts he had held in the past. But he accepted with good grace; asked how it was going, in the early months of the Administration, he answered, "Oh, you know, all these Presidents are the same. You start at the bottom and work your way up." His stock rose steadily in the Administration, but he was furious at the time of the Vienna meeting because he had not been consulted on the planning. That had been left to people like Charles Bohlen, Llewellyn Thompson, and George Kennan, kids really, boys who he had trained. So with the intrusive, audacious style which makes him unique in government ("What makes Averell different from other men?" a reporter once asked one of his very young aides in 1969. "Well, he's the only *ambitious* seventy-seven-year-old I've ever met," the aide answered), Harriman just happened to show up in Paris as Kennedy was visiting De Gaulle, and just happened to see the President's sister Eunice Shriver to let her know that he desperately had to talk to the President. He just happened to get himself invited to a state dinner, just happened to sit one sister and one person away from the President, and just happened to hear the sister say to the President, "Look, Averell is here and I think he has something to say about Khrushchev and Vienna," and Kennedy, well primed, said, "Yes, I hear there is something you want to say to me." Harriman, of course, had practiced what he wanted to say. He had taught all his protégés always to be brief when talking to a President; they have so little time, everyone is always telling them things, keep it short and simple. Having determined to put the lessons of his long sessions with Khrushchev and forty years together in a few sentences, the gist of what he said was: Go to Vienna. Don't be too serious, have some fun, get to know him a little, don't let him rattle and frighten you. Remember that he's just as scared as you are, very aware of his peasant origins, of the contrast between Mrs. Khrushchev and Jackie, and there will be tension. His style will be to attack and then see if he can get away with it. Laugh about it. Rise above it. Have some fun.

That was the sum of the Harriman advice, though the contrary advice had been just as explicit. Stand up to him, show him that you're just as tough as he is, that the Bay of Pigs was an accident and not a reflection of your will. So Kennedy had gone to Vienna, and the meeting was a disaster, harsh and tense. Khrushchev had attacked, and Kennedy, surprised, had finally rejoined. Vienna, like the Bay of Pigs, had increased the tensions in the world.

The Vienna meeting made a powerful impact on Kennedy. James Reston, *The New York Times* columnist and Washington bureau chief, and the most powerful and influential journalist in the capital, had asked for a private meeting with the President after the final encounter. Because of his unique position, it had been granted. Knowing that such a session would enrage his colleagues, Reston spent the day in Vienna hiding from fellow journalists and was smuggled into a special room at the embassy. The blinds were drawn lest anyone see him; he waited there for several hours in the darkness. When Kennedy finally arrived, he could not see Reston at first because of the dark. Finally he spotted Reston, and as the journalist began to rise the President waved him down, came over, sat down on a couch next to him like a beaten man, and breathed a great sigh.

"Pretty rough?" Reston asked.

"Roughest thing in my life," the President answered. He was, Reston thought, genuinely shaken.

Kennedy told Reston, "I think he did it because of the Bay of Pigs. I think he thought that anyone who was so young and inexperienced as to get into that mess could be taken, so he just beat hell out of me. So I've got a terrible problem. If he thinks I'm inexperienced and have no guts, until we remove those ideas we won't get anywhere with him. So we have to act." Then he told Reston that he would increase the military budget (which he did) and send another division to Germany (which he also did). He turned to Reston and said that the only place in the world where there was a real challenge was in Vietnam. (Ironically, a year later, after the Americans had begun their limited commitment to Vietnam, Khrushchev would tell Ambassador Llewellyn Thompson that the Americans were making a major mistake in Vietnam. "In South Vietnam," he said, according to Thompson's cable back to Washington, "the United States has stumbled into a bog. It will be mired there for a long time.")

In retrospect, Reston was convinced that the Vienna bullying became a crucial factor in the subsequent decision to send 18,000 advisory and support troops to Vietnam. It appeared to be part of a derivative link, one more in a chain of events which saw the escalation of the Cold War in Kennedy's first year. The Cold War was still quite real in 1961, on both sides of the Atlantic, and the men who had come to power in Washington were very much a part of it; their own very eagerness to be tested would in fact accelerate it.

Berlin, of course, had dominated their thoughts for some time. They believed that the hopes for war and peace somehow centered around that divided city, and its access routes. Could we maintain our access? Would the Soviets block it? They were the men in power, preoccupied with the tiniest details. When someone questioned the President about spending too much time on Berlin, he answered, better too much than too little, and he did not mind checking too closely on military convoys; he did not, after all, want the world to be blown up because some young captain had a hangover on a given morning. If Berlin had seemed central in early 1961, Vietnam had loomed somehow very distant. Around that time a knowledgeable Far Eastern correspondent named Stanley Karnow had dropped by the Justice Department to talk with the President's brother. In the course of the conversation Karnow began to single out Vietnam as probably the most serious problem there, the one which bore the greatest long-range potential for danger. "Vietnam," said Robert Kennedy, "Vietnam....We have thirty Vietnams a day here."

Thirty Vietnams. From the beginning it had been that way, a tiny issue overclouded by the great issues. Who, in 1945, had time for Indochina, as it was then called? Nineteen forty-five was a time when the problems of Europe were pre-eminent, when the question of the atomic balance with Russia was next, when even China was on the periphery; Vietnam was on the periphery of the periphery.

But it began to go sour for this country as early as July, 1945, when the new and uncertain President of the United States, Harry Truman, made his first major trip abroad, to Potsdam, to come to terms with the enormous problems that seemed to come hurtling at him, great decisions which would decide the immediate wartime and postwar future. He was not particularly concerned with Indochina; but because some of the issues arising at Potsdam might touch on China, Truman had brought along a China and Asian expert, John Carter Vincent, chief of the China division of the State Department.

John Carter Vincent was a charming, social, nominally conservative man who had unusually good connections on the Hill. Having spent a large part of his career in Asia, he felt a distinct empathy for Asian nationalism. By early 1945 he had come to the conclusion that the President in particular believed in indigenous nationalism in Asia and was moving in that direction. Those days, in fact, would be the highwater mark of American support for nationalism in Vietnam, with Roosevelt talking about a trusteeship for the area. It would end with the trip Vincent was on at that moment, the trip to Potsdam. He did not think a great deal about Vietnam at Potsdam because it was not on the agenda.

But a decision was made at Potsdam on Vietnam, without any real consultation. It concerned the surrender; the British would accept the Japanese surrender below the 16th parallel, the Chinese above it. It appeared quite inconsequential, but the matter of who accepts a surrender is a vital one; it determines who will control the turf and who will decide future legitimacy. The British worried about what it might mean for Burma and Malaya, since they were anxious to control future colonial questions in Asia; the British, after all, were not eager to see the dissolution of their empire. Truman, pushed by his military advisers who were wary of what anticolonialism might mean in regard to the future of United States naval and air bases in Asia, urged that we go along with the British. There had been no prior discussion among the Americans (though later evidence would show that there had been a good deal of collusion beforehand between the French and the British on this issue). Having accepted the surrender, the British would permit the French to return, and all subsequent events would flow from this: the French would reassert their authority, they would smile politely at all American requests to deal with the indigenous population, but they would pay no attention; the Americans, after all, had given away the leverage, the French Indochina war would begin, and the Vietnamese would gain their freedom by force of arms.

It was, of course, a minor point clouded over by great issues at the time, and the responsible political officer, John Carter Vincent, did not participate; in fact, he learned of it after the conference was over. A fateful decision unfatefully arrived at. It was, he would acknowledge many sad years later, the turning point, the moment at which it all began to go wrong.

Vietnam up to then had only come into the public's eye through articles in the *National Geographic*. It was filled with exotic but dutiful natives, whom the French were helping to become modern. In Washington it was viewed as a land with vital resources—vital, but not that vital. In 1941, when the United States learned from radio intercepts that the Japanese planned to move against southern Indochina, its reaction had been modest. The military argued against any action which might take us to war with Japan, because of our lack of preparedness. What became clear as events progressed in 1941 and during the war was that Vietnam was important not in itself, but to the extent that the Japanese used it as a gateway to move toward other areas. Europe was the prime theater. "The defeat of

Germany," Roosevelt wrote to Harry Hopkins, George Marshall, and Admiral Ernest King in July, 1942, "means the defeat of Japan, probably without firing a shot or losing a life." So American wartime policy was set. Prime effort in Europe, little effort in Asia—island hopping, securing bases for American air power to be aimed at Japan, rather than the more painful crawling up the mainland.

In Indochina itself, the collapse of the French had given enormous new momentum to political stirrings among the Vietnamese, and there was a belief that somehow the great war was being fought for them as well, a view shared by some Americans, notably their President. Franklin D. Roosevelt was a man before his time: anticolonialism had not surfaced yet as the great global movement, but Roosevelt had strong ideas about colonialism. He was instinctively on the side of the little man, and if he did not like colonialism in general, he did not like French colonialism in particular. The French, Roosevelt was fond of telling people, had been in Indochina for fifty years and the people were worse off than when they had arrived. He had determined that there would be an international trusteeship of Indochina.

At the Yalta meeting between Stalin, Churchill, and Roosevelt in February, 1945, the question of Indochina was discussed. Charles Bohlen's notes record that Roosevelt had a trusteeship in mind; further that the British did not like the idea because of its implications for Burma. Less than a month later, on March 15, 1945, Roosevelt asked Charles Taussig, a State Department adviser on Caribbean affairs, to give him guidance on colonial questions for the forthcoming United Nations meeting. The conversation reflected more clearly than anything else the crystallizing of Roosevelt's feeling about both the French and the area. Taussig recorded the conversation for the Department:

The President said he is much concerned about the brown people in the East. He said that there are 1,100,000,000 brown people. In many eastern countries they are ruled by a handful of whites and they resent it. Our goal must be to help them achieve independence—1,100,000,000 potential enemies are dangerous. The President said he thought we might have some difficulties with France in the matter of colonies. He said that French Indochina and New Caledonia should be taken from France and put under a trusteeship. The President hesitated and then said—Well if we can get the proper pledge from France to assume for herself the obligations of a trustee, then I would agree to France retaining these colonies with the proviso that independence was the ultimate goal. I asked the President if he would settle for dominion status. He said no—it must be independence. He said that is to be the policy, and you can quote it in the State Department.

This was to be the highwater mark of American governmental interest in pure anticolonialism in Indochina. A few short weeks later Roosevelt was dead, and with him any hope for a genuine declared policy of anticolonialism for Vietnam. He was the only high player truly committed to the idea of keeping the French out. Indeed, the State Department moved immediately to present Truman with a *fait accompli* policy in Indochina.

The United States government knew what was going to happen in Vietnam, but committed to its European allies, it could not or would not use any leverage to change the course. The division in the government between its instincts for global power and its brain—a split which would haunt us right through 1965—was spelled out in June, 1945, when Colonel Stimson asked the State Department to prepare a paper on the future in Asia. The paper forecast quite accurately that Vietnamese political aspirations, which had been increasing sharply, would lead the Vietnamese to fight the French, and that the French would have "serious difficulty in overcoming this opposition and re-establishing French control." Knowing this, the United States government did nothing; it already feared French weakness in Europe, and it was not about to pressure a weak and proud ally.

In Vietnam, General Jacques Philippe Leclerc, De Gaulle's favorite general, landed to take charge of French forces. After a tour of the country he was fully aware of the political-military problems that lay ahead. Turning to his political adviser, Paul Mus, he said, "It would take five hundred thousand men to do it, and even then, it could not be done." In France no one listened to either Leclerc or Mus, and in Washington no one listened to the young American political officers warning of the coming struggle. The idea of Asian rebels standing up to a powerful Western army was preposterous at the time. No one had yet heard of political war, of Mao's concept of fish swimming in the ocean of the people, of Asian guerrillas giving the European country the cities and strangling them by holding the countryside; of an army losing battle after battle but winning the people and thus the war. Instead the important thing in Washington was to strengthen France, and in Paris the important thing was to regain France's tarnished greatness. One restored greatness by force. And so in 1945 and 1946 it became increasingly clear that negotiations between France and the Vietminh would fail.

It was all becoming hopeless. Traveling in Indochina in December, 1946, Abbott Low Moffatt, a State Department official, sensed the desperation of the Vietnamese and saw that war was imminent. He cabled Washington, offering his good offices as a negotiator to serve between the French and the Vietminh. The French turned down the offer. Before the week was out, the war was on, and though the Americans began by standing on the sidelines, they would soon find themselves slowly drawn into the conflict, first to support the French, eventually to replace them. Even in the early years, Lauriston Sharpe, a Cornell anthropologist who had served in the area during the war and who remained to work for the State Department, would complain bitterly about the lack of American leadership. One telegram from the United States, he said, and it could all have been avoided, all this bloodshed. Perhaps one telegram would have meant little, but the truth was that United States policy, despite all its commitments to freedom, independence, and anticolonialism, had permitted an ally to start a bitter and foolish colonial war. Without raising a finger or sending any real telegrams.

CHAPTER 5

I n Asia, the first confrontation would take place over Laos. It was the key to the crisis in Southeast Asia, President Eisenhower had told Kennedy, and we must not permit a Communist takeover. If ever anything was an invention of the Cold War and its crisis psychology, it was the illusion of Laos. It was a landlocked country on the China border, a part of the Indochina nation, and it had managed to participate as little as possible in the French Indochina war. Of the Indochinese peoples it was the Vietnamese and particularly the North Vietnamese who were considered warriors, but Dulles had decided to turn Laos into what he called "a bastion of the free world." It was the least likely bastion imaginable. Its people were sleepy, unwarlike, uninterested in ideology. Yet unlikely or not, it bore the imprimatur of American foreign policy of that era: the search for an Asian leader who told us what we wanted to hear, the creation of an army in our image. It was a CIA show, the country perilously close to being a CIA colony (in the sense that the local airline was run by the CIA, and a good many of the bureaucratic jobs were financed by the CIA).

Our man there, so to speak, was a general named Phoumi Nosavan, a right-wing strong man, to use the phrase of that era, but more of a comic-strip figure. Meeting him in Washington for the first time, Kennedy said, "If that's our strong man, we're in trouble." Since 1958,

Phoumi had lived well off the Cold War; he was also in the opium trade, from which he profited considerably. He had an army handsomely paid, but worthless in battle. "Your chief of staff couldn't lead a platoon around a corner to buy a newspaper," the American ambassador, Winthrop Brown, once told him. "I know," Phoumi answered, "but he's loyal."

During the Dulles years, when neutralism was considered somewhat sinful, the Americans had deliberately sabotaged Laotian attempts, led by their ruler, Prince Souvanna Phouma, at neutralism and a coalition government between the various factions. With our money, our CIA men, and our control of the Royal Laotian Army, we had in fact systematically destroyed the neutralist government of Souvanna, eventually forcing the neutralists to the side of the Communist Pathet Lao (though in 1962 we would spend millions and millions of dollars to re-create the very neutralist government we had toppled). One month before Kennedy entered office in 1961, Souvanna had fled to Thailand, and Kong Le, the military leader of the neutralist forces, had joined the Pathet Lao to fight against General Phoumi's army. When the two sides finally met in early February on the strategically important Plain of Jars, Phoumi's army predictably broke and ran. As they ran, the Kennedy Administration had its first Asian crisis.

It was the classic crisis, the kind that the policy makers of the Kennedy era enjoyed. At the White House during the next two months, officials were photographed briskly walking (almost trotting) as they came and went with their attaché cases, giving their "No comments," everything made a little bigger and more important by their very touching it. There were intense conferences, chances for grace under pressure. At the first meeting McNamara forcefully advocated arming half a dozen AT6's (obsolete World War II fighter planes) with hundred-pound bombs, and letting them go after the bad Laotians. Technology and power could do it all. Rusk, who had seen the limits of air power in jungle terrain during the war, gently dampened the idea; the effectiveness of six small fighter-bombers was bound to be limited.

There were other ideas; some of the civilians were interested in the possibility of a quick strike at the Plain of Jars, an airborne landing. Could we get them in there? Kennedy asked the Chairman of the Joint Chiefs. "We can get them in there, all right," General Lemnitzer answered. "It's getting them out that worries me." What quickly became clear was that the military, particularly the Army, were in no rush to fight a ground war in Laos. The Army still felt itself badly burned by its experience in Korea, where it had fought a war which was immensely frustrating for commanders who felt they were sacrificing their men for limited political objectives. This annoyed Kennedy, who felt the Chiefs were not being candid; that they were building a record against him, covering themselves against an invasion and putting the onus on him.

A year later there was a new Laotian crisis, and after a NATO conference in Europe, McNamara went back via Saigon to meet with top United States officials. He asked each one in turn what the United States should do. A limited commitment seemed to be the general response. Then McNamara said, "Let me play the devil's advocate: if we intervene in Laos, if we overfly North Vietnam, will the Chinese let us do it? What will Hanoi do? Will they just sit there or will they come in?" Then he leaned back. What ensued was one of the longest and most appalling silences McNamara had ever sat through. They had all been willing to commit troops, but they had given little or no thought to what the other side might do.

It was in April, 1961, of the Laotian crisis that Harriman entered the picture. He was a man who had lived through most of the past Cold War policies and had helped create them, but he was not tied to them. He was a man who knew that the most dangerous thing about power is to employ it where it is not applicable, and he had serious doubts about the American commitment to Laos. As roving ambassador he had talked with Khrushchev, who had not thought Laos was worth war ("Why take the risk?" Khrushchev told Ambassador Llewellyn Thompson. "It will fall into our lap like a rotten apple."). In March, Harriman had arranged to see Souvanna Phouma, the neutralist leader the United States had succeeded in ousting. They met at an airport in New Delhi. They shared no common language, but Harriman had broken through, and he came away convinced that this was a man you could deal with, that he represented something viable in Laos.

He returned to Washington, and knowing the importance of repetition within a government, he started repeating a litany whenever he could at meetings, dinner parties—Souvanna Phouma, Souvanna Phouma, Souvanna Phouma—until at a certain point close friends were somewhat alarmed; perhaps this time Averell really was showing his age. It was not long after that Kennedy assigned him the job of getting a Laotian settlement at the conference in Geneva in May. He did not think a decent settlement was really possible, but it was a job. Indeed, the way he carried out what he himself would describe as a "good bad deal" so impressed the President that Harriman started an upward journey which might have brought him the Secretary's job itself were it not for the assassination.

In Geneva he worked singlehandedly toward the neutral settlement, trying to convince the Soviets that they had little to lose, that the real problem for them was the Chinese, and that neutralism was more of a problem for the Chinese than for the Russians. At one point during the negotiations, Pat Moynihan, who had worked for him during the Albany days, ran into him in Geneva.

"What are you doing now?" he asked Harriman.

"Oh, I'm just waiting. We've done all the talking we can do. And the Russians are making up their minds and I'm waiting for them. That's all, waiting."

Eventually a neutralist agreement met with all the delegates' approval, much to the anger of the hard liners such as Alsop, who said it reminded him of the White Queen in *Alice in Wonderland* teaching herself to believe six impossible things before breakfast. So the Kennedy Administration had moved away from force in Laos, but not without first a show of force, by stationing United States Marines on Okinawa and in Japan for possible forays into the Mekong Valley, and not without a grand *son et lumière* show, a television spectacular starring Kennedy himself, with maps, charts, clichés about Laotian freedom being tied to American freedom. "The security of all Southeast Asia will be endangered if Laos loses its neutral independence. Its own safety runs with the safety of us all," he said on television, while telling Arthur Schlesinger at lunch of the discrepancy between what he thought he could say and what he believed: "We cannot accept a visible humiliation."

The President would say later that the Bay of Pigs had saved us from going to war in Laos, but what really saved the United States was not the Bay of Pigs, or even Harriman, but the Laotians themselves. If Phoumi was a foolish figure, Souphanuvong, leader of the Pathet Lao, was a Communist counterpart. Neither he nor his people had invested the kind of sacrifice and commitment to the struggle that the Vietcong had in South Vietnam. In Vietnam a dynamic, relentless guerrilla movement was in the fifteenth year of an endless struggle to take over and unify the whole country, and for the leaders of that movement what the United States did or did not do was irrelevant.

With luck the United States had managed to stay out of Laos, and there was one small footnote to the Geneva agreement which in retrospect would take on considerable significance. After the agreement had been reached, Kennedy assigned his own liaison man with Harriman, the young Wall Street lawyer Michael Forrestal, to brief Lyndon Johnson on the settlement. Johnson, of course, already knew of the accords, and Forrestal arrived to find that the meeting had been arranged so that Forrestal would get there about ten minutes after Johnson's masseur had arrived. Forrestal began to discuss the accords, only to find himself blocked again and again by the masseur. Forrestal spoke, the masseur chopped, Forrestal spoke, the masseur rubbed. For ten minutes Forrestal tried to explain the agreement and found no way of getting Johnson's attention; it was, Forrestal thought at the time, and even more so later, Johnson's way of showing contempt for the Laotian accords.

Of all the members of the new Administration only one man besides Chester Bowles had ever shown much interest in the underdeveloped world, or much feel for it. It was not McNamara, nor Rusk, nor Bundy, who was classically a man of the Atlantic. It was, oddly enough, John F. Kennedy. He had been to Indochina twice, in 1951 and 1953, once as a congressman and once as a senator: the first time he was met at the airport by half the French army ready to brief him, to convince him of victory, to introduce him to a few Vietnamese officers bursting from their paratroop uniforms to prove to him how committed the natives were to a French type of freedom. He went to the official briefings, but he also jumped the traces, got the names of the best reporters in town, and showed up unannounced at their apartments, looking so young and innocent that they had trouble believing that he was really a member of the Congress of the United States. There he asked his own questions and got very different briefings from the official ones: the pessimism was considerable, the Vietminh were winning the war, and the French were not giving any real form of independence to the Vietnamese (ironically, a dozen years later in exactly the same situation, on the same soil, Kennedy would rage at the reporters for their pessimism).

Those trips to Vietnam had begun Kennedy's education on the underdeveloped world and colonialism. Later he spoke twice against the French position in Indochina (there was a third speech on Vietnam, which was pro-Diem) and continued with a major address against the French position in Algeria. It was not an expression of great passion, rather it was a reflection of his distaste for colonial callousness and vulgarity. He did not like the French colonial officials; they seemed stupid and insensitive, trying to hold on to something in a world

319

which had already changed. They were bad politicians, living in the past.

It was almost as if the colonialists' lack of style offended him the most, and this was not surprising, because the thirty-fifth President of the United States paid great attention to style; style for him and for those around him came perilously close to substance. He did not like people who were messy and caused problems, nor did he like issues that were messy and caused problems. He would make his own limited commitment to Vietnam in a few short months, not so much to embrace the issue as to get rid of it, to push it away.

Kennedy was committed only to rationality and brains, nothing more. He was almost British in his style. Grace under pressure was that much-quoted phrase describing a quality which Kennedy so wanted as a description of his own behavior. It was very much a British quality: to undergo great hardship and stress and never flinch, never show emotion. He could forgive his opponent Richard Nixon for many of his slurs on the Democratic party, but he could not forgive him for his lack of style and class in permitting Pat Nixon to be shown on election night 1960 close to a breakdown. Kennedy himself was always uneasy with emotion: James MacGregor Burns would note that when, as President, Kennedy visited Ireland and thousands upon thousands of Irishmen wildly cheered, his reaction was to tug self-consciously at his tie and straighten it.

He did not like people who pushed and crowded him, who told him of their cause or their problems. He wanted in his career no one's problems but his own. If the world was changing, he did not intend to accelerate those changes at the risk of his own career; he wanted to keep up with them, but not to be either ahead or behind.

For the thirty-fifth President of the United States was a classic expression of the democratic-elitist society which had produced him in the middle part of the twentieth century. As the country expanded, the old elites in the East had opened up their universities to the best qualified of the new elites, and his education had been superb. He was at once very rich without seeming rich or snobbish and he spent his money judiciously, allowing it to make his political way easier, yet careful not to offend his more egalitarian constituency. So it was not surprising that many of his fellow citizens found reassurance in the fact that he was President. In a country which prized men who were successful, he had always been marvelously successful. He had made no false moves, no votes had been cast in the heat of idealism to be regretted later.

With television emerging in American politics as the main arbiter of candidates, his looks were striking on the screen, and he was catapulted forward in his career by his capacity to handle the new medium. And he was, despite all the advantages, still very hungry. The Kennedys had not grown soft, they still wanted elmost desperately those prizes which were available. It was not by chance that Nelson Rockefeller, the one candidate who probably could have beaten him in 1960, just as photogenic, just as rich, perhaps not quite as bright, was above all a Rockefeller and thus lacked the particular hunger, the edge, and so had allowed himself to be bluffed out by Richard Nixon. Nelson Rockefeller's father had never left one city and moved to another because he felt there was too little social acceptance of his children, but Joseph Kennedy had moved from Boston to Bronxville for precisely that reason when his sons were teenagers.

Yet if many politicians are propelled forward and fed by the tensions and deprivations of their youth, Kennedy was again different. Being Irish may have been an incentive; Jack Kennedy felt no insecurity about it. Lyndon Johnson may never have lost his feeling of insecurity about his Texas background; Richard Nixon, poor and graceless and unaccepted as a young man, the classic grind, became the most private and hidden of politicians, always afraid to reveal himself. Kennedy had been excluded from the top Boston social circles as a young man, but he felt no great insecurity about it. His social friends at the White House tended to be the very people who had ruled those social sets, and he clearly enjoyed having them come to him. But he was unabashedly proud and sure of himself. Someone like John Kenneth Galbraith could note that he had never met a man who took such a great pleasure in simply being himself, and once during the 1960 campaign against Nixon someone had asked Kennedy if he was exhausted, and he answered no, he was not, but he felt sorry for Nixon, he was sure Nixon was tired. "Why?" the friend asked. "Because I know who I am and I don't have to worry about adapting and changing. All I have to do at each stop is be myself. But Nixon doesn't know who he is, and so each time he makes a speech he has to decide which Nixon he is, and that will be very exhausting."

If John Kennedy was cool and above the fray, detached, seeing no irrationality in the awesome Kennedy family thrust for power, he could well afford that luxury, for the rage, the rough edges, the totality of commitment bordering on irrationality belonged to his father. If John Kennedy was fatalistic about life, Joseph Kennedy was not. You did not accept what life handed you and then just tried to make the

321

best of it; instead you fought ferociously for your chance, you pushed aside what stood in your way, the civilized law of the jungle prevailed. Joe Kennedy was a restless, rough genius anxious to shed his semi-immigrant status, anxious to avenge old snubs and hurts; having failed to do so despite his enormous wealth, he was determined to gain his final acceptance through his sons. What better proof of Americanization than a son in the White House, a son running the Justice Department, and a son in the Senate (the last triumph would become somewhat unsettling to the elder boys, who thought perhaps the family was overdoing it, though the patriarch himself knew the code better than they—there was no way of overdoing it). If Joe Kennedy's daughters had been sent to the very best Catholic schools, the better to retain the parochialism and tradition in order to pass it on to his grandchildren, his sons had been educated exactly for the opposite reasons—to shed it. There would be no Holy Cross, or Fordham, or Georgetown Law School in their lives. They were sent instead to the best Eastern Protestant schools, where the British upper-class values were still in vogue. For Jack it had been Choate, not Groton or St. Paul's perhaps, but still a school for proper Christian gentlemen, who understand duty and obligation, and then Harvard. Eventually, after the service in World War II, a political career; the thrust at the beginning was certainly Joseph Kennedy's rather than that of his son, who seemed to be merely pursuing the obligatory career. Later, of course, there was no absence of his own ambition, and he became a remarkable American specimen, carrying in him an immigrant family's rage to get their due, but carefully concealed behind a cool and elegant facade: in the prime of his career in the late fifties as he prepared to run for President, he did not seem an upstart and an outsider raging to get his due, but rather a very fine, well brought up young man dealing with an outmoded unfortunate prejudice. The perfect John O'Hara candidate for President. Once during his Administration a scandal broke out over the fact that the Metropolitan Club, Washington's most elite social and political meeting place, did not encourage Jewish or Negro membership. Many of Kennedy's friends resigned, but not McGeorge Bundy. Kennedy was amused by this and began to tease Bundy, who became irritated and lashed back. Kennedy, he said testily, belonged to clubs which did not have many Jews and Negroes, such as the Links in New York. "Jews and Negroes," laughed Kennedy. "Hell, they don't even allow Catholics!"

It was also symbolic of the era that Kennedy wanted to be his own Secretary of State, not Secretary of Health, Education and Welfare, not Secretary of Labor, not Attorney General. It was symbolic because in the universities, in the journals, and in the intellectual circles it was generally held that the real action was in determining the role America played in the world, rather than redefining America domestically. It was where the excitement was, this competition with the Soviet Union, a competition of politics and of economics and ideas. Kennedy believed in it, and so did other men of ambition in that era. Bright young men off the Eastern campuses went to Mississippi to redefine America in 1964, but in the 1950's they had gone into the CIA and into the State Department. Even as a congressman Kennedy had asked Ted Sorensen what Cabinet post he wanted. Sorensen had talked about HEW, but Kennedy was different, as Cabinet officer he wanted only State or Defense, where the power was.

Yet if there was a problem with the pragmatism of the era, it was that there were simply too many foreign policy problems, too many crises, each crowding the others, demanding to be taken care of in that instant. There was too little time to plan, to think; long-range solutions would have to wait, at least until the second term. And thus it was the irony of the Kennedy Administration that John Kennedy, rationalist, should continue the most irrational of all major American foreign policies, that policy toward China and the rest of Asia.

Early on, when Stevenson and Bowles repeatedly mentioned China to Kennedy, saying that the policy was absurd and that it was urgent to try to change it, Kennedy would smile and agree and say yes, it was a stupid policy, but it would all have to wait.

Above all, John Kennedy did not want to revise America's Asia policy (even in October, 1963, with Vietnam falling apart, he told television interviewers that he did not want to cut off aid to Vietnam because that might start events comparable to those preceding the fall of China, and that was the last thing he wanted). Thus, because he did not look back on America's China policy, it was easier for him, in 1961, to move forward in Vietnam.

CHAPTER 6

The first warning on Vietnam had been sounded in January, 1961, by one of the most unusual members of the United States government. It was as if Brigadier General Edward Lansdale had been invented with the Kennedy Administration in mind. He was a former advertising man, a former Air Force officer, a CIA agent now, deeply interested in doing things in Asia the right way. In the early fifties he had helped Ramón Magsaysay defeat the Huk rebellion in the Philippines, and had become the prototype of the Good American overseas as opposed to the Bad American; he was against big bumbling United States government programs run by insensitive, boastful, bureaucratic, materialistic racists, and for small indigenous programs run by folksy, modest American country boys who knew the local mores, culture, and language.

Lansdale was the classic Good Guy, modern, just what Kennedy was looking for. He had, what better mark of merit, been languishing out of the action during the latter years of the Eisenhower Administration. He was the median man who understood the new kind of war and had helped defeat the Communists in a similar (if far different and simpler) insurgency in the Philippines. He embodied what America had turned into more than anyone realized: the corrosion of the traditional anticolonial instinct had become hard-line anti-Communism. The real question for men like Lansdale, who allegedly knew and loved Asians, was no longer the pure question of what was good for the local people, but what was good for the United States of America and perhaps acceptable locally.

His view of the recent history of Vietnam was comforting, and managed to minimize the role of the Vietminh and the effect of a prolonged war of independence. The Vietminh had less popular support than they imagined; the population had stayed away from both sides, and the French were pictured as fighting for Vietnamese independence.

In 1954, in the last dying days of the French presence in Indochina, the Lansdale group had run around Hanoi putting sugar in the gas tanks of Vietminh trucks, a gesture of no small amount of mindlessness. The war was over, an Asian nationalist army had just defeated a powerful Western nation for its independence, and here was the top American expert on guerrilla war employing the pettiest kind of sabotage—mosquito bites, they were, at a historic moment. In Saigon, Lansdale helped sponsor Ngo Dinh Diem, and played a key role in convincing a very dubious United States government that Diem was worth the risk. He taught Diem how to campaign against Bao Dai, and Diem, ever the worthy student, insisted upon receiving ninety-eight percent of the vote. Lansdale also sponsored other little gestures which seemed somehow to belong to the past: hiring soothsayers—symbols of the suspicious feudal Vietnamese past—to predict bad years ahead for Ho Chi Minh, and good years for Ngo Dinh Diem.

At the tail end of the Eisenhower years, Lansdale had returned to Vietnam and found to his dismay, as reporters there were also discovering in 1960, that the new version of the Vietminh, named the Vietcong, were near victory by fighting guerrilla style in the countryside while the American military mission continued to train the Vietnamese army for a Korean-style invasion. President Diem was almost totally isolated from his former friends and allies, and increasingly dependent on his egomaniacal brother, Ngo Dinh Nhu; Diem and the American ambassador, Elbridge Durbrow, virtually did not speak to each other.

Lansdale wrote a lengthy and very pessimistic report critical of both the Americans and of Diem, but particularly of the former. This was important, because Lansdale was one of the men who had invented Diem, and you do not knock your own invention, but more significant, it was indicative of the Lansdale approach and that of other Good Americans, those sympathetic to Asians. They did not feel that it was deeply rooted historic forces pitted against us which were causing the problems, but rather a failure to supply the right people and the right techniques. Implicit in the Lansdale position was the belief that if the right Americans influenced Diem in the right way, Diem would respond: "Our U.S. Team in Vietnam should have a hard core of experienced Americans who know and really like Asians, dedicated people who are willing to risk their lives for the ideals of freedom, and who will try to influence and guide the Vietnamese towards U.S. policy objectives. . . ." What Lansdale was recommending was, of course, Lansdale.

The Lansdale report was picked up by a friend, who read it in the final days of the Eisenhower Administration and passed it on to the new Administration. Within days it landed with Walt Rostow, who had been looking for something precisely like this. (Lansdale's effect on Rostow is interesting: in 1954 Lansdale had gone around pouring sugar in the Vietminh gas tanks; in 1962, at the height of the Cuban missile crisis, when the clock was ticking off the minutes of a massive confrontation, Rostow was going around Washington talking about sabotage against the Cubans, putting sugar in their oil refineries, which would halt their production and transportation.) Rostow urged Kennedy to read it, but the President seemed reluctant. Was it really that important? Rostow insisted. Kennedy flipped through the pages. "Walt, this is going to be the worst one yet," Rostow recalled him saying. "Get to work on this." Which Rostow quickly did.

Shortly afterward Lansdale found himself hastily summoned to a special breakfast meeting at the White House. As he walked in, Kennedy greeted him graciously and said somewhat casually, pointing to Rusk, "Has the Secretary here mentioned that I wanted you to be ambassador to Vietnam?" Lansdale, caught by surprise, mumbled that it was a great honor and a marvelous opportunity. He was deeply touched, and even more surprised, for it was the first he heard of the idea, and also, as it happened, the last. The appointment never came through; Lansdale would not return to Vietnam for five more years, and by then he seemed a particularly futile and failed figure—the author of how to fight guerrilla wars the right way, being part of a huge American mission which used massive bombing and artillery fire against Vietnamese villages.

Lansdale's more specific proposals were channeled through to Roswell Gilpatric, the Deputy Secretary for Defense (significantly, Vietnam was already being treated as a military problem). The suggestions were essentially antibureaucratic, with Lansdale opposing what he assumed was the inevitable Americanization of the operation, the creation of a mission based on American bureaucratic needs rather than on Vietnamese realities. Gilpatric would head a task force which would oversee the operation in Washington, and Lansdale would be its chief in Saigon, with a minimal increase in personnel. These recommendations made in April were soon pushed aside by bureaucratic needs. Under the revised recommendations the original military mission of 685 men would be increased to around 3,000 in the training group; other agencies would grow proportionately.

The recommendations were brought before Kennedy, who was by no means anxious to send that many more Americans to Vietnam; he had just staggered through the Bay of Pigs, and he was wary of jumping into another confrontation. Years later Gilpatric would remember, more than anything else, Kennedy's reluctance to add anything at that time to Vietnam, particularly men. There would be no 3,000-man military group. On April 29 the President approved a 400-man Special Forces group for training missions. Instead of the Vietnam mission being taken over by Lansdale specialists, it would be run by regular career officials. There would be no Lansdale there.

The first move toward continuing the commitment had, however, been taken earlier without the Administration's even being aware of how fateful a step it was taking. This was the switching of ambassadors to Vietnam on March 15, 1961, when Elbridge Durbrow was replaced by Frederick E. Nolting, Jr. The Durbrow tour had not been a happy one; he had watched the beginning of the Vietcong pressure against Diem, and simultaneously the estrangement of Diem from friends, allies, and reality. Durbrow had insisted on telling Diem how poorly things were going and that candor was now becoming unpleasent. When he suggested that Ngo Dinh Nhu be sent into exile as an ambassador to a foreign country, Durbrow was virtually *persona non grata*. And the Administration decided to replace him. It did not doubt the accuracy of Durbrow's reports, but it could not afford to re-evaluate its policy, dependent as it was on Diem with all his faults. So the change in policy would go from being honest with Diem to being nice to him, hoping that somehow this would create a new confidence and mutuality of trust. To inspire this confidence the Administration picked Frederick Nolting.

Fritz to his friends, who were numerous. A proper man of proper credentials, from a good Virginia family, with a good war record, Navy of course. He was part of that special group of relatively conservative Democrats from Virginia who play a major role in the foreign service and regard it as a gentleman's calling. This hard-working, steady, and solid man had been sponsored by everyone he had ever worked for. Before coming to Vietnam, he had been at NATO, where he was head of the political section. Vietnam was his first ambassadorial post; he had never been to Asia before, and his ideas of Communism had all been fashioned through his European experience.

No one in the Kennedy group knew very much about Nolting; it was an appointment which seemed to slip by them. Only one man seemed to be aware of its potential import, and that was Chester Bowles. He already was arguing for a major change in Asian policy and the neutralization of Vietnam; he alone seemed to see the dangers of continued support of the Diem regime. As Undersecretary of State he was responsible for most of the ambassadorial assignments. He learned of the Nolting appointment at the last minute and tried to intercede against it. Bowles came up with what he thought was a particularly good man for Vietnam, a foreign service officer named Kenneth Todd Young who had served there in the past and gained a reputation for being unusually sensitive to indigenous problems and nationalism. Young had left the State Department during the Dulles years in despair over American policies, then had returned with the Kennedy Administration and was ticketed to be ambassador to Thailand. Bowles, however, was convinced that Vietnam rather than Thailand was going to be the main problem in Southeast Asia, and he wanted his most sensitive man there.

So, after both men had been approved for their respective posts, Nolting for Saigon, Young for Bangkok, Bowles maneuvered to have them switched. He talked with Young about it and found him less than eager to accept the proposition, chiefly because of his reservations about working with the Ngo family. He told Bowles he wanted to sleep on it.

Young thought long and hard that night about all the problems. He knew a good deal about Diem's abilities and liabilities, and he was also a reluctant authority on Mr. and Mrs. Nhu. He thought they were nothing less than poison, and that nothing could be accomplished in Vietnam as long as they were part of the government. One could not hope to work against the Nhus if they were still in the country; each night they would destroy each day's work. The new ambassador would have to establish a relationship of total frankness with Diem, based totally on mutual professional needs. The next day Young told Bowles that he was willing to give it a try. Soon there was a phone call from Lansdale representing Gilpatric saying that Young was to rush over to meetings of the Vietnam Task Force. "The President," Lansdale told him, "has agreed for you to go to Saigon." So it appeared to go through, and then it was stopped, the protocol problems were too complicated. Nolting had reacted badly, finding the switch insulting, which in a way it was. So Ken Young went to Thailand, where from Bangkok he watched Saigon with mounting horror as it became clear that all demands for reform would be dropped and the Nhus would become the dominant figures in the government. And Fritz Nolting in Saigon would find himself under such tension that it finally drove him not just from Vietnam but from the foreign service as well.

If Diem could have designed an ambassador for his country and his regime, he would have come up with Fritz Nolting. He was a fine example of the foreign service officer who commits himself only to the upper level of the host government and the society, not to the country itself. He had looked and listened, and had decided that Diem was the best anti-Communist around (there was, of course, no one else; Diem had systematically removed all other opposition —Communist, neutral, anti-Communist). People who worried about the regime's growing isolation and lack of appeal were, in his words, taking their eyes off the ball: stopping Communism was having your eyes on the ball. He had forbidden the embassy staff to talk to any Vietnamese dissidents; if one did not hear it, it did not exist. His policy was to build credit with Diem by agreeing to everything Diem wanted, hoping that one day he could cash in the due bills. The special significance of Fritz Nolting was that in the very choice of him, and his decision that yes, we could make it with Diem, we were binding ourselves into an old and dying commitment.

In late April, 1961, the bind to that commitment was to be tightened. While deciding not to increase the American mission in Vietnam, Kennedy sought to boost Diem's confidence by a visit from the Vice President of the United States, Lyndon B. Johnson, then somewhat underemployed. Johnson was scheduled to visit a number of Asian countries, and the key stop would be Vietnam. Curiously enough it was not a stop that the Vice President particularly wanted to make. He was so unenthusiastic that Kennedy had to coax him into it. "Don't worry, Lyndon," he said. "If anything happens to you, Sam Rayburn and I will give you the biggest funeral Austin, Texas, ever saw."

The trip came nonetheless at an opportune time for Johnson, who was at the lowest point in his career, being neither a Kennedy political insider nor a Kennedy intellectual. To intimates he would occasionally talk about how his chauffeur had advised him not to leave the Senate to become Vice President, muttering that he wished he had had that chauffeur with him in Los Angeles when Kennedy made the offer. With others, of course, he went to great pains to show that he was deeply involved in the inner decisions of the Administration, that he was the real insider. One day in early 1961, Russell Baker, then a Hill reporter for the *New York Times*, who knew Johnson well, had been coming out of the Senate when he was literally grabbed by Johnson ("*You*, I've been looking for *you*") and pulled into his office. Baker then listened to an hour-and-a-half harangue about Washington, about how busy Lyndon Johnson was, how well things were going. There were these rumors going around that he wasn't on the inside; well, Jackie had said to him just the other night at dinner as she put her hand on his, "Lyndon, you won't desert us, will you?" It was pure Johnson, rich and larger than life, made more wonderful by the fact that if Baker did not believe it, at least for the moment Johnson did.

Now, on the trip all that energy with which he had overwhelmed Washington in his earlier capacity as Senate majority leader, the most influential Democrat in Washington, burst loose. He was away from Washington, he had something to do, barnstorming, finding that all people were alike, that he could reach out by being with them, hunkering down with them, discovering what goals they had in common (eradication of disease, food for all, access to electric power). There he was, campaigning among the villagers, the more rural the better, riding in bullock carts, inviting a Pakistani camel driver to the United States. Johnson loved it all.

As a gesture of the President's concern, Johnson had brought with him Kennedy's sister and brother-in-law, Jean and Stephen Smith. Being a good campaigner, Lyndon did not neglect to show their symbolic value of traditional American concern for Asians. At every stop they were introduced, their importance heralded, their own positions magnified with typical Johnsonian exaggeration: Jean Smith, who started out being "the President's lovely little sister" soon became his "tiny little baby sister." And Steve Smith, perhaps the only member of the family who was *not* in the government, was introduced as "the President's brother-in-law," then as "a State Department official," and finally as "a man who held one of the most important and most sensitive jobs in the State Department."

He had been told to inquire in Vietnam whether Diem wanted troops, but it was not a meaningful query: troops were meant only as a symbol, the way American troops stood in West Berlin, to show the Communists that America was determined to resist, give them something to think about. Johnson found that Diem was in no rush to have Caucasian troops on his soil. Diem knew that it would be a sign of *personal* weakness as far as the population was concerned if he accepted American troops too readily.

Johnson was impressed by Diem; yet the entire episode became an example of gamesmanship. In his report to the President, Johnson wrote that Diem "has admirable qualities, but he is remote from the people, is surrounded by persons less admirable than he. . . ." But if that was Johnson's private view, in public he was hailing Diem as "the Winston Churchill of Southeast Asia." It was a comparison which boggled the mind, but as Johnson confided to a reporter, "Shit, man, he's the only boy we got out there." Kennedy had sent Johnson to Vietnam as a sign of good will; the lasting effect, however, was on Lyndon Johnson himself; *he* had given *our* word. To him, a man's word was important. He himself was now committed both to the war and to Diem personally.

The trouble was that none of the American rhetoric, none of the gestures that the Americans were making to reassure Diem, had had any effect on the most important people in South Vietnam, the peasants. Night after night, the Vietcong, the heirs and linear descendants of the Vietminh, were practicing the same kind of skilled guerrilla warfare and rural recruitment that the Vietminh had used during the French war, growing ever stronger, exploiting the multitude of local grievances against the government. In the field nothing had changed; the Army of the Republic of Vietnam, its commanders all former French officers and noncoms, resembled the French troops which had gone through the countryside in the daytime, using far too much fire power, stealing and looting from the peasants; at night when the ARVN troops were gone, the Vietcong re-entered the villages and spread their skilled political propaganda, against which Diem was particularly impotent. (For a long time he had even refused to concede that a major insurgency was going on, since the very admission would have shown that his government was not perfect. Since he believed in his own rectitude, there could not be an insurgency against him.)

Not surprisingly, though the pressure came from the South Vietnamese, and rural ones at that, Diem turned to white foreigners for help, for more aid, for air power, for a new treaty with the Americans. The idea of Ho Chi Minh needing help or reassurance from the Russians or the Chinese is inconceivable; the idea of Diem, a mandarin aristocrat, being able to understand the needs of the peasants and respond to them in kind is equally inconceivable.

Throughout much of 1961, despite the pessimistic assessments of independent reporters, the American mission remained reasonably optimistic. Diem was doing better, went the line, and the ARVN was fighting better. Others, not in the chain of command, were more dubious. Theodore White, visiting Vietnam on his own in August, wrote to the White House of Vietcong control in the lower Mekong Delta, and of the fact that no American wanted to drive outside of Saigon even during the day without military convoy. Remembering what had happened in China, White sensed history about to repeat itself. In September the Vietcong began to use some of the muscle they had accumulated. They tripled the number of incidents, and after seizing a provincial capital fifty-five miles from Saigon, they publicly beheaded the provincial chief. The latter act had a profound effect in Saigon, where issues of morale and confidence were taken very seriously.

By the end of the month there were strong demands in Washington for new military moves. Walt Rostow, ever enthusiastic and ready to use force (and not particularly knowledgeable about the rural realities), recommended that 25,000 SEATO troops be stationed on the border between the demilitarized zone and Cambodia in order to stop infiltration. (The insurgency, intelligence experts were noting, was almost entirely taking place within the South; all Vietcong troops were southerners; the weapons were captured from government posts. Some southerners, however, were cadre-trained in the North and then repatriated to the South. It was a small part of the war; eighty to ninety percent of the Vietcong were locally recruited, the National Intelligence Estimate said on October 5, 1961.) The Rostow proposal gave military men studying it a chill. It showed so little understanding of the rugged terrain; the 25,000 men would be completely swallowed up and ineffectual. The choice would be left to the enemy to either bypass this thin line of men or systematically eradicate it. Instead, on October 9 the Joint Chiefs of Staff responded to the Rostow proposal with a counterproposal, a commitment of American troops (around 20,000, but it would grow larger) to Vietnam. But the JCS wanted the troops in the Central Highlands and warned that under the Rostow proposal the SEATO troops would quickly be chewed up. Two days later the JCS reported at a National Security Council meeting that it would take only 40,000 American combat troops to clean up the Vietcong; in case the North Vietnamese and the Chinese Communists intervened, then an additional 128,000 troops would be needed.

At almost the same time, as if it were all orchestrated, Diem sent a cable asking for more fighter-bombers, civilian pilots for helicopters, more transport planes, and United States combat units for "combat-training" missions near the DMZ. He also asked that the Americans consider a request for a division of Chiang Kai-shek's troops to support his own army. Ambassador Nolting recommended "serious and prompt" attention to all requests.

Thus the pressures were building. Kennedy and his people had come to power ready to assert American power and they would find ample tests of it. Not just pressures from the Communists, but parallel political pressures at home. Even as Kennedy was about to make his first major move in response to the mounting urgency in Vietnam, he was making a crucial appointment at the very top of his government which reflected not so much his control of the government, but his lack of control. All of these major responses of the Kennedy Administration in the first year were based on two major premises: first, that the Communists were a harsh and monolithic enemy and that relaxation of tensions could only come once the Administration had proven its toughness; and second, that Kennedy's political problems at home were primarily from the right and the center, that the left could be handled, indeed it must accept the Administration's private statements of the good liberal things which might one day come. The Administration still felt itself under pressure to prove its own worth to centrists and conservative Americans, not to the liberal left. Most of the key moves by Kennedy in 1961 reflected this attitude. That he still coveted respectable Establishment support and felt more comfortable with the traditionalists was evidenced in another crucial appointment which he made.

This was Kennedy's choice, on September 27, 1961, of John McCone, an extremely conservative California Republican millionaire to head the CIA. Ever since the Bay of Pigs Kennedy had wanted to change personnel in both the JCS and the CIA; he regarded Allen Dulles as an icon of the past, too imposing for the younger men of the Administration to challenge. Now, in September, Kennedy made his move. He had tentatively offered the job to Clark Clifford, who had impressed him during the changeover from the Eisenhower Administration. But Clifford was not interested; perhaps he sensed that there was not enough power at the CIA to lure him from his law practice. Thus Kennedy, urged on by his brother Robert, turned to McCone.

The appointment caught the rest of the Administration by surprise, and the liberals in the Kennedy group were absolutely appalled by it. One reason the President had been so secretive even within his own Administration (he did not, for example, tell the Foreign Intelligence Advisory Board of his intention) was that he knew the opposition to McCone within the government would be so strong as to virtually nullify the appointment.

McCone came from a wealthy San Francisco family. With the coming of World War II he had become the principal figure in a new shipbuilding company. The business turned out to be an enormous financial success, and there were many contemporaries who felt McCone was nothing less than a war profiteer (in 1946 during a congressional investigation, Ralph Casey of the General Accounting Office, a watchdog of the Congress, testified that McCone and his associates of the California Shipbuilding Corporation had made $44,000,000 on an investment of $100,000. "I daresay that at no time in the history of American business," Casey remarked at the time, "whether in wartime or peacetime have so few men made so much money with so little risk and all at the expense of the taxpayers, not only of his generation but of future generations."). McCone served as a special deputy to James Forrestal, worked with Forrestal in creating the CIA, and later became an undersecretary of the Air Force under Truman. A convert to Catholicism, he believed that Communism was evil and must be stopped—along with Claire Booth Luce, he represented Eisenhower at Pope Pius's funeral in 1958. During the Eisenhower years he was known as the classic hard liner, a believer in massive retaliation and nuclear deterrents.

The liberals within the Administration were appalled, but the appointment was a very calculated move. McCone had been pushed by Robert Kennedy, then very much in his hard-line incarnation, who was also trying to get control of the apparatus of government. Bobby Kennedy wanted movers and doers and activists, men who could cut through the flabby bureaucracy, and McCone had precisely that kind of reputation (which McCone intended to keep—no sooner had he taken over than he called in the various heads of the other intelligence operations, told them that he intended to be the intelligence czar and that if they played ball with him he would increase their power in the government). But in particular, McCone was chosen by Kennedy because he offered one more bit of protection for a young President already on the defensive; having McCone at the CIA would deflect right-wing pressure against his Administration. And it was also a gesture by Kennedy of turning over key parts of his government to people who were in no way part of his domestic political constituency. (In the last months of Kennedy's life, Kenneth O'Donnell, annoyed by the fact that important jobs in the government had gone to people who had not supported the Kennedy political candidacy, or only marginally, was pushing for a new kind of appointment. He wanted to replace John McCone at CIA with Jack Conway, who had been Walter Reuther's main political lobbyist, a man committed to Kennedy on domestic issues and fully capable of making judgments on foreign affairs as well. Had Kennedy lived and made the appointment it would have been almost unique in the entire history of national security appointments, a break in class and outlook of considerable proportion.)

CHAPTER 7

So the appointment of McCone had shown the political center of the Kennedy Administration to be a good deal farther to the right than his original political supporters hoped; now as he moved on Vietnam they would again take minimal confidence. In October, 1961, the President decided to send his own special representatives to Vietnam for an on-site fact-finding trip. He and he alone was responsible for the composition of the team, which would to a very large degree reflect the true outlook of the new Administration toward Vietnam.

The trip was first proposed as a Rostow mission—just Rostow—but Bowles, who had become extremely nervous about Rostow's militancy

("Chester Bowles with machine guns," Arthur Schlesinger said of him), pushed hard for a high representative from State to go along to give the nonmilitary view. It should be someone of genuine rank, perhaps Bowles himself, perhaps Harriman. But Rusk was resistant; he still saw it as a military, not a political problem. Eventually, as something of a concession to the Bowles viewpoint, the President's military adviser, Maxwell Taylor, was added to the mission. Bowles remembered long talks in Korea in 1953, when Taylor had said with considerable emotion that American troops must never again fight a land war in Asia. Never again. And so Bowles and some of the others were pleased by the Taylor presence, but the resulting Taylor-Rostow report would deepen the American involvement in Vietnam from the low-level (and incompetent) advisory commitment of the Eisenhower years to the nearly 20,000 support and advisory troops there at the time President Kennedy was killed. It was one of the crucial turning points in the American involvement, and Kennedy, by his very choice of the two men who had the greatest vested interest in fighting limited antiguerrilla war, had loaded the dice.

Rostow was born in New York in 1916, one of three sons of a Russian Jewish immigrant. Even their names expressed a newcomer's almost naïve love of America. Walt Whitman Rostow, Eugene Victor Rostow, Ralph Waldo Rostow. Walt had always been a prodigy, always the youngest to do something. An unusually young graduate of Yale, a young Rhodes scholar. A young assistant to Gunnar Myrdal. Then a connection with the Eisenhower Administration; then MIT, part of a department which seemed eager to harness the intellectual resources of this country into the struggle against Communism.

In the fifties he had been something of a star in Cambridge, a man who published regularly, whose books were reviewed in *The New York Times*, a man who had a reputation not only in Cambridge but in Washington and New York as well, which was not entirely surprising, for the Rostows were considered by some in Cambridge—a very traditional and somewhat stuffy town—as being quite ambitious socially, perhaps too ambitious. There was one Rostow party which a Cambridge lady remembered well because it was given for Joyce Carey, the great English novelist. Everyone was impressed that the Rostows knew Carey so well, but this dimmed somewhat for the Cambridge lady when Carey very politely took her aside and said, "And now do tell me a little something about our charming host and hostess —I know so little about them."

Kennedy, on the make for an intellectual think tank of his own in the late fifties, particularly liked Rostow, liked his openness, his boundless energy, liked the fact that Rostow, unlike most academics, was realistic, seemed to understand something about how Washington really worked, liked the fact that Rostow mixed well, got on with professional politicians. During Kennedy's Senate days Rostow was always helpful, a demon for work, always producing memos, ideas, a great idea man (Open Skies for Ike, New Frontier and Let's Get This Country Moving Again for Kennedy).

There were those who felt that Kennedy became a little less comfortable with Rostow, a little pressed by him ("Walt," Kennedy said in 1961, not entirely to flatter him, "can write faster than I can read."), but in the 1960 campaign Rostow remained among the advisers, though on the outer periphery.

Rostow entered the new Administration as a genuine certified Cambridge intellectual who had done his part for the greater glory. There were, however, some Kennedy people with reservations about him, and they were not, curiously enough, the professional pols in the group but rather šome of the Cambridge intellectuals themselves. They would, of course, never blow the whistle on Walt, just as the generals would never blow the whistle on a fellow general. But there was a sense of unease about Walt, a concern about his ability to adapt, to change. That feeling would deepen as Rostow went from virtual fellow traveler to militant anti-Communist ideologue, an uneasiness at the facility with which he adapted to fashion, without perhaps even knowing that he was doing it. Some of his colleagues would notice, in the days of the Kennedy Administration, that Rostow sounded a little too much like the President, and that in the subsequent Administration he began to sound like Lyndon B. Johnson, employing the rough, tough language of the Ranch. It was a sense that behind all that bouncy enthusiasm, the Jewish immigrant's son, in his eagerness to make it in the big leagues with the Establishment, had lost sight of who Rostow was.

If there was one thing that bothered Walt's colleagues on the professional level, it was the firmness of his belief in his own ideas (at a given time), a lack of healthy skepticism about them. It was this which made him dangerous, some felt, because he did not know when he had gone too far, when to stop. He was particularly committed to the idea that the United States with its technology and its ideals could play a dominant role in the underdeveloped world and in stopping Communist revolutions, could in fact sponsor our own peaceful revolutions on our own terms. History was on our side if we did it right. Modernization was the key. To him Ho Chi Minh and men like Che Guevara were evil, out to oppress rather than liberate, and his staff would never forget the meeting he called the day Che Guevara was killed. Like a bit of theater, Walt very dramatic: "Gentlemen, I have very important news." Everyone leaning forward. "The Bolivians have executed Che." A pause to let the satisfaction sink in. "They finally got the SOB. The last of the romantic guerrillas." Rostow was, the staff noticed, excited, almost grateful for the news.

In choosing Rostow for the fact-finding trip to Vietnam, Kennedy was picking the one member of the Administration genuinely *enthusiastic* about a guerrilla confrontation there.

The other team member was Maxwell Taylor. Between 1955 and 1959 he had struggled with the Eisenhower Administration as Chief of Staff of the United States Army, during the years when the doctrine of massive retaliation had severely reduced the size and role of the Army (the Kennedy people always thought he had resigned in protest. Quite the opposite was true; though he had presented radically different strategies, he had walked the narrow path. Then he retired and wrote his dissenting book which was so critical of the Republicans that it left the impression that Taylor had, in fact, resigned).

A hero to civilians and soldiers alike, the general seemed almost invented for the Kennedy years. He was cool, correct, handsome, and athletic. As an airborne general, he was more modern in outlook than other generals; he spoke several languages and had written a book. And he was imposing, always in control. Most important of all, his strategic views coincided exactly with Kennedy's. He thought nuclear war unthinkable and that classic conventional war seemed increasingly outmoded. He had written that the next generation of wars would be brush-fire wars which the United States, as keeper of world stability and honor, must extinguish. He *seemed* to be talking about guerrilla wars, though what he apparently meant was the use of highly mobile conventional forces in very limited wars.

To the Kennedy people, then, he was a *good* general, different from the Eisenhower generals, who were simply typical of the military establishment. He had served Kennedy well during the Bay of Pigs, though his reports had been curiously technical in nature and not very astute politically. But Kennedy was inclined to think of Taylor as dispassionate and rational, more like himself than anyone else in the Administration, with the possible exception of Bundy. As if that were not enough, Robert Kennedy constantly promoted him.

So now here was Taylor, chosen for his mission, in the Kennedy eyes independent and modern; above all, a man who had been warning that the great military problem in the world was not nuclear war, but brush-fire wars, and now he was going to a country which contained, if nothing else, the world's most intense brush-fire war.

So they went, Rostow and Taylor; they got on well together. They were both activists, and those who wondered whether America had been taken over by soft, weak men would be reassured by the many photographs sent back from Saigon showing Taylor and Rostow playing vigorous tennis with various Vietnamese.

Also making the trip to Vietnam was one of Washington's most influential columnists (the war would severely damage his credibility and systematically lessen his influence), a man with an enormous vested interest in Asian anti-Communism, Joseph Alsop. He had never quite forgiven the State Department for allowing the United States to stand idly by while China went Communist. He was a forceful advocate of the domino theory, a man skilled in the ways of Washington, and his dispatches made a case for holding the line in a way which implied that manhood was at stake.

All week Alsop encouraged a troop commitment. At a time when the guerrilla war was at a markedly low level, with the Vietcong rarely striking in company units, never in battalion, and with perhaps no more than an estimated 17,000 Vietcong in the country, Alsop found not one but two North Vietnamese regiments preparing to enter the country, some four and a half years before they actually did.

Earlier in the year, as the insurgency in South Vietnam had intensified and the Vietcong moved steadily to larger units and began more and more to join battle (successfully) with the ARVN, there had been talk of combat troops. The Joint Chiefs wanted the troops not so much to engage in combat as to show American firmness (not realizing, of course, that in the particular rhythm of the war, if the Americans upped the ante, so would Hanoi and the Vietcong).

Now in the fall the Chiefs were pushing again, and to their demands was added a new pressure from the South Vietnamese. A year earlier Diem had not even deigned to recognize the Vietcong as a military force. They were bandits and outlaws (the same words Chiang Kai-shek had used to describe the Red Chinese armies, and for the same reason of wanting to have unchallenged legitimacy). As late as May, 1961, he had told Johnson he did not want American troops, but by September the Vietcong muscle had become more obvious. By October, Nguyen Dinh Thuan, who was the Acting Defense Minister and probably, except for the Ngo family itself, the most important senior official in the government, had called Ambassador Nolting in to ask for combat troops. They would be "combat trainer units," Nolting reported to Washington.

The request was something of a surprise to the United States government. It was different from what Diem had been saying before, and there was some suspicion that perhaps it was a trial balloon on the part of Ngo Dinh Nhu. Nevertheless, when Taylor and Rostow went, they were specifically assigned the job of investigating the possible employment of combat troops. There were three specific strategies they were to look into. One was the use of up to three divisions of American troops to defeat the Vietcong. The second was fewer combat troops, for the purpose of making a symbolic gesture and getting an American foot in the door. And the third, a step short of combat troops, was an acceleration of United States assistance and support to the Vietnamese, more equipment, particularly helicopters and light aircraft, to make the ARVN more mobile.

But if it was clear that Taylor's main concern was combat troops, then it followed that it would shortly be John F. Kennedy who either sent or did not send troops. What was also true was that the President was uneasy with the pressure he was already feeling from the men around him.

After the fact-finding mission left Vietnam, it went to the Philippines, where Taylor worked on the central part of the report. In 1954 General Matthew Ridgway, Taylor's predecessor as Chief of Staff, had struggled brilliantly to keep American troops out of Indochina. Kennedy had appointed Taylor partly because he wanted someone like Ridgway, but it would become apparent that Ridgway and Taylor were different men.

Because the Taylor-Rostow mission profoundly changed and escalated the American commitment to Vietnam, and because all news reports at the time said that Taylor had recommended against combat troops, it is easy to underestimate the report. The fact is that Taylor, the dominant figure of the trip—he wrote the crucial report to Kennedy himself—did recommend combat troops. He recommended that up to 8,000 be sent, more if necessary, and most important, that the job could not be done without them. The recommendations shocked Kennedy to such an extent that Taylor's report was closely guarded and in some cases called back (even people as directly concerned with the decision making as Walter McConaughy, the Assistant Secretary of State for Far Eastern Affairs, did not know that Taylor had recommended troops). What was made public was part of the report, the recommendations for the advisory part of the mission and the reform and broadening of Diem's government. In contrast, Taylor's actual cables barely mentioned reform; they dealt primarily with military problems.

Taylor talked in his cables of a "crisis of confidence" because of the growing Vietcong military build-up and because of the United States' neutralization of Laos. Taylor spelled out clearly the mission of the United States troops: it would be a task force largely logistical in makeup whose presence would reassure Diem of the American readiness "to join him in a showdown with the Vietcong or Vietminh." The Taylor cables also outlined the dangers: our strategic reserve was already weak and we would be engaging United States' prestige. If the first increment failed, it would be difficult to "resist the pressure to reinforce," and if the ultimate mission were the closing of the border and the cleaning up of the insurgents, "there is no limit to our possible commitment," unless "we attacked the source in the North." It might increase tensions "and risk escalation into a major war in Asia."

Taylor acknowledged that the risks of backing into a major Asian war were present but (in words that would live longer than he might have wanted) "not impressive." North Vietnam "is extremely vulnerable to conventional bombing, a weakness which should be exploited diplomatically in convincing Hanoi to lay off South Vietnam" (a vulnerability which, if it existed, Hanoi was less aware of than both Taylor and Rostow). Both Hanoi and Peking, he cabled, faced "severe logistical difficulties in trying to maintain strong forces in the field in Southeast Asia, difficulties which we share, but by no means to the same degree." The starvation conditions in China, he found, would keep the Chinese from being militarily venturesome. As for the key question of how American troops would fare, Taylor found South Vietnam "not an excessively difficult or unpleasant place to operate." In perhaps the most significant passage of all, he thought it was comparable to Korea, "where U.S. troops learned to live and work without too much effort. In the High Plateau and in the coastal plain where U.S. troops would probably be stationed, these jungle forest conditions do not exist to any great extent."

This part of the Taylor cables is perhaps the most revealing insight into the way the American military regarded Vietnam and the war. This was the time when unconventional warfare was a great fad in Washington, and here was Taylor, who was supposed to be an expert on it, making a comparison with Korea: we had the same problems there, and we overcame them. In searching for the parallel war, Taylor singled out Korea but without considering the crucial difference between Korea and Vietnam: the nature of the opposing forces. There was a parallel war: the French Indochina war or the Philippine insurrection. But Taylor made the comparison with Korea, and if this general, who was so widely respected, an intellectual who quoted Thucydides, did not see this crucial nuance, who else would?

In his summing up on November 3, Taylor said that the advantages of sending American troops outweighed the disadvantages, and that this was imperative to the success of saving South Vietnam ("I do not believe that our program to save South Vietnam will succeed without it."). Then he asked the same question which Kennedy had posed earlier, whether the suggested program, minus the United States combat task force, could stop further deterioration in the South. He answered that there was no substitute for a military presence to raise morale and "to sober the enemy and to discourage escalation. . . ."

All in all, the Taylor-Rostow report is an extraordinary document, and provides a great insight into the era. It shows a complete misunderstanding of the nature of the war. It was arrogant and contemptuous toward a foe who had a distinguished record against a previous Western challenger. It assumed that the people and the government of South Vietnam were the same thing; yet it also said that a people allegedly fighting for their survival, already overstocked with American aid and materiel, needed reassurance, that the problem was not one of political origin, but of confidence. When Ridgway in 1954 investigated the possibility of United States troops in Indochina, he maximized the risks and minimized the benefits; now Taylor was maximizing the benefits and minimizing the risks.

On the whole, opposition to sending troops was frail. On November 8, Secretary of Defense Robert McNamara, reflecting the pressures from his Pentagon constituency, signed on. In an unusually personalized memo ("The Joint Chiefs, Mr. Gilpatric and I have decided. . . .") he said that the fall of South Vietnam would lead to serious deterioration throughout Southeast Asia, and he agreed that we were unlikely to prevent the fall without sending United States combat forces. He accepted Taylor's judgment that anything less would fail to restore Diem's confidence. However, he noted that even Taylor's 8,000 men would not necessarily impress the other side with the true seriousness of American intent. Such a conviction would only come with a clear statement that we would use more force if necessary, and that if Hanoi continued to aid the Vietcong, we would take punitive action against the North. "I believe we can safely assume the maximum U.S. forces required on the ground in Southeast Asia will not exceed six divisions, or about 205,000 men," McNamara wrote. The basic McNamara summary was in support of the Taylor position.

There were two important men in Washington who had strong misgivings about sending in combat troops. One was John Kennedy; the other was George Ball, Undersecretary of State for Economic Affairs, who was about to be given Bowles' job. Ball was a lawyer who had been willing to defend victims of McCarthy at the height of the witch hunt. He was a forcefully independent man, and the suggestion to use combat troops in Vietnam disturbed him.

George Ball had worked closely with the French during the Indo-china war, and he had seen it all, the false optimism of the generals, the resiliency and relentlessness of the Vietminh, their capacity to exploit nationalism and to mire down a Western nation, the poisonous domestic effect. He wanted no part of it for America. When he read the Taylor cables calling for a small, oh so small, commitment, 8,000 men only, he immediately told Bundy and McNamara that if they went ahead with the Taylor proposals, the commitment would not stay small. They would have 300,000 men in there within five years (he was slightly off; it was 500,000 men in five-plus years) because sending combat troops would change the nature of the commitment and the nature of the war, and the other side would not let us out easily. Besides, this was exactly what Diem wanted; it would stabilize his regime and we would do his fighting for him. Both Bundy and McNamara argued with Ball; they believed in the capacity of rational men to control irrational commitments, and in the end they decided that even at 300,000, a troop commitment was worth a try. Then, Ball said, they must tell the President that it was worth that much blood and resources, and Bundy and McNamara agreed. When Ball himself made exactly the same point to Kennedy—that he would have 300,000 men there in a few short years—the President laughed and said, "George, you're crazier than hell." But it had jarred the President, and had made him even more aware of how long and dark the tunnel might be.

Not that he needed that much jarring; the President had plenty of doubts of his own. He was conscious of the danger of the recommendations, of the facility with which they had been contrived. "They want a force of American troops," he told Arthur Schlesinger at the time. "They say it's necessary in order to restore confidence and maintain morale. But it will be just like Berlin. The troops will march in, the bands will play, the crowds will cheer, and in four days everyone will have forgotten. Then we will be told we have to send in more troops. It's like taking a drink. The effect wears off and you have to take another." He was skeptical about the whole thing. He had been there when the French had 300,000 men and could not control the country, and he wondered aloud how we could do it any better than the French.

On November 11, three days after the McNamara recommendation to introduce combat forces, there was a new McNamara paper, done jointly with Rusk, which reflected the President's position. It was a compromise. Kennedy would send American support units and American advisers, but not American combat troops. We would help the South Vietnamese help themselves. If there really was something to South Vietnam as a nation and it really wanted to remain free, as we in the West defined freedom, then we would support it. We would send our best young officers to advise down to battalion level, we would ferry the ARVN into battle against the elusive Vietcong, and we would, being good egalitarians, pressure Diem to reform and broaden the base of a creaky government and modernize his whole society.

For McNamara to have switched on his recommendations was his normal procedure; his papers were always draft recommendations until the President made up his mind. Then they were tailored to the President's decision so that there would be no record for history of any difference between the Secretary of Defense and the President. He was that loyal. And Kennedy, holding the line on combat troops, told the Joint Chiefs of Staff to go ahead with the planning for a combat commitment, which was a typical procedure: if you do not give them what they want, give them a chance to dream of it. After the Bay of Pigs he had told them to go ahead with the plans for an invasion of Cuba. A little something for everybody, a little nothing for everybody. There was in the final Kennedy package a good deal of emphasis on nation building and reform, and a belief that we could somehow trick Diem into coming round. We would do this by bypassing Diem's government, creating strategic hamlets to protect the people from the Vietcong (on the assumption that they wanted to be protected). We would modernize the state, not necessarily with Diem but in spite of him.

In doing less than what the Taylor-Rostow report called for, Kennedy felt that he was being moderate, cautious. There was an illusion that he had held the line, whereas in reality he was steering us far deeper into the quagmire. He had not withdrawn when a contingent of 600 men there had failed, and now he was escalating that commitment to 15,000, which meant that any future decision on withdrawal would be that much more difficult. And he was escalating not just the troop figure but changing a far more subtle thing as well.

The aid did not come without American military bodies, and the military bodies did not come without journalistic bodies, so by expanding the number of Americans, Kennedy was in every way expanding the importance of Vietnam, making his own country more aware of it. From two full-time American correspondents, the number jumped to eight, including, most dangerous of all, American reporters with television cameras who roamed around discovering things that Diem did not want revealed. Diem's political enemies, who were numerous, finding no outlet through the constitution of Vietnam nor through the American embassy, would for the first time find sympathetic listeners in American reporters, and thus the expansion of the American commitment also meant that there would be an inevitable rise in the pace of domestic Vietnamese turbulence (Diem, totally removed from reality, and almost psychotic at the end, believed that when the first Buddhist monk burned himself to death, it had been arranged for and paid by NBC, despite the fact that there were no television cameras on the scene.). What was true, however, was that the presence of American reporters tended to open up an otherwise closed country; this was the price Diem paid for getting American aid.

The Kennedy commitment changed things in other ways as well. While the President had the illusion that he had held off the military, the reality was that he had let them in. They now began to dominate the official reporting, so that the dispatches which came into Washington were colored through their eyes. Now they were players, men who had a seat at the poker table; they would now, on any potential dovish move, have to be dealt with. He had activated them, and yet at the same time had given them so precious little that they could always tell their friends that they had never been allowed to do what they really wanted. Dealing with the military, once their foot was in the door, both Kennedy and Johnson would learn, was an awesome thing. The failure of their estimates along the way, point by point, meant nothing. It did not follow, as one might expect, that their credibility was diminished and that there was now less pressure from them, but the reverse. It meant that there would be an inexorable pressure for more—more men, more hardware, more targets. They would soon dominate the play. The illusion would always be of civilian control; the reality would be of a relentlessly growing military domination of policy, intelligence, aims, objectives, and means, with the civilians, the very ones who thought they could control the military, conceding step by step, without even knowing they were losing.

The immediate result of the Kennedy decision in December to send a major advisory and support team to Vietnam was the activation of a new player, a major military player, to run a major American command in Saigon. By appointing Lieutenant General Paul D. Harkins to the new command, Kennedy was sending one more potential player against him, a figure who would represent the primacy of Saigon and the war, as opposed to the primacy of the Kennedy Administration.

Harkins, who had been recommended for the command by his old army friend, Maxwell Taylor, began by corrupting the intelligence reports coming in. Up until 1961 they had been reasonably accurate, clear, unclouded by bureaucratic ambition; they had reflected the ambivalence of the American commitment to Diem, and the Diem flaws had been apparent both in CIA and, to a slightly lesser degree, in State reporting. Ambassador Nolting would change State's reporting, and to that would now be added the military reporting, forceful, detailed, and highly erroneous, representing the new commander's belief that his orders were to make sure things looked well on the surface. In effect the Administration had created a situation where it lied to itself.

CHAPTER 8

B y sending its vast advisory and support group—which would eventually number some 18,000 men—the Administration had changed the commitment without changing the war, or the problems which had caused it. It had moved Vietnam off the back burner of crisis quotient. The question was no longer one of Diem's popularity or effectiveness (the answer to that was that he was not popular, but he was *respected*); the real question now was whether the war was being won. And the answer was yes, it was being won, it was going very well. General Harkins was optimistic; he headed what was now a powerful institutional force for optimism. He had been told by his superior, Maxwell Taylor, to be optimistic, to downgrade pessimism, and he would do exactly that. Everything, he assured his superiors, was right on schedule; everyone was getting with the program. The war was being won. He saw victory shaping up within a year.

The only thing wrong was that the war was not being won; it was, in fact, not even being fought. The ARVN was a replica of the past, more arrogant now than ever. All the old mistakes were being repeated in the field; the army still systematically enraged the population by running giant sweeps through peasant villages, with its soldiers stealing chickens and ducks. It still refused to run operations where the Vietcong were known to congregate. Since Diem was afraid that if his army suffered losses he would lose face, he told his commanders not to risk casualties, so they joined battle as little as possible. They made up for it by falsifying after-action reports, creating statistics which were soon on their way to Washington bearing Harkins' imprimatur. All the government optimism was being built on faked reports.

But in the field, things were different. There American officers began to respond to the deceit they encountered daily. It was one thing to sit in Saigon in an air-conditioned room and pass on fake reports; it was another to send young American advisers into combat, knowing that they were risking their lives for what was essentially a fraud. An inevitable confrontation of serious proportions took place.

As the war effort began to fall apart in late 1962 and early 1963, the Military Assistance Command in Saigon set out to crush its own best officers in the field. It was not as if two different and conflicting kinds of military reporting were being sent to Washington, with the White House able to study the two and arbitrate the difference. The Saigon command did not brook dissent or negativism. If a colonel surfaced in a newspaper by name as a pessimist it was the end of his career.

The pessimists included senior advisers to Harkins in the Mekong Delta, and typical of these were Lieutenant Colonel John Paul Vann of the 7th Division (the northern tier of the Delta) and Lieutenant Colonel Fred Ladd, 21st Division (the southern tier of the Delta). They were combat veterans, men who had been specially selected for these slots. They were neither hawks nor doves (those terms did not exist at the time), but they wanted to win the war, they still thought it a possibility, and they understood at least some of the political forces the Vietcong represented. Finally, they were living where the war was taking place, and they thought it was a serious business, sending young men out to die, and if you were willing to do it, you also had to be willing to fight for their doubts and put your career on the line.

Ladd was quickly put down for pessimistic reporting from his area. Vann was even worse; his reporting had caused some problems in the past. Now a major storm would center around him in January, 1963, when the division he advised was badly defeated and performed with great cowardice at the battle of Ap Bac, which, being close to Saigon, was well covered journalistically. Harkins was furious, not at the Vietnamese or their commander, but at Vann for having called it a defeat and for having talked with American reporters. Harkins planned to fire Vann at the time but was talked out of it by staff members who argued that firing him would bring even more adverse publicity. Instead, Vann became a nonperson. Anything he wrote or said thereafter was simply disregarded, and important visitors to the country were steered away from his area.

Vann was the most intense and dedicated of the dissenters, and he came to symbolize the struggle against Harkins and his superior, General Taylor. By the time Vann went home in June, 1963, he was the most informed American in the country. A statistician by training, he had managed to come up with a new kind of statistic. In contrast to the MACV, whose figures reflected only the American willingness to accept inflated ARVN body counts at face value, Vann had managed to compile a different kind of statistical story. Thus he documented the ARVN failure to fight (of the 1,400 government deaths in his sector in one year, only 50 were ARVN). This did not mean that the ARVN was fighting well, as Harkins implied; it confirmed that they were not fighting at all, and that the burden of the war was being borne by ill-equipped local militia who more often than not were being killed asleep in their defensive positions. He was able to prove that commanders got troops from Diem not on the basis of Vietcong pressure, but on the basis of personal ties and their ability to protect Diem against a coup.

Vann went home a very angry man, to find that Saigon had ordered that he not be debriefed in Washington. So he began to give his briefing to friends at the Pentagon. It was very different from the usual Saigon briefings. What made it striking was that it seemed to be based on very hard facts. Vann began to get higher and higher hearings in the Pentagon until finally General Barksdale Hamlett, the Deputy Chief of Staff of the Army, arranged for Vann to meet with the Joint Chiefs. Vann was warned by several high officers that above all he must not appear to be critical of General Harkins, who was the personal choice of Maxwell Taylor (by this time Chairman of the Joint Chiefs). He was also warned not to show his briefing until the last minute to General Krulak, who was the Secretary of Defense's special adviser on guerrilla warfare and who had just returned from a tour of Saigon to report to the Chiefs that the war was going every bit as well as Harkins said.

The Vann briefing was set for 2 P.M. on July 8, 1963. At 9:45 he sent a copy to General Krulak's office. A little later Vann, eager, starched, finally getting his hearing, showed up outside the office of General Earle G. Wheeler, the Chief of Staff, to be on hand in case there were any new developments. He was sitting there when a phone call came in to one of Wheeler's aides. "*Who* wants the item removed from the agenda?" the aide asked. The voice at the other end spoke for a few minutes. "Is this the Secretary of Defense's or the Chairman's office?" There was more talk. "Is that an order or a request?" Then more talk. "Let me get this right. The Chairman *requests* that the item be removed." The aide turned to Vann. "Looks like you don't brief today, buddy." He went to Wheeler's office, returned in a minute, picked up the phone and dialed a number and said, "The Chief agrees to remove the item from the agenda." Thus a major dissenting view was blocked from a hearing at the highest level by Max Taylor (had Vann briefed, it would have been much harder for the high-level military to go into meetings with the President and claim that the war was going well).

There was, however, another outlet for dissent—the American journalists in Saigon. The journalists kept showing up in the countryside, and inevitably they saw how many lies were being told, how fradulent the war was. It was only a matter of time before a version of the war and of the regime, far more pessimistic, began to surface in the American press. But since the official policy now depended for its life on the public relations aspect, the reporters became targets of the Administration, both at home and in Vietnam. They were the one element in Saigon that could not be controlled: Diem controlled his press, his military, his legislature; Harkins his reporting channels, and Ambassador Nolting his. The only people who could be candid were the American reporters. "Get on the team," Admiral Harry Felt told Malcolm Browne of the AP. "Stop looking for the hole in the doughnut," Nolting enjoined reporters.

The reporters were young, without established reputations. Because they were young, their views of the world and of war were not set in a World War II philosophy. Their reporting of the political stagnation in Saigon, of the false promises of Diem, was consistently on target; more honest and accurate than that of the military (eight years later the Pentagon Papers would confirm this through analysis by the Pentagon's own experts).

The Administration countered quickly enough. If the reporters would not write upbeat stories, the Kennedy Administration, facile, particularly good at public relations, would generate its own positive accounts. Thus optimism and optimistic statements became a major and deliberate part of the policy; warfare by public relations, one more reflection of the Kennedy era. High-level Americans were sent over not to learn about Vietnam, not to see Vietnam or to improve what was privately known as a frail policy, but to pump up this weak policy. Their speeches and statements had been written for them before they left, full of praise for Diem, full of talk of a national revolution, of the end of the long war, of victory in sight. One day at the Saigon airport, with television cameras focusing on one of them as he descended the plane and began reading his statement, Neil Sheehan, then a young reporter for UPI, remarked, "Ah, another foolish Westerner come to lose his reputation to Ho Chi Minh."

But in late 1962 Senate Majority Leader Mike Mansfield came through Saigon. The visit was made at Kennedy's request. Mansfield had visited Vietnam many times in the past and had been one of the original liberal-Catholic sponsors of Diem. Now Mansfield was appalled by the deterioration of Diem, the growing isolation of the man, the sense of unreality around the palace, the dominance of Mr. and Mrs. Nhu. Mansfield skipped some of the official briefings provided for him by Nolting and instead spent a four-hour lunch with the American reporters. The next day at the airport, as he prepared to leave, he was handed a statement drafted for him by the embassy (a small courtesy on the part of the ambassador in case the Senate Majority Leader did not know what to say). Mansfield rejected it; his own farewell speech, by its absence of enthusiasm, reflected his disenchantment. When he returned to Washington he gave Kennedy a private account that was blunt and pessimistic about the future of it all. Kennedy had summoned Mansfield to his yacht, the *Honey Fitz,* where there was a party going on, and when the President read the report his face grew redder and redder as his anger mounted. Finally he turned to Mansfield, just about the closest friend he had in the Senate, and snapped, "Do you expect me to take this at face value?" Mansfield answered, "You asked me to go out there." Kennedy looked at him icily and said, "Well, I'll read it again."

But the articles in the daily newspapers, combined with the reports from men like Mansfield, slowly had an effect on the President. By early 1963 Kennedy was unhappy with his team in Saigon; in particular he was dissatisfied with the reporting that was coming in; it was all too simplistic, too confident, and there was too little nuance, too little concern about the population reflected. But it was not so much a distaste for the Harkins and Nolting simplistic reporting as a distaste for the war itself and the problems of Vietnam, a belief that it was not going to be easy, an intuition that it was somehow going to pull us in deeper and deeper. In private he began to voice concern over where we were going. What the President was learning, to his displeasure (once again, the Bay of Pigs had been lesson one), was something that his successor Lyndon Johnson would also find out the hard way: that a policy involving the military, once started, has a life and a thrust of its own, and that its thrust and drive may not be in any way akin to the desires of the President who initiated it.

Starting in mid-1962, this had begun to be true on Vietnam, and there was soon a split between the American military (and Saigon) and the Administration over four main issues: napalm, defoliants, free-fire zones, and the introduction of jet planes instead of outmoded prop fighter-bombers. The military quickly lost on jets, but both Diem and Nhu supported and in fact pushed the American military on all these points, an important insight into the way they regarded their own peasantry. The position of Diem, and particularly Nhu, was that these weapons were vital; they helped support the government, even though they inflicted great pain and death on the peasants. In fact, Diem and Nhu still held to the mandarin psychology that the population would so hate the killing and the awesome force of its government that it would automatically respect the government, and turn on the Vietcong. But the population was simply not that anti-Communist; it resented the force unleashed on it more than it feared the enemy it was allegedly being saved from.

If the military lost on jets, it pushed very hard on the other issues. Napalm was the first one. Harkins liked napalm, Diem and Nhu liked napalm; Harkins said it put the fear of God in the Vietcong. It was just one more weapon in the arsenal, the general said, and perhaps he was right. But it was a weapon that appalled Kennedy. It somehow seemed to be particularly antihuman, and he hated photographs of what it had done to people. Now they want to use it on villages, he would tell his staff. They tell me that it won't hurt anyone, but if no one will be hurt by it, what do they want it for?

Then the military wanted defoliation, and once again the battle started. They wanted to start using it widely, for crop defoliation, but Kennedy did not want crops destroyed, no matter whose crops. Then they pushed for limited defoliation, just on the roads to make it harder for the enemy to ambush the troops. Our boys will be protected. Try it out, MACV said. Just a little bit, it will help win the war. Reluctantly, Kennedy finally approved a limited use of it, just as he approved a limited use of napalm in battles where the population was not nearby.

Then Harkins argued for free-fire zones, a place to drop unused bombs, because to carry those bombs back made it dangerous for the planes on landing. Kennedy asked his staff why they couldn't drop the extra bombs in the sea; the loss of a few bombs into the South China Sea would be no problem. But Harkins wanted the Iron Triangle, no people there; well, no friendly people certainly, and eventually the military gained very limited free-fire zones.

Gradually Kennedy began to hate it, and some of the men around him began to sense that they were losing control. The White House was beginning to see that the people who were in charge of the Saigon mission were more militant than Washington, more committed to Diem than Washington. Kennedy had made the commitment with misgivings, but the commitment was already operative, burning with a special fuel of its own—bureaucratic momentum and individual ambition— men let loose in Saigon and Washington who never questioned whether something was right or wrong, or whether it worked or not.

CHAPTER 9

In Saigon, the Military Assistance Command now functioned as a powerful, organized establishment which could control the loyalty of its people and churn out facts, statistics, and programs to suit the whim of its sponsors at the Pentagon. It had defeated the protests of its own best people, it had determined that things were going well, that there was and would be optimism (at a Honolulu meeting in April, 1963, Harkins was almost euphoric; he could not give any guarantees, but he thought it would be all over by Christmas). And in Washington, the dominant figure on Vietnam was not Dean Rusk, but Secretary of Defense Robert McNamara; it was he who dominated the action, the play. In the growing split between the civilians and the military over Vietnam, McNamara was allowed to be the referee.

That McNamara was by default usurping the role of the Secretary of State, did not faze him. He was intelligent, forceful, courageous, decent, everything, in fact, but wise. This man, whose only real experience had been in dealing with the second largest automotive empire in the world, producing huge Western vehicles, was the last man to understand the problems of a people looking for their political freedom. Yet he was very much a man of the Kennedy Administration. He symbolized the idea that it could manage and control events, in an intelligent, rational way. If McNamara was in charge of something he would run it correctly; if it was a war, it would be a good war.

He was Bob, Bob McNamara, taut, controlled, driving—climbing mountains, harnessing generals—the hair slicked down in a way that made him look like a Grant Wood subject. The look was part of the drive: the glasses straight and rimless, imposing; you looked at the glasses and kept your distance. *Bob got things done*, the can-do man in the can-do society, in the can-do era. He was American through and through, with the American drive and certitude. He sat there behind that huge desk, austere, imposing. A Secretary of Defense of the United States of America, with a budget of 85 billion dollars a year, not to mention a generous supply of nuclear warheads at his disposal, was likely to be imposing.

One was always aware of his time; speak quickly and be gone, make your point, in and out, keep the schedule, lunch from 1:50 to, say, expansively, 2 P.M., and above all, do not engage in any philosophical discussions. *Well, Bob, my view of history is....* No one was to abuse his time. Do not, he told his aides, let people brief me orally. If they are going to make a presentation, find out in advance and make them put it on paper. "Why?" an aide asked. A cold look. "Because I can read faster than they can talk." Those who wasted his time—except of course those above him—would feel his cold stare, and this included even General Maxwell Taylor. The first time Taylor went over to see McNamara, Taylor arrived a little early. He stood outside the Secretary's office while McNamara waited for the exact moment of their appointment. Then Taylor was held up on the phone—a White House call. So McNamara waited for Taylor, and finally Taylor waited for McNamara a bit more, and then he went in and was given one of the icier treatments of his life.

Time was of the essence, to be rationed and saved; time was not just money, it was, even more important, action, decisions, cost effectiveness, power. McNamara, who was under such pressure, always tried to conceal it, to be cool, though there was somehow a price to be paid. He would, for instance, while he was in Detroit, grind his teeth in his sleep, wearing down the enamel until Marg McNamara sent him to a dentist, who had them recapped (a New York dentist just so there would be no gossip in Detroit, which might diminish his legend and thus his power; his legend was his power).

Sometimes, to those around him, he seemed so idealistic as to be innocent. He never talked about power and he did not seem to covet it. Yet the truth was quite different. He loved power and sought it intensely. For all his apparent innocence, he had triumphed in the ferocious jungle of Detroit automotive politics; he was acutely aware of how to gain and hold power.

If the body was tense and driven, the mind was mathematical, analytical, bringing order and reason out of chaos. Always reason. And reasons supported by facts, by statistics—he could prove his rationality with facts, intimidate others. He was marvelous with charts and statistics. Once, sitting at CINCPAC for eight hours watching hundreds and hundreds of slides flashed across the screen showing what was in the pipe line to Vietnam and what was already there, he finally said, after seven hours, "Stop the projector. This slide, number 869, contradicts slide 11." Slide 11 was flashed back and he was right, they did contradict each other. Everyone was impressed, and many a little frightened. No wonder his reputation grew; others were in awe. For it was a mind that could continue to summon its own mathematical kind of sanity into bureaucratic battle, long after the others, the good liberal social scientists who had never gone beyond their original logarithms, had trailed off into the dust, though finally, when the mathematical version of sanity did not work out, when it turned out that the computer had not fed back the right answers and had underestimated those funny little far-off men in their raggedy pajamas, he would be stricken with a profound sense of failure, and he would be, at least briefly, a shattered man.

He was an emotional man as well, weeping at his last Pentagon ceremony, his friends at the very end worried about his health, both mental and physical, about what the war had done to his ethical framework. In 1968 he would go to the World Bank—a job which was the very antithesis of his previous position as head of the greatest war machine in the history of the world, an act which seemed to some to have a touch of penance in it. He was willing to reminisce with old friends about the Defense years, with the exception of one subject which never came up, Vietnam. It still caused him pain and would not go away; there were reminders everywhere of what it had meant. Nor was the split in his own family a unique illustration of what the war had done to this country, in home after home. In the Robert McNamara family there was Bob McNamara, who was one of the great architects of the war, while in 1970 one of the leaders of the California peace movement, attending rallies everywhere, radical, committed, was his young son Craig.

McNamara's growing up had been simple—and enviable. Good parents. Good education. Good marks. He was born in San Francisco in 1916, the son of Robert J. McNamara and Claranell Strange (thus the middle name, Robert Strange McNamara, upon which his critics would so joyously seize in later years). His father, who married late, was fifty when Bob was born; he was a sales manager for a San Francisco wholesale shoe firm. Father Catholic, mother Protestant, McNamara a Protestant. (Later, during the height of Lyndon Johnson's love affair with McNamara, the President thought of the Secretary of Defense as a Vice Presidential possibility and called around to Democratic pols with the idea. "You could even see Lyndon thinking it out—the Protestants will assume he's a Protestant, and the Catholics will think he's a Catholic," one White House aide said.)

When he and his sister were small, the family moved across the Bay to Annerly, a nice middle-class section of Oakland which featured a particularly good school system. At Piedmont High, he was a doer, no jarred nerves, joining all the right clubs, honor societies. He was not yet an exceptional student; an early IQ test put him above the norm, very bright but not exceptional.

From Piedmont he went to Berkeley at a time when Robert Gordon Sproul was turning it into a great university. At Berkeley his proficiency in math was beginning to show through, and his own grades came so easily that he had time to read and work in other courses. His professors assumed that he would become a teacher; he did not seem to have the kind of drive, the hustle, which one felt went with a business career. Those were good years, summers spent gold mining (unsuccessfully), climbing mountains, a sport which he quickly came to love, learning to ski, which he went at in typical McNamara style: find out your weaknesses and keep working on them. Man could conquer all by discipline, will, and rationality.

From Berkeley he went to Harvard Business School, where he was an immediate standout. His unique ability in accounting control became evident, and he began to work at applying that talent to management techniques. He graduated, moved back to the Bay area to work for Price Waterhouse, and in 1939 started seeing an old friend named Margaret Craig. When he was asked back to Harvard Business School to teach accounting, he married Marg (whom everyone would consider a good and humanizing influence on McNamara; much of what was good in Bob, friends thought, came from Marg's generous instincts). At Harvard he was a particularly good teacher, well organized, with good control of his subject and enthusiasm for his work, but he was restless. World War II was approaching and he wanted to play his part; the Navy had turned him down because of weak eyes. He was trying to join the Army when Harvard Business School went to war.

It came about through Robert Lovett who, as Assistant Secretary for Air, was determined to help build the greatest air force in the world, which would wreak massive saturation bombing against the enemy's industrial might. Together with his bright young deputy, Charles (Tex) Thornton, Lovett decided that in order to harness American industry for the great war effort, they needed first and foremost a giant statistical brain to tell them what was needed, and where. They asked Harvard Business School, the most logical place, to train the officers they needed for statistical control. This brain trust would send the right men and the right supplies to the right places and would make sure that when crews arrived at a base there were enough instructors. It was a symbolic step in America's going from a relatively sleepy country toward becoming a superpower (a step which the acceleration in air power and air industry would finalize).

Harvard Business School accepted the proposition, and a group of the best young teachers was sought out. McNamara was among them. He was so effective, such an immediate standout, that Thornton soon pulled him from Harvard and attached him to the Army Air Forces. Finally, for the first time, McNamara had something upon which to fasten that energy, that drive, that curious cold passion. Those traits which would eventually be part of the legend began to emerge. Thornton would recall that the young McNamara of those early days was strikingly similar to the mature McNamara: the same discipline, the concentration, the relentless work all day and night.

Thornton sent him to England to work on the B-17 bomber program, got him a commission as a temporary captain in the Army Air Forces. But when the B-29 was being developed, he was pulled from other programs. This was to become the major project for the Air Force, the long-range bomber which was to prove so vital during the last year of the war. Other men would make their reputations in the development of the B-29, but Thornton later claimed that the genius of the operation was the young McNamara, putting all the infinitely complicated pieces together, doing program analysis, operation analysis, digesting the mass of facts which would have intimidated less disciplined minds, making sure that the planes and the crews were readied at roughly the same time. Since all this took place before the real age of computers, he had to work it out himself. He was the intelligence bank of the project, and he held the operation together, kept its timing right, kept it all on schedule. It was an awesome performance for a man not yet thirty.

McNamara had planned to go back to Harvard after the war. Challenges fascinated him, but not worldly goods or profit as ends in themselves. So why not return to Harvard, the teaching of those beloved statistics, it was awesome to imagine what they might do in the future. The life style of Cambridge appealed to him; he could enjoy the university atmosphere. But Thornton, a man with more imagination than the somewhat reserved McNamara, had other ideas. To Thornton the Air Force had not just been a part of a vast and impressive wartime enterprise but something more, a case study in instant corporate success. It had gone from 295 pilots trained in the year before Pearl Harbor to 96,000 the year after, planes built, flight crews trained, all dovetailed. It had been a staggering task, an enormous success, and they had done it, this group of talented young people that Thornton and Lovett had created, fresh young minds with modern skills.

Now, Thornton knew, there would be a reconversion to civilian production, and the business world would be filled with new opportunities. He took stock of his team: they were without doubt the most talented managerial team of the century, and he began to think of the possibility of selling them as a group, all that expertise and managerial talent bound together. If they were to accomplish something, really create something new and bold in the business world, then their chances were far greater as a group ("If you went in with one or two people you could get lost or chewed up; if you were going to convert a relatively large company quickly you needed a group," he would recall). When he talked it over with his team, they were enthusiastic. Only McNamara had objections, he wanted to return to Harvard. But there were financial problems: he had come down with a mild case of polio, and Marg with a more serious case, necessitating considerable doctor bills. ("I said, 'Bob, you've got those doctor bills and you can't go back there to Harvard on twenty-six hundred dollars a year,' and he thought and said, 'I guess you're right,' and he was on board," Thornton said.)

There were two immediate possibilities; one was Robert Young, the railroad man, and the other was the Ford Motor Company. Ford seemed to offer the most challenge. It would have to be retooled and reconverted; they knew that financially it had not done well, though they did not know how badly it had done during the last twenty years, showing a profit only once since 1927, in the year 1932. The old man's long-time associate, Harry Bennett, had just been ousted and the reins taken over by Henry Ford II, their own age—he was twenty-eight—who now desperately needed to modernize the company that his grandfather had founded and then let slip. They sent Ford a cable which said in effect: bright young management team, ran Air Force, ready to work. Thornton made an early contact; eight of them went out there and impressed Henry Ford and the deal was set. Ford told Thornton to set the salaries—they ranged from $10,000 to $16,000. Thornton gave McNamara the second highest salary. The group became the famous Whiz Kids: Thornton, McNamara, Arjay Miller, J. E. Lundy, Charles Bosworth, Jack Reith, Jim Wright, Ben Davis Mills, Wilbur Andreson, and George Moore. It was an extraordinary decision for young Ford to make; however, at that bleak moment in his company's history he had nowhere to go but up. He was reaching beyond the normally closed auto business for a group of nonauto men whose experience was not in the failure and stupidity of war but rather in the technological success of war. Their chief lesson had been that you could control an organization by converting an abundance of facts and figures into meaningful data and then apply them to industrial production; these men were purveyors of what would be a new managerial art in American industry.

The Ford Motor Company practices, both in production and in personnel, had an almost medieval quality to them. Young Henry had inherited the shell of a company, the name and perhaps not that much more, at a time when General Motors seemed to employ the most up-to-date production and managerial techniques. Young Henry needed, above all else, instant executives; the company was losing nine million dollars a month. But he needed, as one friend would admit, two levels of management. One now, instantly, and one to come along. In hiring the Whiz Kids, he was taking care of the future, so he shrewdly covered all bets and hired a senior level of management from General Motors, men in their late forties and early fifties who could go to work that day and help train his new intellectuals in the auto business. This was to be known in automotive circles as the Breech-Crusoe-Harder group, headed by Ernie Breech, then forty-nine, who had been at General Motors for most of his adult life, and was at the time president of GM's subsidiary, Bendix. He brought with him Lewis Crusoe, another high General Motors executive, now retired, and Delmar Harder, former chief of production of GM.

The arrival of the GM executive group, which the Whiz Kids had not known anything about, slowed down the latter's takeover of Ford (Thornton, restless, left after a year and a half for Hughes Aircraft, where he sensed greater possibilities, finally ending up at Litton Industries). But the system worked very well for Henry Ford. The young men were scattered throughout the company (with McNamara and Arjay Miller, who succeeded McNamara as president of Ford, working in finance). There they worked to convert the incredibly archaic, helter-skelter operation of old Henry to the new classic corporate style used at General Motors, with its highly accountable decentralized units, where each executive would be held directly responsible, and where slippage and failure would be quickly spotted. The lead of General Motors in that postwar period was enormous; Ford had very little in the way of a factory, its machinery was badly outdated, not easily retooled. In contrast, GM had converted to war production, but it had been very careful to establish in its factory and production lines the kind of systems that could be easily converted to peacetime production. Chevrolet thus had a massive lead; it could bring out a car for much less than it actually did, but if it lowered its prices it would kill Chrysler and bring the wrath of the Congress down for antitrust. ("Don't ever hire anyone from the auto industry," Gene McCarthy, one of McNamara's severest critics, later said of him. "The way they have it rigged it's impossible to fail out there.") So Chevy kept its prices higher and produced a much better car than Ford. A two-year-old Chevy sold on the used-car market for about $200 more than a two-year-old Ford, a very considerable gap.

The prime aim of the two new management teams at Ford was to close the gap. Here Breech and McNamara combined their talents; they had to figure out how to produce a car that was at least partially competitive with Chevrolet, and at the same time make enough profit that could be plowed back into the company to build the desperately needed plants. They could not do it by borrowing from the banks, Ford's credit rating simply wasn't good enough, so they did it by skinning down the value of the car, mainly on the inside where it wouldn't be seen. Ford had always been known for styling and speed, so they kept that, and worked on having a modern design, with a zippy car, good for the youth market, though eventually, and sometimes not so eventually, the rest of the car would deteriorate (as was also reflected in the used-car price). The Ford buyers seemed to know it, but curiously enough, continued to buy Fords. By these means Breech got the money to buy and modernize the plants, while it was McNamara's particular genius to raise the quality without raising the cost, a supreme act of cost effectiveness. This was, of course, McNamara's specialty, and he had a bonus system to reward stylists and engineers who could improve the car without increasing the cost. The McNamara phrase—it came up again and again at meetings, driven home like a biblical truth—was "add value rather than cost to the car." And slowly he and Breech closed the gap on the used-car differential while at the same time modernizing the company.

It was at Ford during this period that McNamara was being converted from a bright, hard-charging young statistician into a legend, *McNamara* the entity, someone to respect, someone to fear, a man who rewarded those who met his standards handsomely, and coldly rejected those who did not.

If someone were to be driving with McNamara during work hours, he would see it: Bob was driving, but he was thinking of grilles that day, only grilles existed for him, cheap ones, expensive ones, flashy ones, simple ones, other cars rushing by on their way to lunch, on their way home, and Bob running it through his mind, oblivious to oncoming traffic, frightening his companions. Bob, watch the road, one would say, and if he were in a good mood, he might apologize for his mental absence. McNamara never stopped pushing; in those days he was watching Chevy—how was Chevy doing? The night each year when they got hold of the first Chevy, everyone gathered around in a special room and broke it down piece by piece into hundreds of items, each one stapled to a place already laid out for it, and they concentrated on it—everyone muttering, wondering how Chevy had done this or that for a tenth of a cent less, cursing them slightly—so *that* was how they had done it!

When Thornton left, there was considerable curiosity as to who would emerge as the top Whiz Kid; it soon became clear that it was McNamara. He symbolized a new kind of executive in American business, men who had not grown up in the business, were not part of the family, but who were modern, well educated, technicians who prided themselves that they brought the most progressive analytical devices to business: computers to understand the customers, statistics to break down costs and productions. McNamara was brilliant at systematizing, telling Ford where it was going before it got there.

He rose quickly. Henry Ford was new and unsure of himself, particularly in the field of financial systems. To an uneasy, uncertain Ford, McNamara offered reassurance; when questions arose he always seemed to have the answers, not vague estimates but certitudes, facts, numbers, lots of them. Though his critics might doubt that he knew what the public wanted or what it was doing, he could always forecast precisely the Ford part of the equation. He had little respect for much of the human material around him, the people who claimed, when he reeled off his overwhelming statistics, that they had always done it the other way in the auto business. Such people, when they challenged him, were often proved wrong. Slowly he surrounded himself with men who met his criteria, men who responded to the same challenges and beliefs. This was a formative experience in his life, because years later, when the doubters about Vietnam began to express themselves, they at first tended to be people who did not talk his language and who were very different from his kind of people. They did not think in terms of statistics, or rationalizing systems, and they did not support their judgments with facts as he knew them, but rather by saying that it did not smell right, or that it just did not feel right; he would trust his facts and statistics and instincts against theirs just as he had before at Ford when confronted by the businessmen who had doubted his facts and charts.

In Detroit he was the odd man in. The auto world is a very special segment of America, with the normal American exaggerations blown even larger. Like a mini Texas. It is a world closed in, auto men talk to other auto men, auto traditions passed on in generations of families. Ford people living among Ford people, General Motors among GM people. A Ford country club. A General Motors country club. Cocktail conversations about cars and the company. Dinner conversations about cars and the company. There is a self-belief that what they are doing is not only good for America, it is America. In this atmosphere McNamara was the last puritan. He came to it, met it on his terms, never really changing, conquered it by sheer mathematical and tactical ability, rose to the highest position, a penultimate corporate victory, forcing the head of the company to adjust an entire system to his style. McNamara was never *of* Detroit and never really *of* the auto industry. He preferred to live in Ann Arbor among the eggheads, many of them liberals and Democrats (at Ford executive meetings Henry Ford would occasionally mention contributions to the Republican party and then note with a certain distaste that "Bob here will probably give to the Democrats"), reading books, buying paintings. Indeed it was said that the McNamaras deliberately managed to be elsewhere when Henry and Ann Ford gave great gala parties for their daughters.

But it was more than just a stylistic difference with Detroit, it was something far deeper. In business philosophy as well as personal life McNamara was a puritan, and the auto business is not the place for a puritan, nor for someone who has an abiding faith in man as a rational being. The buying of a car is not necessarily a rational act. Detroit is always happiest when it can foist on a potential customer more than he needs, adding chrome, hard tops, soft tops, air conditioners, speakers, extra horsepower. The auto industry essentially believes the buying of a car is an impulse; McNamara insisted it was a rational decision. It pained him to approve a convertible, the idea that a customer would pay $200 more for a dangerous car that would deteriorate more rapidly offended him (after he left Ford and they made a convertible version out of his beloved Falcon, he wrote a rare message to a friend at Ford: "You must be crazier than hell."). He not only believed in rationality, thought a friend, he loved it. It was his only passion. "If you offended it at a meeting, you were not just wrong, you had violated something far greater, you had violated his sense of the rational order. Like offending a man's religion." If you did show a flash of irrationality or support the wrong position, he would change, speaking faster, the voice like a machine gun, cutting into you: chop chop chop. You miscalculated here. Chop. You left this out. Chop. You neglected this. Chop. Therefore you're wrong. Chop. Chop. Chop.

Yet he was good at Ford, no mistake about that. He brought his system to that declining empire at just the right time; they held the line, they did not decay and collapse as they might have, and they finally grew back, in part owing to his enormous drive and pressure. Eventually, it gained him the presidency of Ford, but it also proved that McNamara was an immensely complicated man. He would have been a simple man had he stayed on in a university, taught there, lived there, sent his students out in the world a little better for their experience with him. But this was different. He who had little material drive of his own was committed to making it in the world of profit and excess and, indeed, greed.

As there was later in Washington, there was something of a split in the McNamara personality during the Detroit years, a switchover after 6:30 P.M. There was the driving, relentless, cost-effective executive of Ford during the day and the resident philosopher of Ann Arbor in the evening, warm, almost gregarious. It was as if he compartmentalized his mind. The deep philosophic thoughts were important, but they were not to be part of the broader outlook; if perhaps he were to stand for some of the good things in business he would do it *after* he took control of Ford. Subvert them first and then announce who you are. If later the immensity of the contradictions between his liberal instincts and the war in Vietnam would cause him grief, similarly the difference between his sense of social conscience and the enormous needs of great industry caused him problems earlier. It was as if the contradictions of our age were all within him.

When McNamara went to Washington, most of his friends in Ann Arbor felt that he left with a sigh of relief, that he had never really liked the auto industry, never found enough fulfillment. It was as if, once he had found that he could make it at Ford and win, he was bored with the world, with the other men who could talk only about cars.

When he was offered the Defense job, his close friends felt they would not really be surprised if he accepted; he had, they thought, been looking for a larger and more satisfying stage. The only thing which would make him stay would be a sense of responsibility to Henry, certainly not to himself. There were people at Ford who were pleased, feeling as they did that the company under this coldly driving, efficient man had been too stifled. In Ann Arbor the pleasant liberals in his circle were pleased too, to see this humane man that they admired so much take on such an important new job as Defense. One of them, Robert Angell, the head of the sociology department, who had admired the breadth of McNamara's mind, went to his classes that morning and talked movingly about McNamara, how lucky the country was to have this kind of man in such a difficult job, a man with a conscience and a human sensitivity. Later, when the Bay of Pigs happened, Angell and the others would receive something of a shock—how could Bob be involved in something like this? Angell, a very gentle man, decided, talking with some of Bob's other friends, that they had made Bob go along. And then McNamara went to Vietnam and came back, and Angell turned on his television set and there was Bob talking about putting people in fortified villages, and Angell wondered what had happened to Bob, he sounded so different. And his friends in Ann Arbor would watch him with his pointer as he crisply explained where the bombs were falling. In 1965 Angell would duly set off for the first teach-in against the war, held at Michigan, and he and the other friends would always wonder what had happened to Bob; they heard that Marg had been sick, that the war had torn Bob up, but they would not talk about it with him because Bob did not come back to visit them.

CHAPTER 10

B ob McNamara took over the Defense Department for a Chief Executive who had run on the promise of getting America moving again (one pictured them always without overcoats and hats, moving quickly through crowds; Kennedy had once gotten angry at Robert Bird, a reporter for the *Herald Tribune* because Bird had written that the reason that this dynamic young man was able to campaign without an overcoat in the cold was that he wore thermal underwear) on the assumption that we were losing our power and manhood, *they* had more missiles. McNamara soon discovered that there was no missile gap. Shortly after the election he told Pentagon reporters this, which caused a considerable flap, particularly among Republicans, who had lost an election partly because of a nonexistent gap. How many Russian-fearing citizens had cast their votes to end the gap and live a more secure life, only to find that they had been safe all along?

But it was true, there was no missile gap, so instead of increasing the might of the United States and catching up with the Russians, McNamara set out to harness the might, to control it and to bring some order and rationality to it, and soon, above all, to limit the use of nuclear weapons. To control the weapons, to limit them, to rationalize their procedures, absorbed his time and his energy; and Vietnam seemed a tiny little storm cloud on the horizon, distant, manageable, far from the real center of man's question of survival or self-destruction. It would be one of the smaller ironies of his years as Secretary of Defense that in making his arguments against nuclear weapons, forcefully, relentlessly, he had to make counterarguments *for* conventional forces, to build up those conventional forces.

McNamara worked hard to change Western thinking about nuclear policy. He set out to educate not just the Pentagon but his European colleagues as well, forming the Nuclear Planning Group for his European counterparts, men who were politicians first, not managers, and thus felt themselves particularly dependent on their generals. He forced them to build a table where only the defense ministers could sit. No prepared papers or set speeches were allowed, and they could not turn to their generals who then turned to their colonels. They came to the meetings, only one person from each country at the table, only four others allowed in the room, he hated crowds. At first it did not work too well because McNamara overwhelmed them, he was too strong a presence, but gradually he forced them to take political responsibility for defense positions, and equally important, build skilled professional staffs which could challenge the technical thinking of the military at the lower levels, point by point, so they would not be forced into blind choices at the highest level.

He worked hard to bring greater control to the entire nuclear system, and he felt himself very much alone, surrounded by hostile forces in his quest. He had no following on the Hill and he felt that his detractors did, so his loyalty to the President, which was strong in any case, was doubly strong, the President was his only patron and protector, and his source of power. But if the President had doubts about him, then he lost power in this savage world in which he was operating. He was already a compromised figure. The growth of the sophistication of weapons and the enormous increase in their price had given the Pentagon a quantum jump in power. Its relationship with the Congress, always strong, was now strengthened by a new loyalty, based on immense defense contracts conveniently placed around the homes of the most powerful committee chairmen.

On how many fronts could he fight? If he had tried to turn the country around on chemical and biological warfare, for instance, Senator Russell surely would have opened hearings. Did you want a fight on everything? By holding them off on the B-70, a bomber which no one needed, he almost brought on a Constitutional crisis, with the Congress passing the money that the executive branch did not want to spend. He was constantly fighting with the Chiefs, but also deciding how much each point was worth. On the test-ban treaty McNamara virtually locked them in a room for a week to fight it out with them. He made them promise that once he had broken an argument they could not go back to it, because he felt that arguing with the Chiefs was a lot like arguing with your mother-in-law; you win a point and go on to the next only to find that they are back at the first. So, for a week, hour after hour, he went through every objection they had, breaking them down point by point, until finally he won. But how many issues were worth this much effort? It should have been the Secretary of State, not of Defense, who was fighting for a nuclear-test ban.

He compiled an awesome record in Washington in those days. He was a much-sought-after figure, a man of impressive qualities. In a flashy Administration which placed great emphasis on style, McNamara was at home. He had always liked style among people at Ford, judging them not only by what they said, but how they said it. He was popular at dinner parties and was considered unusual in that he did not bore women at dinner by talking about nuclear warheads. He was a friend of Jack and Jackie's, of Bobby and Ethel's, and yet he lived simply, driving his own car more often than not, a beat-up old Ford. He was gay when the occasion called for gaiety, sober when it called for sobriety. His congressional appearances were impressive, well prepared, grim, and humorless. McNamara testifying on the Hill was not someone you wanted to cross. Yet he was unbending, he knew too many answers. The Hill didn't like that. His deputy Roswell Gilpatric suggested that it would be a good idea to go over and have a few drinks occasionally, get to know the boys, humanize yourself and your intentions. The oil in the wheels of government was bourbon. But McNamara would have none of it. He had his responsibilities and they theirs, and if they could not see the rightness of what he was doing, he did not think he could woo them by drinking. Probably he was right.

Yet even his enemies added to his reputation; they were the right enemies, the generals, the conservatives on the Hill. And even his liberal critics found something admirable in him, his capacity to change, to follow the evidence, and to keep his ego separated from his opinions. He seemed started on a career as the classic Secretary of Defense. The combination of Kennedy-McNamara seemed to work well. The President had a broader sense of history, a sense of skepticism. Kennedy understood the gaps in McNamara; even if he was brilliant, he was not wise. When Kennedy told him to bring back an answer on a question, McNamara would work diligently, come back, and present the answer. If Kennedy noted that this was not the answer he wanted, McNamara would disappear and come back with the *right* answer. (In 1962 McNamara, always cost conscious, came charging into the White House ready to save millions on the budget by closing certain naval bases. All the statistics were there. Close this base, save this many dollars. Close that one and save that much more. All obsolete. All fat. Each base figured to the fraction of the penny. Kennedy interrupted him and said, Bob, you're going to close the Brooklyn Navy Yard, with twenty-six thousand people, and they're going to be out of work and go across the street and draw unemployment, and you better figure that into the cost. That's going to cost us something and they're going to be awfully mad at me, and we better figure that in too.)

When McNamara began to take charge of Vietnam there was a growing split between the civilians and the military over the assessment of Vietnam. Now McNamara, a civilian heading a military enterprise, was to become the principal figure, in effect the judge of the controversy, a man with civilian attitudes responsible to military pressures and military assessments. But when he moved in on Vietnam he was not, as he was on so many other issues, aided by those bright young civilians from the Defense Department, the Whiz Kids, whom he usually let loose to become his own independent sources of information with which to break institutional information networks. Rather, he took over as if he were the desk officer, with John McNaughton later serving as his own aide. (In 1965 he finally sent the first of the Whiz Kids to Vietnam as a civilian member of the headquarters there. The young man's pessimism differed sharply from Saigon's optimism and had an important effect on McNamara's own doubts. The young man was Daniel Ellsberg.) McNamara, who had unleashed these young men elsewhere in the Pentagon, moved virtually alone in an area where he was least equipped to deal with the problems, where his training was all wrong, the quantifier trying to quantify the unquantifiable. He had no independent information with which to compete with the military's information; he had journalistic accounts, of course, but journalists were not serious people.

Thus he went into Vietnam virtually alone. There was that confidence which bordered on arrogance, a belief that he could handle it. Perhaps, after all, the military weren't all that good; still, they could produce the raw data, and McNamara, who *knew data*, would go over it carefully and extricate truth from the morass. Thus the portrait of McNamara in those years at his desk, on planes, in Saigon, poring over page after page of data, each platoon, each squad, studying all those statistics. All lies. Talking with reporters and telling them that all the indices were good. He could not have been more wrong; he simply had all the wrong indices, looking for American production indices in an Asian political revolution.

There was something symbolic about him during those trips. He epitomized booming American technological success, he scurried around Vietnam, looking for what he wanted to see; and he never saw nor smelled nor felt what was really there, right in front of him. Since any truly factual estimates of the war would immediately have shown its bankruptcy, the McNamara trips became part of a vast unwitting and elaborate charade, the legitimizing of a hopeless lie: McNamara in 1962 going to Operation Sunrise, the first of the repopulated villages, the villagers obviously filled with bitterness and hatred, ready, one could tell, to slit the throat of the first available Westerner, and McNamara not picking it up, innocently firing away his questions. How much of this? How much of that? Were they happy here? On these carefully planned visits, General Harkins, acting as his travel agent, was always at his side. (Years later, when McNamara had turned against the war, he talked with John Vann, the lieutenant colonel who had left the Army in protest of the Harkins policies. McNamara asked Vann why he had been misinformed, and Vann bluntly told him it was his own fault. He should have insisted on his own itinerary. He should have traveled without accompanying brass, and he should have taken some time to find out who the better-informed people were and learned how to talk to them.)

The Harkins briefings were of course planned long in advance; they were brainwashings really, but brainwashings made all the more effective and exciting by the trappings of danger. Occasional mortar rounds going off. A captured rifle to touch, a surly captured Vietcong to look at. What was created on those trips was not an insight about the country but an illusion of knowledge, presented so effectively that he thought he understood Vietnam.

And so he created the base of knowledge, firsthand, on which he would make his judgments and recommendations. It was all based on those terrible trips out there, the unwillingness to accept civilian assistance in challenging the military reporting, the unwillingness to adapt his own standards and criteria. In these crucial middle years he attached his name and reputation to the possibility and hopes for victory, caught himself more deeply in the tar baby of Vietnam, and limited himself greatly in his future actions. It is not a particularly happy chapter in his life; he did not serve himsetf nor the country well; he was, there is no kinder or gentler word for it, a fool.

In the spring of 1963 the war in Vietnam seemed to come to a halt. Then in early May, 1963, Buddhists who were celebrating Buddha's birthday in Hué, the old imperial capital, were told by government troops to disburse. When they refused to break up, armored vehicles opened fire, killing nine people. The government, unable to admit a mistake, blamed the entire incident on the Vietcong. This was the beginning of the prolonged Buddhist crisis which finally brought the Diem government to its knees. It became a full-scale political crisis as the militant, skilled young Buddhist leaders—sensitive to the new political forces and well aware of the changes in psychology and attitudes which twenty years of revolutionary war had brought about—offered the pohulation, for the first time under the Diem government, an outlet for latent nationalist forces. For Diem and his government, sponsored by the Americans, represented, like the French before them, foreign coin, foreign language, foreign style, and the officers of Diem's army were tainted by the Western touch. Now, with the coming of the Buddhists, there was for the first time an outlet for a Vietnamese leadership which had no contact with the Americans, did not take their money and scholarships or visit with their ambassador. The leadership was brilliant, indigenous, nationalist in the true sense, and in no way beholden to the American embassy. The effect of this on the population was potent: the Buddhists became a spearhead for a vast variety of dissident groups, and with their ability made the rigid, unbending, ungenerous government look foolish. Under the press of the Buddhist protest, all the flaws, all the shortcomings, all the intolerance of the Diem regime came to the surface; so, too, did American impotence, the inability of the Americans to move the regime despite the deep involvement with it. To watch the regime stumble through the crisis over a period of five months was like watching it commit suicide; it proved its detractors prophets, its supporters fools.

But one man whose attitude was changed by the crisis was William Trueheart, the deputy chief of the Saigon mission. Trueheart seemed, on the surface, an unlikely candidate to break with the official line. He was a Nolting man, brought to Saigon at the ambassador's personal request; the two were old friends and had stayed in very close touch. Trueheart seemed, if anything, more Nolting than Nolting, a little stiffer at first glance, a product of that same Virginia-gentleman school of the foreign service.

But in late June, 1963, an exhausted and dispirited Nolting went on a prolonged vacation, despite the mounting Buddhist crisis. Nolting chose to sail in the Aegean Sea, where it was difficult to reach him (this became an important point because he felt Trueheart did not try hard enough to reach him and therefore was disloyal; others felt that there had been efforts to reach him but that he had made himself particularly inaccessible). With the crisis continuing to grow, Trueheart followed the straight Nolting line, but after a while, as Diem refused to negotiate and meet any of the Buddhist demands, as the protest mounted and reached deeper and deeper into the society, as unrest mounted in the military, and as the government continued to mislead the Americans regarding its intentions, Trueheart opened up the embassy reporting. Together with Mel Manful, the political officer, Trueheart began to talk to dissidents, to Buddhists, and as embassy officials reached more of the society, the reporting changed. It went from blind support to being skeptical in its appraisal. Doubts were raised, questions asked. The embassy began to doubt that Diem could handle the Buddhist crisis, and it reported that the Buddhists had become the focal point for all sorts of dissidence and that the government was totally isolated. It also cast doubt upon Nhu's sanity, doubts which were accurate; Nhu was more and more on opium in his last years. The embassy saw Diem almost totally a prisoner of his family. The terrible thing, the embassy learned about the Diem regime in that crisis, was that all the clichés about it turned out to be true.

The change in Trueheart was crucial. His reporting was not so much anti-Diem (as opponents charged later) as it was analytical and detached, no longer blindly pro-Diem; it let loose a floodgate of doubts. Five months earlier, only American journalists had been pessimistic about the war and the future; now the State Department people in Saigon were pessimistic, the CIA was pessimistic, the hamlet people were pessimistic, along with the journalists. Only the military held devotedly to the line of optimism. These doubts and divisions of Saigon were reflected in Washington, where Kennedy faced a divided bureaucracy. Earlier in the year he had seemed to be encouraging the Harriman group in its dissent; if not exactly siding with it, at least moving the play in their direction but doing it slowly, trying to prevent an open schism within his Administration, trying to keep from driving the military to the side of the right wing in Congress.

By early July, 1963, Washington knew that it had a major crisis on its hands. Though under great American pressure Diem had finally negotiated a partial settlement with the Buddhist insurgents in mid-June. A couple of weeks later, the intelligence community predicted that Diem would fail to carry out the provisions of the agreement and that it was very likely there would be either a coup against him, or an assassination. Saigon itself became filled with rumors of coups, and by early July at least three major plots had begun to form, reflecting different generational and regional preferences. In Saigon, Trueheart became more and more discouraged with the government. If Diem promised something to him, Trueheart found that it was repudiated the next day in the English-language *Times of Vietnam*, a newspaper controlled by the Nhus; worse, the darker forecasts of the *Times of Vietnam* over a long period of time more accurately reflected the government policy than the official promises of Diem. Thus while Diem was promising one thing to the Americans, in private sessions with his family he reverted to the harder line pushed by his brother and sister-in-law. If Diem promised to be conciliatory about the Buddhists in action and tone, the *Times of Vietnam* would soon charge that the first Buddhist priest who burned himself to death had been drugged. In Washington, Kennedy was again discussing with his advisers the possibility of separating the Nhus from Diem, but it was really too late.

When Nolting went on vacation in early July, the President decided that a new ambassador was needed. Kennedy did not trust Nolting's version of events, but he also realized that part of Nolting's problems was the policy itself, the decision to commit the United States directly to Diem, which had originated in Washington; thus he himself was more than partly responsible. It just hadn't worked and it was time to look around for a replacement, for an ambassador who would become less emotionally involved with Diem. On Rusk's insistence Kennedy chose Henry Cabot Lodge. The appointment of this patrician, symbol of the Establishment, defeated candidate for the Senate by Kennedy himself in 1952, defeated candidate for the Vice Presidency by the Kennedy-Johnson ticket, made the liberals in the Administration uneasy, but the reason for Kennedy's choice was obvious. If Vietnam turned into a disaster, what could be better than to have a major Republican name associated with it?

Since it would take Lodge a certain amount of time to be prepared, Nolting returned in mid-July for one last chance as ambassador. Those were very unhappy days. Nolting found Diem uncommunicative and unresponsive; Nolting, who had acquiesced to Diem on so many things in order to have money in the bank for just such an occasion as this, now found that he had little influence after all. The Nhus, exploiting his loyalty, involved him in a bogus ceremony designed to identify them with the Americans. It was an Orwellian scene: all the strategic hamlets in the country had allegedly competed for the honor of being named after Nolting; they had written essays, describing what the ambassador had done for their country. The winning hamlet had been chosen. Nolting would now visit it. He tried to get out of it; then, trapped, agreed and became furious when reporters said his acceptance

370

was reluctant. He presided at a fake ceremony in front of stone-faced, stoic Vietnamese. The Vietcong soon knocked over the hamlet.

With everything collapsing around him, he turned in his fury on his old friend Trueheart and accused him of having destroyed the trust which Nolting had so carefully built up. Trueheart's protestations that he had worked loyally for the policy, but that the months since May had seen the disintegration of that fragile hope, fell on deaf ears. If Nolting was impotent, then it was Trueheart's fault, not the fault of history or of the policy. So when he went home he would write his final efficiency report about his once trusted deputy, entering into Trueheart's personnel file the most damaging of all assessments, a charge of rank disloyalty, saying that he had brought this man Trueheart to Saigon, had placed his trust in him, and Trueheart had betrayed that trust, had undermined everything Nolting had worked for. It was powerful stuff and it almost destroyed Trueheart's career.

But now events were out of control, no one could do anything. If people, Nolting said, would only keep their eye on the ball, if they would only stop being distracted by all this political activity. Finally it was all over, and on August 15, Nolting, a rather lonely figure at the airport, talked about the mutual traditions of the two countries "of humility and tolerance, respect for others and a deep sense of social justice." The next day another monk burned himself to death, and within a week Diem and Nhu had crushed the Buddhists with a bloody midnight raid on their pagodas, disguising their private security army in uniforms of regular soldiers in order to put the onus on the army (and thus have the society put the blame on the army and turn more against it, in what was of course a political war).

The embassy had been caught unaware by the strike on the pagodas, including John Richardson, the CIA station chief, who was in a state of shock, with many Vietnamese thinking that since it was Nhu who had engineered the crackdown and since Richardson was deeply involved with Nhu, the raid had CIA approval. But the cover story soon faded. It fooled the embassy and Washington for about forty-eight hours, but American journalists had called it right from the moment it happened. It ended an era and a policy, and later, describing those events, John Mecklin wrote: "Thus the Diem regime's final gesture to Fritz Nolting, flagrant abrogation of its solemn last word to this fine man who had staked his career on the regime's defense."

In America, the Buddhist crisis had been a growing embarrassment for the young Catholic President. The photographs of soldiers bringing their billy clubs down on Buddhist monks had been montaged on front pages with stories of the loss of life of young American officers. If Kennedy had worried about right-wing opposition to the loss of part of the free world, now he was worrying about liberal reaction to American blood being spent for a petty family dictatorship. So when Lodge arrived in Vietnam he was already determined to broaden American policy, to move it, at the very least, away from the Nhus, and failing that, away from Diem himself.

With the Vietnamese military pressuring the Americans to absolve the army from responsibility for the crackdown, the Voice of America soon began broadcasting honest assessments, placing the blame on the Nhus. In addition, Lodge received a cable from Washington saying that the Nhus must go, that alternative leadership possibilities be investigated, that the United States would no longer support a government which included the Nhus. It was, in effect, the go-ahead signal for a coup (no one in Washington or Saigon thought Diem would ever drop the Nhus; if it had been unlikely before the crackdown, it was even more improbable now).

The cable had been drafted by Harriman, Forrestal, Roger Hilsman (Assistant Secretary of State for Far Eastern Affairs), and George Ball on Saturday, August 24, at the President's suggestion. Though Rusk was out of town, he was consulted regularly, and he was helpful. McNamara and John McCone, Director of the CIA, were on vacation, and Taylor was out of reach, having dinner at a restaurant. With McNamara out of town, Gilpatric was in charge at Defense, and he said the cable sounded fine, acceptable, he had no objections. At the CIA, Richard Helms, whose doubts on Vietnam had always been considerable, told them that it was about time they moved this way, what had taken them so long in the first place? Forrestal dealt with Krulak, whose job it was to get clearance from General Taylor, which he did, though technically after the cable had gone out (Taylor did not know that it had already left, but disagreed with nothing in it).

Later, when the principals gathered in Washington, there were second thoughts among some of them, particularly as each learned that some of the others had misgivings (it was a stunning example of how the domino theory worked if not with nations in Southeast Asia, then certainly with high government officials who wanted to sense which way the wind was blowing and did not want to be caught alone going against it). Taylor in particular was unhappy about the way it had been maneuvered. He thought everyone else had agreed, but of course they had not, since they had been out of town. The President was furious that some of his closest officials were reneging on a cable he thought they had agreed on. The next time they were gathered he looked at them and said, the voice very cold, very distant, that there had been some doubt about the cable, that it might have been precipitous. Fortunately it was not too late to change. Do you, bmr. Rusk, wish to change? No. Do you, Mr. McNamara, wish to change? No. Do you, General Taylor, wish to change the cable? . . .

There was a flood of cables back and forth between Saigon and Washington about the possibility of a coup, which Vietnamese general to talk to, how to go about it, the extent to which the United States could be involved. Even the CIA station chief, John Richardson, who until recently had been so close to Nhu, was a surprising advocate of a coup. But the generals, who met covertly with the Americans, did not move. The Nhus had caught them off balance with their strike against the pagodas and had tightened control on forces around Saigon. The Americans had switched their support from Diem, but they had switched so quickly they caught the generals unprepared. Saigon, always filled with rumors, seethed with trigue. And the generals did not move. Why hadn't they? State cabled Lodge. "Perhaps they are like the rest of us, and are afraid to die," Lodge told a friend.

But if there was not a coup, it marked the end of our total belief that Diem and Diem alone could be the instrument of American policy, a blind commitment to one irrational family. In the struggle within the American government, there were varying degrees of doubt among the civilians about whether a coup could be staged at all. Some, like Forrestal and Robert Kennedy, were more and more dubious about the whole affair, while Rusk and Lodge viewed an overthrow of the Diem regime as a way of winning the war.

CHAPTER 11

Now suddenly, under crisis conditions, the Kennedy Administration was finding itself confronted with questions it should have faced and resolved almost two years earlier, when it slipped into the larger commitment. The political problems of Vietnam now seemed very real, and they did not go away. The Administration's hopes that there might be an easy coup had dimmed. There was that old illusion, the separation of the Nhus from the government. On September 2 the President himself went on television with Walter Cronkite and tried to disassociate the United States from the harshness of the regime and talk about the limits of the American role in a guerrilla war—it was, he said, "in the final analysis . . . their war. They are the ones who have to win it or lose it." In Saigon at the exact same time, Lodge was with Nhu, trying to get him out of the government, perhaps out of the country. There seemed to be some progress, but four days later Nhu went into a tirade and said that he would not leave the country, though he might leave the government. Experienced Americans in Saigon and Washington realized that there was no such thing as Nhu out of the government as long as he stayed in the country. With this in mind, the National Security Council met again on September 6, and heard the same two factions, ending in the same negated view of policy. The civilians said it was hopeless with Diem and the military said that it was equally hopeless without him. McNamara pressed the military side. Sitting in on the meeting and listening to both sides cancel each other's arguments was Robert Kennedy, and he asked the questions that should have been asked two years earlier.

Perhaps no one reflected the embryonic change in Administration attitudes toward the Cold War as did Robert Kennedy, the change from tough and aggressive anti-Communism toward a sense of the limits and dangers of American power. He was, in mid-1963, in the middle of his personal journey, his own attitudes very much in flux. He had entered the Administration as perhaps the most hard-line member of the entire inner group. The job he had really wanted was not at Justice but at Defense. If he were at Defense, he told friends, he could serve as the ramrod, pushing through newer, tougher programs, and be a watchdog for his brother. He wanted to escape going to Justice, where he feared his reputation as the cop of the family would become permanent.

He was already being haunted by this idea, that no matter what he did or how he served his brother and his country, the public would think of him as the ruthless cop. He had taken Justice against his will, but he had also played a major role in foreign affairs.

It was Robert Kennedy who had been primarily responsible for the counterinsurgency enthusiasm. Toughness fascinated him; he was not at ease with an America which had flabby waistlines. The enemy both at home and abroad was determined; we had to match that determination. If he worked until midnight, and on driving home saw the lights on in the offices of Jimmy Hoffa's Teamsters Union, then he turned around and drove back to his office. The standard by which he judged men was how *tough* they were. He had been a major force in promoting the career of Maxwell Taylor and diminishing that of

Chester Bowles. With almost everyone else he was hard and relentless, but with Taylor he was markedly uncritical. He was in awe of Taylor's war record, the fact that he had dropped by parachute into Normandy and that he had run a special mission for Eisenhower behind the Italian lines. For Bobby Kennedy those were real credentials.

There were several qualities which set him apart in office. The first was total confidence in his relationship with the President. The second was an absolute insistence on being well and honestly briefed. The third was a capacity, indeed an instinct, to see world events not so much in terms of a great global chess game, but in human terms. As such he retained his common sense (when others were talking about a surgical air strike against Cuba during the missile crisis, he said very simply that he did not want his brother to be the Tōjo of the 1960's). Out of all of this came the final characteristic, the capacity to grow and change and to admit error.

In 1962 he had stopped at the Saigon airport long enough to say that we would stay in Vietnam until we won, but he had also learned a very important lesson: that most of the official reporting was mythological. He was supposed to be briefed at the airport terminal by the top members of the mission, all of whom, in one another's presence, assured him that everything was just fine, on target. "Do you have any problems?" he asked. No, said everyone in unison, there were no problems. He looked at them, somewhat shocked by the response. "No problems," he said, "you've really got no problems? Does anyone here want to speak to me in private about his problems?" And then one by one they talked to him at length and it all came pouring out, a brief and instructive lesson in what people would say for the record and what they would say in private.

By 1963, as his perceptions had developed, he was no longer just the President's little ramrod brother with a hard-line view of the world. He had a new reputation, as the best man in government to bring an unconventional idea to. Some of the people working under Harriman, like Forrestal and Hilsman, felt themselves encouraged in their doubts by Robert Kennedy, that he more than anyone else in the upper level regarded the war as a *war* where civilians might be paying a particularly high price. His questions at meetings always centered around the people of Vietnam. What is all of this doing to the people? "Do you think those people really want us there?" he would ask. "Maybe we're trying to do the wrong thing?" His common sense, among other sensibilities, was offended by it.

Now in the early fall of 1963, sitting in these meetings, listening to one side say that it could not be done with Diem, and the other side say that there was no one but Diem, he was appalled. Perhaps, he said, this was the time to consider withdrawing. It was a brief moment, but he was focusing on the central question, which everyone else, for a variety of reasons, had avoided. Perhaps it was symbolic that the first senior official who questioned the overall policy was Robert Kennedy, totally secure in his place in the Administration, and also secure in his credentials as an anti-Communist. The question he raised was not discussed; it was still too sensitive a point. Perhaps that was how he intended it, as a beginning, an airing of a new idea, and giving it just a little respectability.

The stakes were getting higher and the game was getting rougher. In Vietnam, the United States commitment deepened and the Army was beginning to function more and more like a separate organism, responding to its institutional needs, priorities, vanities. Challenged by outsiders, by civilians, it responded by protecting its own senior officers.

In August this reporter did a major survey of the deteriorating military situation in the Mekong Delta. I had been called by two friends who were senior advisers to Vietnamese divisions and who were appalled by the collapse of the ARVN and the appearance of formidable new Vietcong battalions sweeping almost without opposition throughout the Mekong Delta. My story was published and told of big new beefed-up battalions of 600 and 1,000 men, very well armed with captured American weapons. The article suggested that the war was being lost and that the high-level optimism about the Delta was comparable to the French optimism that preceded their debacle at Dienbienphu. The story in *The New York Times* staggered the President, who was an avid newspaper reader, and who took journalists seriously. He asked the military to comment on it, and word was sent through channels from Taylor to General Krulak to General Harkins that this was particularly important, that it was bad enough to be taking heat because of the Buddhist crisis, but if the President thought the war was going poorly as well, the whole game might be over. The assignment was given not to MACV's intelligence section, but to its most gifted general, Dick Stilwell, who thereupon, without consulting his top advisers in the Delta, prepared a massive file, filled with charts, graphs, and statistics, which took the newspaper account apart word by word. The Stilwell account found the journalistic account inaccurate, indeed "the picture is precisely the opposite," he reported. Loyalty was not to the President of the United States, to truth or integrity, or even to subordinate officers risking their lives; loyalty was to uniform, and more specifically, to immediate superior and career.

Nevertheless, Kennedy was convinced that the war was not going well, and that the military reporting was not to be trusted. He told aides that he had to read the newspapers to find out what was going on. But by mid-September he had decided that the problem was not so much the question of information, whether or not the war was being won, as a question of slowly shifting policy and still trying to hold his government together.

On September 17 McNamara asked to go to Vietnam on another trip. Lodge and some other State Department people strongly opposed it. In the past McNamara's trips had not been glowing successes; they had tended to emphasize the dominance of the military over the civilians and to equate statistical results with reality. In addition, the civilians, who normally liked McNamara, had found him surprisingly inflexible on Vietnam. But Kennedy insisted that he be allowed to go; indeed, there were those in the White House who suspected that the idea for the trip had originated with Kennedy. On September 23, McNamara and General Taylor left for Saigon.

Almost literally from the moment he arrived, McNamara found a new Saigon command; instead of the old unified Harkins-Nolting view of the war, he found Lodge and Harkins barely speaking to each other. In fact, as McNamara was descending from his plane Lodge assigned two staff members to block the general so that Lodge could greet him first, leaving an angry Harkins pushing at the human barrier, shouting, "Please, gentlemen, let me through to the Secretary."

It was a fascinating trip; the military controlled the itinerary, but Lodge had McNamara as his house guest. It was there that Lodge worked to change McNamara's view of the war, at breakfast time rushing in people from the provinces who were armed with pessimistic statistics. Then Lodge's time would be up, and McNamara would go off on the prescribed Harkins-Taylor tour, all the young officers geared up long in advance, charts and optimism at the ready: Yes, sir, all programs are go, sir. The young officers briefed Taylor and McNamara, Harkins standing a few feet behind them, the smile on his face, all the curves were up.

It went on like this for several days and finally they reached a province in the Delta where Rufus Phillips, a member of the Saigon mission, had reported enormous Vietcong progress. A copy of the Phillips report had been made available to McNamara in the morning when the military briefing began. Taylor was standing there, impressive, asking helpful leading questions: Major, we know what a good job you're doing and that this situation is under control, and we wonder if you could tell us about it? . . . McNamara had tried to penetrate these briefings in the past without much success, but this time he was prepared; he had read a pessimistic paper on this same province. So finally the entire civilian-military split seemed to have come down to one place, one war, two views of it. Had the major, McNamara asked, read the report of his civilian colleague in the Hamlet program? Yes, sir. Did the major agree with the civilian appraisal? Pause. Finally the officer said yes, he did. Why, then, asked McNamara, hadn't he reported it himself? Because his civilian colleague reported it and because he himself had reported only the military situation as set by guidelines from MACV.

At this point General Taylor looked at the officer very coldly and said that it appeared he had been falsifying reports. No, sir, said the young officer, my report was accurate as far as it went. With that they moved on to the next stop, but McNamara's attitude had changed for the first time; his own doubts had grown, he had penetrated the military reporting.

On the way back the two men, so different in their perceptions and loyalties, worked out their divergent views of Vietnam. Like much of what had come out in the past, and even more of what was to come in the future, two separate attitudes were contained in one report, badly bastardized. It reflected a trade between McNamara and Taylor on a number of things: McNamara accepted Lodge's estimates that we could not succeed with Diem, and got major new doubts about the regime and major new pressures against it into the report ("It is very fortunate for the country to have a man of the breadth and scope of Bob McNamara as Secretary of Defense," said Lodge the day after McNamara left, a big grin on his face, having just swallowed *that* canary). Taylor held the line on the military estimates and optimism, so that the opening line of the report stated that the military program "has made great progress and continues to progress." The programs were going very well, the shooting war was fine, 1,000 Americans would be out by Christmas, and the whole American commitment would be finished by the end of 1965. A lie had become a truth, and the policy makers were trapped in it; their policy was a failure, and they could not admit it.

Back in Washington, McNamara and Taylor went to the White House to read the report. As everything about Vietnam was compromised, so too was this report by McNamara and Taylor, but Kennedy was not that worried. He knew Vietnam was bad and getting worse, but he had a sense of being able to handle it, of having time, that time was somehow on his side.

It was late 1963, and since 1964 was an election year, any delay on major decisions was healthy; if the Vietnamese could hold out a little longer, so could he. Besides, other things were beginning to come together. He had signed a limited nuclear test-ban treaty with the Soviets, the civil rights march on Washington had come and passed—by its grandeur and passion, it had reflected the aspirations of have-not Americans with a sense of majesty that probably had helped his Administration. Kennedy felt that the country's doubts about him were ebbing, that his real popularity, not the visual popularity, but a deeper thing, was beginning to form, that the idea of him as President was beginning to crystallize. So he did not want to rush too quickly, to split his Administration unnecessarily. There was always time. The date of the McNamara-Taylor report was October 2, 1963.

At almost the same time General Duong Van Minh, the most respected military figure in the South, contacted Lou Conein, an old friend of his, and asked if they could talk. Conein had been in Vietnam for eighteen years, mostly with the CIA; he had been one of the first Americans parachuted in at the end of World War II. He knew the non-Communist Vietnamese military well, since they had been his recruits, as he liked to say. Shrewd, irreverent, colorful, he seemed an American sprung to life from a pulp adventure thriller. He knew the country, and the people, and he flirted with danger, it was danger that made life more exciting. Two fingers were missing from one hand, and stories were told all over Saigon as to how those fingers had disappeared, in what noble or ignoble cause. The American command in Saigon despised him; he had, they suspected, been there too long, gone too native. He was erratic, untrustworthy, playing the game of adventurer—the most dangerous kind. He was also one of the very few Americans who had any credibility with the Vietnamese military, who despised Harkins and regarded him as an extension of Nhu.

With Lodge's approval, Conein met General Minh on October 5 and they talked for more than an hour. General Minh said that the war was being lost, that the senior Vietnamese officers (himself, Tran Van Don, and Tran Van Kim, all respected and none of them commanding troops because they had followings of their own and were thus considered dangerous by Nhu) felt that a change had to be made.

He wanted to know what the American attitude toward this was; he did not want American assistance, but neither did he want the Americans to thwart them. They had to move and move quickly, he said, because regimental and battalion commanders were now too restless and were pushing for a coup. Conein said that he could not answer until he had talked to his superiors. Minh mentioned three possible ways of removing the regime: assassination of both Diem and Nhu, a military encirclement of Saigon, or open fighting between loyal and disloyal units. Conein said that the United States would not advise on which plan was best. Minh also wanted to know whether United States' aid would continue if the generals were running the government. Ambassador Lodge immediately answered that the United States would not thwart a coup, would review Vietnamese plans, other than assassination plans, and would assure the generals that United States' aid would be continued to another anti-Communist government.

With this the end was in sight for the Diem regime. Lodge, the dominant player in Saigon, shrewd, forceful, and tough, did not believe anything the government said, nor much of what the United States military said. Lodge felt that all the charges against the Ngo family were true, that Nhu could not be separated from Diem, that the war was being lost, that since there was going to be a coup anyway, the United States position should be to neither encourage it (except perhaps slightly) nor thwart it. He predicted, accurately, to Washington, that Diem would make a request for help, and that the United States attitude should be that its capacities were far less than Diem's.

By mid-October Lodge had convinced the White House, which was in a receptive mood, that a coup was going to take place, led by the generals, unless the Americans openly betrayed them. Three weeks of October passed with coup fever building in Saigon. A form of madness seemed to take over. Having crushed the Buddhists, the government moved against college students, high school students, then finding rebellion in elementary schools, it closed those schools too. In hundreds of homes of government officers, brothers and sisters had been arrested.

Lodge, biding his time, letting the family guess his intentions, began to deal with Diem and found him as unresponsive as ever. Diem asked about reinstatement of American aid, and Lodge parried by demanding the release of hundreds of arrested Buddhists and students. Diem, Lodge later reported, offered a vast number of excuses. Finally Lodge said, "Mr. President, every single specific suggestion which I have made, you have rejected. Isn't there some one thing you may think of that is within your capabilities to do and that would favorably impress U.S. opinion?" According to Lodge, Diem gave him a blank look and changed the subject. It was in fact a tactic which had worked in the past: give the Americans at best a vague promise, count on them to be so committed to you that they would never turn aside.

General Tran Van Don had told Conein that the coup would take place before November 2. On November 1 the Saigon embassy and the CIA predicted in their early reports to Washington that a coup would come that day; MACV, which was supposed to be the best-informed on what the Vietnamese military was doing, said it would not come (when the coup did take place, MACV called up the embassy and asked to have the cable killed).

Shortly after one o'clock in the afternoon, troops committed to the generals began taking over key points in Saigon. Ngo Dinh Nhu had been tipped off earlier by one officer that a coup was coming, and true to form, instead of trying to break it then, he had devised an enormously elaborate countercoup which was designed to lure the plotters into the open, destroy them, destroy the Buddhists and all American sympathizers, and raise such havoc that the Americans would be glad to have the Nhus back in power. As the first incidents took place, Nhu was confident it was his own countercoup set in motion. By the time he realized that he was mistaken and that he had lost control, he and Diem were practically surrounded, only the palace guard remained loyal. Since their situation was almost hopeless, Diem and Nhu asked the generals to call a halt and negotiate demands, as a means of gaining time for loyal units to enter the city. But there were no loyal units.

The fighting continued through the night and into the early morning. By the time the rebels took the palace, Diem and Nhu were gone, having slipped out through a secret tunnel. They fled to the Chinese suburb of Cholon, where they remained in touch with the generals. Reportedly they finally accepted safe conduct out of the country, but were picked up by the insurgents, and on orders of the new junta, killed while in the back of an armored personnel carrier. The body of Ngo Dinh Nhu was repeatedly stabbed after his death.

It was all over. One day photographs and statues had been everywhere, but not just of Diem, of his sister-in-law as well, a personality cult. The next day it was all gone, the statues smashed, the posters ripped through, his likeness left only on the one-piastre coin. In the streets the population mobbed the generals and garlanded the troops with flowers (one combat officer from the Delta later recalled that it was the first time he liked being a soldier, the first time he felt popular with the people).

In Washington almost everyone concerned had seen the coup against Diem as somewhat inevitable. Taylor, reflecting the position he and Harkins had created, had been the most reluctant. But there was one other figure strongly opposed to it, who had rumbled about it, disliked it, and would have fought it, had he exercised the power. He did not exercise the power; perhaps had the issue involved legislation on the Hill or a conflict in Texas politics the others might have paid serious attention to his dissent, but not in the field of foreign affairs, where he was considered particularly inept. His name was Lyndon B. Johnson. He had hated the coup against Diem from the very beginning. All this talk about coups. Cops-and-robbers stuff, he said, coups and assassinations. Why, he and Ralph Yarborough had their differences down in Texas but they didn't go around plotting against each other, murdering each other. When Johnson went to Vietnam in 1961, he had personally symbolized an American commitment to Diem, and part of his allegiance stemmed from this, that he had been the conduit of a promise, so arguing against Diem was arguing against Johnson; but some of it was broader, a somewhat more simplistic view of the world, and of who was a friend and who was an enemy. Friends were real friends, they signed on with you. A contract was a contract, a deal was a deal, you held out your hand and they held out theirs and that was the way it was done.

The talk about the overthrow of Diem hit a very negative chord; Johnson came to dislike and distrust the men who he thought were engineering the pressure against Diem, the young White House types, the brash know-it-alls—all these young people who had not even been through World War II, challenging senior people. Though he usually exempted John Kennedy from all criticism, on this subject he did not; he felt that Kennedy had played too great a role in the whole affair. So in the months of 1963, when Kennedy was so carefully moving the bureaucracy over, the President, who was usually very careful about Johnson, had not worked on his Vice President; he had been preoccupied with moving more central players, and he had simply neglected to work on Johnson. No other word. Neglect. It did not, however, seem important at the time.

The months of September and October were very good ones for John Kennedy, rich in themselves, full of promise for the future. Above all the beginning, perhaps just the beginning of an end to a particularly rigid era of the Cold War. Not the end of the Cold War, the problems were too great and too deep on both sides. Some of the competition was very real and would always remain so; but perhaps turning back the paralyzing effects of it, the almost neurotic quality which had provoked a country to reach beyond its own real interests because of the McCarthy fears which had been set up at home.

There had been the speech at the American University about a reappraisal of attitudes toward the Communists, and he had encouraged and dispatched Averell Harriman to work out a limited test-ban treaty, which was the first break in the almost glacial quality of the Cold War. It had not come easily; the bureaucracy itself was not really prepared for a change, and there was considerable resistance within the government. The Chiefs were opponents (though they finally went along with a limited test-ban treaty in order to kill off pressure for a comprehensive one). On the Hill the vote was very good, better than expected, and the President was pleased. It was a highly personal victory.

The President then left on a tour of Western states that Mike Mansfield had promoted, a conservation tour in essence, where he would praise wide open spaces and high mountains and clean rivers. It was not a subject which particularly interested him (conservation was not yet ecology), and the trip did not start well. He made two poor appearances, then in Billings, Montana, he was scheduled to give another boring speech, boring himself and his audience, and in the middle of it he mentioned the test-ban treaty, and as he did, the crowd responded with force and immediacy. It was a real rapport, not the carefully calculated applause lines which often mark a political speech, hackneyed calls to party or national fidelity, the audience responding faithfully if listlessly on cue. Kennedy was above all a good politician, whose ear was finely tuned. Sensing his audience well, he continued on the peace theme, accelerating the tempo, the intensity, and the crowd responded. He talked of the nuclear confrontations of the last two years, first Berlin and then Cuba, and he said: "What we hope to do is lessen the chance of a military collision between these two great nuclear powers which together have the power to kill three hundred million people in the short space of a day. That is what we are seeking to avoid. That is why we support the test-ban treaty. Not because things are going to be easier in our lives, but because we have a chance to avoid being burned."

From then on through the Far West, the trip was the same; he strayed more and more from conservation and into the test-ban treaty, and everywhere the crowds were very good, and very responsive. He sensed that there was a deep longing for a sane peace and sane world. He knew that Goldwater would be his opponent in 1964 and now he felt that he could beat Goldwater badly and end some of the fears which had haunted American politics since the hardening of the Cold War.

So it had come that in the last months of his life his Presidency had turned, and not by chance, it had coincided with the first major step away from the barren path of the Cold War. It was perhaps not surprising that the first step would take place with the Soviet Union on something like a test-ban treaty. Though it was historically a small break, it was a beginning. By that special irony the problems which had haunted him in his meeting with Khrushchev in Vienna in 1961 were past him now, he had come to terms with them, with his own sense of himself, with Khrushchev's estimate of him, and above all, with his country's estimate of him.

But Vietnam, which he had conceived as a part of the price of making American power and determination credible to the Communists, was coming apart even as the United States-Soviet balance seemed to be stabilizing.

On November 21 Henry Cabot Lodge flew to Honolulu on the first leg of a trip to Washington, where he planned to tell the President that the situation was much worse than they thought; even Lodge, who had been pushing the idea that the war was going badly, was shocked at just how discouraging it really was, and he planned to tell Kennedy that there was serious doubt as to whether any government could make it any more. He never delivered the report; in San Francisco he heard the news of the assassination in Dallas.

John Kennedy was dead. His legacy was a mixed one. He had come in at the latter part of the Cold War; at the beginning he had not challenged it, though he had, in the last part of his Administration, begun to temper it. On Vietnam his record was more than cloudy. More than any other member of his Administration, he knew the dangers of a deep United States involvement, the limits of what Caucasian troops could achieve on Vietnamese soil, and yet he had significantly deepened that involvement, escalated the number of Americans there to 16,900 at the time of his death, with more than 70 dead.

Kennedy had of course in the last couple of months privately expressed a nagging doubt. Could it be done? Was it worth doing? He had always feared the combat-troop idea; the French, he said repeatedly, had not been able to deal with the Vietnamese with 300,000 men, how could we? This was a political war; one could not produce military answers. The men who were close to him in the White House felt that these doubts were growing all the time. And yet, and yet . . . he had worked to conceal the truth about Vietnam from the public and had markedly increased the American commitment there. He had, in a way, always known better. He had preached, both in his book and in his speeches, about the importance of political courage, but his Administration had been reasonably free from acts of courage. In this most crucial area the record was largely one of timidity.

CHAPTER 12

L yndon Johnson seemed in those first few months to be always in motion, running, doing, persuading; if later much of the nation, bitter over its seemingly unscheduled and unchartered journey into Southeast Asia, turned on him and remembered his years with distaste, it was grateful to him then, and with good reason. His mandate seemed to be to hold the country together, to continue to exhort from those around him their best, to heal wounds and divisions. The healer. If later one of the Johnson qualities which caused doubts among the nation's critics was his force, the very *abundance* of it—the great capacity to plead, to bully, to beg, to implore, the capacity to manipulate them to what he considered his interest and the nation's interest—in those early days he was much hailed for it.

The leadership of course was very good. The loss of Kennedy was mourned, and yet Johnson, this new President . . . he was a powerhouse, a mover. He went after the same programs that Kennedy had wanted, but with more force. McGeorge Bundy, sensing grave doubts about Johnson in his White House shop, told the others not to be such Eastern snobs. Perhaps Johnson did not have the elegance of his predecessor, but he got things done, and perhaps, being somewhat weak in foreign affairs, he would need them more; there would perhaps be a greater role to play. And Johnson was impressed by the Kennedy team. He had never had men like them working for him. McNamara, the head of Ford Motor Company. "The ablest man I've ever met," he called him. Bundy, flashingly brilliant, the dean of Harvard College, working for this old boy from San Marcos State Teachers College. He did not really like Bundy, sensing at times a patronizing attitude, though occasionally so delighting in him, in

Mac's style—Mac briefing, tidying up a complicated question, so professional, so clean—that a small amused smile would come to his face, like a hitting coach watching a fine hitter. And Rusk ... Rusk had been the head of the Rockefeller Foundation, a Rhodes scholar.

He was in awe of men like these. This remarkable team that Jack Kennedy had assembled was working for him, Lyndon Johnson, and he accepted judgments from them which he might have questioned from his own men. Years later George Ball, who, having fought with Johnson on the war and lost, retained a considerable affection for him, would say of that period and Johnson's relationship with the Kennedy luminaries that Johnson did not suffer from a poor education, he suffered from a belief that he had had a poor education.

In 1964 the leadership, confident of its professionalism, held back on making decisions on Vietnam and allowed the bureaucracy to plan for war. The men around the President were busy planning for his election campaign, and for the Great Society to come, and they were sure that Vietnam was somehow a stumbling block over which they would not stumble. Yet gradually, even in early 1964, the play was being held closer and closer; the doubters were slowly being cut out of the play. The various dark forecasts of the intelligence agencies were being brushed aside.

McNamara was learning the hard way about Vietnam; when he went there in December, 1963, he had begun to know how to penetrate Harkins' briefings. There was one session when he was questioning a junior officer and he sensed that the junior officer was about to be candid, except that Harkins and General Stilwell kept interrupting, trying to stop the young officer from answering. Suddenly McNamara turned to them, the anger open and visible, his face red—"I asked that Major the question and I want an answer." It was a very tense and bitter scene. On his return to Washington he got together with McCone, who was also bothered by the reporting from Saigon, and they decided to do a CIA-Defense intelligence survey of the situation, which they felt was very bad; at least they ought to serve the President with as honest an evaluation as possible. But the Joint Chiefs of Staff blocked it. Once again the military was able to hold on to its version of reality, this time against the best efforts of the Secretary of Defense.

Above all, there was no real investigation of what kind of a deal might be worked out with Hanoi and the Vietcong, what neutralization might mean. So a year for political exploration was lost, and the reason for this was to be found in the character and outlook of the

Secretary of State of the United States, who was content to wait and let events come to him.

Dean Rusk hated to challenge the military on its needs and its requests because he feared a State-Defense split. In particular, he did not like to be out front on a policy, and he was content to let McNamara surge into the vacuum of leadership, poach on his terrain. All of this was the bane of his subordinates at State, who again and again, when they heard of some projected Defense policy for Vietnam, would go to Rusk and try to get him to intervene. In 1965 when State heard that the military was about to use massive B-52 bombing raids on Vietnam, subordinates pleaded with Rusk to block the bombing. They had argued forcefully and finally Rusk had picked up the phone and called McNamara.

They listened as Rusk relayed their doubts: "Bob, some of the boys here are uneasy about it." Was it really necessary, he asked, he hated to bother McNamara on a question like this . . . Then Rusk was silent and they could almost visualize McNamara at the other end crisply reassuring Rusk. And then McNamara was finished and Rusk was talking again: "Okay, Bob, in for a dime, in for a dollar." And he hung up.

Dean Rusk was a man without a shadow. He left no papers behind, few memories, few impressions. Everyone spoke well of him and no one knew him, he was the hidden man; he concealed, above all, himself and his feelings. All sorts of people thought they were good friends of his. They had known him for a long time—Rhodes scholars, old and intimate friends, called by someone wanting to find out about Rusk, said they would be glad, eager to talk, yes, Dean was a very old friend, and then it would always end the same way, the preliminary insights into Dean, that he was a good fellow, responsible, hard working, intelligent, serious—that and little more. Perhaps a sense finally that he had never been young. And then the faltering admission that on reflection they knew very little about him.

He loved being Secretary of State, the title and the trappings and what it meant. He was aware, to the day, of how long he had held office, and he would say things like "I am now the second oldest foreign minister in the world" . . . "Today I am the second most senior member of NATO." One record that he wanted and never achieved was that of Cordell Hull for American longevity; Rusk held the office for the second longest period in history. Not bad. A small corner of the history books. Many of his critics, the ones in the Kennedy Administration, talked about his imminent departure and denigrated him, but they left after their two years, sometimes voluntarily and sometimes not so voluntarily, to write their books, while Rusk remained. Always the professional. It was an important part of him, that foreign affairs was a profession and he was a professional, a serious man doing serious things. He had studied at it all those years, apprenticed at it under the great men, Marshall, Acheson, Lovett, worked his way up in State, where his rise was nothing less than meteoric (his detractors forgot that at a time right after World War II when the competition at State was ferocious, Rusk rose more quickly than anyone else in the Department). Then he was briefly out of government, went into the shadow-cabinet world of the foundations, and then back to Washington, back to the beloved profession, a chance to hold the torch passed not so much by Roosevelt, Truman, and Kennedy as by Marshall, Acheson, and Lovett, hold it and pass it on to someone else, eight years later, with the world in the same condition, probably not any better, but hopefully not worse, that was all he asked, he would say. No better, no worse.

He was a modest man in an Administration not known for its modesty, self-effacing in an Administration not known for self-effacement. He hated the amateurs, the meddlers, the intellectuals around him playing with power, testing their theories on the world. Quick, glib men dancing around Georgetown cocktail parties, Schlesingers, Galbraiths, Goodwins, Kaysens, people of that ilk. Making their direct phone calls to the President, breaking regular channels with their phone calls and shortcuts.

He worried about the liberals, he was one himself, although not too much of one: did they really understand the Communists, weren't they too likely to come to Washington just long enough to meddle in foreign affairs and fall victim to their own good intentions? Foreign affairs was something special, it was filled with pitfalls for well-meaning idealists. A brief scene: 1962. The Soviets had apparently resumed testing. Kennedy was trying to decide whether to test again. Adlai Stevenson asked what would happen if the United States did not test. Jerome Wiesner answered that American weapons were better, so that if there was a delay in the resumption of testing, what he called a benefit of the doubt delay, it would not make much difference. Then Stevenson (would-be Secretary of State, the man for whom in 1960 Rusk had served as the Scarsdale chairman of "Citizens for Stevenson," Rusk's highest political office) said that perhaps the United States ought to take a small risk in the strategic balance on a question like this, that it ought to try for moral leadership. Rusk interjected at this point: "I wouldn't make the smallest concession for moral leadership. It's much overrated." A young White House aide remembered the conversation, which shocked him, and from then on always thought of Rusk in that context; he thought that when Rusk died that should be inscribed on his tombstone, his epitaph.

A proud man. A poor man. Proud of his poverty in a way, sensitive about it, but that sensitivity showed in his pride (who else in that chic egalitarian Kennedy period, when they were pushing so hard to improve public education, sent his children to public schools?). He was almost defiantly proud of his lack of wealth, mentioning it often to aides in the department, that his job meant a considerable financial sacrifice. Harriman had told him not to worry, there would be plenty of lucrative offers after he finished, but Harriman was wrong. Neither could have foreseen Vietnam and what it would do to Rusk, making him virtually unemployable, making him, because of his decision to ride it through, the prime target for its critics, or the second prime target after Johnson. He would be vilified, but he was proud and refused to answer the attacks, the criticism, he was above it. Friends pleaded with him to answer some of the criticism, to fight back, but he deemed it improper, not so much for himself personally, but for the office.

A controlled man. Always patient. An extremely good diplomat in at least the limited sense of the word, that is, being diplomatic with other human beings. He would go up to the United Nations every year to meet the vast hordes of foreign ministers coming to the opening session, meeting with each one, handling them well, believing that his aides, who thought that this particularly thankless task should go to an underling, were wrong (just as he thought they were wrong in 1962 when he refused to forgo presiding at one of the two huge diplomatic dinners given by the Secretary of State each year to go to Nassau, where Kennedy was meeting with Harold Macmillan to discuss United States and European nuclear defense systems. He sent George Ball in his place, instead of going to Nassau himself and letting Ball handle the dinner, which gave McNamara a chance to play too large—and clumsy—a role at Nassau. Those who knew the role of the Secretary believed, first, that it was typical of his deference to Defense, and second, that Rusk, more cautious, more thoughtful and more reflective than McNamara, might have stopped the decisions of Nassau, decisions which encouraged De Gaulle to go it alone in

Europe and keep England out of the Common Market). When he met all the foreign ministers, he gave each equal time, showing the physical stamina of an old workhorse, great endurance, and always that control. Never, if possible, public or private nakedness of man or spirit or ideas, even at what many thought his greatest triumph, an appearance before a House committee considering civil rights legislation when he startled everyone by giving very strong testimony ("If I were a Negro I thing I might rise up")—one of his finest moments, the committee applauding, the press applauding, his aides proud, delighted. When he left the committee room he turned to a friend and said, "You don't think I went too far, do you?" Control was important, it was part of your discipline, of your attitude; it went with the position. If you lacked it, how could the men below you have it? If an aide walked in on Rusk while he was reading a piece of paper, the Secretary would continue to read it, even as the aide was on top of him. It was a highly disconcerting habit, and Rusk would explain simply that years before, he had vowed that when he picked up a piece of paper to read, he would finish it. Nothing swayed him. Sometimes that conscious quality of his control struck some of the men around him as in part at least a protect on against insecurity; by holding strictly to the form he was protecting himself, not letting himself go.

He was a modest man: a symbol, in personal style, with the control and the sense of the adversity of life, the discipline needed to meet that adversity, of a passing era. You played by the rules of the game and the rules were very strict, you did not indulge in the whim of your own personality, you served at the whim and will of those above you. Dean Rusk did not, so to speak, do his thing. He was the product of an era, and a particularly poor area and harsh culture where exactly the opposite behavior was respected and cherished: the compromising and sacrificing of your own will and desire and prejudices for the good of others, the good of a larger force. Sacrifice was important, and the very act of sacrifice was its own reward. All this was a part of him; he was, the men around him thought, a true Calvinist. Indeed, years later when Senator Eugene McCarthy wondered if Rusk's views on China were real, a friend assured him that they were, that Rusk was very much in the tradition of Dulles, a Calvin come to set policy, but McCarthy, who loved to mix theology and politics, shook his head and said no, not Calvin; Calvin had only written down his philosophy, he had not inflicted it on others. Rusk, McCarthy said, was Cromwell to Dulles' Calvin. He was Rusk, the poor Georgia boy to whom the

Good Lord had given a good mind and a strong body and a great capacity for work, and it was his obligation to use those qualities. This was something that Lyndon Johnson, who had that same sense and came from similar origins, understood completely. Rusk was, in his way, something of a hired hand to these great institutions. His upbringing had taught him to serve, not to question (which immediately set him apart from many of the Kennedy people who had been propelled by their propensity to question everything around them). Once, in an interview in Georgia, Rusk talked of the traits instilled in him by a Calvinist father. He defined it as a "sense of the importance of right and wrong which was something that was before us all the time. I think there was a sense of propriety, a sense of constitutional order, a sense of each playing his part in the general scheme of things, with a good deal of faith and confidence, with a passionate interest in education. . . ." He did not question these institutions; they had become what they were not by happenstance but because wise men who had thought a long time had deliberately fashioned them that way; nor did he severely question their current attitudes, which again had not arisen by happenstance. Indeed he found American and Western institutions admirable in contrast to the disorder which existed in the rest of the world.

He was part of that generation which felt gratitude for what was offered him. It was in that sense generational. His attitudes were close to those of a previous generation, while in the Dean Rusk family the values would change, would be less conservative: a son would work for the Urban League and would be part of the anti-Whitney Young movement because Young was too moderate; a daughter would marry a Negro. In this family, as in many others, children were more confident, more willing to challenge the existing order. "Rusk," said someone at the White House who knew him well and liked and respected him, "was different from the rest of us. He was poor and we had not been, but he really was more of my father's generation. You don't show feelings, you don't complain, you work very hard and you get ahead, and there was a sense that his mind was not his own property, that he was not allowed to let it take him where it wanted to go."

He would regard his own rise as a personification of the American possibilities, and he would see in the American-Rusk story a moral for other people. Cherokee County in Georgia, where he grew up, he would later point out, was an underdeveloped area, with typhoid and other problems, but it had all changed and become modernized.

"I've been able to see in my lifetime how that boyhood environment has been revolutionized with education, with technology, with county agents, and with electricity—all that helping to take the load off the backs of the people who live there. Now I can see that this can happen in one lifetime, I disregard those who say that underdeveloped countries still need two or three hundred years to develop because I know it isn't true. Because I've seen it with my own eyes."

Could there have been a Secretary of State with origins, with traditions more perfectly attuned to Lyndon B. Johnson? It was not surprising that their relationship was different from almost any other in that period of 1964. They felt so comfortable in each other's company that if they were on a plane, they would fall into conversation that was almost giddy, like two schoolboys back together after a summer vacation. And was it not true, thought the men around Rusk, that his accent, which under Kennedy had been somewhat Scarsdale, became more Georgia again? Once Lyndon and Dean were walking around the Ranch, followed by a group of high Washington aides, Johnson taking great pride in showing all the artifacts. One in particular delighted him, an antique piece which he pointed out to the somewhat bewildered Easterners. "You and I know what this is, don't we, Dean?" There was a smile of acknowledgment from Dean of a memory which took him back many years. It was an old indoor potty.

It would become fashionable among Kennedy people to portray Rusk as a man of some mediocrity, and it was a widely shared belief of many Kennedy insiders that usk's greatest problem was simply brain power, he just wasn't as smart as that bright Bundy group. There was an air of patronizing, a sort of winking to each other about Rusk, about the need to check with the good people at State, which did not mean Rusk. Yet in the late forties and early fifties Rusk was considered the most professional officer at State by many who knew the Department well. He rose faster than anyone else; in five years he went from an assistant on loan from the War Department to officer director for the United Nations to director of Special Political Effairs to Deputy Undersecretary of State for Political Affairs, the highest career job. The most striking thing was that he was not associated with any particular policy or viewpoint. It was symbolic of Rusk, the shadow man, that he could have this career and yet not be identified with any policy, so that later he could be a man of NATO, a man of the United Nations, a man of the Rockefeller Foundation, a man of Marshall, a man of Dulles, and a man of Stevenson, all without apparent contradiction.

In his years at State under Marshall, Lovett, Acheson, and Dulles, he was cool, competent, unflappable, carrying out policies which his superiors set, and which were the very basis of great policies of the Cold War. The world, to these architects of policy, was parallel to the one which had existed before the war; a totalitarian force was at work threatening Western Europe, the lines had to be drawn, only force would work. The lessons of Munich were very real and the mistakes would not be repeated. And so the lessons were clear for young Dean Rusk: when confronted by the strength and determination of a just and honorable democracy, the totalitarian forces of the world would have to respect that power.

But it was extraordinary that in this period Rusk avoided the one dangerous issue of the time. The issue was China, the one major place in the world where Communism would become entwined with nationalism and cause major domestic problems for the United States. The fall of China would send American policy—first domestic and then inevitably foreign—into convulsions that would last for more than two decades and give the policy in Asia a hard-rock interior of irrationality, and one tragic aftermath would be Vietnam.

Rusk believed in both the might and the decency of America (having never dealt in the domestic processes, he was uncritical of them). If America was both honorable and strong, and turned that strength in the right directions—which had been charted in the postwar years as containment of the totalitarians—then our side would triumph. Perhaps not easily, perhaps the struggle would be long, but eventually quality and class would tell. In 1965 and 1966, as the Vietnam war began to look more and more difficult and George Ball and others would tell him of their doubts, that it was a lost cause, Rusk would say, again and again, that when a great nation like the United States of America puts its shoulder to the wheel, something has to give. Yes, I know that the French were there and the political situation is bad, and it may be worse than you say, but I can't believe that when a great nation like the United States puts its shoulder to the wheel . . .

So color Rusk neutral, or color him amenable, or hardline. Who was he, which side was he on? He left State for the next best thing, the head of a great foundation at an unusually early age, only forty-three, and there were to be great things ahead. He spent those years of the fifties meeting the wealthy and powerful in New York, making no enemies, waiting for the next phone call from the next President. Making no enemies.

But the Kennedy years were not particularly easy ones; Rusk found himself surrounded by men he considered amateurs, people playing with the processes, interfering with serious men. The Kennedy style upset Rusk, the young men from the White House trying to get their hands into foreign policy, playing at it, looking over at State and finding bright young friends of theirs, bringing them to NSC meetings so that the Secretary, yes, the Secretary of State would be giving advice and have it challenged by some hot young desk officer. This was a recurrent situation, which he found virtually a violation of his office. Rusk had a great sense of the function of the office; he believed in people playing their parts, that and no more. But in all of this there was one curious anomaly; Rusk, who had risen to what was the second most powerful position in the nation, did not really covet power. He liked being Secretary of State, but at the point where you dominate, force yourself and your ideas forward, he shrank back. He really was a modest man in a job which demands that the incumbent fight and dominate an entire area of policy making.

It was factors such as these which led State to play such a dormant role in the year 1964, when the political situation in Vietnam continued to collapse and the strength of the Vietcong became ever more evident. When, under normal procedures, it should have been sending out warning signal after warning signal to the White House about the darkness immediately ahead in the tunnel, saying that the tunnel was getting longer and darker, State simply did not pose deep and probing questions. Instead it geared itself up on straight operational questions: how much fertilizer for this province, how much barbed wire for that. Nineteen sixty-four was a lost year, and much of the loss was attributable to the attitudes and dispositions of Dean Rusk.

CHAPTER 13

In the White House, Lyndon Johnson was in the first stage of becoming a President; he wanted to keep not just Vietnam at arm's length but all foreign problems. In the first months of 1964 he wanted to play from strength, not from weakness; domestic policy was strength, foreign policy was weakness. He was not at ease with the general class of people who made diplomacy their profession, particularly ambassadors. They were, after all, the worst of two worlds, being both State Department people and foreigners. As a result, he almost refused to see the members of the diplomatic corps. "Who are these people?" he would say. "Why do I have to see them? Have Rusk see them. They're his clients, not mine."

A strategy for 1964 slowly began to evolve: fend off the outside world, particularly Vietnam. Keep Vietnam quiet, do not explore its problems, keep them papered over. Make it a functional, factual issue, send more aid, more weapons, a few more men to Saigon. The doubters were to be cleared out. The man in charge was McNamara. Above all, it was not to surface as an issue in 1964; it was to be controlled, kept away from the reaches of Barry Goldwater; it was not to be an issue for the right. Goldwater would be the candidate against Johnson, and he appeared to be a particularly easy mark; he would drive Americans back to political divisions answered years earlier. If anything, Goldwater might propel Lyndon Johnson into his own Presidency with a momentum which Johnson would be hard put to create himself. Anything that diminished the possibility of a real landslide was to be avoided. Vietnam was the most identifiable trouble spot.

Thus if he could keep his people together, the liberals and the Democrats, then he was confident the issue would be Goldwater, and by early 1964 it was clear to him that his real problems—in that they could create serious factional rifts—were, first, his relationship with Robert Kennedy, which was particularly touchy, and second, the broader aspect of handling the Congress, using it in effect as an umbrella, on the question of Vietnam.

The problem of Robert Kennedy was a special one. The relationship between him and Johnson had always been marked by coldness, suspicion, and barely concealed dislike. Now both men were jockeying for the right to be John Kennedy's legatee. Robert Kennedy had the right to it by blood and by emotion, but Lyndon Johnson had it by constitutional right. The last thing he needed or wanted was a split between himself and the Kennedy people; it would divide his party, severely limit his capacity to govern, and sustain the image of Johnson as the usurper. What he wanted, and what he eventually achieved, was to take hold of the Kennedy legacy in 1964, carry out Kennedy programs with Kennedy men, at the same time diminishing the role of Robert Kennedy; then run for President and win on his own, and thus shed the Kennedy mantle. But in order to get rid of the Kennedy mantle he first had to gain control of it. All of this required deft handling. Johnson was partially aided by the fact that all the key men of the previous Administration now worked for him, so the Attorney General could not make an outright challenge against his late brother's closest advisers. Yet at the same time Robert Kennedy had ambitions of his own, and by the spring of 1964 he was openly campaigning for the Vice Presidency, precisely the position Lyndon Johnson did not have in mind for him (a landslide victory against Goldwater would become less of a personal triumph if there was a Kennedy on the ticket. The press, which was Eastern and pro-Kennedy, would give Robert Kennedy considerable credit for the victory). So Robert Kennedy was a serious potential problem in 1964, unlike Barry Goldwater, who was regarded as something of an asset.

The Congress was a more complicated problem: if an issue as fragile and volatile as Vietnam became a major part of the upcoming political campaign, then Johnson wanted some kind of congressional support, for protection. He was very much a creature of Congress: to him the Congress was the country, and he wanted the Congress on board, partly as a way of keeping the country on board. As early as May, 1964, Dean Acheson stopped a White House friend at a cocktail party and said that he thought Vietnam was going to turn out much worse than they expected, that it was all much weaker than the reports coming in—Acheson assumed that if the official reporting was beginning to be a little pessimistic, then it was surely far worse—and that it might be very tricky in the middle of the campaign. He thought the President ought to know this and try and protect himself. Acheson's warnings paralleled the President's own suspicions, and he asked the people around him to start thinking in terms of a congressional resolution. This would protect him from the pressures on the right, and would force Goldwater to support whatever the President was doing on Vietnam, or isolate him even further. Bill Bundy drafted the first copy of the resolution, a document of purposely vague intent and proportions, signifying that all good Americans were behind their President against the invidious enemy.

For a time it was debated within the inner councils whether or not to send the Bundy resolution to the Congress, but Johnson was lying low for the moment. Ernest Gruening of Alaska and Wayne Morse of Oregon were already making waves in the Senate, and Morse in particular was prickly, with that compelling sense of international law and an almost faultless sense of where the weak spot in an issue resided. Morse, Johnson told friends, was a tough one, the kind of man who could hurt you and expose your weaknesses even when he was standing alone. A formidable opponent. "My lawyer," Lyndon Johnson sometimes called him, hoping that a little flattery would rub him the right way. An able and abrasive man. And Johnson knew too that if Gruenino and Morse had surfaced, then there were others hiding in the cloakrooms, more covert in their doubts, but ready to jump if they smelled blood. Even Fulbright, an old friend, was showing signs of independence. And Johnson knew that the more prolonged scrutiny Vietnam received, the more difficult it would be for him. The whole point of the resolution was to paper over tensions, not to increase them. So in June his own intuitive sense of the Congress told him that the time was not right, that he could not just spring the resolution on the Congress, but rather he must mold it to events, and if possible tie it to an issue of patriotism. Something would have to come along.

So he would bide his time on the Congress. In the meantime it was McNamara's job to keep Vietnam in hand to tidy it up. Letting McNamara be the front man for Vietnam was handy in a number of ways. He was at the height of his reputation with liberals, and he was a Kennedy figure in a way that Rusk was not; thus he neutralized potential opposition. Liberal Democrats, by now co-opted by the Kennedys, could not effectively protest the drift of the Vietnam policy without criticizing at least by implication their own people. McNamara was the star of the Administration; he was able to continue his close personal relationship with the Kennedys, his regular visits with Jackie Kennedy, and at the same time receive praise such as Lyndon Johnson had never accorded mortals in the past. He was the ablest man that Lyndon Johnson had ever dealt with, the President told people; there was no one like him for service to his country. "He wields that computer and those figures like King Arthur wielded Excalibur," Jack Valenti told the President.

"Like what?" the President asked.

"Like King Arthur wielded Excalibur," Valenti repeated.

"More like Sam Rayburn with a gavel, I think," the President said.

"Same thing, Mr. President," Valenti answered.

If McNamara was regarded with awe in Washington, there were those in Saigon who had watched his trips to Vietnam with mounting disbelief. They thought that his glib press conferences, the statistics rolling off, were hopefully put-ons, that at least McNamara himself did not believe in what he was doing. Nothing fazed him, he showed no uncertainty, he plunged straight ahead. If he was learning, he was learning too little too late. Indeed, even as he became somewhat more knowledgeable in 1964 and 1965, it was not entirely a blessing. The very process of learning was achieved at the expense of his becoming more deeply involved, more attached to and identified with the problem, and thus more committed to finding a solution. Having helped bring us that far, he felt himself under extra pressure to see it through.

He had learned in late December 1963 and early 1964 that Harkins had seriously misled him and he was furious, and Harkins was in effect finished; the only reason he would be allowed to stay on a few months longer in Saigon was to save face. Not Harkins' face, but the face of the people in Washington who had put him there, not the least of them Robert McNamara. If he were pulled back under the mounting evidence that the war had been going poorly all along, it would be an admission that the Administration had been either taken in by faulty reporting, or worse, had itself been lying. If its past estimates were not to be believed, then how could one fend off critics of present estimates? In addition, when Harkins was finally brought home, the attitude in Washington was again simplistic: a bad general was going to be replaced by a good general; it was not the whole system, the bad war, which had produced such fraud, it was simply the wrong general. Thus one replaced him with the best general around. Individuals *could* make a difference.

In June, 1964, General William C. Westmoreland became the commander of American forces. On June 22 Lyndon Johnson held a ceremony for Harkins at the White House, where he presented him with an oak-leaf cluster for his Distinguished Service Medal. As was the President's wont, particularly in cases where he did not believe what he was saying, he resorted to considerable flattery in his description of Harkins, noting that though the general would soon retire, "I have asked Secretary McNamara, who has such great and unlimited confidence in this great soldier, to have the general remain in the Washington area so that we may benefit from his broad knowledge of and his experience in the various theaters of the world, and particularly Southeast Asia." (McNamara had of course lost confidence in Harkins, in fact was very bitter about him, telling interviewers such as Professor Henry Graff of Columbia that Harkins had failed in Vietnam.)

In May and June things began to look better and better for the President. The polls showed Johnson running well among people who had never liked him before, and cutting in on large segments of Republican voters (one poll taken by Oliver Quayle in the spring of 1964 showed that half of the people who had voted for Nixon in 1960 were now for Johnson). The message confirmed his own intuition.

It was going very well, and he did not need Robert Kennedy on the ticket; if anything, given the restlessness in the South over civil rights, Robert Kennedy, who as Attorney General had been the Cabinet officer most deeply involved, might even hurt him. Now he moved to end the Kennedy threat.

Jack Kennedy had always treated Vice President Johnson courteously and with great sensitivity; Robert Kennedy had not. The antagonism between the two men was very real. Friends thought the origins went back to the 1960 convention, when Johnson attacked Joseph Kennedy personally at a press conference, saying, "My father never carried an umbrella for Chamberlain." Robert Kennedy remembered the incident, as had Johnson, and a year later at a dinner party, Johnson, the Vice President and outsider, took Bobby, the Attorney General and insider, aside and said, "I know why you don't like me. The reason you don't like me is because I made those remarks about your father at the press conference and they were taken out of context and I was misquoted." Kennedy denied that he knew what Johnson was talking about. "Yes, you do," Johnson said, "you know what I'm talking about and that's why you don't like me." None of the tensions had eased after Johnson became President, and Robert Kennedy felt that Johnson was somehow a usurper. Johnson, sensitive to Robert Kennedy's feelings, had worked hard to ease the pain, but he had met little success.

Now in the early summer of 1964 he knew that Robert Kennedy was promoting himself for the Vice Presidency. He tried to head it off, using McGeorge Bundy, among others, as an emissary (the fact that Bundy, nominally a Republican, was willing to run this kind of errand for Johnson particularly infuriated Robert Kennedy, and Bundy's connections with the inner Kennedy group were badly shattered). All of this failed. In late July the President called Robert Kennedy in and told him he would not be on the ticket, that he had a bright future in politics but this was not his year. Johnson would be pleased to have him run the campaign. Their talk seemed to have gone very well, but later Johnson called in three White House correspondents for a leisurely lunch. He described the meeting with Kennedy and could not restrain his talents as a mimic; he demonstrated how Bobby had gulped when the news was broken. Within a few hours the story was all over Washington, complete with Johnsonian embellishments. Robert Kennedy was furious. Johnson soon went on television to say that he had decided against naming any members of his Cabinet to the Vice Presidency. Thus Johnson took care of

Robert Kennedy, and the way was clearer to his own Presidency, but he had paid a price; the tension between the Kennedy people and the Johnson Presidency was more real than ever.

But he still had to deal with the question of the Congress as far as Vietnam was concerned. He wanted that extra protection before he went into the campaign. At the end of July he got his way; an incident in the Gulf of Tonkin provided the factor of patriotism that he had sought for his congressional resolution. It was to be called the Tonkin Gulf incident, and in reality it had begun back in January, when the President and his top advisers gave permission to General Krulak and the restless JCS to go ahead and plan a series of covert activities against the North under the general code name of 34A. These would be run from Saigon under the command of General Harkins (though of course the Vietnamese would be nominally in command), and the purpose would be to make Hanoi pay a little for its pressure on the South, to hit back at the enemy, to raise morale in the South, to show Hanoi we were just as tough as they were, that we understood the game of dirty tricks and could play it just as well as they did. (Which, of course, we could not.)

The people of the United States did not know about 34A, nor did the Congress, but that was of no importance. The covert operations were doubly handy. If no one knew about them, then it bothered no one; if they did become public, if there was a Communist challenge to them, the public and the Congress would be forced between choosing their own side or the Communist side. A question of patriotism then. In the early summer of 1964 the operations under 34A were intensified. The war in the South was not going well, and this was a way of slapping back at the North and also warning Hanoi surreptitiously that its attacks were not going unnoticed, that there was a payment inherent in its war. The subversion attempts proved predictably futile; at the same time, more annoying to the North Vietnamese, though hardly damaging, was the use of unannounced bombing raids along the Laotian border, and the use of South Vietnamese PT boats in hit-and-run commando raids against North Vietnamese naval installations on the coast. Although the latter did not cause much harm, the pressure in the North for some retaliation was building up. The PT raids, though involving Vietnamese crews, had been planned and initiated by the command of MACV, under General Harkins and Mac Bundy. McNamara and Rusk had full knowledge and control of them. In the real sense, these were American operations.

Then, Tonkin Gulf.

On July 30, South Vietnamese patrol boats based in Danang had taken off for a raid on two North Vietnamese bases; the attack took place on July 31. At almost the same time an American destroyer, the *Maddox*, was on its way toward the same coast, its mission to play games with the North Vietnamese radar, to provoke the radar system. Using highly expensive and sophisticated equipment, the *Maddox* could simulate an attack on the North, thus forcing the Chinese Communists and the North Vietnamese to turn on their radar. At this time the Americans could pinpoint more accurately where the other side's installations were located, just in case there was ever a need to have them charted. As the *Maddox* headed toward its mission on July 31, it passed the returning South Vietnamese PT boats; unaware of the other mission, it thought at first they were Soviet boats. On August 1 the *Maddox* began her mission, which was, in North Vietnamese eyes, a provocative act and seemed to be part of the overall assault which had begun on July 31. On August 2 the Maddox sighted three North Vietnamese PT boats, was attacked by them, and destroyed one. Aboard the *Maddox*, radio intercepts of North Vietnamese traffic made clear that it considered the *Maddox* patrol part of the overall 34A operation, and this information was cabled back to the Pentagon (McNamara would soon testify before the Senate Foreign Relations Committee that it "was clear" that the North Vietnamese knew these were separate missions; similarly, on August 6, McNamara would claim that the *Maddox* was attacked when she was thirty miles from the North Vietnamese coast. In truth the attack began when the *Maddox* was thirteen miles from a North Vietnamese island, and earlier in the day much closer to the mainland). Out of this was to come the Tonkin Gulf incident, the first bombing of the North, and almost immediately the Tonkin Resolution.

Johnson's first reaction was that whatever else, we had been fired on in an area where we had a right to be; thus, the *Maddox* and a companion ship, the *C.Turner Joy*, should continue their activities, otherwise we would be pushed farther and farther back. Meeting with Rusk, McNamara, and Bundy, Johnson discussed retaliatory measures. For the moment the President was unwilling to bomb the North; he wanted to know more about what was happening, and he didn't think this episode was worth it. We didn't, he told them, lose anybody in this fight, we had sunk one of their boats. Now we would just show them that we weren't going to move, they couldn't run us out of those waters, and we would kick the hell out of anyone who tried. At the same time Johnson used the hot line to reassure the Soviet

Union that we intended to continue naval operations in that area, but that we did not intend to widen the war. Meanwhile Rusk told his subordinates to go ahead with the drafting of a congressional resolution backing the President in eventualities like this.

Captain John Herrick, who was the commander of the Tonkin Gulf patrol, was cabling back that he thought continuance of the patrol "an unacceptable risk" because of the North Vietnamese sensitivity to the *Maddox* foray; since Herrick was privy to the radio intercepts, he knew what the North Vietnamese were thinking, which was that this and the 34A activity were all one raid. His warning cable had little effect; Washington was in no need to pull back or be cautious. If anything, quite the reverse was true; the Chiefs and some civilians in the Pentagon had been pushing for acts against the North, such as sending low-flying jets over Hanoi in order to create sonic booms, which would push the North to some kind of reaction. Johnson had held the line on that, but he had given permission to go ahead with the radar harassment patrols as well as the 34A missions, and now that had in fact created just the provocation that some of the Joint Chiefs wanted.

The next day, August 3, both the *C. Turner Joy* and the *Maddox* were ordered back into the same dangerous waters as a sign that the United States would not back down. Almost immediately the North Vietnamese appeared to challenge them, in what would become the second Tonkin incident. Whether there had been an attack was somewhat unclear (in fact, much of the Tonkin Gulf controversy centered around whether or not an attack really took place, or whether the two destroyers were firing at each other, or whether in fact the military deliberately faked an incident in order to create the retaliation). The evidence on Tonkin is still clouded, in part because McNamara's story was so filled with old-fashioned lies, but the evidence, clear or not, is peripheral to the real question of what had taken place in the days immediately prior to the incident, and what kind of United States and South Vietnamese provocation had taken place. Because of the secrecy and the covert nature of the operation, because of Administration lies, both the Congress and the public were seriously misled.

On August 4 Captain Herrick radioed back that the intercepts showed the North Vietnamese still thought this was part of a 34A mission. By 8 A.M. Washington time (8 P.M. of the same day in the Gulf) it became clear that some sort of incident was taking place; at 9:52 Washington time, both destroyers signaled that they were under constant attack. Throughout the morning there were unclear and fragmentary reports of combat. By noon Johnson was lunching with Bundy, Rusk, and McNamara (at the same time James Thomson, the specialist on Asian affairs on the Bundy staff, was asking White House staff member Robert Komer what they should do in moments like this. "What we do," said Komer, "is go to lunch. In situations like this the big boys take over."). There would be retaliation this time, Johnson made clear. Bombing most likely. At lunch they continued to discuss the alternatives and gradually firmed it up. American planes would be used, and they would hit bases which harbored the patrol boats. The JCS had provided a list of six sites, but Rusk, who was always worried about the Chinese, suggested eliminating the two northern-most bases because they were too near the China border. Reconnaissance photos showed berths for forty-seven PT boats, with only thirteen of them in the two northern bases. We ought to hit the remaining thirty-four with everything we had, Rusk said, and let the other thirteen be. They would still be there in case we needed to go back and would give us an option for the future. Thus was the list drawn up.

By 5 P.M. Johnson was summoning congressional leaders to the White House; even as the leaders were on their way there, the planning for the retaliation was going ahead. When Johnson met with the congressional leaders at 6:15 he outlined the day's events (without, of course, mentioning the 34A activities) and told them what he intended to do. He emphasized that it would be a limited retaliation, and said he wanted a congressional resolution; he was assured of their support, for both the actions and the resolution. I'm not going in, he told them, unless the Congress goes with me. At 10 P.M., with the Pentagon still sending out urgent messages demanding details of the incident ("Who are witnesses? What is witness reliability? Most important that positive evidence substantiating type and number of attacking forces be gathered and disseminated."), the first planes were leaving the aircraft carriers *Ticonderoga* and *Constellation*. The war planes hit the four PT-boat bases and the oil depot at Vinh. The next day McNamara reported that twenty-five of the thirty boats in the bases had been either damaged or destroyed, and that ninety percent of the Vinh depot had been wiped out; indeed, at Vinh "the smoke was observed rising to 14,000 feet." So in a way it had begun. We had shown ourselves in an act of war. We had perhaps committed ourselves more than we knew.

The day after the meetings, McGeorge Bundy gathered the White House staff together and said that the President had decided to go for a congressional resolution calling for a general posture in Southeast

Asia. Thus if anything more serious happened during the forthcoming election, he would be able to deal with both Hanoi and the Congress. Douglass Cater, a White House adviser on domestic issues, was one of the first to speak up. "Isn't this a little precipitous?" he asked. "Do we have all the information . . . ?"

Bundy said, "The President has decided and that's what we're doing."

Cater, new in the White House, persisted: "Gee, Mac, I haven't really thought it through."

Bundy, with a very small smile: "Don't."

Walt Rostow, still at Policy Planning, though more an enthusiast now of the policies as they became more and more hard line, was very pleased; a few days later friends who lunched with him at State found him almost expansive. Things, he told them, could not have gone better had they planned them exactly this way.

Which seemed to be true at the moment for Lyndon Johnson. As long as he moved ahead toward escalation he had kept the right fairly quiet, and the left had been bothersome but not dangerous. Now a confrontation had taken place where our boys had been fired on, where national patriotism was at stake, and he could lock up both sides. Particularly the right. It would kill Goldwater. In the Senate, people like Morse might try and oppose him, but after an incident like this, it would be much harder. In addition, the hearings would take place in the heat of battle. All the better. He immediately decided to go for the congressional resolution; it was too good an opportunity to miss. He did not miss it, and the first person he co-opted was his old friend Bill Fulbright.

Fulbright was an odd combination of public man and private man, Arkansas and the Senate's link to the Establishment. He was a public official, publicly elected, and yet he seemed to be an ally of the elitists, sharing their view of the private nature of national security. He had good ties to Georgetown and the Metropolitan Club. But if he had believed in the major assumptions of the previous era, he had in 1961 begun to change, as it seemed that the world was changing. He had opposed the Bay of Pigs, and privately he was increasingly unhappy with the direction of the policy in Vietnam—the United States as the anti-Communist policeman of the world. Vietnam and the Dominican Republic intervention would turn him into a major foreign policy critic, but that still lay ahead in August, 1964. He was a particular favorite of the President's, Johnson having engineered the coup against Theodore Green which gave Fulbright his prized Foreign Relations

Committee, and there had been reciprocal favors. Fulbright gave the Johnson operation a little class; Johnson allowed the more reserved Fulbright to rise and hold power without getting his hands dirty. Now, facing Goldwater in the forthcoming election, and faced with the tricky issue of Vietnam, Johnson called in a due bill from Fulbright, and asked him to manage the resolution through the Senate. It was a crucial request and Fulbright accepted, not just because of the threat of Goldwater, though that was the reason he would later give, but largely because, for all his misgivings, and he had plenty of them (he knew that Johnson was not entirely to be trusted, but he also thought that Johnson might manipulate others, but not his old and dear friend Bill Fulbright), he was still part of the old partnership.

So Fulbright, in a move he would spent the rest of his life bitterly regretting, accepted the job of shepherding the Tonkin Gulf Resolution through the Senate. The decision reflected all the ambivalence both of Fulbright's views on foreign affairs and on his view of his own position. He had grave doubts about the war, and he knew the dangers of the wording of the resolution he was pushing through, but he was also willing to take the risk. Having done things and played the game with Johnson in the past, he was willing to try it once more. Though Fulbright was unusually independent and courageous, the stigma of going against the President on an issue of patriotism was not one that any senator sought—which of course was exactly why Johnson was sending his resolution hurtling toward the Hill.

On the night of August 4, while the second Tonkin incident was beginning to wind down and American planes were already on their mission, Senator Wayne Morse received an anonymous phone call from someone at the Pentagon who was reasonably high up and who obviously knew a good deal about destroyers. The caller told Morse that he understood that the Oregon senator was going to oppose the forthcoming resolution. In that case, he should ask the Secretary of Defense two questions. He should ask to see the *Maddox'* log (which would place the ship closer to shore than the alleged site of the incident reflected), and he should ask what the real mission of the ship was. Morse, who had already smelled a rat, was now convinced that the Administration's case was even flimsier than he had suspected, that this was perhaps a provocative incident on our part, and he even suspected that it had been deliberately initiated in order to get the resolution through Congress.

The next day Morse begged Fulbright to hold real hearings on the resolution and warned him that the wording was far too general and far too openended for any President, particularly Lyndon Johnson. Fulbright answered that they didn't have time, that it was an emergency. What emergency? Morse asked. I don't know of any emergency. Instead Morse insisted that this was the proper time to hold real hearings on Vietnam, to summon genuine expertise. He had in mind calling the dovish generals, Ridgway, Gavin, Shoup, Collins, and then some international-law people, and then perhaps witnesses who knew something about the political situation in the South. The sum of the hearing, he was sure, would have been to cast such doubt about any venture in Vietnam as to make any resolution a good deal more limited, if not bottling it up altogether. Morse was absolutely convinced that the instincts of his colleagues were more dovish than was apparent, and that expert testimony by former generals would give them heart. Fulbright turned him down and decided to ram the resolution through in a crisis atmosphere with patriotism a key factor; at a joint meeting of the Foreign Relations and the Armed Services committees, where both McNamara and Rusk testified for forty minutes, Fulbright was a friend of the White House. Morse alone asked unfriendly questions and cast the only dissenting vote.

On August 7 Morse, with Gruening the only two senators to vote against the resolution, said: "I believe that history will record that we have made a great mistake in subverting and circumventing the Constitution of the United States ... by means of this resolution. As I argued earlier today at great length, we are in effect giving the President ... warmaking powers in the absence of a declaration of war. I believe that to be a historic mistake."

Years later a reporter interviewing Wayne Morse, by then an ex-senator, would find him more intense in his retrospective anger toward Fulbright than toward Johnson. Fulbright, Morse thought, had played the game when he should have known, and in fact did know, better. Fulbright would feel that he had been lied to and misled, and finally, with great misgivings—going against the advice of his more conservative Senate staff, and with the urging of his committee staff, he began a series of speeches that would lead to a major break with the Administration. The relationship, once so warm ("To J. William Fulbright, than whom there is no better," Johnson had recently autographed a photo) would become bitter and hostile. Knowing that Fulbright liked to be on the inside, Johnson deliberately tried to isolate him, to mock him in private, calling him "the stud duck of the opposition"; and he would talk to friends of Fulbright's laziness, his vanity. Fulbright in turn dissented first in speeches, and then, by early 1966, with major hearings on the war, calling a series of forceful and eloquent witnesses, Kennan, Gavin, and others. Then the Senate Foreign Relations Committee would become the center of opposition to the war, and it would lead, to a very considerable degree, to Johnson's withdrawal from the 1968 race. For Lyndon Johnson, the Tonkin Gulf Resolution was a victory, but like so many things he was to do in the coming year, it produced short-range gains with far more serious long-range problems.

Although Johnson's success was an illusion, the short-range results were remarkable. The polls were better than ever, the press comment was better than ever (even Walter Lippmann seemed pleased, because Lippmann, a believer in an American policy of blue water and clear skies for the Pacific, that is, staying out of land wars, thought Johnson was signalling the limits of the United States in a Pacific war rather than just the beginning). "In a single stroke Mr. Johnson has, at least temporarily, turned his greatest political vulnerability in foreign policy into one of his strongest assets," wrote Lou Harris, the pollster, on August 10. No less than 85 percent of the nation approved the raids. In July, Harris noted, 58 percent of the nation had criticized Johnson's handling of the war, while after Tonkin, public opinion virtually reversed itself, and 72 percent approved. More and more people, Harris found, wanted us to take the war to the North (though of course there was very little polling about what that meant, whether we should take the war to the North if it meant a prolonged and bloody ground war in the bargain).

Having handled, he thought, the Congress, the people, and the enemy, the way was clear now to Johnson's own Presidency. In late summer he moved away from the shadow of Jack Kennedy, his own legislative program and his foreign problems, to run for the Presidency as his own man, for the Johnson years, and he did it joyously and with zest. It was no wonder that he loved running in 1964, a chance to bask in the kind of national admiration he had never received before. He was frequently described as a healing man; indeed, he would refer to one of his main speeches as the one in which he was "healing the wounds." He was the man who could bring the different regions together, who could overcome his own regional prejudices if the nation would overcome its prejudices against him. Roy Wilkins would say of him, yes, the President seemed to be a great man destined for great things, but that Texas accent did make him, Wilkins, a little uneasy; and no less a figure than Martin Luther King, Jr., saw more hope for him, more commitment from him for Negro rights than from John Kennedy, King seeing in Johnson a desire to cleanse a soul.

His energies became almost mythological; they were our energies, his dreams were our dreams. Business leaders came over to him, made uneasy not by Goldwater's preference for free enterprise, but by their fear that in blowing up the Kremlin men's room, he might blow up their factories as well. The young did not protest him. He sat at a mass rally in Detroit with Walter Reuther on one side of him and Henry Ford on the other. Was it possible? Was this the land where our fathers had struggled? "I never had it so good," he said that day in Detroit. To visitors at the White House he loved to show slides of people reaching out to him at campaign rallies. "Look at them," he would say. "Just look at them." Negroes, in their last year of being content to be known as Negroes, rallied to his side. More than rally—"Those Negroes cling to my hands like I was Jesus Christ walking in their midst," he told friends. He was for one magic moment what he had always wanted to be, the centrist consensus candidate, loved by all his people. He savored it, becoming expansive in the riches that the campaign brought him; he had the issues locked up.

It was all his; Jack Kennedy had started it and Lyndon Johnson had finally put it together and held it together and now he was reaping its dividends. As the campaign progressed, even the greatest sophisticates in the country, the New York jet set, rallied to his cause, opened a discothèque called the LBJ, where chic young people danced beneath giant photos of that somewhat mournful face. Everywhere he campaigned the crowds were good and they responded to him, to the good life he was bringing them. He cast aside the security advice of the Secret Service people, and surged into the throng, and they loved him and he gave back his warmth and his energy. The times were good now and there were better ones, golden years, ahead. His record would make people forget Kennedyism—oh, a few snobs, the Georgetown Ivy Leaguers, might remember how they had danced in those brief years, but the rest of the nation would be reading about the Great Society and Lyndon Johnson and what he had done for all of the people. It was no wonder he tried to keep Vietnam out of his mind, as far from a place of debate as possible. When someone asked him later why he had not involved the public more in the question of Vietnam, he was told: "If you have a mother-in-law with only one eye and she has it in the center of her forehead, you don't keep her in the living room."

Oh, to run against Barry Goldwater, he of the quick tongue and the quick atomic trigger. It was not that he actually advocated nuclear war, it was just that he talked about nuclear war so much that he seemed to be advocating it (reporters covering Goldwater noted that in one thirty-minute speech alone, Goldwater mentioned nuclear weapons, war, and devastation twenty-six times). In the past, Lyndon Johnson knew, there had been doubts in the public mind about him, not doubts about the Johnsonian ability to get things done, but about his ethical sense, doubts about his restraint, doubts stemming from his *Texanisms*. But Goldwater, the man of the real right, cleansed him of his sins; the more Goldwater campaigned, the better it was for Lyndon Johnson, a rare case where exposure of your opponent was a blessing. In case there was any question about what Goldwater might do with the issue of the war, the Administration was careful to send a young naval officer in civilian clothes to Goldwater's headquarters each day to pick up his advance speeches; thus the Administration was prepared to answer any charge on the war almost before Goldwater made it. If Tonkin had tied up the nation, it had also tied up Goldwater, good old-fashioned patriot that he was. So Barry Goldwater made it possible for Johnson to run as he had always wanted and as he felt most comfortable, not as a man of ideology or region, but as someone who simply wanted to do good for all the folks. It was a lovely thing to watch, Lyndon out there, healing the wounds, as he put it.

The signs were good everywhere, in the polls, in the people who came to the White House. He was ebullient; he loved calling people into the White House, showing them the polls, and telling them what it would mean in the next session of Congress. He was going to win and win big, and he was going to get a real Congress, and there was nothing in his way. "We'll have nine, eh, maybe even eighteen months before the Hill turns around on us," he would say. "We have that much time to get it all through." And then he talked of his plans, his dreams, what he would do, the education legislation, the housing program, the domestic vision, and he pushed his domestic staff to work harder and harder on domestic legislation, driving them relentlessly, always aware of the limits of time. "When you win big," he would say, recalling Franklin Roosevelt's experience, "you can have anything you want for a time. You come home with that big landslide and there isn't a one of them who'll stand in your way. No, they'll be gled to be aboard and to have their photograph taken with you and be part of all that victory. They'll come along and they'll give you almost everything you want for a while and then they'll turn on you. They always do. They'll lay in waiting, waiting for you to make a slip and you will. They'll give you almost everything and then they'll make you pay for it. They'll get tired of all those columnists writing how smart you are and how weak they are and then the pendulum will swing back."

At the convention, *his* convention, there had been barely any challenge to his supremacy. Some kids and some Negroes from Mississippi tried to get in, tried to stir up trouble, trouble that would only help Goldwater, so he calmed them down, in his usual way, telling the liberals it was their job to take care of that Mississippi business, or else their man, Hubert Humphrey, would suffer. That was the price. And so they had quieted down the Mississippi people, and Humphrey had been on the ticket ("My link to the bomb throwers," he had called Humphrey in the old days when he used him as an opening to the Senate left, though Humphrey was far from a bomb thrower any more), and it was one more victory for centrist pluralist politics over the extreme fringe.

American politics—the kind of coalition politics he knew best still worked—still delivered. The people might not always like it, but they had no alternative to it. Or did it work? Was it still effective? Or had there been a major change in the attitudes of the people, and in particular among his party's special constituents, the liberal intellectuals, changes which were momentarily obscured by the one issue of 1964, Goldwater? If the benefit of Goldwater was that he dominated the campaign, the price was that he obscured other issues and warning signals, subtle changes in the society, for events and attitudes in America were very much in flux, and if anything, 1964 was a landmark year in American life. The people in power seemed to be very much in control of events; the Cold War still existed and high-level American political attitudes were still shaped by it; the old liberal Democratic coalition still held together, though some of the participants in it were increasingly uneasy with one another. On the surface, things seemed as they had in the past, only perhaps a little bit better. But it was a time when icons were about to be shattered, and when the order was about to change.

There was a growing citizen restlessness which was not reflected in the political order; the politicians and a good many in the population had very different definitions of who the enemies were and what the problems were. For the existing political structure still believed that America was threatened from without, while an increasing number of educated, articulate Americans felt the dangers were from within.

The politicians in Washington were responding to issues which no longer affected large numbers of the people, and as a corollary, increasing numbers of people were bothered about elements of their life which were not defined as political issues. The gap between the politicians and the public, particularly an articulate educated minority, was growing, and nothing would widen it like the war in Vietnam. The government itself was still geared up to hold the lines in the Cold War, but a particularly influential part of the citizenry believed that it was a thing of the past, that the arms race was futile and destructive, that the enemy was really bigness, technology, and the government itself. Liberals had always grown up thinking big and powerful government was good; now for a variety of reasons they were moving back from that position. So there were stirrings in the land; they had not surfaced as political forces and it would have taken a uniquely sensitive political figure to both perceive them and incorporate them into his policies. Lyndon Johnson certainly did not sense them; he saw power residing where it always had in the past and he had little sense of where it might go in the future. Perhaps some of these stirrings might have surfaced earlier, but the sheer charm and style of Kennedy had helped co-opt some of the dissidence and defuse some of the restlessness. Kennedy was intellectual, stylish, liberal, and young, and thus seemed like them and of them; Norman Mailer had seen Kennedy as the existential President whose very presence would somehow make American intellectual and political life better.

Now in 1964 the cracks in the concrete were beginning to show in a variety of places, and the coming of the war would heighten the very restlessness which was just beginning to emerge. Young whites went to Mississippi that summer to attack segregation, but they made it clear that they were attacking the entire structure of American life and that Mississippi was merely the most visible part. Their activity led to the formation of the Mississippi Freedom Democratic party, which caused the one sour note as far as Johnson was concerned at the convention. There they were quickly put down, but what the Freedom Democrats symbolized politically, deep and abiding dissent from the processes and an unwillingness to compromise on terms dictated by the existing power structure, would live and grow. By 1968 many of the people who had helped put them down at the 1964 convention were with them, and the Democratic party itself seemed threatened.

At the same time the civil rights movement itself was winding down; there was a new and growing Negro discontent. There was a new anger in the air, particularly in Northern cities. A sense of bitterness and hate seemed to pervade, and traditional civil rights leaders were pushed aside. Riots started in the ghettos of Harlem, Rochester, Jersey City, and Philadelphia, and other cities would soon follow; as the ghettos burned, the civil rights movement was coming to an end. More alienated and more scarred leaders such as Malcom X rose. They were protesting not just legal segregation, but the very structure of American life. The problem was not a Negro problem, they said, it was a white problem. They did not want In, they wanted Out. They did not want programs; indeed, in the changing mood of the black communities, leaders who were seen cooperating with the white structure soon lost part of their credibility.

In California, at Berkeley, the university that once was a special monument to pluralistic free education, there was a growing student restlessness and a growing dissatisfaction with student and American life. When the protests were put down clumsily by local authorities, the students banded together and formed the Berkeley Free Speech Association; it was the first step in which a new educated youth of America flashed its power and its desire to have a say in political events. Berkeley was the beginning of a growing student protest which sometimes seemed unable to define its exact enemies, but which came together on the issue of the war as Johnson escalated in Vietnam. Even as Berkeley was breaking out, a young lawyer named Ralph Nader was finishing his book on auto safety, and he would come to symbolize the citizen protest against the government and against the corporation, a belief that a citizen, to be effective, had to work outside the government.

Yet for all this change, there was little of it reflected in the political processes. To Lyndon Johnson, the Mississippi Freedom Democratic party was like a gnat to be squashed on his way to the convention, a tiny irritant in a time of great joy, but it would be a symbol of other forces which would have dire consequences.

CHAPTER 14

He was the elemental man, a man of endless, restless ambition. Nothing was ever completed, each accomplishment was a challenge to reach for more. He was a politician the like of which we shall not see again in this country, a man who bridged very different Americas, his early days and attitudes forged by earthy, frontier attitudes, and whose final acts as President took us to the very edge of the moon. He was a man of stunning force, drive, and intelligence, and of equally stunning insecurity. The enormity of his accomplishments never dimmed the hidden fears which had propelled him in the first place; he was, in that sense, the most human of politicians. There was about Lyndon Johnson something compelling; the more he tried to hide his warts, the more he revealed them. His force and power were such that when he entered the White House, the intellectual architects of his own party believed firmly that the greatest political benefits in America were produced by a strong, activist President; it was a negative testimony to him that when he left many of these same people talked of limiting the role of the Chief Executive, of strengthening the powers of the legislature and of local governments. Perhaps there was something of the inherent contradiction of democratic pluralistic America in the contradiction of Lyndon Johnson as President; the country had become so large, so powerful, yet so diffuse and disharmonious that only a man of his raging, towering strengths and energies could harness the nation's potential. That energy, when properly harnessed by him was marvelous, but given his powers, his drives, his instinct to go forward, it was disastrous if he was harnessed to the wrong policies. America then seemed faced with the dilemma of being overgoverned or undergoverned, and no one would ever accuse Lyndon Johnson as President of being content to undergovern. He would never let the history books say of him that he had been content to sit on the sidelines, to be a gentle, leisurely President, letting events take their course. He would control and dominate events, and the history books would tell of the good that he had done. Everything was on a larger scale for him,, the highs were higher, the lows lower. He did not dream small dreams. Nor did he pursue small challenges. He pursued History itself, a place, perhaps, on Mount Rushmore, though there were those who knew him who felt that Rushmore was too small, that it was Westminster Abbey, the history of the West. His speech writers were enjoined to give him a Churchillian twist.

Greatness beckoned him. Even as Vice President he got to meet some elder statesmen when Kennedy dispatched him to Europe. He liked Adenauer, who was warm and pleasant, but he did not like De Gaulle, who was aloof and arrogant. However, he was impresed by De Gaulle, with his sense of grandeur and sense of history. De Gaulle who had greeted him with these words: "What have you come to learn?" That was greatness and that was history.

Later, when he had become President, he never took his eye off history. When an expert on documents warned him against using the auto pen (an automatic pen which reproduces the signature of the busy executive) and said that Jack Kennedy had used it too frequently and promiscuously, and that there were too many Kennedy letters which were not true Kennedy letters in the exact historical sense (including, the historian knew but did not have the heart to say, one from President John F. Kennedy to Vice President Lyndon B. Johnson), Johnson took the admonition seriously. He signed all letters himself; history was history, one did not cheat it, a Johnson letter was a piece of history. Everything was a piece of history, and it was to be treated with proper respect. On board the Presidential jet, he often doodled as he spoke with reporters, and if he left to talk with someone else and noted a reporter moving to pick up a scrap of Presidential doodle, he did not find it beneath himself to walk back and snatch it away. Thus no unauthorized bits of Johnsonian history. He kept everything—letters, photographs, furniture—and it was not surprising that when he left office he speeded his own monument along. The Lyndon Johnson Library rose quickly and massively (while the Kennedy Library was still housed in a warehouse in Boston), and the real curator of the Lyndon Johnson Library would be Lyndon Johnson.

His appetite for achievement was never tempered. Not a contemplative man himself, he was not surrounded by many contemplative men. He preferred men who said yes, it could be done, and they would do it; cut the budget, dam a river, pass the bill, write the speech. He was a doer himself, and one of the most striking parts of the Johnson memorabilia of those Vice Presidential years are his letters from Jackie Kennedy asking Lyndon to please do this, and please take care of that; whenever Jackie wanted something done, accomplished, a job found for a friend, she had turned to Lyndon. And he liked doers around him: McNamara was a man after his own heart; he did not want ideology, he wanted action and energy. Looking at McNamara's fabled excellence at Defense, Johnson decided that one reason for it was the brilliance and drive of one of McNamara's deputies, Joseph Califano, and he set out to bring him to the White House. Eventually Califano joined the White House staff, where he began to submit endless numbers of memos. Sometimes, it was even alleged, he put his name over the work of subordinates, and there was some grumbling about this. When Johnson picked it up, when he heard another trusted staff man imply that Califano was not perfect, he reacted almost fiercely: *Don't you criticize Califano. There's never been a man around me who wrote so many memos.*

He was a man with extraordinary attention to detail, which was very important to him; larger conceptions might not mean that much, but if he knew the details he could control the action, he could control subordinates. So he always knew details about everyone, more about them than they knew of him. Early in 1969, after the election, after it was all over, his attention to detail still lived. An aide wanted to go to New York to look for a job, but Johnson was unhappy about the trip. He did not want any job hunting until after the Inauguration; it was, after all, one more reminder that he was leaving office. So having given his reluctant approval, he remembered later that day to call the White House booking office to make sure that the aide had paid for his own ticket. Always the search for a weakness in another man, always the hunt for something that might be used against him later.

Always that attention to detail, details not just of big things, but little things as well. Nothing was too small for Lyndon Johnson to master and manipulate. Even as Senate leader, when he was about to go back to Texas for the weekend and time was of the essence, a fellow Texas congressman had some constituents in tow who had a problem on soil irrigation. Did Johnson have time for them? Of course, he did, come right in the office, this soil irrigation is a serious problem. In the middle of the conversation, as he listened to them, nodding his head, exchanging views, without changing stride he switched from irrigation to the subject of his aide George Reedy's shirts. "You know, that boy Reedy never packs enough white shirts." He picked up the phone and dialed a number. "Hello, Mrs. Reedy, this is Lyndon Johnson. What size shirt does George wear? . . . No, no, no, he's a bigger man than that. George takes a bigger size." Briefly he argued Mrs. Reedy down, got her to accept *his size* Reedy. He put down the phone, continued talking about water irrigation, picked up the phone again, called a large department store, demanding the manager. "This is Lyndon Johnson and I need four white shirts sent over to my office right away . . . No, no, I need them right away . . . Yes, you can do it, I know you can, you're a can-do fellow. I know you and I won't forget it." He hung up the phone and went right back to irrigation again, without a break in his trend of thought, having done George Reedy's work for him, having assured Mrs. Reedy that she did not know what size shirt her husband wore, and having convinced the store manager that he was a real can-do man.

He was a relentless man who pushed himself and all others with the same severity, and demanded, above all other qualities, total loyalty, not loyalty in the traditional sense, not positive loyalty as John Foster Dulles had demanded, but total loyalty, not just to office or party or concept, but loyalty first and foremost to Lyndon Johnson. Then Lyndon Johnson would become the arbiter of any larger loyalty. Those who passed the loyalty test could have what they wanted. And he always knew who violated that loyalty, who said one thing to him and another thing to a possible enemy. No one could run as good an intelligence network inside Washington as Lyndon Johnson; as President he always knew who had dined with Robert Kennedy. He knew when the loyalty of his followers was waning before they did. No one was more loyal than Lady Bird. Of Marvin Watson, his last political operator, a man of great rigidity and little political sensitivity, Johnson, fiercely protective, could say that there was only one person more loyal than Marvin Watson and that was Lady Bird. High praise indeed. One reason for the long and intimate friendship between Johnson and Abe Fortas was the fact that despite the Johnson inner circle's doubts about the political acumen of Fortas, he was one of the few major Democratic doyens of Washington who was loyal to no other major Washington figure. He was Lyndon's man. Lyndon of course liked to personalize things: his people, his staff, his boys, his bombers. To a young Air Force corporal trying to show him the Presidential helicopter—"This is your helicopter, sir"—he answered, of course, "They're all my helicopters, son."

He was ill at ease with abstract loyalty, loyalty to issue, to concept, to cause, which might lead one to occasional dissent, a broader view, and might mean that a man was caught between loyalty to civil rights and loyalty to Lyndon Johnson. One reason that he was never at ease with the American military was his knowledge that their loyalty was very special, that it was first to uniform and to branch of service, and only then to civilians in the most secondary way. Loyalty was crucial: Washington, after all, was a city with enemies everywhere, with sharks swimming out there waiting for any sign of weakness. Thus the inner circle had to be secure, truly secure; particularly a man with as profound a sense of his own weaknesses and vulnerabilities as Lyndon Johnson wanted men around he could trust.

"How loyal is that man?" he asked a White House staffer about a potential hand.

"Well, he seems quite loyal, Mr. President," said the staffer.

"I don't want loyalty. I want *loyalty*. I want him to kiss my ass in Macy's window at high noon and tell me it smells like roses. I want his pecker in my pocket." When Neil Sheehan interviewed Johnson about McNamara in early 1967, before the break on the war, he was surprised to hear Johnson talk about McNamara in terms not of ability, but of loyalty. "If you asked those boys in the Cabinet to run through a buzz saw for their President, Bob McNamara would be the first to go through it. And I don't have to worry about Rusk either. Rusk's all right. I never have to worry about those two fellows quitting on me." And even two years later, after he had parted from McNamara, after the pressure of the war had become too much for the Secretary of Defense, Johnson could talk with more compassion about McNamara than he could about McGeorge Bundy. In his opinion McNamara had folded, had come apart not just because the war was too much of a problem for his ethical composition but because he had been torn between two great, perhaps even subconscious loyalties: one to the Kennedy family, which had meant a commitment to Robert Kennedy, along with his ambitions and dovishness, and a second to Lyndon Johnson and his Presidency, and that was too much. The other loyalty, Johnson would say, was a prior one. But of Bundy he felt there was no real loyalty to the Kennedys (a judgment in which Robert Kennedy had concurred), nor to Johnson, but only toward self and sense of class. The Kennedys, of course, wanted comparable loyalty, but they were always more subtle about it, and more secure in themselves, and thus less paranoiac; they had a far better sense of touching people by seeming to appeal to higher instincts. The Kennedys demanded loyalty out of confidence, Johnson demanded it out of insecurity. The Kennedys were for civil rights, therefore people who were for civil rights should be for the Kennedys. The Kennedys were for the same things you were for, that was their message; they offered you the best chance of achieving it, and by turning to you, they demonstrated your own excellence. They never presented people of considerable self-esteem with such blatant either-or choice of loyalty as Johnson did, and they somehow managed to put it on a higher plane. They were plagued by fewer doubts about themselves and they had fewer fears that intimates might reveal their shortcomings to a threatening and hostile world at large.

His almost desperate need for loyalty was the other half of the coin of insecurity of this great towering figure who had accomplished so much, was so much a man of Washington, and yet in so many important sections of the city felt himself an alien, the Texas ruffian among the perfumed darlings of the East. It was a profound part of him; his sense of being alien, of the prejudice against him, was never assuaged (in October, 1964, when George Ball handed in his first memo against the war, Johnson turned to an aide and said, "You've got to be careful of these Eastern lawyers. If you're not careful they'll take you and turn you inside out"). He was haunted by regional prejudice, and even the attainment of the Presidency did not temper his feelings. Later, after he had left office, he became convinced that it was his Southern origins, not the war, which had driven him out, that *they* had lain in wait for an issue, any issue, and had used the war, which was their war in the first place, to drive him from office. In July, 1969, he sat in Texas, an ex-President of the United States, and listened to the news of the tragedy of Edward Kennedy and Mary Jo Kopechne at Chappaquiddick, and became convinced by the second day that Teddy Kennedy would get off scot-free. He became almost bitter about the injustice of it all; Kennedy would get off because he was a Kennedy, there was a double standard, "But if I had been with a girl and she had been stung by a bumblebee, then they would put me in Sing Sing," he said. Even as President he had been haunted by these feelings: "If something works out, Joe Alsop will write that it was Bundy the brilliant Harvard dean who did it, and if it falls flat he'll say it was the fault of that dumb ignorant crude baboon of a President," Johnson would complain, and he would remind people again and again that in the chamber where these great decisions were made, there sat the head of the Ford Motor Company, a Rhodes scholar, the dean of Harvard University, and one graduate of San Marcos State Teachers College. He had triumphed over one area of Washington, the doers, the movers, men of the South and West, shrewd insiders, but he had always failed in another area, the taste makers, so much more Eastern, more effete, judging him on qualities to which he could never aspire, all the insecurities confirmed. Hearing in the late fifties that Walter Lippmann was important in the taste making of Washington, that he set and determined everyone else's taste, and knowing that Fulbright knew him well, Johnson had insisted that Fulbright bring him together with Lippmann, which Fulbright with great misgivings had done. It turned out to be a predictably horrendous evening, Johnson giving Lippmann the treatment, an evening of exaggeration and braggadocio, Johnson showing his worst side to the genteel and gentle, self-contained Lippmann, confirming all the worst doubts about the lack of subtlety in this gargantuan figure. Johnson, aware of this, terribly aware of enemies everywhere, of Georgetown's distaste and the Metropolitan Club's distaste, sometimes even as President seemed to want to aggravate the sore, trying to emphasize what the Easterners would consider his own boorishness, trying to inflict some crudity on them, demanding that they accompany him into the bathroom for conversations during the most personal of body demands, virtually driving Douglas Dillon out of the Cabinet by this maneuver alone.

This very earthiness was very much a part of him, and he reveled in it; he was the earthiest man in the White House in a century; his speech was often obscene, shrewd, brilliant. Of one Kennedy aide he could say, "He doesn't have sense enough to pour piss out of a boot with the instructions written on the heel." Trying to get rid of J. Edgar Hoover and then finding it was simply too difficult, he admitted, "Well, it's probably better to have him inside the tent pissing out, than outside pissing in." Asked by reporters why, when he was Senate majority leader, he had not taken a particular speech of Vice President Nixon's seriously, he said, "Boys, I may not know much but I know the difference between chicken shit and chicken salad." And once, driving around the Ranch showing its sights to a CBS television team, he stopped in the midst of particularly rough undergrowth to urinate. "Aren't you afraid a rattlesnake might bite it?" a CBS cameraman asked him.

"Hell," said Johnson, "it *is* part rattlesnake."

He was a man of primal force. Not a man, in the words of James Reston, that you would hand your hat to without thinking twice. His genes were seemingly larger and more demanding than those of other men; he dominated other men, leaning on them, sensing that every man had his price or his breaking point. (Once a young and very ambitious staff member was challenging him on an important point and was being unusually persistent in his opposition. Johnson took it for a while and then said very softly, "You know, Joe, you'd make a great Attorney General." The staff member folded like an accordion.) He knew the uses of force, of flattery and threat, honing in on the weakness like a heat-seeking missile, cataloguing each man's weakness in that incredible memory, to be summoned forth when necessary. Always wanting to know a little more about a potential friend or potential adversary. And everyone was a potential adversary. As President he enjoyed reading FBI files, they gave him lots of tidbits about some of the people he had to deal with. He had, there is no other word, a genius for reading a man instantly, for knowing how far he could go, how much he could push, what he could summon from the man, when to hold on and when to let go. He often took too much, leaving men who had worked for him depleted, exhausted, and feeling that they had been misused.

The people who worked for him lived in mortal fear of him. He humiliated them in front of their peers, then sometimes rewarded them, dressing down one staff member while others watched, then later in the day awarding the staffman a Cadillac, winking and explaining to someone else that it helped bind a man to strike with munificence when he was down. He would call in the press officers from the different departments and chew them out like a drill sergeant, saying they had been doing a terrible job, he hadn't been on the front page in weeks except for lighting a goddamn Christmas tree. Lighting a goddamn Christmas tree! Now he was going down on the Ranch and he wanted them to get him on page one every day; they better dream up something and get it on the first page. On he went, leaving the men in the room, some of them quite distinguished men in their own professions, feeling that they had been crushed and degraded. Or Johnson telling Cabinet members that they wouldn't dare walk out of his Administration, no one was going to walk out on Lyndon Johnson because they knew that if they did, two men were going to follow their ass to the end of the earth, Mr. J. Edgar Hoover and the head of the Internal Revenue Service.

In front of visiting dignitaries he was wont to put up his feet on Jack Valenti's lap and use it as a stool. Similarly, when he was visiting Nehru in 1961 as Vice President and the meeting was breaking up, Johnson turned to an aide and asked if a press conference had been arranged. When the aide said he knew nothing of a press conference, Johnson berated him in the most forceful terms, finally telling the aide, "The only way to deal with you is to handcuff you to my belt, so you'll be there when I need you." His close aide Walter Jenkins in particular lived in terror of Johnson, who had borne down on him so often and so hard that there was little left. Once when an exhausted Jenkins was about to take a brief nap, he told Bill Moyers to guard the office for thirty minutes. Moyers, who like his boss was an excellent mimic, got in the doorway a few minutes later and did a magnificent imitation of Johnson catching Jenkins napping. Jenkins turned first from total panic to total anger: "Don't you ever do that again . . . Don't you ever do that again . . . Don't you ever . . . ."

There was in all of this more than a small element of the bully in Johnson and an occasional misreading of people. Even then he learned quickly. When General Wallace Greene, the Commandant of the Marine Corps, attended his first high-level meeting with the

President, he was appalled by the way the President treated the people around him, abusing them, almost humiliating them, and Greene decided immediately that he would not take this. So the first time Greene spoke up, it was on the subject of Vietnam. Johnson did not like what he was saying; Greene was very hawkish and said he thought too little force was being used, and Johnson began interrupting him: "Speak up! Speak up! I can't hear what you're saying. Speak up!" Greene waited deliberately; then he looked up at Johnson and said in his carefully controlled voice, "You can hear what I'm saying and so can everyone else in this room," and calmly continued to speak. Greene noticed that from then on, whenever he appeared at the White House, Johnson seemed to solicit his advice and opinion, and marked him down for a bully, though of course not many men would enter the National Security Council with the same sense of confidence in himself as the Commandant of the Marine Corps. (General Greene was not the only person who sensed this; Gene McCarthy in 1967 told friends that he thought Johnson was a bully, and that if the early primaries were not good, he would come apart rather than fight back.)

But generally Johnson had that brilliant sense of how far to push and this made him particularly effective in the Senate, where he could employ his knowledge at close-range maneuvering, where his shrewdness, remarkable intelligence, and sheer energy would overwhelm lesser men; totally uncorrupted and never distracted by other pursuits, he considered the Senate, and his maneuvering there, his life. Manipulation of another human being was deemed normal and indeed necessary to the job. But it was a different thing when Johnson was in the White House, where he could extract from people what he needed and wanted, and then when he was finished, when the Johnson stamp was indelibly, and sometimes too indelibly, on them, Johnson would let them go (which often left a bad taste, a feeling after the fact on the part of people that they had been exploited, which was true, they had been, though for the greater good). Once, even before it all went sour on Vietnam, when Johnson was at the height of his accomplishments, he had complained to Dean Acheson about the fact that for all the good things he was doing, he was not beloved in the hearts of his countrymen, and why was that? Acheson looked at him and said simply, "You are not a very likable man." Indeed, those who knew him best (men like Clifford and Fortas, who enjoyed that rarest of things, his respect) were uneasy about working for him. In 1967 Johnson sent an emissary to talk with Clark Clifford about the possibility of his becoming Attorney General, a suggestion Clifford dismissed because he was afraid the job wte that fragile balance between being something of an equal and then overnight a total servant having to bear those tongue lashings.

Johnson would forever quote a maxim of his father's: if a man couldn't walk into a room and tell who was for him and who was against him, then he wasn't much of a politician. Of course Lyndon Johnson could do it like no other man, ipso facto he was a great politician. Thus a key to Johnson was the capacity to move men to his objective and away from their own charted course. That was the way to achieve things: deal with men at close combat, man to man. He believed this deeply, almost too much so. Since he was not a contemplative man, a man who read books, and since he had little belief in the rhythms and thrusts of history, he was convinced that you could accomplish things by reasoning with leaders, by moving them to your goal, manipulating them a little, and that finally, all men had a price. In part this helped bring him into trouble in Vietnam, with his instinct to personalize. He and Ho Chi Minh, out there alone, in a shoot-out. He would find Ho's price, Ho's weakness, whether it was through bombing the North or through threatening to use troops and then offering Ho a lollipop, massive economic aid and regional development, a Mekong River Delta development project. This time he would find himself dealing with a man who was a true revolutionary, incorruptible, a man who had no price, or at least no price that Lyndon Johnson with his Western bombs and Western dollars could meet. But it would take him quite a while to find out that he had met his match. For a long time he thought that he could handle Ho the way he handled senators and bureaucrats, and opponents. Put a little squeeze on him, touch him up a little, then Ho would see the light, know whom he was dealing with, and accept the lollipop.

Nothing existed for Johnson but politics. The idea of his going to a symphony or reading a book was preposterous, and before he took office he would boast of how little he read. When a young Senate staff member named Bill Brammer wrote a brilliant novel about Johnson entitled *The Gay Place*, Johnson did not read the book but was annoyed, not so much about the portrait Brammer had drawn of him, but about the fact that Brammer had written the book at night while working for Johnson, when he clearly should have stayed up late answering Johnson's mail. (If he was not a great reader, in his earlier incarnation, he became sensitive about this failing once he assumed the Presidency.)

Hugh Sidey of *Life*, who had written of Kennedy's reading habits, decided to do a similar article on Johnson's. He started with George Reedy, who told him that yes, Johnson was an avid reader. What books? Sidey asked. All Reedy could think of was Barbara Ward's *The Rich Nations and the Poor Nations*, a book on how the rich should help the poor, which Johnson had liked because it was similar to his own ideas. From there Sidey went to see Moyers. Yes, said Moyers, he was an avid reader. What books? Well, there was Barbara Ward's book *The Rich Nations and the Poor Nations*. And from there to Valenti, who said Johnson read more books than almost anyone he knew. What books? Valenti hesitated and thought for a moment, then his face lit up. Barbara Ward's *The Rich Nations and the Poor Nations*. Even the book he read was of course a can-do book, a book which was about how to make things work; he had little time for light activities. Both his successor and predecessor were sports fans, but Johnson had little interest in football or baseball. Once Lana Turner was promoting a movie in Washington; aides had arranged for her photo to be taken with a group of senators, including Johnson. The schedule for the day was duly shown him, including the appointment with Miss Turner. He looked at it for a moment and then asked, "Who the hell is Lana Turner?"

He was the totally political man, living and breathing for the political act. Yet he was curiously a man of Washington more than of the nation, a man who for most of his career harbored national ambitions, and yet who knew amazingly little about national politics as opposed to Senate politics, perhaps because he was afraid that if he ventured forth, people would treat him as a Texas ruffian. So the Senate had remained his theater, and he had mastered it and orchestrated it, the big things and the little things. Unsure of himself outside, he had remained where he was safe and secure. Because of this he had tended to see the country and its politics through the particular prism of the Senate. He believed in 1960 that since Senator Tom Dodd of Connecticut was for him, this meant that he was doing well in New England, and he did not realize what had happened to him until he reached Los Angeles. The problem there was of course not just that he read the country through the Senate, but he had so terrified his own people that they did not dare tell him bad news. Larry King, now a magazine writer and in those days a legislative assistant to a West Texas congressman, was one of Johnson's area representatives in 1960, assigned the Rocky Mountain area. He went out to work his section, found it very weak and was eventually summoned back to Washington for a meeting of area representatives, all the rest of whom were Texas congressmen. Johnson presided at the meeting, and one after another they made their reports. It was all marvelous: New England was very strong for Johnson, despite the seeming Kennedy strength. New York looked good. The great industrial states were hard and fast. Finally it was King's turn. "Well, I guess I'm working the one part of the country where we've got problems, but things don't look very good at all," he began. "Now, in Wyoming you say Gale McGee is for you, but I'm not so sure. He's staying out of it and telling his people to be neutral but I think they're leaning to Kennedy. And in Colorado. . . ." Johnson gave him a very hard look and cut him off. "Next report," he said.

At Los Angeles he found out what the Kennedys, with their surer sense of national politics, had done to him. Washington and the Senate were his mirrors; he was big in the Senate and Kennedy was small there, usually absent. If he knew this, then others would know it too and know who the real man was. If conservatives and hawks were more powerful in the Senate (which they were, more often than not controlling the key committees, Russell, Stennis, etc.), it was a sign that the conservatives were more powerful in the country. If the liberals were prone to make speeches and never got things done in the Senate (the more they talked, the more of a guarantee it would be that they would be outside the real corridors of power), then it was a sign that they were regarded the same way in the country.

He looked at the East and its politics long after he came to terms with the big-money people of the Southwest with an enduring rural Texas sense of alienation. He did not, for instance, like the big-city bosses as politicians, not liking the culture of the cities they represented, the trailing Catholic priests, the lurking labor leaders who probably didn't like Southern accents; but he was impressed by them as men, with their capacity to control their environment, their sense of presence, their ability to tell him how many votes a given district would produce. In contrast, Kennedy was not impressed by them as men, he knew them all too well; he was spawned by that tradition and wanted not so much to move up in their world as to move out of it, but he was impressed by them as politicians, liking not them but their methods.

Johnson viewed an area of the country not so much in ethnic and social terms but as an area which had sent certain men to Congress. He was best and most effective not as an open politician who seeks the Presidency (Kennedy had absolutely destroyed him there) but as an insider's man, working privately in the great closed corridors, always cloaked in secrecy until the good deed was done. There was a reason for this. He could be an excellent campaigner, and knew his own regions well, but what he had dedicated his career and his working hours to was the accumulation of power as a parliamentarian. Once he had established himself in what was virtually a rotten borough or safe seat (and come to terms with the upper tier of the new Texas power establishment) he proceeded to build up his connections and his possibilities as a Senate parliamentarian, trading his chance of appealing to wide national blocs of voters for the opportunity to work quietly on the inside to influence other legislators in private. He sought due bills on the inside, not due bills to the various great national lobbying groups, except as his and their interests occasionally coincided. He dealt similarly with the press; he held, charmed, and commanded reporters who were intrigued by the inner workings of the institution of the Senate itself (notably his close friend Bill White who had written a biography of Robert Taft and a book on the Senate entitled *The Citadel*, and finally a book on Johnson himself, entitled, not surprisingly, *The Professional*) rather than reporters who were committed more to issues and to ideology, and who, like elements of the public at large, regarded him, because of his great parliamentarian sleight of hand, as something of a wheeler-dealer. Nor did he help himself with reporters by telling them that if they played the game the way he wanted, wrote the stories the way he told them to, he would make them all big men. His view of the press, they soon found, was that in his eyes they were either for him or against him. There was no middle ground. They were either good boys, in which case he felt he owned them, or they were enemies.

Given that safe seat back in Texas, he could concentrate the full force of his attention on his role within the Senate; given regional prejudices against Southerners, he could probably not aspire to a serious race for the Presidency; given the split between the South and the North within the Democratic party, the chance for an ambitious Texan to serve as something of a bridge between the conflicting forces also encouraged him as a man of the inside. The men from the North, for instance, rarely held such safe seats—their constituencies were often too narrowly divided—and had to devote more of their time to coming to terms with their own regions. If they mastered these regions they thought in terms of national ambitions and continued to channel their efforts outside the Senate. He was thus a man of the Senate because it fit his abilities and his possibilities.

In addition, it fit his personality. He did not particularly want to be out in front alone on a policy; he was not by any instinct a loner, and in the Senate, if he did his work well, the responsibility (and potential blame) could be broadly shared. He liked as many other fingerprints on the door as possible (in fact, when Johnson wrote his book on his Presidential years, he spent a great deal of time and effort not discussing the wisdom of his policy, but emphasizing the consensus quality of it, how many others had been on board and wished him well).

He liked to think of himself as something of an Abe Lincoln, the country boy learning by oil lamps, and later, as President, loved to feed his own legend and richly embellished it, taking visitors around the old homestead, describing how simple it had been, a tiny little shack, until finally his mother interrupted him in front of several visitors, and said, "Why, Lyndon, you know that's not true, you know you were born and brought up in a perfectly nice house much closer to town." (In the same way he claimed that an uncle of his stood at the Alamo, which under most conditions would be all right, except that the whole point of the Alamo was how few men stood there, which made it tough on them against the Mexicans but somewhat easy for later historians to check whether a Johnson forebear had been there, and to find that one had not.) He was, in reality, despite the poverty that was around him in those Depression days, a member of a part of the American aristocracy, albeit Texas Hill Country aristocracy. An ancestor was president of Baylor University, and his family gave Johnson City its name. His father had served as a member of the Texas legislature at a time when membership was limited to those who could afford to live in Austin during the biennial session, and Sam Johnson's seat had been held previously by his father-in-law, Joseph Baines. Thus there was a sense of tradition in the family, and if from time to time during the Depression there was not a lot of money, the Johnsons had land, influence, and connections. They were landed aristocrats, though the land was often harsh.

He was a young boy that teachers would pay extra attention to. There was no doubt ever in his family that he would go to college, and when he did, messages about his arrival preceded him and connected him with a job in the office of the president of the school, and almost as soon as he graduated, there was a job in the local congressman's office. Lyndon was a man with some influence and connections, and most of all, respectability. Most of that respectability and much of the drive within him came from his mother, Rebekah Baines Johnson. (In 1968 when Harold Lasswell, pioneering expert on psychology and the political personality, gave an interview on Johnson's personality, he said, "One thing of outstanding interest is the extent to which Johnson had to struggle to achieve independence from his mother. She was an ambitious, domineering woman who thought she had married beneath her. She was determined that this lad would be a great success and she pushed him very hard. . . . It puts the son in a conflict. On the one side there is a tendency to accept domination and on the other hand a rebellious tendency to reassert one's independence and masculinity and sense of adequacy. . . . It is a reasonable inference that Johnson was very much concerned about remaining independent of outside influence. His subsequent political career—with his demand to make his own decisions, and his demand to *control* a situation [italics Lasswell's]—has these very deep roots." This evaluation might have been debatable, except for the fact that when the interview reached the White House, it was immediately Xeroxed and gleefully passed around among some of the President's closest and oldest friends and was much admired for its insights.) For Rebekah Johnson was a person of great force, a great sense of herself, and of her son's destiny; in his own mind she would become a mythological figure. (In a "A Family Album," a brief volume on the Johnson and Baines families which she had written and which was published after her death, with a foreword by the then President, in 1965, there are some signs of her special hold on Lyndon. She told of Lyndon in elementary school reading, as befitted a class leader, a poem of his own choosing, entitled, curiously enough, "I'd Rather Be Mamma's Boy." She also reprinted an essay Lyndon published when he was twenty-two in the college newspaper, entitled "To Our Mothers." ". . . There is no love on earth comparable to that of a mother. Our best description of it is that of all types of earthly love, it most nearly approaches the divine. . . .") Later when he was grown he would talk of his mother to friends: she was the finest, the most intelligent woman he had ever met, and therefore anyone who reminded him of her would have a brighter career ahead of her. Rebekah Johnson had, of course, always believed in Lyndon; all her hopes, which had not been realized in her own life, would be attained through him. When he was elected to Congress, she wrote him:

My darling boy:

Beyond "Congratulations Congressman" what can I say to my dear son in this hour of triumphant success? In this as in all the many letters I have written you there is the same theme: I love you; I believe in you; I expect great things of you. Your election compensates for the heartache and disappointment I experienced as a child when my dear father lost the race you have just won. How happy it would have made my precious noble father to know that the first born of his first born would achieve the position he desired.

The Johnsons were part of the power structure of the Hill Country, the men who had power and who got together with the other men who had power, the Hill Country establishment, so to speak, and they conspired to bring about what was needed. A bridge. A highway. A hospital. Get rid of a bad teacher at the school. Decide who ought to be the candidate for which office. You had your own network of people, your own people arranged and you didn't go public with it until the time was right. (Years later McGeorge Bundy would tell friends that there was one thing you could not do with Lyndon Johnson and that was to go public with it, and by going public, Johnson meant talking to anyone else.) You never talked, not in the open. To do good, to get things done, to help the folks, to be powerful, you stayed private; you didn't go to the people, you helped the people. There was a considerable distinction here; if you were a serious man and wanted to get things done, you had to do them *for* people. Manipulate, but manipulate for their own good. He grew up in that environment and it never left him. In that particular art form there was no one quite like him, the art of doing good for people in spite of themselves. Even when he went to Washington, he mastered the inner corridors of power, getting things done. (Russell Baker, then a young reporter for *The New York Times*, was sent to cover the Senate in the early Johnson years and would recall one of his first meetings with Johnson. "How are you liking the Senate?" Johnson asked. "Well, I like it, but it's not what I thought," Baker answered. "I thought there would be more speeches, more debates, more arguments on the floor." Johnson leaned over, grabbed Baker, looked him in the eye: "You want a speech, you go see Lehman and Pat McNamara. They'll make you a speech. They're good at making speeches." An edge of contempt passes. Johnson now closer to Baker. "You want to find out how things are *done*, and you want to see things *done*? You come to me. I'll tell you all that.")

In Washington his first great mentor was Sam Rayburn, Mr. Sam, who as majority leader held great power, who exercised it wisely, meting it out judiciously, but who was never a public figure, never gave long speeches, never tried to get his name in print. Mr. Sam was the first teacher, and the second was Senator Richard Russell from Georgia, who taught him more about Washington, how to maneuver, how to get people indebted to him. In later years Johnson would tell friends how Dick Russell had operated, Russell the bachelor, always with plenty of time for young bright congressmen when they first arrived, taking them around at night, carefully guiding their careers and their social lives, making profound impressions on them with generosity and intelligence, moving them ever so slightly into his orbit of influence. However, Johnson did not talk about the other half of his particular relationship with Russell, which was similar to that which he had enjoyed with Rayburn and others back in Texas, which was of the bright eager young man who brilliantly cultivates a lonely, forceful, older man of great power (Russell was a bachelor, and Rayburn, briefly married, might as well have been). That was a Johnson specialty, and helped lift him above the average young congressmen of his time. Johnson seemed to be the perfect pupil for both Rayburn and Russell; they were like fathers, he was almost sycophantic, thought some around them, but later, having gone beyond both of them, he could at times be harsh and contemptuous in talking about them. Yet the lessons were clear, these were men who got things done, who did not hang around the fancy men and indulge in the fancy talk of Georgetown dinner parties. These were men.

Like Rayburn, Johnson became an immensely successful parliamentarian, a man of the center able to move slightly to the left or the right depending on his needs and his party's needs, able to accommodate to the Eisenhower years with few problems (leaving Democrats the feeling that the Eisenhower election over Stevenson had upset neither him nor Rayburn; indeed the congressonal leadership was so acquiescent to the Republican White House that the liberals created a Democratic Policy Study group as a means of charting a more independent course). Johnson could move slightly to the left on civil rights as national ambitions began to touch him, but he could also serve as a brake within his party if it moved too far to the left. Similarly, one of the reasons why the Democratic party did so little on major tax reform in the decade of the fifties was the relationship Johnson had with the big money in Texas and their proxies in the Senate (he could say of Senator Paul Douglas of Illinois, a constant critic of the oil-depletion allowance, that Douglas would understand it just a bit better if there were a few oil wells in Cook County).

There were two reasons why he was so successful: his own hold on the Senate, and the fact that, teamed with Rayburn, he controlled both branches of the legislature and could control, through Rayburn, the appropriations aspect of legislation. He could thus, for example, keep the military on a long-enough leash to allow them to plan their new weapons systems, and on a short-enough leash to have them keep coming back for more. His congressional position gave him considerable influence within the party of the fifties, a party caught in the conflict between its Southern-dominated Congress and a Northern-dominated mass. If Richard Russell tried to assert the party leadership through the Congress it would split the party, and someone like Hubert Humphrey, representing the liberal-labor elements of the coalition, did not have the horsepower to stand for the party in the Congress. So Johnson was the go-between; each adversary armed him against the other, their divisions fed his strength, he was the compromise figure. He was acceptable to the Southerners, but not really of them, but the more the Northern wing of the party rebelled, the luckier they felt they were to have Johnson. But if he was regionally acceptable to the South, he was for the same reason probably regionally unacceptable to the rest of the party. But he could, holding power in the Senate, make Humphrey glad to deal *with him*, giving the liberals just enough to keep them from going into open rebellion and asserting independent, though futile, leadership.

He loved the Congress and studied it; he could catalogue the strengths and weaknesses of every man there. The strength of a man put him off, but his weaknesses attracted him; it meant a man could be used. Whereas Kennedy had been uneasy in the face of another man's weakness, it embarrassed him and he tended to back off when a man showed frailty, to Johnson there was a smell of blood, more could come of this. But he understood men only through that one prism, how they performed and handled the Congress (even on the subject of the loss of China, it was the fact that in losing China, Truman had first lost the *Congress* which haunted him. The reaction to the loss had not necessarily come from the population, it had come from the Congress). This attitude was a weakness in itself, for not everyone shared his thirst for congressional work or his opinion that it was the only forum. One reason he misjudged John Kennedy as an opponent was that he did not take Kennedy seriously in the Senate. Kennedy clearly did not care, did not really bother with his congressional work, and was therefore not, in Johnson's eyes, an entirely serious person.

As Lyndon Johnson admired men who got things done, men to be measured by their achievements, surely so too would the nation;

it would choose a doer, a *man*, not a handsome young talker, a *boy*. As congressman and senator he created his own network of power, men who worked through him to move things, and he extracted his particular price and added more layers of power to his original base. But it was always done privately; he went partially public only after it was all done, and even then, when he dealt with the press, he was the private man, calling in a small claque of reporters whom he knew and trusted. He would sit down and explain his great victory, though within certain limits; he would not compromise future victories for the sake of immodesty now. And the reporters would play the game, they knew the ground rules: how much credit would go to Lyndon—never too little, mind you—and how much to the others, perhaps a little extra credit to a particular senator to ensure even greater cooperation the next time. Out of this came his almost neurotic view of the press, two very conflicting views: first, that you owned the press, you summoned them and they wrote good stories, and second, that the press was an enemy, it was disloyal, that if it did not belong to you, then someone else had bought and thus you had to be wary. Rich publishers. Or the Kennedys. Or the big interests. Thus you had to get in there quickly and make your pitch. When Bill White left after covering Johnson in the Senate for *The New York Times* he was replaced by Russell Baker, and Baker heard about the change about six o'clock one evening. A few minutes later there was a telephone call and a booming voice over the phone, and it was, it said, Senator Johnson, what great news that Baker would be covering him, they would get along very well, even better than Johnson had with Bill White. Baker's reputation as a fearless reporter was going to be made; anything Baker wanted to know, his friend Lyndon Johnson would tell him. Anything. Johnson loved the *Times*, admired Baker's work. "For *you*, I'll leak like a sieve," he said.

He was concerned about the reputations of the reporters who covered him and worried about their professional prestige, since it was a reflection of his prestige, particularly during the Vice Presidential years. When *Time* magazine decided to switch the assignment of John Steele, who had long been *Time*'s envoy to Johnson, and replace him with a younger man named Loye Miller, the Vice President was particularly upset. Was this another humiliation? Another taste of Vice Presidential ashes? Steele and others in the *Time* empire rushed to reassure him: it was just the opposite, it was a re-evaluation in *Time*'s eyes of the importance of the Vice Presidency, and Loye Miller was the best they had, their brightest young star, scion of a great newspaper family, his father was a famous editor in Knoxville. There were brilliant things ahead for Loye Miller, and in recognition of the very big things ahead, perhaps the biggest ones, he was being given this choice assignment, this plum, an intimate relationship with Lyndon Johnson. And Johnson smiled and welcomed Miller. It is one of the sad aspects about great flatterers like Lyndon Johnson that among the few things they are vulnerable to is flattery. Shortly afterward Johnson was in New York and of course paid a state visit to the head of the Luce empire, Henry Luce himself. Johnson began with a long tribute to Luce, what a great man he was, how much the communications world of America owed to him, and yet even the greatest men eventually had to step aside and Johnson was delighted by the knowledge that he, Johnson, could vouch for the remarkable young man who would succeed Henry Luce, this fine, handsome, talented, brilliant young man, a scion of a great newspaper family. Some of the *Time* executives noticed a look of surprise and shock on Luce's face as Johnson was carrying on. After the Vice President left, Luce grabbed a high-ranking aide and asked, "Who the hell is Loye Miller?"

The stories of his flattery soon became legendary. He had learned as a congressman that those out of power are surprisingly susceptible to the flattery of those in power, that flattery by someone in power becomes a special form of recognition. As he rose to higher and higher positions he resorted to greater and greater flattery, finding that few resisted it or were offended by it and that, indeed, most people accepted it as God's truth. The Johnsonian view of their abilities was similar to their own. Soon Washington was filled with stories of Johnsonian flattery and exaggeration, of Johnson telling Adlai Stevenson that he should be sitting in the President's chair, of Johnson telling Arthur Goldberg to leave the Court and go to the UN and make peace because the next man who sits in *this* chair is going to be the man who brought peace in Vietnam. But there were some occasions of mistaken identity and problems caused by the flattery. In July, 1967, for instance, after John McNaughton was killed in an airplane crash, Johnson decided, at McNamara's urging, to appoint an able but little-known Washington lawyer named Paul Warnke, who had been working with McNamara as counsel to the Defense Department. Johnson was determined to pass on the news himself, to flatter Warnke and to impress upon him the importance of being Assistant Secretary of Defense for International Security Affairs, and most of all, the importance and goodness of Lyndon Johnson. So he told his secretary to have the switchboard get Warnke. Shortly thereafter the switchboard located John Carl

Warnecke, an architect and social friend of the Kennedys' who was better known in Washington and a frequent visitor to the White House.

Jack Warnecke got on the phone to hear the President of the United States say, "Mr. Warnke, this is Lyndon Johnson, and Bob McNamara has been telling me of all the great things that you have been doing for your country, how much and how generously you have given of your time, and how helpful you have been, and I am calling to say thank you."

Warnecke, who had been doing a little work with McNamara on the Kennedy grave site, quickly answered that that was very kind of the President, but he had really done very little work.

"No, Mr. Warnke, this is not time to be modest. We know all about you. There is no man I hold in higher esteem than Bob McNamara and Bob is saying a lot of fine things, very fine things about you. Mr. Warnke, Bob McNamara is a great American and a great Secretary of Defense."

Warnecke acknowledged that he too admired Bob McNamara and considered him a great American.

"Mr. Warnke, it is refreshing to talk to someone like yourself, a man who could make a great deal of money in private life and yet is willing to give of himself to his country."

Warnecke answered quickly and truthfully that the sacrifice was very small.

"Mr. Warnke, I know better. *I know that you have truly done a fine job for your country* and we are not unaware of it—we know of your dedication, and, Mr. Warnke, Bob McNamara needs you and I need you, and I am calling you today because I am naming you as Assistant Secretary of Defense today and it will be in tomorrow's paper. We are proud of you."

At which point Warnecke understood and felt himself stumbling over the phone: Yes, a great honor, very touched by it, great regard for President Johnson, great regard for Bob McNamara, worked with him on grave sites, but perhaps a mistake had been made, he could not accept. He was an . . . architect, an architect could not run things at Defense. Paul Warnke, a lawyer . . . perhaps they wanted Paul Warnke . . . .

He could hear a slight halt at the other end of the phone, and then Lyndon Johnson, as effusive as ever, saying, "Mr. Warnke, *you too have truly done a fine job for your country*, but it does appear that perhaps a mistake has been made." And so Jack Warnecke did not become an Assistant Secretary of Defense, and the next day when

Paul Warnke received a call from the President naming him to the job, he was puzzled that the President was so brief, almost curt.

Stories like that, about his flattery and about his exaggeration had started out as something of a private joke among the reporters who covered him. It seemed amusing early in the game, when things were going well; they saw it as part of his attempt to control everything in his environment, to make things turn out the way he wanted, his desire to dominate everything, even the official record. At first it had been small things which amused them: his insistence that he drank bourbon, when in fact he drank Scotch; his stories about an uncle who had stood at the Alamo, when no such uncle had existed. His gradual expansion of his own rather thin war record (which brought him one of the least deserved but most often displayed Silver Stars in American military history) to the point where he could tell a somewhat surprised historian named Henry Graff, invited to the White House to report on Vietnam decision making, that he had earned the Silver Star for helping to shoot down twenty Zeros. Later it expanded to versions of whom he would appoint and whom he would not. In 1964 Dick Goodwin, a former Kennedy speech writer, came back to work for Johnson, and not being a blushing violet, immediately let Hugh Sidey of *Life* know he was back, and in fact showed him a draft of a speech. Sidey, looking for a subject for his weekly column, decided to write about the return of Goodwin as Johnson's principal speech writer, only to find that despite the fact that Johnson had been using Goodwin's drafts, the President insisted, in a face-to-face confrontation, that Goodwin had not written for him. Oh, perhaps a little research here and there, but no speeches. Wasn't that right, George? Reedy gurgled slightly, a sound of both yes and no. Finally Johnson took Sidey aside and drew a diagram of White House responsibilities. Nowhere did Goodwin appear. At the last moment Johnson wrote in a category, "Miscellaneous," and penciled in the name "Goodman." At first these anecdotes enlivened the White House press corps and made for fine after-dinner stories; later, as the pressure of Vietnam mounted and the President's credibility problems centered on greater issues, they would not seem so amusing.

He was not a man to be underestimated; he sought power and found it, and relished exercising it; he did not like being out alone on a position and he was brilliant at working others to a position which he intended to take so that they would stand together, there would be plenty of protective coloration. As a man of great force and intelligence, he had mastered a certain kind of power as no one had in Washington in years; he performed in the Senate with such subtlety and skill that there were newspapermen in Washington who would leave their offices to go down to the Hill to watch him when there was a particular scenario coming up, knowing that it would above all be a performance, orchestrated, skilled, and almost joyful.

With all that ability, however, there were limits imposed by the regionalism. What he had exploited also held him back. Even at the 1960 convention, when he was chosen for the Vice Presidency, it was not a recognition of the breakdown of the regional prejudice, but rather a confirmation of it; he could help bind a badly divided party, he could work with the South and try and hold it to what would be a traditionally liberal campaign in the North. It was not that inviting an office; it is a somewhat futile office under the best of conditions, but these were even worse conditions for a man as restless as Johnson, who had been a powerful figure as majority leader and who would serve a strong-willed President younger than he. It had more than the usual elements of being the end of the road, and only Sam Rayburn's deep animosity toward Richard Nixon, toward the Nixon who had called the Democratic party the party of treason, the attack upon the loyalty of an institution that Mr. Sam revered, made him advise Lyndon to take it. That he might help beat Richard Nixon.

Even then his old enemies rebelled and there was talk of a floor fight against him; the liberals and labor leaders from the great industrial states were less than grateful for his leadership in those congressional years. Yet Johnson had been a liberal, perhaps even, it was said, a Texas populist, who had been one of Franklin Roosevelt's most loyal New Dealers, a young man who had been anointed in Washington upon his arrival by none other than FDR himself. FDR, he liked to say, had been like a daddy to him. Was Johnson liberal, or was he conservative? His bitterest enemies were the committed Texas liberals, the Yarborough people, the Texas *Observer* people. They knew him back home. Who was he, anyway? Liberal, conservative, or just very ambitious? He was the kind of man who seemed to be at ease with the power structure of Texas, the richest and most conservative of the rich and conservative, and yet in the spring of 1960 he could tell friends and reporters flying back from a campaign meeting in Binghamton, New York, while complaining about the fat cats he had met that night, "No member of our generation who wasn't a Communist or a dropout in the thirties is worth a damn."

Johnson's first major job in the Depression had been as an assistant to Richard Kleberg, a conservative congressman and owner of the vast King Ranch. This job had brought no great ideological hardship; rather, Johnson seemed more irritated by Kleberg's laziness than his politics. He went back to Texas in 1935 to head the state's National Youth Administration. There, helping to find work for young people, he was also building a political base, and when there was a sudden vacancy in 1937 caused by death of the incumbent congressman, Johnson immediately declared himself a candidate.

It was at the time of the first low point in Franklin Roosevelt's Presidential history. Awed and intoxicated by his own 1936 landslide (46 out of 48 states), Roosevelt had moved to change the one institution in the nation which still blocked his program, by attempting to expand the Supreme Court. He immediately overstepped his popularity; the reaction was quick and intense. All sorts of opposition to Roosevelt which was then dormant suddenly surfaced, and this was particularly true of Texas: the President's enemies were clearly using the Court packing as a means of rallying support against him. (Almost twenty years later Johnson was still acutely aware of this, and after his own landslide victory against Goldwater he was ferocious in pushing legislation through as quickly as he could, always as though time were running out, saying that once the Congress feels it has given too much, it is bound to react and reassert its own independence.) Of the seven candidates running for the Texas seat in the special election, only Johnson wholly committed himself to the New Deal, so when he won, it was a symbol which Roosevelt grasped at.

The President interrupted a vacation to greet the young congressman in Galveston the day after the election, and thus did Johnson start his career twice blessed. Sam Rayburn, his father's old friend from their days in the Texas legislature, had just become House majority leader, a powerful ally for a freshman congressman; now the President himself was committed to him, telling the bright and powerful men of the New Deal to watch out for this young congressman from Texas, he was a hot one. And out of that first year came friendships specifically forged at Roosevelt's direction, which would last Johnson's entire career, ties to men like Abe Fortas, Ed Weisl, William O. Douglas. He was also given a seat on the Naval Appropriations Committee, a choice assignment on a committee which was the forerunner of the House Armed Services Committee. In those days he was Roosevelt's man, straight and simple; it was the height of a new powerful Presidency, and the White House could do more for a young congressman than anyone else.

But Roosevelt's popularity would soon ebb in certain sectors of the country and Texas was one of the first to feel a new conservatism. A young ambitious politician in Texas would not want to look like a prisoner of the New Deal; in 1941 when Johnson made his first race for the Senate he found that Texas was changing, that the New Deal was less popular there and that he was beaten largely because he bore the onus of the New Deal. Too liberal, too much of a spender. He would not make that mistake again. Slowly he began to change his image, and he began to assert a certain independence from the Administration and to concentrate on armed preparedness as an issue, a decision which offended neither Roosevelt nor Texans. He stayed with the New Deal as long as he could, though he declared his independence from it soon after Roosevelt's death.

As the coloration of Texas politics changed, so did Johnson. The new oil money was beginning to dominate the old rural agricultural economy, and an ambitious young congressman who coveted a Senate seat had to come to terms with it. The oil money had gone after Sam Rayburn in 1944 and if it had not cost Rayburn his congressional seat, as the oil people intended, it forced him to stay home and campaign during the 1944 convention, thus depriving him of any chance to get on the ticket with Roosevelt. Lyndon Johnson, who did not intend to stay in the House and who planned a statewide race, had to come to terms with the new money in the mid-forties. He did it by developing close ties to George and Herman Brown, old contracting friends who had moved into oil by getting into natural-gas transmission, buying the Little Big Inch pipe line in 1947. The Browns buffered Johnson with the oil people and eased the transition for what Robert Novak and Rowland Evans in their excellent book on Johnson would call "a lateral movement into the center of the new oil power." He had paid his price. Thus he had become respectable; he had done it to survive, but it was typical of the price the Democratic party in general was paying to stay in power.

At the end of the war and in the immediate postwar years, Johnson made himself even more respectable with the Texas business community by becoming an activist for defense spending. He could be vigilant on the subject of defense spending against the Communist expansion, and simultaneously forge growing links to a massive new industry beginning to flex its muscle in American society. He was typical in that era of many in the Democratic party who were more than glad to change the political subject in the postwar years from the domestic reform of the New Deal to defense and foreign policy. In the House and later in the Senate, Johnson became both an advocate of greater defense spending, and at the same time, with that special duality of his (the kind of duality which allowed him to turn the lights off at the White House while sending the Pentagon budget skyrocketing), became known as a tough critic of potential waste in military spending. He became an advocate of greater air power, breaking with the Truman Administration on this issue, accusing the Administration in effect of not making our air wing adequate (in the postwar years the poor Army could never match the Air Force for congressional support. There was always much more political and business interest in a contract for a multibillion-dollar airplane than there was for an Army contract for new webbing on boots).

His dissent with the Truman Administration never hurt his relationship with the President, who knew exactly the game Johnson was playing; he had played it himself. Yet Johnson's belief in military preparedness and defense spending was a very real part of his outlook, an extension of the way he had felt in 1941 when he helped Roosevelt prepare this country for a war which seemed so distant to many Americans. To be for defense spending in those days seemed to be against isolationism, so in those years he was identified as a great friend of the military. Technically, he was; he helped them get the money they needed, though actually he did not like them or admire many of them. Johnson, who was always so well prepared himself, always better informed than his subordinates, thought they were sloppy in their work, that they left too much to subordinates, and he was uneasy with their parochial view and prejudices, and with their definition of loyalty, which was too limited by his standards. It was to service, not necessarily even to country, and certainly not to Lyndon Johnson. They had to be watched; it was all right when they were temporarily on your side, but they could not really be counted on.

Added to his belief in defense spending and a need for preparedness came a very real belief in the Communist threat. (When he was President and as criticism on the war mounted, he convinced himself that there was a real Communist conspiracy at work in Washington; his feelings about it hardened and became stronger as sentiment against the war—and against him—also mounted during the sixties.) In Texas, as he made this transition, it allowed him to get along with the big boys and show them that that can-do ability didn't just work for the poor and the underprivileged. But this also meant that as a senator committed to greater defense spending, to larger defense contracts, he was not disposed to challenge the prevalent anti-Communism of the day, nor the theories which required such great defense spending. To challenge them, to study them too intensely, might have meant to find them wanting and thus necessitate a cutback in defense spending. So the instinct for force, for greater military might, had been nurtured in and by Johnson; it was at once both very real and very convenient, which was a powerful combination for any politician, and he was a symbolic part of a particular phenomenon of the fifties and sixties which found the military budget dominating American life and the great advocates for even greater spending, the Democrats, ostensible members of the party which was soft on Communism.

Very subtly, in the late forties, he had made the transition from New Deal congressman to sound and respectable senator who did not frighten the big interests of Texas. A change of emphasis really. In the early fifties he made his way up the Senate ladder, not through connections to the national Administration, but rather through connections to Richard Russell and Senator Robert Kerr of Oklahoma, personification of the Southern big-interest wing, and in the late fifties he would undergo another transition. He had never been totally content to be just a senator. Now, as national ambitions stirred him, he became a man who spanned regions. He was not of the South but of the *West*, he could pilot civil rights legislation through the Congress, he could heal, he could understand the heartache of both sides, and also he had genuine ability. In discussing his own Presidential race, Jack Kennedy had said that he had a right to run for it; no one else had more ability except Lyndon, and Lyndon could never make it because he was a Southerner. The prejudice against him never disappeared, and the sense of prejudice, the hurt always remained in Johnson, made him more interesting and, curiously, more sensitive. Even when he was placed on the ticket in 1960 he was put there to help Easterners, first Jack, who would hold office for eight years, and then perhaps Bobby. And he felt the pain of those three years of the Vice Presidency; President Kennedy had been particularly aware of his sensibilities, but not everyone else was so sensitive (except for Rusk, who shared the same origins, humiliations, and enemies). Johnson, who had always known about one thing, power, who held it and who did not, knew that as Vice President he was a living lie, that his title was bigger than his role, that he did not have power. And then suddenly, shockingly, he was President, the awkward easy-to-caricature Southerner replacing the beloved handsome slain Eastern President, shot down in Dallas, a hated city in Johnson's own

Texas. That did not ease his own sense of the prejudice against him as he acceded.

So the perfectly prepared and trained and tuned parliamentary leader moved into the most public office in the world, an entirely different office for which all his previous training was in some ways meaningless, indeed the wrong training; he had learned many of the wrong things. The Presidency is a very different power center; it is not a particularly good place from which to perform private manipulation and to do good things for the folks in spite of themselves. It is at its best when a President identifies what he is and what he seeks as openly as possible, and then slowly bends public opinion toward it. If the President is found manipulating or pressuring a lower figure, putting too much pressure on a congressman, it can easily, and rather damagingly, backfire. Harry Truman was a success in the White House partly because he was openly, joyously, and unabashedly Harry Truman; he was what he was, he gloried in attacks on his inadequacies, they being in general the inadequacies of most normal mortal men, and he made his limitations his assets; the American people had a sense of identification with him and what he was trying to do. Franklin Roosevelt was a fine back-room manipulator, but he always had a sense of the public part of his office, of it as a pulpit, and he used the rhythms of radio expertly in seeming to bring the public into his confidence. Lyndon Johnson never could. His office was above all public, but he could never communicate with the people, never be himself.

Journalist after journalist, politician after politician, businessman after businessman exposed to the private Johnson treatment, the full force of the man, the persuasiveness, the earthiness, the intelligence, came away impressed. Many of Washington's most sophisticated writers regarded Johnson as their favorite politician because of his earthiness, because he was so real that despite all his attempts to be clever and crafty and hide his style and his vanities and faults, he never could; and it was this earthiness, this particular quality to him, to his insecurities, which made him so interesting, so human. It was the lack of ability to control what he was and shield what he was which made him more likable than many politicians who were ideologically more sympathetic. But despite the great capacity to communicate from that office and despite his own enormous capacity to communicate, Johnson was curiously ineffective as a public communicator in the White House. He would not let the real Lyndon Johnson surface, the forceful, dynamic, and very earthy one; not trusting himself, he did not trust the public. He did not feel he could be himself without hurting his Administration. The real Johnson was saved for the private rooms, and the public Johnson was a new Johnson, modest, pious, almost unctuous, and it did not come over very well. The public, which, despite the fact that it did not know Johnson and had never met him, knew instinctively that whatever else, this was not the real man.

This was part of it. The other part was related, the attempt to use the office, to manipulate, but to do so for the good of mankind, which is all right under ideal conditions (in that people do not particularly like being manipulated, even for their betterment, and if it doesn't work out, then they become particularly ungrateful about it, as the Senate did after the Tonkin Gulf Resolution. To a certain degree the Senate knew it was being manipulated, that the wording of the resolution was deliberately vague, that it was not a good idea to take your eyes off Lyndon Johnson; it knew it was not asking hard questions and playing the role it should have, but it was also willing at that point to acquiesce and be manipulated rather than ask the hard questions. But if the war did not work out, and it did not, then there would be a sense of bitterness and even betrayal over the manipulation). Even when Lyndon Johnson passed vast amounts of legislation through the Congress in 1964, there was some uneasiness about him. He was, in the public mind, too much a "politician," he was a wheeler-dealer, you had to watch his hands. Even at his most successful moment there was not that much the public could identify with and say that it had participated in; it was his private act for them; nor could they identify with his personal qualities. So it was in no way inconsistent with his training that in 1964 the public Johnson seemed to campaign in one way while the private Johnson was being pulled in the direction of escalation. (In his memoirs he would clear up the discrepancy between his eventual acts and his campaign rhetoric against having American boys do what Asian boys should be doing. He had, he wrote, simply been implying that he did not intend to get into a ground war with *China*, which had nothing to do with Vietnam because we were already involved there.) If escalation finally was what the people needed and what was good for them, then Lyndon Johnson would make sure they would get it, but it would be better not to frighten them or confront them too openly with it. In 1964, as Lyndon Johnson learned to be President, and for a brief period enjoyed being President, the public man and the private man were doing very different things and going in very different directions.

He might, thought his press secretary and admirer, George Reedy, have been a gigantic figure as prime minister, a man to stand along with Pitt and Disraeli and Churchill, if the parliamentary system had existed here. He was, thought Reedy, particularly well suited for its kind of leadership, a view strikingly similar to that of the man who had been for him in 1960 at Los Angeles and who in 1968 had helped drive him out of office, Eugene McCarthy. McCarthy, questioned in 1968 about his earlier support for Johnson, said he had been for him for prime minister, not for President, because given a particular course, he could get more out of it than almost any other man. But was he a man to chart a course himself? Under the British parliamentary system he would have faced the challenge of his peers, tough, sharp, examining, who feared neither him nor his office. But there was no comparable challenge at the White House, where no one tells the President he is wrong. For the Presidency is an awesome office, even with a mild inhabitant. It tends by its nature to inhibit dissent and opposition, and with a man like Johnson it was simply too much, too powerful an office occupied by too forceful a man (Johnson's own style in the Senate of trying to take the mark of another man from the start to break him quickly was a quality which had served him, if not the others, well. But it did not work so well in the White House. Other men were already too inhibited, they did not need the extra force of the incumbent to put more fear, respect, and awe into them). Now he was too powerful a man with no one to slow him down. He was in an office isolated from reality, with concentric circles of advisers who often isolated rather than informed, who tended to soften bad judgments and harsh analyses, knowing that the President was already bearing too many burdens, that he could not accept more weight, that it would upset him, and also knowing that if they became too identified with negative views, ideas, and information, they too would suffer, their own access would diminish (a classic example of the former of the two problems would be Bob McNamara telling Arthur Goldberg midway through the escalation, when Goldberg raised a negative point to him, that it was certainly a good point but would he please not raise it with the President, it would only upset him).

Now there was a giant of a man in the White House who made the imposing office even more imposing and who personalized the office. Doubts about a policy might seem like doubts about him: were you doubting him, were you disloyal? And Johnson, who in domestic matters reveled in his own expertise (calling in the staff working on a bill and questioning them, matching his own, often superior, knowledge of it against theirs, ventilating the problems), was very different in foreign affairs. He was much more reserved in his participation and was prone to limit the discussion, as if somehow the discussion might show up his weaknesses. He had inherited the Kennedy people, who had always impressed him, but though they were the same men, they were used in a strikingly different way. Kennedy had been aware of the danger of isolation and the inhibitions the office placed on men, and he had deliberately confronted his senior people with young bright nonbureaucratic men from other parts of the bureaucracy, trying to challenge the existing assumptions; Kennedy did not view dissent as a personal challenge. Once Kennedy had played the diverse viewpoints against one another, once there had been an inner debate, he would use some of his own people to filter it down, to analyze it, and then finally make his decision. Even as a Presidential candidate he had sat among his aides as they discussed issues, decisions, positions, all of them equals; as President they were no longer equals but he had encouraged the same diversity, realizing that it was healthy. As President he had been more of a judge than a participant, but he had held it together and set the tone. And it was Kennedy who knew the other players and their weaknesses, that McNamara was a man of great loyalty and force, and of a certain kind of intelligence, but of perhaps limited wisdom, brave in the bureaucratic sense, but that the imposing strength masked equally imposing weaknesses. He liked Bundy too. Bundy seemed so much like him, kept him out of trouble, sometimes he would know better what Kennedy wanted than Kennedy himself did. Only Rusk bothered him, with his reluctance to take strong and forceful positions. He respected Rusk's proficiency, his loyalty, his control, the subtlety of his political instincts, and his performance on the Hill, but he was bothered by his overdependence on the system. He never felt at ease with Rusk, and in the last part of the Kennedy Administration both John and Robert Kennedy were talking with intimates about the possibility of a new Secretary of State.

The Johnson style was very different and it made different men of the chief Presidential advisers. They would bear his stamp, and that made his Presidency different. From the start there was a different atmosphere, a more constrained one, less free, a little more fearful; whether this was deliberate or not, it was the result. (It showed in all sorts of ways, and made the isolated White House even more isolated. Kennedy, for instance, had liked newspapermen and had talked freely to them himself, so freely in fact that Richard Helms of the

443

CIA once called *Newsweek* executives to suggest that perhaps Kennedy's relationship with Ben Bradlee, their Washington bureau chief, was constituting a major security leak. But if Kennedy liked newspapermen and the press, and kept up with what different reporters were writing, then his staff had to do the same, and this in many ways opened up the executive branch. Reporters as such were not necessarily enemies. But Johnson viewed the press, with its different definition of loyalty, darkly; it was in essence a hotbed of enemies. If Johnson did not like reporters and did not see them, then his aides did not either, and they could explain away any critical reporting by the fact that the reporter was personally unfriendly to the Administration.)

So there was a difference in the way the men were used. Johnson did not like the free flow, and did not reach down to younger men in the various offices. He believed that youth in itself was a sign of inexperience. (In 1968, during the great post-Tet events, the Wise Men had arrived to be briefed. What they heard jarred them, and it was reflected in their attitudes. Johnson wanted to know who had briefed them. He was given their names, young men in the various departments, and asked, Who the hell are they, who are these people? When he was told he said, How the hell can they know anything? They weren't even around during World War II.) So the lower-level men did not appear and did not ask the questions which Johnson himself was unable to ask. His was a far more structured government; decisions were made at the very top, in part because of his almost neurotic desire for secrecy. The more men who participate, the more gossip there is going to be, the more rumor that maybe Lyndon Johnson himself didn't make those decisions, that he needed people to make them for him, or worse, that there was disagreement at the top level of government, thus perhaps an inkling, an impression, that the decision was not perfect. So the way to control secrecy was to control the decision making, to keep it in as few hands as possible and make sure those hands were loyal, more committed to working with the President than to anything else. Besides, these were big men who had been given their jobs by Jack Kennedy.

Thus the decisions on Vietnam would be made by very few men, and the players would be different from those under Kennedy. To Johnson, McNamara was not just a forceful statistician and bureaucrat, his judgment and wisdom were invoked; Rusk, who had been something of a liaison man with the Hill before, became a genuine Secretary of State, a wise, thoughtful man, a man not too quick on his horse. So rather than the previous Administration's decision making, where a variety of opinions were sought and filtered down, this was a very structured one, a place where Rusk could feel much more at home, and headed by a man who liked to hold his decisions as close to him as possible and who had an obsession with consensus. That in itself was an illusion as far as foreign policy was concerned. Consensus was primarily the mark of the domestic politician and particularly of someone who was working in the Congress, trying to sign on as many people as possible to a policy (perhaps not the best policy, but a policy which the broadest range found acceptable and bearable; thus it could more readily be pushed through Congress, and more important men could not attack it later on if they had been part of it), but consensus in foreign affairs was likely to be different. Although such a consensus might make the various signatories feel safer and more comfortable, it would not necessarily make the policy any wiser. But to Johnson, a man of some timidity and considerable caution despite the bluster, a consensus was safer, the footprints were covered. He was not a man with a sense of history, a man who had a particular belief in the lone man dissenting, in the man going against the ostensible grain. He was trying to get everyone on board in an office where the best decisions are often the loneliest ones.

CHAPTER 15

Even as the bureaucracy was gearing up its plans for bombing, the upper level of the bureaucracy was meeting in the Pentagon to program war games for Vietnam. It was an elaborate procedure, with the lower-ranking staff people spending two weeks before the arrival of their superiors in planning and setting up the games. The actual scenario reflected the real situation in Vietnam as accurately as possible. The situation in the South was bad, the play was now up to the United States. Would it bomb, and if it did, what would be the North Vietnamese response? Though there was nothing unusual about the idea of having war games—they are constantly being programmed in the game room of the Pentagon—these games were different, and all the players knew it; it was as if this was a dry run for the real thing. The players were some of the great names of the government, men like Curtis LeMay, General Earle Wheeler; and to let everyone know that it was not some light exercise, representing the President of the United States was none less than McGeorge Bundy.

The only problem with the war games was that they did not go well. The real question was to test out what would happen if we bombed the North. It quickly became apparent that very little would happen. The Red (or Hanoi) Team had some very good players, a smart general like Buzz Wheeler, and Marshall Green of the State Department; the Blue Team had men like Bill Bundy and General LeMay. The bombing of the infiltration routes did not seem to bother Hanoi. For every American move, there seemed to be a ready counter-move for Hanoi; the blockade of Haiphong saw the North Vietnamese simply put more pressure on the United States military bases in the South and slip more men down the trail. We bombed and they nudged a few battalions into the South. We bombed some more of the greater military targets, and because we were bombing them we had brought in a surface-to-air (SAM) anti-aircraft missile site to protect the South's cities against North Vietnamese or Chinese bombing. So they put the SAM site under siege, and in order to protect the site, which was staffed by Americans, we had to bring in Marines, at which point they nudged a few more men down the trail. The moment the Marines landed we had more difficult logistic problems, and the Vietcong simply applied more pressure to all supply routes, blowing up railroad tracks, ambushing convoys, making the small bases held by Americans increasingly isolated, dependent upon air supply (because there was little patrolling), and moving their machine guns in closer and closer to the bases, and beginning to shoot down the resupply planes. The enemy was turning out to be very savvy, very clever, and to have just as many options at his disposal as we did at ours. Maybe even more. What was particularly disturbing, the civilians on the Blue Team were discovering, was that he could meet the United States escalations at surprisingly little cost of his own.

North Vietnam had, noted a civilian player, always seemed like such a small country, until you got involved in a war game; then, programmed from their side, their army seemed very large, about 250,000 men, and it was so easy just to send a few divisions down the trails and those divisions somehow did not disturb the mass of troops left behind in the North. The bombing, they soon found out, seemed to have little effect on their military establishment; Hanoi could disassemble it, move it to rural areas, use camouflage, and run on very little logistic support in the American sense. Indeed, the more the Blue Team players pushed, the less vulnerable the North seemed to limited bombing. There was a growing sense of the elephant struggling with the gnat.

It was all very frustrating for the Blue Team and particularly for General LeMay, who was the classic Air Force man and who hated the restraints imposed by civilians. He sensed that a new kind of war was coming and that once again the military would be frustrated, that air power would be misused. At one of the intermissions he began a running dialogue with Mac Bundy which reflected his belief (and later the military's belief) that bombing should be used all out against the North. Bundy's view (the civilians' belief, which would surface in 1964 and again in 1967) was that a limited amount of bombing would do. LeMay continued: they had targets, oil depots, ports, dikes, and if they existed and we were enemy enough to fight them and to die we should tear it all down. "We should bomb them into the Stone Age."

"Maybe," answered Bundy, "they're already there."

The second set of war games went a little better. General Wheeler had switched sides, and though there were certain continuing problems of Asian responses (a massive air attack cut all rail links between North Vietnam and China, but a Chinese general simply released 50,000 men to replace 50,000 North Vietnamese troops who would then move into the South), there was a subtle difference now. That was a greater United States willingness to commit more and more of its resources to the war, and corollary change among the North Vietnamese, a downplaying of their willingness to meet the larger American commitment. Despite the more favorable outcome of this game, however, few of those who played in both of them left sanguine; the real lesson of the games, and it was not a lesson they wanted to talk about, was not how vulnerable the North was to the United States bombing, but rather how invulnerable it was, how much of an American input it would require to dent the North Vietnamese will.

The collapse in the South, the one force which the American leaders could not control, continued unabated. The Americans had always had the illusion that something might turn it around; a new leader in South Vietnam who would understand how to get with the program; a realization on the part of the South Vietnamese that their necks were on the line, that the feared enemy, the Communists, were about to walk into Saigon. But nothing changed, the other side continued to get stronger, the ARVN side weaker. One reason the principals were always surprised by this was that the truth of the war never entered the upper-level American calculations; that this was a revolutionary war, and that the other side held title to the revolution because of the colonial war which had just ended. This most simple fact explained why their soldiers would fight and die and ours would not; why their leaders were skillful and brave, and ours were inept and corrupt. But it never entered into the calculations of the principals. The question of Communism and anti-Communism as opposed to revolution and antirevolution was far more convenient for American policy makers.

Thus did the Americans ignore the most basic factor of the war, and when they did stumble across it, it continued to puzzle them. McNamara's statistics and calculations were of no value at all, because they never contained the fact that if the ratio was ten to one in favor of the government, it still meant nothing, because the one man was willing to fight and die and the ten were not.

So the Americans ignored the real key to Vietnam, only to have successive collapses of the South Vietnamese continue to confront, astound, and disturb the American planners. The inability of the South Vietnamese to behave like Americans was particularly puzzling, and chief among those puzzled was the man who had become the ambassador to Vietnam in July, 1964, Maxwell Taylor, a man who was supposed to be a soldier-intellectual and to understand both the war and the enemy, but who in fact understood neither.

In June, Henry Cabot Lodge had gone home, the call of the Eastern establishment too great upon his ears as Goldwater neared the Republican nomination. He had gone back ostensibly to help the belated campaign of William Scranton as the moderate Eastern challenger to Goldwater, but he was not above hoping that lightning might strike for himself, a hope that would turn a little bitter when he found out later in the year that his old friend Dwight Eisenhower had wanted *Lodge* to run when Lodge had interpreted it as simply the general wanting *someone* from the East to run against Goldwater.

When Lodge came back, there was no dearth of candidates to take his place, including Robert Kennedy, who was still trying to find mission and duty in the postassassination days (Johnson wrote him a compassionate note saying he could not risk the dangers to Kennedy's life inherent in the Saigon job), and the Good Soldier Rusk, ready to resign and take the job of ambassador. When Taylor, who had been serving as Chairman of the Joint Chiefs for the past two years and had accomplished all that could be achieved in that career, also volunteered, willing to peel off his four stars, Johnson gladly chose him. It was a time when he wanted to move things in Vietnam without really touching them, affect events while doing nothing; thus one moves names, celebrities, and what better name than Max Taylor, citizen-soldier, a liberal, an intellectual, a quoter of Greek, a man who knew something about war and politics, and above all a friend of the Kennedys' (thus tying up Robert Kennedy even more; indeed some three years later, when Robert Kennedy began to dissent on the war, the Administration used Taylor to bring him back a step and a half). A cool man in a cool era, Max Taylor.

Which was not the way he saw it. As far as American officials in Saigon were concerned, Taylor gave them their marching orders on July 9, almost immediately upon his arrival. He had summoned the mission council together, that group of a dozen Americans who ran the country, or tried to run it, and he briefed them on what he considered to be American objectives. There were, he said, four alternatives. The first was to throw in our hand and withdraw. The second was accommodation through negotiation, which he said was a sign of political weakness. The third was to take military action against the North, which could be done by the South Vietnamese air force, with or without United States' participation, either in retaliation for specific acts of violence or as part of a general deterrent. These reprisals, he said, would threaten all that Ho Chi Minh had accomplished in his homeland in the last decade and could provide him with a strong incentive to change his mind. The fourth and final option was to improve and expand the in-country pacification program (i.e., within the South Vietnamese borders) with special emphasis on the so-called eight critical provinces. The United States government was, he said, following option four while preparing for alternative three. "No consideration is being given to alternatives one and two, because they are tantamount to accepting defeat," Taylor said. With that he was finished; he had in effect told the men who would be running the operations in Saigon that we were not going to lose Vietnam, that negotiation was out of the question. We would stand. Among the men listening to him, there to get guidance, was his old protégé, the new commander of the United States military mission in Saigon. General William C. Westmoreland, a man who was neither brilliant nor, for that matter, presumptuous, would come away from the meeting with the belief that he had been told to hold Vietnam. Which in fact he had.

So for the third time Max Taylor would become a major player on Vietnam, which had begun in 1961 as a test case for the Administration's new strategies of war, and Taylor more than anyone else had been the author. He had, at the start, been looking more for a limited war than a guerrilla war, but you took what you could get, and he was never too sharp on the distinction and the political significance of the latter. It was his military recommendations which Kennedy had partially followed in authorizing the advisory and support mission. Taylor had handpicked Harkins, so that he himself could control the reporting from Saigon, a reporting system which he had not only orchestrated, but what was worse and more dangerous, come to believe.

In 1964 Taylor's pessimism was not so great as might have been expected; if things were perhaps not going well, he did not see them as going that badly. In the first few months after his arrival in Vietnam he was not as pessimistic as Westmoreland, because he was tied to past optimism, which Westmoreland was not, and because he feared the consequences of the failure of the advisory and support mission, which Westmoreland, ready and just a little eager to be a commander, did not. Taylor did not in mid-1964 particularly believe in the bombing, thinking that it would lack military effectiveness, nor was he particularly enthusiastic about the idea of combat troops. So even before he left for Saigon, Taylor wanted to maintain the kind of commitment which already existed. He talked openly with a handful of Pentagon reporters about the bombing, telling them he was against it (some of the other Chiefs were already pushing it). It was likely to be ineffective, and as far as interdiction went, it was more difficult to interdict than the Air Force thought, he said.

He changed his views on the bombing in the latter half of 1964, and after that to a limited degree on sending combat troops. It was a crucial change in the cast of characters. For as the linear descendant of Matt Ridgway, whose proudest boast was that he had helped keep us out of the French Indochina war, Taylor was, when he became ambassador, the most prestigious American then in uniform. Max Taylor before a Senate committee would have been a powerful advocate for the decision not to escalate, but when he turned, the President lost a compelling reason for staying out. At the very end, in the final rounds of decision making, Taylor voiced doubts about the use of combat troops, but by then it would all be beyond him. He would be replaced by other, more powerful, players, and at the moment when his word carried weight, he had approved the escalation. His role was vital: Washington is a gossipy town both in and outside the government, and the coming of the Xerox machine has made it more so; so when Taylor's cables came in during the last part of 1964 calling for bombing, they had a profound effect upon the bureaucracy.

The reasons why he changed were varied; an awareness of the failure in the South, an irresistible pressure to justify what you are doing. Too much had already been committed, too many men, too much honor, too much prestige, too many white crosses to turn back. And he changed, too, because he had become a spokesman for the American community in Saigon, living in that intense, almost irrational atmosphere of men who talked only to themselves and others like them, and who came to believe that whatever else, Vietnam should not be lost, and for whom the domestic problems of the United States were quite secondary. From Saigon the United States seemed distant and small, Vietnam was the important thing, the center of the universe; the careers and the decisions centered there. So in the last months of 1964 Max Taylor changed; he had not intended to go this far, but there was nowhere else to go, no more forks in the road, even for a supremely detached man like Maxwell Taylor, the Kennedy general.

Taylor had been very helpful to President Kennedy in the early days, Robert Kennedy would say in 1968 (when he was running against the war and reporters haunted him with questions about Taylor and the origins of the war). Which he had. He had come in as military adviser to the President, a filter to the Joint Chiefs, but he had not remained there long. After the Bay of Pigs, Kennedy had relied on him as his chief investigating officer; Taylor had been very thorough in analyzing the failure of the breakdown in planning, though in retrospect his report seemed to deal too little with the political realities of such a venture, instead being concentrated on the technical failings (not enough ammunition; the fact that like most green troops the brigade had fired too quickly and used up too much ammunition). But he had been of value to the Kennedys and McNamara in trying to reshape the grand design of strategy, away from nuclear dependence, and he had given the change in policies a certain respectability; he was an imposing figure to have on your side. In trying to gain some kind of control over the military, Taylor had been a considerable help, and part of the counterinsurgency fad, which Bobby Kennedy promoted in 1961, was an attempt to work outside the existing bureaucracy to Kennedyize the military programs, as if to take some of the decision making away from the Chiefs, who were not Kennedy people.

It quickly became clear to Kennedy that this was not adequate and that he needed more control of the military. Since Taylor as a civilian assistant lacked real leverage, he soon returned to uniform as Chairman of the Joint Chiefs. His was not an easy role, caught as he was between the conflicting pressures of two very different constituencies: the Chiefs with their totality of commitment to the early lessons of the Cold War, the Communists were enemies, the only thing that mattered was force, and maximum application of it; and the Kennedy Administration, nervously and gingerly and slowly beginning to move away from some of the rules of the Cold War. Taylor was particularly valuable to the Administration on nuclear control, and among the White House confidants of the President there was a feeling that if Taylor was not exactly the intellectual he was supposed to be ("He is a very handsome man, and a very impressive one," said Averell Harriman in 1967, "and he is always wrong."), there was genuine warmth toward him based more than anything on the test-ban treaty. He had been very helpful then, and in June, 1963, when Kennedy decided to give the American University speech in which he would announce that the United States would not be the first to test in the atmosphere, a White House staff member had the job of clearing it with McNamara, Gilpatric, and Taylor. He called the general and explained what they were planning to say and what they were doing and suggested that Taylor might want to check with the Chiefs; Taylor answered no, he did not think he needed to check with them, since it was basically a political matter for the President to decide, not a military issue. It was a very special act, a mark of his deference to the President on something the President cared deeply about; Taylor knew that if he asked the Chiefs they would object strenuously, so he decided not to ask them at all. As far as the White House was concerned, Taylor was at his best, and there was a mutuality of gratitude.

This had been a happy time for him, back in uniform, working with a President he liked, on particularly good terms with the President and even better ones with the Attorney General (Jack Kennedy had once said that he would stick with his old friends once in the White House, that the White House, the center of everyone's desire for influence, was not a good place to develop new friends, but McNamara and Taylor were the prime exceptions to that. They were the professional associates who had bridged the gap, which held a certain element of good old-fashioned snobbery to it. In Robert Kennedy's case his friendship with Taylor was even more remarkable, since Taylor was not known for having close friendships of any kind, particularly not with men more than twenty years his junior. Friendship with younger men was not normally something he encouraged, but then, there are exceptions to every rule). After the assassination, Taylor and McNamara would visit Jackie regularly, working very hard to keep her spirits up, visits that she particularly prized. And later, when Taylor became ambassador to Vietnam, the friendship with Bob Kennedy continued, and a friend of Taylor's would remember one moment with the general that was in stark contrast to the everyday Taylor, usually so aloof. The scene was the airport when Taylor was returning to Saigon after a visit to Washington. Bobby and Ethel and innumerable children were there to see him off, arriving a few minutes before Taylor, rushing aboard the plane and leaving notes for him pinned everywhere, hidden here, folded under this seat, and on the ceiling, notes of fondness and trivial jokes. When Taylor, normally so cold and distant, found them, he was absolutely transformed, laughing and affectionate. If there were holes in his discipline, it should not be for anyone below the rank of Attorney General.

But it was no wonder that Robert Kennedy liked him, that Jack and Jackie had liked him; that Lyndon Johnson felt comfortable with him, that he was one more reassuring figure in that era. He was so reasonable and so professional. The very best of the breed. The right officer for the American century. He seemed to embody the American officer of the era; he gave off vibrations of control and excellence and competence, and indeed he seemed to represent something that went even beyond him, the belief of the United States military that they were the best in the business.

If the Kennedy Administration had come to power to be the rationalizers of the great new liberal Democratic empire, then they had found the perfect general; their social and academic hubris was matched by his military self-confidence. His were not the attitudes of a man about to be deterred from his path by a little peasant revolutionary army. Not in the American century.

CHAPTER 16

But the Saigon years would not be happy ones for Max Taylor. After all those years of making control, discipline, the touchstones of his life, Taylor was now confronted by the wild irrationality, the deviousness, and venality of the South Vietnamese. It was somehow unfair; people who are about to be saved from the Communists should feel some element of gratitude, of knowing they were being saved, and more important, wanting to be saved. It was all very puzzling. No common cause. All those years in the military, where there were certain standards and rules, where young men treated their superiors with respect; you gave an order and it was obeyed. Now here in Saigon, all of that meant nothing, medals won on the plains of Europe against the world's mightiest army meant nothing; he was dealing with these boys, most had never heard a shot fired in anger. Everything went so badly; Nguyen Khanh, who had appeared so dramatically on the scene in February as the new prime minister, and whom the Americans had seized upon, the first American-style leader, had turned out to be not American style, but Vietnamese style. Diem's weaknesses without Diem's strengths—neurotic, paranoiac, disliked by both older officers and younger officers, and like his predecessors, totally overwhelmed by the political problems he faced. Khanh and Taylor argued regularly, ever more bitterly.

It was always like that; Max was so organized, disciplined, trying to transfer that rationality and logic to this Alice-in-Wonderland world. The worst thing for him was of course that nothing worked. It was a roller coaster—more advisers, more gear, more threats to the South Vietnamese, more threats to the North. He was at the confluence of it now, the architect of limited war, and particularly this limited war, caught between the failure of it and the threat of a greater war, between his vanities and his beliefs that the United States would not be defeated here, that the loss of prestige for a great power in the face of a small guerrilla army would be a major catastrophe. It had all come home to him, Max Taylor, who had always been able to control things. Now control was getting away from all of them. What they had held on to, the counterinsurgency, was slipping away, and in early August, 1964, he began to grasp almost desperately at solutions. Since the Vietcong could not be defeated in the South, the answers would have to be found elsewhere, and for the first time he began to change on the bombing.

Taylor wanted it for political reasons. In the past he had opposed bombing because he was unwilling to commit the United States to the use of greater power against the North, which meant greater involvement; otherwise, he felt, the United States would find itself at war with the North with a very weak government in the South. Now he was changing. In his August 18 message to the President he said: "Something must be added in the coming months." That something would be bombing; the right time for starting a campaign of reprisal, he suggested, would be January 1, 1965, a time conveniently after the election. Ideally, we should tell Khanh that we would begin to bomb for him and the South Vietnamese if he could show the United

States that he was ready for it and brought a new era of stability to Saigon. Thus the bombing was a political lever, a reward; if they were good and cleaned up their house, we would bomb, and show our greater willingness to commit ourselves.

Events in the fall would turn Taylor completely toward the bombing. Just as the pre-Tonkin covert operations had led to the Tonkin incident and the sense in this country that the other side had provoked us, the principals triggered the situation at Bien Hoa which, when it exploded, filled them with righteousness against the enemy. On November 1 the squadron of obsolete B-57 bombers which had been moved from the Philippines to the air base at Bien Hoa (over State's objections) was hit by the Vietcong; five Americans were killed, seventy-six wounded, and six of the bombers destroyed. Thus the Vietcong had matched their symbols against our symbols; anyone wanting to know what their attitude toward the bombing would be in the future had his answer right there. They would meet our air power with increased pressure against targets in the South.

What was remarkable about the attack was the reaction of Max Taylor. It infuriated him, and his cables back to Washington, which had always in the past been restrained and almost conservative in tone, were now strikingly different, angry, reflecting almost outrage that they could do this to the symbols of the United States of America, of which he himself, as ambassador, was the great symbol. A sign of arrogance on the part of the other side, tinkering with the giant. He wanted to retaliate and retaliate immediately, and he was surprised and a little angry when Johnson, facing an election in two days, did not respond, and he complained openly to friends in the mission and to journalists. But this, as much as anything else, pushed him over on the bombing. From then on he was committed. He was angry at Hanoi and eager to punish, and he wanted not just tit for tat but the major bombing program as well.

Even as Taylor was recommending bombing, he knew that this in itself was not enough, that if you bombed you would need troops. But he was bothered about sending combat troops, and he did not want to cross that bridge if necessary, partly because of the problem of Americans fighting in a political war and turning the population toward the Vietcong, but even more because he felt there was a crossover point at which, as the Americans put in men, the South Vietnamese would let down even more on the job, and the process of Americanizing the war would be accelerated. But if it bothered him, he was still convinced that whatever happened, he could influence American decisions, that he could apply the brake if necessary, that he was at the crucial spot, the ambassador, with Westmoreland under his control. Which would not turn out to be true: as ambassador he was the senior American only as long as there were no American troops; the moment the troops arrived the play would go to Westmoreland.

In late November, 1964, right before Thanksgiving and before his crucial trip back to Washington, where the President was now elected in his own right, Taylor gathered his senior staff together in Saigon. It was, thought one witness, a momentous occasion, Max aware of it, somehow more aloof than other men. Standing there, handsome, reserved—somehow those four stars seemed visible even when he was in civies—he had turned to them and said, "I am going to see the President and I am going to advise him that the way things are going we will need American troops here. I intend to tell him this anyway, but I think it will help, it will make my position stronger, if I could tell the President that all of you here agree as well. I think I should warn you, however, that we may ultimately need as many as one hundred thousand."

The election of November 3, 1964, had gone just the way Johnson wanted, perhaps more so. He had received 43 million votes and Goldwater 27 million; he had sixty-one percent of the vote, the greatest percentage any American President had ever received. He had the Congress, a gain of thirty-seven seats in the House and with an enormous Democratic majority of sixty-eight Senators in the upper chamber. He had carefully camouflaged the question of Vietnam, removing it from debate, from the public eye and from the journalistic eye (Theodore White's coverage of the 1964 campaign, *The Making of the President*, a series known for its thoroughness in backgrounding major issues as well as men, is quite revealing; there are eighteen references to Bill Moyers and fourteen to Kenny O'Donnell, both of whom worked in Johnson's political process, and no references to Bill Bundy or John McNaughton, who were carrying the burden of the preparations for war. Max Taylor, who as ambassador was the central figure in Saigon, was mentioned only twice, a reflection not on White's journalistic ability, but on Johnson's ability to separate the issue of the war from the political process and to hide the decision making). Yet Vietnam had not gone away; even while the President was in the final, hectic, joyous weeks of the campaign, receiving a kind of adulation rarely accorded a political figure, the bureaucracy was grinding away methodically, coming to its positions. The principals had been ready to bomb at the time of the Bien Hoa attack; the pressure to do something, almost anything, was growing.

For the Joint Chiefs of Staff it was an unsettling time. If the intelligence community had a sense that events were getting out of control and that the restraints were being lifted, the Chiefs had a similar feeling from an entirely different viewpoint. They thought it was all moving toward their business, their profession, and yet, even as events progressed, as the inevitability of combat neared, they had too little sense of play. They had assumed that they would move into a larger role: the civilians around the President moved aside, the Chiefs moved to center stage.

But it did not happen that way; instead they found the President, if anything, more nervous than ever about being with them, as if somehow afraid of giving the impression that he was getting into a shooting war, and thus listening to the military, and influenced by the military (they would learn about Lyndon Johnson that he was far more willing to be seen with them and photographed with them later when he was *de-escalating* the war and when he needed their coloration to protect him from the right; whereas in 1964 and 1965 the last thing he wanted was the impression that he was under their spell and influence). They found themselves moving closer and closer to a real war, and yet more and more separated from the President. They did not feel at ease with the President, largely because they were sure he felt uncomfortable with them; they sensed his distrust, the fact that he wanted to keep them at arm's length, and his desire to use both McNamara and Taylor to filter them out.

They neither liked nor trusted McNamara (nor McNaughton, McNamara's chief aide in working with them, who made even less effort to conceal his contempt for them), and they felt that the Secretary was constantly manipulating them, that he did not really represent their position to the President, although he claimed he did. They were sure that he denigrated them, that somehow when he talked with the President they were the enemy, people to be fended off, and that he tried to keep them from seeing the President. ("It's your Constitutional right," he would tell them, "but if I were you I wouldn't do it. He doesn't like you to come over and I can do it better for you.") So they saw the President only twice in the months right before the President made the decision to escalate. Many of them would come to despise McNamara; as the war progressed and the problems mounted he would symbolize their frustrations, the embodiment of all evil. (In August, 1966, at Lynda Johnson and Chuck Robb's wedding, McNamara approached General Wally Greene, Commandant of the Marine Corps, a man who loathed him, and said that he was puzzled, he was losing his influence with the President and he wondered why. Did General Greene know why? Greene thought to himself, You're losing your influence because you've lied to him and misled him all these years. Greene would feel somewhat the same way about Lyndon Johnson by the end of his tour. Asked by a historian to consent to an interview for the Lyndon Johnson Library, he said yes, if they had asbestos tape in the recorder.) The only general that McNamara trusted as late as mid-1964 was Max Taylor.

So there was a strong feeling, even as events were moving ahead toward escalation, that the Chiefs were on the outside looking in. They were General Curtis LeMay of the Air Force, Admiral David McDonald of the Navy, and Wally Greene of the Marine Corps, and they were all very hawkish. The Air Force believed in air power and bombing, old-fashioned, unrelieved bombing; the Navy, anxious to show that the carrier still worked and to get its share of roles and missions in what had been largely an Army show up to now, was hawkish; and Greene was hawkish. They were simple men, products of their training, environment, and era, and they believed in the old maxims of war. If you had to go to war you used force, and if you used force, you used maximum force. If we were going to bomb, then it had to be saturation bombing of every conceivable target, and they would pick the targets. Obliteration of the enemy.

The closer they got to a decision, however, the more they sensed that it was going to be nervous, inadequate, half-hearted bombing. It was exactly the reverse of everything they believed, it signaled the enemy that more was coming, it allowed him to move his resources around and protect himself from bombing, to decrease his losses and increase American ones. All the Chiefs were signed on to a heavy bombing campaign, but LeMay and Greene were the most aggressive; they wanted to hit the irrigation dikes as well. Hit everything there. If it wasn't worth hitting it wasn't worth going to war. If you sent troops in, you sent in enough to do the job, 600,000, 700,000 perhaps; you did it immediately, you went in on a wartime footing; you called up the reserves and you let the nation know it was into something.

What was most striking about this period as events closed in on the principals was how little exploration there was of the consequences of their route, what it might do to the country. And in the same sense, there was a refusal to consider what the alternatives to escalation really were. A question that was almost never raised was whether the Vietnamese might or might not be better off under Ho, and to what degree the success of the Vietcong was a reflection of this. The kind of men who might have the doubts, the men in State—Harriman, Hilsman, Trueheart, Michael Forrestal—had long since been winnowed out. Only one man was left at the top level who had open doubts on Vietnam, and that was George Ball. He had not been a participant in the earlier bureaucratic struggles; he was something of an outsider as far as the Kennedy circle was concerned. He was a man of Europe and he had not considered Vietnam that important. Now, starting in 1964 and through the crucial months of 1965, he argued compellingly, forcefully, and prophetically against the escalation, so prophetically that someone reading his papers five years later would have a chilling feeling that they had been written after the fact, not before.

In arguing against the escalation, Ball was saying that it was doomed. He was alone among the foreign policy people saying this, which did not bother him; he felt he needed only one of Johnson's domestic people to argue for the domestic side, to say that the American people didn't want war, that anti-Communism was ebbing as an issue. If only one more voice . . . If. If.

Ball's pre-election relationship with Kennedy had been marginal, and he had not been in line for a particularly good job. He never became a part of the inner Kennedy group; rather, he existed in something of a no-man's-land for those first years. He was a man of immense pride, and he regarded much of the Kennedy style and dash with considerable skepticism; those snappy young men running around in the White House did not necessarily strike him as brilliant. He was a man of considerable zest, enthusiasm, and egocentricism, and he did not defer to those around him in Washington. He was probably the most traveled man of that group in Washington, the best read, and certainly the most elegant in speech. He was also a good deal more worldly than the others. He was not in awe of McGeorge Bundy, thinking Bundy too much the pragmatist (Bundy in turn would call Ball "the theologian" because of too much belief, and occasionally irritated by Ball's independence and individualism, once said to him, "The trouble with you, George, is that you always want to be the piano player."). Part of the tension between them, of course, was that each saw the other as a possible successor to Rusk. He was less than admiring of McNamara, sensing quite early the weaknesses in him.

A man of genuine intelligence and force, Ball rose at State on his ability. Independence and ability, rather than being the good corporate man, he felt, should bring success in government. He got on particularly well with Rusk during the Kennedy years. The friendship survived remarkably well, despite the vast disagreements over Vietnam. (Years later, when Rusk's reputation was at its lowest, a reporter, interviewing Ball about the war, would mention Rusk and would be stunned by Ball's almost vehement answer, *"I love Dean Rusk."*) Ball had a sense for Rusk as a human being that few others had in that era. Perhaps since both were outsiders in the Kennedy years, Rusk opened up more to Ball than to others. That, plus a certain gratitude to Rusk for permitting him as Undersecretary to dissent so strongly on Vietnam ("I cannot," says one member of that Administration, "imagine McNamara letting Ball dissent like that.") Rusk served as Secretary of State with an overpowering sense of being a civil servant, a superclerk, an attitude which placed strong limits on his individual rights, whereas Ball, with a fierce sense of his own ability and prerogatives, felt that he was there to say what he believed.

Bothered by the direction of the war, and by the attitudes he found around him in the post-Tonkin fall of 1964, and knowing that terrible decisions were coming up, Ball began turning his attention to the subject of Vietnam. He had, at the time of the original Kennedy commitment, warned that 15,000 men would become 300,000; that was his own prediction, and it was not a bad one.

And so now he began, first by writing a memo to Rusk, McNamara, and Bundy expressing his doubts, and expecting that Bundy would pass the memo on to the President. But to Ball's surprise the memo did not reach Johnson, so the next time Ball passed his memo to Bill Moyers, the bright young assistant of Johnson's who showed his own doubts on Vietnam largely by encouraging other doubters to speak and by trying to put doubters in touch with one another. Moyers passed the memo to the President, who encouraged it, and so, beginning in the early fall of 1964, Ball emerged as the voice of dissent. Ball argued that the ground troops would not work, that the United States would repeat the French experience, soon costing us what few friends we had in the South, that the situation "would in the world's eyes approach that of France in the 1950's." But he also argued vigorously against the bombing, saying that if the United States used air power, Hanoi would feel the need to respond, and failing to have air power, they would respond with increased ground forces.

He argued that the bombing would not, as its advocates were claiming, have very much effect on South Vietnamese morale. Rather, he said, it might affect the upper level of the government, and even that rather briefly and impermanently; it would never take root in the country. To Ball, the arguments of Mac Bundy and Taylor that we must bomb to shore up the morale of the South Vietnamese because the government was so frail that it would otherwise collapse was foolishness of a high order. It was all the more reason *not* to commit the power and reputation of the United States to something that weak. The South Vietnamese were, he noted, allegedly a people about to be overrun by their sworn enemies, and if they really cared about the freedoms we were so anxious to protect, why did we have to make a gesture like this to convince them to save themselves?

So Ball made his dissent, and he made it powerfully, and if he was not changing the men around him he was certainly affecting the President, touching those doubts which already existed in the President's mind.

The two sides were supposed to mesh in the late-November meetings. They did not. Lyndon Johnson was still not satisfied that bombing was the answer. Johnson was on the fence, and Rusk, uneasy in his own right about the bombing, was waiting to see which way the President wanted to go. Johnson's own fairly strong political instincts had been stirred by Ball's dissent, and he was discovering that despite the seeming unanimity of his principals, their belief in what they were proposing was not exactly convincing. Of the principals, McNamara and Taylor seemed the most confident, and McNamara, who had a remarkable ability to present answers in terms a superior wanted, was arguing that bombing was not final, it was political, and finally, at a relatively low cost; at the very least it would buy time. The President was becoming skittish. Ball was making him nervous, and the turmoil in Saigon was making him uneasy. How could he bomb the North when some colonel or corporal in a tank might take Saigon the next day? he asked. Couldn't Taylor make it clear to those people that the President wanted to help them, the United States was prepared to play its role, but not unless they got together? Why couldn't they get together? he asked.

So the Taylor mission to Washington, which was supposed to sew everything up, did not; the decisions were still open. Events were closing them down, but the President was unhappy about the trap he found himself in. He was still looking for a way out; if Ball was not changing the direction of the play he was slowing it down. And there would be moments, when after a particular dissent by Ball, the President would turn to him and say, "All right, George, if you can pull me a rabbit out of a hat, go ahead," meaning trying to settle it without losing.

As it got darker, the line was hardening. The winds were blowing in a different way, it was clearer and clearer that they were going to go North. Little signs. A high State Department official who was working on a policy paper was by chance invited to the White House in December. He found the President surprisingly relaxed; stories of his boyhood came flashing out, stories of the Senate, slipping it by them, all punctuated by colorful language, and then suddenly, knowing why the State Department man was there, slipping in the phrase very quickly, as though it were almost unimportant, "Well, I guess we have to touch up those North Vietnamese a litte," and then he was back again regaling his audience, all in the vernacular.

In January it still hung in the balance; the President had decided on the bombing but was unwilling to put his decision into practice. It would be a smaller, almost covert bombing at first; the paper work should go ahead, Bill Bundy should start notifying the various interested allies, and Max Taylor should get the South Vietnamese in line, letting them know that if they could shape up we would bomb the North to help them. And so the bombing decision seemed to have been made, made but not committed, and it was one of the marks of the breakdown in the entire decision-making process that because the bombing was going to be an instrument to prevent the use of combat troops, to win the war cheaply, to flash American technology and will without really using them, the decision was a piecemeal one. Lyndon Johnson liked slicing the salami thin, he could slice a decision as thin as any man around, so he and his decision makers sliced this one very thin: they made the decision on the bombing, and only on the bombing, in a vacuum. The subject of the troops, of the inevitability of them if the bombing failed, was rarely discussed. Even the subject of troops for perimeter defense was barely mentioned. It did not come up for a variety of reasons; for one thing it was not a subject that Lyndon Johnson wanted to hear. It made him very uneasy and unhappy and so he did not encourage it, nor did the people around him, like Mac Bundy (who did not necessarily fully understand the inevitability of it).

So instead of returning to Saigon with a completed bombing package, Taylor returned with instructions in which Johnson stated that he wanted a "stable and effective" government in Saigon before he moved against the North; this was necessary in the South, he wrote, even if Hanoi cut off its aid to the Vietcong. Then, once the government was stable ("firmly in control") and in command, the United States would be willing to start steadily mounting air attacks on the North and "the U.S. mission is authorized to initiate such planning now with the GVN [Government of (South) Vietnam] with the understanding that the U.S. Government does not commit itself now to any form of execution of such plans."

This explained Taylor's fury two weeks later when Nguyen Khanh and the young Turks, including Air Marshal Ky, dissolved the High National Council, a group of civilian elders, and made a large number of political arrests during the night. Taylor was in a rage. They had, he felt, gone against him personally; he had given his word to President Johnson that he could handle them, provide the stability, thus it was a personal insult. He summoned the young generals and lined them up against the wall in his office. When they tried to sit down, he did not permit it, and they were dressed down like West Point cadets. They were lieutenants at best, these young kids, running around playing at governing a country. All the veneer had disappeared. Taylor treated them as he really felt, that they were junior officers in a kids' army, and he read them out. "Do all of you understand English? I told you all clearly at General Westmoreland's dinner we Americans were tired of coups. Apparently I wasted my words. Maybe this is because something is wrong with my French because you evidently didn't understand. I made it clear that all the military plans which I know you would like to carry out are dependent on governmental stability. Now you have made a real mess. We cannot carry you forever if you do things like this. Who speaks for this group? Do you have a spokesman?..." (The idea of Taylor thinking he could speak like this to the Hanoi leadership is inconceivable and shows the difference between the American view of the South and the North. Air Marshal Ky was furious, later telling friends, "He must have thought we were cadets. I've never been talked to in my life like that. I wouldn't let my father talk to me like that.")

The pressure was building to bomb. Lyndon Johnson had to decide. There was going to be no easy way out. A few friends like Dick Russell were warning him not to go ahead, that it would never work; Russell had an intuitive sense that it was all going to be more difficult and complicated than the experts were saying but his doubts were written off as essentially conservative and isolationist, and it was easily rationalized that Russell, like Fulbright, did not care about colored people. Besides, Johnson had bettered Russell in the Senate and now here was Johnson surrounded by truly brilliant men (years later when there were free fire zones in the South—areas where virtually uncontrolled air and artillery could be used—which led to vast refugee resettlement, Russell would pass on his doubts about the wisdom of this as policy to the White House, saying, "I don't know those Asian people, but they tell me they worship their ancestors and so I wouldn't play with their land if I were you. You know whenever the Corps of Engineers has some dam to dedicate in Georgia I make a point of being out of state, because those people don't seem to like the economic improvements as much as they dislike being moved off their ancestral land."). But even Russell was telling the President that he had to make a decision, that he had better move.

He was facing fateful decisions on Vietnam just as he was getting ready to start the Great Society. With his careful assessment of the country, he was sure the resources were there, that the country was finally ready to do something about its long-ignored social problems. The time was right for an assault on them, and he, Lyndon Johnson, would lead that assault, cure them, go down in history as a Roosevelt-like figure. He was keenly aware of these resources, and in late 1964 and early 1965 he began to use the phrase "sixty months of prosperity" as a litany, not just as party propaganda to get credit for the Democrats, but as a way of reminding the country that it had been having it good, very good, that it was secure and affluent, that it now had to turn its attention to the needs of others. Yet he knew he would not have the resources for both the domestic programs and a real war, and as a need for the latter became more and more apparent, he became restless and irritable, even by Johnsonian standards irascible, turning violently on the men around him. Those who knew him well and had worked long for him knew the symptoms only too well; it was, they knew, part of the insecurity of the man, and they talked of it often and guardedly among themselves, since they all were subject to the same abuse. Unable to bear the truth about himself if it was unpleasant, he would transfer his feelings and his anger at himself to others, lashing out at Lady Bird, or George Reedy, or Bill Moyers, or particularly poor Jack Valenti, but really lashing out at himself. And so in early 1965 this great elemental man, seeing his great hopes ahead and sensing also that they might be outside his reach, was almost in a frenzy to push his legislation through, a restless, obsessed man, driving himself and those around him harder and harder, fighting a civil war within himself.

He knew it would not be easy, that the bombing was a tricky business, not as tricky as ground troops, there was, after all, an element of control in bombing. And yet, and yet. "If I don't go in now and they show later I should have gone, then they'll be all over me in Congress. They won't be talking about my civil rights bill, or education or beautification. No sir, they'll push Vietnam up my ass every time. Vietnam. Vietnam. Vietnam. Right up my ass." Cornered, and having what he would consider the Kennedy precedent to stand in Vietnam, a precedent which Kennedy set, but probably never entirely believed, and with all the Kennedy luminaries telling him to go ahead. He was a can-do man surrounded by other can-do men.

So it all came down to Lyndon Johnson, reluctant, uneasy, but not a man to be backed down. No one would push Lyndon Johnson of Texas around. This was Lyndon Johnson representing the United States of America, pledged to follow in the tradition of Great Britain and Winston Churchill—Lyndon Johnson, who, unlike Jack Kennedy, was a believer, not a cynic about the big things. Honor. Force. Commitments.

Machismo was no small part of it. He had always been haunted by the idea that he would be judged as being insufficiently manly for the job, that he would lack courage at a crucial moment. More than a little insecure himself, he very much wanted to be seen as a man; it was a conscious thing. He was very much aware of *machismo* in himself and those around him, and at a moment like this he wanted the respect of men who were tough, real men, and they would turn out to be the hawks. He had always unconsciously divided the people around him between men and boys. Men were activists, doers, who conquered business empires, who acted instead of talked, who made it in the world of other men and had the respect of other men. Boys were the talkers and the writers and the intellectuals, who sat around thinking and criticizing and doubting instead of doing. There were good boys, like Horace Busby and for a time Dick Goodwin, who used their talent for him, and there were snot noses and kids who were to be found at the State Department or in the editorial rooms of the Washington *Post* or *The New York Times* using their talents against him.

Now, as Johnson weighed the advice he was getting on Vietnam, it was the boys who were most skeptical, and the men who were most sure and confident and hawkish and who had Johnson's respect. Hearing that one member of his Administration was becoming a dove on Vietnam, Johnson said, "Hell, he has to squat to piss." The *men* had, after all, done things in their lifetimes, and they had the respect of other men. Doubt itself, he thought, was an almost feminine quality, doubts were for women; once, on another issue, when Lady Bird raised her doubts, Johnson had said of course she was doubtful, it was like a woman to be uncertain. Thus as Vietnam came to the edge of decision, the sides were unfair, given Johnson's makeup. The doubters were not the people he respected; the men who were activists were hawks, and he took sustenance and reassurance that the real men were for going ahead. Of the doves, only George Ball really had his respect. Ball might be a dove, but there was nothing soft about him. He had made it in a tough and savage world of the big law firms, and his approach was tough and skeptical. He did not talk about doing good or put Johnson off by discussing the moral thing to do, rather he too was interested in the exercise of power and a real world that Johnson could understand. He was a doer, an activist, and Johnson would tell him again and again, even as Ball dissented, "You're one of these can-do fellows too, George."

Thus the dice were loaded; the advocates of force were by the very nature of Johnson's personality taken more seriously, the doubters were seen by their very doubts as being lesser men. So he would go ahead, despite his own inner instincts, that the rosy predictions were in fact not likely to be so rosy, that it was likely to be tougher and darker, that George Ball's doubts had a real basis. The thrust to go forward was just too great. Everyone else seemed so convinced of America's invincibility. Even Ball, arguing at the time that it was the right moment to cut our losses, sensed this feeling of American invincibility and will, and would write that by negotiating out, the United States could become a "wiser and more mature nation." But those lessons would have to come the hard way; there were too few restraints. All the training of two decades had been quite the reverse. They had come to the end of one path. They were cornered by bad policies on Asia which they had not so much authored as refused to challenge, both in the fifties when out of power, and in the sixties when in power. And so now they bombed. They did this in place of combat troops, and they believed that it would not last long, perhaps a few months.

On February 22, nine days after the decision to go ahead on a bombing campaign, General William Childs Westmoreland, commander of the United States forces in Vietnam, sent in a request for two Marine corps to provide security for the United States air base at Danang, the base from which more and more raids against the North (and the Vietcong in the South) were being launched.

It was a small request, just two battalions, but it was the beginning, the first time American combat units would arrive as units.

Not many months later, Vice President Hubert Humphrey would have occasion to remark to Senator Gaylord Nelson, "You know, Gaylord, there are people at State and the Pentagon who want to send *three hundred thousand* men out there." Humphrey paused. "But the President will never get sucked into anything like that."

EPILOGUE

The whole basis of the escalation, of using ground forces, was that it would be brief. At least as far as Lyndon Johnson was concerned, but not as far as William Childs Westmoreland was concerned. In the summer of 1965, dissenting senators going to the White House, uneasy with the number of the troops there, and the rumors that more, many more were on their way, were assured by the President that they need not worry. They should just sit still for six months; all we wanted was negotiations, and these would come by Christmas. All we had to do was show them some of our muscle and give them a sense of our determination. Just six months.

If that were true, then the forbidden word in the White House speeches in the summer of 1965 was "negotiations." It was considered a particularly dangerous word, since it would show our weakness, our lack of intent; it would encourage Hanoi to continue the war. Senator Frank Church, making a major speech on negotiations, soon went to a White House dinner with a large group of senators and found himself under personal attack. The President, looking straight at him, began to attack those who were soft and fainthearted. After dinner it was even worse. Johnson singled out Church, backed him into a corner, and went at him heatedly, launching into a tirade on Vietnam. It was a violent discussion, all very explosive, nostril to nostril, and twice Lady Bird, sensing the dangers, tried to separate them, but the President moved her away. Church held his ground and it went on for almost an hour. The next day another senator saw Gene McCarthy and asked how the dinner had gone. "Oh, it wasn't too bad," McCarthy replied, "but if Frank Church had just surrendered sooner we could have all gone home half an hour earlier."

So negotiation was blocked out; the decisions were made, and the troops were on their way. Not just American troops, it turned out, but North Vietnamese troops as well. With the arrival of American combat troops in the summer of 1965, Hanoi moved to match the American escalation. First-line units of the North Vietnamese army, one of the great infantries of the world, began to move down the trails, ready to neutralize the American buildup.

In mid-November, 1965, regiments of the North Vietnamese army stumbled into units of the elite First Cav (the new heliborne division). The result was a bloody and ferocious battle in difficult terrain, which came to be known as the battle of the Ia Drang Valley. It was the first real testing of American men and arms in Vietnam. Official American estimates were that 1,200 of the enemy had been killed, against 200 American losses. To General Westmoreland and his deputy, General William Depuy, it was viewed as a considerable victory. It was a battle which encouraged the American military in its concept that the aggressive use of American force and strike power against the enemy in his distant base-camps could eventually destroy his forces and his will. General Depuy kept talking about the threshold of pain. It was something he believed in, that the enemy had a threshold, and that if we hit him hard enough he would cry out; at this very point, in fact, the North Vietnamese were testing out *our* threshold of pain. They would find that ours was a good deal lower than theirs, that we could not accept heavy casualties as they could. Thus Ia Drang was in a way a kind of closing of the door as far as strategy was concerned. We were convinced that we had dealt the other side a grievous blow and we were now ready to deal him more.

But the battle of Ia Drang had proven beyond doubt one other factor. It had shown graphically that Hanoi would resist the American escalation with an escalation of its own. In the past, despite the prophecies of the intelligence community, the likelihood that North Vietnamese troops would come into the South had been played down. But by the early fall it was clear that Hanoi was taking its regular units, breaking them down into small sizes, and infiltrating them quickly into the South. In July, 1965, when the Americans had decided to send a total of between 175,000 and 200,000 combat troops to Vietnam by the end of the year (with an additional 100,000 ticketed for 1966), the estimate had been that there were still no more than two NVA regiments in the South; by November there were six confirmed North Vietnamese regiments. The bombing, as a weapon of interdiction, had failed. As for affecting Hanoi's will, the bombing and the arrival of American troops had affected it, but not the way the American principals had anticipated. Hanoi was now determined to send men down even more quickly than the Americans could bring theirs in. The American buildup would reach 400,000 by the end of 1965. It was clearly not going to be a short, limited war.

For those who had expected the other side to oblige by folding quickly, the contrary evidence was now in. For McNamara, the new implications were quite obvious. Since he knew there was no easy way out, he had become a frustrated and divided man. As a weapon of interdiction the bombing had failed, and as a weapon to push Hanoi to the table it had failed; yet he had no other answers and had to recommend a steadily ascending rate of bombing—the rate of sorties went up from 2,500 a month to 10,000 a month in the next year, all of it futile. While he was negotiating with Westmoreland for more and more troops, though he sensed the hopelessness of the troop escalation, he was at the same time becoming a leading advocate of negotiations within the government. But even now he could not speak openly about what he really felt, how dark he thought it might all be; he could not lose credibility and say that he had miscalculated, that all his forecasts were wrong. That would cost him his credibility; he would be known as a dove and he would soon be out. So when he pushed for negotiations at the tail end of 1965, he sold it in a particularly disingenuous way—we could have a bombing pause and try to negotiate, and then, after we had shown that the other side was unwilling to be conciliatory, we would have far greater national support. Worse, because he was committed to force and to the war, he could only offer Hanoi what amounted to surrender. So he was pushing doomed negotiations on hopeless terms, and in the very effort to bring about negotiations, he was diminishing his credibility with the President.

So McNamara was boxed in, seeing the darkness, recommending more troops as a means of bringing negotiations which were, given the United States' attitude, hopeless. The real point of it all was that the civilians in Washington, those men who above all else felt they controlled events, had, by the end of 1965, completely lost control. They no longer determined policies, and they did not even know it. One set of reins belonged to Hanoi, the other set to Westmoreland. The future increments were now being determined in Hanoi by the Politburo there, and in Saigon by Westmoreland and his staff. If Westmoreland had enough troops, then Hanoi would send more; if Hanoi sent more, then Westmoreland would want more. The cycle was out of their hands; nor had they set any real limits on Westmoreland as far as his use of troops in-country was concerned. He was the general, he would use them as he saw fit. His projections were for a long war, larger and larger units fighting, a higher and higher rate of combat, the enemy eventually becoming exhausted. But the Commander in Chief of the enemy forces did not have to run for re-election in 1968.

The strategy of attrition would prove politically deadly for Lyndon Johnson, and yet he had slipped into it. He and the men around him did not spend weeks of painful debate measuring both our and the enemy's resources, deciding on the best way to commit American troops, how to get the most for our men. There was in fact remarkably little discussion of the strategy. It had begun as security, had gone to enclave, and then, without the enclave ever being tested, under the pressure of events, they had gone to what would be search and destroy. It was again an almost blind decision to go with the man on the spot, Westmoreland. It was what he wanted, it was what he would get, and so to an extraordinary degree Westmoreland received in-country (as opposed to hitting Cambodian sanctuaries) freedom to maneuver his troops. They were his, to do with whatever he wanted. And out of this came search and destroy, as well as the policy of attrition, a policy which would become one of the most controversial and fiercely debated decisions of the war, a decision that was virtually not even a decision, it was, like so much of the war, simply something that happened. It was Westmoreland's instincts for the use of power, to use it massively and conventionally, and this with Depuy's aid had produced the policy of search and destroy. Westmoreland was after all a conventional man; his background was conventional war, and both his instincts and responses were conventional. Here, almost within sight—his intelligence was getting better and better—were these very big enemy units. The ideal way to shorten this war, to finish it off quickly, was to go after the big units, this enormous prize just within reach. Just smash their big units, teach them it was all over, and they would have to go to the peace table. Westmoreland knew all about the political infrastructure, how the enemy operated through a very clever and complicated political mechanism, and that this was the root of the war; it gave the other side its most precious asset, its capacity to replenish losses, but the conventional instinct, the temptation to go after the big units was too much. It was, he thought, the best thing he could do for Vietnam, handle this burden for them which they clearly were not able to handle themselves. The U.S. forces would be fighting away from the population, and this would lessen racial tension. It was a strategy which appealed to the American

470

military mind, the use of large force and large units, quicker, less frustrating. He was always particularly optimistic about the results of the operations in the base-camp areas, Cedar Falls and Junction City; to him they presaged victory, and it was the sad truth that he, like those before him, underestimated the capacity of the enemy to replenish.

So instead of a limited shield philosophy, we would take over the war. And out of this, the search-and-destroy policy, came the policy of attrition which would prove so costly to Lyndon Johnson. The political implications of such a policy were immense, but he did not think them out, nor did his Secretary of State Dean Rusk nor his Special Assistant for National Security, Mac Bundy. It was perhaps the worst possible policy for the United States of America: it meant inflicting attrition upon the North, which had merely to send 100,000 soldiers south each year to neutralize the American fighting machine. Since the birth rate for the North was particularly high, with between 200,000 young men coming into the draft-age group each year, it was very easy for them to replenish their own manpower (the attrition strategy might have made sense if you could have gone for the whole package, applied total military pressure to the entire country, but the American strategy was filled with limitations as far as that went). So even on the birth rate, the strategy of attrition (which was always based on the belief that the other side had a lower threshold of pain) was fallacious. Add to it the fact that one side was a nation with the nationalist element of unity, and Communist element of control, that the bombing helped unite its people, that its leadership was able and popular, that its people were lean and tough and *believed* in their mission, which was to unify the country and drive the foreigners out, that there were no free newspapers, no congressional dissent, and that this war was not only the top priority, it was the only priority they had.

Against this was a democracy fighting a dubious war some 12,000 miles away from home. The democracy had long overdue social and political programs at home, and there was such uneasiness about a war in Asia that its political leader felt obliged to sneak the country into the war, rather than confronting the Congress and press openly with his decision. The Congress and the press would continue to be free, and doubts about so complicated a war would not subside, they would grow. Television would certainly bring the war home for the first time. The country was undergoing vast political and social changes which would be accelerated by the war itself.

It was, in retrospect, an unlikely match for a war of attrition, and reflecting upon it, one high civilian said later that he longed to take the two men most involved in the strategy, who had such vastly different and conflicting problems and demands, and introduce them to each other; General Westmoreland, meet President Johnson. It was, finally, the problem of limited war which had been so fashionable in the early Kennedy days, the difficulty being that you might be a great power of 200 million people fighting limited war against a very small Asian nation of 17 million, except that unlike you, they decided, as happened in this case, to fight *total* war.

The Administration's policy of hiding the extent of the war, and the extent of its forthcoming commitments, was still successful in early 1966. It was not, as far as the general public was concerned, going to be a large war. The troop figure was consistently hedged so that opponents of the war did not have a firm target. The burden was still seen as being on Hanoi; we were only trying to get them to a conference table. By the time the general public realized the extent of the war, the depth and totality of it all, then the rationale in Washington would change, it would become support of our boys out there. At first the critics were told that they should not be critics because it was not really going to be a war and it would be brief, anyway; then, when it became clear that it was a war, they were told not to be critics because it hurt our boys and helped the other side.

All of which would work for a while. Johnson had successfully co-opted the Congress and to a large degree the press. Time was working against him, but this would only be clear later. In the spring of 1965 the protests against Vietnam had begun on the campuses. In the beginning the Administration was not particularly worried about the challenge; Johnson controlled the vital center, and the campuses were not considered major centers of political activity. Yet these questions should be answered, so Mac Bundy was sent off to a televised teach-in to debate the professors, and the Administration was supremely confident about the outcome. Bundy was at the height of his reputation, the unchallenged political intellectual of Washington, and no one there dared challenge him, for the response would be swift and sharp. But the capital was not the country; what was admired, respected, and feared in Washington was not necessarily what was edmired, respected, and feared in the country, so the teach-in was an omen. In a surprisingly brittle performance he debated Hans Morgenthau, and Edmund Club, one of the exiled China scholars. Club quoted Lord Salisbury on the dangers of adding to a failed policy. Bundy finally Seemed to be saying: We are we, we are here, we hold power, and we know more about it than you do. It was not a convincing performance; rather than easing doubts, it seemed to reveal the frailty of the Administration's policy. The teach-in did not end debate, it encouraged it. It also marked the beginning of the turn in Bundy's reputation; up until then, serious laymen in the country had heard how bright he was, but in this rare public appearance he struck them as merely arrogant and shallow.

In the fall of 1965 Rusk, who had been less than eager for the commitment than most of the others, began to show signs of the toughness, and indeed rigidity, which would later, as the months and years passed, distinguish him from some of the other architects. He was not eager to seek negotiations, and he was uneasy with those on our side who seemed too anxious to talk, afraid they would send the wrong signal, show the Communists our eagerness and our weakness. He felt that the danger in a democracy was that people were spoiled and expected pleasures and were unused to sacrifice, one had to guard against that and he of course would be the guardian. When Adlai Stevenson in 1964 had made his first tentative approach about negotiating with Hanoi to U Thant, it was Rusk who helped keep the discussion of the peace move limited (so limited that his deputy for Asia, Bill Bundy, did not learn of it until the very last moment and was extremely upset). Then, in December 1965, when McNamara began to push for a bombing pause, it was Rusk who was dubious. We should not, he thought, seem too eager for peace; since we had gone to war, we should use our force of arms properly and the other side would have to come to terms with us. A nation as great and as powerful as the United States did not seek war, did not go to war readily, but if it did, then it must be careful not to give away its goals, undermine its own military. There was a consistency to Rusk: he had been the least eager to get in because he had never seen the task as easy, and had few illusions about air power and the quick use of force. In fact, his positions from start to finish, right through to Tet, were remarkably similar to those of the Army generals. His view of the war was a serious one; if we went in we had to be prepared for a long haul, and we had better be ready for it; we had better not flash the wrong signals as soon as we started.

Rusk believed in mutual security, that this was the way to peace; South Vietnam was now linked to mutual security. Thus it must stand; Vietnam had an importance far beyond its own existence. The doubts of the men under him in State did not penetrate his confidence; he was sure of what Americans had to do and sure that they could do it. More than anyone else, more than the military people themselves, he believed what the military said they could do; he took their reports and their estimates perilously close to face value. He told the men under him at State that their job was to wait and watch for the signals from Hanoi, which would give the signal, not the united States. When the signals came, it would be a sign that they were ready to begin; then and only then State's job would begin. "You look for that signal and you tell me when they give it," he told aides. His fault, a deputy thought, was not insincerity, it was the totality of his sincerity. He still believed that the world was the way he had found it as a young man in the thirties, and that good was on our side. Automatically. Because we were a democracy.

His job and State's, then, was to wait. If you were in, you were in. What was it he had told McNamara at the time of the B-52 raids? In for a dime, in for a dollar. So we were in for more than a dollar. And he was different from those around him because they were such rationalists and such optimists, wheras Rusk was always less optimistic, less the rationalist; the others believed that if things did not pan out, they could always turn them around, since they were in control. This was one other reason Rusk was different—he knew his man better.

There were many Lyndon Johnsons, this complicated, difficult, sensitive man, and among them was a Johnson when things were going well and a Johnson when things were going poorly. Most of the Kennedy men, new to him, working with him since Dallas, had only seen Johnson at his best. Moving into the postassassination vacuum with a certain majesty, he had behaved with sensitivity and subtlety, and that challenge had evoked from him the very best of his qualities. Similarly, during the planning on Vietnam, during the time he had been, as a new President, faced with this most terrible dilemma, he had been cautious and reflective. If there was bluster it was largely bluster on the outside; on the inside he was careful, thoughtful, did his homework, and could under certain conditions be reasoned with.

But when things went badly, he did not respond that well, and he did not, to the men around him, seem so reasonable. There would be a steady exodus from the White House during 1966 and 1967 of many of the men, both hawks and doves, who had tried to reason with him and tried to affect him on Vietnam (in May, 1967, McNamara's trusted deputy, John McNaughton, wrote in a memo to McNamara: "I fear that 'natural selection' in this environment will lead the Administration itself to become more and more homogenized—Mac Bundy, George Ball, Bill Moyers are gone. Who next?" The answer, of course, was McNamara himself.). In the late fall of 1965 Johnson learned the hard way that the slide rules and the computers did not work, that the projections were all wrong, that Vietnam was in fact a tar baby and that he was in for a long difficult haul—his commander and Secretary of Defense were projecting 600,000 men by the end of 1967, and even so, as 1968 rolled around, no guarantees. At that time Lyndon Johnson began to change. He began to sulk, he was not so open, not so accessible, and it was not so easy to talk with him about the problems and difficulties involved in Vietnam. McNamara's access was in direct proportion to his optimism; as he became more pessimistic, the President became reluctant to see him alone. Johnson did not need other people's problems and murky forecasts; he had enough of those himself. What he needed was their support and their loyalty. He was, sadly, open minded when things went well, and increasingly close minded when things went poorly, as they now were about to do. In the past, during all those long agonizing hours in 1964 and 1965 when they discussed the problems of Vietnam, they had all been reasonable men discussing reasonable solutions, and in their assumptions was the idea that Ho Chi Minh was reasonable too. But now it would turn out that Ho was not reasonable, not by American terms, anyway, and the war was not reasonable, and suddenly Lyndon Johnson was not very reasonable either. He was a good enough politician to know what had gone wrong and what it meant to his dreams, but he could not turn back, he could not admit that he had made a mistake. *He could not lose* and thus he had to plunge forward. It was a terrible thing, he was caught and he knew it, and he knew he could juggle the figures only so long before the things he knew became obvious to the public at large. The more he realized this, the more he had to keep it in, keep it hidden, knowing that if he ever evinced doubts himself, if he admitted the truth to himself, it would somehow become reality and those around him would also know, and then he would have to follow through on his convictions. There were rare moments when he would admit the truth. Then he would talk with some fatalism about the trap he had built for himself, with an almost plaintive cry for some sort of help. But these moments were rare indeed, very private, and more often than not they would soon be replaced by wild rages against any critic who might voice the most gentle doubt of the policy and the direction in which it was taking the country.

So instead of leading, he was immobilized, surrounded, seeing critics everywhere. Critics became enemies; enemies became traitors; and the press, which earlier had been so friendly, was now filled with enemies baying at his heels. The Senate was beginning to rise up; he knew that and he knew why—it was that damn Fulbright. He knew what Fulbright was up to, he said; even a blind hog can find an acorn once in a while. So by early 1966, attitudes in the White House had become frozen. One could stay viable only by proclaiming faith and swallowing doubts. The price was high; it was very hard to bring doubts and reality to Johnson without losing access. The reasonable had become unreasonable; the rational, irrational. The deeper we were in, the more the outcry in the country, in the Senate, and in the press, the more Johnson hunkered down, isolated himself from reality. What had begun as a credibility gap became something far more perilous, a reality gap. He had a sense that everything he had wanted for his domestic program, his offering to history, was slipping away, and the knowledge of this made him angrier and touchier than ever.

He also took a negative view of negotiations; negotiations meant defeat. He had not been particularly eager for the first bombing pause in late 1965, and the results, in his mind, had justified his doubts (one reason he would turn to Clark Clifford to replace the doubting and disintegrating McNamara in late 1967 was that Clifford had seemingly shown his hawkish credentials by opposing the bombing halt in 1965). Nothing but a propaganda benefit for the other side, nothing but more pressure against him, making it harder and harder to renew the bombing. So in the future when there was talk of other bombing halts, he would react with anger and irritation. Oh yes, a bombing halt, he would say, I'll tell you what happens when there's a bombing halt: I halt and then Ho Chi Minh shoves his trucks right up my ass. That's your bombing halt.

So he was entrapped, and if he was not the same man, then the men around him were not the same men either. In early 1966 Bundy was very uneasy with Johnson. Their relationship, which had never been a natural one, had deteriorated. Bundy was upset by Johnson's disorderly way of running things, by his tendency—when Kennedy would have let Bundy lock up an issue—to turn, after all the normal players had made their case, to people like Fortas and Clifford for last-minute consultation, and though Bundy had been an advocate of escalation, he was enough of a rationalist to understand immediately that Hanoi's counterescalation meant that events were likely to be messy and irrational. And he knew that with Rusk there, the chance of State was now slim. On Johnson's part there was a feeling that Bundy was somehow, no matter how hard he tried to control it, supercilious ("A smart kid, that's all," Johnson later said of him), plus a gnawing belief that when things went well in foreign affairs the credit would be given to Bundy, and when things went poorly they would be blamed on Johnson. In March, 1966, when Bundy was offered the job as president of the Ford Foundation, James Reston at the *Times* found out about it. Bundy, knowing Johnson and fearing his response if there was a story in the *Times*, pleaded with Reston not to run it. The news item was printed and soon there was a story out of Austin, leaked there, that Bundy was indeed accepting, going to Ford. A few weeks later, at a reception in the White House for young White House fellows, Lady Bird Johnson approached a young man and asked him to tell her what his job was.

"Well, I don't really know," he said. "I used to work for McGeorge Bundy, but now I don't know."

"Oh," said Lady Bird, "Lyndon and I are so sorry about Mac's going. We're going to miss Mac like a big front tooth."

If Bundy had doubts about Vietnam, and friends thought that in 1966 and 1967 increasingly he did, then they remained interior ones. Johnson, letting Bundy go, knew that he would not become a critic, that he would be available for any and all errands, that he was anxious enough to return and serve, to play by the rules. Which he did; his doubts were very pragmatic ones, whether Vietnam was worth the time and resources it was absorbing and the division it was creating. Yet they remained closely guarded doubts. There was that quality to him—ferocious pride, belief in self, inability to admit mistakes that kept him from being able to react to the war in a human sense. It was as if the greater his doubts the more he had to show that he did not have doubts. In the months after he left office he seemed at his worst—glib, smug, insensitive. In March of 1966, right after he left office, he went on the Today show, a rare public appearance, and as he walked into the NBC studio early in the morning he was met by a young staff aide named Robert Cunniff, who showed him the makeup room, asked him how he wanted his coffee, and told Bundy he would be on in about fifteen minutes. Then, further trying to put Bundy at ease, realizing that many people are often nervous in television studios, Cunniff tried to make small talk. In some ways it must be a great relief to be out of Washington, Cunniff said, to be away from the terrible decisions involved with Bundy's last job.

"Just what do you mean?" asked Bundy, and there was a small tightening of the mouth.

"Oh," said Cunniff, not realizing what he was getting into, "you know, you must be relieved, getting away from the terrible pressures of the war, making decisions on it."

"Oh, yes," said Bundy, "you people up here in New York take that all very seriously, don't you?"

And Cunniff, who was stunned by the answer, looked quickly to see if it was a put-on, but the face was very cold, and Cunniff realized that McGeorge Bundy was not joking.

There was no dearth of applicants for the Bundy job. Robert Komer, a Bundy assistant, deemed himself available and moved his things into Bundy's office. Bill Moyers, anxious to have experience in foreign affairs, was a quiet candidate, knowing the President well, and knowing that you did not necessarily get what you pushed for with Lyndon Johnson. And then there was the possibility of Walt Rostow, Bundy's former deputy and now the head of Policy Planning.

Gradually the emphasis began to shift to Rostow. The key link here was Jack Valenti, the self-conscious, self-made intellectual, feverishly loyal to Johnson, desperately anxious to improve Johnson's public image (and naturally, with his sycophancy, detracting from it). Valenti, with his desire to improve Johnson's intellectual reputation, was impressed by Rostow, with his enthusiasm, his endless number of theories for almost any subject and situation. But even more comforting was his upbeat spirit, his sheer enthusiasm for the President and his policies, particularly the war policies. Rostow had started giving memos for the President to Valenti; Johnson was impressed and encouraged them, and the two got on well together.

One thing in Rostow's favor was his enthusiasm for the war. At a time when many others were becoming increasingly uneasy about the course of American policies in Vietnam, Rostow was quite the reverse; he did not see failure, he saw inevitable victory. Which was precisely why a good many of his colleagues from Washington and Cambridge began a quiet, discreet campaign against Rostow. As Jack Kennedy had once said somewhat ruefully of Rostow: Walt had ten ideas, nine of which would lead to disaster, but one of them was worth having. So phone calls were made, doubts about him expressed, enthusiasm for others emphasized. But, if anything, it enhanced Rostow's chances. If some of the Kennedy insiders were against him, this was not necessarily a demerit; his loyalty was more likely to be first and foremost to Lyndon Johnson. When Rostow got the job,

Johnson told one Kennedy intimate, "I'm getting Walt Rostow as my intellectual. He's not your intellectual. He's not Bundy's intellectual. He's not Galbraith's intellectual. He's going to be *my* goddamn intellectual and I'm going to have him by the short hairs."

So it was that Walt Rostow moved to the White House and for the second time became a major figure on Vietnam. In the past he had been an advocate and an enthusiast of the war, but he had not been taken altogether seriously. Now he was to move into an important role, the man who was the Special Adviser to the President on National Security, who screened what the President heard and whom he saw, and who gave a special tonal quality to incoming information, an emphasis here, a de-emphasis there. To a President coming increasingly under attack, he was strong and supportive, someone whose own enthusiasm never wavered, who could always find the positive point in the darkest of days. Thus as the policy came under increasing challenge in 1966 and 1967, Rostow helped hold the line; as the President became increasingly isolated, Rostow isolated him more. He was firm and steadfast, and helped load the dice in 1966 and 1967 and 1968 against members of the inner circle having their own doubts. To a Johnson isolated and under attack, Rostow was, said one of his aides, "like Rasputin to a tsar under siege."

In a way George Ball had been counting on the 1966 off-year elections to help him make his case and turn back the American commitment. By mid-1965 he realized he had lost the first part of his battle; from then on he changed tactics. He moved to a fall-back position—to limit the involvement, to hold the line as much as possible, to keep the United States from any miscalculation which would bring in the Chinese. The latter tactic proved particularly effective with Rusk, but it also hurt Ball in the long run. Some of his warnings about Chinese entry (that prolonged bombing of the North would lead to war with Peking in six to nine months) proved false. He was opposing the war, yet kept his legitimacy inside, and he was playing what was essentially a delicate game. He wanted to dissent on the war without provoking emotional resentment on the part of the President or on the part of Rusk. Yet he wanted to make his opposition clear enough to the President, so that if Johnson needed to change Cabinet officers after the midterm election, Ball would be the clear choice. To George Ball, good policies and good politics went together.

He thought that the signs of the war as a major miscalculation would be obvious by mid-1966, and that it would be self-evident that we were bogged down there. Thus the President, in order to prepare himself for the 1968 elections, would have to cut back on Vietnam and rid himself of its architects, which would mean the likely promotion of Ball. He told friends that he thought the President might lose between forty and fifty seats in the 1966 election, largely because of Vietnam. On this judgment Ball was premature. In the fall of 1966 American troops were still arriving, it did not seem like a war where half a million Americans would be involved unsuccessfully, and there was still a general confidence that the war was winnable. The Administration's credibility—that is, its version of the war—had not yet been shattered. The 1966 election results did not show any resentment against the war, and Ball's dissent was premature. Whether, in fact, it might have changed Johnson, even if there had been evidence of dwindling public support, is debatable. Perhaps even with the loss of forty seats, Johnson might have hunkered down just a bit more.

So Ball eventually slipped out of the Administration on September 30, 1966, to be replaced by Nicholas Katzenbach (a typical Johnson move; Johnson wanted Katzenbach out of Justice so he could place Ramsey Clark there, and by moving Katzenbach to the number-two job at State, he was hopefully tying up Robert Kennedy just a little bit more. Thus when in 1967 Robert Kennedy came back from Paris, having possibly heard of a peace feeler there, Johnson could tell Kennedy, critical of State, that it was *Kennedy's* State Department). Later after Ball left, friends like Galbraith and Schlesinger talked with him about using his departure as something of a protest against the policies and the direction. But Ball shrugged it off; a resignation would be a gesture of singular futility in this case, he said, particularly with this President. It would mean a one-day splash in the newspapers, one headline perhaps, and then business as usual, with the President just a little more antagonistic than before to their common viewpoint.

Of the original architects, only one man was undergoing great change, and yet continued to stay in the government to fight for his newer definition of reality—though in a deeply compromised way—and that was Robert McNamara. In a way McNamara was better prepared for the new darkness, since John McNaughton had been preparing him for more than a year on the likelihood of the North Vietnamese responding and stalemating the Americans. The NVA buildup in the South had proven to McNamara, first, that the other side would respond despite the pressure of bombing, and second, that the bombing was hardly an effective way of stopping infiltration. Even as he was feeding men and materiel into the pipelines, he doubted more and more their effectiveness, and he was becoming in effect a critic of his own role. If he had had doubts about the bombing by January, 1966, they would grow even more during the next few months in the controversy over the bombing of Hanoi and Haiphong's petroleum reserves and oil-storage facilities. The Chiefs, increasingly frustrated with the limits placed on them by the civilians, had been pushing for these targets for some time, and wanted them included in the May bombing lists. Now they had a new and powerful advocate within the White House in Rostow.

The President gave the okay, and on June 29 the strikes were launched. At first it appeared that the raids were extraordinarily successful, with all of the Hanoi storage and eighty percent of the Haiphong facility destroyed. McNamara had gone along with the POL [petroleum, oil, and lubricants] raids; it was the last major escalation that he recommended. What became clear in the months that followed was that the air campaign against POL, although seemingly successful, had, like the previous bombing campaigns, failed. The North Vietnamese had learned to adjust to American power, and dispersed their reserves to areas invulnerable to American attack. So at an extremely high cost in American men and planes, we destroyed the surface storage while the North Vietnamese were able to pressure the Soviets into larger and larger petroleum commitments. For McNamara, it helped seal his doubts; he would begin to work to limit bombing. But he was a dissenter operating under considerable limits. For one thing, Rusk was not given to the same doubts, and thus the Secretary of State was to the right of him. In addition, if he was fighting from within, he was accepting the assumptions of his opponents, fighting them on a tactical level, not on a deeper one. This made him particularly vulnerable to the counter proposals of Westmoreland and the Chiefs. He began to give up combat troops to hold down on the bombings, so it would not be too obvious within the government that he was a dove. As such, his half measures always failed.

In October, 1966, with the military asking for troop increases which would bring the American commitment to a minimum of 570,000 troops, McNamara went to Saigon again. This time his sense of pessimism was very real; he was convinced that the other side would match us, that in effect Hanoi was now waging its own special kind of attrition, psychological attrition, against us, slowing down the pace of the war slightly, believing that time was on their side. He was affected considerably by reports by one of his own people there, Daniel Ellsberg, whose own gloom was growing and who told McNamara that most of the official optimism was false. On the way back to Washington, McNamara talked with aides about the developments, and he seemed very down. Things were, he said, worse than a year before. With him was Robert Komer, once the White House aide who had been sent to Vietnam by Johnson to head pacification, a man constantly enthusiastic and upbeat. Komer disagreed with McNamara and insisted that the war was certainly no worse than a year before. McNamara asked Ellsberg whether it was better or worse than a year before. "Pretty much the same," Ellsberg answered.

"You see," said Komer, "at least it's no worse."

"But it is worse," insisted McNamara, "because if things are the same, then they're worse, because we've invested so much more of our resources." (On that same plane ride, McNamara asked Ellsberg for an extra copy of his report, entitled "Visit to an Insecure Province," and then asked him, in the interests of not straining civilian-military relationships, if he would mind *not* showing it to General Earle Wheeler.)

McNamara began to be increasingly appalled by the war itself, what we were doing with our power, the pain inflicted on the civilians. He paid particular attention to stories about the destruction caused by the bombing. When Harrison Salisbury of the *Times* visited Hanoi at the end of 1966, his articles were violently attacked by the Administration, particularly Defense Department spokesmen, but McNamara was fascinated by them and followed them closely. He and Robert Kennedy had remained close friends, and in 1966 they began to feed each other's dissent, McNamara confirming to Kennedy that the war was not going well, Kennedy confirming McNamara's impressions of what the war was doing to this country. He was an intriguing man in this period; almost as if there were a split personality caught between two loyalties, and more, caught between two eras. In those days he could still be part of the planning of the bombing, but be a very different man in the evening, going to dinner parties, raising a glass to someone like Moyers with the toast "Bless the doves—we need more of them." He was able to head the war machine, give the Montreal speech, and then regret giving it. It was as if there was a Kennedy-McNamara who said one thing to Kennedy-type people, and a Johnson-McNamara who said another to Johnson-type people. He was able to come back in October, 1966, and report to Johnson that things did not look good in Vietnam ("I see no reasonable way to bring the war to an end soon"), commenting on how tough and resilient the enemy was, and then conclude that the United States should press on harder militarily and get into a better military position, which would make a war of long duration less attractive to the enemy. The word swept through Washington about his unhappiness; some thought he was being disloyal to Johnson, others began to think he was coming apart. In late 1966 he ran into Emmett Hughes of *Newsweek*, who had just written a hand-wringing piece on Vietnam, and McNamara was very sympathetic about the piece, it certainly wasn't a good situation, was it? "I never thought it would go on like this. I didn't think these people had the capacity to fight this way. If I had thought they could take this punishment and fight this well, could enjoy fighting like this, I would have thought differently at the start. . . ."

In despair and frustration over the war, in 1967 he ordered a massive study of all the papers on Vietnam, going back to the 1940's, a study which became known as the Pentagon Papers. When it was handed in he read parts of it. "You know," he told a friend, "they could hang people for what's in there." His own behavior seemed increasingly erratic as the pressures on him mounted, and close friends worried about his health. In 1967 when there was a possibility of peace negotiations being worked out through the British, Kosygin was in London and a bombing pause had gone into effect. Acting on his talks with the British, Ambassador David Bruce recommended strongly that we not resume the bombing until Kosygin had left London. Bruce pleaded to State that if it valued the alliance at all, it must observe the British request. Rusk, a great chain-of-command man, accepted the Bruce thesis and pushed it. McNamara argued forcefully against it and tore into it at the meetings, but Bruce and Rusk held the day. A few minutes after the last discussion, McNamara was on the phone to Bruce, congratulating him on his victory, how well he had presented his case, and how proud McNamara was of him. At first Bruce was touched by McNamara's warmth and courtesy, but later he was appalled when he learned that McNamara had been his principal adversary, and the story spread through both American and British diplomatic circles in London.

If by 1966, and increasingly in 1967, McNamara was beginning to move away from the policy, then Rusk was, if anything, more steadfast than ever. He not only believed in the policy, he had a sense of profound Constitutional consequences if the President, already at loggerheads with one of his chief advisers, was separated from the other. If Rusk too dissented, if that gossipy town even thought he was a critic, then in Rusk's opinion the country would be in a Constitutional crisis. There must be no blue sky between the President and the Secretary of State, he told aides. Besides, he believed the war could and should be won. So he became a rock, unflinching and unchanging, and absorbing, as deliberately as he could, as much of the reaction to the war as possible. The abuse he took was enormous; he who had been the least anxious of the principal advisers to become involved but who had never argued against it, now became the public symbol of it, a target of public scorn, his statements mocked, so that he would once say in exasperation that he was not the village idiot. He knew that Ho was not Hitler, but nonetheless, there was an obligation to stand. In a pay-phone booth in his own State Department someone in 1967 scratched the graffito: "Dean Rusk is a recorded announcement." As he became a rock, so his own Department was immobilized; the best people in State, increasingly unhappy about the policy, felt they could make no challenge to it.

For Rusk, the job of the Secretary of State seemed to be to absorb pain. That and nothing more. Though there was much to challenge the military on—particularly the political mindlessness of the attrition strategy—State's challenges were few, infrequent, mild, and usually on minor matters. Occasionally there would be quick flashes of the hurt, as when he talked about the journalists who covered the war —which side were they on, were they for their country or against it? Years later, when the ordeal was over, he would tell friends that he did not know how he had lasted through it—if he had not been able to have that drink at the end of the day he could not have survived. There were moments when he did not conceal the anger and the rage, though they were few. Tom Wicker of the *Times* was at a dinner party with Rusk at the Algerian embassy one night in 1966 at a time when there had been a Buddhist crisis in Hué, when suddenly Rusk turned to him and started screaming—there was no other word for it—Why can't *The New York Times* get things right? Why does it always print lies? Which side is it on? Wicker, whose own relations with Rusk had always been pleasant, was stunned by the anger and ferocity of the attack, and it was minutes before he could even understand what Rusk was talking about—a report in the *Times* that day saying that Buddhist dissidents had taken over the Hué radio station. Rusk had read the story and had been so upset by it that he had personally called the American consulate in Hué where of course the American officials had denied the report, and on the basis of this he had proceeded to lecture Wicker on the perfidy of American journalism. The entire episode, particularly the sudden savagery of Rusk's attack—after all, it is not fun to be assaulted by the Secretary of State of the United States of America over coffee and cognac—stayed with Wicker, and six months later when he was in Vietnam, he dropped by the American consulate in Hué and asked a young man on the staff there about the Buddhist crisis. Oh yes, said the young man, the Buddhists had captured the radio station, and Wicker, thinking of Rusk and his obvious sincerity, had decided then that the real problem was that they had created an elaborate machine to lie to them, only to become prisoners of their own lies.

But generally Rusk bore the brunt of it well. He did not complain. He was a proud man and at times it semed as if he took sustenance from the criticism. In the great clubs of New York and Washington his old friends, his sponsors, men like Lovett and McCloy, were worried about Dean being the target of all the nation's anger. One day McCloy stopped Lovett and said that he wished Dean would fight back, answer his critics or yell for help—they would like to get in the fight and help him. But Lovett, who knew Rusk well, said that Dean would never do that, he was too proud. Yet proud or not, at the end the taste, which should have been so good—eight years at the job that he and every other serious young man coveted—was sour, and he was exhausted financially, physically, and spiritually. At the small farewell party for him given by some State Department reporters, the atmosphere was suitably pleasant; these men who had covered Rusk for that long recognized in him qualities of grace, decency, and modesty which were not always obvious from a distance. And Rusk, who had always held together so well, finally broke. He went over to British correspondent Louis Heren and asked why the British had not sent any troops to Vietnam. Rusk knew of course well enough, as they had all known from the start, that this was a war that no one else had wanted, that except for a genuine effort by the Australians and a semimercenary effort by the Koreans, it was virtually a unilateral war. As gently as possible, Heren began to stumble through the usual rationalizations when Rusk, whose own allegiance, whose own lessons of mutual security were derived from England, suddenly cut him off. "All we needed was one regiment. The Black Watch would have done. Just one regiment, but you wouldn't. Well, don't expect us to save you again. They can invade Sussex and we wouldn't do a damn thing about it."

Many of the people around Lyndon Johnson, and many of the people at State had been relatively pleased when Walt Rostow replaced Mc-

George Bundy. In contrast to Bundy's cold, haughty style, Rostow was warm, pleasant, humble, almost angelic, eager to share his enthusiasm, his optimism, with all around. He had time for everyone, he was polite to everyone, there was no element of put-down to him. The real Johnson loyalists were particularly pleased because they had not liked the Bundy-Johnson relationship, and here was Rostow, bearing the same credentials as Bundy, with far more serious books to his credit, a man far more pleasant to work with, and who was joyously, unabashedly pro-Johnson. It was not fake enthusiasm, it was genuine; Johnson had rescued Rostow from the Siberia of Policy Planning, and Rostow was properly grateful, but more important, Rostow genuinely admired Lyndon Johnson. They saw eye to eye on both domestic and foreign affairs, and Rostow thought Johnson the smartest, toughest man he had ever dealt with. As for Johnson, if he had liked about Bill Bundy his willingness to run it in up to the hilt, then Rostow was a man after his own heart.

But the enthusiasm of others for Rostow soon floundered on Rostow's own enthusiasm. He became the President's national security adviser at a time when criticism and opposition to the war were beginning to crystallize, and he eventually served the purpose of shielding the President from criticism and from reality. He deflected others' pessimism and rewarded those who were optimistic. It was not contrived, it was the way he was. Perhaps, too, it was a symptom of the war. A President in a hopeless war did not need, could not accept a chief adviser wringing his hands, an adviser who seemed to reflect the gathering doubts. Maybe the job required a positive thinker. There was no more positive thinker in Washington than Walt Rostow.

His optimism was almost a physiological thing, organically part of him. He always believed in the war and in particular in the bombing. He believed early in what the bombing would do, that it was something quick and dramatic and that the other side would have to give in. Year after year, as the failure of the bombing became apparent, it did not faze him; just a little more bombing. And enthusiastic himself, he was anxious to pass on his enthusiasm. He could always see the bright side of any situation, and in that sense he became legend. In the thousands of items flooding in from Saigon as part of the information glut, he could find the few positive ones, pounce on them, and bring them to his boss, as for instance one morning in 1967 when he told the President *that never had the Boy Scouts of Vietnam gone out to clean up the rubble as they had just done in Danang.* He made his predictions and nothing bothered him. He could grab Dan

Ellsberg in July, 1965, and excitedly pass on the news about the bombing (which to most experts in the CIA had already proven itself a failure): "Dan, it looks very good. The Vietcong are going to collapse within weeks. Not months but weeks. What we hear is that they're already coming apart under the bombing." They did not come apart in a few weeks, but neither did Rostow, and Ellsberg went off to Vietnam, where for two years he became something of an authority on the failure of the Vietcong to collapse. Two years later, tired, depressed, and thoroughly pessimistic about the lost cause in Vietnam, he returned to Washington, where he found Rostow just as upbeat as ever.

"Dan," said Rostow, "it looks very good. The other side is near collapse. In my opinion, victory is very near."

Ellsberg, sick at heart with this very kind of high-level optimism which contrasted with everything he had seen in the field, turned away from Rostow, saying he just did not want to talk about it.

"No," said Rostow, "you don't understand. Victory is very near. I'll show you the charts. The charts are very good."

"Walt," said Ellsberg, "I don't want to hear it. Victory is not near. Victory is very far away. I've just come back from Vietnam. I've been there for two years. I don't want to talk about it. I don't want to see any charts. . . ."

"But, Dan, the charts are very good. . . ."

With the White House under siege, with increasing evidence that the American military commitment to Vietnam had been stalemated, Rostow fought back. In the White House basements, aides culled through the reams of information coming in from Saigon and picked the items which they knew Rostow was following, particularly the good ones. They would send this material up to Rostow, and he would package it and pass it on to the President, usually with covering notes. The notes were similar—there were little touches of flattery: The record of your success indicates . . . Your place in history will bring you. . . . The theme was the greatness of the cause and the immortality of Lyndon Johnson. And Lyndon Johnson, already isolated because of the war and because of his office, was kept even more remote.

By the nature of his office, a President is separated from his natural constituency and from the art of his profession, politics. The office restricts his movements, his access to events and reality, since few want to bring the President bad news. If a politician is a senator, a friend can sometimes tell him the honest truth in a gentle manner. If he is a President there is no such equality, no way of gently and honestly bearing bad tidings. Respect for the office demands that bad news be filtered down. At first Johnson was isolated involuntarily by the nature of the job, but then as the war progressed, the isolation became voluntary. He saw enemies everywhere. He became a figure of scorn. A scurrilous play, *MacBird*, was written about him and enjoyed remarkable critical success. He became a cartoonists' delight: he bombed Vietnam and wept crocodile tears, and the tears turned out to be maps of Vietnam; he showed his famous abdominal scar, and the scar turned out to be a map of Vietnam.

The liberal intellectual community, crucial to the success of a Democratic liberal President, was turning on him. The first signs had come in 1965 when he gave a major festival of the arts—what he hoped would be an intellectual ratification of his great electoral triumph. Instead it turned out to be an intellectual rejection of his Vietnam policies. Some of the writers and artists invited wanted to boycott, others wanted to come and picket and read protests. "Half of those people," Johnson said, "are trying to insult me by staying away and half of them are trying to insult me by coming." But the art festival was the beginning: rather than crowning his legislative victories, it symbolized the intellectual community's rejection of the war. More radical voices, fueled by the war, came to prominence, and in so doing, moved the traditional liberal intellectual center over to the left. The liberals had to move to the radical position on the war or lose influence. The Fulbright hearings came in early 1966, and further legitimized opposition; gradually opposition became increasingly centrist and respectable. Opposition mounted on the campuses; Norman Mailer in 1966 could dedicate a book of essays to Lyndon Johnson with gratitude for having made Americans cheer at the mention of Mailer's name.

With liberal pressure mounting, with Robert Kennedy making the first uneasy gestures toward opposition, Johnson turned ever more inward. He dared not venture out; isolation begot isolation. Someone like Martin Luther King, Jr., could not be a friend on civil rights and a critic on the war; he became in effect an enemy, he had to be kept away. (Of course the price for those who stayed friendly to Johnson was quite considerable, moving them increasingly away from their own people and their own constituencies. At one Negro meeting in March, 1967, Whitney Young of the Urban League defended the war and ended up in a bitter confrontation with Dr. King; Young told King that his criticism of the war was unwise, it would antagonize the President and they wouldn't get anything from him. King, genuinely angry, told him, "Whitney, what you're saying may get you a foundation grant, but it won't get you into the kingdom of truth.")

The protests turned uglier and more personal, neoviolent, and then violent. Attitudes and passions long concealed by the two-party system were now unleashed. More and more trusted staff people left, including some of Johnson's own people—Reedy, Moyers, and even Valenti. The departure of Moyers in 1966 was considered crucial; though he had been the White House press officer and thus a spokesman for the war, he was known on the inside as a doubter, and he had worked to make other doubters available to the President. When Moyers left, feeling himself locked in by the growing inflexibility around him, James Reston wrote that he was a casualty of the war, that he had been wounded at Credibility Gap. Johnson himself was furious when Moyers left. He hated it when anyone left him, anyway, but Moyers was special, he was the proxy son. Johnson raged after he departed—that boy had been using Johnson all this time, out there having dinner with the Kennedys, advancing his own career. Well, Lyndon Johnson wasn't stupid, he knew what Moyers had been doing, he read the clips, and why was it that his press secretary's image kept getting better and better, but Johnson's image got worse and worse?

As the temper in the country grew uglier, the White House became more of a fortress, and security arrangements became more and more stringent. Johnson, aware of the mood and the criticism of him, the highly personal nature of it, told friends, "The only difference between the Kennedy assassination and mine is that I am alive and it has been more torturous." Inside the fortress, Johnson's aides pleaded with him to go out more, to leave the office; they wrote memos saying that even if demonstrators attacked or humiliated him, it would rebound to his credit, and that it was extremely unwise for him to stay locked up in the White House. But the Secret Service people would have none of it; it was far too dangerous, they said, they had never seen the anger and the instability in the country focused as it was on the Chief Executive. They would not permit it.

Nor could Johnson plead effectively for his war. Wars are supposed to unite nations, to rally divided spirits, and Johnson had counted on this in his private political estimates. But this war was different; rather than concealing or healing normal divisions in the society, it widened them, and gaps became chasms. Johnson could not bring a Medal of Honor winner to the White House for a speech without acerbic editorial reaction. He was boxed in. The pressures now seemed to come from both sides, Westmoreland and CINCPAC asking for more troops and greater bombing targets, the civilians asking for greater controls. Limited war was not limited in the pain and dilemmas it brought to a President. In late 1966 the military began to build up pressure for the bombing of Hanoi and Haiphong, blocking the harbor, taking apart the industrial capacity of both cities. The military brought with it evidence that this way the war would be won quicker; that, though drastic, in the long run this would save lives. Doing the hard thing was often doing the right thing. As a way of dramatizing this last point, one of the senior officers brought along projections for what the invasion of the Japanese mainland might have cost the Americans in lives had we not used the atomic bomb. They even had the figure: 750,000 lives saved. Johnson was fascinated and asked the senior military how they had arrived at the figure. The answer was quite simple, they said: some of their bright young men at the Pentagon had fed the right information from the previous landings and battles into a computer, and thus come up with the figure. The President seemed duly impressed and asked to meet the young men who had made the projection. When they were eventually ushered into his office, the President feigned interest in their methodology for a while and then told them, "I have one more problem for your computer—will you feed into it how long it will take five hundred thousand angry Americans to climb that White House wall out there and lynch their President if he does something like that?" Which ended for a time the plan to bomb Hanoi and Haiphong.

But this did not abate the military pressure, which continued to grow. In April, 1967, with support for the war fast dwindling, he brought General Westmoreland home to speak before the Congress and the Associated Press Managing Editors Convention. But the Westmoreland appearances did not ease the pressures against him; if anything, the criticism of Johnson for using Westmoreland, for bringing the military into politics, mounted. Nor did Westmoreland reassure the President in private messages. At this point Westmoreland had 470,000 Americans, and he was asking for an increase which would bring the total to 680,000 men by June, 1968, or at the very least a minimum increase of about 95,000, to 565,000. But even with this increase his forecasts were not optimistic. Without the top figure, he told Johnson, the war would not be lost, but progress would be slowed down; this, he said, was not encouraging but realistic. Then Westmoreland noted that every time we took an action, the other side made a countermove. At this point the President asked him, "When we add divisions, can't the enemy add divisions? If so, where does it all end?" Westmoreland answered that the NVA had eight divisions in the country and had the capacity to go to twelve, but if they did, the problems of support would be considerable. He did note, however, that if we added more men, so would the enemy. But we had finally reached the crossover point, Westmoreland insisted, a crucial point in his war of attrition: we were killing men more quickly than they could add them. Even so, the President was not entirely put at ease. "At what point does the enemy ask for [Chinese] volunteers?" he asked. Westmoreland answered, "That's a good question."

For Lyndon Johnson, a year away from an election, already besieged, already sensing the growing restlessness in the country, hearing these rather dark predictions of his generals, it was hardly a happy occasion.

Two years too late the civilians were finally learning how open ended they had made the war, and how little they had determined the strategy. It was a special irony that the burden of making the case against the war now fell to the civilians at Defense. Nominally the reaction should have come from the White House, from aides to the President anxious to protect their man from false estimates from the military; or from State, a place supposedly sensitive to the political dilemmas of the war. But Rostow made the White House staff supportive, a hotbed of cheerleaders, and at State, Rusk kept his people from analyzing failures.

But if McNamara had lost the first round to limit or stop the bombings, he had decided to continue fighting. He wanted to win within the bureaucracy because that was the battlefield he knew best. He wanted above all to make the case that the bombing could not win the war, that it was a subsidiary part of it at best, and that the limits were greater than the effectiveness. So he prepared his case. He pushed the CIA very hard for judgments on how effective the bombing had been and received in return what were considered some of the best reports ever done by the Agency. In August, when the Stennis committee, primed by frustrated and unhappy generals, was holding hearings on the air war, McNamara was asked to testify. It was exactly what he wanted. He knew about committee hearings by now, and how to make points and make news. He worked mostly by himself with very few aides right up until the last minute, deliberately not clearing his presentation with the White House, knowing that clearance would not come through.

In testifying, he recognized the impact of what he was doing and saying. He did not attack previous bombing; rather, what he sought was to remove bombing as a means of attaining victory. He knew it would infuriate the President, and it did; afterward he was summoned to the White House to receive a full blast of Presidential anger. It was a rare moment for McNamara; he, the compleat corporate man, had broken the corporate rules, and he had acted as an individual, as a man with his own rights and privileges. In a way he lost; eventually the fifty-seven targets which the JCS wanted and which the Stennis committee had criticized him for not authorizing were cleared by the President with, of course, no appreciable change in the war. But he had written into the record a powerful official argument against the bombing, and this would have greater effect in the coming year. In doing this, he paid the price; he separated himself from the military publicly, and he undermined his long-range usefulness. From then on the President made sure that Earle Wheeler was at the Tuesday lunches. A few months later, the President, wanting to make some minor point on the war to a senator, suggested that the senator go by and see Bob McNamara. And then he caught himself: "No, don't go see Bob—he's gone dovish on me."

But a dovish Secretary of Defense in control of a military empire was a political problem for Johnson. It meant that his own house was divided, almost openly so after the Stennis hearings. By mid-1967 Johnson had turned on McNamara (it was not enough that McNamara's earlier 1965 projections had been wrong—what was worse was that he was now trying to act on a new set of calculations); the President still described his Defense Secretary as brilliant, but there was a new sarcastic touch to it. In mid-1967, when McNamara proposed limiting the bombing, gradually reducing it in scale as a means of getting negotiations started, Johnson took the proposals, handed them to an aide, and said "You've never seen such a lot of shit." Clearly, McNamara was no longer an asset; he was a man caught between conflicting loyalties, and Johnson was aware of his very close relationship with Robert Kennedy. Nineteen sixty-eight being a political year, Lyndon Johnson was not about to enter a campaign with a vital member of his official family publicly dissenting on the most important issue. Without checking with McNamara, Johnson announced in November, 1967, that his Secretary of Defense was going to the World Bank. The move came as a surprise to the Secretary, and he did not know whether or not he had been fired. The answer was that he had been.

The protection of the President in an election year of course had been an unwritten, unspoken goal among his principal aides. Even Westmoreland, in wanting larger troop commitments, had seen it as a way of expediting the war, and thus helping the President. In Saigon in the fall of 1967, Robert Komer, the chief of pacification, bumptious, audacious, anxious to show everyone in town how close he was to the President (six photographs of Lyndon Johnson on his office wall, a Saigon record), had gone around dinner parties telling reporters that he had assured the President that the war would not be an election issue in 1968. It was not one of his better predictions.

The President was in fact extremely exposed. The war had become the one issue of his Presidency; it had burned up not just his credibility but his resources as well. He had initiated the Great Society but never really built it; he had been so preoccupied with handling the war that the precious time and energy needed to change the bureaucracy, to apply the almost daily pressure to make the Great Society work, those qualities were simply not forthcoming. As far as the Great Society was concerned he was a father, but finally an absentee father. Nor had he been a very good practicing politician; he had let the Democratic party disintegrate, had not kept in touch with its principal figures, in part because of lack of time, in part because a genuine rapport might have necessitated listening to their growing doubts about the war. So he was isolated from even moderately loyal politicians. Inflation was rampant, and inflation certainly was not easing racial tensions as the country hurtled through racial change. It made vulnerable blue-collar workers feel even more vulnerable, even more resentful of the increasing protest going on around them. Nor was Johnson's position with blacks solidified; he had pushed more and broader civil rights legislation through the Congress than any President in history, and had endeared himself to a generation of older, middle-class blacks. But that was not a visible thing; what was visible was the potent anger of younger, more militant blacks, restless not only with Johnson's leadership, but with their own traditional black leadership, and they were busy linking the peace movement with what had once been the civil rights movement. The country in late 1967 seemed to be more and more in disarray; protest seemed to beget protest. Lyndon Johnson, who above all loved to control events, even little events, had lost control of the country, and he had immobilized himself on the one issue that might allow him to regain it. In 1963 Paul Kattenburg, the young State Department expert on Vietnam, had returned from Saigon to tell Roger Hilsman that Vietnam was poison, and it would poison everything it touched. Now, four and a half years later, the poison was very deep in the bloodstream.

Part of the frustration and bitterness, of course, was the feeling in the liberal community—the political segment most aggravated and most offended by the war—that it was powerless, that Lyndon Johnson was a liberal Democrat and could not be beaten, that they had no real political alternative. For the mythology lived; one could not unseat the sitting President of his own party. Eventually, however, despite the protests of older liberals (some of whom wanted to fight Johnson only on the platform at the forthcoming convention), younger liberals went looking for a candidate. They had only one choice, they thought, and that was to take the issue to the country and make the challenge to the President within the party. Robert Kennedy was the logical choice, but he was torn by the idea. Part of him wanted to go and was outside the system; part of him was still a traditionalist and believed what his advisers said, that you could not challenge the system. In the end he turned it down. Then they went to George McGovern, who was sympathetic and interested, but he faced a re-election race in South Dakota and that posed a problem. But if no one else would make it, then he told them to come back. So they turned to Gene McCarthy of Minnesota, and he accepted. There comes a time, he told reporters, when an honorable man simply has to raise the flag. "What will you do if elected?" a reporter asked, and borrowing from Eisenhower in 1952, he answered, "I will go to the Pentagon."

But if a Robert Kennedy challenge frightened Johnson, one by Gene McCarthy did not. He did not seem a formidable candidate; he had a reputation for being a little lazy. Johnson saw McCarthy enter the race and viewed it as one more way of demonstrating how frail the left really was.

But even as McCarthy was making his lonely way through the small towns of New Hampshire, North Vietnamese General Vo Nguyen Giap was moving his men down the trails for what would be called the Tet offensive. It began on January 31, 1968. Day after day as the battle continued it became clear that the optimism from Saigon had been premature, that the enemy was tough and durable, that journalistic critics had been more correct in their estimates about the war than the government spokesmen. The Tet offensive destroyed Westmoreland's credibility; what crumbled in Saigon now crumbled in Washington and crumbled in New Hampshire. The people of this country were already sick of the war and dubious of the estimates of the government; reading as they did in early March that the generals in Saigon wanted to send an additional 200,000 men, it seemed to symbolize the hopelessness and endlessness of the war. American politics and the war were finally coming together. In New Hampshire,

Gene McCarthy took more than forty-two percent of the vote, pushed Robert Kennedy into the race, and a race by Kennedy was no longer a joke to the President. It was a serious threat.

Nor was the President entirely in control of his own house. He had purged McNamara because he was no longer on the team and because he was a walking reminder of failure, but McNamara's successor, Clark Clifford, was turning out to be even more difficult. Clifford was the prototype of the rich man's Washington lobbyist, the super-smooth, urbane lawyer who knows where every body is buried, the former high official who works for the government just long enough to know where the weak spots are. To Johnson he seemed a reassuring replacement for the idealistic, tormented McNamara. But Clifford was proving to be a new kind of high official for Lyndon Johnson; whatever else, he was not the corporate man. Instead he had a great sense of his own value and did not believe that anyone hired Clark Clifford except to gain the full benefit of Clark Clifford's services. A great lawyer is paid for telling a rich and powerful client the truth, no matter how unpalatable. (The story is told of Clifford's being called by a company president who explained a complicated problem and then asked for Clifford's advice. Clifford told him not to say or do anything. Then he sent a bill for $10,000. A few days later the president called back protesting the size of the bill, and also asked why he should keep quiet. "Because I told you to," Clifford answered and sent him another bill, for an additional $5,000.) When he took office at Defense he was already bothered by the growing domestic turbulence over the war and his own feeling that perhaps it was indeed hopeless. Also, he had just finished a tour of Asia for the President during which he and Max Taylor worked to drum up additional troops for the war from Asian allies. Their report at the end of the trip had been properly supportive, but Clifford was bothered by the fact that the other Asian nations showed no great interest in sending additional men. Oh yes, they thought standing in Vietnam was a marvelous idea, and they certainly gave us their blessing, but it just so happened that they had very little in the way of resources. The threatened dominoes, Clifford discovered, did not seem to take the threat as seriously as we did. Since he was a man of compelling common sense, this offended his sense of reality and proportion.

In addition, he was privy to the forces that McNamara had unleashed at Defense in the last year and a half, the dovishness now prevalent there. John McNaughton was dead, in an airplane crash, but his replacement, Paul Warnke, was a Washington lawyer with no previous experience in foreign affairs, and thus marvelously irreverent and iconoclastic toward all the myths of the period. He was, in fact, a heretic by the era's standards. (Once asked by a reporter when his own doubts about Vietnam had begun, Warnke said, "At the beginning, in 1961. I could never understand why a smart politician like Jack Kennedy was always talking about being against insurgencies when we should obviously have tried to be for them.") Warnke was more open in dealing with his subordinates than McNaughton had been, and the young civilian Defense intellectuals therefore felt themselves encouraged in their doubts. These were unlikely doves; they were all men who had entered the Defense Department convinced that the world hinged on the great struggle between the United States and the Soviet Union. They had been among the most militant Cold Warriors of the period, but now the evidence in the decade was going the other way, and they were for tempering the arms race and limiting the Pentagon's power. Nor were they professional bureaucrats. Most were men with Ph.D.s who could go back to universities and thus did not feel that their careers depended upon subservience to existing myths. So a curious struggle developed as the battle began over the limits of war: State, which was supposed to set the political limits, had no doubts because of Rusk and neither did the military under the Chiefs, and they became allies against the civilians at Defense. (Daniel Ellsberg symbolized the conversion—or reconversion—of the Defense intellectuals, though of course there were others. But Ellsberg seemed to dramatize the great currents of an era. At Harvard he had seemed at first the normal humanist student; serving as president of the literary magazine, more aesthete than warrior. But he had gone from Harvard to the Marine Corps and had drifted, during the years of the fities, into the world of defense studies and theories, believing that the competition between the United States and the Soviet Union was the key to the survival of all values. He had ended up in Washington in the Kennedy years, one of the brightest stars in John McNaughton's constellation of young intellectuals, and he had done some of the early planning on the war. In 1965 he went on assignment to Vietnam and gradually turned against the war; year by year both his doubts and his outspokenness had grown. In 1969 he publicly criticized President Nixon's policies on Vietnam, statements which expedited his departure from Rand, and which were picked up in *The New York Times.* An old friend named John Smail read in the *Times* of Ellsberg's statements and wrote asking: "Are you the Dan Ellsberg I used to know in college?" Ellsberg answered back, in what was an epitaph for many in that era, "I haven't been for a long time, but I am again.")

The Defense civilians had in the past year turned up increasing evidence on the futility of our commitment. Studies made by systems analysis showed that the bombing did not work, that for much of the war, North Vietnam's GNP had risen at the prewar rate of six percent. If the bombing was failing, so, too, claimed the civilians at Defense, was the strategy of attrition. We had, despite three years of ferocious fighting, barely touched their manpower pool. Defense estimates showed that no more than forty percent of the males between seventeen and thirty-five had served in the army, that more than 200,000 North Vietnamese became of draft age every year, and that only about 100,000 had been sent off to the war. Indeed, their main-force army had grown during the war from 250,000 to about 475,000. The war of attrition had barely touched them; we were not keeping up with their birth rate.

All of this had a profound effect on Clifford. Being a good politician and a Democratic party loyalist (he was the principal architect of Harry Truman's election in 1948, which was one additional reason why Johnson had now chosen him), he also knew the political limits of what was going on. He wanted, friends thought, to turn Johnson around on the war. Perhaps, separated from the war, Johnson could run again. But whatever else, Clark Clifford did not intend to see his own reputation destroyed by either Lyndon Johnson or Vietnam. So in the months of February and March, 1968, as the Tet battle raged, as the Joint Chiefs reopened the old Westmoreland request for 206,000 more troops, Clifford fought ferociously to turn the tide, to limit the number of troops and to reduce the bombing. In that battle he was usually alone. Rusk, Taylor, Bill Bundy, Rostow were no help. Nick Katzenbach, Undersecretary of State, worked quietly to help him, but he was limited with Rusk as his superior. Nor did Clifford find the President receptive or pleased by this lonely struggle. Their relationship, once so warm and easy, turned cool and distant. The President did not seek his advice, and Clifford's phone did not ring. He was even cut off from important cable traffic by the White House in ensuing months. But he posed a special problem: when McNamara had gone soft on the war, that could be ascribed to McNamara's idealism, his distaste for blood, his friendship for the Kennedys. But none of this could be said of Clark Clifford. He was no Kennedy enthusiast, no kook, there was nothing soft about him. Slowly, cautiously, painfully, Clifford forced Johnson to turn and look honestly at the war; it was

497

an act of friendship for which Johnson could never forgive him.

And slowly Clifford found allies. Not men in government so much as men outside it, men who had Johnson's respect. In late March, Johnson summoned his Senior Advisory Group on Vietnam, a blue-chip Establishment group. These were the great names of the Cold War: McCloy, Acheson, Arthur Dean, Mac Bundy, Douglas Dillon, Robert Murphy. And over a period of two days they quietly let him know that the Establishment—yes, Wall Street—had turned on the war; it was hurting us more than it was helping us, it had all gotten out of hand, and it was time to bring it back to proportion. It was hurting the economy, dividing the country, turning the youth against the country's best traditions. Great universities, their universities, were being destroyed. It was time to turn it around, to restore some balance. At one of the briefings of the Wise Men, as they were called, it was Arthur Goldberg, much mocked by some of the others, who almost single handedly destroyed the military demand for 205,000 more troops. The briefing began with the military officer saying that the other side had suffered 45,000 deaths during the Tet offensive.

Goldberg then asked what our own killed-to-wounded ratios were.

Seven to one, the officer answered, because we save a lot of men with helicopters.

What, asked Goldberg, was the enemy strength as of February 1, when Tet started?

Between 160,000 and 175,000, the briefer answered.

What is their killed-to-wounded ratio? Goldberg asked.

We use a figure of three and a half to one, the officer said.

Well, if that's true, then they have no effective forces left in the field, Goldberg said. What followed was a long and very devastating silence.

Acheson had told the President earlier that the Joint Chiefs did not know what they were talking about, and the switch in this group, which was saying in effect that the war had to be de-escalated, had a profound effect on the President. Did they know things he didn't know? He demanded to be briefed by the same three officials who had briefed them on the war. Events, and pressure, it was clear, were closing in. He was cornered now. Even in the last days he had fought off those who wanted to stop the bombing, telling Arthur Goldberg angrily, "Let's get one thing clear. I am not going to stop the bombing. I have heard every argument on the subject and I am not interested in further discussion. I have made up my mind, I am not going to do it." He had in late March given particularly belligerent speeches, but now he was caught and he knew it. The Wise Men were telling him what the polls and the newspapers had told him—that the country had turned on the war.

New Hampshire had not been an isolated test. The next primary was in Wisconsin, and the President was entered there as well. The early reports from Wisconsin were very bad. No workers, no volunteers, no enthusiasm. Cabinet members went to Wisconsin in the President's behalf, and drew small crowds. The President himself could not speak in his own behalf—it was too much of a security problem. The polls were bad and getting worse. One night in mid-March there was a sign which the President, hoping against hope, noticed and which he thought might mean there was some change—an upswing. A meeting in one town seemed jammed and enthusiastic. It was actually a small room, but the way the television camera flashed around it made the hall seem like the Roman Colosseum. The President, watching the meeting, called Larry O'Brien, his political operative, to congratulate him and say that it all looked very good. O'Brien, hearing the enthusiasm and excitement in the President's voice, tones and emotions missing now almost four years, thought Johnson was being a little carried away, so O'Brien cautioned him, "Mr. President, it was a good meeting and we had a few hundred people here, but it was in Clem Zablocki's area and he worked hard and the union people worked hard, but it doesn't mean much. To tell you the truth, we're in real trouble here." Later he would tell Johnson not to expect more than thirty-five percent of the Wisconsin vote, and that it might even be below thirty. Lyndon Johnson knew then that he was beaten. He knew he was locked in; he could not do what he wanted on Vietnam and run for re-election. Rather than absorb one more defeat, he withdrew from the race on the eve of the Wisconsin primary and announced that he was pulling back on the bombing. The war was finally turning around; it was time for de-escalation. For Lyndon Johnson it was all over.

In November, 1968, after the election, a group of executives from a New York publishing firm went to the White House to talk with Walt Rostow about publishing his memoirs. The three were important men from the house, and the prospect of Rostow's book was tempting—big figures were in the air. The meeting was pleasant, and Rostow was very friendly. There was some small talk, some reminiscence about the war and the past, and at one point Rostow mentioned that he did not think that the war had been a factor in the 1968 campaign, and he turned and asked his visitors what they thought. One of them,

James Silberman, said that he could not vouch for other states, but in the state he lived in, New York, it most certainly had been an issue, most likely the decisive issue. Silberman noticed that Rostow immediately changed the subject, and also that he did not direct any more questions his way. In fact, when the meeting broke up a few minutes later, the editors noticed that Rostow shook hands pleasantly with two of them and completely ignored Silberman.

Lyndon Johnson had lost it all, and so had the rest of them; they had, for all their brilliance and hubris and sense of themselves, been unwilling to look to and learn from the past and they had been swept forward by their belief in the importance of anti-Communism (and the dangers of not paying sufficient homage to it) and by the sense of power and glory, omnipotence and omniscience of America in this century. They *were* America, and they had been ready for what the world offered, the challenges posed. In a way Lyndon Johnson had known better, he had entertained no small amount of doubt about the course he was taking, but he saw, given his own instincts, his own reading of American politics, his own belief in how he had to look to others, no way of getting off. He and the men around him wanted to be defined as being strong and tough; but strength and toughness and courage were exterior qualities which would be demonstrated by going to a clean and hopefully antiseptic war with a small nation, rather than the interior and more lonely kind of strength and courage of telling the truth to America and perhaps incurring a good deal of domestic political risk. What was it Jack Kennedy had said about Adlai Stevenson during the Cuban missile crisis when he had mocked Stevenson's softness—that you had to admire the way Stevenson was willing to fight for his convictions when everyone else in the room was against him. The irony of that statement was missing for Kennedy and it was missing for Johnson as well.

Nor had they, leaders of democracy, bothered to involve the people of their country in the course they had chosen: they knew the right path and they knew how much could be revealed, step by step along the way. They had manipulated the public, the Congress, and the press from the start, told half truths, about why we were going in, how deeply we were going in, how much we were spending, and how long we were in for. When their predictions turned out to be hopelessly inaccurate, and when the public and the Congress, annoyed at being manipulated, soured on the war, then the architects had been aggrieved. They had turned on those very symbols of the democratic society they had once manipulated, criticizing them for their lack of fiber, stamina, and lack of belief. Why weren't the journalists more supportive? How could you make public policy with television cameras everywhere? The day after he withdrew from re-election in 1968 Lyndon Johnson flew to Chicago for a convention of broadcasters, and he had placed the blame for the failure squarely on their shoulders, their fault being that the cameras had revealed just how empty it all was. A good war televises well; a bad war televises poorly. Maxwell Taylor was the key military figure in all the estimates, and his projections—that the war would be short, that the bombing would be a major asset—had proven to be false, but he had never adjusted his views to those failures; there was no sense of remorse, nor concern on why they had failed to estimate correctly. Rather, even in his memoirs, the blame was placed on those elements of the society which had undermined support for the war; when his book was finished, friends, looking at the galleys, cautioned him to tone down criticism of the press. What was singularly missing from all the memoirs of the period—save from a brief interview with Dean Rusk after the publication of the Pentagon Papers—was an iota of public admission that they had miscalculated. The faults, it seemed, were not theirs, the fault was with this country which was not worthy of them.

So they lost it all. There was a sense of irony here, as if each player had lost, not just a major part of his personal reputation, but much of what he had truly believed in and wanted, much of what he had manipulated for in the first place. Johnson of course had never wanted to go to war, he had become a war President reluctantly, in large part because he feared that otherwise he would lose the Great Society. He had instead gotten the war, but the Great Society was stillborn, it lacked his time, his resources, his second term to bring it to any genuine effectiveness.

For McNamara, the great dream had been of controlling the Pentagon and the arms race, but the war had ruined all that. War secretaries do not limit the power of the military, and to a large degree he had lost control. The war absorbed so much of his time, his energy, his credibility, that he had little to give to the kind of controls he might have wanted. It was not by accident that his name would come more to symbolize the idea of technological warfare than it would civilian control of the military.

McGeorge Bundy was a rationalist in an era which saw the limits of rationalism and which rekindled the need for political humanism; the man of operations and processes in an Administration which seemed to undermine the limits of the processes without moral guidelines. But above all he was a man of the Establishment, the right people deciding on the right policies in the right way; he believed in the capacity and the right of an elite to govern on its terms. The war changed all that; it not only tarnished his personal reputation so that his endorsement of an idea or a candidate had to be done covertly, but it saw a major challenge to the right of the elite to rule. In the Senate, the leading doves believed they had been wiser than the executive branch, and they were beefing up their staffs and playing a larger role in foreign policy. Too, the years had made all the other political groups in the country aware of just how little a part they played in foreign policy, and by the end of the decade the outlanders, Negroes, women, workers, were determined to play a greater role; they had reached the moat and were pressing on.

Dean Rusk had believed not so much in the class as in the policies, mutual security, strong political and military involvement everywhere in the world to stop totalitarians. The war, of course, had brought on a new sense of the limits of power, and with that a growing attitude about the need for the United States to roll back its commitments, which Rusk and others deemed to be a new isolationism. If anything, to a new generation of Americans the war had blurred the differences between the democracies and the totalitarian states. Thus the war, rather than setting the precedent of what the United States had done in the past and would continue to do in the future in the world, had symbolized to growing numbers of Americans what the United States must never do again. It reversed all the traditional directions of American foreign policy, and for Rusk this was a far more bitter thing than the personal abuse which he had suffered.

Max Taylor had always believed in the liberal society and the citizen-democratic army, a professional army respected by its citizenry, the best kind of extension of a healthy society. The Army would contain the finest young men of the society, well-educated civilized young officers, and this very fact would temper old civilian suspicions and alienations. The war of course had ravaged the Army; the kind of officer Taylor sought for the Army suffered because of it and was increasingly driven out of service. A bad war means a bad system; the wrong officers are promoted for the wrong reasons, the best officers, often unable to go along with the expected norm, the fake body count, the excessive use of force, wither along the way. And the gap between the Army and the society as a whole did not close, it widened; there was a growing sense of antimilitary feeling in the country.

The Democratic party too was damaged. It had been hiding from its past at the very beginning of the Kennedy era, unwilling to come to terms with China and what had happened there, and in large part it had gotten into trouble in Vietnam because it accepted the Dulles policies in Asia. But Dulles policies or no, it was the Democrats who had brought us into Vietnam, and the sense of alienation between the party and not just the young but millions of other nominal Democrats was very large. American life was changing very quickly and the party was adjusting very slowly; it seemed increasingly an outmoded institution, its principal spokesmen figures of the past.

Such as Hubert Humphrey, who was one more victim of the war. He had of course always wanted to be the Democratic nominee for the Presidency and he had finally received the nomination one terrible night in Chicago, but by that time it was no longer worth anything. He was nominated in Chicago on a night when police hacked the heads of the young, and Humphrey's only response was to kiss the television set. He had gained the nomination and in so doing lost most of what was left of his reputation.

But it was Lyndon Johnson who had lost the most. He had always known this, even in the turbulent days of 1964 and 1965 when the decisions on the war seemed to press on him; even then he was more dubious than those around him, knowing that of them, he had the most to lose. And he lost it, so much of his reputation, so much of his dreams. He could not go to the 1968 Democratic convention, it was all too painful and explosive; nor did he attend the 1972 convention. There at Miami Beach the Democrats had hung huge portraits of their heroes of the past in the main hall, photos of Presidents and national candidates. But Lyndon Johnson's photo was not among them, rather it could be found in a smaller room where photos of past congressional leaders hung. He had always dreamed of being the greatest domestic President in this century, and he had become, without being able to stop it, a war President, and not a very good one at that.

A FINAL WORD

In the days, weeks, and months after his withdrawal from the race and his decision to cut back on the bombing, Lyndon Johnson was immobilized on the war and so was his Administration. He had been most at ease with a consensus policy, a policy in which all the very great men agreed on the essential wisdom of one centrist idea, and now this consensus was openly and finally shattered, his government totally and irreconcilably divided, and he simply could not come to terms with the division. Events had forced him to set a limit on the American escalation, which he had done reluctantly, though his own generals had warned that even at the current rate of commitment of more than 500,000 Americans, the war might drag on indefinitely. So he had at once limited the war, but he could not make the next step which might see the liquidation of it politically. Perhaps there was simply too much of his own ego involved in it. So the policy on the war was in a kind of suspension.

Clifford at Defense and Harriman in Paris, as the summer of 1968 passed into the fall, were pushing very hard for the kind of political decisions which would see diminishing importance placed on the wishes of the Saigon government, with the United States, if need be, ready to by-pass Saigon. Similarly, in Saigon, Ellsworth Bunker was emerging as a singularly strong proponent of the Thieu regime who felt that in the wake of the Tet offensive we had to strengthen rather than weaken Saigon, and he was arguing forcefully that at this late date we could not let go of Thieu, that the regime was legitimate, and more viable. Bunker, a man with an awesome reputation of his own, was a strong and forceful player, and in a divided bureaucracy his word was crucial. He was picking up the support of both Rusk and Rostow, thereby effectively neutralizing the work of Clifford and Harriman. In March and April, Clifford had won the first round; now the second round, whether or not to keep going on the disengagement of Americans whether Saigon liked it or not, was going to Bunker. This did not stop Clifford from fighting; he was arguing that we had to continue to de-escalate, that it was important not just to limit the commitment but to end it, that Saigon was not in any true sense an ally, that its legitimacy was dubious, that reality was that the United States had overreached itself in Vietnam and now we had to admit it and adjust to it. But Johnson was unable to resolve his new dilemma. With Saigon dragging its feet on negotiations, Clifford prodded everyone along during the fall and publicly criticized the Thieu regime. He was clearly trying to set a new policy for the Administration and move into the vacuum, letting Saigon know that if it wanted any kind of deal at all, it would have to bend as the United States was now bending. Clearly, Clifford was hoping that the President would follow his lead, but Johnson was too deep into the war and he was not that anxious to admit that this ally, for whom he and his country had sacrificed so much (an ally which had in effect cost him his Presidency), was not a worthy ally, not a real government in a real country. In effect, Clifford was arguing the same things that George Ball had advocated four years earlier, but with so many more chips already in the poker game that it was too painful for Johnson to accept the argument of cutting his losses. He could not split off from Saigon, and Saigon was of course holding back on negotiations precisely because it sensed that Nixon would be elected and that he would be easier to deal with than Humphrey (in his memoirs, Johnson would lament Thieu's obstreperous behavior at this point, saying that it was the first time Saigon had failed to come through for him; which it was, though of course it was the first time he had asked them for anything).

Johnson stayed strictly neutral during the campaign. Though Humphrey was in a sense his political protégé, the President seemed less than anxious to do him any special favors, in part because the issue of the war was in his mind so transcending that he did not want to play politics with it, and in part, friends of his sensed, because he had interior doubts about Humphrey's capacity to run the country, at least by Johnsonian standards—was Humphrey tough enough?

It was a view of the campaign not unlike that of Richard Nixon, who had feared a race against Johnson and the White House but who seemed to relax now that his opponent was Hubert Humphrey. It was like running against Johnson without Johnson. Humphrey bore the burden of the Johnson years without the strengths; he had the visible stamp of Johnson, he carried the albatross of the war and the divisions that the war had brought to his party; he seemed, in all, a palpably weak candidate. So Nixon decided to run a do-nothing, say-nothing campaign. The Democrats were divided on Vietnam, the Republicans were not; Vietnam was a problem for the Democrats, not for the Republicans. He did not spell out his policies, in large part because he had none. He contented himself with telling audiences that he had a plan to end the war, even touching his breast pocket as if the plan were right there in the jacket—implying that to say what was in it might jeopardize secrecy. The truth was that he had no plan at all. Throughout the campaign his unwillingness to develop a serious substantive policy on Vietnam, which was, after all, the issue tearing the country apart, was the bane of some of his younger staff members. They were repeatedly pushing him to deal with the war, what it meant, why it had gone wrong, but they found him singularly unresponsive. To the degree that he showed his feelings on the war, particularly early in the campaign, he seemed as hawkish as the Administration. He talked about his belief that the war would be brought to a successful conclusion and that the Tet offensive, which had been launched in January, 1968, was simply a last-ditch effort by an exhausted enemy. His staff soon convinced him to ease off on his support for the Administration, helped, as it were, by the ferocity with which the NVA and the Vietcong were fighting during the Tet offensive. But the issue for him was not the compelling tragedy it was for so many other Americans, something that you had to come to terms with on its own merits, something where the failure had to be traced and explained to a troubled and divided country; rather it was an issue like others, something to maneuver on, to watch Johnson, Humphrey, and Wallace on.

As the Tet offensive dragged on, as dovish and antiwar sentiment mounted in the country even among conservative Republicans (John McCone, Nixon's staff discovered, thought the United States had to get out of Vietnam. What about loss of prestige? McCone was asked. Well, there would be a loss of prestige but it was worse for the United States to stay.), the staff moved Nixon to giving what was a reasonably dovish speech on Vietnam. It was prepared by a talented young writer named Richard Whalen who thought the war a hopeless mistake. The speech was scheduled for delivery in early April, but by that time Johnson had withdrawn on Vietnam, so Nixon felt himself under considerably less pressure and canceled it. From then on, though the country was locked in paroxysms of anguish on the war, Nixon sat it out, and at one strategy meeting when Whalen implored his candidate to be candid about Vietnam, insisting that the American people had been seriously lied to and knew they had been lied to, and that Nixon had to challenge the Administration on the war, Nixon listened to Whalen impassively. But there was no response and Whalen thought to himself: "I might just as well be talking to Humphrey. Nixon looks just the way Humphrey must look when his people tell him to break with Johnson." Discouraged by this attitude, Whalen left the Nixon campaign staff shortly after the Republican convention, but no matter—the Democrats were overwhelmed by problems and the candidate had few of his own. He was convinced that he had Humphrey boxed in on the war; he had a good pipe line to what the Humphrey camp was thinking on the war—pushing the candidate to ask for a bombing halt—and Nixon let Johnson know that he, Nixon, was against the bombing halt. Thus the capacity to split the Democratic party.

In late September the polls showed Nixon leading Humphrey 45 to 30; if he was concerned about anything it was the strength of Wallace, and he was wary of seeming too liberal, too dovish, and thus losing his Southern support. So the campaign was in one sense a repeat of the Tom Dewey campaign, though with far greater technological skill. If Nixon avoided confrontation with the public and with reporters, he nonetheless seemed, by means of carefully controlled televised confrontations with his own supporters, to be meeting people, he seemed to be candid. Meanwhile Humphrey, despite the efforts of his staff to separate him from Johnson, was unable to make the break; he was able to take draft copies of a plan for a new and more independent Vietnam to the President and then unable to show them to the President. "Hubert," said Larry O'Brien, head of the Democratic party, in August, "paid a high price for being a good boy." But then, very late in the campaign, and under constant prodding by his staff and his audiences, Humphrey began slowly, painfully, timidly to dissociate himself from Johnson and the war. Suddenly his campaign came alive, money came in. The final vote in November was extremely close: a fifteen percent edge in the polls had dwindled to less than one percent, Nixon winning 31.77 million to 31.27 million. In part because of his silence and failure to come to terms with such an awesome issue, Nixon had helped turn a potential landslide into a cliffhanger.

So he was President and he had enjoyed a free ride on Vietnam. He had not announced what his thoughts were on the subject, nor would he be in any hurry to. To Republican doves who had supported him during the campaign he had appeared optimistic about the chances for an end. He had told some of them during the campaign that if he was elected he would end the war within six months. After his election that still seemed to be the timetable; in April, 1969, Representative Pete McCloskey of California, who would later challenge Nixon on the war, and Representative Don Riegle of Michigan, who would aid McCloskey in the campaign, went to see Henry Kissinger to plead that the Administration keep its promise and end the war shortly. Kissinger replied that a breakthrough was imminent. "Be patient," he said. "Give us another sixty to ninety days. Please stay silent for the time being." But the first signs of what the Administration's policy would be had already come from Kissinger himself. Even before Nixon took office, Kissinger, who was the vital national security assistant, had gone around Washington telling friends that the most serious mistake the Johnson Administration had made was the public criticism by Clifford and Harriman of Saigon. In contrast, said Kissinger, the

Nixon Administration would move to strengthen the Thieu regime. To many dovish Washington officials who viewed Clifford's attempt to separate Washington from Saigon as the wisest thing the Johnson Administration had done, and felt that it had, if anything, not gone far enough, what Kissinger was saying was ominous. If Nixon was going to strengthen Saigon, then there would be no real change forthcoming in the political objective of the United States and in what the Administration was offering Hanoi. We might lower our troop level there, but the war would continue the same. Though we would probably cut back on American troops in Vietnam (not out of fondness for the other side, but because American political realities demanded it), we were not offering the other side anything new politically.

The answer on the Nixon policies came in November. With antiwar sentiment mounting again, with larger and larger antiwar moratoriums being held, Nixon finally moved. He did not speak to the protesters, he spoke beyond them, to what had become known as Middle America or Silent America, telling them that they were the good Americans who loved their country and their flag, and he summoned them now to support him. He wanted peace, but peace with honor; all Americans would want him to honor the commitment to a great ally. In the speech he seemed to be debating Ho. What was important about the speech was its tone. The rhetoric was harsh and rigid, and there was talk about their atrocities (just a few days earlier Seymour Hersh, a freelance writer, had uncovered the first evidence of the massive American massacre of women and children at My Lai). The rhetoric seemed more like that of the previous Administration than an Administration which intended to end the war; indeed, a few days later Dean Rusk said at a Washington dinner that he was a member of the loyal opposition, but after Nixon's speech he was more loyal than opposed.

At the same time that Nixon invoked the support of Middle America he also unleashed his Vice President, Spiro Agnew, to attack the media and war critics, Agnew in effect becoming Nixon's Nixon. The idea was simple: to freeze critics of the war and the President, to put them on the defensive. Support of the President was patriotic; criticism of him and his policies was not. Eventually Agnew's role became even clearer—to purge the Congress of dissident doves, that is, to remove from the Congress those men most opposed to a war that Nixon was supposed to be ending. By this time Nixon's policy became clear: it would be Vietnamization, we would pull back American troops, probably to 250,000 by 1970, and perhaps to as few as 75,000 by 1972. There would be fewer and fewer Americans on the ground, and greater and greater reliance on American air power. What could be more tempting than to cut back on American troops and casualties and still get the same end result which Lyndon Johnson had sent more than 500,000 men in quest of. So he was dealing with the war without really coming to terms with it; it was the compromise of a by now embattled President who knew he had to get American troops out but who still believed in their essential mission. So now he sought peace with honor. "What President Nixon means by peace," wrote Don Oberdorfer in the Washington *Post*, "is what other people mean by victory."

About the same time, Henry Kissinger, who had emerged as the top foreign policy adviser of the Administration (in part because he, like Nixon, was hard line on Vietnam, whereas both William Rogers, the Secretary of State, and Mel Laird, the Secretary of Defense, had been ready to liquidate the war in the early months of the Administration), was asked by a group of visiting Asians if the Nixon Administration was going to repeat the mistakes of the Johnson Administration in Vietnam. "No," answered Kissinger, who was noted in Washington for having the best sense of humor in the Administration, "we will not repeat their mistakes. We will not send 500,000 men." He paused. "We will make our own mistakes and they will be completely our own." There was appreciative laughter and much enjoyment of the moment. One thing though—Kissinger was wrong. To an extraordinary degree the Nixon men repeated the mistakes and miscalculations of the Johnson Administration, which prompted Russell Baker to describe it all as "the reign of President Lyndon B. Nixonger." For step by step, they repeated the mistakes of the past.

They soon became believers in their policy, and thus began to listen only to others who were believers (they began to believe, in addition, that only they were privy to the truth in reports from Saigon, that the secret messages from the Saigon embassy, rather than being the words of committed, embattled men, were the words of cool, objective observers). Doubters were soon filtered out; the Kissinger staff soon lost most of the talented Asian experts that had come in with him at the start of the Administration. Optimistic assessments of American goals, of what the incursion into Cambodia would do, of what the invasion of Laos would do—always speeding the timetable of withdrawal and victory—were passed on to the public, always to be mocked by ARVN failure and NVA resilience. Most important, Nixon saw South Vietnam as a real country with a real President and a real army, rich in political legitimacy, and most important, capable of performing the role demanded of it by American aims and rhetoric. So there was no tempering of rhetoric to the reality of failure and miscalculation in the South; Nixon himself spoke of the fact that America had never lost a war, precisely the kind of speech a President needed to avoid if he wanted to disengage. Similarly, if there was an overestimation of the South Vietnamese, there was a comparable underestimation of the capacity, resilience, determination, and toughness of the other side. Even in 1972, when Hanoi launched a major offensive, Kissinger called in favored Washington correspondents to be sure that they downplayed the importance of the offensive; like so many French and American spokesmen before him, he saw it as the last gasp—"One last throw of the dice," Kissinger called it.

But the Nixon Administration, like the Johnson Administration before it, did not control events, and did not control the rate of the war; and though it could give Thieu air power, it could not give him what he really needed, which was a genuine, indigenous political legitimacy. While Thieu's regime was as thin and frail as ever, the North Vietnamese were imbued with a total sense of confidence. Time was on their side, they were the legitimate heirs of a revolution; nothing confirmed their legitimacy more than American bombs falling on the country. Eventually, they knew, the Americans would have to leave. What was it a fully confident Pham Van Dong had told Harrison Salisbury of *The New York Times* in December, 1966, in Hanoi: "And how long do you Americans want to fight, Mr. Salisbury . . . one year? Two years? Three years? Five years? Ten years? Twenty years? We will be glad to accommodate you." And the war went on. American air power served its limited purpose; it could, at great cost, keep the South Vietnamese from being routed. Administration sources praised progress in pacification, but there was no real pacification; the 1973 NVA offensive ravaged any frail gains, and Nixon, in frustration, approved an even fiercer bombing campaign against the North, lifting many of the restraints which had marked the Johnson years. In world eyes the bombing, in the name of a losing cause, made the United States look, if anything, even crueler. Peace seemed nowhere near in the summer of 1972, unless the President abruptly changed his policies, and so the American dilemma remained. Time was on the side of the enemy, and we were in a position of not being able to win, not being able to get out, not being able to get our prisoners home, only being able to lash out and bomb. The inability of the Americans to impose their will on Vietnam had been answered in

1968, yet the leadership of this country had not been able to adjust our goals to that failure. And so the war went on, tearing at this country; a sense of numbness seemed to replace an earlier anger. There was, Americans were finding, no light at the end of the tunnel, only greater darkness.